INTRODUCTION TO PHYSIOLOGICAL PSYCHOLOGY

Harper's Physiological Psychology Series
under the editorship of H. Philip Zeigler

INTRODUCTION TO PHYSIOLOGICAL PSYCHOLOGY

Richard F. Thompson

Harper & Row, Publishers
New York, Evanston, San Francisco, London

Introduction to Physiological Psychology

Copyright © 1975 by Richard F. Thompson

All rights reserved. Printed in the United States of America. No part of this book may be used or reproduced in any manner whatsoever without written permission except in the case of brief quotations embodied in critical articles and reviews. For information address Harper & Row, Publishers, Inc., 10 East 53rd Street, New York, N.Y. 10022.

Library of Congress Cataloging in Publication Data

Thompson, Richard Frederick
    Introduction to physiological psychology.

    (Harper's physiological psychology series)
    Bibliography
    Includes index.
    1. Psychology, Physiological.   I. Title.
[DNLM: 1. Psychophysiology. WL102 T468i]
QP360.T48   612'.8   75-2392
ISBN 0-06-046604-9

For Judith, Kathryn,
Elizabeth and Virginia

Contents

**7   MOTOR CONTROL AND SENSORY-MOTOR
INTEGRATION**

8   MOTIVATION

xi

Contents

Preface

This text is written expressly for the first undergraduate course in physiological psychology. It is designed for a one-semester course following a beginning introduction to psychology. The text actually requires no background on the part of the student beyond ordinary high school; all necessary concepts from psychology and biology are discussed and explained when introduced. This book is also well suited for a beginning course in psychobiology in the biology curriculum. Evolution and the genetic roots of behavior are treated, as is the general field of behavioral biology.

The author has been extremely gratified with the very positive reception and success of his earlier text, *Foundations of Physiological Psychology* (Harper and Row, 1967). *Foundations* was written as an upper division or graduate text. In the years since it was published, a great many instructors have stressed to the author the critical need for a shorter and more elementary treatment of the subject. This text is the result. It provides a survey of the important issues and areas of physiological psychology at an uncomplicated level, with emphasis on recent and exciting developments. Biological systems and processes that underlie behavior and experience are presented, with emphasis on brain mechanisms, in the broader context of the fundamental concepts and issues in psychology.

This text is not a revision of *Foundations*. It is broader in scope, considerably more elementary in treatment, and explicitly designed to be maximally useful in teaching an elementary course in physiological psychology. Each chapter ends with a comprehensive summary of the important concepts and information, and a glossary of all important terms is given at the end of the book. A list of suggested readings for each chapter also is given at the end of the book. These readings were selected not only for their clarity and coverage of appropriate material, but also because they are enjoyable and entertaining discussions of the topics. A study guide has been prepared to accompany the text (Roemer, R. *A Study Guide for Introduction to Physiological Psychology*. Harper and Row, 1975).

The author recently published a collection of readings in physiological psychology from the *Scientific American* (Thompson, R. F., Ed. *Physiological Psychology*. Freeman, 1972). This collection of fascinating original articles written by outstanding experts in the field was specifically designed to accompany the present text. Sections I and II of the Reader are for Chapters 1 and 2 of the text, Sections III and IV go with Chapters 3 and 4, Section V goes with Chapter 5, Section VI with Chapters 6 and 7, Section VII with Chapters 8 and 9, Section VIII with Chapter 10, Section IX with Chapter 11, and Section X with Chapter 12.

Although this text and the Reader can, of course, stand alone, the combination of text, Reader, and study guide should provide clear, comprehensive and, we hope, exciting coverage of the field in forms that are most useful to both students and instructors. The subject ultimately of greatest interest to every person is himself and other humans. Physiological psychology is devoted to an understanding of the basic mechanisms underlying human behavior, experience, and awareness. It is surely the most fascinating of all fields. In a very real sense it is the last frontier of science. We know far more about the physical universe than about our own brains and minds.

Recent discoveries in the neurosciences, the sciences relevant to physiological psychology, are numerous and exciting. There are many new and intriguing stories. However, as the reader will see, they often do not yet have endings. The recent explosion of interest in the neurosciences and behavior attests to rapid progress in the field, and to the direct impact it is having on real and practical aspects of human life: the actions of "psychedelic" drugs on the brain and awareness, the problem of drug addiction, the use of "psychosurgery" to control human behavior, the use of electrical brain stimulation to control behavior, genetic and behavioral determinants of criminal violence, biological and behavioral factors in sex, sexual differentiation in humans, the role of inheritance in intelligence, the "memory pill," to name only a few examples. Every person should have a voice in the application and control of these procedures and issues in society. The basic information necessary to develop informed opinions on these and other relevant topics is presented in this text. We hope you will find it both useful and enjoyable.

The author wishes to express his deep and genuine gratitude to the many people who made this book possible. First and foremost to his wife Judith and his three daughters, whose patience and willingness to forego many weekends and holidays created the time for it. Initial versions of several of the chapters were written in collaboration with colleagues: Chapters 1 and 2 with Dr. Edwin Rubel, Department of Psychology, Yale University; Chapters 8 and 9 with Dr. Timothy J. Teyler, Department of

Psychology, Harvard University and Dr. H. Philip Zeigler, Department of Animal Behavior, The American Museum of Natural History; and Chapter 11 with Dr. Michael Patterson, Department of Physiology, Kirksville College of Osteopathic Medicine. However, the author takes sole responsibility for the final version of all chapters—the blame as well as the praise. The Series Editor, Dr. H. Philip Zeigler, has provided constant and helpful feedback, as have a number of academic reviewers. My particular thanks go to Nancy Desmond for an heroic job of shepherding the book to completion. We are deeply indebted to Donna Bradley for elegant art. Thanks also to Nancy Kyle, Rosemary Matich, and Ruth Roemer for assistance on the manuscript.

This book was written for its reader—the student who wishes to learn something about the fascinating field of brain, mind, and behavior. I have tried to convey some sense of the excitement in the field—the new and intriguing findings and concepts—without an overload of detail. I trust the reader will enjoy it.

Richard F. Thompson

Historical note

Psychology is the science of behavior and experience. Its origins as a science can be traced to two major historical traditions, one German and the other British and American. About the middle of the nineteenth century German philosophers and physiologists—men such as Weber, Fechner, and Helmholtz—began to study and measure experience. These efforts led ultimately to the field of *psychophysics*—the study of the relations between properties of physical stimuli and the nature of our experience of stimuli. Psychophysics investigates, for example, why a noise twice as intense as another does not sound twice as loud as the other, but only a bit louder. Psychophysics has been of critical importance for modern understanding of how sensory systems function—how we hear and see and touch. The British empirical philosophers, particularly John Locke and John Stuart Mill, emphasized the role of associations formed by experience. This approach ultimately led to recognition of the importance of *experimental testing of ideas*—of observing facts and conducting experiments to determine whether an idea is correct. In America, this tradition led to the *pragmatic approach* to the study of human behavior—an approach based on the view that the best method of studying a problem is the one that works best.

The coalescence of these traditions into the field of psychology is perhaps best seen in the classic text by William James, *Principles of Psychology*, written at Harvard about 85 years ago. James devoted a large portion of his text to brain function as the biological basis of behavior and experience. The full development of this view, which became physiological psychology, was accomplished by Karl Lashley at Harvard. His 1929 monograph entitled *Brain Mechanisms and Intelligence,* described a series of experiments aimed at finding the location of the engram—the brain substrate of learning. Another approach to the objective study of behavior is represented by the work of Pavlov and his many students in the Soviet Union and other European countries. His analysis of the conditioned reflex was fundamentally biological. He believed, like Lashley, that learning could be explained in terms of brain processes.

While psychology was developing as an independent experimental science of behavior and experience, study of the basic properties of the brain was proceeding in such fields as physiology, anatomy, and chemistry. Sir Charles Sherrington, in England, developed the modern field of neurophysiology. His 1906 text on the integrative action of the nervous system, an elegant analysis of reflex mechanisms, set the stage for modern investigation of how nerve cells interact in the brain.

Still another tradition that has become extremely important in modern psychobiology is *ethology*—the study of the behavior of organisms in their natural environments. It emphasizes the evolutionary determination of behavior in nature. Ethologists usually trace their history back to Darwin, but the field's modern impetus has come largely through the work of such European zoologists as Konrad Lorenz and Niko Tinbergen—both 1973 Nobel prize recipients. Ethology developed within zoology as a method of studying behavior independent of experimental psychology. Both disciplines have the same general goal—an understanding of behavior. When the two first met, the result was often collision rather than synthesis. Ethologists felt that experimental psychologists controlled away most of the important aspects of natural behavior in their laboratories. Psychologists, in turn, felt that ethologists used uncontrolled and unscientific methods, such as simple observations of an animal's behavior in its natural environment. Recently these approaches have combined: Natural behavior is studied analytically in the laboratory and experimental methods are applied in nature.

The modern discipline called physiological psychology represents a coalescence of all these approaches to the study of the biological bases of behavior. Alternative names include psychobiology, biopsychology, neuropsychology, behavioral biology. An apt description is the neurosciences of behavior. All the terms reflect the basic goal: to unveil the biological mechanisms that underlie behavior and experience. We are well on our way to understanding some of the classic problems in psychology—for example, why we experience our visual world as we do—and are even beginning to approach the most fundamental of human problems—such as the nature of consciousness—using the new tools of physiological psychology.

The fundamental questions in physiological psychology are really the questions of psychology. How do we experience sensations and perceive the world? What is emotion? Why are we motivated to behave, both well and badly? To what extent are our abilities and behavior patterns influenced by heredity? Why do we sleep? What is dreaming? How do we learn and remember? How do we think? Why do we possess language? In broader terms these are all questions about the mechanisms and causes of our behavior and experience. In the past few years we have made enormous progress in our understanding of the human brain. This text presents a survey at an uncomplicated level of what is known today about the biological foundations of psychology.

1

Evolution and behavior

1

Man is an animal. This simple fact is all too often ignored in psychology. Man is a biological organism similar in structure, function, and even behavior patterns to other animals, particularly his fellow primates. Further, man is a very recent animal. Modern *Homo sapiens* appeared only about 50 thousand years ago—not a long span in biology's calendar. If you were to trace your ancestral tree back more than about two thousand generations, your forebears would begin to look rather less than human. Man's earliest ancestors began to diverge from other primate lines some two million years ago. During most of this time the overwhelmingly powerful forces of natural selection shaped man as a hunter and food-gathering primate. Raising crops and domesticating animals, activities that led to stable villages and ultimately to civilization as we know it, occurred only in the past ten thousand years, long after man had reached his fully modern form and capabilities. Man is the most awesomely successful species (some would say "carnivorous hunter") ever to appear on the face of the earth, and this past has shaped his present.

The characteristics that set man apart from other primates did not develop by accident. They evolved under the remorseless pressure of natural selection because they have survival value. And the evolution of ape to man included evolution of the biological structure of language. Language use evidently had adaptive value—for example, enabling greater social cooperation in the hunt for food and in the struggle against more powerful carnivores. We must view man in the context of biological evolution if we are ever to understand human nature.

Man is a unique animal—another obvious fact all too often ignored in biology. He is not simply the sexiest primate with strongly developed social and territorial instincts. He is not only a "naked ape." He is occasionally an ethical ape as well. The possession of language sets man apart from all other animals and in all probability did so 50 thousand years ago. Language is the highest and most obviously "learned" of all human capacities. Yet all current human cultures, no matter how primitive, have fully developed and complete languages. There is no evidence that language has evolved only in the recent past. Primitive modern man came with

Written in collaboration with Dr. Edwin Rubel, Department of Psychology, Yale University.

language. The speech areas of the cerebral cortex do not exist in other primates, but they are present as unique biological substrates of language in man.

Man has a seemingly unlimited ability to develop complex and abstract thought, and this ability has led to almost total domination of his environment. Replacement of a chipped-stone hand ax by a stone blade fastened onto the end of a stick may seem a small technological advance, but this material result of abstract thought achieved by modern man about 40 thousand years ago coincided with the total extinction of our ax-wielding cousin, Neanderthal man. Our ancestors took more than a million years to invent this primitive spear, and the accomplishment very likely required the enormous capabilities of the modern human brain. We passed from primitive ideas of the universe to Einstein's theory of relativity and atomic power in a mere five hundred years.

The personality of man has a complexity and richness qualitatively different from that of other animals. He is the only animal to create art deliberately. The cave paintings made by primitive modern man 30 thousand years ago in Spain and France equal or surpass anything done since. Man is the only animal to develop ethical and moral systems and to behave at times with charity to his fellows and to other animals. And his capacity for inflicting suffering and death on his own kind far exceeds that of any other animal. All these characteristics are the result of evolution. They have a biological basis in the structure and function of the human brain. However, most of the human aspects of human nature, both humane and inhumane, differ in kind from characteristics of infrahuman animals. It is misleading and often plain wrong to extrapolate simple inferences from the behavior of nonhuman animals to the behavior of man.

Man is the supremely interesting subject, at least to us. Physiological psychology is the study of man as the world's most extraordinary animal. It is concerned with the biological basis of behavior and experience—in essence, the study of the brain. For many of us it is the most exciting and challenging field of study that exists. The human brain is the most complex structure in the known universe. If we could fully understand its organization and functioning, we should understand all human behavior and experience.

EVOLUTION

The fact that organisms resemble one another to greater or lesser degrees was recognized long before the time of Charles Darwin. Carl Linnaeus, the Swedish naturalist, established much of the basis of our present classification system in his monumental work, *Systema Naturae*, published in 1735. Linnaeus, however, assumed that each species was separately and uniquely created and that in the process of classifying species into groups he was discovering the logic of their creator. While modern taxonomists have abandoned these assumptions, they have retained the broad outlines of his system of classification. The system works in a hierarchical fashion, classifying organisms first in general categories (phyla) and gradually in narrower categories (class, order, family, genus, and finally species). For example, the lion belongs to the phylum Chordata and the subphylum Vertebrata, along with fish, frogs, birds, and all other creatures that have backbones; to the class Mammalia, with other vertebrates that bear their young alive and suckle them; to the order Carnivora, with flesh-eating mammals such as bears, dogs, and weasels; to the family Felidae, with the cheetah and other typical cats; to the genus *Felis*, with other cats such as the leopard, tiger, and domestic cat, all of which have fully retractable claws; and the species *leo*. This classification system is continually being revised as more is learned about the relations between organisms.

Species is the key category in classifying animals. And interestingly, species of animals sometimes can be distinguished most clearly by their behaviors. Physical appearance and morphology (form) are obvious characteristics; behavior may seem less so. For example, animals of different species do not normally interbreed, but this is not always because they are physically incapable of doing so. Lions and tigers can be crossbred to produce viable offspring (ligers), but do not normally exhibit such wanton behavior in nature. The mule, the misbegotten child of horse and donkey, is itself a healthy and vigorous animal, but is sterile and cannot produce offspring. These examples illustrate the complexity of the genetic and experiential factors that determine both the forms and behaviors of animals. Are lions and tigers separate species because they are so determined by their genes or because they are so disposed in their behavior? If the latter, is their behavior in mate selection determined by genetic factors or by experience? Lions, after all, grow up with lions. The causes of behavior are complex and in higher animals always involve both genes and experience.

This issue will recur in various guises throughout the book. In some cases, genetic factors are overwhelmingly important. In others, experience plays the deciding role. More commonly, both kinds of influences are important and interact in complex ways. Study of the causal factors in any aspect of behavior is difficult. Reduction to purely genetic or purely experiential effects is rarely possible, and such analyses are extraordinarily complex.

Natural selection and species development

The theory of evolution—that all living things are descended from one or a few simple organisms—also had its pre-Darwin proponents. However, in this early form, the theory had little power, since it failed to provide a mechanism whereby an organism could become adapted to its environment. This gap Charles Darwin filled in 1859 with the publication of *Origin of Species,* in which he proposed and documented the evidence for the theory of natural selection. In its original form the theory of natural selection stated that adaptations favoring the reproductive success of an individual tend to be passed on from generation to generation. Thus, adaptations of the individuals in a population are constantly perfected to meet the demands of the environment. It is now known that selection acts upon the reproductive success of *populations* rather than individuals. This point is best exemplified by the social insects, such as ants or bees, of which few individuals reproduce and the success of the population depends on the nonreproductive members. This seemingly minor point is also important for populations in which a great deal of behavorial or structural diversity is advantageous, as in human populations (Simpson, 1958).

The relations between behavior and evolution provided the first controversy in evolutionary thought. In the early 1790s a French zoologist, Jean Baptiste Lamarck, proposed that as an animal strove to adapt to its environment, the behavior modified its physical form and these modifications were passed on to succeeding generations. The giraffe, by continually stretching its neck into the trees, acquired the long neck that was passed on to its progeny. This view, later stressed by the Russian botanist Lysenko, is called the theory of inheritance of acquired characteristics. Darwin himself saw little objection to this theory, but it was soon shown that selection does not act directly on behavioral modifications but acts to ensure that characteristics that prove advantageous are propagated—giraffes with long necks survived, birds that could learn the correct song found mates, and primates that could learn to use tools "inherited the earth."

We know today that evolution is largely the result of natural selection acting on genetically predetermined characteristics. Genetic variation is the rule in higher species, and with the trivial exception of identical twins, every human being has a unique genetic composition. This variation and mutation (sudden or accidental change) of the genetic material constitute the basis for evolution because they provide the diversity of individuals within a species that enables different responses—some more successful than others—to environmental pressures.

The genetic basis of evolution and behavior will be considered further in Chapter 2. We are concerned here with the general issue of how species form and evolve. Darwin was first able to explain the manner in which separate species develop from his studies of the finches living on the Galápagos islands, 600 miles off the western coast of South America (Lack, 1947). Apparently a flock of typical seed-eating finches reached the islands at a time when they were unoccupied by most other birds common on the mainland. With few other birds to compete for the food supply, the finches developed into a total of 13 different species in different islands, occupying various ecological niches normally filled by other birds on the mainland. One developed into a warbler finch closely resembling the true warbler in habits. Another developed into a woodpecker finch, which, like the woodpecker, climbed tree trunks and excavated holes in search of insects. However, lacking the long tongue of the true woodpecker, the finch developed a "tool-using" habit of poking insects out of the holes with twigs.

The finches illustrate two mechanisms of species development. One is *isolation*. Whenever a population is isolated from others of its kind, it adapts to the unique features of its environment and forms a new species that does not interbreed with the original stock. The other mechanism is *adaptive radiation*. In the absence of competition from other organisms, a given form evolves to fill all the available ecological niches. The woodpecker finch evolved because there were no true woodpeckers on that island to occupy that particular niche. A more familiar example is the evolution of marsupials (mammals that carry their young in an external pouch) in Australia. With only a few more advanced mammals to compete with, marsupials evolved into carnivorous (flesh-eating) types such as the Tasmanian devil and the native cat, as well as familiar herbivorous (plant-eating) forms such as the kangaroo, the phalanger, and the koala bear.

Vertebrate evolution

Vertebrates arose from the free-swimming larval forms of primitive marine organisms that in their adult forms are sessile (immobile) filter feeders. From this new mobile filter feeder, which had primitive eyes, developed an organism something like the modern amphioxus (a primitive fish). Amphioxus' nervous system consists of a central nerve cord lying dorsal to the digestive tract. This cord widens slightly at the anterior end to form a "brain." Amphioxus also possesses primitive eyes and an olfactory pit; however, it is a sedentary creature incapable of invading the fresh water where vertebrates are known to have evolved. From the primitive form resembling amphioxus arose filter-feeding fish—the jawless fish—that invaded the fresh water. These organisms were ancestors of the modern lamprey, considered the most primitive of living vertebrates.

The next great evolutionary achievement was the development of jaws, which could be used for eating new types of food or for seizing prey. From these jawed fish many radiations (i.e., evolutionary developments) occurred, one leading to the cartilaginous fish such as sharks, a second to the bony fish (teleosts) that are most common today and that use their eyes as the dominant sensory structure, and a third to the predatory fish that use their sense of smell to find prey. This last type of fish, the Crossopterygia arose some 390 million years ago and may have been our far distant but direct forebears. From them developed fish with lungs, fish with lungs and modified fins to serve as legs, and finally the first amphibians. Although they could traverse the land, these amphibians were mainly aquatic, as were their primitive reptilian descendants. Later, with the ability to produce eggs with protective membranes enclosing the young, terrestrial life became common and the age of reptiles began. Some primitive reptilian forms took to the air and later split into two main lines—the flying reptiles, which became extinct, and the birds. Another group of reptiles became specialized for size and evolved into the dinosaurs that ruled the earth for more than 100 million years. Yet another radiation from the early reptiles led to the ancestors of mammals.

The oldest known mammals lived some 200 million years ago, but the mammals did not begin to flourish until the end of the reptilian dynasty, around 65 million to 70 million years ago. Early mammals were small carnivores, the size of a mouse or a rat. They ate mainly insects and other small invertebrates. Although small, their bodies had become adapted for speed and agility, thermal regulation had evolved along with an insulating coat of hair, and their olfactory systems became extremely sensitive. It is even possible that the evolution of a dominant and powerful olfactory system mediated by the frontal part of the brain is responsible for the continual elaboration of the cerebral cortex in more advanced animals. Another factor in the evolution of the larger mammalian brain is the development of better hearing. Extra bones in the reptilian jaw migrated and became miniaturized to form the middle-ear bones of mammals. At the same time, the auditory (hearing) structures in the brain became larger and more elaborate. Jerison (1973) has suggested that mammals first evolved to fill an empty ecological niche— nocturnal (night) land dwelling. The suggestion is based on the assumption that dinosaurs had excellent vision, as do modern reptiles and amphibians. However, as we will see later in our discussion of the visual system of the frog (Chapter 6), visual analysis of the world is done in the eye rather than the brain in lower vertebrates. In contrast, the auditory system had to expand within the brain rather than in the ear. If dinosaurs were visually oriented beasts, they must have occupied daylight niches, and if the forerunners of mammals were to survive, they must have been active at night when detection of distant stimuli would best be done by hearing and smell.

Early mammals were probably egg layers that nursed their young, like the monotremes (e.g., duck-billed platypus) of today. Soon two other related adaptations of major importance evolved: retention of the young within the uterus until they could climb into a pouch where they could be protected and nursed; and, development of placental circulation, enabling retention of the young in the uterus until an even more advanced stage. These last adaptations proved to be of monumental importance. Although reptiles produce many eggs, relatively few hatch, and of the young that hatch, few survive. Intrauterine development of the fetus and postnatal nursing afforded the young protection at their most vulnerable stage. Producing only a few eggs, but ensuring their survival, guaranteed a small but continual population gain. Suckling the young had other far-reaching effects—mammals were evolving as animals continually under attack by the reptilian dynasty. Speed, agility, and the ability to adapt to environmental change were of primary importance; natural selection favored brain over brawn. Keeping the young to nurse established the family and allowed "education" of the young through imitation and practice before they became independent. Throughout mammalian evolution a recurring theme is the importance of this early training period for the establishment of adaptive behavior. This period reaches its apogee in primates. Romer (1958, p. 72) emphasizes this fact; "It is perhaps an exaggeration, but not too great a one, to say that our modern educational systems all stem back to the initiation of nursing by ancestral mammals."

With the extinction of the dinosaurs, the age of mammals began. They radiated into all the forms we know today as well as many that are now extinct. The primitive insectivores were one of the many radiations of the placental mammals. Of these, an animal like the tree shrew (*Tupia*) is thought by most investigators to be the ancestor of modern primates.

Human evolution

The study of evolution has as an ultimate goal a clearer understanding of the fundamental biological nature of man. The same selective pressures that resulted in the development of the relatively large-brained mammals are evident in the evolution of man from lower primates. From the time our early primate ancestors descended from the trees, some 30 million years ago, until the development of agriculture, about ten thousand years ago, man was a hunter. During the entire course of evolution from ape to modern man, natural selection operated on a being who hunted to survive. The physical characteristics, abilities, and even behavior of modern man have been shaped by the overriding selective pressure to survive as a hunter. *Proconsul*, an early ancestor of modern great apes and man, was smaller and slighter of build than a modern baboon. The trend toward larger physique is seen throughout the evolution of man. Indeed, man is among the larger and more powerful predators, and is perhaps the most vicious. This may help to explain the distressing fact that man is far more aggressive and destructive, particularly to his own kind, than are other primates or, for that matter, other mammals.

Physical size and strength, however, have not been the critical factors in human evolution. *Gorilla*, an even larger and stronger genus, is not particularly successful, at least by the criterion of numbers. The ancestors of man were far more successful and adaptive hunters than other primates. There are several obvious reasons for this. Man has been the only primate to develop true bipedalism—an upright posture that frees the hands for using tools and weapons. But hands are not enough. "The hands of the higher monkeys would be perfectly capable of the finest skills had they a mind to set them to work; monkeys could be watchmakers had they ever conceived the notion of time" (Hawkes and Woolley 1963, p. 104).

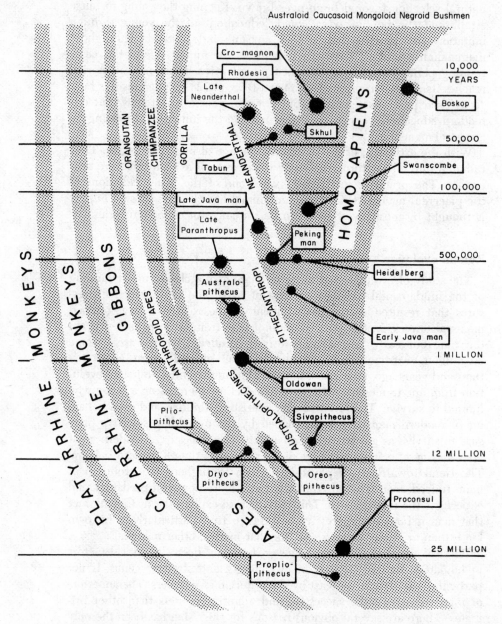

Figure 1.1 The mainstreams of human evolution. Great ape and human lines diverged at least 25 million years ago. (From Hawkes, J. and Woolley, Sir L., *History of Mankind: Prehistory and the Beginnings of Civilization*, Vol. I. Copyright © 1963 by UNESCO. Reprinted by permission of Harper & Row, Publishers, Inc.)

The use of tools requires a brain capable of conceiving them. Even primitive forms of tool using are not common among modern monkeys and apes. The chimpanzee, man's closest living relative, is the exception. Van Lawick-Goodall (1971) describes how wild chimps select sticks or reeds of appropriate size, clean them of side branches, and shape them to insert in termite nests. If the stick has the correct shape, a procession of delectable termites rich in fatty tissue will crawl up the stick to be eaten by the chimp. Young chimps were seen attempting this with inadequate sticks and gradually learning to manufacture the proper "termite tool." There appears to be no necessary evolutionary sequence for development of tools; rather, selection pressure favors general tendencies and abilities to use tools. The necessary substrate for tool use is an adequate brain. Even in terms of sheer motor skills, the motor cortex region of the human brain has a much larger representation of the thumb than does the chimpanzee's brain.

Stages of human evolution. The various stages in the physical evolution of man are now moderately well documented. His early cultural evolution must remain forever shrouded in mystery. The mainstreams of primate evolution are indicated in Figure 1.1, and some of our representative ancestors are shown in Figure 1.2. The terms used to name these creatures are often confusing and contradictory. All belong to the order Primates and the superfamily Hominoid, which also includes the great apes (chimpanzee, gorilla, gibbon, orangutan, and baboon). From *Australopithecus* on, they belong to the family Hominidae. Beyond this, authorities disagree. The next step after *Australopithecus* is represented by a group of fossil ape-men called *Pithecanthropus* (from the Greek word *pithēk*, meaning apelike) or *Homo erectus* (upright man). The most recent modern form of extinct primitive man is Neanderthal, named from

Figure 1.2 Artist's impression of man's ancestral evolution: A, *Proconsul,* a monkey-like ape; B, *Australopithecus,* the earliest ape-man; C, *Pithecanthropus;* D, Neanderthal man, modern in brain capacity but primitive in appearance; E, *Homo sapiens.*

the Neander valley near Düsseldorf, Germany, where his remains were first discovered in 1856. Our species is somewhat optimistically termed *Homo sapiens* (thinking man). Essentially all fossil remains of early man can be grouped into *Australopithecus, Pithecanthropus,* or *Homo sapiens* —the three major forms leading from ape to man.

The Proto-Apes. Some authorities believe that *Proconsul* is the most recent proto-ape that might resemble the common ancestor of the great apes and man. Even at the time of *Proconsul,* some 25 million to 35 million years ago, the great ape line had begun to specialize for tree living, developing long hands and arms—longer than those of either modern monkey or man—and retaining the earlier primate characteristics of the opposable big toe. Although differerent species of *Proconsul* varied in size, the most widespread form was a relatively small and generalized monkeylike ape that could live both in trees and on the ground. The ecology of Africa at the time of *Proconsul* was much like that of East Africa today—clusters of trees in open grassland, a savanna type of country that might have exerted selective pressure favoring ground living. *Proconsul* was of somewhat lighter build and had smaller canine teeth than modern apes of similar size. It forecasts the directions of the human line.

Ramapithecus, the earliest manlike primate yet known, lived about 12 million to 15 million years ago. Fragmentary remains have been found in Africa and India. Were we to see the creature today, we should judge it an ape, but its teeth and jaws show a distinct transition in the direction of the human line.

Australopithecus. Australopithecus appeared in Africa about two million years ago. It is of interest that the time required for the evolution of the ape-man *Australopithecus* from the ape *Ramapithecus* is about eight to ten million years. Simpson (1953) has estimated that the average rate of evolution for a new genus of mammals is about this length of time. Washburn and Shirek (1967) have noted that if the creatures occupied about two million square miles and there was a density of ten per square mile —reasonable estimates based on distributions of modern monkeys—there would have been 20 million animals in the transitional population at any one time. Approximately 800 thousand generations separate *Ramapithecus* from *Australopithecus,* a much longer span than separates *Australopithecus* from us.

Australopithecus is the missing link of popular science. He had an upright posture and was truly bipedal, in contrast to all great apes. The skull was balanced above the spinal column in modern human fashion. The ape-man was small, about the size of a modern pygmy, and slightly built. The body bears a striking resemblance to that of a small modern man. However, the skull capacity was very small—about 600 cc, the size of the cranium of a modern great ape—in contrast to the modern human skull capacity of about 1500 cc. The face was apelike with a low forehead, prominent brows, a flat nose, and a protruding muzzle (Fig. 1.3).

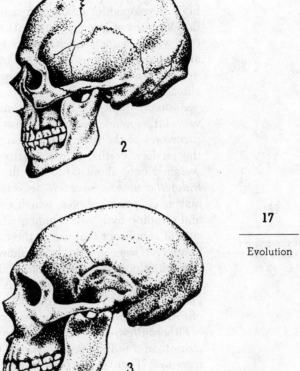

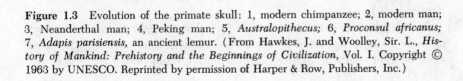

Figure 1.3 Evolution of the primate skull: 1, modern chimpanzee; 2, modern man; 3, Neanderthal man; 4, Peking man; 5, *Australopithecus;* 6, *Proconsul africanus;* 7, *Adapis parisiensis,* an ancient lemur. (From Hawkes, J. and Woolley, Sir. L., *History of Mankind: Prehistory and the Beginnings of Civilization,* Vol. I. Copyright © 1963 by UNESCO. Reprinted by permission of Harper & Row, Publishers, Inc.)

It is of great importance that *Australopithecus* had an upright human posture and a small brain. One of the classic arguments in evolution concerns the development of the brain. The older view was that a large brain developed for unknown reasons and thus enabled tool using and the development of human culture. However, natural selection does not work that way. Characteristics evolve very gradually from normal variations and minor mutations under selective pressure. In the case of man, an upright posture came first, perhaps as a necessary adaptive response to climate and ecology.

A small, slight ape-man with an upright posture would seem to have very little going for him against the much larger and more powerful carnivores of the time. But although his brain was no larger than that of the modern gorilla, it was relatively larger. An adult *Australopithecus* weighed only about 60 to 100 lb; a gorilla weighs 600 lb. In fact, *Australopithecus* was smarter; he was a tool user and possibly even a tool maker. Chipped pebbles, which could be used as weapons or as cutting and scraping tools, are commonly found with his remains. This is the first sign of significant tool use in the evolution of man. Already his small but relatively larger apelike brain showed glimmerings of the enormous and overriding power of the human brain. Judging by the animal bones found with his remains, *Australopithecus* was a successful hunter. Two million years ago selective pressure was shaping a bipedal hunter whose most effective weapon lay inside his skull.

Pithecanthropus. Various species of *Australopithecus* were prevalent for more than a million years. During this period his physical size gradually increased. Then, in the next million years, possibly as a result of increased selective pressure occasioned by changing climatic conditions, the development of man proceeded at a rate unparalleled in evolution. *Pithecanthropus* appeared about 800 thousand years ago and *Homo sapiens* entered the scene about 270 thousand years ago. Compare this incredibly rapid evolution with the 8 to 10 million years separating *Ramapithecus* and *Australopithecus*. The most significant change from later *Australopithecus* to *Homo sapiens*, incidentally, was in the size of the brain. Although we might judge their *appearances* to be vastly different, facial features are of less biological significance. The reasons for this rapid recent evolution are unknown. Geologically, this was the ice age. Four separate times glaciers extended down over much of Europe. It may be that changing climate and the severe stress of the ice ages exerted a much greater selective pressure. Another factor was the isolation produced by the climate changes—small groups could develop in different ways. Whatever the reasons, human evolution occurred with unprecedented speed.

Pithecanthropus is intermediate in form between *Australopithecus* and modern man. In physique he resembled modern man, although perhaps a bit smaller, with a slightly more primitive hand—the thumb was not quite so well developed—and a skull capacity ranging from 750 to 1000 cc. This brain size covers the range from just larger than *Australopithecus* to the lower limit of modern *Homo sapiens* (volumes of less than 1000 cc are found among some living men), but is still well below the 1500-cc average for modern man. Remains of *Pithecanthropus* have been unearthed in Africa, where he apparently first developed, and in Asia, where he apparently lived in relative isolation well beyond the period of his African cousins.

In the caves of Choukoutien in North China, fossil records indicate that *Pithecanthropus* lived in more or less continuous occupation for a period that may extend over several hundred thousand years. The main site was occupied while some 50 meters of cave deposits accumulated on the floor! His "culture" represented a distinct advance over that of *Australopithecus;* he chipped rough stone tools, particularly choppers and scrapers, and possessed fire. However, his culture was static and unprogressive, the stone tools show no improvement or change during this long period of time. The prevalence of cracked human bones suggests he may have been a cannibal with a particular fondness for human, or rather pithecanthropoid, brains. There is no evidence of artistic endeavor or ritual burial associated with *Pithecanthropus*. Nonethless, his widespread distribution and achievements as a hunter demonstrate clearly that he was an adaptive success.

Although it is evident that modern man developed from one or another species of *Pithecanthropus,* the particulars are not yet known. One view suggests that an early species of *Pithecanthropus* began the succession to *Homo sapiens* and other species developed into more regressive, simian-featured evolutionary blind alleys. Another view suggests a gradual progression. In any event, the earliest remains of true *Homo sapiens,* found in England, Germany, and France, are over 200 thousand years old. By this time *Pithecanthropus* had largely disappeared.

Neanderthal. Neanderthal man lived from about 100 thousand to 50 thousand years ago. Many authorities argue that he shows retrogressive development of certain apelike features and is not in the direct line to *Homo sapiens*. One view places him as the final development of the pithecanthropoid line and another as a side branch of the *Homo sapiens* line. In either event he was a rather remarkable fellow. A bit shorter than modern man, he was broad, heavy, squat, and brutish looking, with a low sloping forehead, enormous brow ridges, a receding chin, and heavy jaws with large teeth (Fig. 1.4). Although his skull looked simian, it was thoroughly modern in capacity. His brain was as large as or slightly larger than that of modern man. It is not known whether his brain differed from ours in structure, but it certainly did in shape. The frontal regions were smaller and the posterior occipital regions were larger.

Neanderthal developed a vigorous and thriving culture that apparently arose in Eastern Europe and spread throughout Europe, North Africa, and the Near East. He possessed a characteristic tool culture identified

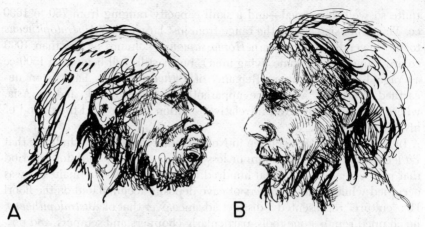

A   B

Figure 1.4 Profiles of Neanderthal man, A, and *Homo sapiens,* B. The drawing of Neanderthal is, of course, hypothetical.

by flaked stone tools—choppers and scrapers—and typically primitive hand axes. Except for his tools, Neanderthal left no evidence of artistic activity, but he did exhibit signs of religion. The grave of a young Neanderthal child who had been buried within a ring of goat horns was found in Uzbekistan.

Homo sapiens. Between 50 thousand and 40 thousand years ago modern *Homo sapiens* appeared in Europe, and Neanderthal became abruptly extinct. It seems indeed to have been a confrontation. Neanderthal and related descendants of the pithecanthropoid line inhabited much of the Old World and possessed a common hand-ax culture. Modern *Homo sapiens* appears to have developed initially in a limited region of Southwest Asia. His culture included the stone blade, which spelled extinction for Neanderthal:

An apelike breed in possession of one well-defined cultural tradition [ax] was directly confronted and dispossessed by men of modern type and with a totally different material culture. Two breeds, we think two species, met face to face and their faces were strikingly unalike [Fig. 1.4]. However much mixed cultural and physical traits had been in the past, in the early Upper Pleistocene there was some centre or centres where men entirely of our own kind had created the beginning of the high hunting cultures [blade] of the Upper Palaeolithic, a tradition almost wholly new, remarkably inventive, and, as history was to prove, immensely potent for future growth.

(Hawkes and Woolley, 1963, page 81)

Early modern man is exemplified by Cro-Magnon (named for a cave in France where he was discovered), a tall, vigorous, muscular race with an unusually large cranial capacity who established its culture in Europe. The contemporary races of man appear to have developed in the past 40 thousand years from common ancestors such as Cro-Magnon. Although a good deal of uncertainty exists, modern races seem to be relatively minor recent adaptations to climatic conditions: Mongolian characteristics are specialized for extreme cold; Negro characteristics for warm, damp climates; and Caucasian characteristics for climates with relatively little sunlight (Dobzhansky, 1962). It is certain, however, that all modern races evolved from common origins in the recent past. Those who make much of racial differences would do well to remember this fact.

Homo sapiens spread out from his origins in western Asia to conquer the Old World, then crossed through Alaska to occupy the New World. The earliest remains of man in the Western Hemisphere date back about 30 thousand years. Thus in the short span of some 20 thousand years, modern man occupied the entire world and set the stage for rapid cultural evolution. Judged against the earlier forms of man, modern *Homo sapiens* showed incredibly rapid cultural evolution from his first appearance. The stone blade became the spear, the spear thrower, and the bow and arrow. Painting and sculpture were practiced, animals were tamed, wild grains were cultivated—independently in the Old World and New World—and modern civilization was born.

The extreme rapidity with which civilization developed, and its seemingly independent development in many places in the world, suggest that, in common with language, it may represent an almost biological given of the species *Homo sapiens,* the inevitable result of the human brain. An appreciation of the time scales involved in the successive evolution of vertebrates, man, and man's culture is provided in the following quotation from Maynard Smith (1958, p. 290):

If a film, greatly speeded up, were to be made of vertebrate evolution, to run for a total of two hours, tool-making man would appear only in the last ten seconds. If another two-hour film were made of the history of tool-making man, the domestication of animals and plants would be shown only during the last two minutes, and the period between the invention of the steam engine and the discovery of atomic energy would be only three seconds.

BEHAVIOR

It seems inconceivable today that anyone would object seriously to describing man as a genetically determined biological organism. Structurally, man is obviously a primate; as we have seen, his evolutionary history can be traced back to the cellular origins of all life on earth. However, man's evolutionary heritage is still not seriously considered as a determinant of his behavior. Only a few years ago many behaviorists still insisted, with Watson, that man's mind is a blank slate upon which anything can be written and that it has no biological limits or even propensities. Even today discussions of the physiological bases of behavior often ignore its evolutionary and genetic background.

Behavior determinants: genes and experience

Perhaps the most obvious physiological determinants of behavior are genetic. The study of behavior genetics is a new and exciting field that is already providing us with tantalizing hints about basic mechanisms underlying behavior. An example is the "supermale" syndrome, a genetic mistake that *may* provide an explanation for certain types of criminal violence. A supermale has two male sex chromosomes (XYY) instead of the usual one (XY). Preliminary data suggest that such an individual may be physically large, mentally retarded, and given to crimes of violence. Behavior genetics will be discussed in greater detail in Chapter 2.

A few years ago, pitched arguments raged over the extent to which particular characteristics, traits, and behavior patterns were genetically determined or were learned. This nature-nurture controversy was resolved when both sides admitted two obvious facts: (1) behavior does not occur in a vacuum, but rather develops and occurs in an environment from the time the egg is fertilized and forced to interact with environmental factors; and (2) the organism is not a blank slate but rather a genetically determined animal possessing biological structures, capabilities, and limitations. Insistence on either extreme is not profitable. The genetic base cannot be ignored, but while many behavior patterns and tendencies are fixed, many others are modifiable by environmental influence. Indeed, behavior examples can be cited that range from the seemingly purely innate to the apparently entirely learned. It has been said that flies live from birth to death without ever exhibiting any sign of learning anything; all their behavior patterns are inborn. On the other hand, human culture and knowledge are obviously learned.

Innate behavior patterns imply a significant degree of genetic determination. Genes do not directly produce behavior. In fact, as we shall see in Chapter 2, the direct action of genes is simply to determine the synthesis of proteins. This step initiates the events in development that lead to the formation of the brain. The basic properties of the sensory-motor patterns responsible for innate behavior patterns are formed in the developing nervous system as a result of genetic determination. Environmental cues are necessary to elicit innate behavior patterns. These can be external cues (a fly won't eat unless food stimuli are available), internal cues (a female rat builds a nest as a function of hormone levels in the blood), or combinations of these.

Experience can condition or shape many innate behavior patterns. If experienced mother ring doves are injected with appropriate hormones to duplicate those of the reproduction cycle at a time other than the cycle, they will care for and hatch eggs. However, female ring doves that have not yet experienced their first reproductive cycle cannot be made to care for eggs by hormonal injections. One normal experience of the reproductive cycle is necessary to condition the bird so that hormone injections can initiate the appropriate innate behavior sequence (Lehrman, 1955).

Dilger (1959) has provided a striking example of the other extreme in nest-building patterns of certain species of African parrots. These birds are quick to learn many behavior sequences and are often used in circus bird acts where they have been trained to ride trains, wash clothes, push little wagons, etc. However, when it comes to nest building, a rather necessary adaptive behavior, they seem unable to learn anything at all. One species builds the nest by retrieving many strips of leaves, tucking them in its tail feathers, and taking them to the nest. Another species carries one strip at a time to the nest in its beak. Dilger crossbred the two species. The hybrid females exhibited striking maladaptive intermediate nest-building behaviors ranging from trying to tuck leaves in the wrong feathers or tucking improperly to attempting to get leaves into the tail feathers by running backward at the leaves. It appears that the two different sequences of nest building behaviors got mixed up in the hybrids. The birds were unable to learn to build nests even after two years of practice.

In general, animals with larger brains exhibit behavior that is more subject to modification or learning. The trend of evolutionary adaptation for survival seems to have gone in the direction of increased plasticity or adaptability of the individual. Simple stereotyped behavior patterns are not characteristic of higher mammals. However, this does not mean that genetic factors are unimportant in the behavior of man. Our large brains are the result of genetic determination. Further, the limits and potentialities of behavior are genetically set. Neither rat, monkey, nor man normally exhibits behavior indicating it can solve complex visual discrimination problems. However, the genetically determined brain structures of monkey and of man are sufficiently complex so that these animals can solve the problems when challenged. Rat cannot.

Recent evidence suggests that genetic factors may play a far more profound and subtle role in determining human behavior than merely setting the upper limits. As we shall see in Chapter 6, nerve cells in the visual area of the mammalian brain respond only to very abstract aspects of visual stimuli, such as edges, lines, and angles. Those complex stimulus-coding neurons apparently exist in the newborn animal prior to visual experience. Our perception of visual forms may at least in part be wired into the brain as a result of genetic determination.

Language seems to be one aspect of behavior that is obviously learned through experience. A child can learn any language with equal facility.

The structure and sounds of any particular language appear to be an artificial product of culture history without any biological determinants. However, many modern linguists now feel that language has many universal properties, which are the result of the genetically determined brain organization of the species *Homo sapiens*. The fundamental structure of language itself may in some manner be wired into the brain by the actions of the genes. We shall explore this further in our discussion of language in Chapter 12.

The ethological view of behavior

Ethology, the study of organisms' behavior in their natural environments, emphasizes the evolutionary determination of behavior. Ethologists have sought to understand behavior through studying animals in natural or seminatural environments. At the core of this approach is the notion that the behavior of an organism can be analyzed as a number of relatively fixed motor sequences that, through natural selection, come to be triggered by specific stimuli in the internal and external environments of the organism. Thus, the emphasis has been on *innate* or *instinctive* behavior patterns that can be directly linked to natural selection. The sequences of motor acts most often described by ethologists are called *fixed action patterns*. They are (1) extremely stereotyped within a species (at least in members of the same sex), (2) presumably innate, (3) alike every time they are repeated by an individual, (4) completed whenever activated, and (5) resistant to modification.

A great deal of ethological research has concentrated on identifying specific environmental stimuli that trigger the fixed action patterns. These stimuli are called *sign stimuli* or *releasers*. Like fixed action patterns, the releasers are assumed to be species specific. That is, the same releaser triggers similar fixed action patterns in all like-sexed members of a species. Sign stimuli may be the structures, sounds, odors, or even behaviors of another organism, particularly another member of the same species. An obvious example is the odor of a female dog in heat, which serves as the sign stimulus for the male to initiate mating behaviors. In many animals sign stimuli and fixed action patterns are chained together so that in social behaviors a fixed action pattern in one member serves as the releaser for another fixed action pattern in a companion. In some cases ethologists have been able to construct artificial stimuli that are more effective than natural stimuli in eliciting a particular response (Fig. 1.5). For example, a ground-nesting bird, the herring gull, if given a choice between her own nest and one with similarly colored eggs double the normal size, selects the latter. Presumably, this is because the oversized eggs serve as a supernormal sign stimulus. Although the concept of a supernormal stimulus is not highly important for the natural behavior of most organisms, Lorenz contends it is crucial to the understanding of

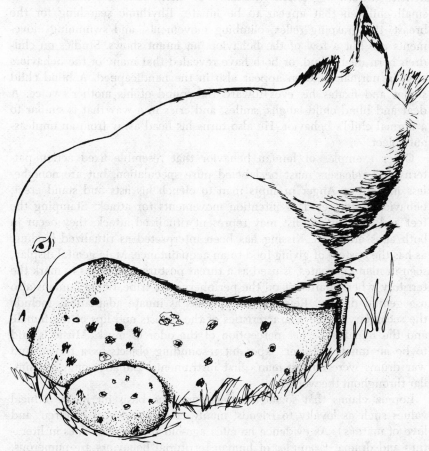

Figure 1.5 Herring gull illustrating its preference for the supernormal stimulus. Both eggs are wooden. One is normal size, the other 20 times as large. The gull ignores the normal-size egg and attempts to incubate the giant one, even though it keeps falling off the egg!

human ethology, since man, through his intelligence, has been able to construct supernormal stimuli for releasing many behaviors. Advertising, in this view, may be the game of trying to find the *most* supernormal stimuli.

The emergence of public as well as scientific interest in the ethology of man is an indication that literate people throughout the world have finally come to accept Darwinian evolution. Man is as much a product of evolution as are other organisms. Ethological views of human behaviors have ranged from interpreting the seemingly trivial behavior of scratching one's head as a displacement activity to interpretations of wars as inevitable because of man's innate, genetically determined tendencies toward aggression. We know of many behaviors in infants and small children that appear to be innate. Rhythmic searching for the breast, the grasping reflex, climbing movements, and swimming movements are but a few of the behaviors an infant shows. Studies on children born deaf, blind, or both have revealed that many of the behaviors seen in normal children appear also in the handicapped. A blind child smiles and fixates his eyes toward the sound of his mother's voice. A deaf and blind child laughs, smiles, and cries in a way that is similar to a normal child's behavior. He also turns his head away from an unpleasant object.

Other examples of human behavior that resemble fixed action patterns and releasers must be labeled pure speculation, but are nonetheless intriguing. Anger prompts man to clench his fists and stand erect, behaviors interpreted as intention movements for attack. Stamping the feet and banging the fist may represent ritualized attack; they occur in both apes and man. Kissing has been interpreted as ritualized feeding, as has the custom of giving food to an acquaintance. Male genital display, seen in many primates, is used as a threat posture and serves to mark the territory when guards sit on the periphery of a tribe. Some humans also use genital display. Releasers interpreted as innate adaptations include the secondary sexual characteristics of the breasts and lips of the female and the female's keener perception of the odor of musk. Music is said to be an innate releaser: Apes hit resounding objects as a threat, and war drums were among man's first instruments. Lullaby songs are similar throughout the world.

Lorenz claims that social releasers form the basis for innate ethical values such as loyalty to friends, manly courage, love of children, and love of mate(s). As evidence he cites age-old recurrent themes in literature and drama. Examples of human territorial behaviors are numerous. Man builds fences, separates his house into rooms for individuals, and appeases with gifts others whose territory he enters. Children are said to develop "individual distances" at the same time they develop a feeling for property. Man is also gregarious and forms social groups with definite dominance relationships. The dominance hierarchy is formalized in the formation of armies, and the need for authority is exemplified in religious practices.

Cross-cultural studies show that many emotional expressions are uniform across societies. Smiling, laughing, flirting, and greeting expressions of the eyes and mouth appear identical in most cultures even when analyzed by slow-motion photography (Fig. 1.6). Gestures, such as bowing and nodding, are also fairly stable and have been interpreted as submissive behaviors. Raising an open hand is a common greeting.

Although it is entertaining to view such aspects of human behavior as innate or fixed action patterns, the view is, we emphasize again, only speculative. The apparent universality of certain behaviors among humans does not prove their genetic basis. The cross-cultural occurrence

a   b   c   d

Figure 1.6 Many human facial expressions may be universal species traits. Examples of the eyebrow flash during greeting for the Balinese (upper row), the Huni tribe of New Guinea (middle row), and the Woitapmin tribe of Papua (lower row). Stop-frame photographic analysis reveals the time sequence of the eyebrow flash is essentially identical in all three cases. (From I. Eibl-Eibesfeldt, *Ethology: The Biology of Behavior*. Tr. by E. Klinghammer. New York: Holt, Rinehart and Winston, 1970.)

can also be explained on the basis that the long period of dependence on parents, common to all human infants, enforces a prolonged parent-child interaction during which the behaviors are learned. The same explanation applies to the similarities between our behaviors and those of our primate relatives, since other primates share with man a long period of infant dependence. In fact, recent studies on primates show vast differences in aggressiveness, not only among species but among races and tribes of the same species and indicate that much of this variability may be culturally determined. Learning—the ability to profit from experience—has developed to its highest degree in man. There is no reason to believe this ability evolved for the fulfillment of the trivial aspects of life. It evolved because it proved adaptively successful for the species.

If any clear statement can be made about *Homo sapiens* as an animal, it is that he is a very generalized animal. Many other animals are more specialized—some see better, some hear better, most smell better, some run faster, some climb better. In evolutionary terms, man is biologically the most generalized of the primates. Nothing about us is specialized except our brains. To overstate the case, we are the first species to evolve independently of environment. Unlike other animals we did not evolve specialized characteristics to deal with particular environmental pressures. Instead, we evolved the capability to control the environment. In this sense we are unique. We are the first animal to evolve the general ability to evolve our own environment. The ultimate consequences of this possibly fatal step in the evolution of organic matter remain to be determined.

Summary

Physiological psychology is concerned with the biological bases of behavior. It emphasizes the study of brain structure and function. Numerous disciplines—biology, anatomy, physiology, chemistry, psychology—have contributed to the development of physiological psychology as a science.

If human behavior is to be viewed in perspective, man must be considered in relation to his evolutionary history. While many scientists were aware of the apparent relation among organisms before Darwin proposed a theory of evolution in 1859, his theory attempted to explain the mechanisms responsible for environmental adaptation. The theory of evolution states that all living organisms are descended from a few organisms. Natural selection acts upon the reproductive success of populations and ensures that advantageous characteristics are continued in subsequent generations. Therefore, evolution can be viewed as the result of natural selection acting upon genetically predetermined characteristics. Mutation and variation of genetic material constitute the basis for evolution. They provide the diversity of individuals within a species that is essential for differential responses to environmental pressures.

The development of species is an important aspect of evolution. Two mechanisms, isolation and adaptive radiation, are utilized to explain species development. When a population is isolated, it adapts to the unique aspects of its environment and forms a new species that does not interbreed with the original population. Adaptive radiation occurs when a species encounters no competition from other organisms in an environment and, therefore, evolves to fill all the available ecological niches.

Hominoids evolved from early vertebrate forms. Vertebrates evolved from primitive, filter-feeding marine organisms, first in the form of a creature resembling the modern amphioxus, which was characterized by a central nerve cord. Freshwater, jawless, filter-feeding fish were the next development. From these jawless fish evolved jawed fish, from which there were many radiations. Eventually, the first amphibians evolved. Thousands of years later development of the ability to produce eggs with protective membranes enclosing the young made terrestrial life possible. The reptiles were the major development following this adaptation to life on dry land.

There were many radiations from the reptile forms—birds, the extinct dinosaurs, and the ancestors of mammals. The earliest known mammals were carnivorous beasts, well-adapted for speed, agility, and thermal regulation, and possessing a well-developed olfactory system. Two major adaptations then occurred that proved of great importance in the evolution of man: retention of the young within the uterus until they were able to climb into their mother's pouch and nurse, and development of placental circulation, which allowed retention of the young in the uterus until an even more advanced stage. These two adaptations ensured the protection of the young during a vulnerable period and enabled continuous population gains.

In man's evolution from his more recent ancestors, the critical factors were not physical size and strength. They were the development of true bipedalism, which freed the hands for other uses, and the development of a brain capable of conceiving of tool use. This second factor is especially important: Even primitive forms of tool using are uncommon among monkeys and apes.

The physical evolution of the three major forms of early man—*Australopithecus, Pithecanthropus*, and *Homo sapiens*—has been fairly well documented. *Australopithecus* was truly bipedal, and his body resembled that of a small modern man. His brain was relatively small compared with that of modern *Homo sapiens. Pithecanthropus*, one of the intermediary forms, possessed a more highly developed culture. Archaeologists have found choppers and scrapers with the remains of *Pithecanthropus*, as well as evidence that he possessed fire. Although it represents the first sign of significant tool use in the evolution of man, pithecanthropoid culture is considered to have been static and unprogressive.

The most significant change from *Australopithecus* to *Homo sapiens* is the development of the brain. The cranial capacity of *Australopithecus* is about 600 cc; that of *Homo sapiens*, about 1500 cc. This striking increase in size occurred over approximately 750 thousand years.

Concomitant with the physical evolution of modern *Homo sapiens* was his unprecedented cultural evolution. In about 20 thousand years modern man occupied the entire world. Many different tools developed: the stone blade, the spear, spear throwers, the bow and arrow. Painting and sculpture were practiced, and the cultivation of grains began. These developments were important in the rapid cultural evolution of modern *Homo sapiens*.

In studying man's behavior, it is important to remember that man is a genetically determined biological organism. However, the effect of environmental influences upon behavior should not be overlooked. Perhaps the most productive course is to consider man's behavior as a complex interaction between environmental influences and the biological structures, capabilities, and limitations that are genetically determined.

We need to assess the extent to which behavior patterns are fixed or modifiable by environmental influences. Research has shown that even innate behavior forms, such as the reproductive behavior of female ring doves, can be conditioned by experience. However, the behavior of organisms with large brains is more amenable to modification or learning than that of smaller-brained organisms. This underlies the trend of increased plasticity evident in evolution, but should not be misconstrued to mean that genetic factors are unimportant in the determination of the behavior of large-brained organisms.

Ethological research has influenced physiological psychology. Ethologists are interested in examining the evolutionary determination of natural behavior through the observation of animal behavior in natural environmental settings. They analyze behavior in terms of fixed action patterns and sign stimuli. Fixed action patterns are (1) stereotyped within one species, (2) presumably innate, (3) identical when repeated by the same animal, (4) completed every time they occur, and (5) resistant to modification. Sign stimuli are species-specific environmental stimuli that trigger the fixed action patterns. By analyzing animal behavior in terms of these two constructs, the ethologists hope to understand behavior patterns of animals within their natural environments.

2

Genetic and
developmental bases
of behavior

2

The dominant features associated with the presence of an extra Y chromosome include unusual height, excessive episodic aggressiveness, and borderline intelligence. Not surprisingly, an extra Y chromosome has been detected in some of the most renowned murderers of our time. One of the first such cases was that of Robert Tait, an Australian who was convicted in 1962 of bludgeoning to death an 81-year-old woman in a vicarage where he had gone seeking a handout. In 1965, Daniel Hugon, a 31-year-old French stablehand brutally strangled a Paris prostitute, with no apparent motivation. During the course of his trial in 1968, he was found to have an extra Y chromosome. In April, 1969, six-foot, eight-inch, 240-pound John Farley, nicknamed "Jolly Green Giant" because he was good-natured and "Big Bad John" because he was subject to fits of violent temper, confessed to having beaten, strangled, raped, and mutilated a Queens, New York, woman. He was defended on the grounds that due to the presence in his cells of an extra Y chromosome, he had no control over his actions or his judgment, and should therefore be found not guilty "by reason of insanity resulting from a chromosome imbalance."

(Jarvik et al., 1973, page 675)

These gruesome examples provide a striking demonstration of the importance of genetic factors in behavior, not to mention the eccentric character of our legal system. Individuals possessing the XYY genotype are males with one Y chromosome too many. The normal male genotype is XY; the normal female genotype, XX. Evidence now supports the view that this extra Y chromosome is far more common among men convicted of crimes of violence than among men in the general population.

Genetic makeup does influence behavior, as the XYY syndrome suggests. Further, it can be argued that human aggression may "reside" in the Y chromosome. Women are far less aggressive than men, at least in terms of physical violence. There are two possible explanations: (1) men are more and women less aggressive because society teaches these social roles, and (2) there is an inherent genetic determination of violence in men. The data on the XYY syndrome seem to provide some support for the genetic hypothesis.

The significance of the XYY syndrome extends well beyond the issue of violence per se. Previously discovered chromosomal abnormalities have been related either to physical abnormalities or to mental retardation—gross and global kinds of defects. The person with Klinefelter's syndrome (genotype XXY) is a "female" with many male characteristics—the very masculine "woman" athlete. The person with Down's syndrome (mongolism) has an extra non-sex chromosome and as a result is severely mentally retarded and has certain characteristic physical features and defects. These are relatively gross physical and intellectual abnormalities. However, the XYY genotype yields an abnormality that is primarily *behavioral* —aggression.

How does the Y chromosome lead to violence? Chromosomes are, after all, simply strands of chemical substances. The Y (male) chromosome, incidentally, is physically much smaller than the X (female) chromosome. It can be described as regressive or more dominant, the view depending perhaps on one's own chromosomes. In any event, the XY combination yields a normal male and the XX combination yields a normal female, with all the normal physical and behavioral differences. The extra Y chromosome exaggerates several male characteristics—for example, height and muscular build (some might add reduced intelligence as well)—in

Written in collaboration with Dr. Edwin Rubel, Department of Psychology, Yale University.

33
—————

Genetic and developmental bases of behavior

addition to aggression. This suggests that physical build and glandular activity are somehow controlled by the X and Y chromosomes. Brain development itself—the growth and structure of the nervous system—is under genetic control and influenced by hormones. However, there are still wide gaps in our understanding of how the chromosomes, the genetic material, control the growth and development, and ultimately the behavior, of human beings.

Each chromosome is composed of a great many *genes,* the ultimate structural unit of heredity. The structures and functions of all organisms are determined by the genes. Actually, genes merely determine the structures of chemical substances called *proteins.* Proteins are of two types: structural proteins and enzymes. The structural proteins form the structure of the organism, and the enzymes control the physical-chemical reactions of the organism.

In theory, all biological and behavioral functions can be traced back to gene action. In practice, however, as the organism develops, from the time the egg is fertilized, gene effects interact with environment. The critical distinction is made between the *genotype* (the underlying genetic makeup of an organism) and the *phenotype* (the outward expression of gene action as a result of interaction with the environment). All behavior among higher animals is phenotypic.

In this chapter we shall examine the fundamentals of genetics, the genetic bases of behavior (the subject matter of a fascinating new field called behavior genetics), the development of the nervous system, and the relative influence of genetic makeup and environment on behavior.

BASIC GENETICS

The laws of heredity

Although Darwin postulated that natural selection works by the inheritance of characteristics that proved adaptive, the mechanism was obscure. Around the time Darwin was formulating the final version of *Origin of Species,* an Austrian monk, Gregor Johann Mendel, was experimenting with the hybridization of peas. Mendel's findings, published in 1866, led him to hypothesize (1) that heredity is transmitted by independent, inheritable units; (2) when each parent contributes the same kind of unit, the progeny show this character, but when each parent furnishes a different kind of unit, a *hybrid* forms, and when the hybrids form their own reproductive cells, the two different kinds of units are "liberated" again; and (3) that the hereditary units are not affected by the experience of an individual.

In these hypotheses Mendel formulated the basic laws of heredity—the notion of genes—but for over three decades his work went unnoticed. Within five months of one another, in the year 1900, three European botanists rediscovered Mendel's work and brought it to the forefront of biology. The best known of these was Hugo De Vries, who stressed the concept of mutations as responsible for the development of new species. Modern geneticists do not stress mutation to the extent De Vries and his followers did. All realize, however, that although a population's genetic material is continually being reshuffled by mating, the only way for entirely new characters to be introduced is through mutation.

The basis of heredity

The science of genetics began with the rediscovery of Mendel's work. It was already known that the nucleus of every cell contains a number of pairs of tiny threadlike structures that reproduce themselves when the cell divides. These were called *chromosomes*. Different species were known to possess different numbers of pairs—the fruit fly, 8 chromosomes or 4 structurally similar pairs; the normal human, 46 chromosomes or 23 pairs (Fig. 2.1). It was also known that when an egg or a sperm cell is formed, only one chromosome of each pair is incorporated in the new sex cell, so that fertilization of egg by sperm produces a new individual with a full complement of chromosomal pairs.

In succeeding years it became apparent, through the efforts of such men as Thomas Hunt Morgan and H. J. Muller, that Mendel's units of heredity, the genes, must lie in the chromosomes. It was found that if

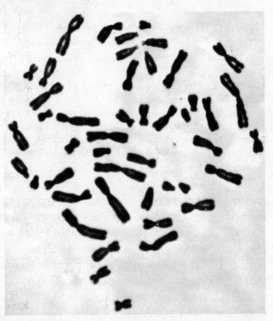

Figure 2.1 Chromosomes from a white blood cell of a human male. A staining procedure was used that selectively stained only the chromosomes in the cell. These chromosomes are in the process of division. The homologue for each of the chromosomes is located somewhere in the photomicrograph. (From Stern, C. *Principles of Human Genetics.* 3d Ed., San Francisco: W. H. Freeman and Co., 1973; original photomicrograph by Dr. Margery Shaw.)

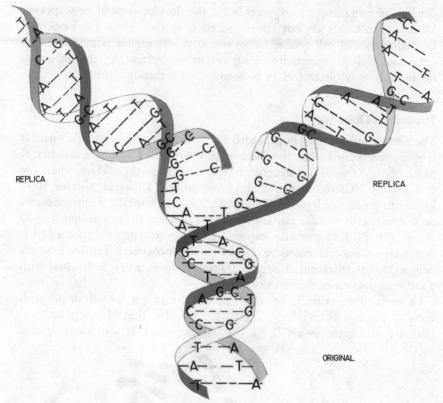

REPLICA

REPLICA

ORIGINAL

Figure 2.2 The double helix model of DNA replication proposed by Watson and Crick. The two strands coil around each other to form the double helix. During division, the DNA molecule unwinds, the base pairs separate, and one base of each pair remains attached to each strand. As shown here, a complementary strand is formed, resulting in two molecules of DNA following replication. (From Stent, Gunther S. *Molecular Biology of Bacterial Viruses*. Copyright © 1963 by W. H. Freeman and Co.)

mutations of the genes are produced by radiation, aberrant organisms are formed. The chromosomes were shown to consist mainly of two substances: *deoxyribonucleic acid* (DNA) and proteins. Of the two, DNA is the most stable, never leaves the nucleus, and is capable of self-replication. It has the fundamental property of genes. Further studies disclosed that all DNA has the same chemical composition. It consists of a simple sugar (deoxyribose), phosphate, and four bases: adenine, guanine, thymine, and cytosine (A, G, T, C).

The next great advance came with the discovery by J. D. Watson and F. H. C. Crick of the structure of the DNA molecule. Using x-ray crystallography, Watson and Crick proposed the double helix model (Fig. 2.2). According to this model the molecule consists of two strands wound around each other in a spiral. The backbone of each strand consists of a

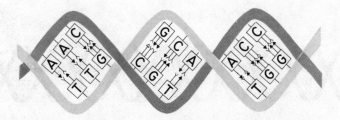

Figure 2.3 A segment of a DNA molecule showing the bonding combinations of the four bases—adenine, guanine, thymine and cytosine. As shown here, adenine bonds only with thymine and guanine only with cytosine. (Redrawn from Lerner, I. Michael. *Heredity, Evolution, and Society.* Copyright © 1968 by W. H. Freeman and Co.)

continuous sugar-phosphate-sugar-phosphate arrangement. The bases A, G, T, and C are attached to these backbones and in turn bond to each other, thereby attaching the two strands. Although the bases can occur in any sequence along a single strand, there is a fixed relation between the complementary strands. Adenine always bonds with thymine and guanine always with cytosine. The genetic code is contained in the sequence of bases. This code determines the properties and effects of each gene. The ability of DNA to reproduce itself lies in the specific bonding combination of the bases (Fig. 2.3). When the strands separate during cell division, they are able to produce identical copies of the original DNA molecule by picking up their appropriate partners.

The mechanisms of heredity

DNA never leaves the nucleus. Genes exert their direct effect by determining what proteins are to be produced in the *ribosomes* (specialized structures lying outside the nucleus in the cytoplasm of the cell). The mechanism for translation of the genetic code (base sequence in the DNA molecule) into a protein involves *ribonucleic acid* (RNA), a substance structurally similar to DNA but occurring throughout the cell. A special kind of RNA, called *messenger RNA*, transfers the code from the DNA to the ribosome, where another RNA, *transfer RNA*, probably acts in assembling the particular amino acids required to make the protein coded for by the DNA (Fig. 2.4). The types of proteins made, the places they are made, and the times they are made determine the sex of an individual, the color of its skin, and indeed whether it is an earthworm, a fruit fly, a mouse, or a man.

Normally formation of RNA takes place at times when cells are directing physiological functions but are not replicating. During these periods the two strands of the DNA helix are unwound. Only one strand actively produces RNA. It does this by picking up complementary bases from cellular material, but substitutes uracil (U) for thymine (T). When the chain of RNA is finished, it detaches from the DNA, leaves the nucleus

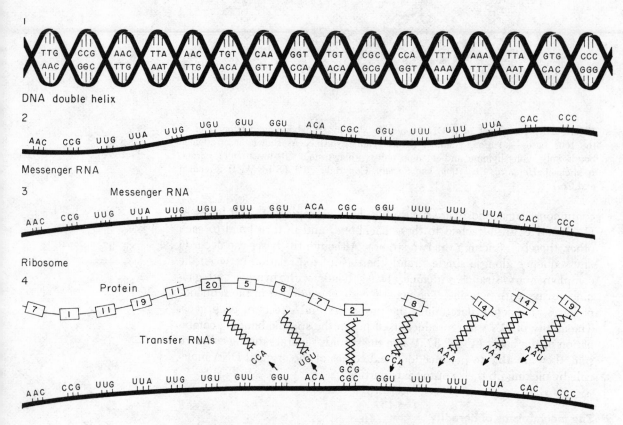

1 DNA double helix

| TTG | CCG | AAC | TTA | AAC | TGT | CAA | GGT | TGT | CGC | CCA | TTT | AAA | TTA | GTG | CCC |
| AAC | GGC | TTG | AAT | TTG | ACA | GTT | CCA | ACA | GCG | GGT | AAA | TTT | AAT | CAC | GGG |

2 Messenger RNA

AAC CCG UUG UUA UUG UGU GUU GGU ACA CGC GGU UUU UUU UUA CAC CCC

3 Messenger RNA

AAC CCG UUG UUA UUG UGU GUU GGU ACA CGC GGU UUU UUU UUA CAC CCC

Ribosome

4 Protein

7 1 11 19 11 20 5 8 7 2 8 14 14 19

Transfer RNAs

CCA UGU GCG CCA AAA AAA AAU

AAC CCG UUG UUA UUG UGU GUU GGU ACA CGC GGU UUU UUU UUA CAC CCC

Figure 2.4 Mechanism involved in the translation of the genetic code into a protein. Information on the DNA molecule is transcribed onto an RNA molecule (1). By a process of base pairing, a complementary RNA strand (called messenger RNA) is formed (2). Messenger RNA transfers the code from DNA to the ribosomes in the cytoplasm (3). The ribosomes are the sites of protein synthesis. Transfer RNAs and their attached amino acids (shown as boxed numerals in the figure) line up on the messenger RNA in a particular sequence (4). These amino acids combine to form polypeptide chains that make up proteins. (Adapted from Nirenberg, M. W. The genetic code: II. Copyright © 1963 by Scientific American, Inc. All rights reserved.)

of the cell, and attaches itself to the ribosomes (Fig. 2.4). This is the messenger RNA. Transfer RNA brings amino acids to the ribosome sites, where the amino acids are assembled into proteins—essentially long strings of amino acids hooked together. There are 20 amino acids that make up most proteins. There are four different bases in RNA, and it takes three bases to specify one amino acid. Thus the four bases taken three at a time permit a total of 64 different amino acids—considerably more than the actual 20 needed. Finally, the structural proteins and enzymes are formed at the ribosomes.

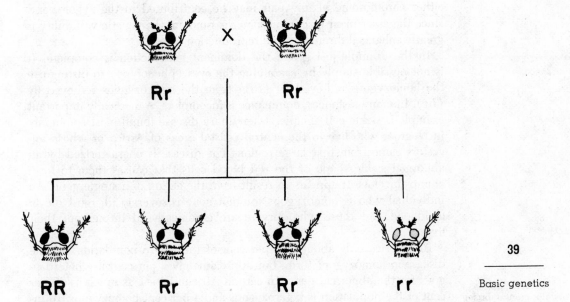

Rr   X   Rr

RR   Rr   Rr   rr

Figure 2.5 Example of the action of dominant and recessive genes in the determination of eye color (phenotype) in the fruit fly. When two flies heterozygous for eye color mate, the ratio of phenotypes of their offspring is 3:1, with three out of four flies having red eyes. However, the ratio of genotypes is 1:2:1, so that while three flies have red eyes, only one of them is homozygous for red eye color.

Genes for a particular trait occur at specific locations on specific chromosomes. The two chromosomes making up each pair contain *homologous* loci. When the egg or sperm cell is formed only one chromosome from each pair is included, and thus only one of the two genes present in the homologous loci of the parent is included. When fertilization occurs the cell again possesses paired chromosomes, but 50 per cent of the genes are from each parent. The various genes (base sequences) that may occur at any one locus are called the *alleles*. If the newly formed *zygote* (fertilized egg) inherits the same allele at a particular locus on the two homologous chromosomes, the individual is said to be *homozygous* for that gene; if different alleles are present on the two homologous loci, the individual is *heterozygous* for that gene. In the simplest case, when one gene at a particular locus is dominant (R) and another is recessive (r), the genotype of any member of the population can be RR, Rr, or rr. Suppose that R produces red eyes and r yields gray eyes in the fruit fly. When two heterozygotic members of the population, each with red eyes, mate ($Rr \times Rr$), the expected ratios of the offspring genotypes will be 1:2:1 (RR:Rr:rr) and the ratio of phenotypes will be 3:1 (i.e., three out of any four will have red eyes; Fig. 2.5). The important thing to note here is that the variability in the population is retained. Further, since either chromosome of any pair may be contributed to the zygote, and since the assortment of chromosomes is random, the genetic variability is greatly enhanced through sexual reproduction.

In the example just given, the dominant gene action is complete. It is not possible simply by examining the eyes (phenotype) to distinguish the homozygous red-eyed fly (*RR*) from the heterozygous red-eyed fly (*Rr*). In many instances, dominance is incomplete. A medically important example is sickle cell anemia, a hereditary disease found most commonly in Negroes who live in the central coastal areas of Africa or whose ancestors came from that large region. The disease is characterized by an abnormal sickle shape of the red blood cells that causes them to form clumps or clots. It appears to result from the action of a single gene. An individual who is homozygous for that gene is severely ill; most die in childhood and those who survive are chronically ill throughout their lives.

In America only about 0.25 per cent of the Negro population has the disease in homozygous form, but approximately 9 per cent are heterozygous for the abnormal gene. In certain African tribes, as much as 40 per cent of the population is heterozygous and 4 per cent homozygous. In individuals heterozygous for the sickle cell gene, the dominance of the normal gene is incomplete. Under ordinary circumstances these persons appear completely healthy, but they become ill at high altitudes where the blood does not receive enough oxygen. Thus the *carriers,* who have one normal gene and one sickle cell gene, ordinarily are not affected, but do respond abnormally to the stress of low oxygen.

The puzzling feature of the disease is its high incidence in certain regions of Africa. All we know about evolution suggests that such a debilitating gene should not exist in such a high per cent of the population. The reason for its persistence became clear when it was noticed that the regions of Africa where sickle cell anemia is most common are also the regions where malaria is most widespread and severe. The correlation is very close. Even in the central belt of Africa, tribes living in nonmalarial regions have virtually no sickle cell anemia. Individuals heterozygous for the sickle cell gene are resistant to malaria. Apparently the slightly different shape and properties of the abnormal red blood cells make it more difficult for the malarial organism to infect them (a necessary part of the malarial life cycle). In terms of survival in the malarial belt of Africa, individuals heterozygous for the sickle cell gene have a better chance of survival than do normal persons or those homozygous for the abnormal gene. An encouraging postscript to this story is the fact that the incidence of the sickle cell gene is steadily dropping among Negroes in America, where the abnormality has no adaptive value. This is in fact a striking example of human evolution occurring today.

Genetic variability is important in any population. It is necessary not only for the development of new species, but for the survival of an existing species in the face of a continually changing environment. The variability of a population's gene pool is increased by such processes as random assortment in reproduction, mutations (the rearrangement of the bases of the DNA molecule), crossing over (chromosome breakage and the exchange of parts between the pairs, permitting new combinations of genes on a particular chromosome), and the existence of more than two alleles for a given chromosomal locus.

GENETIC BASES OF BEHAVIOR

Genes do not act directly on behavior. They act only to regulate the production of proteins responsible for the structure and enzymatic activities of an organism. However, in most cases we are ignorant of the structural basis of behavior. For example, we know that a horse cannot run without legs and we know certain aspects of bone and muscle morphology that correlate with faster running in horses. But these are not enough; no horse breeder would stay in business if he based the breeding exclusively upon anatomical features of the animals' legs. Other features—temperament, neuromuscular coordination, stamina—make for a good race horse. Instead of considering only the legs, breeders attempt to mate horses that have proved successful on the turf. Similarly, investigators of the genetic bases of other behaviors pursue their studies either by examining individuals that display a particular behavior or by analyzing the ancestry of individuals that differ in a particular behavior.

Two points regarding the study of behavior genetics should be stressed. First, this approach does not disregard environmental effects upon behavior. On the contrary, it studies the interaction of genes and environment by attempting to quantify how much of the observed variability of a trait within a population results from genetic differences among individuals and how much results from environmental differences. The percentage of trait variance that is due to genotype differences has been termed the heritability of a trait. Heritability is a numerical measure or index indicating the extent to which a trait, characteristic, or behavioral tendency is inherited. Second, the vast majority of behavioral characteristics do not depend on a single gene that acts in an all-or-none fashion. Rather, behaviors depend on many loci where the contribution of each gene is small and cumulative. These systems are called *polygenic*.

Experimental studies on genetic manipulation

With animals it is possible to arrange laboratory conditions so that the environment is held reasonably constant and to practice artificial selection by (1) measuring a particular behavioral characteristic in a laboratory population, (2) selecting animals from the high and low extremes

TOTAL BLIND ALLEY ENTRANCES IN 19 TRIALS

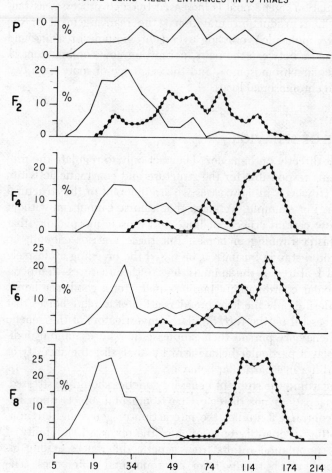

Figure 2.6 Selective breeding for maze-learning ability in rats. Maze-learning ability was measured in terms of the total number of blind alley entrances during 19 trials. There is a progressive differentiation in maze-learning ability between the "maze brights" and "maze dulls" from the F_2 to the F_8 generation. (Adapted from Tryon, R. C. Individual differences. In Moss, F. A. (ed.) *Comparative Psychology.* New York: Prentice-Hall, 1942, pp. 330–365.)

and mating animals within the extremes (high scorers with high scorers and lows with lows), and (3) testing offspring and in each subsequent generation continuing to mate within the extremes. If, under these environmental conditions, there is a genetic influence on the variability of the behavior, the two populations will diverge with each successive generation until the range of genetic variability is exhausted.

Pioneering studies using artificial selection were conducted by Robert Tryon at Berkeley. Tryon selected for maze learning in rats. After mea-

42

Genetic and
developmental bases
of behavior

suring maze performance in an unselected sample, he mated the fastest learners ("maze brights") with each other and the slowest learners ("maze dulls") among themselves. By the time this procedure had been continued for eight generations the two strains showed almost no overlap (Fig. 2.6).

Selective breeding experiments on rats and mice have shown that a wide range of behavioral traits can be varied by genetic manipulation. Characteristics studied include maze learning, emotionality as measured by tendency to defecate in an open-field situation, activity as measured by amount of running in a rotating wheel, aggressiveness, rate of avoidance learning, and susceptibility to sound-induced seizures. Many investigators have recently turned to the fruit fly *Drosophila* for the study of genetic influences on behavior. *Drosophila* can be bred for phototactic behavior—approach versus nonapproach to a light source—or for geotactic behavior—tendency to go up or down at a choice point. In one study of phototaxis in the fruit fly, Hirsch and Boudreau (1958) interbred animals that tended to approach a light source (positive phototaxis) and interbred animals that avoided the light. After 29 generations they estimated that even in this relatively simple organism only 57 per cent of the variance was genetically determined.

In addition to artificial selection experiments, much of our knowledge about genetic influences on the behavior of animals (including man) comes from comparisons of different strains or races. Consider the behavioral differences among breeds of dogs you have known. Scott (1964) compared five breeds of dogs on 34 behavioral traits and estimated the percentage of variability (heritability) attributable to breed differences. The mean heritability score for the 34 traits was 27 per cent, which was exactly the same as for the 10 physical traits he measured.

A large number of inbred mouse strains have been developed to enable examination of strain differences in behavior. By isolating a population and continually mating close relatives, the genetic variability of a population can be drastically reduced. After continual isolation and inbreeding, strains in which the individuals are genetically uniform, and distinct from other strains, can be produced. Inbred mouse strains have been found to differ on a number of behavioral traits including aggressiveness, locomotor activity, learning, alcohol preference, hoarding behavior, litter size, exploratory behavior, resistance to stress, and mating behavior. Although there are many criticisms of the inbreeding approach, mostly stemming from the fact that the amount of homozygosity produced could never occur in a successful natural population, this method has contributed immensely to our understanding of genetic influences on behavior.

Degree of locomotor activity provides a clear example of an inherited behavioral characteristic in inbred mouse strains (Fig. 2.7). General activity levels of six strains were tested by placing the animals on a grid floor marked off in squares. Activity was determined by the number of

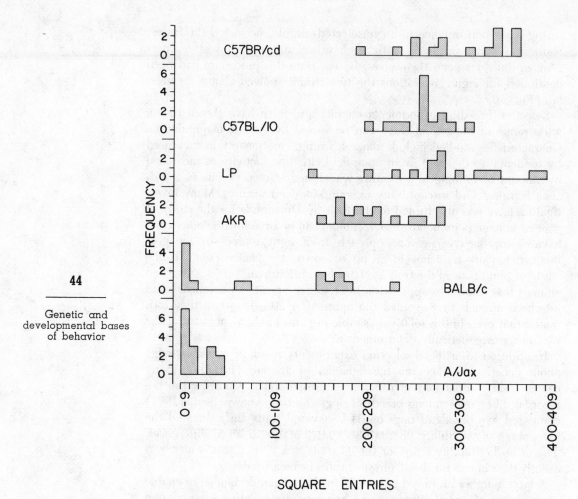

Figure 2.7 Degree of locomotor activity in six different inbred mouse strains. Loco-motor activity was defined as the number of squares crossed in 5-minute periods. Frequency indicates the number of animals from each strain that made a given number of square entries. Note the differences in degree of locomotor activity among various strains and the differences in the variability of activity within the strains. (McClearn, unpublished data.)

squares crossed in a 5-minute period. As shown in Figure 2.7, the six strains differed widely in degree of locomotor activity. They also differed in the amount of variability in activity within a strain. The strain plotted on the top graph shows virtually no activity and little variability. In contrast, the strain plotted on the lowest graph shows low activity but considerable variability. Thiessen (1972) has demonstrated that such strain differences in activity are maintained in a wide variety of testing situations over years of breeding. Activity appears to be a stable, genetically determined behavioral trait.

Emotionality would seem to be a much more complex aspect of behavior than activity. However, using amount of defecation in an open-field test situation as a simple index of emotionality, Lindzey et al. (1960) were able to show that emotional responsiveness differs for different strains of mice and remains so over years of breeding. Emotionality, at least in inbred strains of mice, is a relatively stable trait strongly determined by genetic factors.

An intriguing example of inbreeding is provided by the waltzing mouse. The strain was believed to have been developed as early as 80 B.C. in China and it probably has a continuous pedigree extending to the present. The behavior of the waltzers is quite striking: the animals whirl rapidly for long periods, but exhibit no sign of dizziness. The genetic defect is apparently expressed in damage to the vestibular system and inner ear.

Susceptibility to audiogenic seizure is another example. Certain strains of mice develop full-blown epilepsy-like seizures, often resulting in death, when exposed to particular sounds. The sound need not be loud; jingling of keys is an effective seizure stimulus. This trait appears to be under the control of several genes.

Effects of inbreeding

As the reader has no doubt realized, waltzing and audiogenic seizures are not adaptive. In general, inbreeding tends to result in the expression of both physical and behavioral defects. For every ten inbred strains of mice that are begun by breeders, at least nine die, and the deleterious effects of inbreeding are apparently even greater in man than in mouse. In general, the degree of relationship between human mating partners is directly related to deleterious effects on the children. In the general population, the death rate in children by age ten is 24 per 1000. For children of cousin marriages it is 81 per 1000 (Thiessen, 1972). An extensive study of Japanese schoolchildren found that children of first-cousin marriages are less fit on essentially all measures (17 were used) than control children from genetically unrelated parents (Schull and Neel, 1965). Table 2.1 presents these data. Compared with controls, children of first-cousin marriages began to walk and talk at a later age, showed less physical vitality, scored lower on intelligence tests, and performed less well in school. Even more striking are the deleterious effects on the unfortunate children of so-called nuclear incest matings (brother-sister or father-daughter). Adams and Neel (1967) compared 18 such children with children of nonrelated parents matched for age, weight, intelligence, and socioeconomic status. Among the children of incest, 5 died, 2 were mentally retarded, 1 had a cleft palate, and 3 showed only borderline intelligence. Only 7 of the 18 seemed moderately normal. Among the controls, 1 child showed a minor physical defect and all the others were normal.

Table 2.1 Effects of inbreeding on the behavior of Japanese schoolchildren

Characteristic	Sex	Average control value	Average offspring of first cousins	Inbreeding effect
Age when walked (months)	M	14.06	14.19	0.13
	F	13.62	14.07	0.45
Age when talked (months)	M	11.81	12.60	0.79
	F	10.38	10.82	0.44
Intelligence scores				
Performance score	M	57.37	54.94	2.06
	F	55.10	52.52	2.06
Verbal score	M	58.67	55.34	2.76
	F	57.01	53.46	2.76
School grade: language	M	3.09	2.95	0.10
	F	3.28	3.10	0.10

Data from Schull, W. J., and Neel, J. V. **The Effects of Inbreeding on Japanese Children.** New York: Harper and Row, Publishers, Inc. (1965).

Genetic and
developmental bases
of behavior

The devastating effect of close inbreeding on the viability, health, and intelligence of children seems to have been recognized by most primitive societies. Indeed, no society or culture of which we have knowledge condones incest. The pharoahs of ancient Egypt, who produced a remarkably defective line of rulers by incest, were the exception in their culture. Lindzey (1967) makes the interesting point that the universal taboo on incest may have been the result of natural selection acting on primitive human cultures. All those tribes that did not prevent incest died out long ago.

Effects of hybridization

Hybrid vigor is the opposite of inbreeding. When two separate strains mate, the offspring tend to be healthier than the parents. This hybrid vigor has long been known by agriculturists. All corn produced today is hybridized. Hybrid corn is healthier and has longer ears than the parent strains. There is no clear evidence on hybrid vigor in man. The author is tempted to cite the peoples of Polynesia as an example, but there are no real data. Sickle cell disease, discussed above, is a rather special example. In the malarial areas of Africa, children heterozygous for the sickle cell gene have a reproductive advantage over both homozygous and normal individuals. A more puzzling case is Tay-Sachs disease, a devastating form of infantile mental deficiency in the individual homozygous for the appropriate gene. It occurs primarily among the Ashkenazic Jewish population. Oddly enough, individuals heterozygous for the gene show a slight (6 per cent) reproductive advantage over normals (Dobzhansky, 1964).

Studies on twins

Most research on genetic influences in human behavior has utilized twins, usually comparisons between identical or monozygotic (MZ) twins and like-sexed fraternal or dizygotic (DZ) twins. The rationale for this approach is that MZ twins are genetically identical, while DZ twins are genetically no more similar than ordinary siblings. Thus, any differences between MZ twins must be entirely environmental, while differences between DZ twins are both hereditary and environmental. With the assumption that the effects of environment are equal in the two groups, differences between MZ twins can be subtracted from those between DZ twins, and the result should be a measure of the effects of genetic differences. Numerous studies have been conducted in this way on intelligence test scores as well as personality variables. Typically, investigators have found a small but reliable genetic component in personality variables and a larger genetic component in intelligence test scores. We shall return to this topic later in the chapter.

Behavioral consequences of single gene defects

Certain types of severe mental deficiency result from defects at a single gene locus. For example, a disease known as *phenylketonuria* (PKU) is characterized by severe mental retardation and the presence of phenylpyruvic acid in the urine. Phenylketonuria results from the inheritance of a double recessive gene. The individual who is homozygous for the gene produces insufficient amounts of a substance required for the normal conversion of phenylalanine (a common amino acid present in many protein foods) to tyrosine. The disease process itself is believed to result from increases in tissue and blood levels of phenylpyruvic acid and other nonnormal by-products of phenylalanine, which act as toxins on the developing brain. By the time the affected infant is four to six months of age, severe and irreversible brain damage has resulted. It is now possible to detect phenylketonuria within hours after birth and to prevent serious mental deficiency by feeding the child a diet low in phenylalanine. Most hospitals routinely test every child for phenylketonuria within two days of birth. It is now possible also to identify heterozygous carriers of the recessive gene and, through genetic counseling, to warn such persons of the danger to their offspring before birth or even conception.

A host of other metabolic diseases causing mental deficiency are now known to be genetically transmitted. Two of these, *infantile amauratic idiocy* (Tay-Sachs disease) and *juvenile amauratic idiocy*, result from inheritance of a double recessive gene at a single locus and involve malfunction of lipid metabolism. Effects of the former are noticeable at a few months of age; those of the latter at two to ten years of age. *Huntington's chorea,* a condition characterized by progressive mental impairment as well as involuntary movements, illustrates the fact that genetically caused mental deficiency need not arise early in life. This disease is transmitted by a dominant gene and its onset is usually between the ages of 30 and 50 years.

Behavioral and physical consequences of chromosomal abnormalities

Abnormality in the chromosome complement is responsible for certain mental and physical disorders. The best known example is *Down's syndrome* (also called mongolism because the victims have slanted eyes). In addition to the slanted eyes and other morphological features, persons afflicted are severely retarded (IQ usually between 20 and 60). Down's syndrome is the most common single definable cause of mental retardation in the world, occurring in approximately 1 out of every 500 to 600 births and accounting for about 10 per cent of the persons currently institutionalized for mental retardation in the United States. It is caused by a chromosomal abnormality called trisomy-21. Sometimes, instead of the usual complement of 46 chromosomes (23 pairs), the person has 47, including an extra chromosome of pair number 21. Sometimes parts of chromosomes 21 and 15 have been exchanged during formation of the sex cells and the afflicted person carries the extra twenty-first chromosome as part of pair number 15. Although the reasons for occurrence of this extra genetic material are unknown, it has been shown that Down's syndrome is more likely to occur in offspring of women who are older than the average child-bearing age.

The effects of abnormalities in the number and kind of sex chromosomes on human structure and personality have attracted great interest. Normally, a male has one X chromosome and one Y chromosome, much shorter than the X. The normal female has two X chromosomes. The person with *Klinefelter's syndrome* has one Y and two X chromosomes (genotype *XXY*) and is phenotypically male with some degree of feminization, reduced sexual drive, and sometimes mental retardation. Some Soviet "female" athletes with physical abilities superior to those of normal females have been shown to have Klinefelter's syndrome—a situation that creates problems both of definition and of international relations. Although many persons with Klinefelter's syndrome have been reported to have personality problems, cause and effect cannot be disentangled and the data are not clear. Klinefelter's syndrome is surprisingly common, appearing in 1 out of every 400 births.

The person with Turner's syndrome has a normal X chromosome but lacks the Y chromosome (genotype *XO*). Such an individual is phenotypically female, but is short in stature and has diminished sexual characteristics. She appears normal in general intelligence, but shows a specific deficiency in spatial discriminations. The syndrome is rather rare, occurring in 1 out of 3000 births.

Perhaps the most intriguing of the sex chromosome abnormalities is the *XYY* syndrome (page 33). Individuals with *XYY* genotype tend to be tall, muscular, retarded, highly aggressive males. The syndrome was originally found among prison inmates and many studies have restricted their samples to tall prisoners with violent histories—a limitation that obviously introduces sampling bias. Nonetheless, most surveys of tall prisoners reveal an incidence of *XYY* genotype of from 2 to 12 per cent. In the normal population the incidence appears to be about 0.1 per cent (McClearn, 1970; Jarvik et al., 1973). Despite inadequate data, there is a factual basis for believing that an extra Y chromosome increases both maleness and aggressiveness. It is not hard to extrapolate from this extreme syndrome to much more subtle genetic influences of the normal Y chromosome on aggressive behavior.

In general, abnormal numbers of sex chromosomes result in abnormalities of both physique and behavior. It would be surprising if this were not so. Research attempting to correlate chromosomal abnormality with behavioral deviation has only barely begun and so far has dealt only with additions and deletions of entire chromosomes. Many abnormalities undoubtedly exist at the level of individual genes that cannot yet be detected with the microscope.

Polygenic behavioral characteristics

When a property or characteristic exhibits a continuous or quantitative distribution in a population, it likely results from occurrences at more than one gene locus. It is polygenic. The field of quantitative genetics is concerned with the study of such characteristics. The basic approach is to determine the degree of relation or correlation in performance on quantitative measures such as IQ or personality tests for individuals who are or are not related. The most valuable comparisons have been of identical (MZ) and fraternal (DZ) twins and unrelated individuals. Results of these comparisons indicate quite clearly that such traits as schizophrenia, manic depressive psychosis, and intelligence are highly heritable (McClearn and DeFries, 1973).

Schizophrenia. The data make it increasingly clear that schizophrenia is a genetic disease. Schizophrenia is the most widespread and severe form of mental illness. It occurs in about 1 per cent of the population in all countries and all cultures in the world, no matter how advanced or primitive. Schizophrenia is characterized by varying degrees of disordered thought processes, hallucinations and delusions, and personality disintegration. Although there is disagreement over exact diagnostic criteria, the most widely agreed-upon characteristic is disordered thinking. We have no knowledge at present of the possible chemical, neural, or biological abnormalities that result in schizophrenia; nonetheless, there is no question that they exist. Although environmental, cultural, and social factors may be important, particularly in precipitating schizophrenic episodes, the disease is fundamentally psychobiological.

The great majority of studies of identical versus fraternal twins has indicated a much higher concordance for schizophrenia in identical twins. Typical values range from 42 to 86 per cent for identical twins and from 9 to 15 per cent for fraternal twins (McClearn, 1970). Thus, if an identical twin develops schizophrenia, the chances are at least even that his twin will also develop the disease.

A most convincing study of the heritability of schizophrenia in unrelated, adopted children was done by Heston (1966). He identified 47 children born to mothers who were diagnosed schizophrenic patients in a state hospital. The children were all separated from their mothers within a few days of birth and placed in adoptive homes. A comparable sized group of children adopted at the same age from nonschizophrenic mothers was used as a control. Of the 47 children of schizophrenic mothers, 5 themselves became schizophrenic, and half of the children exhibited clear psychosocial disabilities. The control children showed no schizophrenia and a much lower incidence of psychosocial difficulties.

Although we have characterized schizophrenia as a disorder caused by polygenic abnormalities, not all authorities agree with this definition. Some believe it can be accounted for by a single recessive gene; others think it represents several different single gene abnormalities all diagnosed together as schizophrenia; and still others believe it results from defects in two or more genes. Finally, it must be admitted that some authorities persist in questioning the extent to which schizophrenia has a clear genetic basis (see McClearn and DeFries, 1973, for a careful discussion of these possibilities).

Intelligence. Much heated debate in recent years has been concerned with the degree to which intelligence is inherited. Much of the emotion stems from assertions that there are genetic racial differences in intelligence. These two issues must be separated. A review of the data can lead only to the conclusion that intelligence, as measured by standard intelligence tests, is significantly determined by genetic factors. In contrast, the data on race and intelligence are impossible to interpret at present.

Several obvious points must be made in any discussion of the genetic basis of intelligence. First, intelligence is an idea—a theoretical construct with almost as many meanings as the number of authorities who have written on the subject. To measure intelligence we must measure performance of some sort. The most widely used measures are standard IQ tests such as the Stanford-Binet. Intelligence measured by such an IQ test is nothing more or less than a test score. It has no independent meaning. It does, however, have relations and correlations with other kinds of performance.

Second, the IQ score is a general test score and does not, per se, specify particular kinds of abilities. It is not *necessarily* a prediction of success in life. Many successful persons do not have high IQs and many individuals with high IQs are strikingly unsuccessful. There is, however, a gross general relation between IQ test performance and life performance. An individual with an IQ far below normal will not perform in most situations as well as a normal person. The correlation between IQ and school grades is about 0.5—a significant but not a terribly close relation. The general relation between IQ and adaptive success is indicated in the long-term study of gifted children begun by Terman in 1921. He followed the careers of 1500 children, all of whom had IQs of 140 or higher. As a group, they were definitely superior to the average in health, development, literary and scientific achievement, and income, and did not differ from the average in terms of mental health or emotional adjustment.

Third, environment significantly influences IQ test performance. If an individual is tested at several times over a period of years, changes in IQ as large as 20 points are not uncommon. Children moved from impoverished to enriched environments show increased IQ scores. A significant portion of IQ performance is dependent on cultural experience and learning. Many items on standard IQ tests assume familiarity with middle-class western culture. Children are assumed to be familiar with such things as money, stores, cars, and houses. Another factor of critical importance is maturation. Children suffering from chronic malnourishment perform poorly on IQ tests. None of these factors is surprising. IQ is a performance test and is influenced by all factors that influence human performance. Given all these qualifications, it actually is rather surprising that IQ test scores show highly significant heritability. That they do suggests a profound role for genetic factors in the determination of IQ test performance.

A summary of data on intelligence of MZ and DZ twins is given in Table 2.2. Identical twins raised together are identical on school performance and nearly identical in IQ. The correlation for IQ remains high when they are raised apart (from at least six months of age), but school performance is more variable. A common criticism of such data is that MZ twins raised apart are placed for adoption in homes of similar socioeconomic level. Burt (1966) evaluated this by correlating occupational status of the two families in which each MZ twin pair was raised. The correlation was slightly negative. Thus the high correlation in IQ for MZ twins raised apart cannot be explained by similar socioeconomic levels in the adoptive homes: the socioeconomic levels were not similar.

Recent work on the genetic basis of intelligence has emphasized the heritability of different kinds of abilities. The abilities, loosely defined, that seem to show strong genetic determination are those measured by the subtests Information, Vocabulary, Picture Arrangement, and Digit

Table 2.2 Correlations of behavioral and physical phenotypes

		Phenotype			
Group	N	Stanford-Binet IQ score	General school achievement	Height	Weight
MZ reared together	95	.92	.98	.96	.93
MZ reared apart	53	.86	.62	.94	.88
DZ reared together	127	.53	.83	.47	.59
Siblings reared together	264	.50	.80	.50	.57
Siblings reared apart	151	.42	.53	.54	.43
Unrelated reared together	136	.25	.54	—.07	.24

Data from Burt (1966), as cited in McClearn (1970). Reproduced, with permission, from "Behavioral Genetics" by G. E. McClearn, **Ann. Rev. Genetics 4.** Copyright © 1970 by Annual Reviews, Inc. All rights reserved.

Symbol Substitution of the Wechsler Intelligence Scale for Children (WISC), a widely used IQ test. In contrast, results on the subtests Memory and Reasoning showed these abilities to have little or no heritability (Vandenberg, 1967, 1968). These results are based on a careful statistical analysis of the occurrence of a significant difference between MZ and DZ twins on the various subtests.

In terms of underlying genetic factors, Vandenberg's work suggests that there are at least four different genetic units corresponding to the four heritable abilities. However, the number of genetic components varies with the type of test used. Estimates of the total number of gene loci involved in intelligence vary from 3 or 4 to more than 70. The issue is clearly unresolved. In contrast, extremely high IQ scores may be under the control of single genes, and abnormally low IQs may also represent single gene actions, as in the case of children with phenylketonuria.

An issue of potential concern for the future evolution of man has to do with the possibility that intelligence is declining in the human race. Many studies have shown that there is a significant inverse relation between IQ and family size. The apparent conclusion is that more individuals are continually being born with lower IQs, and it leads to the estimate that the mean IQ should decline from 2 to 4 points per generation. Since mankind has existed as modern *Homo sapiens* for at least two thousand generations, either our remote ancestors were incredibly intelligent or there is something wrong with the inference. In fact, the data from long-term testing of children indicate no decrease in IQ. Table 2.3 provides the explanation. Individuals with low IQs have significantly fewer children: many with extremely low IQs are institutionalized since childhood and have no opportunity to mate. On balance, the IQ of the population as a whole appears relatively stable.

Table 2.3 Reproduction rates of individuals with varying IQ levels

IQ range	0–55	56–70	71–85	86–100	101–115	116–130	131+
Number	29	74	208	583	778	269	25
Average no. children	1.4	2.5	2.4	2.2	2.3	2.4	3.0

Data from Higgins et al. (1962). Reproduced, with permission, from "Behavioral Genetics" by G. E. McClearn, **Ann. Rev. Genetics 4.** Copyright © 1970 by Annual Reviews, Inc. All rights reserved.

Importance of genetic makeup to behavior

Genetic makeup influences a number of human behavioral characteristics. In the case of severe mental disturbances, such as schizophrenia or Down's syndrome, genetic makeup appears to play a large role. But to what extent does it account for the variability of human behavioral characteristics in the normal population? Obviously, a precise answer to this question is impossible, but all evidence indicates that its role may not be overriding. In the evolution of mammals, especially man, natural selection has stressed behavioral plasticity. Man has been selected in part for the ability to change his behavior rapidly in accordance with small environmental changes. Further, the effectiveness of these behavioral changes are remembered. In a very real sense, selection pressure on man has been upon the ability to learn.

DEVELOPMENT OF THE NERVOUS SYSTEM

Physical growth, development, and aging are under strong genetic control from the time the egg is fertilized until the organism dies. Environment also plays a role. At birth, the importance of the external environment increases abruptly. Prior to that time, the environment external to the mother has little effect on the developing fetus, so long as no major catastrophe occurs. But the intrauterine environment of the embryo is believed to be highly important from the time of conception, although little is at present known about its influence on either normal or abnormal development.

About eight days after the human ovum is fertilized, it attaches to the lining of the uterus and divides into two cells. From this time on, the rate of cellular multiplication becomes rapid. The embryo differentiates into three germinal layers of cells—*endoderm, ectoderm,* and *mesoderm.* Cells of the endoderm eventually form internal organs, those of the mesoderm form the skeletal muscles, and those of the ectoderm become skin and the nervous system.

The developing human is termed an *embryo* for the first two months of development and is called a *fetus* from that time until birth. The heart begins to beat at the end of the first month, the kidney starts excreting urine by the third month, and by the fifth month vigorous skeletal movements—kicking, squirming, jerking—begin to occur. The lungs develop early, but are filled with fluid and essentially nonfunctional until birth. A premature infant can survive, with help, if it is seven months or older and weighs about 5 lb.

Embryonic development

Cell differentiation. The growth and differentiation of the nervous system illustrates the fact that at all stages of development both structure and behavior represent a complex interaction of genetic makeup and environment. Early in the life of an embryo, the cells of tissues destined to become the nervous system look similar to other cells. Then, during the process by which the embryonic cells are divided into endoderm, mesoderm, and ectoderm layers (Fig. 2.8), a rod-shaped structure of mesodermal tissue forms just beneath a portion of the ectoderm and stretches from the head almost to the tail end of the embryo. This axial rod, called the *notochord*, serves as a trigger for the overlying ectoderm cells to differentiate into nervous tissue. Without the notochord the ectoderm cells remain undifferentiated. If a piece of notochord is placed beneath other tissues—for example, presumptive belly tissues—a second nervous system begins to form. Alternatively, presumptive nervous tissue can become belly tissue if transplanted appropriately. Thus, the nervous system at its very start is dependent on its environment.

Cells at this stage are said to be undetermined, in that they can be made to develop in a number of directions. Once these cells come into

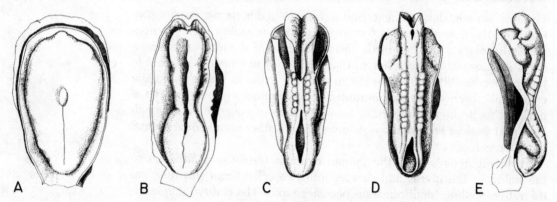

A B C D E

Figure 2.8 Early development of the neural groove and tube in the human embryo. A, The beginning of the neural groove formed from an infolding of the ectodermal layer. B, Further development of the neural groove. C, The neural groove is beginning to close. D, Continuation of the closing of the neural groove from the midline in both rostral and caudal directions. E, A lateral view of the embryo showing nearly complete closure of the neural tube. (Adapted from Buchanan, A. R. *Functional Neuro-anatomy.* 4th Ed. Philadelphia: Lea & Febiger, 1961.)

contact with the notochord, however, *determination* occurs and they become nervous tissue, even if transplanted. The process whereby the notochord causes determination is called *induction:* the notochord induces the overlying ectoderm to become nervous tissue. Induction, although little understood, appears to be one of the most pervasive phenomena in development. In all cases it acts to limit or specify the developmental opportunities of one group of cells through their interaction with another group. As cells become more and more determined, they slowly differentiate into the tissues and organ systems that constitute the adult organism. *Differentiation,* then, is this entire process during which a relatively unspecialized group of cells is molded into a heart, a kidney, a stomach, a muscle, or a brain.

Stages of development. In 1842 Karl Ernst von Baer, a pre-Darwinian evolutionary theorist, stated the principle that the young stages of higher animals resemble the young stages of lower ones. Two decades later Ernst Haeckel reformulated this principle into the view that an individual during its ontogeny (growth) goes through a series of forms resembling its adult ancestors; hence the expression "ontogeny recapitulates phylogeny." The phrase implies that evolutionary history (phylogeny) can be directly studied through the development of an individual organism. Current evidence indicates that von Baer was to some extent correct: animals of the same phylum usually develop similarly up to a point, where they diverge according to their own specializations. The gill pouches of a mammalian embryo never develop into functional gills like those of an adult fish, but they clearly resemble the gill pouches of an embryonic fish. Similarly, the brain development of a human embryo and that of a fish, an amphibian, or a bird resemble one another very closely until a time when each begins to develop its own specializations.

The early stages of nervous system formation are quite similar in all vertebrate embryos (Figs. 2.8 and 2.9). Soon after the upper ectoderm comes into contact with the notochord, a *neural plate* becomes the prominent feature of the upper surface. Gradually a longitudinal groove forms in the middle part of the embryo and spreads slowly toward both ends, while the edges of the plate become elevated. The edges become progressively more elevated and the groove deepens until these edges meet and fuse, forming the *neural tube* (Fig. 2.8). The closure of the tube, like the formation of the groove, proceeds from the middle of the embryo simultaneously toward both ends. As the tube closes, small groups of cells on the edges are not incorporated into the tube and split off, forming the *neural crest*. At its early stages, the neural groove is made up of a single layer of rapidly dividing cells. As the neural tube closes, cell division still occurs primarily at the inner space of the tube, but an increasing number of the new cells begin to migrate toward the outside of the tube, thereby forming three distinct layers. The internal layer con-

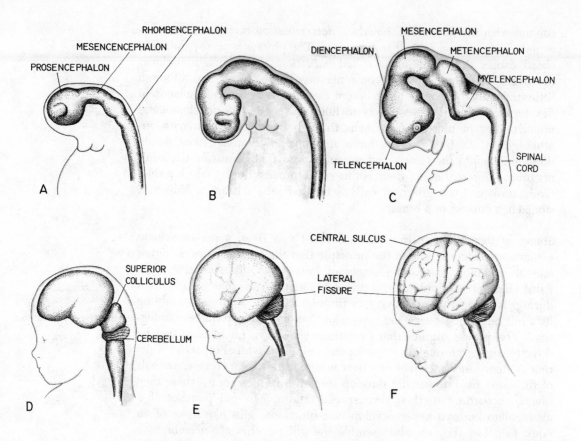

Figure 2.9 Development of human brain from 3 weeks to birth, lateral view. A, 3-week embryo, the three primary brain regions are formed. B, 4-week embryo, the forebrain, midbrain, and hindbrain are increasingly developed. C, 7-week embryo, the forebrain is now differentiated into the telencephalon and diencephalon, and the hindbrain into the metencephalon and myelencephalon. D, 11-week fetus, the cerebellum is clearly differentiated. E, 6-month fetus, the cerebral hemispheres are further developed. F, newborn infant, the sulci and gyri can be seen on the cerebral hemispheres. (Adapted from Patten, B. M. *Human Embryology.* 2d Ed. New York: McGraw-Hill, 1953.)

tains cells that are still dividing. The middle layer consists of cell bodies that are beginning to form the gray matter or nuclear regions of the nervous system. In most cases these cells never divide again; this region contains the same cells that are found in the adult organism. The outside layer is temporarily cell-free, containing the fiber processes of cells in the other two zones. Soon, however, in some areas of the brain, this layer will contain cells that have continued their outward migration.

From the time the neural plate is forming, its anterior (front) end is wider, and as the tube closes three bulges appear, called the three primary brain regions (Fig. 2.9). The most anterior region, the forebrain, gives rise to the cerebral cortex and other higher brain regions (Fig. 2.9; see also Chapter 3, where these anatomical terms are explained). The midbrain remains undivided and gives rise to the adult midbrain. The hindbrain gives rise to the cerebellum and lower brain stem regions.

Through differential growth in these regions, the brain slowly takes its adult shape. Even at these early stages, the parts of the brain are not completely independent of one another, and they depend on the surrounding structures to induce normal differentiation. For example, in early stages, if the posterior (back) region is removed entirely, rotated 180 degrees, and replaced, so that the anterior end is now in contact with the spinal cord and the posterior end abuts the midbrain, a normal brain develops. These cells can be induced by their environment to form quite different nuclear regions having different functions.

While cell division is still rapidly occurring at the surface, the migrating neurons begin to form into groups, making up the nuclei of the adult brain. During this phase of development, differentiation is occurring at a rapid rate throughout the nervous system. Not only are brain nuclei forming, but fiber tracts are beginning to connect the nuclei; some of the neural crest cells are forming into spinal ganglia, sending their processes into the spinal cord as well as out toward the skin; and the optic stalks have grown out of the diencephalon to form eye cups at their ends. These eye cups induce formation of a lens from the overlying ectoderm. The eye is thus formed directly from the brain tissue.

Regulation of development. Much of this differentiation appears to be self-controlled. Muscle movements begin even in the absence of sensory input, and brain nuclei will mature when isolated from their respective sensory or motor organs. However, after the basic pattern of the nervous system has been established, its periphery becomes more and more important. For example, neural centers form with an excess of cells over that seen in the mature organism. About the time when a region forms connections with the periphery (i.e., organs and receptors outside the brain), many of the cells degenerate so that the final number of cells is the normal one. However, if the peripheral organ (e.g., eye) is removed, an even greater number of cells degenerate so that the brain region atrophies (shrinks); conversely, if the peripheral organ is somehow enlarged over its usual size, fewer than normal cells degenerate. This effect has been shown in the brain stem and spinal cord for both motor and sensory nuclei in many vertebrates.

It is interesting to note that the time at which the periphery begins having this influence on neural development appears to correlate with the time at which the peripheral organs become functional. This observation does not, however, allow the conclusion that in all cases function is necessary for the establishment of neuronal connections. If parts of the nervous system are grown in tissue culture, connections among many neurons will form.

The role of functional activity in sensory and motor systems in regulating the future development of the nervous system and behavior is, at present, one of the most controversial topics in developmental neurobiology. One view states that there is primarily a unidirectional relation in which nervous system development is not dependent on feedback from the environment, but is preprogrammed to develop in an autonomous fashion along a particular course. The other view envisions a reciprocal relation in which nervous system development is continually modulated by environmental stimuli, and the normal development of the nervous system *depends* on this modulation.

Victor Hamburger and his colleagues, through experiments on the behavior of chick embryos, have stressed the autonomous aspects of behavior development. By starting with careful descriptions of the types and rates of movement at each stage of pre-hatching development, these authors have been able to describe effects of various operations. For example, by removing part of the spinal cord or sectioning it near the brain, they found that each level of the cord can initiate behavior in the associated body structures. The main effect of these operations was to reduce the total amount of activity without substantially changing the pattern of movements. The influence of sensory stimulation from the skin and muscles was studied in deafferentation experiments. Removing input from the skin and muscles does not seriously affect behavior patterns from embryonic day 3, when behavior begins, to day 17, three days prior to hatching. Although these experiments cannot rule out the effects of early stimulation on hatching or post-hatching behavior patterns, they do show that a great deal of behavior development can occur in the absence of sensory stimulation.

Hormonal influences on brain and behavior development are of critical importance. Several studies have shown that excess of the thyroid hormone thyroxine stimulates abnormally early maturation of some neural areas and premature development of many reflexes. Too little thyroxine early in life can lead to such devastating effects as a delay in the maturation of many reflex behaviors, reduced neuronal growth, abnormal brain wave patterns, and reduced learning ability. Most of the effects of thyroxine depend on an adequate supply of the hormone during a specific *critical period* in the organism's development (in rat, the first 15 days after birth). If the hormone is not present at this time, the deficiencies cannot be overcome. (This contrasts with the situation in adulthood. The behavioral deficits produced by removal of the thyroid gland in an adult can be overcome by hormone replacement.)

The presence of male sex hormones, *androgens*, during a critical period in embryonic development, influences neural processes that determine whether male or female behavioral characteristics will emerge. One of the most dramatic demonstrations was produced by Young and his co-workers by injecting female monkeys with androgens during pregnancy.

In three such cases, the genetically female offspring were pseudohermaphroditic (possessed incomplete male sex organs as well as female sex organs). These experiments will be discussed further in Chapter 9.

Postnatal development

At birth, the infant possesses a number of reflex behaviors and a brain that is largely, if not entirely, functional. However, the reflexes are not yet under control of the cerebral cortex, the highest brain region. For example, the grasp reflex is very strong at birth: A newborn baby can support its entire weight by gripping a bar. However, by the end of one month, the grasp reflex is considerably weakened. An infant monkey has a similarly strong grasp reflex, but its grasp remains strong and apparently comes under voluntary control by about 20 days after birth. In monkeys, and no doubt the early ancestors of man as well, this reflex is critical for survival. If the infant does not hold onto its mother's fur, it will fall from its riding position when the mother moves about and may be left behind to die.

The brain waves generated in the cerebral cortex (Chapter 4) can be recorded from the scalp overlying the brain of a newborn infant. In fact, a fetus's brain waves can even be recorded from the mother's abdomen. However, structural maturation of the cerebral cortex requires several years, and the cerebral cortex and other higher brain structures change continually throughout the entire life span of man.

THE NATURE-NURTURE CONTROVERSY

Developmental psychobiology is the study of the growth and development of brain and behavior. Since all organisms grow from single cells, all aspects of biology and behavior have a developmental history. A complete survey of developmental psychobiology amounts to a complete review of psychobiology. Partly for this reason, many psychologists feel that development per se does not really constitute a separate field of study. Rather, if one is interested in a particular phenomenon, such as instrumental learning, the development of the behavior as a result of both growth and experience is simply a part of the topic.

A somewhat contrasting view is held by many biologically oriented psychologists, who tend to favor the notion the a significant part of behavioral development is preprogrammed, that is, dependent on the growth and development of the nervous system. Particular kinds of learning can occur only when the appropriate brain and body substrates have developed. The following passage from Daniel Lehrman illustrates this view:

A newborn kitten can withdraw from an electric shock, and it can show a motor response to a tone; but attempts to develop a simple condi-

59

The nature-nurture
controversy

tioned association between the tone and the withdrawal to shock fail until the kitten is a couple of weeks old. It would, however, be premature to conclude from this that the kitten cannot learn very much during its first 10 days. My colleague Jay Rosenblatt, while watching kittens with their mothers, noted that by the time the kittens are 2 or 3 days old each kitten is feeding from a particular nipple of the mother and has developed a particular route for getting to that nipple. Under some circumstances it can be demonstrated that by the time the kitten is 7 or 8 days old, it has even developed what looks like territorial rights to the nipple; it shows a tendency to cling to its "rightful" nipple when challenged by a sibling, while being willing to give up a "wrong" nipple if it has latched onto one.

Now, that is a rather important, and rather complex, kind of learning that can be seen in the kitten during its first few days of life. The difference between the scientist who cannot demonstrate learning in a kitten until it is more than 10 days old, and the one who can show it when the kitten is 3 days old is, I think, the difference between the investigator who is trying to find out when the kitten can learn something that the **experimenter** wants it to learn and one who is trying to find out when the kitten can learn something that the **kitten** wants to learn! (Lehrman, 1971, page 465)

These contrasting views of the importance of growth and development find their origins in the nature-nurture controversy. Behavioral psychologists tend to emphasize the importance of past experience and learning; psychobiologists stress the role of genetically controlled growth and development of the organism. Many modern students of development would like to bury the nature-nurture issue. Thus, the organizers of an outstanding symposium on developmental psychobiology (Tobach, Aronson, and Shaw, 1971) hoped to avoid the "pseudo-dichotomous conceptualization of nature and nurture." They were appalled at the "unplanned-for emphasis on the heredity-environment problem" that developed during the conference.

The reason the nature-nurture issue persists is simple. It is perhaps the most fundamental and important of all human questions. Philosophers and scholars have debated the issue from the beginnings of history. It *does* make a very real difference. If violent and aggressive behavior in humans is primarily learned through experience, it can be controlled through proper learning. If it is primarily genetic, social control must be quite different. Genetically violent individuals must be isolated (e.g., in prisons) from their potential victims. All the good-hearted social rehabilitation in the world will not help. Violence can be eliminated from the human race only by genetic techniques—by selective breeding (*eugenics*) or ultimately by *genetic engineering* (direct physical alteration of the genes, the fundamental germ plasm itself).

Mental illness provides another good explanation for the fact that the nature-nurture controversy will not go away. Current thinking favors the view that many forms of neurosis, ranging from mild conditions such as excessive blushing to severe and persistent fears that can completely incapacitate a person, are primarily learned through experience. They can presumably be treated by the application of learning principles and techniques. Severe psychoses, on the other hand, appear to be largely genetic. Treatment and prevention of schizophrenia cannot be accomplished solely by learning therapies. Biological, biochemical, and ultimately genetic methods must be used.

Many fundamental issues in psychology and psychobiology can be traced to nature-nurture arguments about human development. This applies to virtually all complex psychological processes such as perception, sensory-motor integration, thought processes, and even language. One extreme view holds that the infant brain is a blank slate, a *tabula rasa*, upon which experience writes the human mind. The opposite extreme holds that the adult human mind is preprogrammed in the infant brain to unfold and develop with growth, independent of experience. The truth, as with all truths, is somewhere in between. We shall explore these issues of development at greater length in appropriate subsequent chapters.

The major objection to the nature-nurture issue is that it is an oversimplification. No human trait is completely genetic, and none results completely from experience. Genes and environment interact from at least the time the egg is fertilized. Violent criminals are not always violent; schizophrenics are not always disoriented. All life is a continual interaction between the germ plasm and the world. Modern psychobiology is more interested in investigating all the sources of behavior than in choosing between nature and nurture. Analysis in terms of the heritability of characteristics, as is done in contemporary behavior genetics, provides a more realistic picture of the relative importance of hereditary and environmental influences, and their interactions, in the growth and development of human abilities, behavior, and personality. However, we are still a long way from understanding the genetic basis even of such simple and fixed behaviors as the song pattern of the cricket. We cannot yet describe the chain of events from gene to cricket song, let alone from gene to complex human behaviors like violence, schizophrenia, or intelligence.

Summary

Genes are the structural units of heredity. By determining the structures of proteins produced in the ribosomes, the genes determine the structures and functions of an organism. Genes also interact with the environment. The genotype of an organism expresses its underlying genetic makeup.

The phenotype is the outward expression of gene action that results from the interaction with the environment.

The three hypotheses formulated by Mendel are the basic laws of heredity: (1) Heredity is transmitted by independent, inheritable units (the genes); (2) when each parent contributes the same kind of unit, the offspring also manifest this characteristic, but when each parent contributes a different kind of unit, a hybrid offspring forms; and (3) the experience of an organism does not affect the genes.

DNA is the fundamental substance of genes. DNA is composed of deoxyribose, phosphate, and four bases: adenine, guanine, thymine, and cytosine. Watson and Crick proposed the double helix model for the structure of DNA. The molecule is composed of two strands wound around each other. The bases attach to the backbone of each strand and then bond to each other. Although the bases may occur in any sequence along a single strand, there is a constant relation between the two complementary strands so that adenine always bonds with thymine and guanine with cytosine. The genetic code is contained in this sequence of bases. The ability of DNA to reproduce itself lies in the specific bonding combinations of the bases.

The mechanism for the translation of the genetic code into protein involves RNA. Messenger RNA transfers the code from DNA to the ribosome. At the ribosome, transfer RNA acts to assemble the amino acids needed to make the proteins coded for by DNA.

Genes for a specific trait occur at specific loci on particular chromosomes. Each pair of chromosomes contains homologous loci. A zygote is characterized as homozygous if the same allele is inherited at a particular locus on both chromosomes. It is said to be heterozygous when two different alleles are located on the homologous loci.

Several different processes contribute to the variability of the gene pool. Random assortment during reproduction, mutation, crossing-over, and the existence of more than two alleles for a given chromosomal locus all serve to increase the variability of the gene pool. This genetic variability is crucial for the development of new species and for the survival of a species in a continually changing environment.

While genes do not directly affect behavior, they do serve to regulate the production of proteins, which are responsible for the structure and enzymatic activities of an organism. The primary concern of scientists working in the field of behavior genetics is the interaction between genes and the environment. These scientists attempt to quantify the amount of observed variability of a trait within a population that results from genetic differences among individuals and the amount that results from environmental differences. Most behaviors are polygenic; they are dependent upon many chromosomal loci where the contribution of each gene is small and cumulative.

Many studies using animals have been conducted in laboratory situations where the environment is held relatively constant. In this way, it is possible to practice artificial selection and to determine the effects of genetic makeup upon various behaviors. Selective breeding experiments have shown that many behavioral traits can be varied by genetic manipulation. Comparisons have also been made between different strains or races of animals.

In addition to experimental investigations of the effects of genetic manipulation on animal behavior, a great deal of productive research has been concerned with the genetic bases of severe mental deficiency. Phenylketonuria, infantile amauratic idiocy, juvenile amauratic idiocy, and Huntington's chorea are abnormalities involving a single gene locus. For example, phenylketonuria results from the inheritance of a double recessive gene that produces a deficiency in the production of a substance that converts phenylalanine to tyrosine. Defects in the chromosomal complement also produce mental deficiencies. The individual with Down's syndrome, for example, carries 47 chromosomes instead of the usual 46, and the result is severe mental retardation. Abnormalities in the numbers and kinds of sex chromosomes also affect human structure and personality. Kleinfelter's syndrome, Turner's syndrome, and the XYY syndrome are thought to be the result of abnormalities in the sex chromosomes.

Polygenic characteristics, those produced by actions at more than one gene locus, appear to be important in traits such as schizophrenia and intelligence. Polygenic characteristics have been studied by determining the degree of relation on quantitative performance measures between individuals who are or are not related. Comparisons of MZ and DZ twins with unrelated individuals have been helpful in examining the degree of heritability of various traits. Evidence now indicates that schizophrenia is genetically based. Intelligence, as measured by standard IQ tests, also seems to be significantly determined by genetic factors. However, environmental factors such as cultural experience, learning, and stage of maturation all significantly affect performance on IQ tests.

Although environment plays an important role after the organism is born, physical growth and development are under strong genetic control from fertilization of the egg until death of the organism. The embryonic development of the nervous system illustrates the interplay of gene action and environment in the development of structure and behavior. The cells of the tissue that becomes the nervous system are originally similar to all other cells in the embryo. When the three germinal layers (ectoderm, endoderm, and mesoderm) form, the notochord also develops. The notochord triggers the differentiation of ectoderm cells into nervous tissue by a process called induction, in which the development of a group of cells acts to specify the development of another group of cells through their interaction.

In the early stages of vertebrate brain development, a number of structures are formed. When the upper ectoderm comes into contact with the notochord, the neural plate develops along the upper surface. With the elevation of the edges of the neural plate, the neural tube is formed and three layers of cells form. As the neural tube closes, the three primary brain regions (forebrain, midbrain, and hindbrain) develop. The forebrain develops into the cerebral cortex and other higher brain regions. The midbrain remains undivided, and the hindbrain develops into the cerebellum and lower brain stem. With differential growth in these three regions, the brain takes on its adult form.

Rapid differentiation also occurs throughout the nervous system. Brain nuclei form, the fiber tracts begin to connect nuclei, spinal ganglia form from neural crest cells, and the eye forms from brain tissue. Much of this differentiation seems to be self-controlled. However, once the basic pattern of the nervous system has been established, its periphery becomes more important. It is interesting to note that when the periphery begins to affect neural development, the peripheral organs also become functional.

Hormonal influences on brain and behavior development are highly important. An excess amount of thyroxine has been shown to stimulate abnormally early maturation of some neural areas and many reflexes. A reduced amount of thyroxine has a negative effect upon brain and behavior development. Normal development depends upon an adequate supply of thyroxine during a critical period in development. If the hormone is absent during this critical period, deficiencies cannot be overcome at a later time.

One of the perennial controversies in neuropsychology concerns nature versus nurture. The nurture viewpoint, in its extreme manifestation, stresses that the infant's brain is a *tabula rasa* upon which experience constructs the human mind. The extreme of the nature view argues that the adult human mind is preprogrammed in the infant brain to develop with growth, independent of experience. The stark contrast between these two viewpoints is an oversimplification, since no human trait is completely genetic or completely the product of experience. Genes and environment interact from the time of conception.

3

Neuroanatomy:
the structural basis of
behavior and
awareness

3

The physical basis of mind encroaches more and more upon the study of mind, but there remain mental events which seem to lie beyond any physiology of the brain. When I turn my gaze skyward I see the flattened dome of sky and the sun's brilliant disc and a hundred other visible things underneath it. What are the steps which bring this about? A pencil of light from the sun enters the eye and is focused there on the retina. It gives rise to a change, which in turn travels to the nerve-layer at the top of the brain. The whole chain of these events, from the sun to the top of my brain, is physical. Each step is an electrical reaction. But now there succeeds a change wholly unlike any which led up to it, and wholly inexplicable by us. A visual scene presents itself to the mind; I see the dome of sky and the sun in it, and a hundred other visual things beside. In fact, I perceive a picture of the world around me. When this visual scene appears I ought, I suppose, to feel startled; but I am too accustomed to feel even surprised.

(Sir Charles Sherrington, 1950, page 3)

Perhaps no question in history has been more persistent, more trouble-some, and more influential in human affairs than the nature of the human mind. All religions are the result of certain assumptions about the nature of mind, consciousness, or spirit. What is consciousness or awareness? No simple answer can yet be given. However, modern psychobiology has contributed greatly to our understanding of certain aspects of the nature of human consciousness in the context of the structure and organization of the brain.

Most normal persons readily assert that they are conscious; they ex-perience stimuli and sensations and claim to be aware of their own ex-periences. Opinions about the nature of mind and consciousness range from materialism (there is no such thing as mind) through dualism (mind and matter exist as totally different entities) to monism (there is only mind). Science cannot deal in concepts so general and vague. How-ever, the neural basis of mind and consciousness is a subject of vital in-terest in science today. For fascinating discussions, the reader is urged to consult two recent books by leading brain scientists—an eminent neuro-physiologist, John Eccles (*Facing Reality: Philosophical Adventures by a Brain Scientist*, 1970) and an eminent neuropsychologist, Karl Pribram (*The Languages of the Brain*, 1971).

One fact has long been clear: mind and consciousness, whatever their precise definitions, are products of the brain. A blow to the head can cause a person to lose consciousness. Severe brain damage can reduce a person to a reflex machine that shows no signs of consciousness or mind. Damage limited only to the cerebral cortex, the highest region of the brain, appears to abolish completely all human characteristics, abilities, and awareness. Further, damage to certain regions of the brain can cause loss of particular functions or abilities, and even of particular aspects of awareness or consciousness. Clearly, the brain is the physical substrate of mind and consciousness.

Neuroanatomy, the subject of this chapter, is concerned with the phy-sical structure of the brain—its shape and form, and the interconnections of its elements, the individual neurons (nerve cells). Neuroanatomy deals with the physical basis of mind. The human brain (Fig. 3.1) is the most complex structure in the known universe. It consists of approximately 10 billion to 12 billion neurons and even more glia (nonneural brain cells).

67

Neuroanatomy:
the structural basis
of behavior and
awareness

68

Neuroanatomy:
the structural basis
of behavior and
awareness

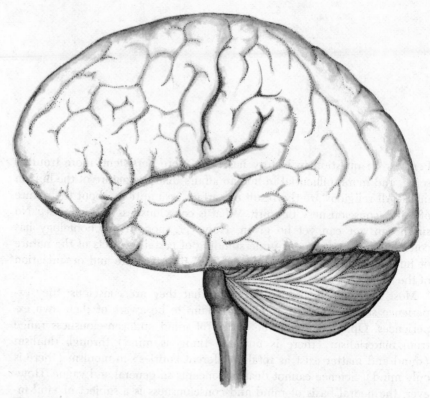

Figure 3.1 Lateral surface of the human brain showing the cerebral cortex and the fissure patterns.

The number of possible interconnections among the neurons in a single human brain is greater than the number of atomic particles that constitute the entire universe.

Fortunately, the brain is not a random structure; if it were, we could never begin to identify all the possible interconnections. Rather, it is organized according to relatively simple principles, whose analysis supplies an uncomplicated overall view of anatomical relation within the brain, particularly in terms of *input* (sensory) and *output* (motor) systems. The overview presented here emphasizes the organization of the cerebral cortex. This structure, the most recent to develop in the course of evolution, is concerned with mediation of the more complex aspects of behavior and is perhaps of greatest interest to psychologists. Gray (1948) has put it well:

This roof brain [cerebral cortex] is the supremely distinctive organ of the human species. What goes on within its network of cells makes the fundamental difference between man and brute. The functioning of the cerebral cortex not only distinguishes man from the animals, but more than any other faculty it distinguishes man from man. It marks the fateful difference between the meek follower and the dynamic leader, between the scholar and the artist, between the genius and the moron.

THE CEREBRAL CORTEX:
FUNCTION IN COMPLEX MENTAL PROCESSES

Hemispheric allocation of functions

The first clues that certain regions of the cerebral cortex are specialized for complex abilities and aspects of consciousness came from medical studies of patients suffering various types of brain damage. Damage to a part of the left hemisphere of the cerebral cortex in a right-handed person essentially abolishes the ability to understand or speak language intelligently. Damage to the corresponding part of the right hemisphere has no such effect. However, a right-handed person with right hemisphere damage has great difficulty in performing spatial tasks: he may lose his way, forget a well-traveled route, and have difficulty understanding complex diagrams and pictures. In left-handed persons speech ability seems to be localized almost as often in the left as in the right hemisphere. However, the number of left-handed persons studied is too small for the reliability of this estimate to be certain.

69

The cerebral cortex:
function in complex
mental processes

Patients who have had portions of the left or right cerebral cortex removed surgically as treatment for severe epilepsy have been studied by Brenda Milner and associates at McGill University in Montreal. Her findings are clear. Verbal abilities and speech require a region of the left posterior or parietal cortex (these terms are explained later in this chapter). Spatial and complex perceptual abilities depend on the comparable region of the right cerebral cortex. Musical ability seems also to depend more on the right hemisphere. Ability to handle mathematics and symbols depends more on the left hemisphere. Table 3.1 summarizes the functions allocated to the two sides of the cerebral cortex by various scientists.

Studies on split-brained patients

The most remarkable studies on brain substrates of human awareness have been those of Roger Sperry and associates at the California Institute of Technology. Certain patients suffer from a form of epilepsy that begins with abnormal electrical activity on one side of the brain and spreads to the other side, producing severe seizures. Neurosurgeons found that some of these patients could be helped greatly by severing the nerve fibers that interconnect the two hemispheres, particularly the cerebral cortex. This large band of fibers, called the *corpus callosum*, is shown in Figure 3.2. In

Table 3.1 Functions controlled by the left and right hemispheres of the cerebral cortex

Suggested by	Left hemisphere	Right hemisphere
Jackson (1864)	Expression	Perception
Jackson (1874)	Audito-articular	Retino-ocular
Jackson (1876)	Propositionizing	Visual imagery
Weisenburg and McBride (1935)	Linguistic	Visual or kinesthetic
Anderson (1951)	Storage	Executive
Humphrey and Zangwill (1951)	Symbolic or propositional	Visual or imaginative
McFie and Piercy (1952)	Eduction of relations	Eduction of correlates
Milner (1958)	Verbal	Perceptual or nonverbal
Semmes et al. (1960)	Discrete	Diffuse
Zangwill (1961)	Symbolic	Visuospatial
Hécaen, Ajuriaguerra, and Angelergues (1963)	Linguistic	Preverbal
Bogen and Gazzaniga (1965)	Verbal	Visuospatial
Levy-Agresti and Sperry (1968)	Logical or analytic	Synthetic perceptual
Bogen (1969)	Propositional	Appositional

From Bogen, J. E. The other side of the brain: an appositional mind. **Bltn. of the Los Angeles Neurol. Soc. 34,** July 1969, pp. 135–162.

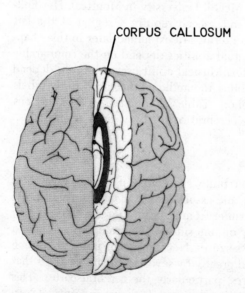

CORPUS CALLOSUM

Figure 3.2 View of the cerebral hemispheres with the right hemisphere retracted to reveal the corpus callosum, which connects the two hemispheres.

the figure, we are looking down on the top of the brain, the front of which is facing the top of the page. The two hemispheres have been separated to show the corpus callosum, a structure consisting of many millions of nerve fibers, each crossing from one hemisphere to the other. This massive transverse band of fibers extends perhaps half the length of the brain from front to back, interconnecting corresponding regions of the cerebral cortex on the two hemispheres.

The most surprising thing about this drastic surgical intervention in the human brain is that at first glance it seems to have no bad effects on the patients. Indeed, when the operation succeeds in abolishing the epileptic seizures, the patients are much improved. They show no loss of intelligence and none of the typical signs of brain damage, in spite of the fact that the two cerebral hemispheres have been disconnected from each other.

Roger Sperry's brilliant studies of these patients involved procedures for testing the functions of the two hemispheres separately and independently. To understand the implications of Sperry's experiments, you must know the following:

1. Each side of each eye projects visual information through nerve pathways to both sides of the cerebral cortex. The left side of the left and right eyes projects to the left cerebral cortex and vice versa.
2. The right half of the visual field projects to the left half of each eye. If you look at a particular point on the wall opposite you, everything you see to the right of that point projects to the left hemisphere of the cerebral cortex, and everything you see to the left of your point of gaze projects to the right hemisphere of the cerebral cortex. These two areas of cortex are normally interconnected by the corpus callosum, and you experience a unified cohesive visual world rather than two half-worlds. The split-brained patients have quite different experiences, as Sperry and his associates found.
3. Control of movement is crossed from brain to muscles. The left hemisphere of the cerebral cortex controls movements of the right side of the body (in Sperry's experiment, the right hand), and the right hemisphere of the cerebral cortex controls movements of the left side of the body. The output from each of the two hemispheres can be evaluated by measuring actions—for example, by testing each hand behind a screen that blocks the patient's view of them.

Figure 3.3 diagrams the input pathways from the visual field to the two hemispheres. The experimental test situation is shown in Figure 3.4. The patient (all were right-handed, so that the speech area was in the left hemisphere) looked at a fixation point, and visual information—words, drawings, pictures—was flashed briefly to his left or right cerebral cortex. He could respond verbally or with movements of either hand behind the screen. Remember, the corpus callosum has been severed in these patients.

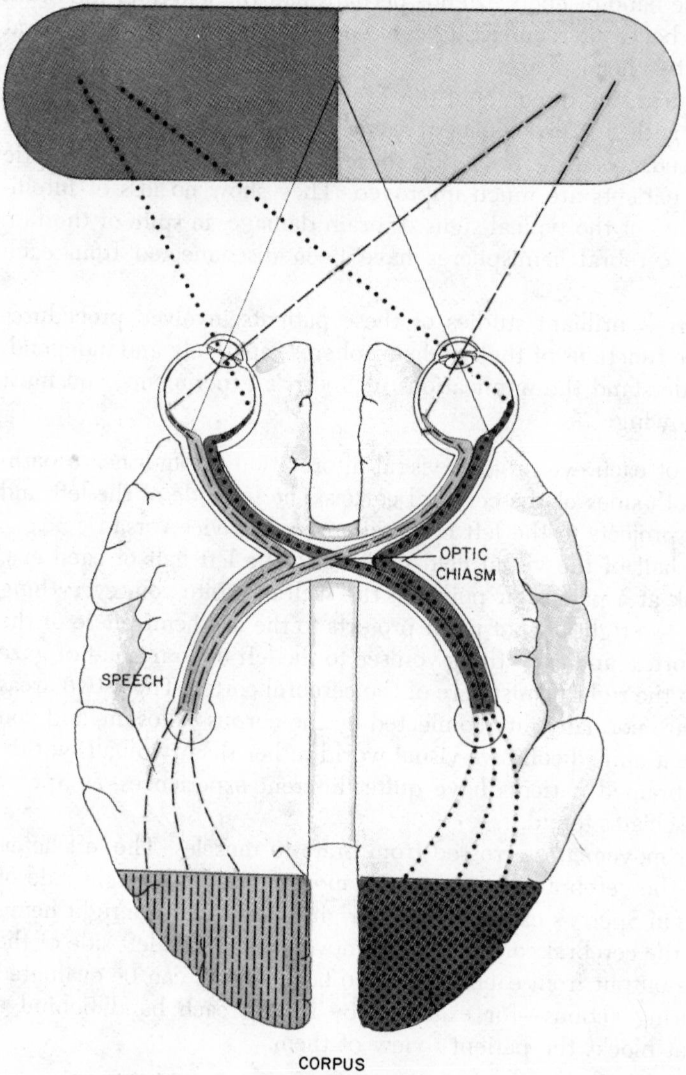

72

Neuroanatomy:
the structural basis
of behavior and
awareness

Figure 3.3 View of the brain illustrating the way visual input from the right and left visual fields projects to the cortex via connecting nerve pathways. Information crosses to the opposite hemisphere at the level of the corpus callosum and optic chiasm. Through the optic chiasm, information from the left and right visual fields of each eye is projected to the left and right hemispheres. The result is that the *left* half of the visual field for each eye (right half of each retina) project together to the *right* hemisphere of the brain, and vice versa. The corpus callosum interconnects the two hemispheres to permit visual information to be exchanged.

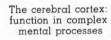

Figure 3.4 Experimental situation used to evaluate output from the two hemispheres. When the subject's gaze is fixated on a dot marking the center of the visual field, the examiner flashes a word or a picture of an object on a translucent screen to either side of the fixation dot. As shown, the information projects to the right hemisphere. Either a verbal (reading the flashed word) or a nonverbal (selecting the object named among the many objects on the table) response may be required. The objects are screened from the patient's view and can be identified only on the basis of touch.

73

The cerebral cortex:
function in complex
mental processes

The results of these experiments were strikingly clear. If a word was flashed to the left hemisphere, the patient could immediately say it and write it with his right hand. He appeared to be functioning normally. In marked contrast, if the word was flashed to the right hemisphere, the patient could neither say it nor write it. In spite of this, it soon became apparent that the right hemisphere was quite capable of recognizing objects. The trick was to find a way for it to tell the experimenter. If, when a picture of a fork was flashed to the right hemisphere, the left hand was allowed to feel many different objects behind the screen, including a fork, it would immediately select the fork and hold it up. The right hemisphere was nonverbal, but not incompetent. Having correctly identified the fork, the patient still could not say what it was. However, if the right hand was allowed to take the fork from the left, the patient immediately said "fork."

Actually, the right hemisphere did show some limited verbal comprehension. If simple words rather than pictures of objects were flashed to it, the patient could often identify the object by touching it with his left hand. Similarly, if an object like a pencil was placed in his left hand behind the screen, and a series of words, including pencil, was flashed to the right hemisphere, the patient could correctly signal with his left hand the word *pencil*. However, he still could not say the word. Gazzaniga (1967) reported:

In one particularly interesting test the word "heart" was flashed across the center of the visual field, with the "he" portion to the left of the center and "art" to the right. Asked to tell what the word was, the patients would say they had seen "art"—the portion projected to the left brain hemisphere (which is responsible for speech). Curiously, when, after "heart" had been flashed in the same way, the patients were asked to point with the left hand to one of two cards—"art" or "he"—to identify the word they had seen, they invariably pointed to "he." The experiment showed clearly that both hemispheres had simultaneously observed portions of the word available to them and that in this particular case the right hemisphere, when it had had the opportunity to express itself, had prevailed over the left.

(From "The split brain in man," M. S. Gazzaniga, page 26. Copyright © 1967 by Scientific American, Inc. All rights reserved.)

74

Neuroanatomy:
the structural basis
of behavior and
awareness

The patients became adept at cross communicating between hemispheres by using peripheral cues:

We had a case of such cross-cuing during a series of tests of whether the right hemisphere could respond verbally to simple red or green stimuli. At first, after either a red or a green light was flashed to the right hemisphere, the patient would guess the color at a chance level, as might be expected if the speech mechanism is solely represented in the left hemisphere. After a few trials, however, the score improved whenever the examiner allowed a second guess.

We soon caught on to the strategy the patient used. If a red light was flashed and the patient by chance guessed red, he would stick with that answer. If the flashed light was red and the patient by chance guessed green, he would frown, shake his head and then say, "Oh no, I meant red." What was happening was that the right hemisphere saw the red light and heard the left hemisphere make the guess "green." Knowing that the answer was wrong, the right hemisphere precipitated a frown and a shake of the head, which in turn cued in the left hemisphere to the fact that the answer was wrong and that it had better correct itself! We have learned that this cross-cuing mechanism can become extremely refined. The realization that the neurological patient has various strategies at his command emphasizes how difficult it is to obtain a clear neurological description of a human being with brain damage.

(From "The split brain in man," M. S. Gazzaniga, page 27. Copyright © 1967 by Scientific American, Inc. All rights reserved.)

In marked contrast to verbal performance, the right hemisphere was distinctly superior in spatial tasks such as arranging blocks or drawing a cube in three dimensions. Examples of drawings of simple designs

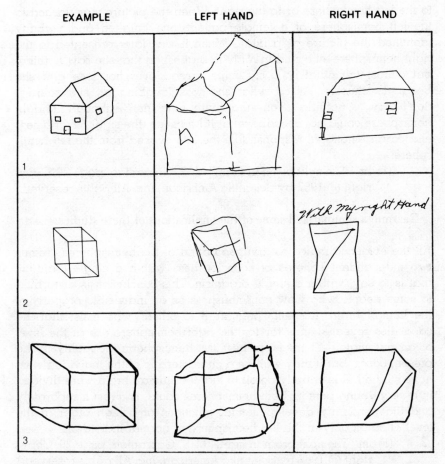

EXAMPLE	LEFT HAND	RIGHT HAND

With my right Hand

75

The cerebral cortex:
function in complex
mental processes

Figure 3.5 Drawings made by split-brained patients using the right hand and the left hand. The left-hand drawings are clearly superior to the right-hand ones for all three patients (who were all right-handed!). These drawings illustrate the superiority of the right hemisphere in spatial or visual-constructional tasks. (Courtesy, Michael S. Gazzaniga.)

made separately by each hand show this strikingly (Fig. 3.5). In each case the picture was presented only to the appropriate hemisphere (right hemisphere for left hand). The left-hand drawings are clearly much superior even though all the patients were right-handed.

Finally, emotional perception and responsiveness were handled quite well, although nonverbally, by the right hemisphere.

In one of our experiments we would present a series of ordinary objects and then suddenly flash a picture of a nude woman. This evoked an amused reaction regardless of whether the picture was presented to the left hemisphere or to the right. When the picture was flashed to the left hemisphere of a female patient, she laughed and verbally identified the picture as a nude. When it was later presented to the right hemisphere, she said in reply to a question that she saw nothing, but almost immediately a sly smile spread over her face and she began to chuckle. Asked what she was laughing at, she said: "I don't know . . . nothing . . . oh—that funny machine." Although the right hemisphere could not describe what it had seen, the sight nevertheless elicited an emotional response like the one evoked from the left hemisphere.

(From "The split brain in man," M. S. Gazzaniga, page 29. Copyright © 1967 by Scientific American, Inc. All rights reserved.)

Gazzaniga summarized some of the implications of these studies:

All the evidence indicates that separation of the hemispheres creates two independent spheres of consciousness within a single cranium, that is to say, within a single organism. This conclusion is disturbing to some people who view consciousness as an indivisible property of the human brain. It seems premature to others, who insist that the capacities revealed thus far for the right hemisphere are at the level of an automaton. There is, to be sure, hemispheric inequality in the present cases, but it may well be a characteristic of the individuals we have studied. It is entirely possible that if a human brain were divided in a very young person, both hemispheres could as a result separately and independently develop mental functions of a high order at the level attained only in the left hemisphere of normal individuals.

(From "The split brain in man," M. S. Gazzaniga, page 29. Copyright © 1967 by Scientific American, Inc. All rights reserved.)

Implications of the right-left dichotomy

In his book *The Psychology of Consciousness*, Robert Ornstein, a research psychologist at Langley Porter Institute in San Francisco, has developed a controversial but most interesting view of consciousness. His starting point was the work reviewed above concerning the functions of the two hemispheres of the cerebral cortex. Drawing on several different cultural histories, Ornstein made the point that in most human cultures "right" is considered to be rational and analytic, and "left" to be intuitive, dark, and mysterious. The French word for law is *droit*, "right." The Mojave Indians believe the left hand is passive and maternal while the right hand is the active father. Our word *sinister* comes from the Latin word for "left."

Ornstein has proposed that there are two different modes of consciousness. Table 3.2 illustrates this tentative dichotomy. It further suggests

Table 3.2 The two modes of consciousness: A tentative dichotomy

Source	Mode 1	Mode 2
Many sources	Day	Night
Blackburn	Intellectual	Sensuous
Oppenheimer	Time, history	Eternity, timelessness
Diekman	Active	Receptive
Polanyi	Explicit	Tacit
Levy, Sperry	Analytic	Gestalt
Domhoff	Right (side of body)	Left (side of body)
Many sources	Left hemisphere	Right hemisphere
Bogen	Propositional	Appositional
Lee	Lineal	Nonlineal
Luria	Sequential	Simultaneous
Semmes	Focal	Diffuse
I Ching	The Creative: heaven masculine, Yang	The Receptive: earth feminine, Yin
I Ching	Light	Dark
I Ching	Time	Space
Many sources	Verbal	Spatial
Many sources	Intellectual	Intuitive
Vedanta	Buddhi	Manas
Jung	Causal	Acausal
Bacon	Argument	Experience

From **The Psychology of Consciousness** by Robert E. Ornstein. W. H. Freeman and Company. Copyright © 1972.

that the rational mode is the left hemisphere and the intuitive mode is the right hemisphere. Further, different cultures and religions have emphasized one or the other mode. Western rational culture and science are "left hemisphere," and the meditative mystical religions and culture of the East and certain American Indian tribes are "right hemisphere."

Ornstein has suggested we attempt to integrate the two approaches to wisdom—the rational and the intuitive. Indeed, there is an old cultural tradition in the Western world of the two sides of man, often at war with one another, epitomized by Freud's concept of the conscious versus the unconscious and personified as Robert Louis Stevenson's Dr. Jekyll and Mr. Hyde. Sperry's studies have provided striking descriptions of Jekyll and Hyde behavior in split-brained patients. A man might, for example, grab a woman roughly with his left hand, only to have his right hand seize the left and pull it away.

These are fascinating speculations, but a scientific "right-sided" view can merely note that the data demonstrate differences in performance between the left and right hemispheres of the cerebral cortex. These data seem to suggest that the nature and functions of consciousness may be quite different for the two hemispheres.

THE CEREBRAL CORTEX:
STRUCTURE AND ORGANIZATION

The cerebral cortex is the outer covering of the brain. A layer about 2 mm thick, it overlies the lower brain regions and is composed of neurons (nerve cell bodies and their fiber processes) and various nonneural cells. When you see a picture of the human brain (Fig. 3.1), the surface you see covering the two brain hemispheres is the cerebral cortex.

Evolutionary relations

The cerebral cortex represents the most recent evolutionary development of the vertebrate nervous system. Fish and amphibians have no cerebral cortex, and reptiles and birds only a rudimentary indication of cortex. Much of the cerebral cortex in these lower forms is *paleocortex* or *archicortex*, having close interrelations with the more primitive olfactory and limbic systems. However, it must be noted (1) that cells in the archicortex and other brain regions in lower animals appear to have many of the connections and properties of neurons in mammalian cerebral cortex, and (2) that older forms of cortex are present in certain areas of the mammalian brain. In this discussion we are concerned with the new cortex, the *neocortex*, that has become elaborated more recently in evolution.

Within the mammalian series, the more primitive mammals, such as the rat, have a relatively small, smooth cortex. In the progression from more primitive to more complex mammals, following the general course of evolution, the amount of cortex relative to the total amount of brain tissue increases in a fairly regular manner. Within primates, this same relation is seen. More primitive monkeys, such as the marmoset and squirrel monkey, have relatively small, smooth cortical surfaces compared with higher forms. More advanced primates, such as the rhesus monkey, the chimpanzee, and man, have an enormous and disproportionately increased amount of cerebral cortex. Of the approximately 12 billion neurons in the human brain, 9 billion are in the cerebral cortex. In general terms, there is a correlation between the extent of cortical development for a species, its phylogenetic position, and the degree of complexity and modifiability characteristic of its behavior.

All incoming (afferent) sensory systems send information to the cortex, each to a specific region. Outgoing (efferent) motor systems controlling ultimately the activity of muscles and glands arise in other regions of the cortex. Interestingly, the basic organization of the cortical sensory and motor areas does not appear to differ markedly from rat to man. However, in the ascending mammalian scale of evolution, the relative amount of *association cortex* (cortex that is neither sensory nor motor and has often been assumed to be involved in higher or more complex behavioral functions) increases strikingly. Approximate scale drawings of

Neuroanatomy:
the structural basis
of behavior and
awareness

the cerebral cortex in rat, cat, monkey, and man are shown in Figure 3.6. Note both the remarkable increase in absolute brain size and the increase in relative amount of association cortex. Man, incidentally, does not have the largest brain. Porpoise, whale, and elephant all have larger brain masses, although the packing density of cells may be less.

The cortical fissures

The increased amount of cerebral cortex in higher forms is largely contained in *fissures* (or *sulci*), in foldings of the cortical surface such as would occur if you pressed the skin of an orange inward with the edge of a ruler. Cortical tissue is present on both banks (sides) of a fissure and is of normal thickness except at the bottom, where it is usually thinner. The development of fissures has permitted an enormous increase in the amount of cortex without undue enlargement of the rigid skull casing. Comparison of the fissure patterns for squirrel monkey, rhesus monkey, and man (Fig. 3.7) illustrates this point. It has been estimated that more than three-quarters of the total amount of cerebral cortex in the human brain lies within fissures.

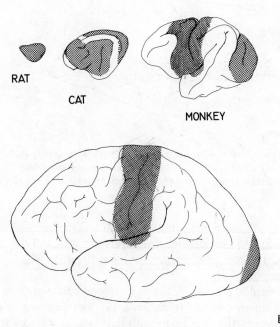

RAT

CAT

MONKEY

MAN

▨ SENSORY OR MOTOR AREA

☐ ASSOCIATION AREAS

Figure 3.6 Approximate scale drawings of the cerebral hemispheres of four mammals. Note the increase in absolute brain size and the increase in the relative amount of association cortex from rat to man.

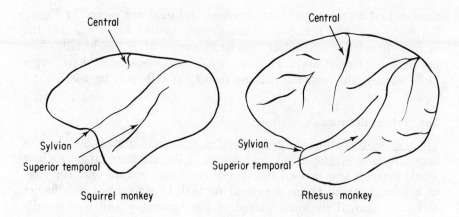

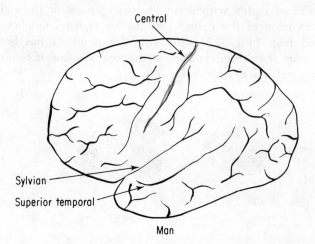

Figure 3.7 Development of the fissure patterns in squirrel monkey, rhesus monkey, and man. The central, sylvian, and superior temporal fissures are present in all three primate brains. The brains shown here are not drawn to scale and are all facing left.

80

Neuroanatomy:
the structural basis
of behavior and
awareness

Two fissures serve as major cerebral landmarks: the *central fissure* (fissure of Rolando), which divides the cerebrum into anterior and posterior halves, and the *temporal fissure* (sylvian fissure), which serves to demarcate the temporal lobe.

Some rather complex terminology has developed to designate various regions of the brain in relation to fissures. For our purpose it is necessary to remember only the few major subdivisions shown in Figure 3.8. The anterior portion of the cortex lies in front of the central fissure. It is customarily divided into precentral and frontal regions, the frontal lobe extending from the front of the brain backward to the precentral cortex. The temporal lobe lies below and behind the temporal (sylvian) fissure.

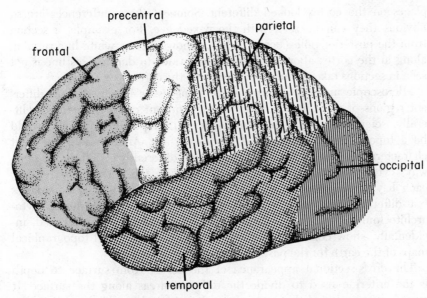

precentral

frontal

parietal

occipital

temporal

Figure 3.8 Major subdivisions of the brain in relation to the fissures.

The remaining postcentral cortex is usually divided into the occipital lobe, which is the posterior portion, and the parietal lobe, which extends from the occipital lobe to the central fissure. To help remember these subdivisions, it is useful to keep in mind the following somewhat oversimplified set of relations between cortical structure and function:

Occipital lobe = vision
Parietal lobe = skin and muscle senses
Part of temporal lobe and temporal fissure = hearing
Precentral cortex = motor or movement control

All remaining parietal, preoccipital, temporal, and frontal areas that seem to be neither sensory nor motor in function have been called silent or association areas.

Cortical organization: Cytoarchitectonics

If a cross section is cut through the cerebral cortex from surface to depth (at a right angle to the surface) and viewed under a microscope, a number of characteristics can be distinguished. It is usually possible to see six layers or regions of nerve cell bodies from surface to depth that seem to differ from one another in appearance. Even before the days of careful microscopic analysis, it was noticed that sections taken from different places on the cortex looked different. Some of these differences are so obvious they can be seen with the naked eye. For example, a section from the posterior pole (occipital lobe) shows a clear white line running along in the cortex about halfway from surface to depth. This line is not seen in sections taken from other regions of the cortex.

Microscopic analysis of cross sections of tissue obtained from different regions of the cortex constitutes the study of *cytoarchitectonics* (literally, science of the architecture of cells). A possible analogy would be a topographical map of the earth's surface. Areas having different characteristics (mountains, hills, plains) are differently coded. In the same way, cytoarchitectonics attempts to subdivide the cortex into regions, each having a similar cross-sectional appearance within its boundaries but differing from other regions. The boundaries of the various cytoarchitectonic maps of the human cortex that have been published, incidentally, show considerably more variability than would topographical maps of the earth for the past few thousand years.

Neuroanatomy:
the structural basis
of behavior and
awareness

The cross-sectional appearance of the cortex from surface to depth is the criterion used to divide the different areas along the surface. It must be remembered that neurons in almost any layer of the cortex may possess fibers extending to or beyond all layers. The division is made primarily in terms of appearance and distribution of nerve cell bodies. *Layers* of cortex refer to the surface-to-depth appearance; *areas* are the various cytoarchitectonic regions laid out over the hemisphere. The six layers from surface to depth into which the cortex can be subdivided are, of necessity, somewhat arbitrary and qualitative. In the latter part of the nineteenth century many authorities subdivided the cortex into eight or more separate layers. Today it is commonly described in terms of six layers, after Lorente de Nó's analysis (1938), which in turn is the outgrowth of previous work by Korbinian Brodmann, Santiago Ramón y Cajal, and many others.

Figure 3.9 illustrates a general schema of the cortical laminations, showing a few typical cell bodies and their processes on the left, the distribution of cell bodies in the middle, and the fiber distribution on the right. A photomicrograph of a section stained (by the Nissl method) to show nerve cell bodies from human visual cortex is shown in Figure 3.10. To appreciate the difficulty in identifying and dividing laminations, see if you can subdivide the section of cortex in this figure into six layers according to the diagram in Figure 3.9.

The cortical layers from surface to depth may be named and described as follows:

1. *Molecular layer* (plexiform layer). Consists of many fibers but only a few cells, mostly horizontal cells of Cajal and granule cells.
2. *External granular layer* (layer of small pyramids). Consists mostly of small pyramidal cells and Golgi type II cells.

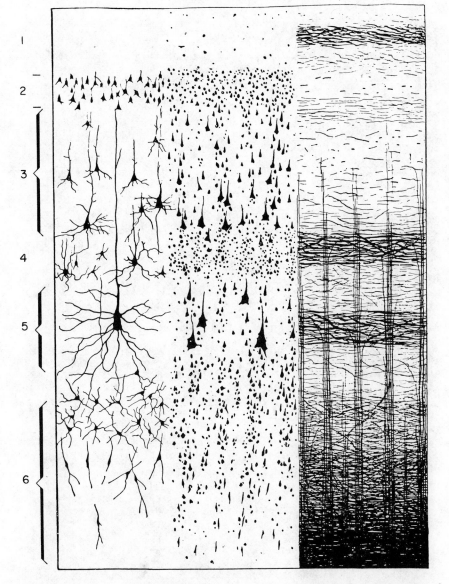

Figure 3.9 General schema of the six layers of cerebral cortex. A few examples of typical nerve cells are shown on the left, the distribution of the cell bodies in the middle, and the distribution of fiber processes on the right. (From Ranson, S. W., and Clark, S. L. *The Anatomy of the Nervous System.* 10th Ed. Philadelphia: W. B. Saunders Co., 1959; after Brodmann.)

84

Neuroanatomy:
the structural basis
of behavior and
awareness

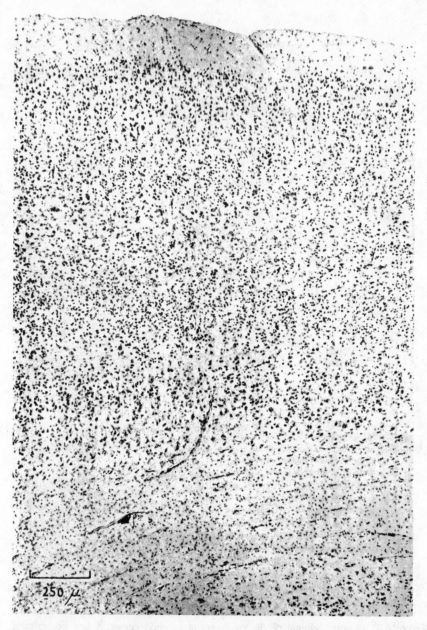

Figure 3.10 Photomicrograph of a cross section from human occipital lobe of the cerebral cortex stained by the Nissl method. The Nissl method selectively stains cell bodies. (From Sholl, D. A. *The Organization of the Cerebral Cortex.* London: Methuen, 1956.)

3. *Medium pyramid layer.* Consists of medium-sized and larger pyramidal cells.
4. *Internal granular layer.* Consists mostly of Golgi type II granule cells with fewer smaller pyramidal cells.
5. *Large pyramid layer.* Consists of medium-sized or large pyramidal cells.
6. *Spindle cell layer* (fusiform layer). Consists mostly of spindle cells.

The names of the cells most commonly found in the various layers are simply descriptive of their appearance (Fig. 3.9). The cells are discussed in greater detail later in this chapter. In terms of interconnections, the various types of cells can be divided into four basic groups (Lorente de Nó, 1938):

1. Small cells with horizontal dendrites and axons are called horizontal cells of Cajal in layer 1 and spindle cells in layer 6 (axons of the latter bend and penetrate into white matter).
2. Granule cells (stellate cells) are cells with short branching axons and many branched dendritic trees. They include the granule cells of layer 1 and the Golgi type II cells of layers 2 and 4.
3. Pyramidal cells are pyramid-shaped cells that send axons down into white matter below the cortex and long apical dendrites toward the cortical surface. In addition they have many short dendrites nearer the cell body. Pyramidal cells are found primarily in layers 2, 3, and 5.
4. Cells sending axons toward the surface of the cortex, although not named as such above, are found in essentially all layers of the cortex.

Although the details of organization vary considerably from place to place in the cortex, the basic points listed above appear to hold. Two simple generalizations may be made that should help to keep this organization in mind and suggest possible functions associated with different types of cells. First, afferent fibers projecting into the cortex from the modality-specific sensory systems (auditory, visual, and somatic) appear to terminate on granule cells in layer 4. In primary sensory areas of the cortex this layer is consequently much enlarged. Second, pyramidal cells of layer 5 are much enlarged in the region of the motor cortex (here they are called giant pyramidal cells or Betz cells) and send their axons all the way to the spinal cord, where they influence the motor nerve cells that control muscle activity.

Regional subdivisions of the cortex are based on the relative changes in the appearance of the six cortical layers in different areas of the cerebral cortex. Since no two pieces of cortex are exactly the same in histological (microscopic) characteristics, it is possible to make a good many subdivisions. Campbell described 20 areas, Elliott Smith increased this to 50, and in 1919 the Vogts described over 200 separate cortical fields.

Brodmann's map, which is still used most widely today, has about 50 areas. For a time it was hoped that such detailed architectonic studies would permit analysis into elementary functional units of the cortex. However, more recent work makes it seem unlikely that this goal will ever be achieved. Nonetheless, many regions can reliably be differentiated using histological criteria.

ANATOMICAL TERMS, DEFINITIONS, AND METHODS OF STUDY

Terms. Anatomists have developed a number of standardized directional terms to indicate the relative locations of bodily structures (Fig. 3.11). While these terms may be unfamiliar and seem perhaps unnecessarily complicated at first, they have the advantage of being unambiguous. These terms tell us whether a given section of the brain is located at the top or bottom, front or back, middle or side of the brain, and from what direction it is viewed in a particular drawing or photograph. *Dorsal* refers to the back, *ventral* to the front, *medial* is toward the middle, and *lateral* to either side. The head end is termed *anterior, cephalic,* or *rostral*; the tail end is referred to as *caudal* or *posterior*. Dorsal and ventral are sometimes confusing. In a four-legged animal such as the frog, rat, or cat, dorsal refers to the back of the animal and the top of its head.

86

Neuroanatomy:
the structural basis
of behavior and
awareness

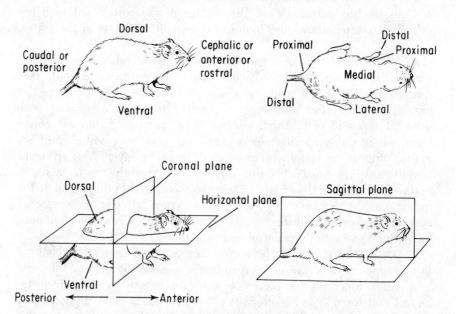

Figure 3.11 Anatomical terms utilized to describe position and location in reference to the axes of the body.

As can be seen in Figure 3.11, the top of the rat's head is a continuous extension of the animal's back. However in a two-legged animal like man, the top of the head is at right angles to the back of the body. Rather than switch terms (so that the back of the human head would be called dorsal and the top anterior), anatomists have chosen to put a right-angle bend in the directions. This allows us to use the same directional term for all brains, be they rat or human. The top of the human brain (Fig. 3.1) is termed dorsal, the bottom ventral, the back posterior, and the front anterior, just as with the rat, even though the human brain is at a right angle to the body axis.

Definitions. It is necessary also to learn a few simple definitions. The *brain* refers to the enlarged collection of cells and fibers inside the skull at the head end of an animal: it becomes the *spinal cord* as it leaves the skull. The *central nervous system* (CNS) includes both the brain and the spinal cord and is composed of *neurons* (nerve cell bodies and their characteristic fiber processes), *glia* (nonneural cells), and a variety of other types of cells making up blood vessels, membranes, etc. The word *nerve* refers to a collection of nerve fibers (not including the cell bodies). Collections of nerve cell bodies are called *nuclei* if they are inside the central nervous system and *ganglia* if they are outside. *Gray matter* consists of cell bodies and small fibers, and *white matter* is made up of tracts of large fibers covered with fatty *myelin sheaths.* They are so-called because in fresh brain they have these respective colors. The central nervous system is bilaterally symmetrical in that most structures are duplicated on the two sides. A number of central nervous systems are *crossed*, so that neural structures on the left are functionally related to body structures on the right, and vice versa.

Methods of study. A wide variety of procedures have been developed for the study of structural characteristics of the nervous system. These procedures range from gross anatomical dissection of the entire brain, through microscopic analysis of the detailed appearance of thin slices of the tissue, to electron microscopy of minute portions of individual nerve cells.

Gross anatomy is the naming and describing of the structural aspects of organs that can be seen with the unaided eye. Historically this was naturally the earliest branch of neuroanatomy to develop. While gross anatomy is a necessary starting point (agreed-upon names for structures are a prerequisite for further study), its value as an analytic method is limited. This is particularly true for the nervous system, where the most important structural characteristic is interconnections among fibers that are too small to be visible without a microscope.

A large variety of *histological* procedures have been developed for microscopic analysis of the tissues of the nervous system. These in turn can be subdivided into descriptive methods used with normal tissues and analytic methods used to trace fiber connections. If a region of brain is damaged, degenerative changes occur in both the bodies and the fibers of nerve cells injured. Histological examination allows the connections between cells to be traced. When a thin slice of untreated brain tissue is viewed in a microscope, little can be seen except a complex jumble of cellular elements. The appearance and nature of neural tissue seen through a microscope depends entirely upon the techniques used to prepare the tissues, particularly the stains used to color the various cellular elements.

Electron microscopic study of very fine details of nerve cells is the most recent and important development in the analysis of structural features of the nervous system.

88

Neuroanatomy:
the structural basis
of behavior and
awareness

COMPARATIVE ASPECTS OF THE VERTEBRATE BRAIN

The basic organization of the vertebrate brain and spinal cord is perhaps most easily seen in certain invertebrates, particularly worms. A series of brains ranging from the earthworm through primitive vertebrates to the primate is shown in Figure 3.12. The fundamental plan is that of a segmented tube. This is evident in the earthworm, where each body segment has nerves going into and out from the corresponding segment of the tubular nervous system. Even in the worm there is an enlargement of the head end in relation to specialized receptors. The human brain maintains the basic tubular organization from spinal cord up to about the middle of the brain (midbrain). However, the front end of the tube is enormously expanded and laid back over the core tube to form most of what we normally call the brain.

It is convenient in comparing brains of different vertebrates to divide the brain up into regions. Neuroanatomists normally use five subdivisions ranging from the front end to the spinal cord, but in terms of embryological development (Chapter 2), it is more correct to divide the brain into two regions: a *hindbrain* (induced to develop by the notochord and a *forebrain* (induced to develop by the primitive oral gut). Table 3.3 summarizes the divisions of the vertebrate brain and the major structures in each division.

Most of the structures listed in Table 3.3 are indicated in the drawings of the human brain in Figures 3.13 and 3.19. The lightly shaded *cerebrum* overlies brain stem structures, as does the cerebellum. The posterior portion of the brain stem is called the *medulla*; the portion just above it with an enlarged ventral region is the *pons*, with the cerebellum overlying it, and the upper portion of the brain stem is called the *midbrain* (*mesencephalon*). Above or anterior to the brain stem are the *thalamus* and *hypothalamus,* and the structures of the cerebrum, in-

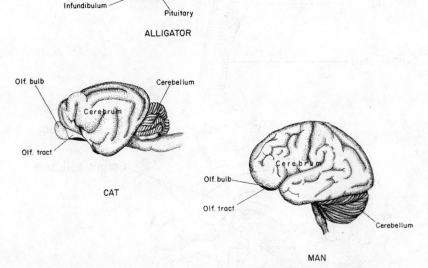

Esophageal connective
Subpharyngeal ganglion
Ventral nerve cord
Brain (Suprapharyngeal ganglion)
Segmental ganglion

WORM

Optic lobe
Cerebrum
Olf. bulb
Cerebellum
Olf. tract
Pituitary
Inf. lobe

CODFISH

Optic lobe
Diencephalon
Cerebellum
Olf. bulb
Cerebrum
Olf. tract
Infundibulum
Pituitary

ALLIGATOR

Olf. bulb
Cerebellum
Cerebrum
Olf. tract

CAT

Cerebrum
Olf. bulb
Olf. tract
Cerebellum

MAN

Figure 3.12 Development of brain from earthworm through man. Note the progressive growth of the cerebral cortex from alligator to man, and the changes in size of cerebellum among the various vertebrate brains shown here. The drawings are not shown in scale. (Modified from Truex, R. C. and Carpenter, M. B. *Strong and Elwyn's Human Neuroanatomy.* 5th Ed. Baltimore: Williams and Wilkins, © 1964.)

cluding the *cerebral cortex, basal ganglia,* and *rhinencephalon.* The hindbrain of the human, particularly in the medulla and midbrain, is a continuation of the tubular organization of the spinal cord, and resembles the worm's nervous system. In mammals the tubular portion of the nervous system is, of course, only relatively tubular. There is a very small central canal filled with fluid (*cerebrospinal fluid*). The tube is thus

90

Neuroanatomy:
the structural basis
of behavior and
awareness

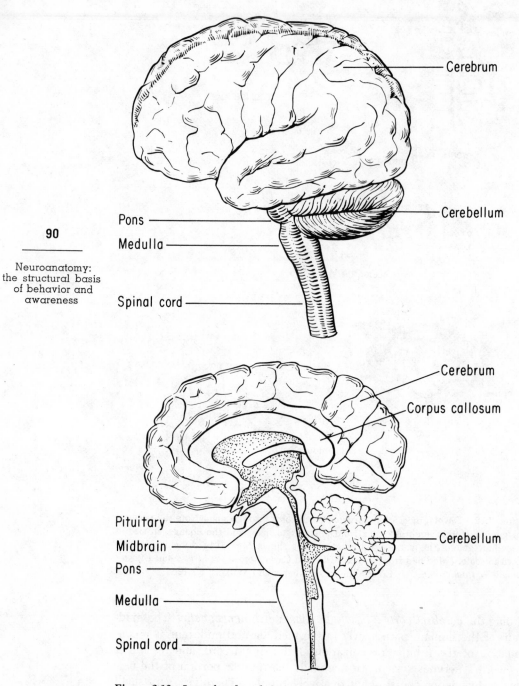

Cerebrum

Cerebellum

Pons

Medulla

Spinal cord

Cerebrum

Corpus callosum

Pituitary

Midbrain

Pons

Cerebellum

Medulla

Spinal cord

Figure 3.13 Lateral and medial views of the human brain. The lower drawing shows the midsagittal plane.

Table 3.3 General subdivisions of the brain

General division	Major structures included
Myelencephalon	Medulla
Metencephalon	Pons
	Cerebellum
Mesencephalon	Midbrain
Diencephalon	Hypothalamus
	Pituitary gland
	Optic tracts
	Subthalamus
	Thalamus
Telencephalon	Cerebral hemispheres
	Basal ganglia
	Olfactory bulb and tracts

mostly wall and is composed of neurons, nonneural cells, such as glia, and blood vessels. However, the forebrain of the higher mammals is, as we noted earlier, so enlarged that it becomes most of the brain. It is worth emphasizing again that the forebrain differs embryologically from the hindbrain. The relative enlargement of the forebrain is what distinguishes men from monkeys and monkeys from lower mammals.

BRAIN CELLS AND THEIR CONNECTIONS

The brain is composed of two quite different kinds of cells: neurons (nerve cells) and glia. There are, of course, also blood cells and other cells found in all tissues. Descriptions of the elements of brain have tended to emphasize neurons, with good reason. They are, we believe, the ultimate functional elements, although glia may play important roles as well. While there are perhaps 12 billion neurons in the brain, there are 120 billion glia. The glia outnumber the neurons by 10 to 1!

Drawings of a neuron and a glia are shown in Figure 3.14. As will be described later, neurons have receptive regions and fibers that connect to other neurons. They have a unique structural organization that permits them to act on one another electrically and chemically. Glia do not have this kind of organization.

Initially it was thought that glia served only to provide a supporting matrix to hold the neurons in place, as do connective tissue cells in many organs of the body. However, we now think they do much more than that. There are many complex chemical interactions between neurons and neighboring glia, including exchanges of ions and possibly of nutritive elements. It even appears that in some systems, such as the retina

92

Neuroanatomy:
the structural basis
of behavior and
awareness

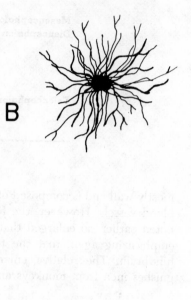

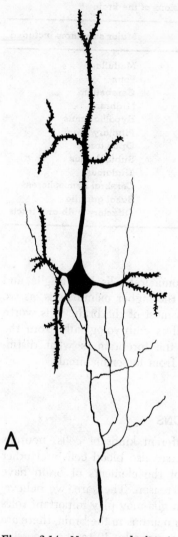

Figure 3.14 Neurons and glia. A, Pyramidal cell from visual cortex; B, Astrocyte (glial cell) from the white matter.

(the light-sensitive region at the back of the eye), electrochemical activity of glia can directly modify the electrical activity, and hence the information transmissions of neurons. It is quite possible that the ubiquitous glia will eventually be found to play critical roles in control of neuron activity in the brain, and hence in higher processes such as perception and learning.

A typical neuron has several characteristic features. The cell shown in Figure 3.15A is a type having a relatively long fiber. The main *cell*

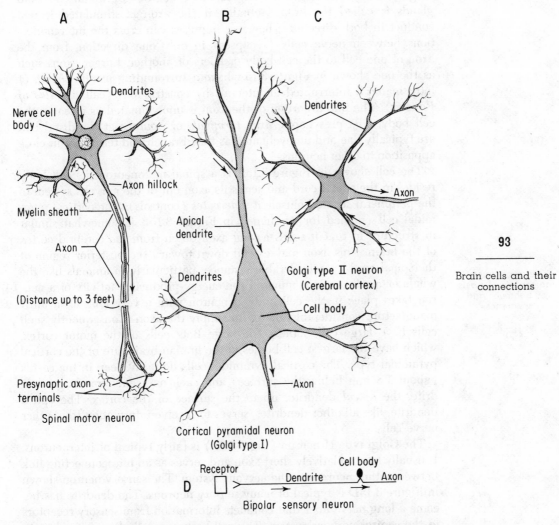

A

- Dendrites
- Nerve cell body
- Axon hillock
- Myelin sheath
- Axon
- (Distance up to 3 feet)
- Presynaptic axon terminals

Spinal motor neuron

B C

- Dendrites
- Apical dendrite
- Dendrites
- Golgi type II neuron (Cerebral cortex)
- Cell body
- Axon
- Axon

Cortical pyramidal neuron
(Golgi type I)

D

- Receptor
- Dendrite
- Cell body
- Axon

Bipolar sensory neuron

Figure 3.15 A, A typical nerve cell (spinal motoneuron). Dendrites receive activity from nearby cells and conduct this information to the soma. The axon conducts activity from the soma to other neurons or to muscle fibers and glands. B, Cortical pyramidal cell, which has short dendritic processes and a long apical dendrite extending to the cerebral cortex (see Fig. 3.14A). C, Golgi type II neuron, typical of interneurons, has relatively short dendrites and axon. D, Bipolar sensory neuron with its specialized shape; the soma generally lies close to the CNS and the dendrite and axon may form a single nerve fiber as shown here.

body contains the cell nucleus and is referred to as the *soma*. Many short fibers (*dendrites*) extend out from it and serve to receive activity from adjacent cells and conduct this activity to the cell body. The long fiber that transmits activity to other neurons or to muscles and glands is called the *axon*. Actually, if the axon is stimulated it will conduct in both directions; however impulses can cross the interconnections between nerve cells (synapses) in only one direction, from the axon of one cell to the cell body or fibers of another. Larger axons such as the one shown in Figure 3.15A have a surrounding *myelin sheath* of fatty material interrupted at intervals by constrictions (called *nodes of Ranvier*). The initial portion of the axon is unmyelinated as it leaves the cell body. The presynaptic *axon terminals* or *boutons* at the distal end are typically fine and unmyelinated as they branch and terminate in close apposition to other neurons.

The cell shown in Figure 3.15A is a spinal motoneuron; its cell body resides in the spinal cord and sends its axon out of the nervous system to the peripheral striated muscle it *innervates* (controls). The cortical pyramidal cell (named for its shape) in Figure 3.15B is somewhat similar in structure in that it sends a long axon down from the cerebral cortex of the brain. This axon may extend down toward the posterior region of the spinal cord (a considerable distance, particularly in animals like the whale or giraffe). Since much of the energy-producing activity of a neuron takes place in the cell body, a neuron with a very long axon must manufacture considerable energy to supply the axon. Consequently such cells have large cell bodies. The large Betz cells of the motor cortex, which have the largest cell bodies in the human brain, are of the cortical pyramidal type. The cortical pyramidal cells lie fairly deep in the cortex (about 1.8 mm below the surface) and each one sends one large dendrite, the *apical* dendrite, up to the surface of the cortex. The apical dendrite, like all other dendrites, serves to receive information from other nerve cells.

The Golgi type II neuron (Fig. 3.15C) is fairly typical of interneurons. It usually has a relatively short axon and serves as an interconnecting link between other neurons in the nervous system. The sensory neuron shown in Figure 3.15D is typical of many sensory neurons. The dendrite has become a long nerve fiber that conducts information from sensory receptors to the central nervous system. The cell body typically lies quite close to the CNS. The dendrite and axon may form a single nerve fiber, with the cell body offset to the side (as in sensory nerves from the skin); or the cell body may simply form an enlarged portion of the continuous fiber (as in the auditory or vestibular nerves).

To summarize, sensory input nerves are bipolar, interneurons are often of the Golgi type II, and output neurons are of the pyramidal or motor type. There are a variety of other, rather specialized neuron forms not shown in Figure 3.15.

The *synapse* is the key to the brain. It is the site of the functional interaction between neurons. So far as we know, the only places where neurons can influence other neurons are synapses. The synapse is not an actual, physical connection, but rather a close approximation to one. The synaptic space between the terminal *bouton* (ending) from one neuron and the cell body of another neuron is about 200 angstroms (20 millionths of a mm; 1 Å = 1/10,000,000 of a mm). A typical neuron in the brain has thousands of synaptic terminals from other neurons forming synapses on it, and it in turn may form synapses on many other neurons. Synapses occur mostly on the soma (cell body) and dendrites of a neuron. The synaptic terminals a neuron forms on the soma and dendrites of other neurons are the endings of small branches of the axon (see Chapter 5).

ORGANIZATION OF THE NERVOUS SYSTEM

The organization of the central nervous system is best understood in terms of groupings of nerve cell bodies and the fiber tracts interconnecting them. We shall examine this organization in general terms here and in more detail where relevant in subsequent chapters.

General principles of organization

In the spinal cord, nerve cell bodies forming nuclei lie in the central core and are surrounded by fiber tracts. Those tracts traveling the farthest tend to lie more toward the outside, while short tracts lie closer to the central core. This generalization tends to hold for the pons and medulla as well. However, in the cerebellum and cerebrum the outside covering is composed of nerve cell bodies in a layer about 2 mm thick, which surrounds the more centrally lying fiber tracts. In each case several nuclei are buried within the central core region—the thalamus and basal ganglia within the cerebrum and the cerebellar nuclei within the cerebellum.

Interactions among neurons occur largely in the vicinity of the nerve cell bodies, where axon terminals synapse on the cell bodies, dendrites, or other axon terminals. Thus the gray matter, consisting of nerve cell bodies forming the cerebral cortex and subcortical nuclei, is the site of neuronal interactions. White matter is made up of fibers that simply connect different regions of gray matter. Throughout the spinal cord and brain stem, nerve cell bodies and fibers concerned with sensory input tend to lie dorsally, and those concerned with motor output tend to lie ventrally.

Peripheral nervous system—somatic nerves

The nerves lying outside the spinal cord are termed *peripheral* or *somatic*. They innervate the striated skeletal musculature (somatic or body muscles) and a variety of sensory receptors. Throughout most of their length in the body they are *mixed;* that is, they contain both incoming (*afferent*) sensory fibers carrying information from receptors of skin, muscle, and joints to the spinal cord, and outgoing (*efferent*) motor fibers conveying

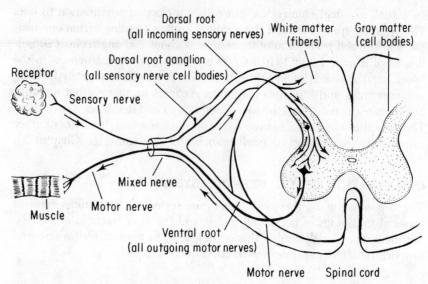

Dorsal root
(all incoming sensory nerves)

White matter
(fibers)

Gray matter
(cell bodies)

Dorsal root ganglion
(all sensory nerve cell bodies)

Receptor

Sensory nerve

Mixed nerve

Muscle

Motor nerve

Ventral root
(all outgoing motor nerves)

Motor nerve   Spinal cord

Figure 3.16 Organization of peripheral nerves viewed in a cross section of spinal cord cut at right angles to the cord. Afferent fibers transmit information to the spinal cord via the dorsal root. The motor nerve fibers have their cell bodies in the ventral portion of the gray matter of the spinal cord. All outgoing motor nerves from the cord pass through the ventral root and then continue outside the spinal cord via peripheral nerves to muscles.

96

Neuroanatomy:
the structural basis
of behavior and
awareness

activity from the spinal cord and brain stem motoneurons to muscle fibers. Figure 3.16 illustrates this arrangement in a cross-sectional view through the spinal cord at right angles to it.

The motor nerve fibers have their cell bodies in the ventral part of the central gray matter within the cord. Their axons go out through the ventral root, which contains *only* motor fibers, and then together with sensory fibers form mixed nerves, which travel to various body structures. As they approach the regions where they terminate, the motor and sensory fibers again separate and go to their appropriate locations.

The sensory nerve fibers are somewhat different from the motor nerves, having their cell bodies in a series of separate ganglia (*dorsal root ganglia*) outside the spinal cord. Sensory fibers are activated by peripheral receptors (e.g., touch, pain, temperature, pressure, joint movement), and convey information to the spinal cord through the dorsal root.

Peripheral nervous system—autonomic nerves

The *autonomic* nerve fibers are those concerned with structures such as smooth muscle, heart muscle, and those glands involved in autonomic aspects of responding (e.g., lacrimation, sweating, activity of stomach

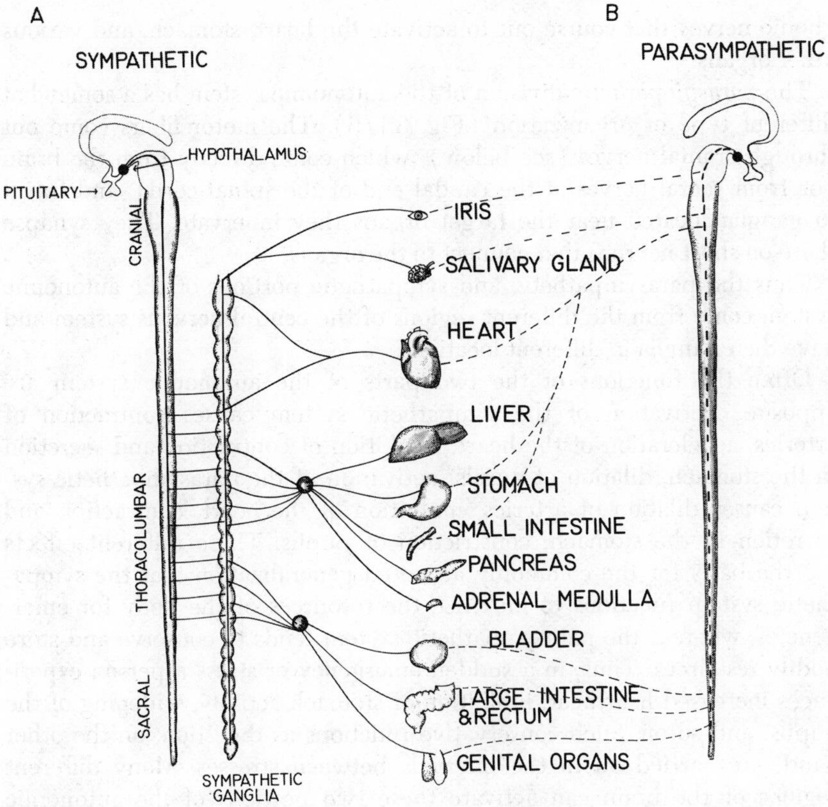

A   B

SYMPATHETIC   PARASYMPATHETIC

HYPOTHALAMUS

PITUITARY→

CRANIAL

IRIS

SALIVARY GLAND

HEART

THORACOLUMBAR

LIVER

STOMACH

SMALL INTESTINE

PANCREAS

ADRENAL MEDULLA

SACRAL

BLADDER

LARGE INTESTINE
&RECTUM

GENITAL ORGANS

SYMPATHETIC
GANGLIA

Figure 3.17 A, Organization of the sympathetic division of the autonomic system.
The cell bodies of sympathetic fibers are located in the spinal cord and pass through
the ventral root to the sympathetic ganglia. The sympathetic ganglia form a connected chain running parallel to the spinal cord. The fibers then synapse on postganglionic fibers, which innervate the heart and other organs. B, Organization of the parasympathetic division of the autonomic system. Parasympathetic fibers travel from the
cranial nerves directly to ganglia located near the target organ which they innervate.
These fibers then synapse on short neurons which connect to the target organ.

and heart) commonly related to emotional behavior. There are two divisions of the autonomic system; the sympathetic (thoracolumbar) and the
parasympathetic (craniosacral), which have somewhat different connections.

The *sympathetic* fibers (Fig. 3.17A) have their cell bodies in the
spinal cord and run out through the ventral root and a brief portion of
the mixed nerve to the sympathetic ganglia. These form a connected
chain that runs parallel to the spinal cord but lies outside the spinal bony
vertebrae. In the sympathetic ganglia these fibers synapse on postgan-

glionic nerves that course out to activate the heart, stomach, and various other organs.

The *parasympathetic* division of the autonomic system has a somewhat different type of organization (Fig. 3.17B). The motor fibers come out through cranial nerves (see below), which come directly from the brain (or from sacral nerves at the caudal end of the spinal cord), and travel to ganglia located near the target organs they innervate. They synapse there on short neurons that connect to the organs.

Thus the parasympathetic and sympathetic portions of the autonomic system come from the different regions of the central nervous system and have their ganglia in different locations.

Often the functions of the two parts of the autonomic system are opposite. Activation of the sympathetic system causes contraction of arteries, acceleration of the heart, inhibition of contraction and secretion in the stomach, dilation of pupils; activation of the parasympathetic system causes dilation of arteries, inhibition of the heart, contraction and secretion in the stomach, constriction of pupils. These different effects are the basis for the commonly accepted generalization that the sympathetic system functions to mobilize the resources of the body for emergencies, whereas the parasympathetic system tends to conserve and store bodily resources. Thus, in a sudden emergency or stress a person experiences increased heartbeat, inhibition of stomach activity, widening of the pupils, and so on. Such conservative functions as digestion, on the other hand, are carried on in the intervals between stresses. Many different regions of the brain can activate these two portions of the autonomic system. A number of these central nervous system regions have been linked together descriptively as the *limbic system*, believed by many to control motivation and emotional aspects of behavior. We shall consider this further in Chapter 9.

In summary, motor fibers have their cell bodies in the ventral regions of the gray matter in the cord and run out to muscles or autonomic ganglia. Sensory fibers have their cell bodies in the dorsal root ganglia and enter the spinal cord to convey information from receptors either directly to motoneurons (in reflexes) or to more central regions of the system for further information processing and control.

Cranial nerves

The cranial nerves are not really different in principle from the spinal nerves, except that they enter and leave the brain rather than the spinal cord. Table 3.4 lists the 12 nerves and some of their characteristics. Those of greatest interest to the psychologist are the optic (II) and the auditory (VIII), conveying information from receptors of the eye and ear.

98
_____

Neuroanatomy:
the structural basis
of behavior and
awareness

Spinal cord

Two general categories of activity—spinal reflexes and supraspinal activity—are handled by the spinal cord. *Spinal reflexes* are muscular and autonomic responses to bodily stimuli that occur even after the spinal cord is severed from the brain, as in a paraplegic accident victim. In addition, a wide variety of *supraspinal activity* is channeled through the spinal cord. The cerebral cortex and other brain structures controlling movement of the body convey activity down the spinal cord to motoneurons, and all bodily sensations are conveyed up the spinal cord to the brain. Analogous sensory and motor relations for the head are handled directly by the cranial nerves and brain (Table 3.4).

Table 3.4 The cranial nerves

Number	Name	Functions (s, sensory; m, motor)	Origin or end in the brain
I	Olfactory	(s) Smell	Cerebral hemispheres (ventral part)
II	Optic	(s) Vision	Thalamus
III	Oculomotor	(m) Eye movement	Midbrain
IV	Trochlear	(m) Eye movement	Midbrain
V	Trigeminal	(m) Masticatory movements	Midbrain and pons
		(s) Sensitivity of face and tongue	Medulla
VI	Abducens	(m) Eye movement	Medulla
VII	Facial	(m) Facial movement	Medulla
VIII	Auditory vestibular	(s) Hearing	Medulla
		(s) Balance	
IX	Glossopharyngeal	(s, m) Tongue and pharynx	Medulla
X	Vagus	(s, m) Heart, blood vessels, viscera	Medulla
XI	Spinal accessory	(m) Neck muscles and viscera	Medulla
XII	Hypoglossal	(m) Tongue muscles	Medulla

A schematic cross section of the spinal cord is shown in Figure 3.18. The incoming dorsal root fibers and the outgoing ventral root fibers separate each half of the cord into dorsal, lateral, and ventral regions of white matter. Remember that white matter is composed simply of nerve fibers. Note that the dorsal region of white matter is almost entirely taken up by ascending fibers conveying sensory information to the

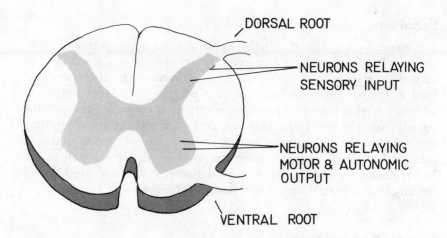

DORSAL ROOT

NEURONS RELAYING
SENSORY INPUT

NEURONS RELAYING
MOTOR & AUTONOMIC
OUTPUT

VENTRAL ROOT

Figure 3.18 Schematic cross section of the spinal cord illustrating the organization of sensory and motor neurons within the gray matter of the spinal cord.

Neuroanatomy:
the structural basis
of behavior and
awareness

brain, whereas the more lateral and ventral portion is taken up almost entirely by descending (motor) fiber systems.

The descending fiber systems all terminate in some fashion upon the various types of motoneurons in the cord. As we shall see later, different tracts tend to exert somewhat different types of influences on movement. For the present, we need simply distinguish between the *pyramidal tract fibers,* coming mostly from cerebral cortex, and the *extrapyramidal fibers,* composing the other tracts.

The gray matter of the cord (Fig. 3.18) contains nerve cell bodies whose axons connect to closely adjacent cells, others whose axons make up descending and ascending fiber tracts, and the motoneurons whose axons go out to muscles and autonomic ganglia. The larger cells of the dorsal portion are sensory in function, relaying incoming information from sensory receptors both upward to the brain and through the spinal gray matter to form reflex connections to the motoneurons of the spinal cord.

Brain stem

The term *brain stem* technically refers to everything between the spinal cord and the cerebral and cerebellar cortices. The major subdivisions, going from cord to cortex, are medulla, pons, midbrain, thalamus, and the basal ganglia. More often than not brain stem is used to mean only the medulla, pons, and midbrain. Actually these three structures appear as a somewhat enlarged continuation of the tubular spinal cord and contain a large number of nuclei and fiber tracts. The pons is overlaid ventrally by large fiber bundles that give it its characteristic appearance and

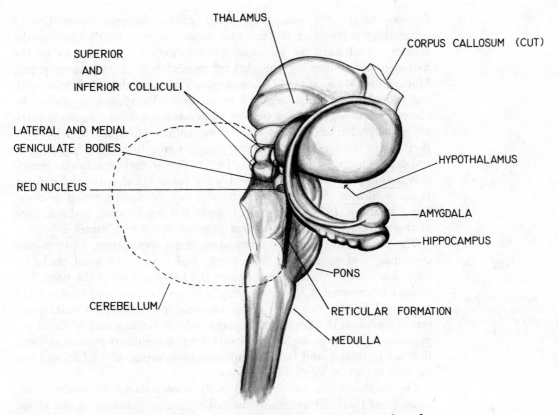

THALAMUS

CORPUS CALLOSUM (CUT)

SUPERIOR
AND
INFERIOR COLLICULI

LATERAL AND MEDIAL
GENICULATE BODIES

HYPOTHALAMUS

RED NUCLEUS

AMYGDALA

HIPPOCAMPUS

PONS

CEREBELLUM

RETICULAR FORMATION

MEDULLA

Figure 3.19 Gross appearance of the brain stem with the cerebral hemisphere dissected away. Note the organization of brain stem structures in relation to the cerebral hemisphere. Lateral view.

name (i.e., bridge). Figure 3.19 illustrates the gross appearance of the brain stem with the cerebral hemisphere dissected away.

The *medulla* is the continuation of the spinal cord in the brain and contains all the ascending and descending fiber tracts interconnecting brain and spinal cord, together with a number of important nerve cell nuclei. The majority of the cranial nerves have their entrances and exits from the medulla and the bordering region of the medulla and pons. In addition, several vital autonomic nuclei concerned with respiration, heart action, and gastrointestinal function are located in the medulla.

The brain stem *reticular formation* has extremely important functions that have only recently been appreciated. Anatomically it is a complex mixture of cell bodies, fibers, and nuclei (a reticulum) extending from the spinal cord to the thalamus, generally occupying a somewhat ventral location in the brain stem. The two major aspects of the reticular formation concern descending influences on motoneurons and ascending influences on the thalamus, cortex, and other structures. Stimulation of descending portions of the reticular formation may result either in decreases (inhibition) or increases (facilitation) in the activity of the motoneurons controlling the skeletal musculature. In a classic paper, Moruzzi and Magoun (1949) demonstrated that stimulation of the ascending reticular formation resulted in an arousal response as shown by electroencephalography—a pattern of low-voltage, high-frequency cortical activity characteristic of the waking animal (Chapter 10). Destruction of the midbrain reticular formation tends to yield a sleeping or stuporous animal (Lindsley et al., 1949). The ascending reticular formation thus appears crucially involved in the control of sleeping and waking. It seems also to play a fundamental role in behavioral alerting or attention (Lindsley, 1958). We shall consider the organization and functions of this extremely important system in more detail in Chapter 8.

The *pons* is the upward continuation of the brain stem, and contains ascending and descending fiber tracts and many additional nuclei. A large bundle of crossing fibers lies on the lower aspect of the pons. The bundle interconnects the brain stem and cerebellum, and contains the pyramidal fibers going from cortex to spinal cord. Several cranial nerve nuclei found in the pons play a major role in feeding and in facial expression. In addition, higher order relays for the auditory system, neurons that act to inhibit and facilitate spinal motoneurons, and additional respiratory nuclei are located in the pons.

The *midbrain* (mesencephalon) is the most anterior extension of the brain stem that still maintains the basic tubular structure of the spinal cord. It merges anteriorly into the thalamus and hypothalamus. The dorsal portion of the midbrain (the *tectum*) contains the superior and inferior colliculi, two pairs of important relay nuclei for the visual and auditory systems. These nuclei appear as four bumps on the dorsal surface of the midbrain (Fig. 3.19). The ventral portion of the midbrain (the *tegmentum*) contains nuclei for cranial nerves that control eye movement, all the ascending and descending tracts interconnecting the upper and lower portions of the brain, and the rostral portion of the reticular formation. A large nucleus (the *red nucleus*) is found here, as is a collection of dark, heavily pigmented cells, the *substantia nigra*. These structures are believed to be involved in the control of movement.

The medulla, pons, and midbrain developed early in the course of evolution and are surprisingly uniform in structure and organization from fish to man. There are, of course, some variations among species. Lower vertebrates such as the shark or frog, who have little cerebral cortex, have essentially no pyramidal tract and fewer ventral fiber bundles in the pons. A general principle of neural organization states that the size and complexity of a structure is related to the behavioral importance of that structure. In fish, which have no cerebral cortex, the superior and inferior colliculi are the important centers of seeing and hearing, and

102

Neuroanatomy:
the structural basis
of behavior and
awareness

are relatively large. Among mammals, the bat, for example, has a much enlarged inferior colliculus (auditory relay nucleus), correlated with its extensive use of auditory information. (The bat employs a sonar-like system. It emits high-frequency sound pulses and determines the location of objects in space by the echo sounds of the reflected pulses.) This principle of the relation of structure size to behavioral importance has supplied a number of clues about possible functions of brain structures (Chapter 6, Fig. 6.23).

In summary, the brain stem contains all fiber systems interconnecting higher brain structures and spinal cord; it also contains the cranial nerves and their nuclei (except for the olfactory and optic nerves), nuclei subserving vital functions and emotional expression, and many higher-order nuclei concerned with various sensory modalities. When all brain tissue above the midbrain is removed in an animal such as the cat, the animal can still exhibit an amazing variety of behaviors. Such animals can live for long periods, can walk, vocalize, eat, sleep, exhibit some components of emotional expression, and may even be capable of very limited learning (Bard and Macht, 1958).

Cerebellum

The cerebellum is a phylogenetically old structure and was probably the first to be specialized for sensory-motor coordination. It overlies the pons (Fig. 3.19) and typically presents a much convoluted appearance, having a large number of lobules separated by fissures. As in the cerebral cortex, the nerve cell bodies form a surface layer about 2 mm thick that covers the underlying white matter and the cerebellar nuclei. In terms of organization of nerve cells, the cerebellar cortex presents a remarkably similar appearance everywhere, in contrast to structures like the cerebral cortex, which exhibit marked regional characteristics.

The cortex and underlying nuclei of the cerebellum receive connections from the vestibular system, from spinal sensory fibers, from the auditory and visual systems, from various regions of the cerebral cortex, and from the reticular formation. The cerebellum sends motor fibers to the thalamus, reticular formation, and several other brain stem structures. Although it is probably involved in a number of other functions as well, the cerebellum is primarily concerned with the regulation of motor coordination. Removal of the cerebellum produces a characteristic syndrome (set of symptoms) of jerky, uncoordinated movement (Chapter 7).

Thalamus

The thalamus is a large grouping of nuclei located just anterior and dorsal to the midbrain. In gross appearance it is shaped somewhat like two small footballs, one within each cerebral hemisphere.

The many nuclei of the thalamus have been differentiated and named on the basis of several different sets of criteria, including histological appearance, anatomical location, and connections. The simplest classification is in terms of input and output connections. The three classes are sensory relay nuclei, association nuclei, and intrinsic nuclei.

Sensory relay nuclei receive projections from specific ascending sensory pathways and in turn project (relay) to specific sensory regions of the cerebral cortex. One major nucleus in this class receives visual fibers and relays to the visual cortex, another receives auditory projections and relays to the auditory cortex, and a third receives projections from the somatic-sensory system and projects to the somatic-sensory areas of the cerebral cortex. If the cerebral cortex is removed, all these nuclei degenerate completely because their axon terminals in the cortex are destroyed.

The *association nuclei* also project to the cerebral cortex and degenerate completely after removal of the cortex. However, these nuclei do not receive direct projections from ascending pathways, and they project to association areas of the cerebral cortex rather than to specific sensory regions.

104

Neuroanatomy:
the structural basis
of behavior and
awareness

The *intrinsic nuclei* are often classified as midline and intralaminar on the basis of anatomical location. They have interconnections with other thalamic regions, with the reticular formation, with various structures of the limbic systems (see below), and with some areas of the cerebral cortex. They appear to play a significant role in the regulation of spontaneous electrical activity in the cortex and are involved in the control of such processes as sleep, waking, and attention. They are sometimes viewed as composing a diffuse thalamic system.

The thalamus is an extremely complex structure. The above discussion indicates only a few of its major regions and their connections. Thalamic nuclei projecting up to the cortex also appear to receive projections *from* the cortex, and many project to lower brain regions as well. A great deal remains to be learned about the organization and functions of the thalamic nuclei, particularly the association and intrinsic groups. The sensory relay group may be thought of as *relatively* simple relay stations transmitting sensory information from lower regions of the brain to the cerebral cortex.

Hypothalamus

The term *hypothalamus* refers to a grouping of small nuclei that lie generally in the ventral portion of the cerebrum at the junction of the midbrain and thalamus. It is not possible to convey diagrammatically a clear picture of their rather complicated spatial layout. The various nuclei lie along the base of the brain (above the roof of the mouth) and are contiguous with the pituitary gland, which is innervated by neurons from the hypothalamus. These hypothalamic-hypophyseal interrelations have been found to be of crucial importance in the neural regulation of endocrine gland function. It is difficult to stress sufficiently the importance of the minute nuclei composing the hypothalamus. They are crucially involved in eating, sexual behavior, drinking, sleeping, temperature regulation, rage and violence, and behavior generally. The hypothalamus is the major central brain structure concerned with the functions of the autonomic nervous system, particularly with its sympathetic division.

The hypothalamus interconnects with many regions of the brain. A number of these structures, including the paleocortex (old cortex), portions of the rhinencephalon (nosebrain), the hippocampus, the septal area, and the hypothalamus itself, are viewed by many anatomists as composing an integrated network of structures called the limbic system. Many of these structures seem to be involved in aspects of behavior such as emotion, motivation, and reinforcement. Two separate chapters (Chapters 8 and 9) are devoted to the emotional and motivational aspects of behavior and their brain substrates.

Basal ganglia

These are a group of large nuclei (the term *ganglia* is a misnomer) lying in the central regions of the cerebral hemispheres. They partially surround the thalamus and are themselves enclosed by the cerebral cortex and cerebral white matter. The *amygdala*, sometimes included as well, has quite different connections and probably different functions from the other nuclei of the basal ganglia and is usually grouped in the limbic system. The remaining nuclei, collectively termed the *corpus striatum,* appear to play a role in the control of movement and form the major part of the extrapyramidal motor system. They have connections with the cortex, thalamus, hypothalamus, reticular formation, portions of the midbrain, and the spinal cord. It should be noted that the substantia nigra and the red nucleus of the midbrain, which are usually included in the extrapyramidal motor system, also have connections with corpus striatum.

The basal ganglia seem to be involved in motor activity and certainly have indirect connections with motoneurons. However, the specific functions they subserve remain a mystery. Animals display no particular motor dysfunctions after removal of the basal ganglia. In man, clinical evidence suggests that damage to the extrapyramidal system may produce two syndromes: hypertonia (an increased muscle tone that tends to restrict bodily movement and facial expression) and abnormal repetitive movements.

CAVEAT

The overall rapid trip through the brain we have just completed can lead to very erroneous notions about the nature of brain organization and functions. Many structures in the brain have distinct physical shapes and appearances and have been given particular names. It is easy for the student to visualize the brain as a very complicated hi-fi system with many components—an amplifier here, a tuner there, and so on. The brain is really not like that at all. It is a continuous series of interconnections among neurons. Many of the nerve cell bodies are grouped into clusters and shapes, but it is a mistake to think that a given "thing" in the brain, for example, the red nucleus, is in fact a structure with a particular function.

Much of our general information about the possible functions of brain structures still comes from the crudest of techniques. A given portion of the brain is damaged or destroyed and the associated loss of ability or the behavioral defects are noted. To jump from this kind of observation to the conclusion that particular structures have particular functions is wrong, particularly for higher regions of the brain. It is like trying to determine the function of one part of a TV circuit by smashing it with a hammer and noting how the TV set misbehaves.

Paradoxically, we began this chapter with a description of the speech area localized in association cortex of the left hemisphere. However, the inputs and outputs of this rather large region of brain, and the interrelated activities of many other parts of the brain, are necessary for speech and other higher functions. Abilities, complex behavioral processes, and consciousness do not live in particular pieces of neural tissue. They are the end result of the interrelated activities of the human brain, the most complex machine in the universe and seemingly the only machine that has ever attempted to understand itself.

106

Neuroanatomy:
the structural basis
of behavior and
awareness

Summary

Neuroanatomy focuses on the physical description of the brain—its shape, form, and structure, and the interconnections among neurons.

The cerebral cortex is the most recent evolutionary development of the vertebrate nervous system. If one examines the brains of successively more complex mammals, one finds a fairly regular increase in the amount of cortical tissue in relation to the total amount of brain tissue.

The cerebral cortex is the outer covering of the brain. Incoming (afferent) sensory systems project to specific regions of the cortex. Outgoing (efferent) systems, which control muscular and glandular activity, arise in other cortical regions. While the organization of cortical sensory and motor areas does not differ markedly in rat and man, the relative amount of association cortex is much greater in man.

The development of numerous fissures in the human brain serves an important function. These fissures have allowed a large increase in the amount of cortex in higher primates without any significant enlargement of skull. Two important fissures are the fissure of Rolando, which demarcates the cerebrum into anterior and posterior halves, and the sylvian fissure, which demarcates the temporal lobe.

The brain may be differentiated into various regions in relation to the fissures. In front of the central fissure lies the anterior portion of the brain. Both the frontal and precentral regions are located here. The frontal lobe extends back to the precentral (motor) cortex. The temporal lobe lies below and behind the sylvian (temporal) fissure. The occipital lobe is located in the posterior portion of precentral cortex. The parietal lobe lies between the occipital lobe and the central fissure.

A better understanding of the layers and areas of the cortex has been gained from the study of cytoarchitectonics—the microscopic analysis of cross sections of the cortex. In terms of nerve cell body appearance and distribution, six layers of cortex are identified: (1) molecular layer; (2) external granular layer; (3) medium pyramid layer; (4) internal granular layer; (5) large pyramid layer; and (6) spindle cell layer. Cortical cells are classified into four groups on the basis of their interconnections. The small cells with horizontal dendrites and axons are termed horizontal cells of Cajal if located in layer 1. The other three groups are the granule cells, pyramidal cells, and those cells that send axons toward the surface of the cortex.

Two generalizations hold for the organization of the cerebral cortex: (1) afferent fibers that project into the cortex from modality-specific systems terminate on granule cells in layer 4; (2) the pyramidal cells of layer 5 are enlarged in the region of the motor cortex and send their axons out to other brain areas.

The basic organization of the vertebrate brain is that of a segmented tube. This tubal organization of the brain is best seen in the earthworm, where nerves project into and out of each body segment from the corresponding segment of the tubular nervous system. In the earthworm there is also an enlargement of the cephalic end of the tube which is related to specialized receptors. In the human brain this tubular organization is maintained from the spinal cord to the midbrain.

Neurons and glia are the two major types of brain cells. While the functions of neurons are fairly well established, the function of the glia is uncertain. Neurons have a unique structural organization that allows them to act upon one another both chemically and electrically. The major characteristic structures of a neuron are the nerve cell body (soma), which contains the nucleus; the dendrites, which receive activity from adjacent cells and conduct activity to the soma; and the axon, which conducts activity out to other neurons or to muscles and glands. The synapse is the site of functional interaction between neurons. Synapses occur mainly on the soma and the dendrites of a neuron.

Three basic principles aid understanding of the structure of the nervous system: (1) in the spinal cord, cell bodies forming nuclei are located in the central core and are surrounded by fiber tracts; (2) those tracts

Summary

lying toward the outside tend to be ones that travel the farthest, while those lying toward the central core are shorter tracts; (3) in the cerebellum and cerebrum the fiber tracts lie more centrally and the layers of cell bodies are on the outside. However, many nuclei are buried within the central core of the cerebellum and cerebrum. Interactions among nerve cells occur mainly around the cell bodies where the axon terminals synapse on dendrites and cell bodies. Neuronal interactions occur within the gray matter; the white matter is composed of fibers connecting different regions of gray matter.

The peripheral nerves are those nerves that lie outside the spinal cord. They contain both afferent and efferent fibers. The cell bodies of afferent fibers are located in the dorsal root ganglia. These fibers are activated by peripheral receptors and convey information to the spinal cord through the dorsal roots.

The autonomic nerve fibers are involved with structures such as smooth muscle, heart muscle, and glands, which are concerned with autonomic aspects of responding. The autonomic system has two divisions: the sympathetic system and the parasympathetic system. In the sympathetic system, the motoneuron bodies are located in the spinal cord and run through the ventral root to the sympathetic ganglia, which run parallel to the spinal cord. Generally, the sympathetic system functions to activate bodily resources for emergencies. In contrast, the parasympathetic system motoneuron fibers come out through the cranial nerves, travel to the ganglia near the organs they innervate, and synapse there on short neurons that connect to these organs. The parasympathetic system in general functions to store and conserve the resources utilized by the sympathetic system. The brain regions that activate the autonomic nervous system are grouped together to form the limbic system.

It is important to distinguish between the structure of motor and sensory fibers. The cell bodies of the motor fibers are located in ventral regions of gray matter in the spinal cord and run out to muscles or autonomic ganglia. The cell bodies of the sensory fibers lie in dorsal root ganglia and enter the spinal cord to transmit information from receptors to spinal cord or to higher brain regions for additional processing.

Two basic categories of activity are handled by the spinal cord: spinal reflexes and supraspinal activity. In the spinal cord the dorsal regions of white matter contain the ascending fibers, which convey sensory information to the brain. Descending fiber systems are located in the lateral and ventral regions of white matter. These fiber systems all exert their influence ultimately upon motoneurons in the cord. The pyramidal tract fibers are entirely from the cortex. The extrapyramidal tract fibers are from the cortex and other brain regions.

The major subdivisions of the brain stem are the medulla, pons, midbrain, thalamus, and basal ganglia. The medulla contains the descending and ascending fiber tracts that interconnect the brain and spinal cord.

The reticular formation, located in the brain stem, plays an important role in activity. If the descending portions of the reticular formation are stimulated, the activity of the motoneurons controlling skeletal musculature is either inhibited or facilitated. The ascending reticular formation is involved in the control of sleep and wakefulness. The pons is the upward continuation of the brain stem that contains ascending and descending fiber tracts. The midbrain anteriorly merges into the hypothalamus and thalamus. The dorsal portion of the midbrain is termed the tectum and contains the superior and inferior colliculi. The tegmentum, the ventral portion of the midbrain, contains the red nucleus and the substantia nigra, which are believed to be involved in movement control.

The cerebellum is a phylogenetically old structure with a similar appearance throughout in terms of the organization of nerve cells. The cerebellum is primarily involved with the regulation of motor coordination.

The thalamus is located anterior and dorsal to the midbrain. In terms of input and output connections, there are three classes of thalamic nuclei: sensory relay nuclei, association nuclei, and intrinsic nuclei. The thalamus is a complex structure. Apparently, thalamic nuclei that project to the cortex also receive projections from the cortex.

The hypothalamus is a group of small nuclei located in the ventral portion of the cerebrum. These nuclei are crucial for the regulation of eating, sexual behavior, drinking, sleeping, temperature, and violence. The hypothalamus is the major central brain structure involved with the functioning of the autonomic nervous system, in particular the sympathetic branch.

The basal ganglia are groups of large nuclei found in the central regions of the cerebral hemispheres. The amygdala is occasionally included with the basal ganglia, although its connections and functions are different from those of other nuclei of the basal ganglia. The other nuclei are termed the corpus striatum; this structure forms a major part of the extrapyramidal motor system. While the basal ganglia appear to be involved in motor activity, their specific functions are unclear.

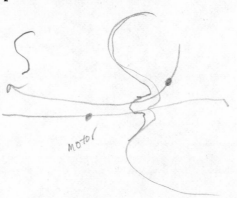

4

The electrical signs of
brain activity

4

The brain is an enchanted loom where millions of flashing shuttles [nerve impulses] weave a dissolving pattern, always a meaningful pattern though never an abiding one; a shifting harmony of sub-patterns.

—Sir Charles Sherrington

In the previous chapter we saw that the cerebral cortex, the highest and most recent region of the brain to develop, is expanded in humans to overshadow and dominate the entire brain. Three-fourths of the neurons in the human brain are in the cerebral cortex. Except in unusual circumstances, like brain surgery during which abnormal tissues must be found and removed, it is not possible to insert electrodes in human brain tissue.

ELECTROENCEPHALOGRAPHY

Perhaps the simplest method of recording and studying the electrical signs of human brain activity is by use of the electroencephalogram (EEG). Wires are glued to the surface of the scalp to record the electrical activity (voltage) generated by the underlying brain (Fig. 4.1). Because the signals are weak, in the microvolt (millionths of a volt) range, they are first amplified and then displayed on a polygraph—usually an ink record made on moving paper.

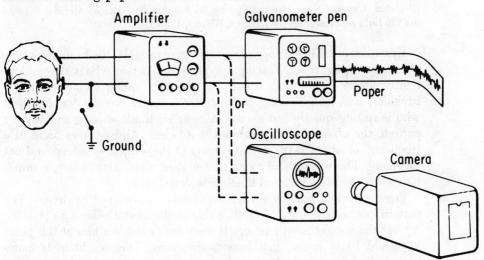

Figure 4.1 Block diagram of EEG recording system. The scalp electrode is the active one which records the voltage generated by the brain. The indifferent electrode comes from a neutral point such as the ear. The signals from the brain are amplified and then are displayed on a polygraph. (From Thompson, R. F. *Foundations of Physiological Psychology.* New York: Harper & Row, 1967.)

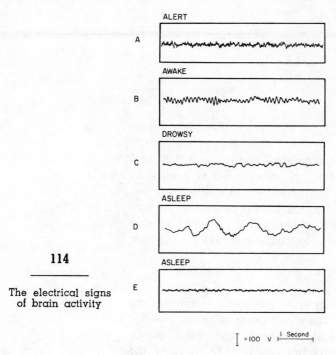

ALERT

A

AWAKE

B

DROWSY

C

ASLEEP

D

ASLEEP

E

I =100 V $\vdash\!\!\overset{\text{I Second}}{\underline{\qquad}}\!\!\dashv$

Figure 4.2 Typical human EEG records during different states. Alpha waves (8-12/sec) are commonly observed in resting awake state (B). In D, the wave pattern is called slow-wave sleep and exhibits large slow delta waves. In E, deep sleep, the record resembles the alert waking state. (Modified from Brazier, Mary A. B. *The Electrical Activity of the Nervous System.* 3d Ed. London: Pitman Medical Publishing Co. Ltd., and Baltimore: Williams & Wilkins, 1968.)

Examples of EEG tracings of voltages generated by the brain over time are shown in Figure 4.2. Tracing A, typical for a person who is alert and attentive, shows few obvious waves; the activity (voltage change) is small, irregular, and fast. Tracing B illustrates a typical record for a subject who is resting quietly but awake. A clear rhythmic waxing and waning pattern, the *alpha rhythm,* becomes quite clear. Alpha waves occur at a frequency of about 8-12/sec. In tracing D the subject is asleep and not dreaming. The waves tend to be slower than alpha and of larger amplitude (this condition is called *slow-wave sleep*).

Tracing E is a pattern for a subject who has started to dream. The pattern has become much more like that of the alert awake state (tracing A) but the subject is still asleep. If we were to awaken him at this point he would likely report that he was dreaming. This condition is sometimes called "paradoxical" sleep because the person is deeply asleep by behavioral criteria but his EEG is that of the alert waking state. It is also referred to as REM (from *Rapid Eye Movements*) sleep; the eyes show irregular bursts of movements as though the subject is looking at objects in his dreams. In slow-wave sleep these rapid eye movements are not present. If we were to wait until the subject awakened naturally, he would probably be unable to tell us whether or not he was dreaming at the time we noted the occurrence of paradoxical sleep. Most dreaming is reported to occur in REM periods, a fact which was discovered by awakening subjects during periods of REM and non-REM sleep. Thus an EEG can tell us with a good degree of accuracy whether or not a sleeping person dreamed during the recording of the brain waves. However we cannot yet tell with any certainty *what* he dreamed about. The topic of sleep and dreaming will be treated in more detail in Chapter 10.

Historically, the EEG was the first kind of electrical activity to be recorded from the brain. An English scientist named Caton, working in 1895 with anesthetized animals, not humans, reported that the brains showed variations in voltage. Because the available electrical recording device was primitive, Caton was unable to draw specific conclusions about the brain activity of the animals. Interestingly, the first meaningful recording of EEG was performed on a human subject. Hans Berger, a somewhat obscure German psychiatrist in Jena, placed large metal discs on the head of a human volunteer and connected them to a primitive recording device, a galvanometer. In his first paper, published in 1929, Berger noted that, for a relaxed adult subject, there were regular sequences of waves at about 10 per second. Berger, who named these the alpha waves, noted that they were best observed when the subject's eyes were closed and he was relaxed. He also noted smaller amplitude waves that were faster in frequency, ranging from about 18 to 50 per second, which he called the beta waves. Berger's discovery, at first ignored by most scientists, was imitated in the 1930s. Animals were used as subjects at that time. With the development of vacuum tube amplifiers, the field literally exploded.

Some sense of the excitement and enthusiasm of that period comes through in the writings of Dr. Donald B. Lindsley of UCLA, one of the pioneers in the study of EEG.

It is difficult to explain to a modern generation of research workers in neuroscience and electrophysiology what the early days of electrophysiology and electroencephalography were like! Today we are heirs to 30 years of vast technological development, with many choices of fine amplifying and recording equipment and ample funds to buy it ready-made. The 1930s was an era of economic depression with almost no funds available for research, and even if money had been available, the equipment, or the parts to make it, would not have been, for radio and electronics were in their infancy and there were few manufacturers of electronic parts and equipment. Consequently, the period of the early 1930s was one of "blood, sweat, and tears" for the electrophysiologist and electroencephalographer. But they were days of hope and inspiration and improvisation; and they were days of cooperation and collaboration.

115

Electroencephalography

Figure 4.3 Modern electroencephalography laboratory. 1. Tektronix 502 Oscilloscope; 2. Tektronix Polaroid Camera; 3. Grass Kymograph Camera; 4. Grass Physiological Stimulators; 5. Tektronix Power Supply, Waveform and Pulse Generators; 6, Moseley X-Y Plotter; 7. Massey-Dickinson Control and Programming Equipment; 8. Power Supply; 9. Hewlett-Packard Counter; 10. Tapereader; 11. Oscilloscope Monitors; 12. Mne-motron Computer of Average Transient (CAT) and Accessories; 13. Preset Controller and Tape Coder; 14. Ampex FR-1300 7-channel FM Tape Recorder; 15. Grass Model 6 8-channel EEG. (Lindsley, Donald B., and Wicke, J. D. The electroencephalogram: autonomous electrical activity in man and animals. From Thompson, R. F., and Patterson, M. M. (eds.). *Bioelectric Recording Techniques*, **IB.** New York: Academic Press, 1974, pp. 3–83.)

One "begged or borrowed" condensers, tubes, resistors, and other components necessary to build an amplifier. The input tubes of the amplifier were not very noise free and had to be carefully shock mounted against building vibration and even sound waves; the amplifiers often had to be shielded in a copper lined and sound attenuated box and suspended by screen door springs. Voltage amplifiers were operated from batteries, with separate batteries for filament, plate, and screen grid-voltages. The batteries were large and cumbersome; the transformers supplying voltage for the power stages of the amplifier were large and heavy and together with the vacuum tubes generated much heat.

(Lindsley and Wicke, 1974, page 9)

A photograph of a modern electroencephalography laboratory is shown in Figure 4.3. A bewildering array of equipment is necessary for special-

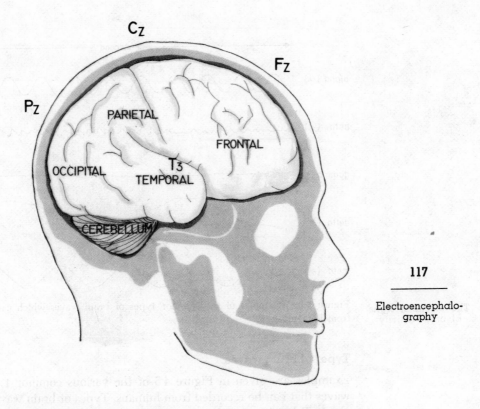

Figure 4.4 Schematic drawing of the human brain *in situ* in the head and some typical electrode placement locations.

ized purposes. The basic method of recording the EEG, indicated in Figure 4.1, is simple. Wire electrodes, with an application of conducting jelly, are glued to the surface of the scalp. Wires connect the electrodes to an amplifier. The amplifier simply increases the amplitude of the voltage recorded by the wires. Then the amplifier is connected to a polygraph, a device that records with an ink pen on moving paper. It displays a plot of the changes in voltage over time of the electrical activity of the brain. A schematic drawing of the human brain *in situ* in the head and some typical electrode placement locations are shown in Figure 4.4. Today, clinical electroencephalographers follow a standardized placement of electrodes set forth by the so-called 10/20 system; this allows reliable determination of brain activity, both normal and abnormal. It should be noted here that the major use of electroencephalography has been in clinical studies of human brain dysfunction. It has been a very powerful and successful tool in the diagnosis and localization of certain forms of epilepsy and brain damage. However, it is also a widely used research tool for the study of the normal functions of the human brain.

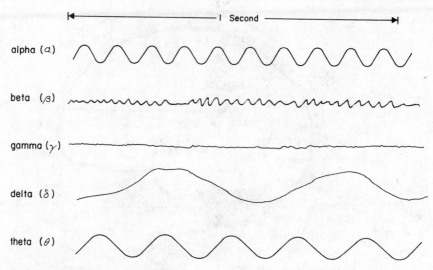

	|←————————— 1 Second —————————→|
alpha (α)	
beta (β)	
gamma (γ)	
delta (δ)	
theta (θ)	

Figure 4.5 Examples of the common types of brain waves which can be recorded from humans.

The electrical signs
of brain activity

Types of brain waves

Examples are given in Figure 4.5 of the various common type of brain waves that can be recorded from humans. Types of brain waves are listed also in Table 4.1.

Table 4.1 Types of brain waves in the human electroencephalogram, their frequencies, and conditions when present

Type of wave or rhythm	Frequency per second (range)	Condition when present
Alpha	8–12	Awake, relaxed, eyes closed
Beta	18–30	Awake, no movement
Gamma	30–50	Awake
Delta	0.5–4	Asleep
Theta	5–7	Awake, affective or stress
Kappa	8–12	Awake, problem solving (?)

Adapted from Lindsley, D. B., and Wicke, J. D. The electroencephalogram: autonomous electrical activity in man and animals. From Thompson, R. F., and Patterson, M. M. (eds.) **Bioelectric Recording Techniques, IB.** New York: Academic Press, 1974, pp. 3–83.

Alpha waves. The alpha waves, first observed by Berger on an EEG of a human, are the 10-per-second variation present from widespread regions of the brain when the subject is awake and physically relaxed in an environment free of sudden stimuli. Alpha waves can be recorded for people over 12 years old. The size or amplitude of the alpha wave can range from a few microvolts to a few hundred microvolts (one microvolt equals one millionth of a volt). The more relaxed and at ease the subject is, the larger and more prominent are the alpha waves. Interestingly, some people do not show clear alpha waves, although they are present for the majority of subjects. During an EEG in which alpha waves are being displayed, the startling or sudden arousal of the subject causes the alpha waves to stop. This is called *alpha blocking*. One way to cause alpha blocking is simply to shine a light in the subject's eyes. The alpha immediately stops. In other words, alpha seems to be inversely related to arousal. If the subject is not aroused, alpha is likely to occur. If he is aroused, alpha will stop. Consequently, alpha bears an inverse relationship to the general state of arousal or alertness of the individual and must therefore be related to brain mechanisms concerned with arousal and alerting. The reticular activating system (RAS), the major brain system involved in arousal, is treated in a later section. Indeed, the blocking of the alpha response by any kind of arousing stimulus is often called an activation or an *arousal response.*

Beta and gamma waves. Although Berger first defined beta waves as fast, with a low voltage rhythm of about 20 to 50 per second, this category was later subdivided. Jasper defined *beta waves* as those ranging from 18 to 30 per second, and *gamma waves* as those ranging from 30 to 50 per second. Beta and gamma waves have not been studied as much as alpha waves, and less is known about them. They occur at higher states of arousal or alerting than alpha.

Delta waves. Very slow, large amplitude waves of about two or three per second, delta waves normally occur only in slow-wave sleep where the EEG shows the very large, slow synchronized waves and rapid eye movements do not occur. Delta waves are also common in unconsciousness induced by anesthesia, by head injury, or by convulsions. Certain types of brain injury can cause a prominent display of delta waves. If present in a waking subject, they may indicate severe brain malfunction or brain damage.

Theta waves. Slightly slower than the alpha wave, the *theta wave* has a frequency of about five to seven per second. Theta waves are observable particularly over temporal (sides) and frontal (front) regions of the head, and are particularly prominent in adolescents and children. These waves are very characteristic of one particular brain structure, the hippocampus, and other portions of the so-called limbic system, as well as of the frontal and temporal regions of the cerebral cortex. In animal studies the data suggest that theta waves from the hippocampus may occur at the same time that alpha is blocked in the cerebral cortex. In other words, when an animal is aroused his cortical alpha stops and his hippocampal theta becomes intensified. Under many circumstances these two rhythms seem to show a reciprocal relationship. When alpha stops, theta becomes larger, and vice versa. One interesting aspect of theta waves is that they seem to be much more common in children with behavioral disorders.

Kappa waves. One form of EEG wave surrounded by controversy is the so-called *kappa wave*. J. L. Kennedy and associates (1948) described an alpha-like rhythm at the temples which they thought was associated with intellectual processes. With a frequency of about 8 to 12 per second, the same as the alpha rhythm, kappa waves tend to occur in spindle-shaped bursts. They are reported to increase when a subject is reading, doing mental arithmetic, making difficult discriminations, memorizing material, and solving problems. Some authorities attribute the so-called kappa wave largely to artifacts from eye movements. The voltage gradients across the various chambers of the eye record voltage changes on the EEG when the eyes move. Simply by looking at the EEG record it is not possible to distinguish between eye movement voltages and brain EEG voltages. Since eye movements can occur at about these same rhythms in bursts, they may contribute to the so-called kappa response. However, a recent study by Chapman (1972) suggests that some subjects may show a reliable kappa rhythm correlated with mental activity which cannot be attributed to eye movements.

Brain waves as indicators of behavior disorders

Pioneering studies relating brain waves to behavior problems were made by Donald Lindsley and his associates some years ago (Lindsley and Cutts, 1940; Lindsley and Henry, 1942). Figure 4.6 illustrates brain waves in the EEG of a normal child (A) and two children with behavior disorders (B and C). Record A from an 11-year-old boy with no apparent disorders shows well-regulated alpha waves of about 10 per second in the occipital, parietal, and central regions and a mixture of alpha and faster beta waves in the frontal region. Record B, the EEG of an eight-year-old boy with a behavior disorder, shows abnormal slow-wave activity in all regions but especially in the parietal region. Record C is the EEG of a 10-year-old boy with a behavior disorder. The frontal EEG tracings show prominent bursts of 6 per second theta activity. Both children with this abnormal slow brain wave activity had severe behavior problems. Otherwise, both were healthy and responded normally in physical and neurological examinations. Lindsley summarizes this work:

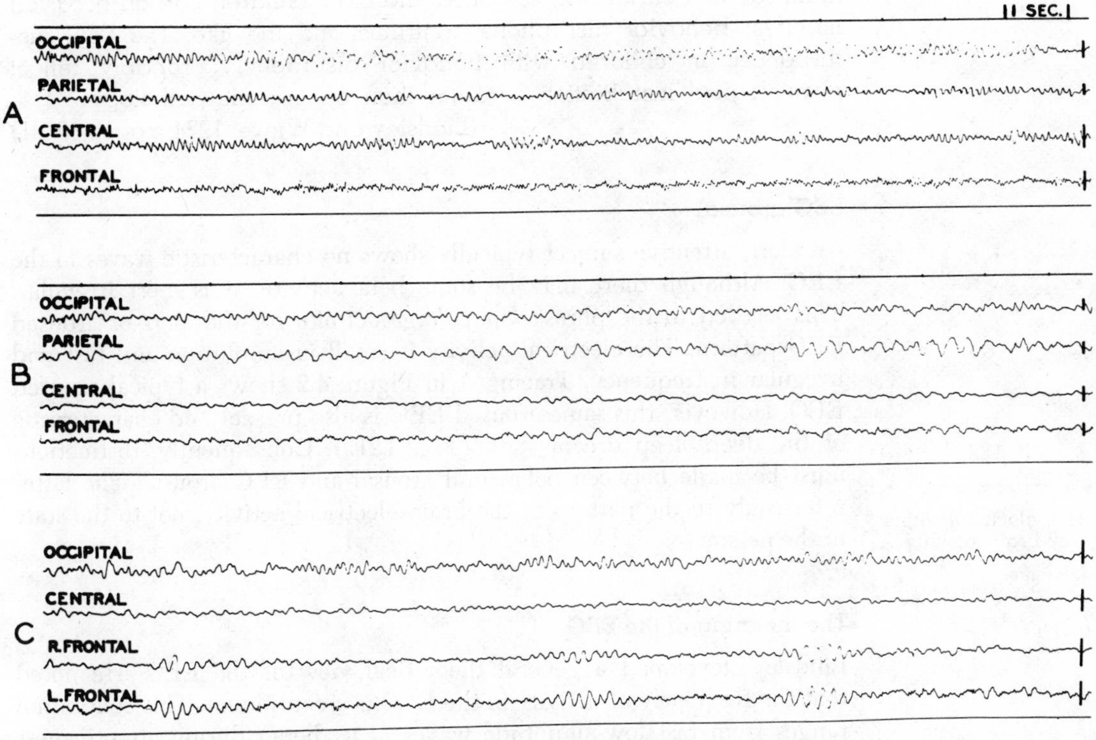

|1 SEC.|

Figure 4.6 EEG waves of a child with no apparent disorders and of two children with behavior disorders. A, EEG of normal 11-year-old boy showing well-regulated alpha rhythms and no abnormal waves. B, EEG of an 8-year-old child with a behavior problem, which shows abnormal delta waves particularly in the parietal region. C, EEG of 10-year-old child with a behavior problem, which shows abnormal theta activity in frontal areas and normal alpha activity in the occipital region. (From Lindsley, D. B., and Cutts, K. K. Electroencephalograms of "constitutionally inferior" and behavior problem children. *Arch. Neurol. Psychiat.* 44, 1940, pp. 1199–1212. Copyright 1940, American Medical Association.)

Several studies have shown that approximately 75 percent of children with behavior disorders will manifest one of these types of "abnormalities" in their EEG. The aberrant waves and rhythms are much less prominent both in voltage and in percent of time present than in children with convulsive disorder or other types of neurological problems. The EEGs of "normal" children show a small amount of these slower than alpha rhythms, but generally they form a sharp contrast with the behavior problem groups in terms of the incidence and amount. Much of the time behavior problem children appear like normal children, but their behavior may be rather intensely disturbing at times and aberrant behavior seems to have a lower threshold for the effects of environmental stress, both physiological and psychological. On the other hand, as is well known, so-called "normal" children can on occasion manifest behavior disruptions, tantrums and the like. The EEG disturbances in children with behavior disorders...probably reflect physiological instabilities...rather than an organic pathology.

(Lindsley and Wicke, 1974, pages 30–31)

EEG arousal

An alert, attentive subject typically shows no characteristic waves in the EEG. Although there may be some beta activity, it is most irregular. This has led to the phrase *low-voltage activity* for the alert or aroused EEG pattern. The electrical activity is small in amplitude and fast and irregular in frequency. Tracing A in Figure 4.2 shows a typical aroused EEG. However, this same aroused EEG is also present and characteristic of the deep sleep dream state (Fig. 4.2E). Consequently, distinctions must be made between behavioral arousal and EEG arousal. The latter refers only to the pattern of the brain electrical activity, not to the state of the person.

The meaning of the EEG

Lindsley developed a general theoretical view of the EEG. He noted that the frequency of activity in the EEG is a continuum. This continuum ranges from fast low-amplitude waves (e.g., beta) during attentiveness and arousal, to the slower alpha waves of the normal waking relaxed state, to waves of gradually lower and lower frequency as sleep and its deeper stages follow, and ends with the slow delta waves of slow-wave sleep. However, do not forget that in very deep or REM sleep with rapid eye movements and dreaming, the EEG pattern shifts to the aroused waking type of beta and fast activity waves. Nonetheless, Lindsley's general model has a good deal of empirical validity. Table 4.2 represents Lindsley's summary of behavior and EEG phenomena in terms of the continuum of arousal.

EEG development in children. The EEG has been used to follow the development of children. Figure 4.7 shows the EEG recorded from a child subject from infancy up through young adulthood. [Incidentally, Dr. Donald Lindsley recorded these waves, with his son, David Lindsley, as the subject. David is now a well known neurophysiologist.] No regular brain rhythm is obvious at all in the newborn, and no alpha waves in infants. The onset of a regular brain rhythm over the occipital region first occurs at three or four months of age with a frequency of three to four waves per second. The frequency increases to about five or six per second

Table 4.2 Psychological states and their EEG and conscious correlates

Behavioral continuum	Electroencephalogram	State of awareness
Strong, excited emotion (fear) (rage) (anxiety)	Desynchronized: Low to moderate amplitude; fast, mixed frequencies	Restricted awareness; divided attention; diffuse, hazy; "confusion"
Alert attentiveness	Partially synchronized: Mainly fast, low-amplitude waves	Selective attention, but may vary or shift. "Concentration" anticipation, "set"
Relaxed wakefulness	Synchronized: Optimal alpha rhythm	Attention wanders—not forced. Favors free association
Drowsiness	Reduced alpha and occasional low-amplitude slow waves	Borderline, partial awareness. Imagery and reverie. "Dreamlike states"
Light sleep	Spindle bursts and slow waves (larger). Loss of alphas	Markedly reduced consciousness (loss of consciousness). Dream state
Deep sleep	Large and very slow waves (synchrony but on slow time base). Random, irregular pattern	Complete loss of awareness (no memory for stimulation or for dreams)
Coma	Isoelectric to irregular large slow waves	Complete loss of consciousness, little or no response to stimulation; amnesia
Death	Isoelectric: Gradual and permanent disappearance of all electrical activity	Complete loss of awareness as death ensues

From Lindsley, D.B. Psychological phenomena and the electroencephalogram. Electroencephalog. Clin. Neurophysiol. 4, 1952, pp. 443–456.

123

Electroencephalography

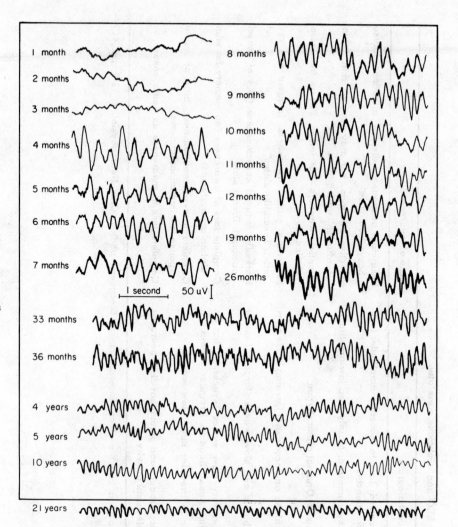

1 month

2 months

3 months

4 months

5 months

6 months

7 months

|—— 1 second ——| 50 uV

33 months

36 months

4 years

5 years

10 years

21 years

8 months

9 months

10 months

11 months

12 months

19 months

26 months

Figure 4.7 Development of EEG in children. Recordings are from age 1 month to 21 years in same child. The frequency of activity gradually increases to reach the adult alpha frequency level of about 10/sec by about 10 years of age. (From Lindsley, D. B. Attention, consciousness, sleep, and wakefulness. In Field, J. (ed.) *Handbook of Physiology-Neurophysiology,* III. Washington, D.C.: American Physiological Society (1960), pp. 1553–1593.)

at the end of the first year. After this, frequency gradually increases until by about 10 years of age the adult alpha frequency level of about 10 per second is reached. Indeed, the 10-year-old child exhibits an essentially adult pattern of EEG.

The EEG and biofeedback. There is much popular discussion of the alpha wave today. Some companies now sell devices to allow a person to "control" his own alpha. These devices are simply poor men's electroencephalograms which are purported to record the brain EEG in the alpha range from surface electrodes on the scalp. They provide *biofeedback* to the subject about the state of his brain waves. A tone or other signal to the subject indicates that he is generating alpha. The subject's task is to attempt to keep the tone on as much as possible, that is, to train his alpha to occur more frequently. Absurd claims are made for these devices and for the value of the alpha state. In fact, alpha is a correlate of normal, relaxed waking. If you are able to generate more alpha, it means simply that you are able to relax. Induced relaxation may be very beneficial for people who normally are so tense that they cannot relax. However, there is nothing mystical about EEG alpha; it is simply an index of relaxed wakefulness. Interestingly, in the state of so-called "transcendental meditation," EEG alpha intensifies and may become slower in frequency. Whether transcendental meditation is merely a relaxed, wakeful state or something more remains to be determined. However, when you turn on by tuning in your alpha, you are simply relaxing.

THE AVERAGED EVOKED POTENTIAL

With the development of computers a new form of brain recording became possible in human subjects. If you were to present a sudden stimulus like a "click" or a weak shock to a finger of a subject while you were recording his EEG on a standard EEG machine, you might or might not see a tiny blip on the EEG record. The example in Figure 4.8

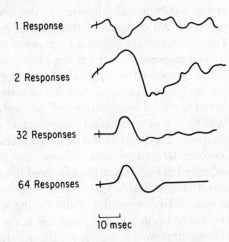

1 Response

2 Responses

32 Responses

64 Responses

|— 10 msec

Figure 4.8 Use of an average response computer to average out spontaneous background noise. The trace is a gross EEG record from the scalp overlying the somatic-sensory area of man and the stimulus is a brief shock to the finger. A single evoked response (top trace) can be seen emerging from the noise (positive up). (From Thompson, R. F. *Foundations of Physiological Psychology.* New York: Harper & Row, 1967.)

(top trace) shows a brain potential evoked by the stimulus. The small blip is buried in ongoing EEG activity, perhaps alpha or faster beta activity, and is nearly impossible to distinguish from the background activity. The background activity has been occurring before the shock is felt and has no relation to the shock. It is random in time in relation to the shock and could be anywhere from highly positive to highly negative. Consequently, it washes out the small evoked response of the brain to the shock stimulus. It is very simple to give a number of trials of the shock stimulus and average the results with a computer. An example of what happens when the EEG is averaged is shown in Figure 4.8. Initially you see activity random in relation to the shock, perhaps alpha activity, so that the shock-evoked potential cannot be seen. However, more and more alpha and other background brain responses average out to zero because they bear no relation to the shock. They could be either positive or negative at any time but the net average is no activity or zero. However, the small blip that occurred to the shock, initially much smaller than alpha, will gradually get larger and more prominent. It always occurs at the same time after the shock. In fact, only 10 to 20 trials are needed to obtain a clear averaged scalp-recorded evoked potential from the human brain. An average of 10 cancels out enough of the background brain activity and allows you to see the evoked potential.

The current study of evoked potentials reveals many fascinating relations between the characteristics of the potentials and psychological processes like attention and perception. Donald Lindsley was one of the pioneers in this field. He first showed that the state of attention of the subject, i.e., whether you instruct him to attend to the stimulus or not, makes a substantial difference in the size and form of the average evoked potential. An example of this kind of experiment is shown in Figure 4.9. The subjects were given a long series of faint light flashes and the brain evoked responses recorded from the occipital region of the scalp over the visual area of the cerebral cortex. The subjects were required to press a key each time they detected the occurrence of a light flash. It may be inferred that they were "attending" properly when they detected the flash (the light flash was of constant intensity and above perceptual threshold). The computer then sorted the brain responses to the constant light flash into "correct detections" and "misses" and averaged the response to each. As indicated in Figure 4.9, the averaged brain-evoked response to the correctly detected light flash was significantly larger than the averaged brain response to misses. In comparable studies using a weak sound stimulus (click) and recording brain activity from the scalp overlying the auditory region of the cerebral cortex, similar results occurred—the brain response was larger for detected clicks than for missed clicks. When both types of stimuli—light flashes and clicks—were given and the subjects instructed to attend only the flashes or only to clicks, brain responses were always larger for the stimulus to which the subjects were attending. Here, then, is a kind of brain measure that is very sensitive to relatively subtle differences in the subject's "instructional set" or attentive state.

126

———

The electrical signs of brain activity

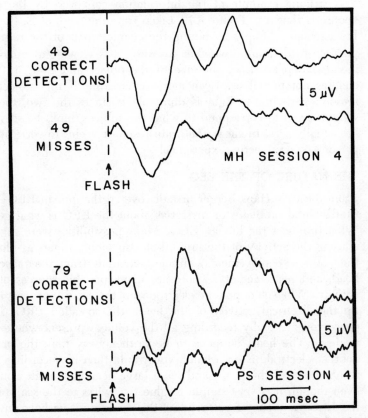

49
CORRECT
DETECTIONS

5 μV

49
MISSES

MH SESSION 4

↑
FLASH

79
CORRECT
DETECTIONS

5 μV

79
MISSES

PS SESSION 4

↑
FLASH

100 msec

Figure 4.9 Computer-averaged evoked responses to faint light flashes for two subjects (M. H. and P. S.). The responses are sensitive to differences in the subjects' attentional state. The brain potentials were separated into two categories—those flashes detected by the subject (that is, he is attending successfully to the task) and those missed. The brain potentials are larger for detected flashes than for missed flashes. (From Haider, M., Spong, P., and Lindsley, D. B. Attention, vigilance, and cortical evoked potentials. *Science* **145**, 1964, pp. 180–182. Copyright 1964 by the American Association for the Advancement of Science.)

Figure 4.10 Averaged brain responses from two separate sessions by the same subject. Note the similarities in responses to the same object of different sizes and the differences between responses to squares and diamonds. Negative deflections upward. (John, E. R., Herrington, R. N., and Sutton, S. Effects of visual form on the evoked response. *Science* **155**, 1967, pp. 1439–1442. Copyright 1967 by the American Association for the Advancement of Science.)

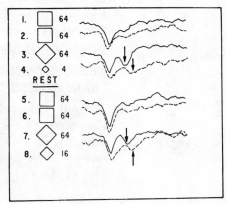

1. □ 64
2. □ 64
3. ◇ 64
4. ◇ 4
REST
5. □ 64
6. □ 64
7. ◇ 64
8. ◇ 16

A striking example of the information conveyed by the evoked response is shown in Figure 4.10, taken from the work of E. Roy John and his associates. Simply by noting the characteristic of the responses, it is possible to determine whether the subject is viewing a square or a diamond, independent of the size of the object and even if the subject chooses not to tell us. Even more remarkable, if the subject for some reason (perhaps the light is dimmed) mistakes the two, the brain responses seem to correspond to what the subject thinks he sees, not what he actually sees. In short, the brain response seems to correlate with the person's own subjective experience!

THE NATURE OF THE EEG

From the time Hans Berger first discovered the human EEG, one of the fundamental problems or mysteries about the EEG is what generates it. What produces the human EEG? Many possibilities were suggested, including the activity of the brain, but also such artifacts as blood flow in the scalp, eye movements, muscle potentials from the muscles of the head, and heart activity. There are many possible sources of electrical activity. When you put an electrode on the head, you can easily pick up the electrical activity of the heart, the so-called EKG. This is because you are really recording all the voltages present where your electrode is. The heart happens to be farther away than the brain, but if another electrode is on a hand, you would then be recording from head to hand, across the heart, and see a large heart potential. Consequently, even though it is very simple to glue two wires to the scalp and record the EEG (any one of you reading this could do it without any trouble), it is difficult to be sure you are not recording other sources of potential, like heart muscle activity. With modern techniques and care, it is possible to record activity from the scalp which is generated almost entirely from the brain. To oversimplify a very large research literature, most of the EEG activity recorded from the surface of the scalp in a normal human being is generated by the cerebral cortex. This means that it is presumably generated by the neurons in the cerebral cortex. What aspect of the electrical activity of neurons is recorded in the EEG? This turns out to be a somewhat complicated question. To address the question properly, we must first consider the basic processes of information transmission in neurons.

NEUROPHYSIOLOGY—THE CONDUCTION AND TRANSMISSION OF INFORMATION IN NERVE CELLS

Neurophysiology, literally the functions of the nervous system, emphasizes study of the electrical aspects of brain function. There are many different ways of recording electrical activity from the central nervous system. These range in complexity from simply gluing wire on the surface of the scalp, as described above, to inserting very tiny microelec-

trodes inside single nerve cells. The resulting record is a plot of voltage changes over time. Every nerve cell in the brain generates voltages. A gross averaged recording, such as that of Figure 4.10, sums many different kinds of neural activity. From the point of view of understanding how the brain works, it is necessary to understand the types of electrical activity characteristic of single nerve cells.

In higher organisms all behavior is a reflection of the activity of the brain. Viewed in these terms, each of us is simply a brain together with a few minor input and output appendages. The brain itself is essentially a set of interconnecting elements, the neurons. Each neuron receives information from other neurons or sensory receptors and transmits information to other neurons or muscles. All stimuli impinging upon us, all sensations, thoughts, feelings, and actions of a person must be coded into the "language" of the neuron. Every neuron transmits information in two quite different languages or codes. A given neuron is activated, in a continuous fashion, by other neurons. This is the *graded decision-process language* of the neuron. The activated nerve cell transmits this activity along a fiber by an all-or-none spike or action potential to act on other neurons. This is the "action" language that transmits activity to other neurons.

The basic events involved in conduction and transmission, and the portions of the neuron involved in each, are sketched in Figure 4.11. The *action potential* or *spike discharge,* which conducts information along the nerve cell fiber, is probably most familiar to the reader. This is the all-or-none impulse that travels down the axon of the nerve cell and produces effects on other nerve cells at synapses (Fig. 4.11). The size of a given spike discharge is constant, and once started it travels all the way down the axon to the synapses. The statement that nerves conduct in an all-or-none fashion refers to this spike discharge event. An analogy is often made with a *digital* computer; just as the spike discharge either does or does not occur, each element in the digital computer can be in only one of two possible states (Yes or No). This decision made by a neuron to fire or not fire, however, depends upon an entirely different kind of activity, often termed *synaptic* or *graded* activity. When the nerve cell body and dendrites are activated or stimulated by other nerve cells (at synapses on the cell), small shifts are induced in the electrical potential of the cell membrane (Fig. 4.11). The amount of these shifts is proportional to the amount and kind of incoming activity. In fact the size of the graded potential varies in a continuous fashion. If the change in the graded potential is sufficiently large, the *spike discharge threshold* of the cell is reached and an all-or-none spike discharge travels down the axon. If the graded potential does not reach spike discharge threshold, *no activity* is conducted down the axon. The occurrence of these graded potentials in the nerve cell body can be likened to a decision-making process. The neuron considers all incoming activity, and depending on

129

Neurophysiology
—the conduction
and transmission of
information in nerve
cells

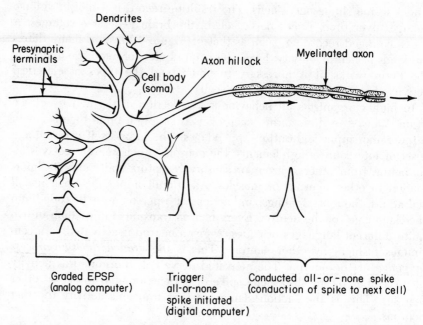

Dendrites

Presynaptic
terminals

Cell body
(soma)

Axon hillock

Myelinated axon

The electrical signs
of brain activity

Graded EPSP
(analog computer)

Trigger:
all-or-none
spike initiated
(digital computer)

Conducted all-or-none spike
(conduction of spike to next cell)

Figure 4.11 Summary diagram showing locations on the motor neuron of the events responsible for impulse initiation. Dendrites and cell body give graded *excitatory post-synaptic potentials* (EPSPs); the action potential is triggered in the initial segment (axon hillock) and travels down the axon. (From Thompson, R. F. *Foundations of Physiological Psychology*. New York: Harper & Row, 1967.)

the amount and type of this activity, "decides" to fire or not fire. These graded potentials often have been compared to the operation of an *analog* computer, which processes signals that vary in amplitude continuously.

Although somewhat overworked, firing a gun provides a simple analogy to activating a nerve cell. A small squeeze on the trigger produces nothing. A squeeze that is sufficient to activate the firing pin causes the cartridge to discharge a bullet. Two smaller squeezes given close enough together in time (so that the second squeeze occurs when the trigger is maximally pulled by the first squeeze) may also activate the firing pin (temporal summation). Alternatively, if the safety is on, the effect of the squeeze is nullified (inhibition). The velocity of the bullet has no relation to the strength of the trigger squeeze; it is dependent only upon intrinsic characteristics of the cartridge and gun. In the analogy no axon discharge occurs in a neuron until the spike discharge threshold is reached. When the graded potentials induced in the cell cross this threshold, a spike discharge is fired down the axon. The characteristics of the spike, such as its amplitude and velocity, have nothing whatever to do with the graded potentials that trigger the spike; the size of the graded potentials is determined by intrinsic characteristics of the axon (primarily its size and the presence or absence of myelin).

The nerve membrane potential

It has been known for a good many years that two types of electrical events are associated with the membrane potential of the nerve axon. When a nerve is at rest, not conducting, there is a steady *resting membrane potential*. If could measure the voltage across the resting nerve cell membrane (the structure that forms the boundary between the inside and outside of the neuron), we would find that it is nearly one-tenth of a volt. This resting membrane potential is analogous somewhat to the potential difference that exists across the two poles of a battery. The resting membrane potential is not unique to nerve cells; most living biological cells maintain a voltage difference across the cell membrane.

In addition to the resting potential, nerve cells also exhibit the *propagated* (that is, traveling) *action potential*, sometimes called the spike potential. When a nerve cell is activated, a change in voltage develops and travels along the axon. This action potential is not simply an electrical current that flows down the axon. Currents in wires can propagate at close to the speed of light; the action potential travels down the axon at the very much slower speed of a few feet per second. Electric currents are, of course, involved in the action potential, but the actual sequence of events is much more complicated, involving movements of various ions across the nerve membrane.

The resting potential

The existence of a steady potential difference across the nerve membrane may seem puzzling. There are no obvious batteries or other sources of current flow, and yet a steady potential exists. As a matter of fact, such a membrane potential is a necessary result of basic physical-chemical processes and is characteristic of all *semipermeable* membranes separating different ionic solutions. Semipermeable means that some molecules can pass through the membrane and others cannot, usually dependent upon the size of the molecule. Most semipermeable membranes behave as though they are filled with small holes. The size of the holes allows small molecules to pass through fairly easily and excludes larger molecules.

In the resting state, when the axon is not conducting action potentials, essentially all the sodium ions are excluded by a sodium "barrier" (the existence of this sodium barrier has been well demonstrated but we do not yet know the actual mechanism of the barrier or how it works). However, other small ions like potassium and chloride can pass relatively freely in and out of the axon. The axon membrane can be analyzed as though it were a simple physical system. For example, any semipermeable membrane, such as colloidin or a sausage skin, that holds large protein ions inside could allow potassium and chloride ions to cross the membrane freely. Under these conditions a steady potential difference develops across the membrane. Two forces act together to produce this

potential. Ions tend to diffuse through the membrane until there are an equal number of each type of ion inside and outside. However, the negatively charged protein molecules are too large and cannot cross. Consequently, if the potassium and chloride ions were distributed equally inside and outside, a greater negative charge would be contained inside. This interior negative charge tends to hold the positively charged potassium ions inside the axon. The actual distribution of potassium and chloride ions is a compromise between these diffusional and electrical forces. The net result is a steady potential difference across the membrane. The inside is more negative than the outside, typically about −70 mV (mV stands for a millivolt) which is equal to 70/1000 of a volt or nearly −1/10 volt, about one-fifteenth of the potential difference of a flashlight battery.

To summarize, the resting nerve membrane potential is about −70 mV. This steady potential results because the nerve membrane is permeable to potassium ions but not to sodium, which is kept outside, and protein, which is kept inside. The actual value of the resting membrane potential is the result of the differential concentration of potassium ions inside and outside the axon.

132
───────────
The electrical signs
of brain activity

The action potential

An example of a propagated (traveling) action potential recorded from the the squid giant axon is shown in Figure 4.12B. This was obtained in an experiment, illustrated in Figure 4.12A, in which a stimulus is applied to one portion of the axon, and changes in the potential across the membrane recorded at another locus on the fiber. The stimulus marker indicates the time when a stimulus was applied (Fig. 4.12B); the time, about 1 msec, between the stimulus and the onset of the response is the time required for the action potential to travel from the stimulating electrodes to the recording electrodes. Remember that the action potential is propagated (that is, it travels) down the axon at a fixed and relatively slow speed (several meters per second) and is nondecremental; wherever it is recorded along the nerve it has the same amplitude. The propagated action potential is not itself directional, incidentally. If a nerve fiber is stimulated at a given point, action potentials will develop at that point and travel out along the fiber in both directions from the stimulus site. As you will learn later in the chapter, directionality of conduction in the nervous system is the result of one-way transmission across the synaptic interconnections between cells.

An example of an action potential recorded from the squid giant axon fiber is shown in Figure 4.13. Hypothetical processes believed to result in the action potential are drawn schematically. During the initial rising phase of the action potential, the barrier to sodium ions that normally exists across the membrane suddenly breaks down and sodium rushes

DonE

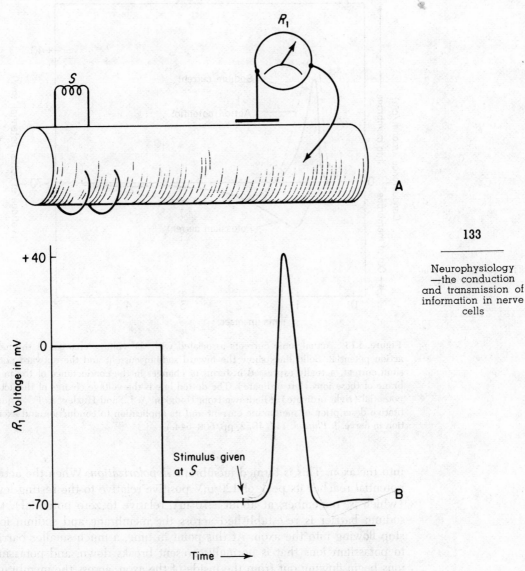

133

Neurophysiology
—the conduction
and transmission of
information in nerve
cells

Figure 4.12 A, Idealized experiment for measuring the resting membrane potential and the action potential of a nerve fiber. Stimulus is applied at one portion of the axon, and changes in the potential across the membrane are recorded at R_1. B, The graph shows the voltage changes over time measured at R_1. Initially both electrodes are resting on the outside surface of the membrane and the potential difference is zero. When the voltage drops from zero to −70 mV, one electrode has been pushed through the membrane; the steady −70 mV potential is the resting potential. After the electrical stimulus is given at another point (S), an action potential develops which travels along the nerve and is recorded at R_1. (From Thompson, R. F. *Foundations of Physiological Psychology.* New York: Harper & Row, 1967.)

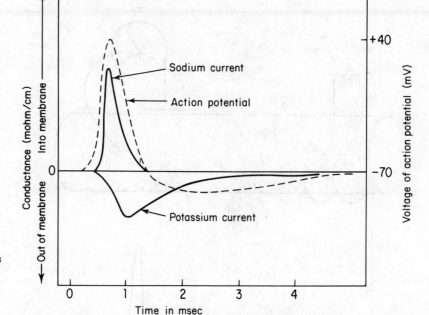

Figure 4.13 Actual ionic currents associated with the voltage changes of the nerve action potential. Solid lines show the inward sodium current and the outward potassium current, actually expressed in terms of changes in the conductance of the membrane of these ions (left ordinate). The dotted line is the voltage change of the action potential (right ordinate). (Redrawn from Hodgkin, A. L., and Huxley, A. F. A quantitative description of membrane current and its application to conduction and excitation in nerve. *J. Physiol.* **117**, 1952, pp. 500–544.)

into the axon. This is termed membrane *depolarization*. When the action potential reaches its peak of 120 mV positive relative to the resting level (which is, remember, at about −70 mV relative to zero potential), the sodium barrier is re-established across the membrane and sodium ions stop flowing into the axon. At this point in time, a much smaller barrier to potassium ions that is normally present breaks down, and potassium ions begin flowing out from the inside of the axon, across the membrane. This phase in the action potential is the negativity following the positive response. It is termed the period of *hyperpolarization* (polarization *more* than normal), hence the membrane is somewhat *more* negative than the resting level.

What is the mechanism that starts the breakdown of the sodium barrier, permitting the action potential to develop? The answer to this problem is very simple. The strength of the sodium barrier is directly related to the value of the membrane potential. In the normal resting state, with a membrane potential of about −70 mV, the barrier is virtually complete. However, as the membrane potential is depolarized (moved toward zero), the sodium barrier weakens and sodium ions begin to move into the axon. At a critical threshold value of about −55 mV to −50 mV, the sodium barrier breaks down completely. This threshold effect is easily explained. The inward movement of sodium ions is termed a *self-regenerative* process. The more that occurs, the more that will occur. A simple analogy is the explosion threshold of a heated gas mixture. If hydrogen and oxygen gases are mixed and heated, above a threshold point the gas will explode to form water (that is, the reaction goes to completion). If the gas mixture is heated nearly to the explosion threshold, the reaction will fluctuate and may or may not explode. The membrane potential controls the sodium reaction, the influx of sodium, in an analogous manner. When the threshold is crossed at about −50 mV, sodium rushes in across the membrane and this leads to a positive action potential of about 50 mV.

At the same time that the sodium ions rush into the axon, the potassium ions begin to move out. The outward flux of potassium stops the influx of sodium. Further, the outward movement of potassium is a negative feedback system. It tends to hyperpolarize the membrane potential (for example, moves it to about −75 mV) which, in turn, stops this outward movement of potassium. The reaction is self-limiting. Consequently, the membrane potential returns to the resting level, ready to conduct another action potential.

The fact that the action potential travels (is propagated) downward along the axon also depends upon the inward movement of sodium which, in its turn, depends upon the membrane potential. At the point on the axon where the action potential occurs—where the sodium rushes into the axon—a local current flow produces a shift toward zero in the membrane potential of the axon close to that point. The shift toward zero is sufficient to cross the sodium barrier in the membrane immediately adjacent to the point where the action potential occurs. Consequently, the action potential moves down along the axon at a constant velocity, dependent upon the axon diameter, and a constant amplitude, determined by the high external concentration of sodium.

Conduction in myelinated fibers

Most nerve axons in vertebrates are surrounded individually by a covering of fatty material termed the *myelin sheath* (the squid giant axon has no such covering). This sheath begins a short distance from the cell body or *soma* and covers all of the axon except for the fine axon terminals that synapse on other nerve cells. Very small diameter fibers have no myelin sheath, but all larger fibers both inside and outside the CNS are covered with this insulating material. The sheath is interrupted frequently

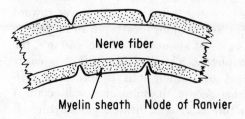

Figure 4.14 Longitudinal section of a myelinated nerve fiber. (From Thompson, R. F. *Foundations of Physiological Psychology*. New York: Harper & Row, 1967.)

by constrictions termed *nodes of Ranvier,* where myelin is either very thin or absent. A longitudinal section of a myelinated axon is shown in Figure 4.14. In brief, the myelin sheath appears to act primarily as an insulator. If a nerve fiber is activated by electrical stimulation at a given node, the action potential with its associated currents resulting from the ion flows described above develops at that node. In nonmyelinated fibers breakdown of the nerve membrane barriers to ion flows move progressively along the axon. However, in myelinated fibers the myelin sheath effectively insulates the fiber from these currents. Current flows in and out of the nerve fiber only at the nodes. Conduction along the nerve occurs when the ionic currents are large enough to cause a breakdown of the axon membrane barriers at the *next* node of Ranvier.

The time required for the action potential to travel from one node to the next is essentially only the time required for the action potential to develop at the next node. As though the intervening myelinated region does not exist, conduction jumps along the fiber from node to node. Thus this process is very much more rapid in myelinated fibers than in nonmyelinated fibers. The effects of anesthetics verify this hypothesis. Anesthetic agents applied on the myelin between nodes are relatively ineffective in blocking transmission. However, they are very effective when applied at the nodes of Ranvier (Tasaki, 1953).

Synaptic transmission

One great achievement of 20th century neurophysiology involved determination of how information is transmitted from nerve cell to nerve cell at the synapses (which are the only points of functional contact between neurons). Although a great many scientists have contributed to the study of synaptic transmission, Bernard Katz and John Eccles have been dominant figures in the field, both having received Nobel Prizes for their work.

It might be well to review briefly the general features of the synapse at this point (Chapter 3). Each neuron sends out one major axon, the output fiber from the nerve cell body. This axon subdivides into small

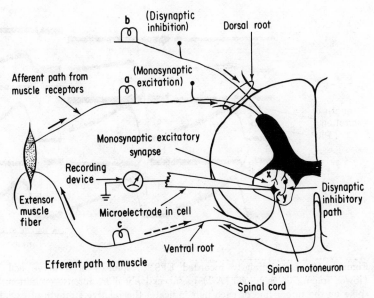

Figure 4.15 Schematic drawing of the type of experiment used to study synaptic transmission. Stimulation of different peripheral nerves (a and b) permits monosynaptic excitation (x) or disynaptic inhibition (y) to be included in the motoneuron. Its activity is recorded by an intracellular microelectrode. The motoneuron can also be activated antidromically by stimulation of the ventral root (c). (From Thompson, R. F. *Foundations of Physiological Psychology.* New York: Harper & Row, 1967.)

137

Neurophysiology
—the conduction
and transmission of
information in nerve
cells

axon terminals which typically go to a number of target neurons in a given region. When the action potential reaches the terminal (Fig. 5.5), packets of chemical transmitter substance are released across the synaptic space to act on the target or postsynaptic neuron. To avoid confusion with terminology here, synapse generally refers to the space and the associated specialized membranes. The *presynaptic* portion is the structure before this space—the axon terminal bouton. The *postsynaptic* portion is the membrane of the cell after the space.

The basic type of experiment used to study excitatory synaptic transmission is shown in Figure 4.15. It involves recording the membrane response of a neuron to direct synaptic activation by axon terminals from other neurons, using a small microelectrode inserted inside the nerve cell. The neuron first used to study synaptic transmission in the CNS (schematized in Fig. 4.15) was the spinal motoneuron, the neuron in the spinal cord that sends out its axon to control the muscles (Chapter 3). Some sensory nerves from muscles have direct synaptic connections on motoneurons (a in Figure 4.15). This direct synapse of nerve fibers on a neuron, without any intervening neurons, is termed a *monosynaptic* (one synapse) connection. It is important to remember that in any monosynaptic system each fiber forms many synapses (many fiber terminals); there are many fibers, and they synapse on many neurons. For each fiber

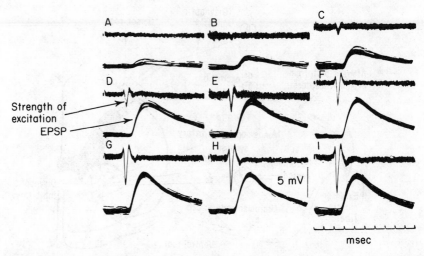

Figure 4.16 Intracellularly recorded EPSP responses of a nerve cell membrane (lower tracing of each pair, A-I) to successively more intense excitation. The sharp spike on the upper line of each pair indicates the relative strength of excitation. Note that the EPSP increases with stronger stimulation in a graded manner, and that following excitation the potential rises rapidly and decays more slowly. (From Eccles, J. C., Eccles, R. M., and Lundberg, A. Synaptic actions on motoneurones in relation to the two components of group I muscle afferent volley. *J. Physiol.* **36**, 1957, pp. 527–546.)

terminal, however, there is only one synapse to cross to go from the sensory input to the motor output.

In the experiment shown in Figure 4.15 a microelectrode is inserted inside the motoneuron and the cell membrane potential is recorded, very much like the axon membrane potential was recorded in the squid giant axon. When the microelectrode is pushed through the cell membrane, a potential of −70 mV is recorded, just as with the squid axon. If now a few fibers (at point a in Figure 4.15) are stimulated, a weak excitatory response is evoked in the motoneuron. This response is a brief slight decrease, or depolarization, of the membrane potential; it shifts a small amount toward zero. A series of such responses to progressively stronger stimuli are shown in Figure 4.16. Note that as the stimulus strength is increased, which means here that more fibers are activated, the potential recorded from the motoneuron increases. The response is not a spike but rather a graded potential often called a *synaptic potential*. This potential develops only in the cell body (and associated dendrites and at the beginning of the axon), but does not travel down the axon as a spike. This response is somewhat like the weak subthreshold response of the squid axon membrane. Remember that if a weak electrical stimulus was given to the squid axon a small potential developed, but if it was below spike threshold, it simply decayed and no spike was generated.

In the motoneuron, as in the squid axon, the spike threshold is about 10 mV less than the resting level. Thus if the resting potential is −70 mV, it has to be shifted to about −60 mV before a spike will develop. The stronger the excitation of the motoneuron by the fiber synapses (i.e., the more synapses that activate the motoneuron), the larger the graded response (Fig. 4.16). If enough synapses are activated for the graded response to reach −60 mV, a spike develops in the motoneuron, travels down the motoneuron axon, and causes the muscle to contract.

It appears that the spike action potential actually develops first at the beginning of the axon in a region termed the *axon hillock* (see Fig. 4.11) and travels down the axon. The sequence of events involved in generating a spike in the motoneuron axon is indicated in Figure 4.11. The graded synaptic potential that develops in the cell body and dendrites of the motoneuron as a function of the amount of synaptic activation is termed the *excitatory postsynaptic potential,* usually abbreviated as EPSP. The most important point to remember is that the EPSP is *graded.* The size of the EPSP is a continuous function of the amount and kind of synaptic actions on the cell. It is important to bear in mind that a given nerve cell may have thousands of synaptic endings from other cells. In normal function the cell is constantly bombarded through these synapses. The cell integrates all this incoming information continuously in time. The net result is a kind of overall average of the information and is expressed by the cell in terms of the membrane potential level. When the synaptic influences on the cell are such that this "average" membrane level shifts to spike threshold (about 10 mV less negative than the resting potential) an all-or-none spike is triggered and fires down the axon. The EPSP, then, reflects the graded "analog computer" portion of the nerve response, which continuously adds activity in time until spike threshold is reached.

We have used the motoneuron of the spinal cord as the experimental system to study synaptic excitation. However, the basic phenomenon of excitatory synaptic transmission appears to be the same for all neurons in the mammalian central nervous system. In all cases, excitatory synaptic activity impinging on a neuron induces a brief small decrease or depolarization in the membrane potential. Similarly the spike threshold of about 10 mV depolarization from the resting level of −70 mV appears to hold for most neurons. However, the duration of the EPSP may differ somewhat for different neurons. In all cases it appears to have the same shape—following excitation the potential rises rapidly and then decays more slowly (Fig. 4.16). The total duration of the EPSP in the spinal motoneuron is about 10 msec (1/100 of a second). However in some neurons in the brain EPSPs may last one-tenth of a second or longer.

It appears that whenever a cell is bombarded by an excitatory synaptic action, the result is a brief and limited short-circuiting of the membrane barrier that normally maintains the unequal distributions of ions. All small ions (e.g., sodium, potassium, and chloride) flow down their concentration gradients. Since the short-circuit is brief, partial, and limited, these ion flows last for only a short time and die away as the barrier is re-established. The graded character of the EPSP results from the fact that the degree of short-circuiting of the cell membrane is a direct function of the degree of synaptic bombardment. Although the graded EPSP of the nerve cell often is referred to as the decision-making response of the cell, there is no active decision process, simply a passive response to synaptic bombardment that has a predictable amplitude from physical-chemical laws of ion exchange.

There appears to be no selectivity in the type of ions that flow in producing the EPSP. The brief short-circuiting of the membrane barrier apparently opens the membrane to free passive diffusion of all small ions. Ionic flows then are determined entirely by the electrochemical gradients resulting from differential concentrations and membrane potentials. Sodium, potassium, and chloride ions may all exchange—probably in that order of significance, since sodium ions have greatest imbalance in the resting state and chloride ions, the least.

Inhibition: the control of synaptic transmission. It can be demonstrated theoretically that if the brain were composed entirely of excitatory synapses, any stimulus that induced neural activity would immediately cause a runaway buildup of excitation to the point where the brain would be in a permanent state of massive discharge, as in an epileptic seizure. Indeed, certain drugs that block inhibition, like strychnine, produce just such an effect—massive epilepsy-like discharges of neurons. It is therefore necessary to involve processes of inhibition to account for the neural functioning of the brain.

Perhaps the simplest possible way that an inhibitory synapse could act would be to do just the opposite of an excitatory synapse, namely to increase the negativity of the membrane potential beyond that of its resting level. As noted above, the resting membrane potential is normally about −70 mV, and an excitatory change of about 10 mV to the threshold level of −60 mV initiates spike discharge. If, for example, we could shift the membrane potential in the opposite direction to a value of −73 mV, then an EPSP of 10 mV that had previously caused discharge of the cell would now only shift the membrane potential back to −63 mV—still 3 mV below the spike discharge threshold. This is essentially what takes place during inhibition; there is a brief *increase* in the negativity of the membrane potential.

The experiment that was used to study this type of synaptic inhibition, called *postsynaptic inhibition,* is shown in Figure 4.15. Stimulation of an input nerve (b) that exerts an inhibitory effect on the spinal motoneuron activates the small inhibitory interneuron through an excitatory synapse. When the action potential in the interneuron reaches the synapse on the

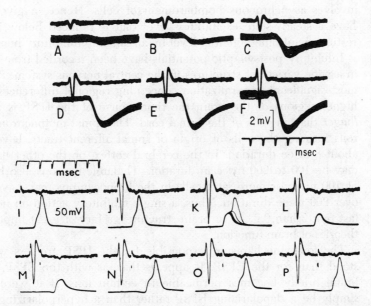

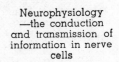

Figure 4.17 Examples of IPSPs produced in a spinal motoneuron by increasingly strong volleys in an inhibitory nerve. The cell membrane potential shows a brief hyperpolarization (IPSP) which increases with increasing inhibitory activation. Upper trace in each is the size of the nerve volley eliciting the IPSP. (From Eccles, J. C. The behavior of nerve cells. In Wolstenholme, G. E. W., and O'Connor, C. M. (eds.) Ciba Foundation Symposium, *Neurological Basis of Behavior*. London: Churchill, 1958, pp. 28–47.)

141

Neurophysiology
—the conduction
and transmission of
information in nerve
cells

motoneuron (y in Fig. 4.15), a small amount of an inhibitory transmitter substance is released. This diffuses across the synapse to act on the postsynaptic membrane of the cell body. Up to this point, the mechanism is identical to excitation. However, in inhibition the cell membrane potential is shifted toward a greater degree of polarization—that is, the cell membrane becomes hyperpolarized. As we noted, the actual membrane potential may shift from -70 mV to -73 mV. This is termed the *inhibitory postsynaptic potential* (IPSP). When an IPSP occurs, an excitatory action that previously depolarized the cell to firing threshold no longer produces a depolarization sufficient to reach spike threshold. Examples of IPSPs produced in a spinal motoneuron by increasingly strong volleys in an inhibitory nerve are shown in Figure 4.17. The IPSP appears to be roughly a mirror image of the EPSP. Note that it grows in a *graded* fashion with increasing stimulus strength. Note also that it has a relatively short time course, approximately 10 msec. An excitatory volley to the cell would be inhibited only if it reached the cell within a few milliseconds of the inhibitory volley. Again, however, this picture holds only for synchronous volleys. The normal state of the central nervous system involves asynchronous bombardment of cells. Hence, a given cell can have a steady-state excitability level that is reduced below the normal resting membrane potential level by an ongoing inhibitory bombardment.

Inhibitory postsynaptic potentials have been recorded from nerve cells in a wide variety of structures in the central nervous system. Perhaps the most significant generalization concerning regional differences is that in higher regions of the brain the time course of the IPSP is *very much longer* than in cells of the spinal cord. The spinal motoneuron, and neurons forming the cells of origin of spinal afferent tracts, have IPSPs of about 8 msec duration. In the cerebral cortex, on the other hand, IPSPs may be 100 to 200 msec in duration. Thalamic neurons also have IPSPs of 100 msec or more, and cells in the hippocampus may have IPSPs of over 200 msec duration. Thus, a single inhibitory action on neurons can last more than 0.2 sec in brain structures, a fact of great importance for theories of brain function.

The ionic mechanisms responsible for the IPSP are less well understood than for the EPSP. It appears that, as with the EPSP, the membrane briefly becomes permeable to certain ions. If it were, it would simply be a depolarizing EPSP rather than a hyperpolarizing IPSP (as noted above, the EPSP results from a brief increase in permeability to all small ions). Since the IPSP is a further increase in the negative potential of the membrane, opposite in direction to the decreased negativity of the EPSP, the current (ion flow) must be in the opposite direction. Hence, the membrane must become selectively permeable to only certain ions. The most logical candidates are chloride and potassium. The equilibrium potentials of both these ions are more negative than the resting membrane potential. In fact, the equilibrium potential of chloride is about 5 mV more negative than the resting membrane potential, which is just about the size of the maximum IPSP that can be induced. If the membrane did become permeable only to chloride, for example, chloride ions would now flow down their concentration gradient and shift the membrane potential briefly to a more negative level, exactly as during the IPSP. The membrane does not become permeable to sodium during the IPSP.

Indicated in Figure 4.15 was a small inhibitory interneuron between the receiving afferent fiber and the motoneurons that acted to produce the IPSP in the motoneuron. It appears that in many places in the brain, whenever postsynaptic inhibition occurs on a cell, a small inhibitory interneuron is present that actually induces the inhibition (the IPSP) on the cell in question. The presence of such interneurons makes very good sense in view of the chemical nature of synaptic transmission. All afferent nerves conveying sensory information to the CNS, and most major tracts and pathways within the nervous system, are basically excitatory in nature. They convey information by activating other cells. If a particular axon causes excitation of a given neuron by releasing a particular and excitatory type of chemical transmitter substance, then it ought to produce only excitation at all its terminals on other neurons. Consequently, it could not produce inhibition. The simplest solution to the problem, the one commonly adopted by the brain, is to have a small inhibitory interneuron itself excited by the axon terminal. The interneuron, in turn, acts to inhibit another cell by releasing a different type of substance, an inhibitory chemical transmitter, to produce an IPSP in the cell. Thus, an excitatory afferent fiber can produce inhibition of a given neuron by activating an inhibitory interneuron that, in turn, induces inhibition in the neuron. As always seems to be true in nature, there are exceptions to this general rule. The *Purkinje cells* of the cerebellum are large, with long axons that exert direct postsynaptic inhibition on all cells they influence, without the interposition of inhibitory interneurons.

Synaptic interactions among neurons

Almost all interactions among neurons in the mammalian nervous system occur at synapses. The two types of synaptic interaction described in this chapter, the excitatory postsynaptic potential (EPSP) and the inhibitory postsynaptic potential (IPSP), are the major kinds of synaptic processes that have been demonstrated for mammals.

Other types of synaptic interactions are known to occur in the mammalian brain, for example, *presynaptic inhibition*. An axon terminal ends on another axon terminal instead of ending on a neuron soma or dendrite. It reduces the excitation normally produced by the target terminal on the postsynaptic neuron. In an analogous fashion, *presynaptic excitation* involves one axon terminal ending on another terminal. It increases the excitation normally produced by the target terminal on the postsynaptic neuron. Presynaptic influences, particularly presynaptic inhibition, are prominent in various ascending relay stations on the major sensory systems. Such influences provide mechanisms whereby higher brain regions can act on lower regions to influence the nature of ascending information.

We have talked of synaptic transmission as though it were definitely known to be a chemical process involving release of chemical transmitter substance across the synaptic space. Actually, there are many examples of electrical synaptic transmission in the nervous systems of invertebrates, and even in some vertebrates. Electrical synapses work much like an electrical transformer. Electrical activity in the presynaptic terminal directly induces electrical activity in the postsynaptic cell. Many of these electrical synapses have a characteristic appearance in the electron microscope—they are called *tight junctions* because the pre- and postsynaptic membranes appear to contact one another directly. To date, electrical synapses have not been found in the mammalian brain. However, this by no means rules out the possibility that electrical synapses, and still other quite different kinds of synaptic processes and interactions among neurons (and glia), may occur in the brain. We have only scratched the surface in understanding how neurons interact in the human brain.

Virtually every nerve cell body and dendrite has an essentially continuous covering of synaptic terminal knobs. In the normal state the cell is bombarded continuously with excitatory and inhibitory synaptic influences, and many excitatory inputs themselves are altered by presynaptic influences. The extent to which the cell fires or does not fire all-or-none spike potentials down the axon is determined by the dynamic balance among the classes of synaptic events. This complexity of organization makes it very clear that the simple diagrams of the nervous system, in which each neuron synapses on only one or two other neurons and all are excitatory synapses, commonly shown in discussions of neural models and networks fail to prescribe the complexity of behavior of the real nervous system.

THE ELECTRICAL SIGNS OF NERVOUS ACTIVITY

Much of this chapter has been devoted to the electrical activity of single nerve cells—the action potential of the nerve cell axon and the graded synaptic potentials of the nerve cell body and dendrites. At the beginning of the chapter some examples were given of recording electroencephalograms by means of electrodes placed on the scalp. Evoked responses often are termed *gross* responses because they are recorded by

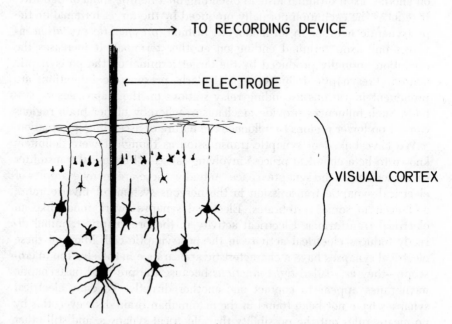

Figure 4.18 Schematic drawing of the experimental situation used to record the electrical activity of neurons directly from visual cortex.

large or gross electrodes that pick up activity from many thousands of cells. What relationship do these gross averaged measures—which seem correlated with behavioral or psychological variables such as arousal, attention, and meaning—have to the action potentials and synaptic potentials of individual nerve cells? This question reflects a presently very active area of research and, of course, cannot be answered completely—not enough is yet known. The problem can be simplified somewhat by stating it as a simple experimental situation. Instead of putting a wire on the surface of the scalp, a small insulated wire is inserted into the cerebral cortex in an anesthetized animal, for example, monkey or cat. As was the case in Figure 4.9, activity in response to a light flash is recorded, but now the wire is placed directly in the visual cortex rather than on the scalp above it. The situation is shown schematically in Figure 4.18, and not quite to scale—there will be hundreds or thousands of neurons in the vicinity of the electrode.

The gross evoked response to light-flash stimulation is in many ways similar in this situation. The main difference is that in the anesthetized preparation here some of the later components that seem particularly related to psychological variables are not prominent. In any event the "raw" gross response to light flash is shown in Figure 4.19A. By using a device called an electronic filter, we can selectively record only slower waves or only the fast spike action potentials, or both. In Figure 4.19B we filtered out the spikes and recorded only the slower waves. In Figure 4.19C we changed the filter so only the spikes are recorded, not the slower waves. In Figure 4.19A the filter is open so we record both on the same tracing; the spikes are seen as blips riding on the gross slow wave. In other words, the gross evoked response looks the same whether or not the spikes are recorded. This would seem to suggest that the spikes are not involved in generating the gross evoked response.

We have not previously discussed the recording of spikes as it is done in Figure 4.19. The spikes are the action potentials generated by the axons and cell bodies of single nerve cells. In our earlier discussion of the action potential we recorded across the membrane of a single axon (the squid giant axon), and recorded a potential of about one-tenth of a volt (110 mV). Here we record outside the cells at a distance and from a good many cells. Consequently, the action potentials are much lower in amplitude, ranging in Figure 4.19 from about 1 μV (1/1,000,000 of a volt—the activity shows up as "fuzz" in the baseline) to 1 mV (1/1000 of a volt—the largest single spike). Each different amplitude or height of spike is the action potential from a different cell. We can differentiate among the larger amplitudes but not among the very small amplitude spikes. Action potentials recorded in this way are referred to as *extracellular spike discharges* or *extracellular spikes*. It should be clear that they are action potentials from single axons and cell bodies, recorded extracellularly (outside the cell membrane).

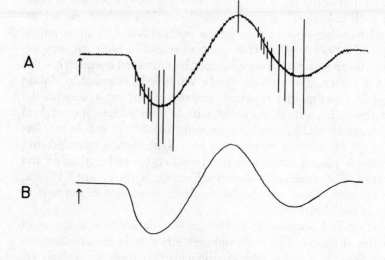

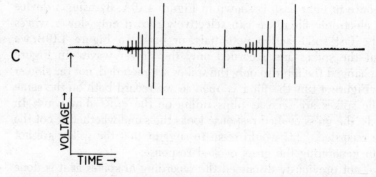

VOLTAGE →

TIME →

Figure 4.19 Electrical activity recorded by electrode in Fig. 4.18 from visual cortex in response to light flash. A, The "raw" electrical record consisting of slow-wave field potentials and single neuron action potential spike discharges. Both slow waves and spikes are generated from a number of neurons close to the recording electrode (Fig. 4.18). B, The action potential spikes are filtered out to record only the slower field potential waves. C, The slower field potential waves are filtered out to record only the action potential spike discharges.

Do the spikes relate to the gross response? Many investigators have noted relationships. A particularly clear example was provided in a study by Fox and O'Brien (1965). For a long succession of light flashes, they recorded both the gross evoked response and the spike response of a single neuron in the visual cortex on two separate channels. The averaged gross response is shown in Figure 4.20B. On the spike discharge they computed what is called a *poststimulus histogram,* where the probability

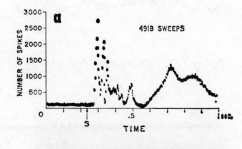

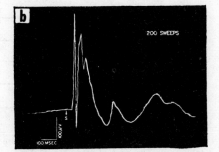

Figure 4.20 Relation between probability of firing of a single cell in visual cortex and evoked potential waveform. A, A "post-stimulus-histogram" of the frequency or probability of spike discharge at various times after the light flash. B, The averaged gross slower wave field potential waveform in response to the light flash. (Fox, S. S., and O'Brien, J. H. Duplication of evoked potential waveform by curve of probability of firing of a single cell. *Science* **147**, 1965, pp. 888–890. Copyright 1965 by the American Association for the Advancement of Science.)

of the spike discharge is plotted against the time after the stimulus—the higher the line the greater the probability of discharge. This is shown in Figure 4.20A. The two graphs appear almost identical. This result would seem to imply that the spike has a great deal to do with the gross evoked potential.

We noted earlier that the spike discharges seemed not to be involved in generating the gross evoked response (Fig. 4.19). This is seemingly a paradox, but there are several possible explanations. For example, assuming that the gross potential is the sum of the graded synaptic potentials of many cells, we would expect these cells to tend to fire spike discharges during periods of membrane depolarization. The gross response and the spikes would both be "caused" by the graded synaptic potentials. The gross response and the spikes would then be highly correlated but have no causal relationship (another example of the fact that correlation need not imply causation). Another possibility is that the gross response is, in significant part, an "envelope" of all the spike discharge activity recorded

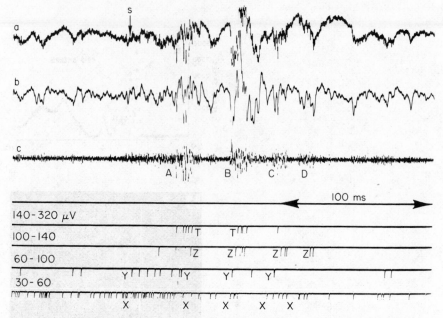

Figure 4.21 Recording of activity from visual cortex of cat. A, Gross evoked response. B, The plot of the rate of change of activity in A. C, Everything but the neuronal spikes have been filtered out. The neuronal spikes are shown in progressively higher amplitude ranges such that the smallest amplitude spikes fire first and the largest amplitude spikes fire last. (Verzeano, M. Evoked responses and network dynamics. From Whalen, R. E., Thompson, R. F., Verzeano, M., and Weinberger, N. M. (eds.). *The Neural Control of Behavior.* New York: Academic Press, 1970, pp. 27–54.)

by the electrode. Even if the large spikes were filtered out (see Fig. 4.19) the influence of the more numerous very small spikes would remain. Other interpretations are possible as well.

Perhaps more important at present is the extent to which it is possible to predict spike discharge activity from the gross potential. Gross evoked responses and spontaneous EEG activity technically are very easy to record—single or even multiple unit activity is much more difficult. The data of Fox and O'Brien indicate a clear relationship; however, they were lucky. Any one cell may not give an adequate picture of the relationship between the population of unit discharges and the gross response. Marcel Verzeano and associates have completed a number of studies in which activity of several or many different spike discharges are compared with the gross response. Their findings, strikingly clear and consistent, are schematized in Figure 4.21. Assume the recording is in visual cortex, as has been the case. The gross response shows an initial negativity followed by various positive and negative components (positive and negative relative to a zero, or ground, potential level). The smallest amplitude spikes fire first, then the next larger amplitude spikes, and so on until the largest amplitude spikes fire last. This sequence, surprisingly enough, appears to hold in a number of experiments in various brain loci under various conditions. It leads to a clear correlation—the smallest units tend to fire during the steepest portions of the negative slopes of the gross response, the intermediate units next, and the largest units tend to fire at the peak of negativity or on the period of positive slope, as indicated in Figure 4.21.

The reason these relations hold is not known; however, because they do, a great deal of information about patterns of unit activity in the brain is provided. With appropriate recording conditions, the gross evoked response or EEG (as in Figs. 4.20 and 4.21) allows us to deduce the patterns of unit discharge that occur in the relevant brain regions.

This discussion may seem to have gone somewhat afield. The main point to be made, of course, is the interrelation of the kinds of electrical activity seen at the level of the single neuron (graded synaptic potentials and unit spike discharges) with the kinds of gross neural activity such as evoked responses, EEG, and multiple unit activity more commonly (and easily) measured in studies attempting to relate brain activity and behavior. When looking at gross recordings it is important to remember that the gross response is not generated by a single source but rather by thousands or millions of anatomically and functionally discrete individual generators, the individual neurons. So far as we know, the only way in which information is transmitted through the brain to influence behavior is from nerve cell to nerve cell, crossing a synapse at each junction. Thus a postsynaptic potential is induced, which, in turn, leads to a spike discharge that travels down the axon to influence another cell. The brain is a computer composed of roughly 12 billion individual computers, each of which is a "hybrid" analog-digital computer of very great complexity interconnected in intricate ways with many other similar computers.

Summary

The electroencephalogram is one means of studying the electrical signs of brain activity. Various wave patterns are obtained in EEG recordings of brain functions. Alpha waves are related to the general state of arousal. These waves are found in a variety of brain regions when the subject is awake, physically relaxed, and in an environment in which there are no sudden stimuli. Alpha blocking takes place when an alpha response is blocked by an arousing stimulus. Both beta waves and gamma waves occur at higher states of arousal than alpha waves. Delta waves, slow large-amplitude waves, usually occur only in slow-wave sleep, although they are common also during unconsciousness. Theta waves are visible in children and adolescents, most notably in children with behavior disorders. In many situations, theta waves and alpha waves show a reciprocal relationship to each other. Theta waves are characteristic of the hippocampus, limbic system, and the frontal and temporal regions of the cerebral cortex. Kappa waves occur at the same frequency as do alpha waves. It is thought that these waves may be related to mental activity in some way.

As a child matures, the possibilities of EEG recording gradually develop. In the newborn infant no regular brain rhythm is apparent, and during infancy no alpha waves are found. Around three to four months of age, the onset of regular brain rhythm over the occipital regions takes place. The frequency of brain rhythm increases until the basically adult EEG pattern is present at about ten years of age.

The averaged evoked potential, one form of brain recording, has proven to be a useful means of examining brain activity in humans. If a click stimulus is presented to a subject, the brain potential evoked by the stimulus is indistinguishable because of the ongoing EEG activity. The background activity covers the evoked response to the click. If about ten trials of the click stimulus are presented, and the results averaged by a computer, the background activity averages out to zero so that the evoked response to the click becomes much more prominent. With this type of averaging, it is possible to obtain a clear averaged evoked potential recorded by EEG electrodes attached to the scalp. Several studies suggest that the averaged evoked potential may be affected by attentional states and verbal or cognitive meaning of the stimuli.

In the field of neurophysiology a large body of research is devoted to determination of the various types of electrical activity associated with single nerve cells. The action potential is a "digital" event which consists of an all-or-none impulse that moves down the axon and affects other nerve cells at the synapse. The action potential is dependent upon synaptic activity. If the shift in electrical potential is sufficient when the soma and dendrites are activated at a synapse, the spike discharge threshold is reached, and the action potential is propagated down the axon. This is the "analog" event of brain activity. The characteristics of the spike are not related to the size of the graded potentials that trigger the spike. They are determined by intrinsic characteristics of the axon, its size and the presence or absence of myelin.

Two kinds of electrical events are associated with the nerve membrane potential of an axon, the steady resting membrane potential and the propagated action potential. The resting membrane potential difference is characteristic of semipermeable membranes which separate different ionic solutions. Sodium ions are effectively kept out of the axon by a sodium barrier, and potassium and chloride ions pass relatively freely in and out of the axon. Under these conditions, a steady potential difference develops across the membrane.

Two forces act to produce this potential. Ions tend to diffuse through the membrane until there are equal numbers of each type of ion inside and outside. However, negatively charged protein molecules are too large to cross the membrane. Consequently, if potassium and chloride ions were distributed equally inside and outside of the membrane, there would be a greater negative charge inside than outside. This interior negative charge tends to retain the positively charged potassium ions inside the axon. The net result of these forces is a steady potential difference across the membrane of approximately -70 mV. The steady potential results because the nerve membrane is permeable to potassium ions but not to sodium ions or protein molecules. The actual value of the resting membrane potential is the result of differential concentration of potassium ions inside and outside of the axon.

The action potential is propagated down an axon at a fixed and relatively slow speed and is nondecremental. The action potential itself is not directional; the directionality of conduction results from the one-way transmission across the synaptic interconnections between cells. Several processes are hypothesized to be involved in the activity of an action potential. Membrane depolarization occurs when the sodium barrier breaks and sodium ions rush into the axon during the initial rising phase of the action potential. When the action potential reaches 120 mV positive in relation to the resting level, the sodium barrier is re-established across the membrane, and sodium ions stop flowing into the axon. During the period of hyperpolarization which follows, the potassium ions begin to flow out across the membrane. This outward movement of potassium ions stops the influx of sodium ions. This tends to hyperpolarize the membrane potential so that the outward movement of potassium is terminated. The action potential moves along an axon at a constant velocity, dependent upon axon diameter, and at a constant amplitude.

In vertebrates, most nerve axons are coated with a myelin sheath which begins near the soma and covers the entire axon except for the axon terminals which synapse on other nerve cells. The nodes of Ranvier are constrictions on an axon where the myelin is either thin or absent. The myelin sheath primarily acts as an insulator. In myelinated fibers the current flows in and out of the nerve fiber only at the nodes of Ranvier. Conduction occurs when the ionic currents are large enough to cause a breakdown of the axon membrane barriers at a node of Ranvier. Since the conduction moves along the fiber from node to node, it is much more rapid in myelinated fibers than in nonmyelinated ones.

The synaptic potential is a graded potential which develops in the cell body but which is not propagated down the axon as a spike. A spike action potential first develops at the axon hillock and travels down the axon. Excitatory postsynaptic potentials (EPSP) are graded synaptic potentials which develop in cell bodies and dendrites as a function of the amount and kind of synaptic actions on the cell. The EPSP reflects the graded "analog" portion of nerve response, which continuously adds activity until spike threshold is reached. Excitatory synaptic activity impinging on a neuron induces a small decrease or depolarization in the membrane potential. The basic phenomenon of excitatory synaptic transmission appears to be the same for all neurons in the mammalian central nervous system although the duration of the EPSP may vary slightly among neurons. The graded character of the EPSP is a result of the degree of short-circuiting of the cell membrane.

Processes of inhibition are essential in order to account for neural functioning of the brain. During inhibition there is a brief increase in the negativity of the membrane potential which is termed postsynaptic inhibition. When an inhibitory postsynaptic potential (IPSP) occurs, an excitatory action that previously depolarized the cell to firing threshold no longer produces depolarization sufficient to reach spike threshold. An IPSP is a rough mirror of an EPSP and grows in a graded manner with increasing stimulus strength. In higher brain regions the time course of an IPSP is much longer than in cells of the spinal cord. The ionic mechanisms responsible for IPSP are not as well understood as those for EPSP. The membrane seems to become briefly permeable to certain ions, probably chloride and potassium. Essentially all interactions among neurons in the mammalian nervous system occur at synapses. The EPSP and IPSP are the major types of synaptic processes which have been demonstrated for mammals.

With appropriate recording conditions, gross evoked responses allow us to determine the patterns of unit discharge that occur in the related brain regions. Gross responses are generated by thousands of anatomically and functionally discrete individual neurons.

5

The chemistry of
behavior and
awareness

5

"I'm a hard-headed, conservative, Midwestern, Republican businessman. Under no circumstances would I consider myself a person who goes around taking strange drugs.

"But my wife took LSD at a friend's house, and in order to get her to agree to come home, I took the stuff myself.

"We got in the car, and I had only driven about three blocks, when suddenly the pavement in front of me opened up. It was as though the pavement was flowing over Niagara Falls. The street lights expanded into fantastic globes of light that filled my entire vision. I didn't dare stop.

"It was a nightmare. I came to traffic lights, but I couldn't tell what color they were. There were all sorts of colors around me anyway. I could detect other cars around me, so I stopped when they stopped, and went when they went.

"At home I flopped in a chair. I wasn't afraid. My conscious mind was sort of sitting on my shoulder—watching everything I was doing. I found I could make the room expand—oh, maybe a thousand miles— or I could make it contract right in front of me. All over the ceiling there were geometric patterns of light. To say they were beautiful is too shallow a word.

"My wife put on a violin concerto. I could make the music come out of the speaker like taffy, or a tube of toothpaste, surrounded by dancing lights of colors beyond description.

"A friend showed up. He was talking to me, and I was answering, all in a perfectly normal way. Then, I saw his face change. He became an Arab, a Chinese, a Negro. I found I could take my finger and wipe away his face and then paint it back again.

"I made a chocolate sundae and gave it to him for a head. A great truth appeared to me. The reason he had all those faces was this: he was a reflection of all mankind. So was I.

"I asked myself, 'What is God?' Then I knew that I was God. That really sounds ridiculous as I say it. But I knew that all life is one, and since God is Life, and I am Life, we are the same being.

"Then I decided to examine my own fears, because I wasn't really afraid of anything. I went down into my stomach and it was like Dante's inferno—all steaming and bubbling and ghastly. I saw some hideous shapes in the distance. My mind floated to each one, and they were horrible, hideous.

"They all got together in a mob and started to come up after me—a flood of bogeymen. But I knew I was stronger than all of them, and I took my hand and wiped them out.

"Now, I think there lies the real danger with LSD. Anyone who motioned with his hand and couldn't wipe out those creatures. He has to stay down there with them, forever."

(Barry Farrell, Life Magazine, pages 8–9. Copyright © 1966 Time, Inc. Reprinted with permission.)

Neurochemistry, the study of the chemical basis of experience and behavior, has undergone a major revolution in the past few years. One unfortunate facet of this has been what the popular press terms the "psychic" revolution—the widespread use of "mind" drugs. We have become a drugged society. The quotation given above is typical of thousands from persons who have taken LSD or other psychotogenic agents. The study of these and other types of drugs and chemicals that influence experience and behavior has provided us, however, with fundamental new insights into the workings of the biological machinery of the mind. It has been recognized that in the human brain all nerve cells interact with other nerve cells by means of chemical processes at the *synapses*, the points of functional contact between neurons (Chapter 4). This has enormously important implications—chemical processes must play a fundamental role in learning, thinking, and other complex and significant aspects of human behavior. Because the interactions between neurons are chemical, drugs like LSD can exert a potent influence on human experience and underlying brain activity.

Neurochemistry usually refers to the chemistry of the nervous system. However, much of this chemistry is the same for nerve cells, liver cells, muscle cells, and, in fact, for most living cells. Metabolism, respiration, synthesis of proteins and other substances are processes carried on by all cells. The major difference between the chemical processes of the neuron and other cells is that neurons manufacture and release synaptic transmitter substances. In this chapter we review briefly the general types of chemical processes that occur in nerve cells, then consider the chemicals believed to be involved in neuronal synaptic transmission, and conclude with a review of the effects of drugs on brain function and behavior.

THE CHEMICAL SYNAPSE

A nerve cell (shown in Fig. 5.1), in common with all other living cells, has several kinds of specialized structures or organelles within it. Some of these are particularly relevant to synaptic transmission. First, a nerve cell has a *cell membrane*, A. This membrane, as we saw earlier, conducts information in the form of spike potentials. The nerve cell membrane is a complicated chemical structure composed largely of fat and protein. Despite its specialized function of transmitting information, it does not

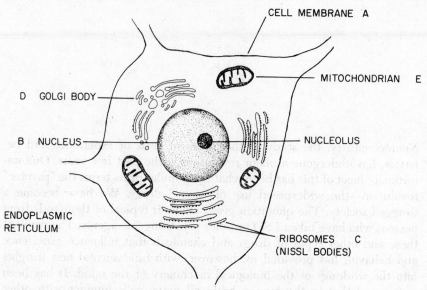

CELL MEMBRANE A

MITOCHONDRIAN   E

D GOLGI BODY

NUCLEOLUS

B NUCLEUS

ENDOPLASMIC
RETICULUM

RIBOSOMES   C
(NISSL BODIES)

Figure 5.1 Simplified drawing of a nerve cell, showing the cell membrane, the nucleus, the Nissl bodies, the Golgi bodies, and the mitochondria.

appear grossly or chemically different from other kinds of cell membranes.

Nerve cells, in common with most other cells, contain a *nucleus*, B. The nucleus, characteristically quite large in nerve cells, contains the genetic material, the chromosomes. These are composed of DNA, a complex type of biochemical substance called a nucleic acid. The nucleus also contains another kind of nucleic acid, RNA, which forms the basic mechanism to manufacture proteins for the cell. In essence, the DNA chromosomes tell the RNA the kinds of proteins and other substances to make, and RNA makes them. RNA also is present outside the nucleus of the cell in structures called the *ribosomes*. In nerve cells the ribosomes are very numerous and are called *Nissl bodies* (see Fig. 5.1C).

A structure found only in nerve cells and certain types of secretory cells is called the *Golgi body* (D in Fig. 5.1). Golgi bodies are very common in cells that are specialized to secrete substances, such as the cells in the pancreas that secrete insulin or the cells in the pituitary gland that secrete hormones. Indeed, simply because nerve cells have many Golgi bodies, it might be concluded that their basic function is to secrete chemicals, in this instance, chemical transmitter substances to work at synapses. It is probable that the Golgi bodies are the site of manufacture of the synaptic transmitter substances.

The remaining organelle common in nerve cells and other cells as well is the *mitochondria* (E in Fig. 5.1). These are closely formed ovoid bodies about 7 microns in length and 1 micron in diameter (1 millimeter equals 1000 microns). Energy metabolism occurs at the mitochondria in

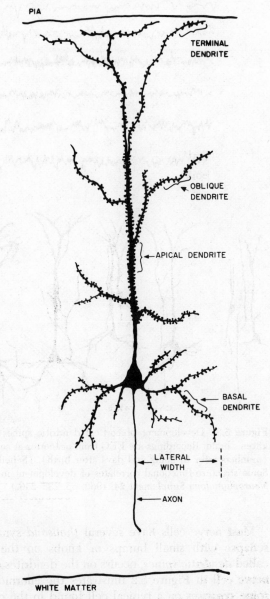

PIA

TERMINAL
DENDRITE

OBLIQUE
DENDRITE

APICAL DENDRITE

BASAL
DENDRITE

LATERAL
WIDTH

AXON

WHITE MATTER

Figure 5.2 A neuron in rat occipital cortex illustrating the large numbers of dendritic spines on the dendrites. (Globus, A., Rosenzweig, M. R., Bennett, E. L., and Diamond, M. C. Effects of differential experience on dendritic spine counts in rat cerebral cortex. *J. Comp. Physiol. Psych.* **82**, 1973, pp. 175–181. Copyright 1973 by the American Psychological Association. Reprinted by permission.)

the cell. Here the cells convert foodstuff such as glucose and oxygen into biological energy to run the cells and the body. The mitochondria can be termed the energy factories in the cell.

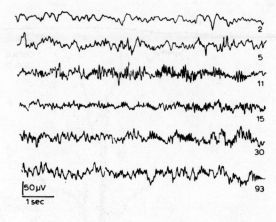

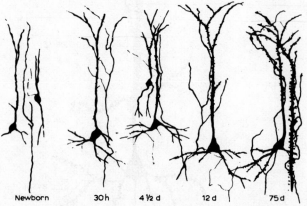

Newborn   30h   4½d   12d   75d

Figure 5.3 Development of cortical dendritic spines and of electrical activity of a kitten's brain. Recordings are EEG from neocortex at successive phases of development (numbers refer to hours and days after birth). (Scheibel, M. E., and Scheibel, A. B. Some structuro-functional correlates of development in young cats. *EEG and Clinical Neurophysiology Supplement* 24, 1963, pp. 235–246.)

Most nerve cells have several *thousand* synapses on them. A type of synapse with small bumps or knobs on the postsynaptic membrane, called *dendritic spines*, occurs on the dendrites of nerve cells. The cortical nerve cell in Figure 5.2 illustrates the enormous profusion of dendritic spine synapses on a typical cell found in the cerebral cortex. Spines are shown as small thorn-like protrusions covering the dendrites. Each tiny spine on the dendrites is a separate synapse. First described by the great neuroanatomist Ramon y Cajal in 1888, the significance of dendritic spines went unappreciated until recently. Each spine on the neuron is the site of a synaptic terminal. These dendritic spine synapses are believed to be excitatory in nature—they act to cause the neuron to fire a spike discharge.

158

The chemistry of
behavior and
awareness

Figure 5.4 Photograph of a "rich" rat environment. (Bennett, E. L., Diamond, M. C., Krech, D., and Rosenzweig, M. R. Chemical and anatomical plasticity of brain. *Science* **146,** 1964, pp. 610–619. Copyright 1964 by the American Association for the Advancement of Science.)

Perhaps the most intriguing aspect of dendritic spines is that their occurrence may be related to behavioral experience. Typically, they develop after birth in the cerebral cortex. The degree of development of cortical dendritic spines seems to correlate with the developing electrical activity of the brain. Figure 5.3 indicates the development of the cortical brain-wave activity (see Chapter 4) and the concomitant development of cortical dendritic spines in the kitten's brain. Further, restriction of the visual experience of an animal can result in fewer than normal cortical dendritic spines (Globus and Scheibel, 1967).

Studies by Mark Rosenzweig and his group at Berkeley have demonstrated that the environment of a growing rat can have powerful effects on the growth and development of its brain. In their classic experiment, rats were raised in enriched or impoverished environments, somewhat analogous to children who are raised in advantageous or disadvantageous surroundings, the rich and the poor. The "poor" rats lived in the standard small wire rat cage. The "rich" rat environment is shown in Figure 5.4.

The effects of environment on the rat's brain were quite striking. First, the rich rats had bigger and heavier brains. The cerebral cortex actually was thicker in the rich rats. There were also more subtle chemical differences. AChE, the enzyme that breaks down the transmitter ACh, was present in greater amounts in the rich rat brains. This implies that more ACh transmitter was also present. In addition, the rich rat brains had many more glial cells present. Finally, a recent study by Globus and Rosenzweig demonstrated that the nerve cells in the cerebral cortex of the rich rats had *more dendritic spines* than did the poor rats. Presumably they had more synapses.

These fundamental studies on effects of environment on brain development are important. They suggest that the growth and complexity of development of the brain is enhanced by a rich environment and/or retarded by a poor environment. The inference that mental abilities and

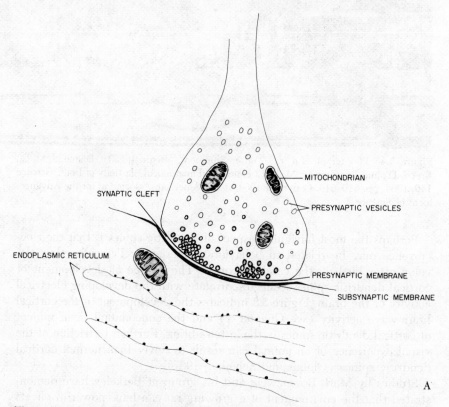

SYNAPTIC CLEFT

ENDOPLASMIC RETICULUM

MITOCHONDRIAN

PRESYNAPTIC VESICLES

PRESYNAPTIC MEMBRANE

SUBSYNAPTIC MEMBRANE

A

Figure 5.5 A, Schematic of a synapse with the presynaptic knob terminating on the cell body of a postsynaptic neuron. (Modified from Noback, C. R. *The Human Nervous System.* New York: McGraw-Hill, 1967.) B, Electron microphotograph of a synapse from frog spinal cord showing the termination of an axon on the cell body of a neuron. C, Drawing of B.

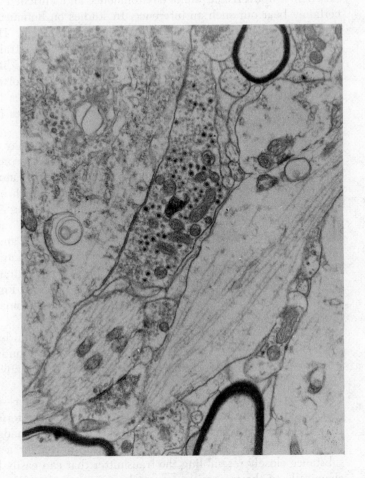

B

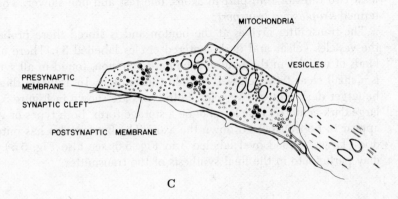

MITOCHONDRIA

VESICLES

PRESYNAPTIC
MEMBRANE

SYNAPTIC CLEFT

POSTSYNAPTIC MEMBRANE

C

capacities are enhanced by a rich environment and retarded by a poor environment may also be noted. Studies of mental abilities of children raised in impoverished slum environments and enriched environments certainly bear out such an inference. In studies on humans, it is difficult to factor out influences of heredity and environment. However, rich and poor rats were litter mates from the same genetic strain. Their genetic background was the same; only their environments differed.

To return to synapses, the neuron in the cerebral cortex (Fig. 5.2) with its thousands of dendritic spine synapses illustrates the real complexity of the brain. Each spine is a synapse, and involves (roughly) ten processes of synaptic transmission (described below).

Each of the 12 billion neurons in the human brain may have up to 5 thousand synapses on it. The number of possible interconnections in a single human brain is greater than the total number of atomic particles that compose the entire universe. It would seem a much easier task for the human brain to understand the physical universe than ever to understand itself.

A synapse is shown diagrammatically in Figure 5.5A and an electron microscope picture of a synapse is shown in B. What is actually shown is the termination of an axon as a presynaptic knob (bouton) at the cell body of a postsynaptic neuron. Compare the drawing, Figure 5.5C, to Figure 5.5B. The photograph happens to be from frog spinal cord, but it illustrates many common features of synapses.

The process of chemical synaptic transmission can be described by a sequence of about ten steps (Fig. 5.6). Although this sounds formidable, it is really quite simple, partly because the details of many of the steps are still unknown.

The first step involves getting the synaptic transmitter—the chemical that actually crosses the synapse—down the axon to the terminal bouton. It is believed that transmitter chemical is synthesized (made) in the cell body, probably at the Golgi bodies. The transmitter, or a precursor—a substance closely resembling the transmitter that can easily be converted chemically to the transmitter—must be transported or moved down the inside of the axon to the terminal. It is known that there are actually at least two rates of transport in axons, one fast and one slower. These are termed *axoplasmic transport*.

The transmitter arrives at the bouton and is stored there probably in the vesicles (clear and dark centered circles labelled 3). There are two kinds of vesicles in the bouton. The most common, found in all synapses, is a small clear type believed to hold transmitters. In addition there may be larger dark-centered vesicles. Both types are shown in Figure 5.5. The large dark-centered vesicles may be a storage form. Both types of vesicles appear to be transported down the axon. The bouton also has mitochondria (larger shaded oval labeled 3 in Fig. 5.6; see also Fig. 5.5) which may participate in the final synthesis of the transmitter.

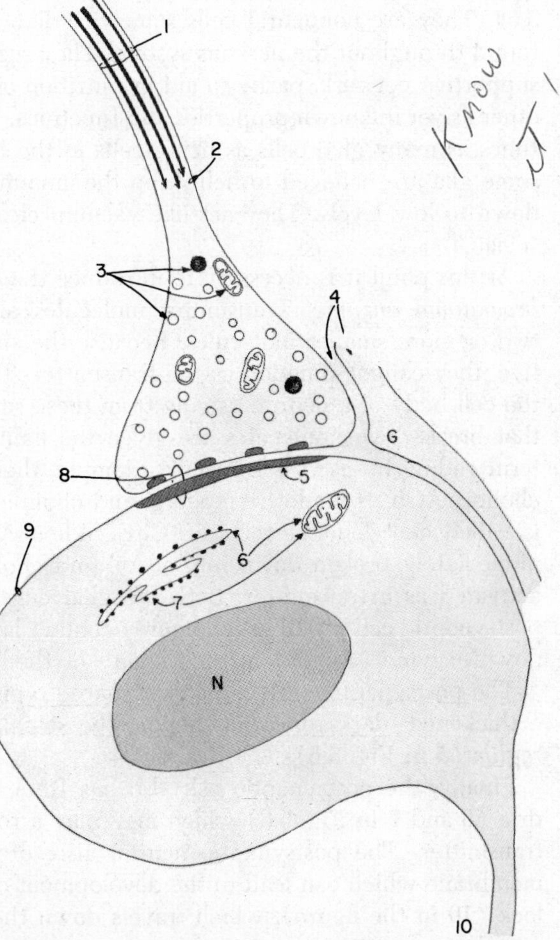

Figure 5.6 Ten steps in the synaptic transmission process as indicated in the schematic. Step 1 is transport of the chemical transmitter down the axon to the terminal bouton. Step 2 is the action potential in the membrane of the axon. Step 3 involves the organelles and enzymes present in the nerve terminal for synthesizing, storing, and releasing the transmitter, as well as for the process of active re-uptake. Step 4 includes the enzymes present in the extracellular space and within the glia (G) for catabolizing excess transmitter released from nerve terminals. Step 5 is the postsynaptic receptor which triggers the response of the postsynaptic cell to the transmitter. Step 6 shows the organelles within the postsynaptic cells which respond to the receptor trigger. Step 7 is the interaction between genetic mechanism of the postsynaptic nerve cell and its influences on the cytoplasmic organelles which respond to transmitter action. Step 8 includes the possible "plastic" steps modifiable by events at the specialized synaptic contact zone. Step 9 includes the electrical portion of the nerve cell membrane which, in response to the various transmitters, is able to integrate the postsynaptic potentials and produce an action potential. Step 10 is the continuation of the information transmission by which this postsynaptic cell sends an action potential down its axon. (Cooper, J. R., Bloom, F. E., and Roth, R. H. *The Biochemical Basis of Neuropharmacology.* 2nd Ed. New York: Oxford Univ. Press, 1974.)

Most synapses between neurons also have glial cells close by (G in Fig. 5.6). They are nonneural cells somewhat like connective tissue and are found throughout the nervous system. They seem to function in part as a supportive network, partly to aid in nutrition of the brain, and may have other as yet unknown properties and functions. Interestingly there are ten times as many glial cells as nerve cells in the human brain. At synapses, some glia are believed to help keep the amount of transmitter substance down to low levels. They act like vacuum cleaners to keep the synapse "clean."

At this point it is necessary to introduce the concept of the *transmitter breakdown enzyme*. Transmitter molecules are composed typically of two or more smaller molecules. Because the smaller molecules are inactive, they cannot function as the transmitter. The transmitter is made in the cell body of a neuron usually from these smaller molecules. Enzymes that break down molecules are given the name of the molecule plus a term ending in *-ase*. As a specific example, the transmitter called acetylcholine, ACh, is made from acetyl and choline. The breakdown enzyme is called acetylcholinesterase, AChE. When ACh contacts AChE, it is immediately broken down into acetyl and choline and consequently inactivated as a transmitter. Both the glial cells (4 in Fig. 5.6) and the postsynaptic cell (5–10 in the figure) contain large amounts of the breakdown enzyme (AChE) in the vicinity of the synapse.

The postsynaptic surface of the synapse typically, but not always, has a thickened, dark-appearing region, the so-called *postsynaptic receptor region* (5 in Fig. 5.6).

Finally, the postsynaptic cell also has RNA ribosomes and mitochondria (6 and 7 in Fig. 5.6) which may play a role in the final rate of the transmitter. The postsynaptic neuron also, of course, has an excitable membrane which can lead to the development of a spike, at the axon hillock (10 in the figure), which travels down the axon to act at synapses on other neurons.

The events in synaptic transmission are summarized as follows: The transmitter moves down the axon (1) and is stored in the vesicles of the bouton (3). Any transmitter that "leaks" from the bouton is destroyed by the enzyme in the glial cells (4) and postsynaptic cell (5). When a spike action potential travels down the axon (2) to the bouton, the chemical transmitter is released into the synapse (8). How this happens is unknown but the critical event is an inward movement of calcium ions ($Ca++$) into the bouton. The inward calcium movement is triggered by the membrane spike potential, and in turn triggers release of the transmitter. This role of calcium, incidentally, appears to account for calcium being essential in the human diet to assure normal brain function. The synapse proper is the pre- and postsynaptic region labeled 8 in Figure 5.6.

When the transmitter reaches the chemical receptor in the postsynaptic membrane (5 in Fig. 5.6), a change in the membrane results in a postsynaptic potential (in 9 in Fig. 5.6). This can be either an excitation, which moves the membrane potential toward the spike threshold (a depolarization) or an inhibition that moves the membrane potential farther away from spike threshold (a hyperpolarization). If it is a depolarization and the spike threshold is crossed, a spike potential develops at the axon hillock (10) and travels down the axon of the postsynaptic cell. The ribosomes and mitochondria in the postsynaptic cell (6 and 7 in Fig. 5.6) may further act on transmitters, but do not participate in the actual development of the spike potential. Finally, the breakdown enzyme inactivates the transmitter at the postsynaptic receptor membrane (5 in Fig. 5.6).

To recap: The transmitter moves down the axon to be stored in the terminal. An action potential arriving at the terminal causes transmitter to be released into the synapse. It travels across by diffusion to the postsynaptic membrane, where it activates receptors that cause the postsynaptic cell membrane to develop a potential change. The transmitter is then broken down or inactivated and the synapse is ready to function again.

Chemicals and drugs can act at least on any one or more of the ten steps in synaptic transmission shown in Figure 5.6. This should make clear the reason for so many different kinds of drug effects on the brain. Presumably there are many kinds of synaptic transmitter chemicals in the brain at various regions and synapses. The interested student is urged to consult a very readable account by Cooper, Bloom, and Roth (1974) for more detailed treatment.

Synaptic transmitters

Acetylcholine (ACh). The best understood synaptic transmitter is ACh. It has been *proven* to be the transmitter at the neuromuscular junction— the synapses made by motor nerves on skeletal muscle fibers and at certain peripheral autonomic synapses. It is *believed* to be a transmitter in certain brain regions, for example, regions of the hypothalamus and the cerebral cortex. The main reason so much is known about ACh is that it is easy to remove a neuromuscular junction (together with a piece of the nerve and muscle) and study its functions *in vitro*—that is, in a dish.

ACh is formed in the cell bodies of neurons and transported down axons to synaptic terminals (neuromuscular junctions). When an action potential arrives at the junction, ACh is released, crosses the synapse and activates the muscle fiber just as we described above for the transmitter action of a nerve cell. The breakdown enzyme AChE then breaks down ACh into acetyl and choline, which are reabsorbed into the nerve cell to be reformed into ACh (see Fig. 5.7).

Some common drug actions on the ACh synapse are indicated in Figure 5.7. The best know drug is curare, the poison used by South American Indians on their arrows. Curare prevents ACh from activating the postsynaptic receptor. It is believed that the curare molecules occupy on the receptors the site that is normally activated by ACh. Curare itself does

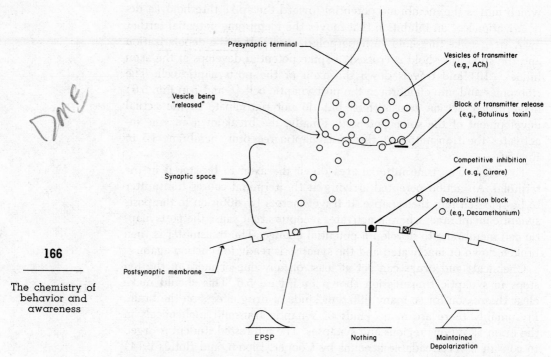

DME

Presynaptic terminal

Vesicles of transmitter
(e.g., ACh)

Vesicle being
"released"

Block of transmitter release
(e.g., Botulinus toxin)

Competitive inhibition
(e.g., Curare)

Synaptic space

Depolarization block
○ (e.g., Decamethonium)

Postsynaptic membrane

EPSP   Nothing   Maintained
                                Depolarization

Figure 5.7 Schematic diagram of some of the common drug actions on ACh synapses and the means by which they affect these synapses.

not activate the postsynaptic receptors (i.e., muscle fibers). Consequently ACh is blocked from acting. The effect of curare is total paralysis. The muscles no longer respond to nerve commands; the transmission of the commands is blocked at the synapse between nerve and muscle.

Another kind of blocking action at ACh synapses is produced by the deadly food poison, botulinus toxin. It appears to block the release of ACh from the presynaptic bouton (Fig. 5.7). As with curare, total paralysis is the result—transmission at the synapse between nerve and muscle is again blocked. However, the mechanism of blocking is quite different. Curare and botulinus toxin, chemically quite different, have quite different actions. Curare blocks ACh from postsynaptic receptors and the toxin blocks ACh release from the presynaptic terminal. Yet they have exactly the same final effect, paralysis. This illustrates how difficult it is to determine drug actions on unknown synaptic transmitters. Very different drugs can act in quite different ways on synapses and yet produce similar effects.

LSD (a synthetic substance) and mescaline (from cactus peyote buttons) are quite different chemicals and may act very differently, yet they produce similar effects on awareness—bizarre hallucinations and psychotic-like experience. Further, they show cross-tolerance. With repeated usage of, for example, LSD, more is required to produce the same effect (tolerance). More than normal dosage of mescaline is then also required, even though it had not been used before (cross-tolerance). It may be that both LSD and mescaline act in different ways on the same particular brain synapses to yield the same net effect.

Still another way to influence the ACh synapse is to block the action of the enzyme AChE. A drug called Prostigmin does just this. What do you think the behavioral effect of Prostigmin would be? It leads to prolonged and uncontrollable muscle contractions. The ACh is not broken down because AChE is blocked; hence ACh continues to act on the post-synaptic receptor to cause repeated activation of the muscle.

Another mechanism that must be considered in any discussion of how drugs act on the brain is the *blood-brain barrier*. Many drugs have no effect on the brain because they cannot get into the brain. A special barrier —believed to be just outside the small blood vessels and capillaries in the brain and probably composed of glial cell elements—prevents many drugs from getting to the brain. Such drugs penetrate all other organs with ease but cannot enter the brain. This is very fortunate, since blood levels of many substances vary widely and could have catastrophic effects on the brain.

The blood-brain barrier proved embarrassing to some early investigators of chemical treatment of presumed brain dysfunction. Several studies in the 1940s reported marked improvement in the intelligence of mentally retarded patients after treatment with high doses of glutamic acid (one normal constituent of many protein foods). The enthusiastic conclusion was drawn that glutamic acid acted directly on the brain. Subsequently, however, it was found that glutamic acid cannot cross the blood-brain barrier and hence could not have acted on the brain. The "improvement" noted very likely resulted from increased protein in the patients' diet.

To return again to ACh—some drugs can cross the blood-brain barrier and result in an increase in brain content of ACh. Some of these reportedly have produced nightmares, confusion, and hallucinations. Other evidence suggests that ACh in the brain may be involved in perception of pain. However, for the most part, the central synaptic actions of ACh remain a mystery.

Biogenic amines. One other substance known to be a synaptic transmitter is noradrenalin or *norepinephrine*. It is the transmitter at certain peripheral autonomic synapses and is also released by the adrenal glands. Chemically, norepinephrine is a type of compound called an amine. Two other amines also are believed to be synaptic transmitters: *dopamine* and *serotonin*. Actually, norepinephrine is made in the body directly from dopamine, which in turn is manufactured from an amino acid, tyrosine, common in protein foods. Serotonin is made from another amino acid, tryptophan.

Norepinephrine is found in high concentrations in the hypothalamus and midbrain and, in general, in brain structures that have their influence primarily on the autonomic nervous system. Norepinephrine may be the brain transmitter most involved in the motivational and emotional aspects of behavior.

Dopamine is found in a particular brain system involving the substantia nigra, a dark-appearing collection of cells in the midbrain that project to the basal ganglia in the forebrain. The basal ganglia are large masses of cells in the cerebrum that seem to have motor functions. Interestingly, Parkinson's disease, a disorder that causes forced repetitive "pill-rolling" movements of the hands, is generally associated with deterioration of cells in the substantia nigra. Recently it has been treated with some success by administering dopamine. Reported side effects include alleviation of depression and marked increase in sexual drive and desire.

Serotonin is a most intriguing substance. It has its highest concentrations in the pineal gland, a very mysterious gland that appears somewhat regressive in man but seems to have important, but as yet unclear, functions in lower animals. In the higher vertebrate and human brain, serotonin is found only in one system, the *raphé-nuclei* in the midbrain. These "serotonin" nerve cells send their axons to wide areas of the forebrain, particularly the hypothalamus, septal area, and other regions of the limbic system. The raphé-nuclei have been implicated as a major brain control system for regulation of sleep. It has been said that the raphé cells are a very ancient system with their own transmitter, serotonin, concerned with primitive aspects of behavior such as sleep and basic emotion. Recent studies by Aghajanian, Bloom, and others indicate that direct application of LSD to raphé cells causes them to cease activity. The powerful tranquilizer, reserpine, causes brain serotonin content to decrease markedly.

Schildkraut and Kety (1967) noted that a great many drugs that seem to influence mood and emotion also have effects on brain levels of biogenic amines. Specifically, drugs that cause sedation or *depression* also cause decreases in brain content of biogenic amines. Drugs that combat depression and cause euphoria or elation also cause increases in brain biogenic amines. They suggested that human depression may be due to a deficiency of brain biogenic amines. In short, "happiness is brain biogenic amines." This is only a suggestion at present, but it may have very important implications for our understanding of the depressive illnesses.

DRUGS AND BEHAVIOR

Drugs usually are defined as chemicals that have effects on animals. This definition would seem to include almost every substance as a drug, which is probably not far from being true. Even water, taken to excess, has potent harmful effects. The field concerned with the study of drugs is called *pharmacology;* the study of drugs that influence experience and

know what
each drug generally
does.

behavior is termed *psychopharmacology*. Almost any drug that affects man also influences his experience and behavior, so psychopharmacology, broadly conceived, is almost synonymous with pharmacology. Drugs may be classified in many possible ways—they can be categorized in terms of chemical structures, in terms of the places they act in the organism, etc. No category is entirely satisfactory—drugs with different chemical structures have similar effects; drugs with similar structures have very different effects; the places where many drugs act are unknown, beyond the obvious fact that they act on the nervous system; and so on. Interestingly, most pharmacology texts actually classify drugs in terms of their effects on experience and behavior, e.g., as anesthetics, stimulants, depressants, etc.

Although psychopharmacology has existed as a field for only about 20 years, the oldest historical references to drugs are to those that affect experience. Cuneiform tablets from ancient Assyria refer repeatedly to drug recipes that have psychological effects. According to Homer, Helen of Troy was an opium addict; alcohol is at least as old as western society; Herodotus described how the ancient Scythians heated hemp seeds on hot stones, inhaled the vapors (marijuana) and "shouted for joy." Endless examples can be found. Probably it is safe to generalize and say that every primitive culture in the world has discovered and developed its own brand of "trip" from naturally occurring substances.

Some of the major classification categories for drugs are indicated in Table 5.1, together with examples and information regarding addiction. We will discuss each category briefly. Since these groupings are based on the general biological or behavioral effects of the drugs, and also in part on the ways the drugs are used, some drugs fit into more than one category. For example, barbiturates are used primarily as sedatives but can also function as general anesthetics; amphetamine is used as a stimulant but in larger doses acts as a psychotogenic drug.

General anesthetics

A wide variety of drugs can act as general anesthetics. Three types generally distinguished on the basis of physical properties are *gas anesthetics* such as nitrous oxide ("laughing" gas) and cyclopropane, *volatile anesthetics* which are liquids that evaporate rapidly like ether and chloroform, and *intravenous anesthetics,* which are solid substances like barbiturates that must be dissolved in solution and injected in a vein. However, the effects of these different types of general anesthetics are similar.

Drugs like alcohol and opium were used in ancient times to dull the pain of surgery, but today's use of anesthetics in conjunction with medicine is only about 100 years old. The anesthetic properties of nitrous oxide were discovered by Priestley in 1776 and the similar effects of ether noted by Faraday in 1818; however, neither drug was used in surgery until the mid-19th century when Horace Wells, a dentist in Hartford, Connecticut,

Table 5.1 Major categories in the classification of drugs based on general biological or behavioral effects.

Drug Class	Group	Trade or Common Name	Example	Evidence of Addiction?
Sedatives and Hypnotics	General		alcohol	yes
	Barbiturates	Luminal	phenobarbital	yes
	Bromides		potassium bromide	no
	Chloral derivatives		chloral hydrate	yes
Stimulants	Analeptics	Metrazol	pentylenetetrazol	no
	Nicotinics		nicotine	yes
	Psychotogenics	(See Psychotogenics, below)	lysergic acid diethylamide	
	Sympathomimetics	Benzadrine, speed	amphetamine	yes
	Xanthines		caffeine	yes
Anesthetics, Analgesics, and Paralytics	Analgesics	morphine, heroin	opium derivatives	yes
	Local anesthetics	coca	cocaine	yes
		Novocaine	procaine	no
	General anesthetics	"laughing gas"	nitrous oxide	no
			diethyl ether	no
			chloroform	no
	Paralytics	curare	d-tubocurarine	no
Psychotogenics	Cannabis sativa	hemp, hashish	marijuana	no
	Ergot derivative	LSD, "acid"	lysergic acid diethylamide	no

Drug Class	Group	Trade or Common Name	Example	Evidence of Addiction?
	Lophophora williamsii	peyote buttons	mescaline	no
	Psilocybe mexicana		psilocybin	no
Psychotherapeutics	Anti-anxiety:			
	Propanediols	Miltown	meprobamate	yes
	Benzodiazephines	Librium	chlordiazepoxide	yes
	Barbiturates	(See Sedatives, above)	phenobarbital	
	Anti-depressant:			
	MAO inhibitors		tranylcypromine	no
	Dibenzazepines	Tofranil	imipramine	no
	Anti-psychotic:			
	Rauwolfia alkaloids		reserpine	no
	Phenothiazines	Thorazine	chlorpromazine	no
	Stimulant:	(See Stimulants, above)	amphetamine	

Table 5.2 Stages and planes of anesthesia

STAGES OF ANESTHESIA		RESPIRATION		PUPIL SIZE			EYE-BALL ACTIV-ITY	SOMATIC MUSCLES	APPROXIMATE EEG PATTERN
		THORACIC	ABDOMINAL	NO MEDICATION	MORPHINE AND ATROPINE	MORPHINE			
I ANALGESIA				○	○	○	VOLUN-TARY	NORMAL TONE	
II DELIRIUM				○	○	○	+ + + +	UN-INHIBITED ACTIVITY	
III SURGICAL	PLANE I			○	○	○	+ + + + / + + + / + + / +	RELAX-ATION • SLIGHT	
	PLANE II			○	○	○	FIXED	• MODERATE	
	PLANE III			○	○	○	FIXED	• MARKED	
	PLANE IV			○	○	○	FIXED	• MARKED	
IV MEDULLARY PARALYSIS								• EXTREME	

Adapted from Guedel, A. E. **Inhalation Anesthesia.** 2nd Ed. New York: Macmillan, 1951.

began using nitrous oxide to extract teeth and William T. G. Morton introduced ether for general surgery. At that time ether was known primarily as a dangerous curiosity; it was not uncommon for medical students to hold ether parties or "jags," not unlike the marijuana parties of today, where they sipped or inhaled ether to become high. Interestingly, Morton faced very strong opposition when he proposed the use of anesthesia in surgery and childbirth. Opposition came particularly from the churches, which apparently believed that pain and suffering were somehow virtuous. It is difficult to imagine that anyone could favor continuing the unbelievable agony of, for example, major abdominal surgery in a fully awake patient who had to be strapped to the table and held down by four strong men, the standard surgical team of the day. (Speed was the prime requirement of a surgeon in those days—it is said there were some who could amputate a leg in six seconds flat.) However, the objections of the church were effectively silenced when it was pointed out that, according to the Bible, God anesthetized Adam when He took out a rib to make Eve.

When a general anesthetic is administered slowly, the patient progresses through several stages of consciousness (see Table 5.2). The stages are roughly similar for most general anesthetics, although some, like barbiturates, take the subject (i.e., patient or experimental animal) down so rapidly from the waking state to the third stage, surgical anesthesia, that the intervening stages are not easily seen. The table indicates the characteristic patterns of respiration, pupil size, eye movement activity, muscle tone, and approximate EEG pattern in the various stages. In the first stage, *analgesia,* the subject can be brought to a point where he is still "conscious" in the sense that he can respond to questions, but reports no pain. Pain, the reason why anesthetics were developed, is still very poorly understood. It is surely the most immediate and compelling subjective experience, and in an evolutionary sense is essential for adaptive survival. Patients with diseases or lesions that destroy pain pathways in the nervous system such that, for example, they experience no pain in their legs, must be extremely careful of injury. Such persons commonly develop severe infections simply because they do not feel cuts and bruises and the subsequent irritation associated with infections. In a primitive hunting-and-gathering society a person who could not feel pain would not survive more than a few days.

During the second stage of anesthesia, *delirium,* the subject is unconscious but extremely active, and may laugh, shout, sing, thrash about, and struggle violently. In barbiturate anesthesia this state is rarely seen because the subject goes through it so rapidly to *surgical anesthesia.* This, the third stage of anesthesia, is subdivided into various "planes" or levels, with increasing depth. One of the major reasons for taking the subject to a deep level for operations, incidentally, is to obtain sufficient relaxation of the muscles to facilitate surgery. The fourth and final stage of anesthesia involves respiratory paralysis and ultimate death.

The mechanisms of action of general anesthetics are not well understood, particularly at the cellular level. One hypothesis is that anesthetics change the permeability of nerve cell membranes; another theory suggests that they cause a decrease in cellular respiration, that is, uptake of oxygen by neurons. Others theorize that anesthetics combine with water in the brain to form very tiny crystals which impede synaptic transmission. Little conclusive evidence exists to support any of these views. In fact, it is entirely possible that different anesthetics have quite different basic modes of action on nerve cells. The fact that most general anesthetics produce the same effects in terms of stages of anesthesia could still be explained if the net result of different cellular effects were always decreased neuronal activity.

At a more general level there is growing evidence that anesthetics may differentially block or impair the ascending reticular activation system (Fig. 5.8). As you will learn in Chapter 6, there are two general types of sensory systems—the specific systems concerned with vision, hearing, touch, etc., and an older nonspecific system involving the reticular core of the brain stem. The reticular system is influenced or activated by all varieties of stimuli and is concerned more with regulating the general

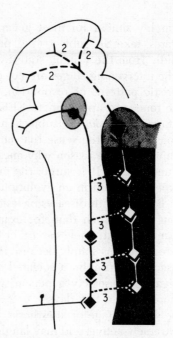

▨ Thalamic nuclei

■ Reticular formation

— Specific afferent pathways

- - - Diffuse projection systems

······ Afferent collaterals

Figure 5.8 Diagram showing possible sites of action for various drugs within the CNS: 1, reticular formation; 2, diffuse thalamic projection system; 3, afferent collaterals to reticular formation. Barbiturates might act directly on 1, cholinergic drugs on 2, and chlorpromazine and LSD-25 on 3. (Bradley, P. B., The central action of certain drugs in relation to the reticular formation of the brain. In Jasper, H. H. (ed.), *Reticular Formation of the Brain.* Boston: Little, Brown and Co., 1958, pp. 123–149.)

level of activation or arousal of the organism than with the details of sensory information. Pain, in contrast to other types of sensory input, is relayed primarily through the reticular system and is not represented by a separate specific pathway in the higher regions of the brain.

If anesthetics selectively inactivate or block the ascending reticular system, then it ought to be possible selectively to block the transmission of pain information, and hence the experience of pain. At the same time, experiences of other types of sensation, such as vision and hearing, still should occur. This is, of course, exactly what happens in the first stage of general anesthesia. It is not necessary to assume that anesthetics have a specific action on the reticular system. Specific sensory systems have long nerve fiber pathways and relatively few neurons in series in the chain from receptors to the cerebral cortex. Naturally, the total number of neurons is not small, there are simply few levels (Fig. 5.8). Thus to go from the optic nerve of the eye to the visual area of the cortex involves only two synaptic levels or relays. There are millions of neurons in this system but only two levels or synaptic relays from eye to cortex. The reticular system, on the other hand, is characterized by many more neurons in the ascending chain (Fig. 5.8). Consequently if a general anesthetic produces the same partial depression in activity of all neurons, it will have a much greater effect on transmission through the many-neuron chain of the reticular formation than on the few-neuron long-fiber chains of the specific sensory systems.

Local anesthetics

Local anesthetics are drugs that act at the site of application to block nerve activity. Cocaine, the first local anesthetic to be discovered, occurs naturally in high concentrations in the leaves of the cocoa bush that grows in higher elevations of the Andes. For centuries the natives who live in the Andes in Peru have eaten the cocoa leaves—they now consume several million pounds annually. This is not because of the local anesthetic properties of cocaine but because it acts as a stimulant centrally, as do most specific local anesthetics, and produces a sense of well-being and freedom from care. It is addictive when consumed in this manner but apparently only moderately so. Cocaine addiction is relatively rare now in the United States but at one time was more common. In pure state cocaine is white and flaky in appearance (hence the name "snow"). This substance is sniffed, like snuff. Occasionally it is taken intravenously in combination with heroin (a mixture called a "speedball").

Sigmund Freud was the first to study cocaine in detail, both as a local anesthetic and as a centrally acting stimulant. He used it successfully to wean a colleague away from morphine addiction (so successfully that the man became the first cocaine addict in western society). Cocaine is not used today as a stimulant but rather as a local anesthetic. A number of synthetic substitutes for cocaine have been developed, of which the best known is procaine (trade name, "Novocaine").

Local anesthetics act directly on nerve fibers to block conduction. Most readers have experienced local anesthetics either for dental work or minor skin surgery. Since procaine, for example, can act anywhere it is injected on a nerve, it is possible to anesthetize relatively large surface areas if desired. Thus a nerve with all sensory input from a large portion of the hand can be blocked by injecting procaine in it in the wrist or arm, producing total anesthesia for that portion of the hand supplied by the nerve. If you have been administered procaine for dental work, you may have noticed that although a probe being pushed into the gum could be felt, it did not hurt. The blocking action of local anesthetics is differential; pain is the first sensation to be blocked, followed by cold, warm, touch, and lastly, deep pressure. We will discuss the manner in which skin receptors and nerves code this kind of sensory experience in a later chapter. For now it is sufficient to note that the sequence of blocking by cocaine corresponds closely (and inversely) to the sizes of the different nerve fibers. In nerves in the skin, pain fibers are the smallest, and touch and deep pressure fibers the largest. Interestingly, if the blood supply to a nerve is reduced, the sequence of blocking tends to be just the opposite. For example, when your leg "goes to sleep," light touch disappears first and pain last.

The action of a local anesthetic appears to be directly on the membrane of the nerve fiber. As we noted in Chapter 4, when the action potential develops at a given point on a nerve fiber there is an abrupt increase in the inward movement of sodium ions from the outside to the inside of the fiber, and a slower outward movement of potassium ions. It appears that local anesthetics decrease the tendency of the membrane to allow these ion movements. Stated technically, the permeability of the nerve membrane to sodium and potassium ions is decreased. How this happens is not yet known.

Sedatives and hypnotics

The most widely used types of drugs in this category are *barbiturates*. These substances are general depressants; indeed the barbiturates in larger doses act as general anesthetics. Barbiturates, however, do not impair the sense of pain without impairing consciousness. That is, in order to produce a significant anesthetic effect it is necessary to produce unconsciousness with barbiturates. One barbiturate of particular interest is sodium pentothal, the so-called "truth serum." In appropriate doses, this drug can produce a kind of twilight state in which the subject responds much as he would if he had been hypnotized. The subject responds to questions and describes events, yet he has no memory of it afterward. Actually this effect is common to most barbiturates; pentothal simply has convenient dose-effect properties to obtain the hypnotic-like state. Narcoanalysis, or narcotherapy, as it has been called, has been widely used. It is often possible to elicit statements and feelings from subjects under the drug that they would not normally make.

Other commonly used sedatives include bromides—at one time the most widely used sleeping pill—and chloral hydrate, so-called "knockout drops."

The actions of the sedatives are not known in detail but there seems to be general agreement that they are totally nonspecific in the sense that they depress a wide range of biological functions. The degree of depression, of course, is proportional to the relative potency of the particular sedative and, obviously, the amount given. The main point is that a larger dosage produces more general depression; there seems to be no particular effect on anxiety, tension, or other specific aspect of experience.

Alcohol is the most widely used of all sedatives. Contrary to popular opinion it is not a stimulant, but rather is a depressant, like other sedatives. The general effects of alcohol are too well known to require discussion. For some individuals it is a severely addictive drug.

Addiction to barbiturates is widespread; indeed, barbiturates comprise the groups of drugs that seem to result in particularly severe addiction. Addiction will be treated separately at the end of this section on drugs; suffice it to say here that both psychological and physical dependence develop with repeated use of barbiturates.

Paralytics

Curare is the best known paralytic agent. There are a variety of synthetic analogues now, the most widely used being *d*-tubocurarine and Flaxedil. Curare, a drug with well understood actions, blocks transmission at the neuromuscular junction (between motor nerve axons and striated muscles) producing paralysis, and other ACh synapses (as noted previously). With sufficient dosage the intercostal muscles of the chest are paralyzed, breathing stops, and death ensues. Curare is used clinically primarily to increase muscle relaxation during surgery. Curare has had most important use in certain types of behavioral experiments, particularly in testing hypotheses relating to the extent to which muscle movements are essential for learning or thinking. An heroic experiment by the pharmacologist Goodman and his associates (Smith et al., 1947) is a classic. One of the experimenters took repeated doses of curare until totally paralyzed. He was, of course, placed on a respirator under careful medical supervision. A number of stimuli were given—lights, sounds, verbal questions, pin pricks, etc. He was then taken off curare, and reported accurately all stimuli that he had received, the verbal questions, and noted that the pin pricks hurt. In brief, his sensory experiences and ability to perceive and think seemed relatively unchanged by total muscular paralysis. This is a most important point—it discounts all theories of perception and thinking that require essential participation of muscle responses.

Narcotic analgesics

Morphine, heroin, and other opium alkaloids are among the most severely addictive of all drugs. For centuries they have been used to ease pain; indeed morphine continues to be one of the most widely used drugs in medicine. The modes of action of the narcotics are unknown. In moderate doses they produce a sense of euphoria (feeling of well-being), drowsiness, and most important, marked analgesia. Even the most severe chronic pains, ranging from toothache to terminal cancer, often are markedly and completely relieved by morphine. It is important to note that although chronic pain is eliminated, awareness is not. The pain threshold and the feeling of unpleasantness from a pin prick seem relatively unchanged after analgesic doses of morphine. Commonly, it is said that morphine does not alter the immediate sensation of pain but rather alters the reactions of the patient to that sensation. Although this may convey the essential character of the morphine syndrome, it probably is not a scientifically tenable distinction. Further, under many conditions, narcotics may reduce response to pain in man and animals.

The most striking feature of the narcotics, of course, is the very strong addiction that develops with repeated use. It is sufficient to note here that heroin and other narcotic addiction are among the most serious social problems at present in the United States.

Stimulants

A wide variety of substances can be categorized as stimulants in terms of their general effects on behavior. Strychnine, picrotoxin, and Metrazol (pentylenetetrazol) are potent central nervous system stimulants that lead to convulsions and death in overdoses. Strychnine and picrotoxin, incidentally, are among the very few drugs whose actions on nerve cells are, to some degree, understood. They block particular forms of neural inhibition, and thus lead to runaway excitation and convulsions. These three drugs and related substances are of particular interest to physiological psychologists because of their facilitative effect on certain kinds of behaviors, particularly learning. We will explore this further in the chapter on learning and memory (Chapter 11).

Mild stimulants widely used include caffeine (in coffee, tea, and cocoa) and nicotine (in tobacco). One cup of coffee, incidentally, contains about 200 mg (0.2 grams) of caffeine, a dose sufficiently high to produce central stimulation (i.e., activation of the brain). The effects of caffeine and nicotine as stimulants are relatively mild. Caffeine, in particular, appears to be an almost ideal stimulant; it seems to allay drowsiness and fatigue, increases the "flow of thought," increases motor activity, and for most people has few or no side effects. Never has a death been attributed to an overdose of caffeine.

Amphetamines and related drugs are the most widely used and perhaps abused of the potent stimulants. *Amphetamine* is one of the most potent sympathomimetic amines as a central nervous system stimulant (sympathomimetic means that a drug mimics the actions of the sympathetic portion of the peripheral autonomic nervous system—see Chapter 2). Amphetamine lessens depression, increases performance, can increase alertness, decrease fatigue, lessen the need for sleep, lessen the appetite, elevate the mood leading to elation and euphoria, increase motor and verbal activity, etc. Both simple mental tasks and athletic performance are improved. However, these positive effects are followed by a letdown, fatigue, and depression that can be severe following large doses of amphetamines.

Amphetamine is most commonly used medically as a stimulant for patients who tend to be sleepy (for example, women during pregnancy) and for weight reduction. The latter effect seems to result primarily from decreased appetite and is quite variable in humans. A dog, given a dose an hour before feeding, will refuse food. Repeated such dosages can lead to a dog starving to death. However, humans often show little or no effect of amphetamine on appetite.

Amphetamine is strongly addictive, and contributes heavily to the overall serious social problem of drug abuse in the United States. Of great interest and possibly of great theoretical importance is the fact that amphetamine is the only drug that can produce a psychotic state indistinguishable from a "normal" psychosis. In particular, in some people continued usage of amphetamine produces a state that is clinically indistinguishable from paranoid schizophrenia. In this context it is of interest that the chemical actions of amphetamine lead to an increased action of norepinephrine, a synaptic transmitter in the peripheral autonomic nervous system and very likely a synaptic transmitter in the brain as well. In addition, it is an MAO inhibitor—it inhibits the action of monoamine oxidase, the enzyme that breaks down norepinephrine. We will discuss MAO inhibition below when we consider psychotherapeutic agents.

Psychotherapeutics

Psychotherapeutic agents are drugs used in the treatment of psychological disorders. These drugs have led to a genuine revolution in the care and treatment of the mentally ill. Many thousands of patients who just a few years ago would spend their lives in the back wards of institutions now are able to live and function in society, thanks to psychotherapeutic drugs.

There are three general categories of these drugs, the *anti-psychotic* drugs like reserpine and chlorpromazine used to treat the major psychoses, such as schizophrenia, manic depressive psychosis, and senile psychosis; the *anti-anxiety* drugs, mild tranquilizers like meprobamate (Miltown) and chlordiazepoxide (Librium) used to treat neurotic conditions and reduce psychological stress, and the *anti-depressants* such as imipramine and MAO inhibitors used to treat severe psychological depression and phobic-anxiety states.

It must be emphasized that these psychotherapeutic drugs do not cure mental illness. They are successful to varying degrees in different patients in treating and controlling the symptoms and, perhaps in the case of the anti-depressants, come close to effecting a temporary cure. However, this does not mean that we understand the causes of mental illness or that we understand why the drugs have the effects they do. Much of the work, particularly in the original forms of the drugs, was empirical and accidental. The psychotherapeutic effects of reserpine were discovered as a more or less unexpected side effect when it was being used to control hypertension (a form of high blood pressure).

Anti-psychotic drugs. There are two major categories of these drugs, the *phenothiazine derivatives* (e.g., chlorpromazine), and the *Rauwolfia alka-*

loids (e.g., reserpine). The phenothiazine derivatives grew out of biochemical work on antihistamines and related substances. Although there are a great many similar substances now available, chlorpromazine, synthesized in 1950, is still most widely used. The Rauwolfia alkaloids are derived from a natural plant that grows in India. Interestingly, ancient Hindu writings recommended the use of Rauwolfia for both hypertension and insanity—its two modern applications. Reserpine is the purified synthetic form of Rauwolfia in use today. Although chemically unrelated, many of the general behavioral effects of chlorpromazine and reserpine are similar. Chlorpromazine is more effective and more easily controlled and is consequently much more widely used today than reserpine. Reserpine produces marked depression of mood, whereas chlorpromazine does not. Interestingly, reserpine also causes a significant decrease in brain norepinephrine, serotonin, and dopamine. As is true for most drugs, the mechanisms and modes of actions of the anti-psychotic drugs essentially are unknown. The general behavioral effects of chlorpromazine are well described in the following early report by Delay and Deniker (1952):

... Sitting or lying, the patient is motionless in his bed, often pale and with eyelids lowered. He remains silent most of the time. If he is questioned, he answers slowly and deliberately in a monotonous, indifferent voice; he expresses himself in few words and becomes silent. Without exception the response is fairly appropriate and adaptable, showing that the subject is capable of attention and of thought. But he rarely initiates a question and he does not express his anxieties, desires, or preferences. He is usually aware of the improvement induced by the treatment but does not show euphoria. **The apparent indifference or the slowing of responses to external stimuli, the diminution of initiative and of anxiety without a change in the state of waking and consciousness or of intellectual faculties constitute the psychological syndrome attributable to the drug.**
(Delay and Deniker, 1952, as quoted in Jarvik, 1970, page 156)

(See Jarvik, 1970, for an extensive discussion.) Interestingly enough the sedative effects quickly decrease or adapt out with repeated use but the drug continues to produce marked improvement in the psychotic condition. If any drug can truly be called a "wonder drug" for severe mental illness it is chlorpromazine, in spite of the many side effects, some of which can be severe.

Anti-anxiety drugs. Most properly considered as tranquilizers, anti-anxiety drugs are of little value in treating psychosis but produce a pleasant, drowsy and anxiety-free state somewhat similar to that produced by alcohol and barbiturates, without the marked sedative effects of the latter. Two common but chemically unrelated anti-anxiety drugs are meprobamate (Miltown) and chlordiazepoxide (Librium). Meprobamate was developed initially as a muscle relaxant and its tranquilizing properties discovered later. The usual clinical dose has no effect on psychological test performance, produces a mildly pleasant feeling, alters the EEG slightly in the direction of that seen during sleep, and seems, according to subjective reports, to reduce anxiety. The mechanisms of action of the anti-anxiety drugs are unknown.

Anti-depressant drugs. Anti-depressants are a particularly interesting group of drugs that are effective in providing rather dramatic relief from certain forms of severe depression. Although amphetamine might be included here, its action is of much shorter duration so it is usually classed as a stimulant. Its mode of action, however, in some ways resembles certain of the anti-depressant drugs. There are two general types of anti-depressants, *MAO inhibitors* and *imipramine*, that are chemically unrelated. Both seem to have effects on norepinephrine, one of the biogenic amines. The MAO inhibitors are substances that prevent MAO (monoamine oxidase) from breaking down catecholamines, particularly norepinephrine. If this seems fairly confusing, simply remember that norepinephrine is probably a synaptic transmitter substance in the brain and that these anti-depressants all act in such a way as to produce more norepinephrine in the brain by blocking the breakdown action of MAO on norepinephrine. Imipramine, the other main type of anti-depressant, inhibits the uptake inactivation of norepinephrine, thus leading in a different way to increased norepinephrine in brain. Amphetamine, on the other hand, causes release of norepinephrine, leading to higher levels by still another mechanism. Thus these three chemically quite different substances, acting in different ways, all lead to increased norepinephrine in brain and all have stimulating or anti-depressant actions. These and similar observations have led Schildkraut and Kety to develop the "norepinephrine" or "biogenic amine" theory of emotions noted above. Those drugs like reserpine which decrease brain amines lead to tranquilization and drugs that increase brain amines, like MAO inhibitors, imipramine, and amphetamine, produce stimulation or anti-depression. Hence general level of emotional state may be determined by brain levels of biogenic amines, particularly norepinephrine, in regions of brain, such as hypothalamus and limbic system, involved in emotional and motivational aspects of behavior.

Psychotogenic drugs

These are drugs that induce psychotic ("insane")-like symptoms in people. The most widely known of these are LSD ("acid"), mescaline (from the peyote cactus), psilocybin (from mushrooms), and marijuana. A number of words have been used to describe the effect of these drugs

Don

A

—psychotomimetic (imitating psychosis), hallucinogenic (producing hallucinations), psychedelic, etc. Psychotogenic, a term suggested by Jarvik (1970) is perhaps the better term—it simply means that the drugs produce psychotic-like effects, without inferring that those effects are the same as "normal" psychosis.

LSD (lysergic acid diethylamide, also called "acid") is one of the most potent and dangerous drugs known. The effective dose is as low as 100 micrograms (1/10,000 of a gram). As the reader is no doubt aware, LSD produces a variety of bizarre subjective experiences and behavior that in many ways resemble insanity. For a time, it was hoped that LSD would provide a good model of psychosis for experimental study. Unfortunately,

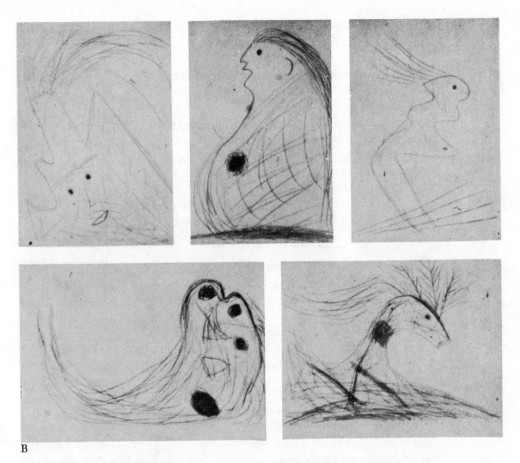

B

Figure 5.9 Two sets of drawings by a schizophrenic patient: A, before administration of LSD_{25}; B, three hours after administration of LSD_{25}. (From Vittorino, M. A., and Trabucci, C. Graphic modifications using LSD_{25} in a schizophrenic group. In Volmat, R., and Wiart, C. (eds.). *Art and Psychopathology.* Amsterdam; Excerpta Medica Foundation, 1969, pp. 275–284.)

however, this does not seem to be the case. The type of hallucination (experiences of stimuli that are not physically present in the external world) induced by LSD is primarily visual. Psychotic individuals predominantly tend to have auditory hallucinations (i.e., hearing voices that are not there).

The quotation at the beginning of this chapter (p. 154) was from a normal individual who had taken LSD for the first time. A normal individual under the influence of LSD is aware of the fact that he is a normal person who has taken LSD. A psychotic individual does not believe he is psychotic.

The potent psychological effects of LSD were discovered accidentally by Hofmann, who with Stoll had earlier synthesized the substance for another purpose. As Hofmann describes it:

In the afternoon of 16 April 1943, when I was working on this problem, I was seized by a peculiar sensation of vertigo and restlessness. Objects, as well as the shape of my associates in the laboratory, appeared to undergo optical changes. I was unable to concentrate on my work. In a dreamlike state I left for home where an irresistible urge to lie down overcame me. I drew the curtains and immediately fell into a peculiar state similar to a drunkenness, characterized by an exaggerated imagination. With my eyes closed, fantastic pictures of extraordinary plasticity and intensive color seemed to surge towards me. After two hours this state gradually wore off.

(Hofmann, 1959, pages 244–245)

Hofmann suspected a relationship between his experience and LSD, which he had accidentally inhaled from his laboratory bench. To settle the matter he deliberately took what he thought was a very low dose of LSD—0.25 mg, now known to be ten times the effective dose. As a result, Hofmann perhaps holds the record for a "bad trip."

As this is written, we do not know why LSD has the effects it does. It is the most potent psychotogenic drug in existence, suggesting not only that the effect on brain function is profound but also that it may mimic or block substances that normally are active in the brain in very low concentrations. LSD is known to exert a powerful antagonistic effect on serotonin, it exerts strong inhibition or blocking of the activity of the raphé-nuclei cells which are believed to form the brain serotonin system (see the earlier section on the biogenic amines), and causes subtle changes in the electrical activity of the brain. However, none of these phenomena accounts for its fantastic effects on human (and other primate) experience.

Apparently, LSD is not severely addictive, although marked tolerance for it develops. Interestingly, this tolerance extends to certain other psychotogenic drugs such as mescaline and psilocybin, even though chemically they are quite different. This is termed *cross-tolerance*. If you take one of these drugs several times you must take progressively larger amounts of any drug to produce the same effect.

LSD is extremely dangerous, not only because of its immediate effects on brain and experience, but also because the individual's behavior becomes so abnormal and bizarre. People on "bad trips" have committed suicide, or injured themselves and others. It does not seem possible to predict whether a person will have a good trip or a bad trip from a given dose of LSD; however, the higher the dose the greater the likelihood of a bad trip. Further, it has been reported that bizarre symptoms may recur at a later date in the absence of LSD. Reports of chromosome damage from LSD are conflicting at present but remain a possibility. This is not a very pretty collection of side effects. An intriguing example of the influence of LSD on one patient's perception of the world is shown in the drawing (Fig. 5.9) done under the influence of LSD.

Marijuana ("grass") is the most widely used psychotogenic drug. In the low doses normally used, its effects seem relatively mild; however in higher doses it is a severe psychotogenic agent, inducing pronounced psychotic-like behavior. One of the early terms for marijuana, *hashish*, is indicative of this. The word comes from an Arabian group of murderers who called themselves *hashashi* (the origin of the English word *assassin*). They took marijuana to build up their courage to assassinate. Marijuana seems to produce a feeling of well-being, at least in some individuals, and tends to result in lowered activity levels. Although the drug itself may be relatively harmless, and this is not yet known for certain, it has indirect effects that may be considered socially harmful. Thus an individual who takes marijuana tends not to do much else; his level of performance drops.

DRUG ADDICTION

Addiction, a complex phenomenon, is a very real and relevant problem in our society. Marijuana, LSD, and other psychotogenic agents do not appear to be addictive, at least not in terms of the development of strong biological needs. The patient may, however, develop a strong psychological need for them. This distinction is confusing. Addiction to heroin, barbiturates, amphetamine, alcohol, and other severely addicting drugs produces extreme biological needs. An addicted person who tries to stop taking the drug suddenly (i.e., "kick the drug cold turkey") will experience severe *withdrawal symptoms*; he may become seriously ill or die. In contrast, if a person who is a regular marijuana user stops taking it, he experiences no particular biological effects. Nonetheless, many users of marijuana continue to use it because they "like" it. This could be said to constitute a psychological addiction. However, since we know that "likes" are fundamentally biological phenomena, indeed they are the result of brain processes, the distinction between psychological and biological addiction is very unclear. It may be a matter of degree.

An important distinction must be made between *tolerance* and *addiction*. Tolerance means that when a drug is repeatedly given, progressively higher doses must be used to produce the same effect. All biologically addicting drugs produce marked tolerance. A heroin addict must take doses of heroin that would kill a normal person in order to experience any effect at all! However, many drugs that are not biologically addictive also have marked tolerance. LSD is a case in point. Not only tolerance but cross-tolerance to other psychotogenic drugs develops with repeated doses of LSD (see above). However LSD seems not to be biologically addicting.

Sharpless, Jaffe, and others have developed a most intriguing and important theory of biological drug addiction, the _hypersensitivity_ theory, which explains many effects. The idea is that whatever the effects of taking the drug have been, just the opposite effects will occur during withdrawal. If stomach contractions are decreased by the drug, they may become abnormally strong and produce stomach cramps during withdrawal. Amphetamine produces a sense of well-being; the person becomes severely depressed during withdrawal. All these effects would occur if the biological systems that are decreased in activity by the drug compensate while the person is on the drug so that their base levels of activity are much higher than normal. In other words, biological systems strive to maintain constant levels of function. If these levels are depressed by a drug, the systems will compensate by becoming much more active. Then when the drug is withdrawn, the biological systems are hyperactive and produce the symptoms of withdrawal.

The duration of withdrawal symptoms corresponds to the duration of action of the drugs themselves. Heroin is relatively short acting; the withdrawal symptoms are relatively brief and extremely severe. The synthetic drug, methadone, has effects similar to heroin but is much longer acting. A person can be shifted from heroin to methadone without difficulty. If he is then taken off methadone his withdrawal symptoms are of much longer duration but much _less_ severe. This fact provides a basis for what may be a promising approach to the treatment of heroin addiction.

Summary

The major difference between the chemical processes of neurons and other cells concerns the manufacture and release of the synaptic transmitter substances by neurons. A nerve cell contains many structures which are common to all living cells. One important structure is the Golgi bodies which are found only in nerve cells and some types of secretory cells. The Golgi bodies are the probable site of the production of the synaptic transmitter substances.

There are thousands of synapses on each nerve cell. Each dendritic spine on a neuron is the site of a synaptic terminal. Dendritic spines are believed to be excitatory in nature. Research has indicated that the number of dendritic spines may be related to behavioral experience. They develop after birth in the cerebral cortex, and the degree of development of cortical dendritic spines is correlated with the developing electrical activity of the brain.

The environment has also been found to affect brain growth and development. Comparisons of the brains of rats reared in enriched and impoverished environments showed differences in the chemical composition, weight, size, and thickness of the cerebral cortex, and in the number of dendritic spines on cortical nerve cells. These studies suggest that the growth and complexity of development of the brain is enhanced by an enriched environment and/or retarded by an impoverished environment.

The process of chemical synaptic transmission is complex and involves a number of chemical substances and structures within neurons. First, the synaptic transmitter moves down the axon to the terminal bouton where it is stored in vesicles. When the spike action potential travels to the bouton, the chemical transmitter is released into the synapse. The critical event in the release of the chemical transmitter is the inward movement of Ca++ into the bouton. The membrane spike potential triggers the movement of Ca++, and this, in turn, triggers the release of the transmitter chemical at the synapse. The transmitter diffuses across the synapse to the chemical receptors in the postsynaptic membrane. These receptors are activated, and the postsynaptic membrane consequently develops a postsynaptic potential of either an excitatory or inhibitory nature. If the membrane potential is depolarized sufficiently, a spike potential develops at the axon hillock and travels down the axon of the postsynaptic cell. Ultimately, the breakdown enzyme inactivates the transmitter at the postsynaptic receptor membrane, and the synapse may again function.

There are several different synaptic transmitter chemicals which act in different ways on the nervous system. Acetylcholine (ACh) is a transmitter at neuromuscular junctions. ACh is also thought to be a transmitter in the hypothalamus and cerebral cortex. AChE, the breakdown enzyme for ACh, breaks it into acetyl and choline which are then reabsorbed into the nerve cell to be reformed into ACh. There are several drugs which act on ACh synapses with the same result (total paralysis), but their mechanisms of blocking are very different. Curare blocks ACh from activating the postsynaptic receptor. It is thought that curare molecules occupy the sites on the receptors which are normally activated by ACh. Botulinus toxin is thought to block the release of ACh from the presynaptic bouton. Another way ACh synapses are influenced is through the blocking of the action of AChE. Prostigmin acts in this way and results in prolonged muscular contractions. By blocking the action of AChE, ACh cannot be broken down and continues to act on the postsynaptic receptor.

Three biogenic amines, norepinephrine, dopamine, and serotonin, all act as neurotransmitter substances. Norepinephrine is a transmitter at certain peripheral autonomic synapses and is also released by the adrenal glands. Norepinephrine is found in high concentrations in the hypothalamus, midbrain, and in other brain structures which influence the autonomic nervous system. It is believed to be a transmitter involved in motivational and emotional aspects of behavior. Dopamine may be involved in motor functions and is found in the substantia nigra and basal ganglia. In the higher vertebrate brain serotonin is located only in the raphé-nuclei, which have been implicated as a major brain control system for sleep regulation.

The field of psychopharmacology is relatively new. Although the behavioral effects of various drugs are known, little is known about the modes of action of these drugs. The categories used to classify drugs are based upon their behavioral effects. The three types of general anesthetics are based upon their physical properties: gas anesthetics, volatile anesthetics, and intravenous anesthetics. The behavioral effects are similar for all three types of anesthetics. When a general anesthetic is administered, four stages of anesthesia are evident: analgesia, delirium, surgical stage, and the final stage involving respiratory paralysis and ultimate death. The mechanisms of actions of general anesthetics are not well understood. At a general level, it appears that anesthetics may differentially block the actions of the ascending reticular activating system.

Local anesthetics act on the nerve fibers at the site of application to differentially block conduction of nerve activity. Local anesthetic action appears to be directly on the membrane of the nerve fiber. Cocaine possesses local anesthetic properties. The sequence of blocking of cocaine corresponds closely and inversely to the sizes of different nerve fibers.

Barbiturates are the most commonly used sedatives. These drugs are general depressants which may result in severe psychological and physical dependence. Bromides, chloral hydrate, and alcohol also are classified as sedatives. The action of sedatives is nonspecific, depressing a wide range of biological functions.

Drugs such as morphine, heroin, and other opium alkaloids are classified as narcotic analgesics. The mode of action of narcotics is unknown; strong addiction occurs with repeated usage.

Central nervous system stimulants, such as strychnine, picrotoxin, and Metrazol, appear to block particular forms of neural inhibition. Overdoses of these stimulants may lead to convulsions and death. Mild stimulants such as caffeine and nicotine are widely used and produce very mild effects. The amphetamines are one of the most potent sympathomimetic amines as a central nervous system stimulant. Amphetamine is strongly addictive. It is the only drug which produces a psychotic state indistinguishable from "normal" psychosis. The chemical action of amphetamines leads to an increased action of norepinephrine. Amphetamines are also an MAO inhibitor.

The three categories of psychotherapeutics are anti-psychotic, anti-anxiety, and anti-depressant drugs. Although these drugs do not cure mental illness, they do help in the treatment and control of symptoms. The two major categories of anti-psychotic drugs, phenothiazine derivatives (chlorpromazine) and Rauwolfia alkaloids (reserpine) are chemically unrelated substances, but their general behavioral effects are similar. The anti-anxiety drugs are tranquilizers, whose mode of action is unknown. The two most common tranquilizers are meprobamate and chlordiazepoxide. The anti-depressant drugs often provide dramatic relief from certain forms of severe depression. The MAO inhibitors and imipramine are chemically unrelated but both affect norepinephrine. The general levels of emotional states may be determined by brain levels of biogenic amines, in particular norepinephrine, in the hypothalamus and the limbic system. Therefore, drugs which decrease the level of brain amines lead to tranquilization while drugs which increase the level of amines produce stimulation or anti-depression.

The psychotogenic drugs induce a variety of psychotic-like symptoms. LSD is the most potent existing psychotogenic drug. Its potency suggests that it may block substances that are normally active in the brain in low concentrations. LSD exerts an antagonistic effect on serotonin. The strong inhibition of activity of the raphé-nuclei causes subtle changes in the electrical activity of the brain. In very large doses, marijuana also acts as a severe psychotogenic agent.

Although the psychotogenic drugs do not appear to be addicting, users may develop a psychological need for them. The distinction between tolerance and addiction is an important and sometimes confusing one. Tolerance refers to the situation where a drug is taken repeatedly and progressively larger doses must be taken in order to produce the same effect. All biologically addicting drugs produce a marked tolerance. However, drugs which are not biologically addictive can also produce marked tolerance.

Summary

6

Sensory processes—
the basis of sensation

6

So I was in the park just now. The roots of the chestnut tree were sunk in the ground just under my bench. I couldn't remember it was a root any more. The words had vanished and with them the significance of things, their methods of use, and the feeble points of reference which men have traced on their surface. I was sitting, stooping forward, head bowed, alone in front of this black, knotty mass, entirely beastly, which frightened me. Then I had this vision.

It left me breathless. Never, until these last few days, had I understood the meaning of "existence." I was like the others, like the ones walking along the seashore, all dressed in their spring finery. I said, like them, "The ocean _is_ green; that white speck up there _is_ a seagull," but I didn't feel that it existed or that the seagull was an "existing seagull"; usually existence hides itself. It is there, around us, in us, it is _us_, you can't say two words without mentioning it, but you can never touch it. When I believed I was thinking about it. I must believe that I was thinking nothing, my head was empty, or there was just one word in my head, the word "to be." Or else I was thinking . . . how can I explain it? I was thinking of belonging, I was telling myself that the sea belonged to the class of green objects, or that the green was part of the quality of the sea. Even when I looked at things, I was miles from dreaming that they existed: they looked like scenery to me. I picked them up in my hands, they served me as tools, I foresaw their resistance. But that all happened on the surface. If anyone had asked me what existence was, I would have answered, in good faith, that it was nothing, simply an empty form which was added to external things without changing anything in their nature. And then all of a sudden, there it was, clear as day: existence had suddenly unveiled itself. It had lost the harmless look of an abstract category: it was the very paste of things, this root was kneaded into existence. Or rather the root, the park gates, the bench, the sparse grass, all that had vanished: the diversity of things, their individuality, were only an appearance, a veneer. This veneer had melted, leaving soft, monstrous masses, all in disorder—naked, in a frightful, obscene nakedness.

(Jean-Paul Sartre, _Nausea_. Translated by Lloyd Alexander, 1964, pages 126–127. Copyright © 1964 by New Directions Publishing Corporation. All rights reserved. Reprinted by permission of New Directions Publishing Corporation.)

How we experience the world around us is one of the fundamental problems in psychology. Why do we identify and experience one stimulus as a red light, another as a Beethoven symphony, and still another as an interesting painting? When you look at a chair you see a chair. The chair obviously does not exist inside your head—it is in the external world. However, some kind of representation or "image" of the chair must occur inside your head. Somehow, the pattern of light energy reflected from the chair activates something in your eyes which in turn activates neurons to convey a pattern of nerve impulses into your brain. This pattern of impulses is changed or transformed as it ascends to the cerebral cortex. Shortly after this point in time you have the experience of "seeing the chair."

193

Stimulus coding—
a common problem
for sensory systems

Psychologists often use the terms *sensation* and *perception* to refer to the experience of seeing the chair. For some, sensation is restricted to pure experience in the absence of learning, as suggested in the passage from Sartre above, while perception is held to be a more complex interpretation of sensations in the light of past experience. This distinction is untenable. We cannot even begin to describe sensations without using words, a process that entails a great deal of past learning. Even a newborn infant appears to *perceive*—at least he looks at some stimuli, such as faces, much more than others. The terms are useful only in reference to the degree of interpretation of stimuli. We will use *sensation* to mean the most immediate experience of stimulation. As will become evident in this chapter, immediate sensations bear a very close relationship to certain aspects of neuronal activity. In the past few years we have made enormous progress in understanding basic processes of *stimulus coding* in the nervous system.

STIMULUS CODING—A COMMON PROBLEM FOR SENSORY SYSTEMS

The fundamental problem of how physical stimuli are coded by sense receptors and brain into patterns of neuronal activity that lead to sensations and experience is extremely complex. We are immediately landed in the midst of the "mind-body" problem. Suppose you see a red light. The light waves (or particles, the photons—the physical stimulus is not simple

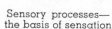

in the case of light) are converted by receptors in your eyes into nerve action potentials which influence progressively higher regions of the brain. So far the story is straightforward, although not simple. The actors in the story are all physical events: light waves, receptors, and neurons. As it happens, we know enough about vision to describe most of these steps, at least from the eye to visual areas of the cerebral cortex. Beyond this point the story is not yet told. Somehow, the complex higher levels of sensory coding in the brain result in behavioral responses: "I see a red light." This part of the story is unknown but the actors are still physical events: brain actions and behavioral responses. It will someday be known.

The step from these physical brain events to subjective experience, your *experience* of red, is the source of much difficulty. This step is completely unknown; some authorities would argue that it cannot ever be known, or even that the first sentence of this paragraph has no meaning. The problem is that subjective experience is often labeled as nonmaterial or nonphysical by definition. If so, the actors in the chain of events that comprise experience are nonmaterial and cannot be studied by the known methods of science. We discussed consciousness at some length in Chapter 3. Perhaps the most important point to reiterate here is that the initial assumptions made about the nature of mind and consciousness determine (or exclude) the methods of analysis used. We can, for example, assume that they are purely physical events or entities and proceed with a conventional scientific analysis. Alternatively, we could adopt a dualist position, and attempt to work out the relations between brain and mind. The dualist position is essentially that of the pioneering scientists like Weber and Fechner who founded the field of psychophysics— study of the relations between properties of physical stimuli and human judgments about stimuli. They attempted to measure and analyze the nature of human consciousness.

In this chapter, we will sidestep the issue of consciousness. Whenever we use terms like experience (i.e., experience of stimuli) here we will refer to subjects' reports, either verbal or other behaviors like pushing a button. We do not mean to imply any position on the larger mind-body problem. We can present a story that is complete in itself, without any appeal to mind. It is sufficient that human (or infrahuman) observers tell us what they experience: "the light is red." We can analyze the receptor processes and brain mechanisms that underlie such judgments. It would be relatively easy to attach photoelectric cells to a computer such that whenever a red light is turned on the computer would say "the light is red." There is no need to assume the existence of subjective awareness or consciousness inside the computer to analyze the way it processes and identifies the stimulus.

The actors in this chapter are receptor cells and nerve cells and the relations between activities of these and human judgments about stimuli. We will review the nature of stimulus coding in the three major sensory

Table 6.1 The kind of correlation matrix
relating sensory judgments to neural responses

Sensory Judgments	Neural Response Dimensions (The Candidate Codes)				
	Place	Topographic Pattern	Number of Activated Units	Frequency	Pattern of Discharge
Quality					
Quantity					
Relative Temporal Order					
Temporal Acuity					
Duration					
Spatial Localization					

Simplified from Uttal, W.R. **The Psychobiology of Sensory Coding.** New York: Harper & Row, 1973.

Stimulus coding—
a common problem
for sensory systems

systems—visual, auditory, and somatic-sensory. However, before plunging into the details of particular sensory systems, it is best to consider some of the general and common aspects of sensory coding. Look up from the book at your world. What aspects of visual experience can you distinguish? Perhaps the most immediate are brightness, color, and form. If you listen to music you note loudness, pitch, and temporal order (for example, melody). An obvious dimension shared by all kinds of stimuli is *intensity* or *quantity*—how loud, how bright, how strong, or how large a stimulus seems. Color and pitch are examples of another dimension, *quality*. Intensity and quality of stimuli are independent, at least in the sense that quality, for example, red or middle C, seems the same over a wide range of stimulus intensities. Visual form is an example of spatial localization and melody is an example of temporal order. In short, human judgments about stimuli can be categorized into a relatively small group of dimensions which are common to most or all particular sensory systems. These categories are shown in the left-hand column of Table 6.1, taken from Uttal's recent and elegant text on the psychobiology of stimulus coding. These aspects of human judgment must be explained in terms of sensory receptors and brain processes.

A given nerve cell in the brain can do only two things to influence other nerve cells and hence behavior—fire a spike, that is, generate an action potential, or not fire a spike. Somehow this simple all-or-none event can serve to code all aspects of sensory experience. The spike action potential is constant in amplitude. All that a single nerve cell can do to code changing influences upon it is vary the frequency and pattern of its spike discharges. We must construct the dimensions of sensory experience from this elemental neuron behavior. A group of neurons can produce a larger or smaller population response, depending on how many fire. A neuron at a given place can fire or not fire. This provides us with at least five different possible substrates of coding: place (in the brain), topographic pattern, number of units firing, frequency of discharge, and pattern of discharge (Table 6.1). All aspects of our sensory experience must somehow be coded in these neuronal terms. Try to keep these various possibilities in mind as you read about the particular sensory systems. At the end of the chapter we will attempt to summarize the decoding of the sensory codes in the nervous system in relation to human judgments about stimuli.

Stimulus transduction

There are really two aspects to stimulus coding in sensory pathways of the brain. One concerns the manner in which neurons code the properties

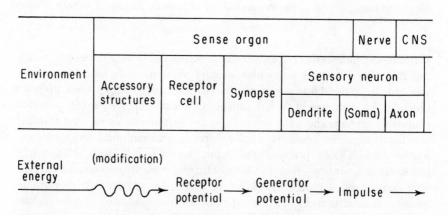

Figure 6.1 Generalized scheme of common features of sensory receptors and their action (not all features shown here are present in all sense organs). (Modified from Davis, H., Some principles of sensory receptor action. *Physiol. Rev.* **41**, 1961, pp. 391–416.)

of stimuli, as we noted above. The other aspect is the transformation of physical stimuli into nerve impulses at the sensory receptors. This process is termed *transduction*. Most receptors share a number of common features, schematized in Figure 6.1. External energy, in the form of light, sound, pressure, heat, soluble molecules, etc., impinges on receptors, which in turn initiate spike discharges in sensory nerve cells. Some receptors have *accessory structures*, such as the lens of the eye, the Pacinian corpuscle of the pressure receptor or the tectorial membrane of the ear, which serve to focus, alter, amplify, or localize the particular stimulus. The stimulus or accessory structure then activates the *receptor cell*. Examples of receptor cells are the rods and cones in the retina of the eye and the hair cells in the cochlea of the ear.

Activation of receptor cells produces graded electrical activity, the *receptor potential* (Fig. 6.1). In turn, this activates the dendrite of the sensory neuron by transmission across the synapse between the receptor cell and the sensory neuron. Activation of the sensory neuron dendrite produces a graded response in the dendrite, just as in the dendrites and cell body of any neuron. The graded dendrite response, if sufficiently large to cross firing threshold, initiates an all-or-none spike discharge in the sensory neuron, which is conducted along the sensory nerve fiber into the CNS.

THE VISUAL SYSTEM

Most organisms, including single-celled animals, can respond to light energy. However, the vertebrate visual system is designed to do much more than simply signal the presence or absence of light. A detailed image of the external world is projected on the *retina* (the layers of receptors and nerve cells at the back of the eye). The retina transforms and codes the image into nerve impulses which carry a representation of the external visual world to the brain. The precision of detail vision is surprising: the image of the full moon on the retina has a radius of about 0.1 mm. Considerable detail can be seen within this image. Lines that are much narrower than the single receptor cells of the retina can easily be seen. In addition to detail vision, the vertebrate visual system is particularly sensitive to movement of objects in the visual world. The faster a predator normally moves, and the faster its prey moves, the more acute must the movement vision of each be to insure survival. Man, incidentally, is a predator in terms of the arrangement of his eyes. Typically, the eyes of predators are close together in the front of the head to permit good depth vision. The eyes of prey animals, such as rabbit or deer, are set far apart and on the sides of the head to detect movements (of predators) to the sides and behind them. In the following discussion of the visual receptors and pathways, try not to lose sight of the basic coding problems involved in delivering a representation of the external visual world, and particularly movements in that world, to the brain.

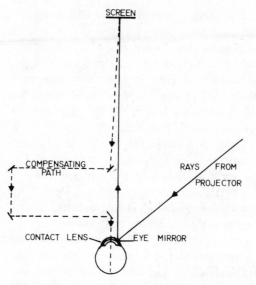

SCREEN

COMPENSATING PATH

RAYS FROM PROJECTOR

CONTACT LENS — EYE MIRROR

Sensory processes—
the basis of sensation

Figure 6.2 Diagram of the method for counteracting the effects of eye movements. The viewing path is effectively double the distance from the eye to the screen. The compensating path includes two dove prisms and an arrangement for providing fixation at the center of a bright annular field. (From Riggs, L. A., Ratliff, F., Cornsweet, J. C., and Cornsweet, T. N. The disappearance of steadily fixated visual test objects. *J. Opt. Soc. Am.* **43**, 1953, pp. 495–501.)

The retina is far more sensitive to stimulus *change* than to the presence of a fixed, unmoving pattern of light. Experiments by Riggs, Ratliff, Cornsweet, and Cornsweet (1953) demonstrated that if an image is stabilized on the retina it fades away (Fig. 6.2). Normally the eye is continuously making small and very rapid movements, so that all retinal images continuously shift back and forth on the retina. Riggs and his associates devised an optical system in which the visual object was reflected to a viewing screen from a small mirror attached to the side of a contact lens on the cornea of the eye. The image moved with the eye ball and thus was always projected on the same retinal elements. Under these conditions, most objects tend to fade out in a few seconds. This rather striking adaption does not normally occur because the image is shifted to different receptor cells by rapid eye movements.

The retina

The basic organization of receptors and nerve cells in the retina is indicated in Figure 6.3. *Rods* and *cones,* the two basic types of light-sensitive receptor cells in the eye, are in close apposition to the dendrites of the bipolar nerve cells. These, in turn, synapse on *ganglion* cells whose axons form the optic nerve. In addition, the receptors are interconnected

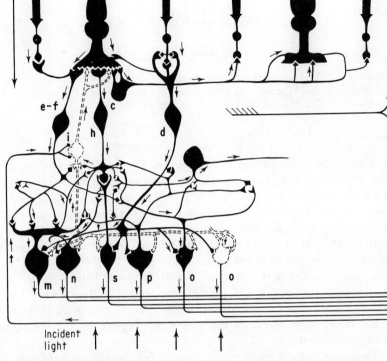

Incident
light

Figure 6.3 Diagram illustrating the basic organization of the neural connections in the retina: a, rods; b, cones; c, d, e, f, h, i, bipolar cells; m, n, o, p, s, ganglion cells. Note the efferent cell (light dots) conducting neural activity back to the receptor cells. (Redrawn from Polyak, S. L. *The Retina*. Chicago: Univ. of Chicago Press, 1941.)

by several varieties of *amacrine* or association-type *neurons*. The retina, actually a very complex neural system, is perhaps best thought of as a "little brain" lying between the photoreceptors and the optic nerve. Embryologically, the retina grows out from the brain rather than being formed peripherally. Although there is only one cell (the bipolar cell) in the main line between the receptors and the ganglion cells, the various interconnecting association cells add a great deal of complexity to the system.

Rods and cones appear to serve rather different functions. The rods are sensitive to very dim illumination (*scotopic vision*), whereas the cones require greater intensities of light and are more involved in acuity and color aspects of visual function (*photopic vision*). Although not always structurally distinct in invertebrates, rods and cones are easily differentiable in mammals. This differentiation of structure and function in rods

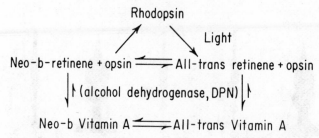

Figure 6.4 The major steps involved in the breakdown and formation of rhodopsin. (Hubbard, R. and Wald, G. Cis-trans isomers of vitamin A and retinene in the rhodopsin system. *J. Gen. Physiol.* 36, 1952–53, pp. 269–315.)

and cones is of fundamental importance. The center of the visual field, that is, the region we see most clearly when we look at an object, projects upon the *fovea*, which is composed entirely of cones. The foveal cones have an almost one-to-one relation to outgoing nerve fibers. The rods have their greatest density about 20° of visual angle (the angle in degrees between the direct line of sight projecting to the fovea and the projection of any other position in the visual field) away from the fovea. Thus you can see a dim star best if you look about 20° away from it. In the human retina, there are about 125 million rods and 6 million cones, but only about 1 million optic nerve fibers. Hence many receptors activate each nerve fiber, particularly in the peripheral regions of the retina where rods predominate.

There are at least two visual pigments (chemicals responsive to light) in receptor cells of the mammalian retina, *rhodopsin* in the rods and *iodopsin* in cones. When light falls on a rod, the rhodopsin immediately breaks down into *retinene* and *opsin* (Fig. 6.4). Retinene has a relatively simple chemical structure closely related to Vitamin A (thus the need for Vitamin A for adequate night vision), and opsin is a complex protein. There are two different biochemical pathways by which rhodopsin can be resynthesized, either from retinene and opsin, or from Vitamin A back to retinene and then combination with opsin. The important point is that when rhodopsin is broken down by light, the retinene and Vitamin A produced are in *isomeric* forms (particular structural arrangements of the molecules) which do not recombine. They must be altered enzymatically to other isomeric forms for resynthesis of rhodopsin.

The visual pigment of the cones, iodopsin, breaks down upon exposure to light into two substances: retinene, in the same form as that from rhodopsin, and a different protein termed *photopsin*. In other words the visual pigments of the rods and cones are both composed of retinene and a protein, with only the protein differing, and the chemical reactions of both are comparable.

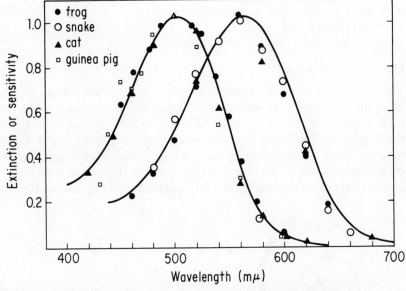

Figure 6.5 Spectral sensitivity curves of rhodopsin (left) and iodopsin (right), determined chemically. Points are Granit's (1947) determinations of spectral sensitivity measures from various animals using microelectrode recording from retinal cells in dark and light adaptation. (Wald, G., Brown, P. K., and Smith, P. H. Iodopsin. *J. Gen. Physiol.* **38**, 1955, pp. 623–681.)

We have spoken of two visual pigments, rhodopsin and iodopsin. Actually, there appear to be a great many different pigments in vertebrates, depending upon the species and upon whether the receptor is a rod or a cone. However, in all cases the pigment is composed of retinene and a type of protein opsin. It is the opsin that differs. As Wald puts it, "one retinene and many opsins." In fact it appears that most organisms with eyes, including squid and lobster, as well as vertebrates, have the same retinene, namely neo-b-retinene, in combination with some type of opsin. However, each species has a different opsin. In human rods there is one rhodopsin, composed of neo-b-retinene and a particular opsin, and in human cones there are three iodopsins, the latter made up of neo-b-retinene and three different opsins (Wald, 1961).

A number of aspects of visual sensation, particularly relating to brightness and color phenomena, can be deduced very accurately from the biochemical properties of rhodopsin and iodopsins. Foremost among these is the virtually perfect correspondence between *spectral sensitivities* (i.e., sensitivity to different wavelengths of light—as you may know, your eyes are more sensitive to green than to red or blue light) for rod and cone vision and the chemical absorption spectra of the rod and cone pigments (Fig. 6.5). In other words, by studying the light absorption properties of the rod and cone pigment chemicals in a test tube, we can predict with great accuracy the sensitivity of human eyes and visual experience to various wavelengths of light.

The visual pathways

The anatomical relations of projection from visual field to retina to brain are a bit complicated in mammals. In lower vertebrates such as the frog there is complete crossing, so that all input to the right eye (right visual field) goes to the left brain, and vice versa (Fig. 6.6). Such animals have no *binocular vision*. In lower mammals, like the rat or rabbit, the visual fields from the two eyes partially overlap. Here there is incomplete crossing; about 80 per cent of the left retina and 20 per cent of the right

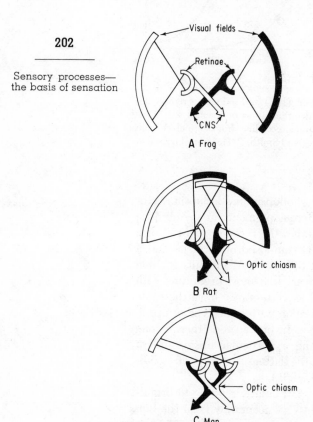

Figure 6.6 Degree of binocularity of visual projections to cortex for different species. In frog the optic tracts are completely crossed; the left visual field projects entirely to the right optic lobe and vice versa. In rat there is some crossing, with some degree of binocular vision. In man the degree of "mixing" is virtually complete; most of the visual field is binocular. (Thompson, R. F. *Foundations of Physiological Psychology.* New York: Harper & Row, 1967.)

retina project to the right brain. The projection from the two retinas overlap, so that perhaps 30 per cent of the visual area has input from both eyes and hence can mediate binocular vision. In the dog and cat there is about 80 per cent overlap, so that they have considerable binocular vision. Primates, including man, have virtually total binocular vision; the left half of each retina projects to the left visual cortex and the right half of each retina projects to the right visual cortex (Fig. 6.7). This means, of course, that the right cortex receives input from the left visual field, and vice versa. Removal of the left visual cortex eliminates all visual input from the entire right half of the visual field of both eyes.

In primates, optic nerve fibers from the left half of each retina (representing the right half of each visual field) project to the left *lateral geniculate body* of the thalamus and fibers from the right half of each

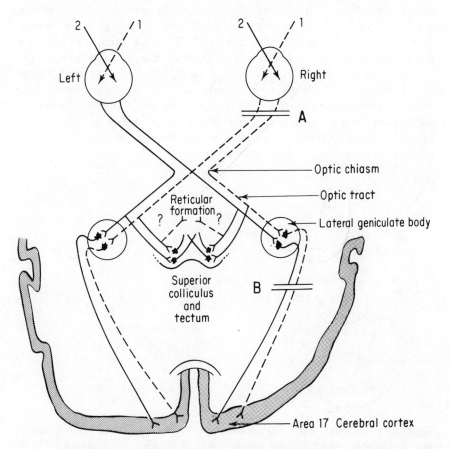

Figure 6.7 Schematic of the primate visual system showing the major afferent pathways. Section at A eliminates input from the right eye, but section at B eliminates input from the right half of each eye. (Modified from Gardner, E. *Fundamentals of Neurology.* 5th Ed. Philadelphia: W. B. Saunders, 1968.)

retina project to the right lateral geniculate body (Fig. 6.7). The resorting of fibers takes place at the *optic chiasm*, the point at which the two optic nerves come together. Although the retina grows out from the brain embryologically, and the optic nerve fibers are at the very least second-order fibers (receptors, bipolar cells, ganglion cells) convention dictates that the fibers from retinas to chiasm are called optic nerves and those from chiasm to CNS are called optic tracts. The optic tracts synapse in the lateral geniculate body, the thalamic relay nucleus, with projections to the visual region of the cerebral cortex. Although the projections from the optic tract to lateral geniculate body to cerebral cortex constitute the main visual pathways in higher vertebrates, there are several other pathways of importance in lower vertebrates.

The visual cortex. The primary visual area of the cerebral cortex, termed the *striate cortex*, is in the occipital lobe in the posterior region of the cerebral hemisphere. It corresponds to Brodmann's area 17 of the human cerebral cortex and is often referred to as VI (visual area I). There is a *retinotopic projection* of the retina on the cortex, essentially a "point-to-point" representation of retinal regions on the occipital cortex. Cortical representation of the foveal area is relatively large, occupying nearly half of the primary visual cortex. This is to be expected since the fovea, although only a small region of the retina, is the central focal point of the eye, and mediates detail vision (i.e., it is the region of maximum visual acuity).

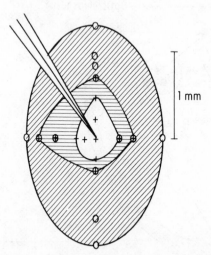

1 mm

Figure 6.8 Cat retina illustrating the receptive fields for optic nerve fibers. Distribution of discharge patterns within receptive field of ganglion cell (located at tip of electrode). Exploring spot was 0.2 mm in diameter, about 100 times threshold at center of field. Background illumination approximately 25 mc. In central region (crosses) *on* discharges were found; in diagonally hatched part only *off* discharges occurred (circles). In intermediary zone (horizontal hatching) discharges were *on/off*. (Thompson, R. F. *Foundations of Physiological Psychology*. New York: Harper & Row, 1967.)

Coding of visual stimuli

Responses of the ganglion cell neurons in the retina (whose axons course out of the eye to form the optic nerve) in vertebrates ranging from cat to monkey, and presumably man, exhibit common, relatively simple, properties. Illumination of a small central region of the field of a given neuron on the retina causes the cell to respond (discharge spike action potentials up the optic nerve) and illumination of an area immediately around this central region inhibits firing of the cell. Examples of receptive fields for optic nerve fibers in the cat are shown in Figure 6.8, from the work of Kuffler (1953).

Not all cells respond when a light is turned on. In fact there are three general types or categories of optic nerve fibers: *on* fibers, that fire when the light is turned on; *off* fibers that fire only when the light is turned off; and *on-off* fibers that fire both when it is turned on and off. These illustrate the common elementary properties of optic nerve fibers in terms of coding the presence or absence of light.

Response to visual form. The simple categories of response to light by optic nerve fibers described above would seem to imply that the retina does little more than transmit activation resulting from turning a light on or off. Actually, a great deal of information processing takes place in the retina. For example, discharges of optic nerve fibers do not necessarily bear a direct relationship to the simple activation of rods and cones by light. An observation that emphasizes this point is that optic nerve fibers of the cat exhibit spontaneous discharging in the absence of light stimulation of the retina. The total amount of activity in optic nerve fibers may be greatest when the eye is in total darkness!

Information processing in the retina appears to be more pronounced in lower vertebrates. Thus the degree of coding that can occur in the retina of the frog is particularly striking (Lettvin et al., 1959). The ingenious experimental arrangement used by these investigators is illustrated in Figure 6.9. Activity of single optic nerve fibers was recorded by microelectrodes. A variety of stimuli were used, including lines, edges, dots of various sizes, checkered patterns, etc., which were moved about the frog's visual field by the simple magnet device shown in Figure 6.9.

The experimenters found that the optic nerve fibers of the frog responded in terms of particular and rather complex features of the stimuli. Some responded only to the continued presence of a light or dark edge, others responded only to an edge moved across the retinal receptive field (region of the retina that activated the fiber being studied), and still others responded only to a general darkening of the stimulus. Perhaps the most interesting category of fibers were those that responded only to a small dark object moved irregularly across the field. The authors termed these fibers "bug perceivers"—they respond best to stimuli that most resembled a bug moving in front of the frog's eye!

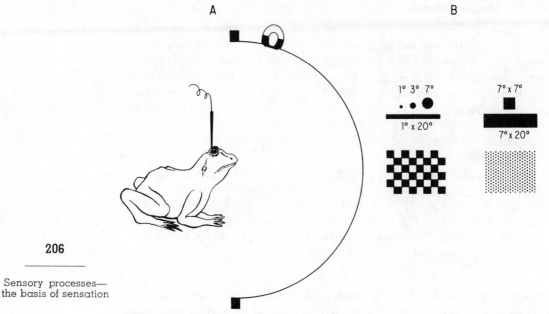

1° 3° 7°

1° x 20°

7° x 7°

7° x 20°

Figure 6.9 A, Schematic drawing of experimental arrangement used to test information coding in frog retina. B, Scale drawings of some of the objects used as stimuli.
The degrees indicate their diameter when placed inside a hemisphere of the same
radius as represented in A. The actual hemisphere used was larger, 14 in. in diameter. (From Maturana, H. R., Lettvin, J. Y., McCulloch, W. S., and Pitts, W. H. Anatomy and physiology of vision in the frog *(Rana pipiens). J. Gen. Physiol.* **43**, 1960,
pp. 129–175.)

Perhaps the most impressive finding of these beautiful experiments is
that the categories of effective stimuli resemble those usually characterized as *complex perceptual processes.* Selective response to bug-like
objects moving in a bug-like fashion does not require "awareness," or
even learning. The transformations are done at the level of the retina. It is
not necessary to invoke any mysterious perceptual processes to account
for the frog's perception of a bug.

Important studies by Hubel and Wiesel (1959, 1965) have provided a
great deal of information about the manner in which cells in the visual
cortex of higher mammals code visual form. In contrast to the frog, the
simple receptive fields and response patterns (*on, off, on-off*) described
above for the optic nerve fibers of mammals seem to be maintained even
at the level of the lateral geniculate body in the cat. Complex information
coding processes occur in cells of the visual *cortex* in cat. Although cortical cells do have receptive fields, their organization can be detected only
by presentation of very small spots of light and visual forms. Many cells in
the visual cortex will not respond at all to a light flash or large diffuse
spot of light.

In general, the receptive fields of cells in the visual cortex (area 17) are not concentric or circular but tend instead to be rectangular or "edge-shaped." An example of such a receptive field is shown in Figure 6.10A. In addition to shape, the orientation of the receptive field, and movement of the appropriate shape across the field, are crucial variables. Figure 6.10B illustrates the importance of orientation. The cell fires when the stimulus rectangle is at a particular orientation. Figure 6.10C shows that for this cell, movement of a stimulus rectangle in one direction through one angle is the most effective stimulus. The rectangular shapes of receptive fields are analogous to edges. In more general terms, cells of the visual cortex respond to edges or boundaries of particular shapes, sizes, positions, and orientations, and often only if they move in particular directions. Hubel and Wiesel differentiate between *simple* and *complex* receptive fields. Simple fields are those with responses to form that could be predicted from the asymmetric regions of excitation and inhibition. The properties of complex fields could not be so predicted. In general, complex fields differ from simple fields in that a stimulus is effective whenever it is placed in the field, provided that the orientation is appropriate. Simple fields require the stimulus to have a specific location as well.

Even more complex and abstract types of receptive fields exist for neurons in the prestriate cortex (cortical areas 18 and 19 bordering the primary VI area 17 in the occipital region of the cortex). Most cells in area 18 and about half the cells in area 19 are complex. Some cells in 18 are *hypercomplex* and many cells in 19 are hypercomplex or *higher order hypercomplex*. These terms simply mean that the organization or form of the receptive field that discharges the cell most effectively is progressively more complex. An example of a hypercomplex cell in area 19 is shown in Figure 6.11. This cell is a right angle "detector"; it responds best to a right angle anywhere within the field and at two different orientations, but will not respond to a straight edge.

Another striking finding by Hubel and Wiesel was the existence of a columnar organization in the visual cortex. If the microelectrode penetrates through the cortex in a path perpendicular to the surface (i.e., at right angles), all the cells in that penetration will respond only to a stimulus edge of the *same orientation*. Different columns of cells respond to stimuli having different orientations. A small region of the retina projects to each square millimeter of cortex. Within that area of cortex are many different columns of cells, each column with cells that respond to a different stimulus orientation. This vertical columnar organization appears to be a very general principle in cortex; actually it was first discovered by Mountcastle in somatic-sensory cortex (see below). A great many different types of columns in the visual cortex are responsive to different stimulus orientations. Further, the neural organization required for this columnar "abstraction" of stimulus orientation in the visual system occurs at the cortex. No such organization is found for cells of the lateral

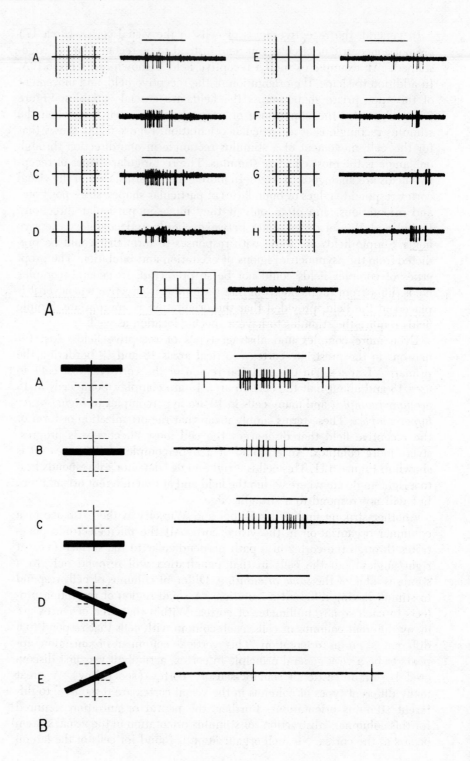

Sensory processes—
the basis of sensation

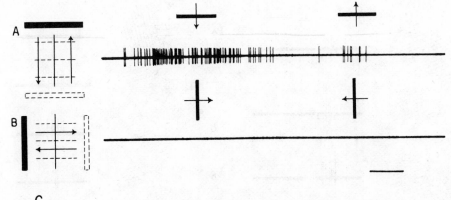

Figure 6.10 Examples of types of visual stimuli that will activate cells in visual cortex. In all three cells (A, B, and C) the stimulus patterns are shown on the left (and also above in C) and the cell discharges on the right. The horizontal line above each spike discharge base line (in A and B) indicates a stimulus presentation. Horizontal bar in lower right (in A and B) represents 1-sec time calibrations. A, Example of an "edge detector" cell. Labels A–H indicate responses of the cell to a stimulus edge placed in different locations (no edge in I). B, Example of an "orientation detector" cell. Labels A–E indicate responses of the cell when the stimulus bar is presented in different orientations. C, Example of a "direction of movement detector" cell. The cell fires a great deal when the stimulus bar moves down and very little when it moves up (A) and does not fire at all when the bar moves from left to right (B) over the same region of the retina. (From Hubel, D. H., and Wiesel, T. N. Receptive fields, binocular interaction and functional architecture in the cat's visual cortex. *J. Physiol.* **160**, 1962, pp. 106–154.)

geniculate body. Presumably, orientation coding by columns of cells in visual cortex plays a role in the neuronal reconstruction of visual space. As Hubel and Wiesel put it (1965), "far from being a mere aggregation of cells with common characteristics, the column emerges as a dynamic unit of function."

The reader probably has noted the many similarities between responses of the frog optic nerve fibers and responses of the cortical visual cells of the cat. In both cases, the cells respond to objects, shadows, and movements in the visual field, but these responses cannot be predicted from the responses to diffuse light flash. Indeed, the characteristics of stimuli effective in activating cells are those often said to be mediated by "higher" processes such as perception. Perhaps the most fundamental importance of these experiments is that they remove much of the mystery from *perception*. Abstract aspects of stimulus quality are coded by single nerve cells and do not require mysterious gestalt fields, a "scanning sensor," or a "man-within-a-man" to do the perceiving. The transformations of stimulus characteristics from retina to cortex result from neural interconnections, and often are predictable from the elementary response properties of the receptive fields (as in the "simple" cells of Hubel and Wiesel). Perception

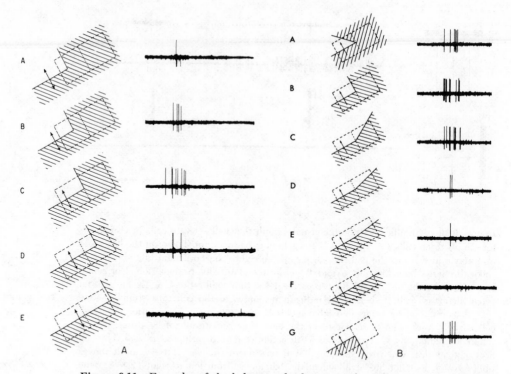

Figure 6.11 Examples of the behavior of a hypercomplex cell in area 19 of the cat. The stimuli are shown on the left and the cell discharges on the right. This cell appears to function in general terms as a "right angle detector." In A, responses of the cell are shown to a right angle stimulus moved across different regions of the field (A–E). In B, various stimulus angles are moved across the field (A–G). Angles closest to right angles produce the greatest response. (From Hubel, D. H., and Wiesel, T. N. Receptive fields and functional architecture in two nonstriate visual areas (18 and 19) of the cat. *J. Neurophysiol.* **28**, 1965, pp. 229–289.)

of simple visual forms may be a direct result of the structure of the cells; it is built in.

Color vision. In addition to the spatial and temporal aspects of visual stimuli considered so far, response to differences in the wavelength of light, or color, is a very fundamental aspect of vision. Indeed it is one of those immediately given experiences or sensations that is impossible to express verbally. You cannot describe *red* to a congenitally (from birth) blind person. Very young children can match different colors to samples correctly long before they can learn the names of the colors. Interestingly, the same appears to be true for congenitally blind cataract patients whose sight has been restored in adulthood (Hebb, 1949). Such patients immediately sort objects into categories correctly on the basis of color but may require several weeks of training to learn to use the correct *name* for each color.

An understanding of color vision is often complicated by discussions of the extensive literature on the various physical aspects of color stimuli such as the effects of mixing different paint pigments. The fact that any color can be matched by suitable proportions of three basic colors such as red, green, and blue has no necessary relationship to the way in which the nervous system codes the wavelength of light. Historically, there are two major theories of color vision, both based on hypotheses concerning the types of color receptors (cones) in the retina. In 1802, Thomas Young suggested that there were three different color receptors, one for red, one for green, and one for blue, in the retina. Each receptor is not assumed to be sensitive only to one color, merely most sensitive in that particular region of the frequency range of visible light. This theory accounts very nicely for color mixing and a great many other phemomena of color vision. An alternate theory proposed in the 19th century by Hering assumed that receptors worked in an opponent fashion such that one receptor complex coded red and green, another blue and yellow, and a third black and white. More recently, this theory has been forwarded in terms of relations between photochemical receptors and neurons (see Hurvich and Jameson, 1957). Thus a blue cone and a yellow cone could mutually influence a pair of neurons such that blue causes inhibition and yellow excitation of the output of the neuron pair. Hurvich and Jameson suggested an alternative model that reconciles Young's three receptor theory with Hering's opponent theory. The three color receptors (red, green, and blue) are assumed to be interconnected with neurons so that the output of the neurons act in an opponent manner—one excited by blue and inhibited by red, another in just the opposite way, and so on. Recent evidence suggests that this compromise view may be closest to the true situation.

We noted earlier that there were three different types of iodopsin in the cones of the human retina. Ingenious experiments by Stiles (1961), Rushton (1961), and Wald (1961) provide some very strong indirect evidence concerning the *absorption spectra* (wavelengths of light that are absorbed) of the three types of iodopsin found in human cones. In brief, the method is as follows. A very narrow beam of light is shone in the eye. The light passes through the foveal portion of the retina (only cones), is reflected from the back of the eye, passes again through the retina, and out of the eye. The amount of light reflected out of the eye can be measured and the amount absorbed calculated from measurements and careful consideration of other factors. The amount of light absorbed depends upon the degree of bleaching of the cone pigments in the retina. Hence the degree of cone-bleaching resulting from pre-exposure to various wavelengths of light can be measured. Although the techniques are exceedingly difficult, and many possible sources of error exist, results seem fairly consistent. There appear to be three types of cone pigments, with absorption maximal at about 440 (blue), 540 (green), and 590 (red) $m\mu$. These findings constitute a very real triumph for Young's three-receptor theory of color vision.

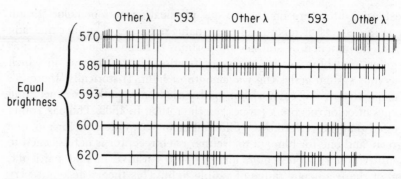

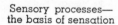

Figure 6.12 Example of responses of an *opponent* cell from the lateral geniculate body of the monkey. The cell is of the type that normally increases firing rate to green and decreases firing rate to red. In this experiment responses of the cell to shifts from various other wavelengths (other λ) to a standard (593) and back were studied. Note that when the cell is firing (to green—570) it decreases firing to 593, but when its firing rate is low (to red—620) its firing rate increases to 593. (DeValois, R. L. Analysis and coding of color vision in the primate visual system. From *Sensory Receptors*. Cold Spring Harbor, NY: Cold Spring Harbor Laboratory of Quant. Biology, 1965, pp. 567–580.)

Microelectrode studies of the responses of single neurons in the visual system to different wavelengths of light have markedly increased our understanding of the neural bases of color vision. DeValois and his colleagues (DeValois and Jacobs, 1968) demonstrated in behavioral studies that color vision of the Old World monkey rhesus macaque is identical to human color vision. They completed a very extensive series of experiments on the manner in which nerve cells in the lateral geniculate body of the macaque code color. In brief, there are two general categories of cells. One category is influenced by all visible wavelengths of light and the wavelength threshold curve agrees closely with the scotopic (rod) threshold curve for rhodopsin. DeValois terms these *nonopponent* cells. Actually there are two types of nonopponent cells, one type that is inhibited and one type that is excited by all visible wavelengths (see Fig. 6.12). The other category of cells responds to much narrower bands of wavelengths and behaves in an *opponent* manner such that a given cell is excited by blue and inhibited by yellow, another is excited by yellow and inhibited by blue, a third is excited by green and inhibited by red, and the fourth is excited by red and inhibited by green. These are the only four types of opponent cells found by DeValois. Responses of the different types of cells to various wavelengths of light are indicated in Figure 6.12.

No doubt you have noted the remarkable correspondence between DeValois' findings for cells in the visual relay nucleus of the thalamus and Hurvich and Jameson's reformulation of Hering's opponent theory of color vision. It is likely that the coding of color into opponent categories occurs in the retina.

In summary, it appears that the theories of both Young and Hering are partially correct. The studies on human retinal pigments indicate that there are three types of photosensitive chemicals in the cones—red, green, and blue (Young's theory). However, neural (and possible glial) interactions recode the activity from receptors such that neurons in the higher visual centers respond in an opponent manner (Hering's theory). The two opponent categories are red-green and blue-yellow, some cells being excited by one color and inhibited by the other, and vice versa. In addition, of course, the nonopponent cells are either excited or inhibited by all visible wavelengths of light.

THE AUDITORY SYSTEM

In contrast to the million or so fibers in the optic nerve of man, each auditory nerve has only about 28,000 fibers. Nevertheless, the total number of single tones discriminated on the basis of frequency and intensity is about 340,000. Curiously enough this is approximately the same as the total number of single visual stimuli discernible on the basis of frequency (wavelength) and intensity of light (Stevens and Davis, 1938). The nature of the mechanisms underlying this efficiency in the auditory system has puzzled investigators for many years. Historically, two major theories of auditory pitch discrimination have been put forth. (1) The *place* theory (Helmholtz) assumes that each tone frequency activates a different portion of the auditory receptors. (2) The *frequency* theory proposes that the frequency of the tone is reflected in the frequency of auditory nerve fiber discharges (Rutherford). Recent developments in the field (Davis, 1961, 1965) show that the more correct view lies somewhere between these extremes.

The distinction between the terms *pitch* and *frequency* often is a source of confusion. Frequency refers to a physical characteristic of the *stimulus*: the actual frequency of vibration of the sound waves in the air, commonly expressed in cycles per second (Hz)—(Hz is short for Hertz, a pioneering scientist in acoustics—the older term was *cps* for cycles per second. 1 cps = 1 Hz). Pitch refers to the "subjective sensation" or behavioral response correlated with the frequency of a sound. The relationship between pitch and frequency, depicted in Figure 6.13, tends to be logarithmic rather than linear or one-to-one. Note that while the pitch scale (in mels) on the right ordinate is linear, the frequency scale on the abscissa is logarithmic. Because the curve that relates the two functions is approximately linear throughout most of its extent, pitch and frequency are related logarithmically. To give an example—middle C is 256 Hz and the C one octave above middle C is 512 Hz, twice as high in frequency. However it *sounds* a good deal less than twice as high in pitch to us.

A similar dichotomy exists between the physical and "subjective" scales in the case of sound intensity. The relationship between the judged *loud-*

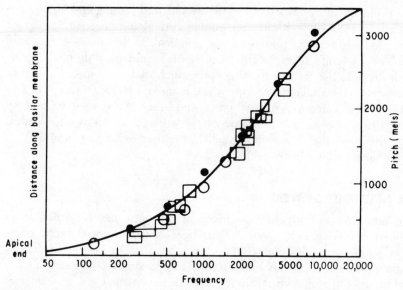

Figure 6.13 The logarithmic relation between pitch and frequency is shown. Pitch-function is compared with data locating the positions on the basilar membrane stimulated by tones of various frequencies. The linear extent of the basilar membrane is represented by the left ordinate and the pitch scale is along the right ordinate. The curve represents the pitch-function; the hollow rectangles and circles and the filled circles show the locations in the cochleas of guinea pigs of stimulation by various frequencies. (Stevens, S. S., and Volkmann, J. The relation of pitch to frequency. *Amer. J. Psychol.* **53**, 1940, pp. 329–353.)

ness (subjective measure) of a tone and the amount of physical *energy* in the tone is approximately logarithmic. This relationship was described a number of years ago by the development of the decibel (db) scale for measuring sound intensity. The decibel scale is based on the logarithm of the sound energy level (actually ten times the logarithm of the ratio of a given sound energy to the lowest threshold of sound energy). Consequently, the judged *loudness* of sounds corresponds in an approximately linear fashion with the decibel scale of sound intensity. The relationships between pitch and frequency and between loudness and intensity are examples of *psychophysical functions*: relations between psychological or behavioral judgments of stimuli and physical characteristics of stimuli.

Receptor processes

The anatomy of the auditory receptor system is somewhat complicated (see Fig. 6.14). In brief, the external ear canal ends in the *tympanic membrane* (ear drum). This connects through three small bones (*ossicles*) of the middle ear to a membrane covering the end of the *cochlea*. This structure is a coiled tube shaped much like a snail shell. The tube

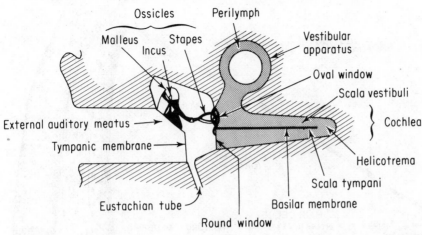

Ossicles

Perilymph

Malleus   Stapes
      Incus

Vestibular
apparatus

Oval window

Scala vestibuli
} Cochlea

External auditory meatus →

Tympanic membrane →

Helicotrema

Scala tympani

Eustachian tube

Basilar membrane

Round window

Figure 6.14 Schematic of the human ear. The coiled cochlea has been straightened to give a clear view of the basic anatomical relationships. (From von Békésy, G., and Rosenblith, W. A. The mechanical properties of the ear. From Stevens, S. S. (ed.). *Handbook of Experimental Psychology.* New York: Wiley, 1951, pp. 1075–1115.)

is filled with fluid and contains within it a smaller tube, the *cochlear duct,* which contains the sense organ proper. A cross section through the tube of the cochlea is shown in Figure 6.15. Sound vibrations transmitted through the ossicles cause movement of fluid, which in turn produces vibrations of the *basilar membrane.* This rather stiff membrane bends relative to the *tectorial membrane,* thus bending and activating the *hair-cell* receptors lying between. These receptors are innervated by fibers of the auditory nerve, whose cell bodies lie in the spiral ganglion embedded in the skull. Axons of these fibers enter the CNS and synapse in the *cochlear nuclei* in the medulla.

Identification of the particular receptor and neural processes that determine various aspects of sensory experience or behavior is one of the fundamental goals in the analysis of sensory processes. The absolute loudness threshold is a good case in point. In humans, the total range of audible frequencies is about 15 to 20,000 Hz. However the ear is most sensitive to tones between 1000 Hz and 4000 Hz. As frequency is increased or decreased beyond this range of maximum sensitivity, increasingly greater sound energy is required to make the tone audible. The curve relating absolute threshold and frequency is shown in Figure 6.16. Several lines of evidence (Davis, 1959) indicate that the physical characteristics of the external and middle ear structures, such as elasticity and inertia, determine the form of the frequency-threshold curve.

The acoustical and mechanical properties of the ear canal, ear drum, and the middle ear bones determine the efficiency with which sounds of various frequencies are converted to mechanical vibrations and trans-

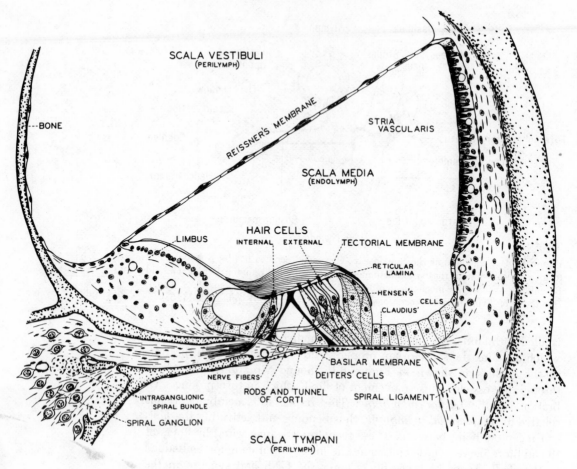

SCALA VESTIBULI
(PERILYMPH)

BONE

REISSNER'S MEMBRANE

STRIA VASCULARIS

SCALA MEDIA
(ENDOLYMPH)

LIMBUS

HAIR CELLS
INTERNAL   EXTERNAL

TECTORIAL MEMBRANE

RETICULAR LAMINA

HENSEN'S

CELLS

CLAUDIUS'

BASILAR MEMBRANE

NERVE FIBERS

DEITERS' CELLS

RODS AND TUNNEL
OF CORTI

SPIRAL LIGAMENT

INTRAGANGLIONIC
SPIRAL BUNDLE

SPIRAL GANGLION

SCALA TYMPANI
(PERILYMPH)

Figure 6.15 Cross section of the cochlear duct. The actual receptors are the hair cells lying in the spiral organ (of Corti) on the basilar membrane. (Davis, H. et al. Acoustic trauma in the guinea pig. *J. Acoust. Soc. Amer.* **25**, 1953, pp. 1180–1189.)

mitted to the cochlea. In humans, these structures have greatest efficiency in the 1000 to 4000 Hz range, and drop off in efficiency as the frequency becomes higher or lower. Because the absolute threshold curve is determined by the physical properties of these accessory auditory structures, it might be expected that the size of an animal's external and middle ear structures would influence its threshold curve. In general this seems to be true. Among mammals, elephants have the lowest frequency curve and small animals like the rat or mouse have very much higher frequency sensitivity curves. Man, incidentally, has a relatively "middle" frequency range. Cats can hear sounds ranging from about 30 Hz to 70,000 Hz. Some exceptional animals are bats and porpoises, both of which can hear sounds of up to about 100,000 Hz. However these animals make use of a

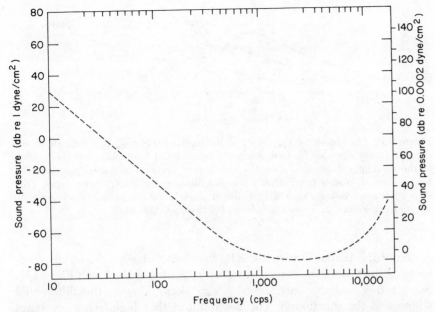

Figure 6.16 The absolute auditory threshold curve for humans. This is an average based on results from a variety of different types of measures. (Modified from Licklider, J. C. R. Basic correlates of the auditory stimulus. In Stevens, S. S. (ed.). *Handbook of Experimental Psychology.* New York: Wiley, 1951, pp. 985–1039.)

very specialized echo location system. They emit very high frequency pulses of sound and determine the position of objects in space by the characteristics of the reflected sound pulses.

The ear is about as sensitive as it can be to sound energy, at least in the frequency region of best threshold (around 2000 Hz in humans). The degree of sensitivity of the human ear is quite remarkable; a movement of the ear drum of less than one-tenth the diameter of a hydrogen atom can result in an auditory sensation! If the ear were more sensitive than this the random Brownian movements of air molecules would produce a constant roaring sound, which would tend to mask auditory stimuli. Thus, paradoxically, if the ear were more sensitive it would be less sensitive. As a matter of fact, persons with very good hearing are able to detect Brownian movement under ideal listening conditions (e.g., in a soundproofed anechoic chamber).

The movements of the basilar membrane in the cochlea related to auditory stimuli were analyzed in a series of elegant experiments by von Békésy (von Békésy and Rosenblith, 1951), who was awarded the Nobel prize in 1962 for his work. In essence, he showed that when a tone of given frequency is presented, a traveling wave of fluid is set up in the cochlea. The traveling wave causes a maximum displacement in a given

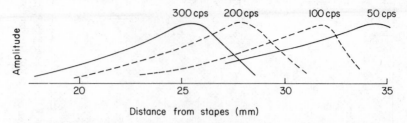

Figure 6.17 Amplitude of movement of the basilar membrane as a function of the distance from the stapes for four different frequencies of tone. Note that the location of the maximum displacement on the membrane is related to the frequency of the tone; higher frequency tones show a maximal displacement closer to the stapes. (Redrawn from von Békésy, G. The variation of phase along the basilar membrane with sinusoidal variations. *J. Acoust. Soc. Amer.* **19**, 1947, pp. 452–460.)

region of the basilar membrane. The location of this maximum displacement on the membrane is related to the frequency of the tone (Fig. 6.17). Some rather complex mechanical effects occur, due to the differential stiffness of the membrane. The net result is that high-frequency tones selectively distort regions of the basilar membrane close to the base of the cochlea, intermediate tones distort a portion of the membrane from the base to an intermediate region, and low frequency tones tend to distort the entire membrane. These response characteristics all can be predicted from analogous physical models of the cochlea (e.g., a fluid-filled tube containing a semielastic membrane). The cochlea acts simply as a complex mechanical analyzer of the auditory stimulus. The region of greatest distortion of the basilar membrane produces the greatest amount of bending of hair cells and consequently the greatest differential activation of the auditory nerve fibers.

At this point it might be well to recall the two major theories concerning pitch coding, namely *place* and *frequency*. The findings of von Békésy actually seem to offer some support for each. A given frequency of tone tends to produce greatest distortion at a given region of the basilar membrane. The original place theory proposed by Helmholtz assumed that the basilar membrane was a very large series of highly tuned elements much like tuning forks, or the strings on a harp. Von Békésy's data, particularly for high frequencies, support this view if modified to the extent that small differences in degree of distortion of the membrane can serve as "tuned elements." In general the higher the frequency, the closer the distortion is to the base of the cochlea. The large open circles of Figure 6.13 and the left ordinate refer to the relative location of the place of maximum distortion along the basilar membrane as a function of frequency (for both guinea pig and man). The relative locations correspond almost exactly to the relationship between pitch and frequency!

On the other hand, von Békésy observed that low frequency tones tend to activate the entire basilar membrane equivalently, and intermediate tones activate a substantial portion of the membrane. The differential distortion of the membrane does not seem great enough to provide for our very sensitive ability to discriminate pitch, and there is no differential distortion to code low frequency tones. Human psychophysical studies provide some interesting corollary data on this point. If a steady "white noise" (all frequencies equally represented in the stimulus) is presented it has a "sssssh" sound somewhat resembling an air jet. No particular frequency or pitch is associated with the sound. Since all frequencies are present in the stimulus, the basilar membrane exhibits no differential distortion. If the noise is now presented as a series of brief pulses of white noise, the sound takes on a pitch related to the frequency with which the pulses are delivered (Miller and Taylor, 1948). This relationship holds only for low frequencies. Thus, for low frequencies a pitch can be heard even though there is no differential distortion of the basilar membrane. It would appear that at least for low frequencies some type of frequency coding occurs in the cochlea and auditory nerve other than the analysis into place of distortion along the basilar membrane.

If a gross recording electrode is placed on the cochlea near the auditory nerve, several types of signals can be recorded. The most noticeable of these is the *cochlear microphonic,* discovered by Wever and Bray (1930). This is an electrical response that follows the frequency and intensity characteristics of the auditory stimulus *exactly.* If a Beethoven symphony is played into the ear of an anesthetized cat and the electrically recorded cochlear microphonic is amplified and connected to a speaker you will hear the symphony with essentially no distortion. The cochlear microphonic is, literally, a microphone; sound waves are converted to electrical pulses in exactly the same manner as in a microphone.

The discovery of the cochlear microphonic seemed to provide very strong evidence favoring the frequency theory of pitch coding. It was initially believed that the electrical pulses of the cochlear microphonic were spike discharges of the auditory nerve. This would mean that the frequency of discharges in the auditory nerve exactly follow the input frequency of any sound. However, it soon became apparent that the cochlear microphonic did not represent nerve activity. In the cat, for example, it can follow sound frequencies up to 70,000 Hz, which is a great deal faster than any nerve fiber can respond (2000 Hz is about the highest frequency recordable from a nerve fiber). Further, it can be recorded after death, is not affected by anesthetics, and does not fatigue. It appears that the cochlear microphonic is produced by the hair cells in the cochlea and may represent a receptor or generator potential. The hair cells are bent with a frequency that follows the input sound frequency. The cochlear microphonic seems to result from a transducer action of the hair cells quite analogous to the conversion of mechanical vibrations into electrical pulses by the crystal in a phonograph cartridge. It has been suggested that the same kind of *piezo-electric* effect may be involved in both (Stevens and Davis, 1938). Although the cochlear microphonic has been considered by many as merely an accidental electromechanical by-product resulting from bending of the hair cells, Davis, Tasaki, and many other authorities favor the view that the terminals of the auditory nerve fibers are directly activated by the flows of current associated with the cochlear microphonic, i.e., it is a generator potential.

The fibers of the auditory nerve do follow the frequency of low frequency tones. Thus if a tone of 500 Hz is given, some fibers in the auditory nerve will discharge 500 times per second. This following breaks down above about 1000 Hz. A most interesting *volley* mechanism seems to take over at this point. When a high-frequency tone, for example, 2000 Hz, is given, one group of fibers may fire 1000 times per second and another group may also fire at 1000 times per second directly out of step with the first group. A central brain nucleus receiving this input from the auditory nerve would "see" 2000 discharges per second, even though no single fiber responds faster than 1000 times per second.

It appears that both *place* of excitation on the basilar membrane and *frequency* of nerve response are important in coding tone frequency. For high frequencies, place is most important but for lower frequencies (below 4000 cps) synchronous discharges in nerve fibers also play a role. Intensity may be coded both by total numbers of fibers activated and by activation of high threshold fibers (i.e., nerve fibers that require considerable bending of the hair cells to be stimulated). The nerve fibers are stimulated by the bending of the hair cells, possibly as a direct result of generator potentials, such as the cochlear microphonic produced by the hair cells.

Coding of auditory stimuli

The details of the auditory pathways are complex and beyond the scope of this text (see Thompson, 1967; Uttal, 1973). Activity from the auditory nerve relays in the cochlear nucleus and in turn at several other nuclei as it ascends the brain to reach the auditory area of the cerebral cortex. The most fundamental principle of organization in the auditory system is that tone frequency has a clear spatial representation at all levels from the basilar membrane to the cerebral cortex. As in other sensory modalities the receptor elements are represented in a spatial manner at each relay in the auditory system. In fact there appear to be several such representations of the cochlea at some levels. The most important aspect of stimulus coding in the auditory system is that single neurons code the frequency or pitch of sounds. Most nerve cells in the auditory system from the auditory nerve to the cerebral cortex have a limited range of "best frequencies." When the activity of a single cell has been isolated by a microelectrode, the tuning curve is obtained by presenting a wide range of tones of various frequencies and intensities. Typically, the threshold intensity that

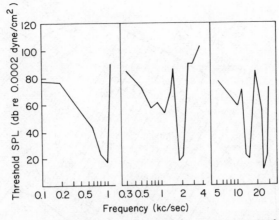

Figure 6.18 Tuning curves for three cells in primary auditory cortex of cat. Each curve shows the minimum energy (sound pressure level, SPL) that will activate the cell plotted as a function of frequency. The cell on the left has only one best frequency, but the cell on the right has two best frequencies separated by about one octave. (Redrawn from Hind, J. E. et al. Unit activity in the auditory cortex. In Rasmussen, G. L., and Windle, W. L. (eds.). *Neural Mechanisms of the Auditory and Vestibular Systems.* Springfield, Ill.: Charles C. Thomas, 1961, pp. 201–210. Courtesy of Charles C. Thomas, Publisher.)

causes the cell to fire is determined at each of a number of different frequencies. The tuning curve is thus a frequency-threshold curve, plotted in an analogous fashion to the human frequency-threshold curve of Figure 6.16. The best-frequency range is the range of tone frequencies at which the cell is fired by the lowest intensity stimuli. Examples of the best-frequency tuning curves for single nerve cells in the auditory cortex are shown in Figure 6.18.

One difficulty noted above for a place theory of pitch was that the distortion pattern of the basilar membrane was much too broad to account for differential frequency sensitivity. However, the data of Figure 6.18 suggest that neural processes serve to sharpen the discriminatory ability of cells in the auditory system. The effect probably results from inhibitory synaptic interactions among cells at all levels of the system.

The auditory cortex. The general location of the auditory cortex on the temporal lobe (and buried in the sylvian fissure in man) has been known for many years. However, electrophysiological analysis of cortical auditory areas is relatively recent. The organization of auditory projection fields seems to be rather complex; at least six different regions have been described for the cat (see Woolsey, 1961; Thompson, 1967). We will consider here the detailed organization of the major auditory field, the primary auditory cortex (AI).

Studies of tone frequency representation in the auditory cortex (Figure 6.19) indicate that high frequencies project to the anterior portion of AI

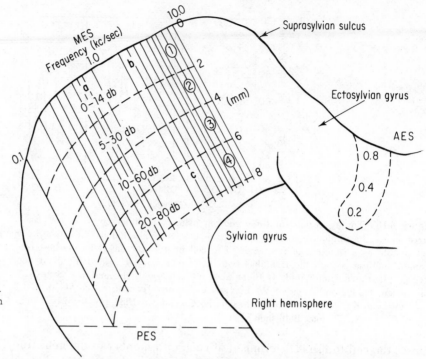

Figure 6.19 The spatial representation of tone frequency along the auditory cortex of the dog (brain facing right). MES, middle ectosylvian area; PES, posterior ectosylvian area; AES, anterior ectosylvian area. Solid lines on MES are best-frequency lines: a given frequency evoked maximum responses on a single line. Frequency expressed in kilocycles per second. For example, the line labeled 1.0 is the region of the cortex showing maximum evoked responses to a 1000 cps tone. The layout of frequency appears to be a logarithmic function of distance above the cortex. Intensity of tones appears to be represented at right angles to frequency, at least for the contralateral ear. (From Tunturi, A. R. A difference in the representation of auditory signals for the left and right ears in the iso-frequency contours of the right middle ectosylvian cortex of the dog. *Amer. J. Physiol.* **168**, 1952, pp. 712–727.)

and low frequencies to the posterior portion. Indeed, the representation of tone frequency is "laid out" along the auditory cortex. The parallel lines running from top to bottom in Figure 6.19 are "equal frequency" lines. To take a specific example, suppose we record evoked responses from the small region on the line labeled 1.0 Kcps (KHz in current terms—K stands for 1000 so 1 Kcps=1000 cycles=1 KHz) to weak tones of various frequencies. Large potentials will be obtained from this region only for tones close to 1000 Hz (1 KHz=1 Kcps=1000 cps=1000 Hz) (actually from about 950 Hz to 1050 Hz). If we record from another region, say in the (between 1.0 Kcps and 10.0 Kcps) (5000 Hz) line, only tones of around 5000 cps yield large potentials, and so on. The auditory cortex appears to be very

Sensory processes—
the basis of sensation

selectively tuned to frequency. It is as though the basilar membrane has been unrolled and laid down along the auditory cortex.

As indicated in Figure 6.18, single neurons in auditory cortex typically have best frequencies, at which the threshold intensity of the tone necessary to fire the cell is much lower than for the other frequencies. Several rather interesting phenomena have been described for single units in auditory cortex (Hind et al., 1961). For example, in many cells, if the best frequency used to stimulate the cell becomes increasingly loud, the cell ceases firing. Thus there is not a simple increasing relationship between tone intensity and discharges of the cell. Another finding of interest is that some cells have more than one best frequency. These are often octave multiple, that is, if one best frequency were 1000 Hz the other would be 2000, if one were 5000 the other would be 10,000, and so on. This suggests a possible basis for the common observation that tones separated by octaves sound "more alike" than tones closer together or farther apart in frequency.

In general terms, the auditory region of the cerebral cortex seems to be involved in analysis of the more complex aspects of auditory stimuli. Whitfield and Evans (1965), for example, found single neurons in the cortex that will not respond to any single tone but only to a tone that changes frequency, such as a "warble." Neff (1961) has emphasized that auditory cortex seems particularly concerned with the temporal aspect of sounds, the patterning of sound in time, as in human speech.

THE SOMATIC-SENSORY SYSTEM

Receptor processes

A wide variety of different forms of sensory receptors have been found in the skin. You might expect that after 100 years of study there would be some agreement on the functional properties of these variously formed structures, but such is not the case. The classical view was that the four basic modalities of cutaneous sensation were subserved by four specific types of receptors: pain by free nerve endings, cold by Krause endbulbs, warmth by Ruffini corpuscles, and touch by Pacinian and Meissner's corpuscles. However, more recent work by Weddell and co-workers has shown that all these sensations can result from appropriate stimulation of the cornea, which apparently has only free nerve endings (Lele and Weddell, 1956). Nevertheless, there is solid evidence showing that many skin receptors are "tuned" to respond to only one modality. Direct measurements on *Pacinian corpuscles* (pressure receptors) show them to be exquisitely sensitive to mechanical displacement. Pacinian corpuscles, very sensitive to pressure, are insensitive to thermal stimuli. Other skin receptors are sensitive primarily to heat or cold, still others respond to both thermal and mechanical stimuli, and finally, some respond to all types of stimuli. Touch stimuli tend to activate the largest diameter cutaneous afferent fibers, as well as smaller fibers. The small diameter C fiber group tends to respond to all varieties of stimulation.

In somewhat simplified terms, there are two categories of skin receptors and two different types of pathways or systems in the CNS that mediate quite different aspects of skin and deep tissue sensations. Henry Head proposed the two systems, which he termed *epicritic* (specific sensations of touch and pressure) and *protopathic* (diffuse and vague touch sensation, pain, and temperature). Specific epicritic receptors exist for pressure, Meissner's corpuscles in the outer layers of skin, hair root pressure receptors, Pacinian corpuscles in deeper tissue, and pressure receptors in joints that code position of the limbs. In the CNS this system is called the *lemniscal system*. The protopathic receptors are primarily free nerve endings mediating pain, temperature, and diffuse touch. In the CNS this is technically termed the *spinothalamic system*.

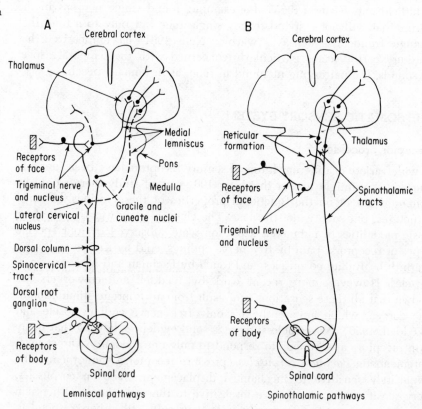

Figure 6.20 Schematics of the lemniscal or specific (A) and spinothalamic or diffuse (B) pathways of the somatic-sensory system. (From Thompson, R. F. *Foundations of Physiological Psychology.* New York: Harper & Row, 1967.)

Central pathways of the somatic-sensory system

As noted above, there are two distinct pathways in the spinal cord and brain stem carrying cutaneous information to the cerebral cortex. The lemniscal system is best understood. As indicated in the diagram of Figure 6.20, afferent fibers from tactile and kinesthetic receptors enter the spinal cord, turn upward in the dorsal columns and ascend to make their first synapse on cells in nuclei in the lower medulla. This is the first central synapse of the specific system. Fibers from these nuclei then *cross* and ascend in a tract, called the *lemniscal tract,* to synapse in the thalamic relay nucleus, the *ventrobasal complex.* Fibers from these thalamic nuclei project to the somatic-sensory areas of the cerebral cortex.

Afferent fibers of the *spinothalamic system,* carrying pain and temperature information, and some tactile information as well, synapse on large cells in the dorsal horn of the spinal cord. Many of the secondary fibers cross and ascend the spinal cord, probably in several different pathways, relay through interneurons in the brain stem *reticular formation,* and reach the thalamus (Fig. 6.20). Many of the fibers appear to end in the *ventrobasal complex* of the thalamus, thus relaying to somatic-sensory areas of the cortex. It appears that there may be an ipsilateral component of the spinothalamic tract as well. Indirect evidence suggests that many fibers of the spinothalamic tract end in a somewhat different region of the thalamus. This is an area lying between the ventrobasal complex and the medial geniculate body (the auditory relay in the thalamus), which has been termed the *posterior nuclear group* (Rose and Woolsey, 1958). This thalamic region is known to have connections to somatic-sensory area II of the cortex (see below).

Coding of somatic-sensory stimuli

Functional properties of the lemniscal system. The somatic-sensory system appears to make use of both spatial representation and spike discharge frequency in solving the problem of coding sensory information. We will examine the specific system first; more is known about its anatomical relations and physical characteristics than for the protopathic spinothalamic system. There is a clear spatial segregation of different regions of the body surface at all levels of the lemniscal system from skin to cerebral cortex; indeed, there is a complete regional layout of the skin surface on the cerebral cortex.

Microelectrode studies, particularly those of Mountcastle and his colleagues (Poggio and Mountcastle, 1963; Mountcastle, Poggio, and Werner, 1963), demonstrate that a subtle refinement of the principle of spatial representation can serve to code the various submodalities of somatic sensation in the thalamus. Within a given block of tissue in the ventrobasal complex representing a particular region in the body surface, small blocks or cubes of cells are responsive to different submodalities. There are three basic submodalities, light touch to the skin, deep pres-

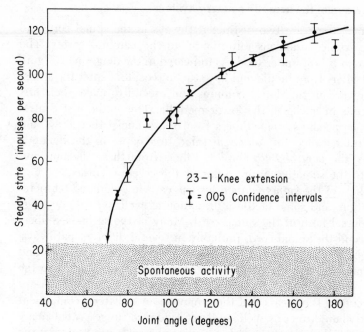

Figure 6.21 Graph showing activity of a ventrobasal neuron driven by extension of the contralateral knee of a monkey. Nerve impulses per second (dots) in the steady state are plotted against angle for a ventrobasal neuron (lines and bars include 99.5 per cent of the data around each point). The rate of spontaneous activity is the means of many different records of it, obtained over a 3-hour period of study. The intercept of the curve with the spontaneous activity level is defined as the threshold, or the edge of the excitatory angle, for the cell. (From Mountcastle, V. B., Poggio, G. F., and Werner, G. The relation of thalamic cell response to peripheral stimuli varied over an intensive continuum. *J. Neurophysiol.* **26,** 1963, pp. 807–834.)

sure to the fascia below the skin, and joint movement. Within the block of thalamic tissue representing a finger of one hand, some small blocks of tissue contain cells activated only by light touch, other blocks have cells responsive to only deep pressure, and still other blocks have cells responding only to joint movement.

Cells of the ventrobasal complex in the thalamus are very specific. Any given cell is responsive to only one of the three modes of stimulation, regardless of the condition of the animal. In the monkey, roughly 42 per cent of the ventrobasal cells respond to skin stimulation, 32 per cent to deep pressure, and 26 per cent to movements of the joints. Thus the type of submodality of the somatic-sensory stimulus is specifically and rigidly coded in the thalamus in terms of spatial representation. The region or extent of skin area stimulated that activates a given cell in the ventrobasal complex is relatively small. In the monkey, the average area of skin ranges from 0.2 cm² on the fingers and toes to 20 cm² on the back. The areal extent of the receptor region (i.e., skin) that activates a given neuron is called the *receptive field* of that cell.

Mountcastle, Poggio, and Werner (1963) demonstrated that cells of the ventrobasal complex responsive to joint movement *code* the degree of movement precisely in terms of spike discharge frequency. Figure 6.21 is a graph that shows the activity of a ventrobasal neuron driven by extension of the contralateral knee of a monkey. The graph relates the steady-state frequency of spike discharges (impulses per second) of the cell to the number of degrees of angular movement of the knee joint. Each dot is an average of many determinations. All the dots appear to fall rather close to the smooth curve drawn through them. Note that the spontaneous discharge rate in the absence of stimulation is about 24 impulses per sec. Threshold for this cell is a joint position of about 70 degrees; when the angle is increased beyond this, the discharge frequency of the cell increases above the spontaneous activity level.

Functional properties of the spinothalamic system. As described above, afferent fibers conveying pain, temperature, and diffuse touch synapse either directly or via interneurons on the cells of the dorsal horn of the spinal cord. These cells give rise to contralateral (and probably ipsilateral) ascending pathways, which synapse in many regions of the brain stem and midbrain, particularly in the reticular formation. At least a portion of the system eventually terminates in the thalamus, partly in the ventrobasal complex and partly in the posterior nuclear group.

Poggio and Mountcastle (1960) undertook an extensive investigation of the response properties of the cells in the posterior nuclear group of the thalamus in the cat. Cells in this region can be activated by ipsilateral (same side) skin stimulation, in contrast to the purely contralateral projection of the leminiscal system. From this fact, it can be inferred that the posterior group serves as a relay for at least a portion of the spinothalamic system. Cells in the posterior thalamic group could hardly differ more from those of the ventrobasal complex. First, there appears to be no somatotopic representation of the body surface in the posterior region. Second, there is no spatial representation of submodalities. Third, the receptive fields are extremely large, sometimes including virtually the entire body surface. Finally, some cells respond to both mechanical and painful stimuli. Some cells respond only to painful stimulation and not to mechanical stimulation; however, they are scattered throughout the posterior nuclear region rather than being organized into only one portion. It would appear that this region of the thalamus may play a basic role in the elaboration of painful sensation, but the nature of this role is obscure.

Somatic-sensory-motor cortex. At about the turn of the century, Sir Charles Sherrington proposed a separation between motor and sensory cortex. With the central fissure taken as the dividing line, cortex just anterior to it (Brodmann's areas 4 and 6) was believed to be primarily concerned with the control of movement and was termed the *motor cortex* (see Fig. 6.22; and Fig. 3.7 in Chapter 3). The sensory cortex just posterior to the central fissure (Brodmann's areas 1, 2, and 3), which receives the primary projections of the system conveying information from the skin receptors (leminiscal system), was termed the *sensory* or *somatic-sensory* cortex. Research in more recent years has emphasized the fact that the distinction between somatic-sensory and motor areas is very much a relative matter. Each area seems to share most functions of the other.

The degree of overlap of functional organization of the sensory and motor areas led Woolsey (1958) to propose a most appropriate terminology, which is used here. He labels the entire region *somatic* cortex. The portion posterior to the central fissure, the traditional somatic-sensory area, is called the *sensory-motor* area, and that portion anterior to the central fissure, the classical motor region, is called the *motor-sensory* area. We have separated our discussion of the two regions, and emphasize the primary sensory-motor area (SI) here. The extent of SI corresponds to the postcentral gyrus (Brodmann's areas 1, 2, and 3) in primates. Cortex in this region contains representation of the skin, muscle, and joint receptors. The system is extremely sensitive; rapid bending of a single hair produces a measurable activity in the cortex.

The representation of the body surface on the cerebral cortex in area SI is given in Figure 6.22 for rat, cat, and monkey (Woolsey, 1958, 1964).

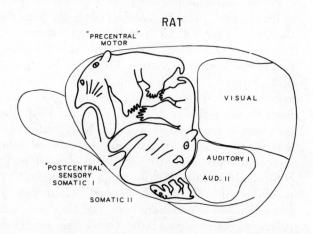

RAT

Figure 6.22 Somatic-sensory and motor area "anamunculi" for rat, cat, and monkey. SI, somatic-sensory area I; SII, somatic-sensory area II: *M*I, primary motor area; *M*II, supplementary motor area. In all three animals, the orientation of the anamunculi is similar, but the monkey anamunculus is distorted by the large hand and foot areas. (From Woolsey, C. N. Organization of somatic sensory and motor areas of the cerebral cortex. In Harlow, H. F. and Woolsey, C. N. (eds.) *Biological and Biochemical Bases of Behavior.* Madison: Univ. of Wisconsin Press, 1958, pp. 63–81.)

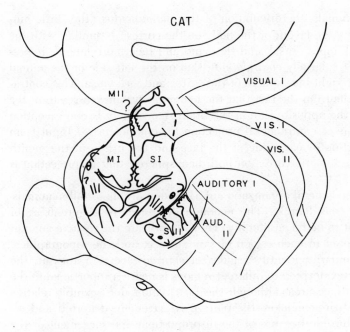

CAT

MII
?
MI
SI
III
SII
VISUAL I
VIS. I
VIS. II
AUDITORY I
AUD. II

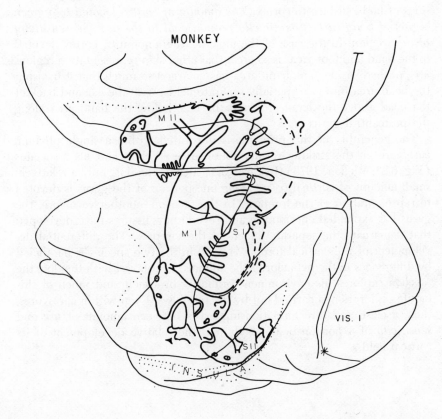

MONKEY

M II
?
MI
SI
?
SII
VIS. I
I N S U L A

In all three animals, the orientation of the *anamunculus* (the "little animal" formed by the layout of the body on the cortex) is similar, with the foot and trunk more dorsal, and the hand and face more lateral. Representation in SI is largely *contralateral*; skin on the left side of the animal projects to the right hemisphere of the cortex and vice versa. This contralaterality results from the fact that the lemniscal system crosses from the input side to the opposite side in the brain stem. There is one exception to the principle of contralateral projection to somatic cortex. Input from the lower portion of each side of the face and the inside of the mouth projects to the somatic cortex on both hemispheres, that is, projection is bilateral.

Although the general organization of SI is comparable for all mammals, details differ considerably. The anamunculi shown in Figure 6.22, of course, are not to be taken literally. They do indicate the relative amount of cortex devoted to each region of skin surface, and the topographical relations. Boundaries identify regions of skin surface. For the rat, the amount of cortex devoted to different regions is nearly proportional to the actual skin surface area, although the face region does exhibit relative enlargement. In the monkey the pattern is extremely distorted and almost unrecognizable because of the disproportionate enlargement of the cortical hand and foot areas.

A very fundamental generalization may be made concerning projections of body surface to cortex: *The amount of cortex devoted to a given region of body surface is directly proportional to the use and sensitivity of that region.* In the case of the monkey, the amount of cortex devoted to the hand and foot areas is so great that other skin representation regions are "pushed" aside. The hand area has enlarged so much that it has split the head area into two spatially separate fields, with the ear and back of the head above the hand area and the face below the hand area along the postcentral gyrus.

The generality of this principle is illustrated within a single phylum, carnivore, in the striking results obtained by Welker and his associates (Fig. 6.23; Welker, 1973). In carnivores such as the dog, only a relatively small amount of cortical tissue along one portion of the gyrus is devoted to representation of the forepaw. In the raccoon, another carnivore, the gyrus has expanded enormously and several new fissures have developed that demarcate the separate fingers of the forepaw. The differential development of the cortical forepaw region in the two species is paralleled by differences in the behavior of the animals. In contrast with the dog, the raccoon explores his environment primarily by touch, and much of this tactile exploration is carried out by the forepaws. Even within carnivores, then, a close and direct relationship exists between amount of *use* and *sensitivity* of a portion of the body and the relative development of its cortical field.

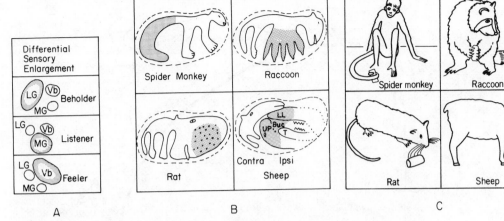

Figure 6.23 Illustrations of the close correspondence in specialization of somatic-sensory *behavior* and brain structures, particularly the ventrobasal nucleus (Vb) of the thalamus. A, The sizes of different thalamic nuclei relative to behavior. In a beholder (i.e., visual animal like primate and man) the lateral geniculate body (LG—visual relay nucleus in thalamus) is large. In a feeler (e.g., raccoon) the ventrobasal nucleus (Vb) is large. B and C show the relative enlargement of areas in the ventrobasal nucleus (B) in relation to behavioral specializations (C) in four animals. Spider monkey is a tail feeler, raccoon is a forepaw feeler, rat is a whisker feeler, and sheep is a lips and tongue feeler. (From Welker, W. I. Principles of organization of the ventrobasal complex in mammals. *Brain, Behav. Evol.* 7, 1973, Basel: S. Karger, pp. 253–336.)

These same relations for man were determined by Penfield and Rasmussen (1950). In the course of necessary neurosurgical procedures, Penfield electrically stimulated different regions of the human cortex and determined response characteristics from verbal report of the patient (use of local anesthetics allows such a procedure with a minimum of discomfort for the human patient). The sensations reported by most patients, incidentally, were a numbness, tingling, or feeling of "electricity" localized to the appropriate skin regions. All body sensations were localized to the contralateral body surface. The representation of body surface on the cortex of SI along the postcentral gyrus is shown in schematic cross section in Figure 6.24. Here the exaggerated size of the fingers is even more pronounced and the face is also much enlarged. It would appear that so far as the cortex is concerned, man is mostly fingers, lips, and tongue. This of course corresponds closely to human behavior. A comparison of Figures 6.22 and 6.24 shows that the relative development for cortical projection of skin can be traced from that of the rat, in which there is little distortion of the anamunculus, to that of man, in which differential enlargement of important skin regions has produced considerable distortion of the cortical homunculus ("little man").

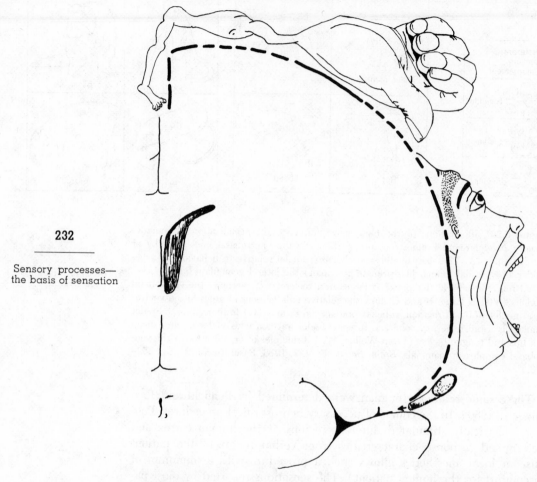

Figure 6.24 Homunculus for human SI (postcentral gyrus) shown on a cross section through the hemisphere. So far as the cortex is concerned, man is mainly fingers, lips, and tongue. (From Penfield, W., and Rasmussen, T. *The Cerebral Cortex of Man.* New York: Macmillan, 1950.)

Penfield and Jasper (1954) report that 25 per cent of the points that elicit somatic sensations lie in front of the central sulcus. The nature of the sensation appears to be the same regardless of whether the stimulus is applied in front or behind the sulcus. Apparently, however, there is a desire to move the extremity when precentral stimulation is delivered, but not following postcentral stimulation. The somatotopic organization of the sensory projection to the motor-sensory cortex appears to be more or less a mirror image of that projecting to the somatic-sensory area lying behind the sulcus. It corresponds, as we will see later, to the homunculus found on the motor cortex for representation of muscles and movement.

Microelectrode studies of single neurons have provided critical information concerning the detailed organization and stimulus coding mechanisms of the somatic cortex. Mountcastle and his colleagues (Mountcastle, 1957) have analyzed the cortical representation of the various modalities of somatic-sensory stimulation. Within a particular region of body representation, say a finger area, a given cell usually can be activated by only one type of stimulus. Thus one cell might respond to light touch, another to pressure, and another to joint movement. Further, cells responding to a given type of stimulus tend to lie in a column from surface to depth of cortex. Columns representing the different modalities lie close together within the cortical region representing each small area of body surface. This spatially distinct representation of the various somatic-sensory modalities is termed *columnar organization*. Columnar representation of modalities is a further elaboration of the principle of receptotopic organization of the cerebral cortex. It is a striking example of the extent to which spatial localization of input can provide a basis for stimulus coding. Different modalities of stimulation activate separate and discrete columns of cells within the cortex, which in turn can serve as the basis for the somatic sensations of touch, pressure, and joint position.

STIMULUS CODING AND HUMAN JUDGMENT

In our survey of the visual, auditory, and somatosensory systems we described the major kinds of coding of stimulus properties by neurons. To take one simple example, joint angle (e.g., of the elbow) is coded by frequency of firing of the appropriate neurons in the thalamus and cortex. Actually, this is an example of stimulus intensity or "how much" (see Table 6.1). As the arm bends at the elbow it exerts progressively more pressure on the joint receptor, which is a pressure receptor. We called this *coding of joint angle*. In more technically correct terms, it is described as a *candidate code*—a reasonable candidate for the neural coding of joint angle. To prove that this candidate code is the necessary and sufficient neuronal code of joint angle is a much more complicated issue. The interested reader is urged to consult Uttal's text (1973) for an extended discussion.

Let us review briefly the candidate codes for the three major sensory systems. Remember that these are candidate codes, the best guess at present about neuronal coding of stimulus characteristics. A word of apology, incidentally, is due to those with particular interests in the chemical senses, taste and olfaction. Both the receptor transduction processes and neuronal codes are poorly understood and adequate discussion would take us too far afield for this text. The interested reader may consult Thompson (1967) and Uttal (1973) for discussion of these senses.

Visual candidate codes. *Visual space* is projected in a relatively precise manner over the retina. It is preserved in a topographically accurate manner to the primary visual cortex. All receptor surfaces project in a topographic fashion to their appropriate primary sensory areas of the cerebral cortex. For vision, the retina represents visual space. Insofar as the visual cortex is concerned, topographic projection really means place on the cortex, which in turn means different neurons. An object at your center of gaze projects to the fovea, which is represented in the foveal area of the visual cortex. *Visual orientation* is coded by separate columns of cells in the visual cortex. Each small areal representation of each region of retina has many small columns of cells. All the cells in a given column code a particular orientation or angle of stimulus. Different columns code different angles. Each small area thus has columns coding many orientations. To make a considerable inference from the data of Hubel and Weisel, *visual form* is coded in the same way, by groups of neurons that respond to angularity, rectangularity, etc. Again both orientation and form are coded basically in terms of the activation of different neurons. *Color* is coded by different neurons at the thalamus and cortex. Some are activated by red and inhibited by green, and so on. Again, different neurons for different colors. Visual *intensity*, or brightness, is coded by frequency of spike discharges in optic nerve fibers and number of fibers activated at least in lower vertebrates and invertebrates. Surprisingly, almost nothing is known about visual intensity coding in the mammalian central nervous system (see Uttal, 1973).

Excluding visual intensity we can summarize the candidate codes for visual experience quite simply because there is basically only one: different neurons. Each aspect of the visual stimulus, place, orientation, form, and color, is coded by activating different subgroups of neurons in the visual cortex. The extent to which these subgroups form separate or overlapping sets is unknown.

Auditory candidate codes. As in the visual system, the auditory receptor surface projects in a topographically accurate manner to the auditory cortex. However, the receptor surface (i.e., hair cells along the basilar membrane) does not represent auditory "space" but rather *tone frequency*. Tones of different frequencies activate different regions, and hence different neurons, in the auditory cortex. Most neurons in auditory brain structures are tuned, and respond best only to a narrow range of frequencies. There may be columnar organization in the cortex in the sense that most neurons in a small region respond best to a particular range of tone frequencies, but this is not entirely clear. An extreme complication in the auditory system concerns coding of *low frequencies* of tone. Lower levels of the auditory system (auditory nerve) fire at the same frequency as the tone. This would be an example of stimulus quality (pitch) coded by frequency of nerve discharge, a most atypical case.

However, this nerve frequency coding of tone frequency is lost by the auditory cortex where cells exhibit tuning curves for low frequencies just as for higher frequencies.

The location of sound in space is a complicated issue—it depends in part on alterations in loudness and in phase at each ear and the two ears together. Neurons in different auditory brain regions exhibit possible candidate codes by responding differentially depending upon the properties of the sound stimulus at the two ears—for example, act as comparators. Finally, some neurons in auditory cortex respond best to constantly changing tones or "warbles."

The coding of stimulus intensity in the auditory system seems related to total amount and frequency of nerve discharge, at least at the level of the auditory nerve. However, this simplicity is lost at the auditory cortex. Many cells exhibit loudness tuning, responding best to a particular narrow range of loudness as well as a narrow range of frequency.

In sum, the characteristics of sounds appear to be coded primarily by activating different neurons in the higher auditory brain regions. This may even be true for loudness.

Somatic-sensory candidate codes. The body surface projects in a topographically precise manner to the somatic-sensory area of the cerebral cortex. Localization of *body place* is coded by the area of cortex, and hence, by which neurons are activated. Within each small region of cortex in this somatotopic projection are columns of cells that respond only to one or another modality—touch, pressure, joint movement. Of course, a major segregation exists even in the spinal cord between the pathway concerned with pain and temperature and the pathway concerned more with touch and pressure. In the somatosensory system stimulus intensity is clearly coded by frequency of nerve discharge.

The various properties of somatic-sensory stimulation, except intensity, are coded by activating different neurons in the somatic-sensory cortex.

It should be obvious by now to the reader that there are only two types of coding that serve to code and represent all aspects of sensory stimuli. Frequency of discharge serves to code stimulus intensity and particular neurons, or regions of neurons, serve to code all the other qualities of sensation. This latter is simply a restatement of the *law of specific nerve energies* formulated by Müller in the 19th century—stimulus quality is determined by the particular place activated in the nervous system, as a result of the particular peripheral stimulus quality. What intervenes between this neuronal coding in the sensory areas of the cerebral cortex and behavioral response (not to mention subjective experience) is unknown. How are the patterns of activity in particular subgroups of neurons read, and read out, into behavior? What or "who" reads them? How is stimulus quality preserved from sensory cortex to motor (i.e., muscle) response? These are questions that remain to be answered.

PSYCHOPHYSICS AND INTENSITY JUDGMENT

The neuronal coding, or more properly candidate codes, we have discussed are concerned with the relations between stimulus properties and neuronal responses. A major aspect of sensory processing concerns behavioral judgments about stimuli. If the reader prefers to think subjectively, sensory processing relates actual stimuli and our *experience* of stimuli. In any event, human judgments about the properties of stimuli are measured in terms of behavioral responses—judging the intensity of a stimulus, whether a stimulus is or is not present, and so on. This is the subject matter of *psychophysics*, the first aspect of modern scientific psychology to develop.

In the middle 19th century, Weber made the empirical discovery that the amount the magnitude of a stimulus had to be increased to be of just noticeably greater magnitude was proportional to the absolute magnitude of the initial stimulus. We are all aware of this fact in simple experience. If a sound is loud, it has to be made considerably louder in physical terms before it is perceived as louder. A very weak sound is detected as louder after only a small increase in intensity. Fechner, who developed the first formulation of the psychophysical law from Weber's observation, provided a more dramatic illustration:

> A dollar has, in this connection, much less value to a rich man than to a poor man. It can make a beggar happy for a whole day, but it is not even noticed when added to the fortune of a millionaire.
>
> (Fechner, 1860; cited in Uttal, 1973, page 261)

At this point we must emphasize an important distinction between the physical intensity or magnitude of a stimulus and human judgment about its intensity. A number of specialized terms refer to judged stimulus qualities. For sound, sound wave intensity (actually pressure or energy) is judged as loudness, and sound frequency is judged as pitch. The intensity of a light is judged as brightness. The reason for the distinction, as the reader will soon see, is that physical intensity and judged intensity scales usually are quite different from each other. Indeed, psychophysics is concerned primarily with the relations between the two types of scales, one physical and one based on human judgment.

We will use the symbol ϕ to stand for the physical intensity of a stimulus and the symbol ψ to stand for the judged intensity of a stimulus. A delta (Δ) preceding the symbol means a just noticeable difference in the stimulus intensity. Thus $\Delta\phi$ is the amount of increase in the physical intensity necessary for ϕ to seem just noticeably more intense. Weber's law can be written very simply as $\Delta\phi/\phi = c$, where c is a constant. In words, the amount a physical stimulus intensity ϕ must be increased to be just noticeably more intense, $\Delta\phi$, is represented by a constant c.

come back to.

Sensory processes—
the basis of sensation

Fechner developed this simple relationship into the first formulation of the psychophysical law by making one seemingly simple assumption: the subjective size of the just noticeable difference is always the same. An intense tone must be increased considerably in physical intensity to make the sound just noticeably louder. The physical intensity of a weak tone needs to be increased only a little for it to sound just noticeably louder. The amount of added sound energy to the loud tone is of course much greater than that needed for the weak tone. However, in both cases the resulting sound is just noticeably louder to human subjective experience. Hence it seems natural to assume that the size of this just noticeably subjective increase is always the same—after all, it is always the *just noticeable* increase, no matter how much or how little the physical stimulus must be changed. To put it in symbols, Fechner assumed that the subjective size of the just noticeable difference ($\Delta\psi$) is a constant—it is always the same. Since Weber's law states that the ratio of increase in physical stimulus to initial stimulus intensity is constant, the two are equivalent:

$$\Delta\psi = c = \frac{\Delta\phi}{\phi}.$$

By use of simple calculus, this equation can be rewritten in logarithmic form as the psychophysical law:

$$\psi = c \log \phi.$$

In words, the judged intensity of a physical stimulus is equal to a constant times the logarithm of the physical intensity of the stimulus. This is a semi-log equation. The left side, judged intensity, is in simple numerical units and the right side, physical intensity, is in logarithmic units. Many judged stimulus scales, like the decibel scale for loudness, are of this form.

S. S. Stevens of Harvard University (see 1957) developed a different and very important form of the psychophysical law. He challenged Fechner's assumption that all just noticeable differences (jnds) are equal. In fact he made the drastically different assumption that the size of the subjective jnd is proportional to the judged intensity of the stimulus. In symbols:

$$\frac{\Delta\psi}{\psi} = c.$$

In terms of our earlier example, this means that if a loud tone is increased until it sounds just louder, the increment, even though just noticeable, seems subjectively larger than the just noticeable increase in a weak tone. The reader should attempt to determine whether this seems to be true for his or her own subjective experience. In any event, the consequences of this assumption are very different. Since Weber's law states that the

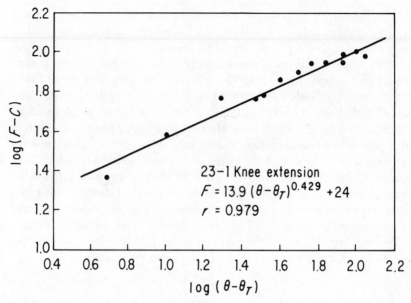

Figure 6.25 A replot of the data of Figure 6.20 after logarithmic transformation. The Pearson product moment correlation coefficient $= r$. The straight line is the best fit to these values. Note the nearly perfect fit. (From Mountcastle, V. B., Poggio, G. F., and Werner, G. The relation of thalamic cell response to peripheral stimuli varied over an intensive continuum. *J. Neurophysiol.* **26**, 1963, pp. 807–834.)

ratio of increased intensity to initial intensity is constant, the two ratios can be equated:

$$\frac{\Delta\psi}{\psi} = c\,\frac{\Delta\phi}{\phi}.$$

By use of calculus this becomes

$$\psi = k\phi^n,$$

when n, the exponent, is another constant. This form of equation is termed *power law*. Put in logarithmic terms, this becomes

$$\log\psi = n\log\phi + k,$$

a log-log equation. Stevens' formulation of the psychophysical law appears to have more generality and fits more kinds of stimulus properties than Fechner's.

We will take one example here to illustrate. First, it should be noted that if Stevens' law applies to a set of data, when data are graphed on a log-log plot, where both the ordinate and the abscissa are in logarithmic scales, the graph should be a straight line. Turn back to Figure 6.21, which plotted frequency of discharge of a neuron in the thalamus as a function of joint angle. It is plotted on a linear graph—frequency of discharge vs. joint angle. These data are replotted in a log-log graph in Figure 6.25. Note that they form an almost perfect straight line (the correlation coefficient r is a measure of the goodness of fit of the straight line; a perfect fit would be $r = 0.999$). Thus, this kind of relationship between neuron firing and joint position, a form of stimulus intensity relation as we noted above, fits Stevens' formulation of the psychophysical law perfectly.

Note that we have shifted the discussion from judgments about stimuli to frequency of nerve discharge. It is a very fundamental and important fact that the two seem to be identical, at least insofar as stimulus intensity is concerned. Frequency of nerve firing can be substituted exactly for subjective experience of stimulus magnitude. Both have the same power law relationship to physical stimulus intensity for a wide variety of stimuli. This is perhaps the most profound thing to be said at present about the nature of stimulus coding in the brain. The candidate code for stimulus intensity, nerve discharge frequency, agrees almost perfectly with our subjective judgments of stimulus intensity.

To state the relationship another way, insofar as stimulus intensity is concerned, what we actually "experience" are the frequencies of neuronal discharge in the sensory nerves and pathways that carry information about the world to the higher regions of the brain. Human perception of stimulus intensity is not a direct reflection of stimulus intensity, but bears a power law relationship to it. Humans do not experience the world as it is but only as a power function of what it is. Further, in most cases the power law relationship between stimulus intensity (of, for example, touches, tones, or lights) and perceived intensity is a "compression." That is, the doubled physical intensity of a stimulus is perceived as an increase that is much smaller than twice as great. A wide range of physical intensities is compressed into a narrower range of subjective experience.

The threshold problem and the theory of signal detection

It was generally taken for granted in classical psychophysics that a real absolute threshold existed. There is some particular weak intensity of sound below which the sound will not be heard. This assumption that a real absolute threshold exists was challenged by a different approach to the measurement of signal in noise. Signal detection theory was an outgrowth of the work of communications engineers who grappled with applied problems of the detection of signals in very noisy electronic systems, as in the modern telephone. The engineers assumed that noise always exists, as indeed it does in any sensory threshold experiment conducted with real human subjects. Consequently, a signal is always embedded in noise. More important, the criterion of judgment adopted by the observer in detecting a weak signal plays as important a role in this "threshold" as does the intensity of the signal, per se. Sometimes the observer detects noise and calls it signal, other times he detects signal and calls it noise (examples of false positive and false negative judgments). At other times he correctly detects signal and noise.

The theory of signal detection is complex and beyond the scope of this book. The key issue is that it emphasizes the psychological state of the observer, and that judgments are influenced by many variables interacting to determine criteria of judgments about signals in noise. The interested reader is urged to consult the classic text by Green and Swets (1966) for a detailed treatment and Uttal (1973) for a clear discussion of the applications of signal detection theory in the psychobiology of sensory processes. It is likely that new and valuable insights into the nature of stimulus coding in the brain will come from applications of signal detection theory.

Perception, as we noted at the beginning of the chapter, refers to our interpretation of sensations. One of the most fundamental problems in psychology concerns how we develop our complex integrated perceptions and awareness of the external world. Much recent experimentation indicates that movement and responding are essential for the development of normal perception. The completely passive observer may be a senser, but would never become a perceiver. The control of movement and the development of perception are treated in the next chapter.

Summary

In the visual system, the retina, a complex multiple layer of receptive and nerve cells at the back of the eye, transforms and codes visual images into nervous impulses. These impulses transport a representation of the external visual world to the brain. The vertebrate visual system is most sensitive to details and movements of objects in the visual world. The retina is more sensitive to stimulus change than to the presence of a fixed, unmoving pattern of light.

Rods and cones are the two basic kinds of light-sensitive receptor cells in the retina. These cells serve different functions: the rods are involved with scotopic (dim black and white) vision while the cones are concerned with photopic (brighter light, color and detail) vision. In mammals, the rods and cones are structurally distinct entities. The rods predominate in the peripheral regions of the retina; the fovea, at the center of gaze, is composed entirely of cones. These cones bear almost a one-to-one relation to the outgoing nerve fibers.

Vertebrates have many visual pigments, depending upon the species and upon whether the receptor is a rod or cone. In all cases the pigment is comprised of retinene and a type of protein opsin which varies from pigment to pigment. Rhodopsin and iodopsin are the two major visual pigments in the receptor cells of mammalian retina. Many aspects of visual sensation can be determined from the biochemical properties of these two pigments. There is a correspondence between the spectral sensitivities for rod and cone vision and the chemical absorption spectra of rod and cone pigments. In addition, there is a correspondence between the time courses of rod and cone dark adaptation and the chemical recovery processes of the pigments.

Binocular vision develops as one moves to successively higher vertebrates. In frogs there is a complete absence of binocular vision while in primates one finds virtually total binocular vision. The left half of each retina projects to the left visual cortex and the right half of each retina projects to right visual cortex. In primates the optic nerve fibers from the left half of each retina project to the left lateral geniculate body of the thalamus while fibers from the right halves of the retinae project to the corresponding right lateral geniculate body. The major visual pathways in the higher vertebrates consist of the projections from the optic tract to the lateral geniculate body to the cerebral cortex.

Striate cortex is the primary visual area of the cerebral cortex and is located in the occipital lobe. There is a retinotopic projection of the retina on the cortex in mammals. The cortical representation of the foveal area is relatively large in comparison to the actual size of the fovea. Visual stimuli are coded in terms of the presence and/or absence of light. Three general categories of optic nerve fibers have been distinguished: *on* fibers, *off* fibers, and *on-off* fibers which fire differentially with respect to the presence and/or absence of light.

Information processing in the retina is much more pronounced in lower vertebrates than in primates. In the frog, for example, it has been found that optic nerve fibers respond in terms of particular complex features of the stimuli. In the cat, complex information coding processes occur in visual cortex cells. The receptive fields of cells in visual cortex tend to be "edge-shaped." Shape, orientation of the receptive field, and movement of the appropriate shape across the field are three important variables in complex information coding processes.

The visual cortex is organized in a columnar manner. Different columns of cells respond to stimuli with different orientations.

Experiments indicate that the true answer to the manner in which the nervous system codes the wavelength of light lies between Hering's and Young's theories, perhaps closest to Hurvich and Jameson's model. Three types of cone pigments, red, blue, and green, are found in the *retina*. There also appear to be two general categories of *nerve* cells related to color vision: nonopponent cells which are influenced by all visible wavelengths of light, and opponent cells which respond to much narrower bands of wavelengths. The nonopponent cells are divided into two types, one which is inhibited and the other which is excited by all visible wavelengths. This evidence closely corresponds to Hurvich and Jameson's model of color vision.

Psychophysical functions relate psychological judgments of stimuli and the physical characteristics of these stimuli (human judgment). The relationship between pitch and frequency (physical property) is roughly logarithmic. Similarly, there is a logarithmic relationship between loudness of sounds (the decibel scale) and the physical sound intensity. In more general terms, the psychophysical function is a power law relationship between human experience of stimuli and the physical properties of stimuli, for all modalities and types of stimulation.

The anatomy of the auditory receptor system is complex. The external ear canal terminates on the tympanic membrane which is connected through the ossicles (middle ear bones) to the cochlea. The sense organ proper, the basilar membrane, is located within the cochlear duct. Sound vibrations transmitted through the ossicles result in a movement of fluid, producing vibrations of the basilar membrane. The bending of the basilar membrane and of the tectorial membrane activates the hair-cell receptors which lie between the two membranes.

The cochlea acts as a complex analyzer of the auditory stimulus. When a tone of a particular frequency is presented, a traveling wave of fluid originates in the cochlea. This wave results in a maximum displacement in a particular region of the basilar membrane. The location of this displacement is relative to the frequency of the tone. The cochlear microphonic represents a conversion of sound waves to electrical pulses which then follow the frequency and intensity characteristics of the auditory stimulus. The cochlear microphonic appears to be produced by the hair cells on the cochlea and may represent a receptor or generator potential.

Both place of excitation on the basilar membrane and frequency of nerve response seem to be significant in the coding of tone *frequency*. For high frequencies place is most important, while for low frequencies, synchronous discharges in nerve fibers also play a role. Both Helmholtz' place theory and Rutherford's frequency theory are partially correct. *Intensity* of a tone is coded both by the total number of fibers activated and by the activation of high threshold fibers.

When auditory stimuli are coded, activity from the auditory nerve relays in the cochlear nucleus and at other nuclei. The activity thus ascends to the auditory regions of the thalamus and cerebral cortex. In the auditory system there is a clear spatial representation of tone frequencies at all levels from the basilar membrane to the cerebral cortex. Auditory cortex is located in the temporal lobe, and in man is also located within the sylvian fissure. In general, the auditory region of the cerebral cortex appears to be involved in analysis of the more complex aspects of auditory stimuli.

Within the somatic-sensory system, many skin receptors are attuned to respond to only one modality. The lemniscal system is one of the central pathways of the somatic-sensory system which transmits cutaneous information from the spinal cord and brain stem to the cortex. In this system, which codes discrete touch and pressure sensations, afferent fibers from tactile and kinesthetic receptors enter the spinal cord and after turning upward in the dorsal columns, ascend to synapse on cells in the nuclei in the lower medulla. Fibers from these nuclei then cross and ascend to synapse in the thalamic relay nucleus, the ventrobasal complex. Fibers from this complex then project to the somatic-sensory areas of the cortex.

The spino-thalamic system of the somatic-sensory system is arranged much differently. Here, afferent fibers synapse in the dorsal horn of the spinal cord. Secondary fibers then cross and ascend the spinal cord, relay through interneurons in the reticular formation and terminate in the thalamus, again predominantly at the ventrobasal complex.

Spatial representation and spike discharge frequency are utilized by the somatic-sensory system in the coding of sensory information. Within the specific system, there is spatial segregation of the different regions of body surface at all levels of the lemniscal system. Cells of the ventrobasal complex are very specific and are responsive to only one of three modes of stimulation. The relationship between stimulus intensity and neural response follows a power function. Human perception of stimulus intensity is not a direct reflection of stimulus intensity, but bears a power law relationship to it. Perception of intensity corresponds to frequency of nerve discharge.

Somatic-sensory-motor cortex is located posterior to the central fissure. Here cortex contains representations of skin, muscle, and joint receptors. The representation in the cortex is contralateral. In general, the amount of cortex devoted to a particular region of body surface is directly proportional to the use and sensitivity of that region. Microelectrode studies of single neurons in somatic cortex have shown that within a particular region of body representation, a given cell usually can be activated by only one type of stimulus. There is also columnar organization of cells representing different modalities within somatic cortex.

Perception

In this chapter we have focused on basic sensory processes and their anatomical and physiological substrates. By the study of sensory receptors and the responses of neurons in sensory pathways, it has been possible to trace the conversion of physical stimuli into patterns of neuronal activity in the higher regions of the brain. This is a very satisfying field of inquiry. Many of the problems have been solved. Indeed, we can show a clear basis for the fundamental relationship between stimuli and sensations. The power law psychophysical function describes the relation between stimulus intensity and our experience or sensation of intensity for all stimulus modalities. There is an essentially identical, or at least linear, correspondence between the neural code (the firing of neurons) in sensory pathways and our experience or sensation of stimulus intensity. The power law transformation between stimulus intensity and the neural coding of intensity, incidentally, appears to occur largely in the receptors. However, it is a considerable jump from sensations of the intensity of stimuli to perception.

7

Motor control and sensory-motor integration

7

Stimulate 17. Patient made a vowel sound which was repeated rhyth-
mically. After electrode withdrawn she explained that she thought
she was starting to say something but "it" (the stimulation) had
forced her to repeat.

Stimulate 17. Repeated while patient was counting. Stimulation arrested speech completely. Patient added, "It (the stimulus) raised
my right arm." The arm had actually raised itself.

Stimulate 18. Patient counting. Stimulation caused her to vocalize in
a continuous sound. She explained afterward that she was sorry
she could not count. There was some movement in the right arm
also.

Stimulate 19. Patient counting. She made an exclamation and then
was silent, but the whole body moved. This movement caused the
head to turn a little to the right. There was not much movement of
the arm. When asked whether she had felt as she did before one of
her attacks, she said "Yes." When asked why, she replied, "Because I repeated my speech."

Stimulate 20. Patient counting backward. Stimulation caused the
counting to stop. Two or three seconds after withdrawal she continued counting backward. The observer noted no change during
her silence except that she looked surprised.

Stimulate 19. Approximate repetition of 20. Vocalization was produced, somewhat rhythmical. There was some movement of both
arms and both legs.

Stimulate 18. Repeated without warning. Stimulation produced vocalization which sounded like "da, da, da."

Stimulate 21. Stimulation while patient was counting. She hesitated
and then continued. There was movement of right arm, the shoulder
being drawn posteriorly. The right leg was extended and raised
off the table. When asked what she had noticed, she said her right
arm. When asked if she could prevent the movement, she said, "No."

Stimulate 22. Patient said, "Oh." There were generalized movements.
When asked what she noticed, she said her body seemed to rise up
but she did not seem to be doing it.

(Penfield and Jasper, Epilepsy and the Functional Anatomy of
the Human Brain. Boston: Little, Brown, 1954, page 97.
Copyright © 1954 by Little, Brown and Company.)

THE BASIS OF RESPONDING AND PERCEIVING

The brain control of movement is graphically illustrated in the quoted protocol from a brain operation described by Penfield and Jasper (1954). The patient was a right-handed woman of 39 whose symptoms suggested a tumor in the left hemisphere of the brain. The motor region of the left hemisphere was exposed and various points of the cerebral cortex stimulated electrically to aid in localizing the abnormal tissue (see Fig. 7.1). The patient was under only local anesthesia so she could respond and describe her sensations and feelings (the brain itself has no pain receptors —stimulation of the brain does not hurt). The stimulation numbers given in the protocol are simply arbitrary labels for the locations on the brain of the points stimulated.

Essentially all aspects of behavior that we can observe in other people and animals are muscle movements. Walking, running, fighting, tightrope walking, ballet dancing, piano playing; the list of people's movements is virtually endless. All these are simply sequences of skeletal muscle contractions and relaxations. To the same extent that psychology is the study of behavior, it also is the study of muscle movements.

The most important movements of people, indeed the movements that are uniquely human, are the movements of the tongue, lips, and throat associated with speech. Handwriting, typing, and even reading may be considered of secondary importance; vocal movements come first. It is likely that most thought processes have as an essential component some degree of movement of the vocal apparatus. Speech and language are mediated by the cerebral cortex. We will explore the neural basis of language in more detail in Chapter 12. The main point here is simply that speech and language are movements produced and controlled by the motor systems of the brain, particularly the cerebral cortex. More often than not, these crucially important movements are ignored in discussions of motor systems.

Make a "simple" voluntary movement such as picking up a pencil or a cup of coffee. Try to analyze your experiences as you make the movement. Initiation of the movement of your arm as you reach seems purely voluntary. You decide to reach and your arm reaches. We have no understanding at present of the mechanisms underlying this initiation of voluntary

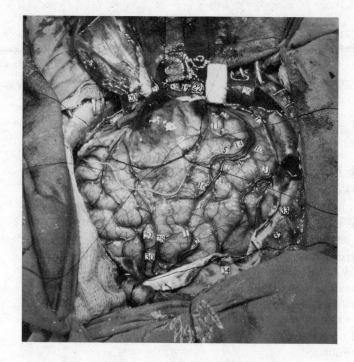

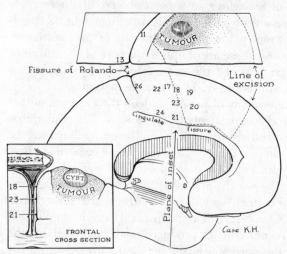

Figure 7.1 Upper figure is a photograph of left human frontoparietal cortex with tumor. White thread indicates proposed boundary of excision. Position of tumor and line of excision are shown in the lower figure. The fissure of Rolando is between tickets 10 and 14. The inset in the lower figure shows position of the tumor. Points from which stimulation produced responses in the supplementary motor area are indicated by the numbers on the mesial surface of the hemisphere. (From Penfield, W., and Jasper, H. *Epilepsy and the Functional Anatomy of the Human Brain*. Boston: Little, Brown and Co., 1954.)

movement. Once your arm movement begins, you look at the object to be picked up—you utilize visual cues or feedback to guide the movement. As your arm moves you are aware of where it is in space. This awareness is only partly due to visual information. If you close your eyes and reach for the object, your movement still will be fairly accurate if you remember where the object is in space. The sensory information that tells you where your arm is moving comes from several specialized types of pressure and stretch receptors in muscles, joints, and tendons. When your fingers first encounter the object, touch sensations guide your hand and fingers. As you pick up the object you are aware of how it feels (touch), how it is shaped (often called *stereognosis*), how heavy it is, and where you are holding it in space. A great amount of sensory information of different kinds continually guides your movements. Much of the sensory information that guides movement is the result of the movement—changes in muscle tension, changes of joint angles, touch sensations—and is fed back to the brain from the sensory receptors. This aspect of sensory control of movement is called feedback control or *biofeedback*. Even visual guidance of movement is partly biofeedback—where your hand is moving forms an essential part of the visual control of the movement. There is much interest in the general topic of biofeedback today. It appears that human movement control and even performance in very complex perceptual-motor tasks can be improved significantly by providing a person with increased or enhanced biofeedback. We will return to this topic later in the chapter.

Biofeedback plays a critical role in all movements, including the simplest reflexes that are mediated at the level of the spinal cord. One of the most elegant examples of biofeedback control is the *gamma system,* a spinal mechanism regulating the degree of contraction of muscles as a function of how much and in what way they are stretched. The gamma system is described in more detail below. Biofeedback control is not limited to reflexes or even to sensory information from the receptors. There is good evidence that the brain, once it issues a command to move, "knows" where the hand is moving even in the absence of sensory biofeedback information from the hand and arm. There appear to be higher order biofeedback systems within the brain itself that help to guide movements.

The ongoing movements that form the smooth and continuous behavior characteristic of higher animals are the result of a constant interplay between sensory biofeedback and muscle actions. This interaction of sensory input and motor output occurs at all levels from the spinal cord to the motor-sensory cortex. Recent evidence indicates that even highly specific aspects of sensation, such as visual orientation, act on neurons in the motor-sensory cortex. *Sensory-motor integration* is the term used to describe this continual and recurrent interplay between sensation and response.

The role of sensory information and feedback in the control of movement has been stressed. The issue can also be considered in reverse. What role does movement or responding play in determining sensory input? At a simple level it is obvious that what you see depends on where you look. In general terms the issue relates more to the role of behavioral responding in the development of perception. A human infant constantly waves his arms and hands when awake. A long period of learning and development is necessary before he can reach smoothly and grasp an object he sees. Do we learn to perceive the world as a result of our transactions with it? This aspect of sensory-motor integration, one of the fundamental questions of perception, will be dealt with later in the chapter.

MOTOR SYSTEMS—A BRIEF OVERVIEW

The number and variety of brain structures that relate to the control of movement are somewhat bewildering, to say the least. The English neurologist, Hughlings Jackson, stated many years ago that the basic function of the nervous system is movement. In a certain sense this is, of course, true. All movement is behavior, and behavior is merely the outwardly visible sign of brain activity. However, it is common practice to identify as motor systems those structures and pathways that can exert fairly direct influences on muscle (and gland) responses.

Essentially all muscle responses that would normally be termed behavior (i.e., activity of skeletal muscles) are solely and exclusively controlled by the motoneurons of the spinal cord and cranial nerve nuclei. These are Sir Charles Sherrington's "final common path." To produce muscle contractions, and hence movement, it is necessary to excite the motoneurons. The spinal motoneurons have their cell bodies and dendrites in the grey matter of the spinal cord and send axons out to form synapses on the muscles (see Chapter 3). Of course, the motoneurons of the cranial nerve nuclei are analogous, except that their cell bodies lie within nuclei in the brain stem rather than in the spinal cord and control muscles of the face and head. Since the only way to produce movement is to influence the motoneurons, all motor systems must act ultimately on the motoneurons. Basically, only two types of synaptic actions can occur directly on the motoneurons, namely excitation and inhibition. However, there are many different *ways* that various motor systems can exercise influences on the motoneurons. Activation of a given pathway might excite inhibitory interneurons that induce inhibition on the motoneurons. Another pathway might activate inhibitory interneurons that act to inhibit other inhibitory interneurons that normally inhibit the motoneurons, thus producing a net excitatory effect on the motoneurons. These and many more complex possibilities exist. Again, however, it is well to keep in mind that all motor systems must ultimately act on the motoneurons. The net balance of excitation and inhibition existing on the

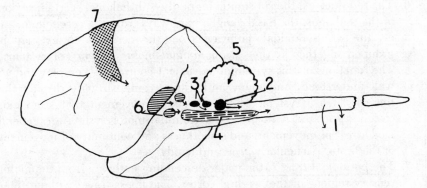

Figure 7.2 Diagram of the major motor regions of the primate brain. The numbers in the figure refer to the structures discussed in the text.

motoneurons of the spinal cord and brain stem completely determines the nature and extent of behavioral responding at any given moment.

The principal motor regions are indicated in the sketch of the generalized primate nervous system in Figure 7.2. With sufficient oversimplification, certain of these structures and systems may be grouped in terms of interrelations and functions:

1. The spinal reflex pathways stand more or less alone as a basic system, some of them exhibiting features of organization of our primitive ancestors whose nervous systems were little more than a spinal cord. Sensory information from muscles, tendons, joints, and skin has immediate and profound influences on the state of motoneuron activity, particularly on such aspects of behavior as postural adjustment, coordination of contractions and relaxations of groups of muscles that act together to produce movements, rapid withdrawal of limbs from painful stimuli, etc. All descending motor systems must of course "play" on those basic reflex patterns.

2. The vestibular nuclei and an old portion of the cerebellum function to maintain balance, no easy matter for an unstable, top-heavy biped-like man, and even more difficult for animals such as birds that live in a three-dimensional world of movement.

3. The pathway from the midbrain tectum appears to mediate certain postural adjustments in relation to auditory and visual stimuli.

4. Various regions of the descending reticular formation exert powerful excitatory and inhibitory influences on motoneurons, particularly those controlling muscles concerned with postural adjustments.

5. The cerebellum exerts powerful descending influences on brain stem motor systems and also has very potent actions on the motor area of the cerebral cortex.

6. The red nucleus, the substantia nigra, the subthalamus, certain regions of the thalamus, the basal ganglia, pathways from the cerebellum, and certain extrapyramidal pathways from the cerebral cortex may be grouped together as the *extrapyramidal motor system* (or systems). The functions of this system in movement control are complex and not well understood, and many authorities would strongly dispute that there is such a system. Those aspects of movement that seem most closely associated with the extrapyramidal motor system are generalized arrest of movement, and smoothness and continuity of movements of the limbs, particularly arms and hands.

7. The *pyramidal tract* is the major descending pathway from the motor-sensory regions of the cerebral cortex. The fibers travel without interruption from the cerebral cortex to the cranial nerve nuclei and spinal cord. The pyramidal tract appears to mediate precise and skilled movements in man, particularly those that involve a good bit of training such as athletic activities, playing of musical instruments, etc.

These various motor systems do not, of course, function in isolation. The activity of the higher systems modulates and is modulated by activity of the lower systems. For the most part, a human being functions as an integrated organism, not as a collection of separate systems. This is nowhere more evident than in the interaction of the motor systems that produce the integrated movements we call behavior.

THE NEUROMUSCULAR SYSTEM

The structure and actions of muscle

In terms of structural characteristics there are three general types of muscle tissue: striated, smooth, and cardiac (Fig. 7.3). Smooth muscle and cardiac muscle are under the control of the autonomic portion of the nervous system and striated muscle is controlled by the somatic portion of the nervous system (see Chapter 3). Further, smooth and cardiac muscle continues to function after all neural control is eliminated, while striated muscle is useless after nerve section. Biologists sometimes classify striated muscle activity as "voluntary" and smooth and cardiac muscle activity as "involuntary." Although these terms often carry surplus meanings, they can be approximately defined in operational terms. For example, we might use the label *voluntary* for all muscle actions a person can make upon request. Using this criterion we would include some smooth muscle actions as voluntary (i.e., bladder control) and some striated muscle responses as involuntary (i.e., postural adjustments) but there is a general correspondence.

In gross appearance muscle seems to be made up of many small fibers all running lengthwise. The fibers range in diameter from about 0.01 to

A

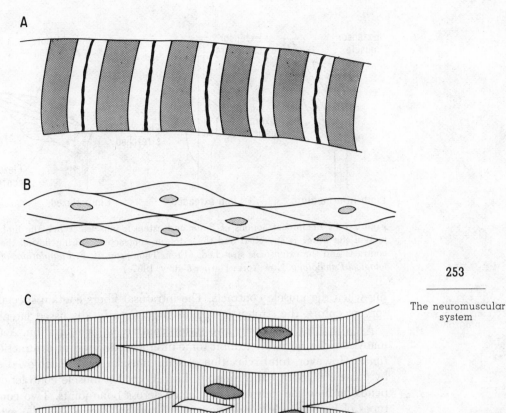

B

C

Figure 7.3 The three major types of muscle fibers: A, striated or skeletal muscle; B, smooth muscle; C, cardiac (heart) muscle. (From Thompson, R. F. *Foundations of Physiological Psychology*. New York: Harper & Row, 1967.)

0.1 mm in man, and no individual fiber is longer than about 12 cm. If the muscle is shorter than this length all fibers run the entire length; if it is longer, individual fibers attach to other fibers along the muscle. The gross muscle attaches to the bone at each end by tendons or fascia of very tough connective tissue. Each muscle fiber is a separate entity but not necessarily a single cell, there being a number of cell nuclei in each fiber. Striated muscle fibers are of two types, *extrafusal* and *intrafusal* (see Fig. 7.8, below). The extrafusal fibers are those that actually do the contract-

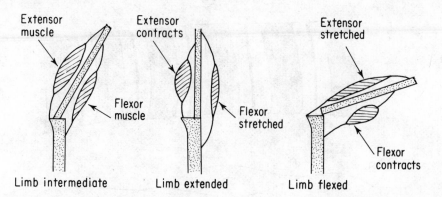

Extensor muscle

Flexor muscle

Limb intermediate

Extensor contracts

Flexor stretched

Limb extended

Extensor stretched

Flexor contracts

Limb flexed

Figure 7.4 Reciprocal actions of flexor and extensor muscles. When the limb is extended the flexor is stretched and the extensor contracted. During flexion the flexor contracts and the extensor is stretched. (From Thompson, R. F. *Foundations of Physiological Psychology*. New York: Harper & Row, 1967.)

ing when the muscle contracts. The intrafusal fibers contain special sensory receptors, the stretch or spindle organs, to be discussed later.

A given muscle has only two states, contraction or relaxation. Actually many muscles normally exhibit some intermediate level of contraction, or *tonus*. However, total relaxation of some muscles can be achieved easily by conscious control and training. The effect of a muscle contraction depends on how the muscle is connected across bone joints. Two common types of limb muscle connections are shown in Figure 7.4. The *extensor muscle* is connected across the joint so that contraction of the muscle causes extension (straightening) of the limb. The *flexor muscle* is connected so that contraction causes flexion or contraction (bending) of the limb. Essentially all joint movements are controlled by both types of muscles. (Other types of muscle actions are, for example, lateral and rotational movements of limbs.) Each muscle or set of muscles that acts in one manner is balanced by another set that acts in the opposite manner. This is often referred to as *reciprocal control*. Muscles that act in an opposite fashion are called *antagonists;* those that act to produce the same type of movement are called *synergists*.

Two types of muscle contraction, in terms of limb movements, are usually called *isotonic* (during contraction the muscle tension is relatively constant and the limb moves) and *isometric* (the muscle tends to change its degree of tension without actually moving the limb or changing its own length). Exercises currently in fad that do not involve actual movement are thus termed isometric exercises. Isometric contractions are crucially involved in the control of posture. If two antagonistic muscle groups both contract to the same degree, there may be little movement of the limb and the contraction tends to be isometric. If one group contracts more than the other, both muscles move and the contraction tends more to be isotonic. In more general terms, it is worth noting that changes in the isometric contraction strength of muscles can increase or decrease the tendency or probability that the organism will make a given response without actually producing any overtly measurable movement or response.

Muscular fatigue is a common experience, but a rather complicated matter. In ordinary humans fatigue following exercise is partly "psychological." In a classic demonstration a student was required to write his name repeatedly on a sheet of paper as fast as possible. Eventually he complained of such severe fatigue that he simply could not write it again. He was then asked to turn the paper over and sign it, which he promptly did, with no evidence of fatigue. Studies of electrical activity of muscles (*electromyography*) indicate that muscle fatigue is a neuronal phenomenon; the muscle fibers themselves never fatigue under conditions of normal health and use. Somewhat unexpectedly, muscular fatigue discomfort is attributable largely to tendons rather than muscles. In fact, if you hold a heavy weight with your arm hanging straight down, the muscles across the shoulder and elbow joints relax completely—all the stress and subsequent discomfort involves only the tendons and ligaments (Basmajian, 1967). Similarly, when you stand at rest, the muscles of the foot that are supposed to support the arches are relaxed and inactive. The fatigue and ache that develop are due to the load-bearing ligaments in the foot.

The innervation of muscles

In the normal organism striated muscles are activated by nerve fibers. After the muscle nerve is cut, the muscle can no longer be activated. Each efferent nerve fiber to muscle branches and innervates several muscle fibers. The basic unit of action of the neuromuscular system is the *motor unit*, a single efferent nerve fiber that comes from a single motoneuron, together with the muscle fibers it innervates. The innervation ratio (number of muscle fibers per nerve fiber) ranges from about 3:1 for small muscles concerned with fine movement control to over 150:1 for large muscles. A spike discharge conducted along the axon of a single motoneuron travels out all the axon branches and activates all the muscle fibers receiving the branches. The whole set of muscle fibers acts as a unit; all contract or none contracts.

Humans easily can learn to exert conscious control over the activity of single motor units. The experimental arrangement used to train single motor unit control is shown in Figure 7.5. A fine needle electrode is inserted in the muscle, or placed over its surface, and connected to an amplifier and other devices. The activity of a single motor unit is recorded electrically as a spike (Fig. 7.6). A critical aspect of this training is the biofeedback provided to the subject from the oscilloscope and loud-

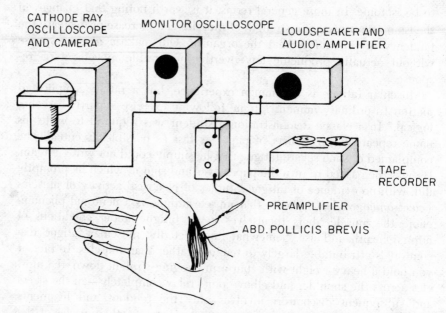

CATHODE RAY
OSCILLOSCOPE
AND CAMERA

MONITOR OSCILLOSCOPE

LOUDSPEAKER AND
AUDIO-AMPLIFIER

TAPE
RECORDER

PREAMPLIFIER

ABD. POLLICIS BREVIS

Figure 7.5 Experimental arrangement for training a subject to control single motor units in his own muscles. A small electrode needle is inserted in a muscle that controls movement of the thumb (abductor pollicis brevis). It is amplified and displayed on an oscilloscope and photographed (data shown in Fig. 7.6) and also shown to the subject on another oscilloscope and heard from a loudspeaker (each discharge of the motor unit generates a spike discharge and the oscilloscope makes a brief *pop* sound in the loudspeaker). The subject learns quickly to make the unit fire at will even though he cannot "feel" it responding. (Basmajian, J. V. *Muscles Alive: Their Functions Revealed by Electromyography.* Baltimore: Williams and Wilkins, © 1967.)

speaker. He sees and hears the spike discharge of the single motor unit and learns to make it fire or not fire at will. No detectable movement is generated by activating a single motor unit in this manner. Basmajian (1967), who has done much of this work, provides the following description:

Subjects are invariably amazed at the responsiveness of the loud-speaker and cathode-ray tube to their slightest efforts, and they accept these as a new form of "proprioception" without difficulty. It is not necessary for subjects to have any knowledge of electromyography. After getting a general explanation they need only to concentrate their attention on the obvious response of the electromyograph. With encouragement and guidance, even the most naive subject is soon able to maintain various levels of activity in a muscle on the sensory basis provided by the monitors. Indeed, most of the procedures he carries out involve such gentle contractions that his only awareness

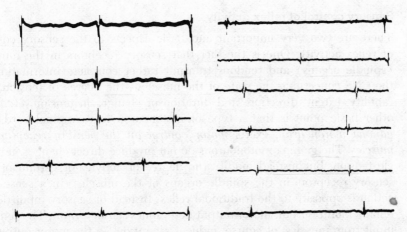

Figure 7.6 Examples of precisely controlled generation of a single motor unit response by a subject trained as in Figure 7.5. Each vertical spike is a "willed" motor unit response. (Basmajian, J. V., Baeza, M., and Fabrigar, C. Conscious control and training of individual spinal motor neurons in normal human subjects. *J. New Drugs* **5**, 1965, pp. 78–85.)

of them is through the apparatus. Following a period of orientation, the subject can be put through a series of tests for many hours . . .

Once a person has gained control of a spinal motor neuron, it is possible for him to learn to vary its rate of firing. This rate can be deliberately changed in immediate response to a command. The lowest limit of the range of frequencies is zero, i.e., one can start from neuromuscular silence and then give single isolated contractions at regular rates as low as one per second and at increasingly faster rates. When the more able subjects are asked to produce special repetitive rhythms and imitations of drum beats, almost all are successful (some strikingly so) in producing subtle shades and coloring of internal rhythms. When tape-recorded and replayed, these rhythms provide striking proof of the fineness of the control.

(Basmajian, 1967, pages 107, 109)

It is even possible to learn simultaneous control of several motor units from different muscles of the hands if immediate and adequate biofeedback about the activity of the muscles is provided to the subject. In one such experiment a subject was taught a simplified alphabet by generating different combinations of motor unit responses in the absence of overt movements. She was able to learn to generate words in this manner faster than a skilled typist (Teyler, Roemer, Thompson, Thompson, and Voss, 1974). It appears that humans have much more rapid and fine-grained control over muscles of the hand than had earlier been thought possible.

✳ Sensory control of reflex activity

There are two very important and basic aspects to the sensory control of reflex activity. One is the fact that sensory receptors in the muscles (spindle organs) and tendons transmit rather complete information to the CNS concerning the state of the muscles—the degree of tension, the rapidity, extent, direction, and duration of changes in tension, etc. The other basic point is that a type of motoneuron in the spinal cord, the *gamma motoneuron*, exerts *motor control on the sensory receptors in muscles*. The gamma motoneurons do not produce direct changes in muscle tension, but instead modify the degree of activity of certain of the sensory receptors in the spindle organs of the muscles. In a sense this action is opposite to the traditional reflex. Instead of sensory input determining motor output, motor output determines sensory input. The sensory input from muscles, of course, induces alterations in the motor output as well, which in turn will modify sensory input, and so on. The system represents a rather complex and elegant example of feedback control.

✳ Sensory information from muscles: the spindle organ and Golgi tendon organ

Figure 7.7 illustrates a few of the muscle bundles making up a given muscle. At each end they are attached to bone by tendons composed of very tough connective tissues. Individual muscle bundles are of two types, the regular muscle bundles made up of extrafusal fibers, which are the contractile elements of the muscle (Fig. 7.7), and the *spindle organs*, each consisting of several *intrafusal* fibers. Throughout muscles, the spindle organs are intermingled with regular muscle bundles, and are attached to tendons or to regular muscle bundles. Spindle organs always lie *parallel* to the regular muscle bundles. Although spindle organs have been a recognized entity for many years, a clear appreciation of their significance has been attained only in recent years through the work of such scientists as Matthews, Kuffler, Hunt, Granit, and others. Although the intrafusal fibers of the spindle organ are muscle fibers and do contract, they contract very weakly and contribute nothing to the overall pull of the muscle, which is due entirely to contraction of the extrafusal fiber bundles. Instead, they influence the activity of the spindle organ receptors. The intrafusal fibers of the spindle are innervated by the γ (*gamma*) *motoneurons*. Motoneurons innervating regular contractile muscle fibers are termed α (*alpha*) *motoneurons*.

The afferent (sensory) fiber terminals from the spindle organ are found in the enlarged central region (Fig. 7.7). The other type of muscle receptor of importance here is the *Golgi tendon organ* or receptor. This is simply an afferent nerve fiber whose terminals lie in the tendon joining muscle and bone. The terminals proliferate in the tendon fibers close to the muscle-tendon junction (Fig. 7.8).

draw sterno (handwritten)

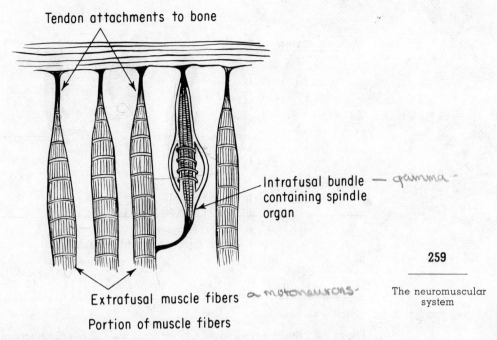

Tendon attachments to bone

Intrafusal bundle — *gamma* (handwritten)
containing spindle
organ

Extrafusal muscle fibers *α motoneurons* (handwritten)

Portion of muscle fibers

Figure 7.7 Anatomical arrangement of extrafusal (contractile) muscle fibers and an intrafusal muscle bundle containing a spindle organ. (Thompson, R. F. *Foundations of Physiological Psychology.* New York: Harper & Row, 1967.)

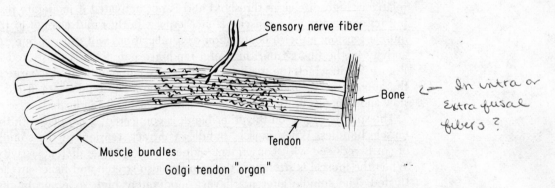

Sensory nerve fiber

Bone — *In intra or Extra fusal fibers ?* (handwritten)

Tendon

Muscle bundles

Golgi tendon "organ"

Figure 7.8 Schematic drawing of the Golgi tendon organ. Nerve fibrils of the sensory nerve fiber are distributed to the tendon fibers. (After Patton, H. D. Reflex regulation of posture and movement. From Ruch, T. C., and Fulton, J. F. (eds.). *Medical Physiology and Biophysics.* Philadelphia: W. B. Saunders Co., 1960, pp. 167–198.)

In physical terms the tendon organs are in *series* with the muscle bundles. They stretch when the muscle contracts, because the muscle exerts pull on the tendon attachments when it contracts. In like manner if the muscle is stretched by a passive pull (as when antagonistic muscles contract) the tendon organ also stretches. However, the tendon organ has a

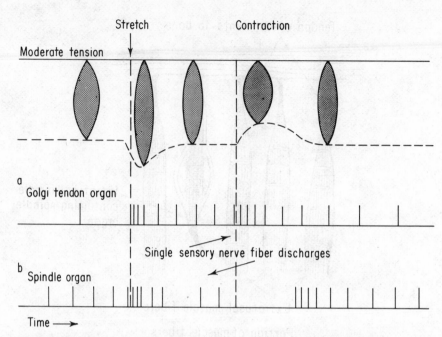

Figure 7.9 Response patterns of sensory nerve fibers from a Golgi tendon organ (a) and a spindle organ (b) to stretch and contraction of a muscle. The small spikes on the baseline indicate discharge in the afferent nerve fiber. (After Granit, R. *Receptors and Sensory Perception.* New Haven: Yale Univ. Press, 1955.)

relatively high discharge threshold and is not activated if moderate resting tension exists on a muscle. Hence only a fairly rapid change in the muscle tension, either a contraction or a relaxation, will cause a burst of activity in the fibers from the Golgi tendon organ. This is illustrated in Figure 7.9, in which the small spikes on the baseline indicate discharge in the afferent nerve fiber from the tendon organ. The tendon organ has a slow spontaneous firing rate under constant tension, as indicated.

The spindle organ, on the other hand, is connected in *parallel* with the muscle bundles. When muscle bundles contract, tension on the spindle organ is reduced with consequent reduction of spindle afferent activity. When the muscle is stretched, the spindles also stretch and hence are activated. The spindle afferents have a moderately high spontaneous discharge rate, higher than the Golgi organ fiber rate when the muscle is under a given amount of constant tension. Further, *the rate of spontaneous firing of spindle afferent fibers is directly related to degree of muscle tension.*

If we consider the actions of the tendon and spindle fibers together, rather complete information is transmitted to the CNS about the state of muscles. Suppose a muscle is under moderate tension. The Golgi tendon fibers will fire at a slow steady rate and the spindle fibers at a somewhat

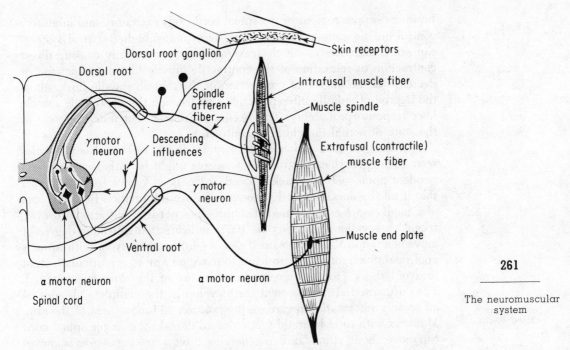

Figure 7.10 Summary diagram of the gamma motor neuron system. (See text for explanation.) (Thompson, R. F. *Foundations of Physiological Psychology.* New York: Harper & Row, 1967.)

faster steady rate. When the muscle tension is increased suddenly and held at a high level, the Golgi fibers show a brief burst of activity and then return to the slow spontaneous rate, whereas the spindle fibers give a rapid burst and then stabilize at a higher rate. When the muscle tension is reduced, the Golgi fibers again show a brief discharge, but the spindle fibers cease firing briefly and then stabilize at a lower rate. *The Golgi fibers signal change in muscle tension and the spindles signal the degree, direction, and rate of change.*

The gamma motoneuron

As if the system were not already sufficiently complex, an additional mechanism must also be considered, the *gamma motoneuron*. Remember that these motoneurons of the spinal cord activate and cause contraction of the intrafusal fibers of the spindle organ, which in turn stretch and activate the spindle afferent fibers. These fibers, in turn, play back on the alpha motoneurons to the muscle to cause changes in muscle tension (Fig. 7.10).

The gamma system has a general significance that extends beyond its role in spinal reflex activity. A number of descending pathways from the brain and upper regions of the spinal cord exert excitatory and inhibitory control on the gamma motoneurons. Thus many higher control systems can exert influence on muscle tension without necessarily causing direct contraction or relaxation of the contractile muscle fibers. An increase or decrease in the degree of contraction of the muscle spindle fibers alters the degree of spindle afferent activity and hence the contractile muscle fiber response probability. This occurs to some extent independently of the state of actual muscle fiber contraction.

The complex and elaborate sensory feedback systems from muscles seem to suggest that controlled movements might be rather crucially dependent upon such feedback. Indeed, it has been known for many years that if all the dorsal roots that convey sensory information from one arm of a monkey are cut, the animal simply does not use that arm. However, recent observations (Taub et al., 1965) indicate that a striking degree of movement control can develop if sensory information from both arms is abolished. Such monkeys can learn to move an arm to a particular extent to avoid shock (to ear), even when viewing of the arms is prevented. Thus a learned arm movement can develop in the complete absence of *all* sensory information regarding the position and movement of the arm. Monkeys with total bilateral section of *all* dorsal roots in the spinal cord can move about, climb, and, in general, exhibit a striking degree of movement control. These and related studies have important implications for mechanisms underlying perception, the integration of sensation and response.

MOTOR-SENSORY AREAS OF THE CEREBRAL CORTEX

Earlier in this chapter it was noted that the most complex aspects of movement control are mediated by the cerebral cortex. The protocol of the patient undergoing brain surgery gave dramatic evidence of the complex and highly organized nature of cortical influence on responding—complex movements and even vocalizations were elicited by electrical stimulation of the "motor" areas of the cerebral cortex.

Several observations must be emphasized in regard to that protocol quoted at the beginning of this chapter. First, the movements elicited by stimulation of the cortex were organized. Stimulation did not produce random twitching of muscles, but rather well integrated movements, even to the point of producing recognizable vocalizations. Second, the patient seemed to have no control over the movements; the electrical stimulus preempted her voluntary control of movement. Finally, the patient did not describe any experiences, memories, or even strong sensations other than the movements that resulted from the stimulus. In other words, the motor-sensory cortex appears to be a region of the brain that controls complex integrated movements.

Most of the analytic work on the organization of the motor-sensory cortex has, of course, been done on animals. The location of the primary motor-sensory cortex (MI) has been known for nearly 100 years. Fritsch and Hitzig (1870) showed that stimulation of the anterior portion of the cerebral cortex in the dog elicited muscle movements of the opposite side of the body. This cortical region contains giant Betz cells and is primarily concerned with control of movement.

The analytic method used to study the motor-sensory cortex is quite simple (Woolsey, 1958). After an animal is deeply anesthetized (barbiturate), he is suspended to permit free movement of the extremities. The motor-sensory cortex is exposed and an electrical (60 cycle) stimulus lasting about one second is delivered to a discrete point on the surface of the cortex. This stimulus is similar to that used in the work on human patients. If muscular movements are elicited, the stimulus intensity is reduced to a value just above threshold and the movement response observed and recorded. A summary of the findings of such experiments was indicated in Figure 6.22 in Chapter 6 (pp. 228–229) for rat, cat, and monkey. The diagrams indicate the region of the body that moves following cortical stimulation. As can be seen, the primary motor cortex is in many respects a mirror image of the somatic-sensory-motor cortex. The primary motor-sensory cortex controls muscles on the contralateral side of the body (i.e., right motor-sensory cortex to left side of body). The pattern of representation of movement on the motor-sensory cortex of man shows marked enlargement of the hands, lips, and tongue control areas, as is the case in the somatic-sensory-motor cortex (Fig. 7.11; Fig. 6.24 in Chapter 6).

The type of movement elicited by electrical stimulation of the primary motor-sensory cortex in the deeply anesthetized animal is of considerable importance in understanding central control of movement. If a somewhat supra-threshold stimulus is used (the stimulus, remember, being a relatively long duration 60-cycle current), an organized movement such as flexion of the arm, rotation of the wrist, or flexion of the finger occurs. Such results led to the dicta that "movements, not muscles" are represented in the motor-sensory cortex (Walshe, 1943). Chang, Ruch, and Ward (1947) completed a very careful study on the cortical control of eight individual muscles acting on the ankle joint of the rhesus monkey. They found that with just threshold stimuli a single muscle sometimes would contract without activity of any other muscle. Each separate muscle had a slightly different cortical locus, which would yield contraction of that muscle alone. In general, extensor muscles were more responsive than flexors. Thus it appears that *muscles as well as movements* may be represented in the motor-sensory cortex. However, the fact that stronger stimuli do yield "movements" rather than disorganized and conflicting contractions in the separate muscles involved suggests that the cortex is superimposing organization on the control of movement.

Motor-sensory areas
of the cerebral cortex

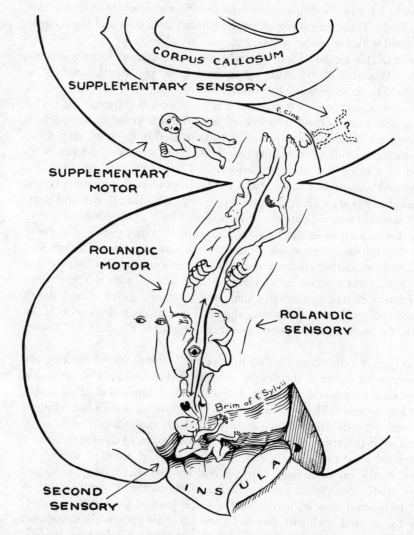

Figure 7.11 Somatic figures drawn on the left hemisphere showing the pattern of representation of movement on the motor-sensory cortex of man. The size and position of the Rolandic figures correspond roughly with the extent of Rolandic cortex concerned with sensation or movement of those parts. The representation of the second sensory figure is primarily contralateral. Of the supplementary figures, the motor figure is in the posture most often produced by stimulation, but no fixed topographical localization of the parts of the body or of vocalization, autonomic sensation, or inhibition have been established. The exact position of the parts of these figures is not topographically accurate. (From Penfield, W., and Jasper, H. *Epilepsy and the Functional Anatomy of the Human Brain.* Boston: Little, Brown and Co., 1954.)

Strong evidence that supports the view that the motor-sensory cortex superimposes organization on lower motor systems has been provided by the work of Phillips and his associates (Phillips and Porter, 1964). In brief, this work examined the area of *motor-sensory cortex* that would influence the activity of a *single* spinal motoneuron and found it to be quite large, approximately 20 sq mm in the baboon. Further, the areas of the motor-sensory cortex controlling different spinal motoneurons overlap extensively. Consequently, in motor-sensory cortex the neurons that project to spinal motoneurons controlling different muscles are themselves extensively intermingled. The fineness of voluntary motor control is not due to a very fine-grained separate anatomical representation of separate muscles in the motor-sensory cortex, but rather to complex integration of overlapping control systems in the cerebral cortex.

Function of motor-sensory cortex

Our discussion of motor-sensory cortex thus far has been concerned primarily with the kinds of movements elicited by electrical stimulation. Such a technique by itself does not necessarily specify the essential role of the motor-sensory cortex in the control of movement. In fact, removal of the primary motor-sensory cortex in man produces loss of the most delicate and skilled movements, particularly those of the fingers and hand. Removal of the motor-sensory cortex has little or no permanent effect on the movements produced by electrical stimulation of the cortex of man. These movements, which consist largely of flexion and extension of the arms and legs, opening and closure of the fist, and vocalizations, have the same character whether the patient is a child of 8, a man of 60, a skilled pianist, or a manual laborer (Penfield and Jasper, 1954). Further, these are the same movements of which the newborn baby is capable. The crucial matter at hand, of course, is to determine the nature and organization of the higher order central control systems that play upon the motor-sensory cortex. This determination cannot begin to be made at present; essentially nothing is known about such systems.

We have emphasized the movement control function of the motor-sensory cortex. Actually, it could equally well be called a sensory cortex. You may remember from Chapter 6 that Woolsey proposed to call both somatic-sensory and motor areas of the cortex the *somatic* cortex. We adopted his terminology of *motor-sensory* for the primary motor cortex and *sensory-motor* for the primary somatic-sensory cortex. On the motor-sensory cortex a detailed representation of the body skin surface is a virtual mirror image of the representation, just behind it, in the sensory-motor cortex. Further, it corresponds closely to the representation of muscles and movements on the motor-sensory cortex. Another point of great importance is that movements can be elicited by stimulation of the somatic-sensory-motor cortex. Woolsey's terminology most appropriately

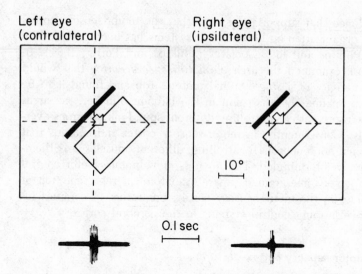

Left eye
(contralateral)

Right eye
(ipsilateral)

10°

0.1 sec

Figure 7.12 Responses from a pyramidal tract neuron from the motor cortex of the cat. This cell responded best to movement of a diagonal black bar moving downward and to the right. The records of action potentials from the unit, photographed from an oscilloscope, are shown below a plot of the receptive field. The cell responded to the same sort of target shown to each eye separately although it was more sensitive to stimuli presented to the contralateral (left) eye.

emphasizes this dual representation. The "motor" area and "somatic-sensory" area of the cerebral cortex are both sensory and motor in organization and in function.

The work of Vernon Brooks and associates (Brooks and Stoney, 1971) has shown that many neurons in the motor-sensory cortex have detailed somatic-sensory receptive fields. A given "motor cortex" neuron might be activated by a very specific and small region of skin. Another might be activated by a large region of the body surface. This well organized projection of sensory information to the motor-sensory cortex provides many opportunities for sensory-motor integration in the control of behavior.

In addition to somatic-sensory information, other sensory modalities also project to the motor-sensory cortex. Some of the neurons in the motor-sensory cortex even behave like neurons in the visual cortex. They have very specific visual receptive fields. An example is shown in Figure 7.12. This neuron was a cell of origin of a pyramidal tract fiber (see below), a cell that would be classed as an "upper motor neuron." The cell has a very specific visual receptive field—a bar moving across the eye at a particular angle and velocity was an extremely effective stimulus (Teyler, Roemer, and Thompson, 1972). A neuron of a type that has been believed to be purely motor in function has a visual receptive field very much like neurons in the visual cortex! The existence of these visual-motor neurons in the motor-sensory area of the cerebral cortex raises many possibilities for sensory-motor integration at the level of the cerebral cortex.

DESCENDING CORTICAL CONTROL SYSTEMS

From the cerebral cortex, two major descending systems mediate the cortical control over movement. One, the *pyramidal tract*, has its cell bodies largely in the motor cortex and sends axons down to the regions of the cranial motor nuclei and motor regions of the spinal cord without intervening synapses. Many of these pyramidal tract axons do, however, send off collateral branches at many subcortical levels to influence other regions of the brain. All other descending pathways are defined by exclusion—arbitrarily grouped together under the label *cortical extrapyramidal system*. The existence of these pathways is demonstrated by the fact that stimulation of the cerebral cortex can induce movements after complete bilateral destruction of the pyramidal tracts.

The pyramidal tract

The pyramidal tract is composed of fibers passing through the *pyramids*, large pyramid-shaped fiber bundles in the medulla. The cell bodies of the pyramidal fibers lie in the cerebral cortex, primarily in the motor and somatic-sensory areas, and the fibers end in the spinal cord. The fibers of the pyramidal tract are the longest single fibers in the mammalian central nervous system, extending in man some 2 feet and in the whale 20 feet or more. The pyramidal tracts are predominantly crossed: the tract originating in the left cortex, for example, descends on the left side to the lower medulla, crosses to the right at the *decussation* of the pyramids, and descends on the right side of the spinal cord. In primates there is also an uncrossed portion, comprising about 20 per cent of the pyramidal fibers, which descends to the ipsilateral portion of the spinal cord.

It is important to note that the pyramidal tract sends fibers out into various brain regions as it descends from the cerebral cortex to the spinal cord. These collateral (branching) fibers can serve as feedback loops to provide to lower brain regions information about what the pyramidal tract is "telling" the cranial and spinal motoneurons to do. These lower brain regions in turn can act back to influence the motor-sensory cortex and pyramidal tract. This kind of recurrent or feedback organization is a very common property of brain systems. In the case of the pyramidal tract, the branching fibers provide information back to the brain about the movement commands being issued from the motor-sensory cortex. If the movement, say an arm motion, goes as planned, the brain "knows" where the arm is without any peripheral sensory feedback from the arm.

The pyramidal tract has occasioned interest because of its late appearance in the course of evolution. It is best developed in mammals and reaches its maximum elaboration in primates. These facts parallel the general characteristics of the phylogenetic development of the cerebral cortex, a not-too-surprising observation in view of the cortical origin of the pyramidal tract. It is of particular interest that in primates, but not in lower forms, there is a significant proportion of direct monosynaptic

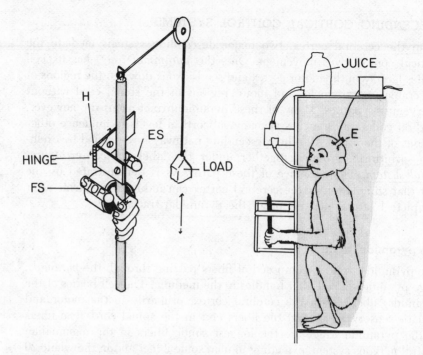

Figure 7.13 Initial training was carried out in the monkey's home cage. Here the monkey's left hand is seen to be protruding from a tube in a Lucite panel attached to the front of the cage. In order to receive a juice reward, the monkey was required to grasp the vertical rod attached to a hinge and to move it back and forth from one stop to the other. The stops are labeled FS (flexor stop) and ES (extensor stop). The monkey was required to contact the FS and then move the handle through the arc between the stops until the ES was reached. If the period between breaking contact with the FS and making contact with the ES was between 400 and 700 msec, and if the previous movement in the other direction also fell within these time limits, a reward was delivered. A narrow slit, just large enough to accommodate the monkey's wrist, was placed so as to prevent side-to-side arm movements and require that movements of the handle result from alternate flexion-extension at the wrist. An electrode is implanted at E. (From Evarts, E. V. Relation of pyramidal tract activity to force exerted during voluntary movement. *J. Neurophysiol.* **31**, 1968, pp. 14–27.)

connections of pyramidal tract fibers to spinal motoneurons (i.e., the pyramidal tract fiber synapses directly on the spinal motoneuron). As you may recall from the previous discussion of the motor-sensory cortex, Phillips and his colleagues found that in the baboon rather extensive and overlapping *colonies* of cortical pyramidal cells have monosynaptic connections to given spinal motoneurons. Phillips and Porter (1964) compared monosynaptic pyramidal actions on motoneurons of hand and forearm vs. upper arm muscles. They found that the cortical pyramidal cell colonies, projecting to motoneurons controlling hand muscles, tended to occupy smaller cortical areas and induce larger monosynaptic actions than did those to motoneurons of upper arm muscles. These findings have clear implications for the cortical-pyramidal control of fine hand movements:

It is probable that such versatile but precise control (of the hand) depends in part on a special development of the monosynaptic corticospinal pathway to the motoneurones of the distal muscles of the upper limb. The directness of this pathway should increase the accessibility of hand motor units to the complex intracortical neuronal systems lying upstream of the corticofugal pyramidal neurons.

(Phillips and Porter, 1964, page 242)

The functions of pyramidal tract neurons in the performance of skilled movements have been studied in elegant experiments by Evarts (1966). These neurons, with cell bodies in the motor cortex and with axons that make up the pyramidal tract, are often referred to as *PT neurons*. Evarts trained monkeys to move a handgrip rapidly in either a flexion or extension movement following a signal to obtain an orange juice reward (see Fig. 7.13). The lever had to be moved to the correct position ("flexor stop" or "extensor stop" in Fig. 7.13) and the amount of force required to make the movement could be varied ("load" in the figure).

When an animal was well trained, a chronic microelectrode recording chamber system was affixed to the skull overlying a small exposure of the motor cortex (E in Fig. 7.13). During a recording session a microelectrode was lowered into the motor cortex and the activity of PT cells studied during performance of the skilled movements.

Examples of responses of a PT cell during the performance of the rapid wrist movement are shown in Figure 7.14. The responses were recorded with three different degrees of load. The top record is with 400 grams opposing flexion, the middle record with no load, and the lowest record with 400 grams. The thin line below each tracing of the cell responses indicates the actual position of the lever (down is extension and up is flexion). This is a flexor-type cell—it discharges when a flexor movement must be made against a load. However, the cell does not discharge (except for one spike) when the load favors the flexion movement. In other words, the cell fires whenever the monkey has to exert force to make a flexion movement and the rate of firing is proportional to the degree of force required.

Evarts found both flexor- and extensor-type PT cells. In all cases the crucial factor that determined the discharge rate of a cell during movement was the actual *force* required to make the movement. The movement, per se, was not as important. Whether or not a cell fired depended on the force of the movement and not on the movement itself. This is a further example of the organizational control imposed by the motorsensory cortex on movement or responding.

The pyramidal tract appears to play an essential role in the performance of highly skilled movements. Tower (1940) completed extensive

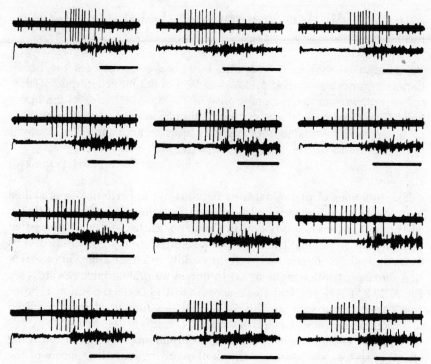

Figure 7.14 PT neuron response (top trace of each group of three), extensor EMG response (middle trace), and reaction time (bottom trace). Figure shows a series of 12 trials for a PT neuron which was silent during flexion and which consistently discharged prior to extension of the contralateral wrist. All traces begin at the onset of the light. Minimum response latency for this PT neuron was about 120 msec. In general, the shortest latency PT neuron responses were associated with the shortest latency EMG responses. Time marks are 50 msec apart. The bottom line of each set of traces indicates when the contact opened. (From Evarts, E. V. Pyramidal tract activity associated with a conditioned hand movement in the monkey. *J. Neurophysiol.* **29**, 1966, pp. 1011–1027.)

studies of the possible role of the pyramidal tract in movement control. She sectioned the pyramidal tract bilaterally in monkeys and chimpanzees, and observed the subsequent behavior of the animals for long periods of time following lesion. She found the extremities lost the finer qualities of aim and precision in movements. During the course of execution of a movement the animals were not able to modify the movement smoothly. Skilled movements were performed very much more poorly. The selective destruction was of the "least stereotyped, most discrete, movements or elements in movement." Thus the fine control of movement is seriously impaired after bilateral section of the pyramidal tract.

In this regard, it is worth recalling Lashley's early experiments (1924) indicating that, although the motor-sensory cortex (and therefore much of the pyramidal tract) is necessary for skilled movements, it plays no essential role in the *learning* or *retention* of particular sequences of movements. Monkeys were trained to perform skilled acts such as opening a puzzle box to obtain food. The motor-sensory cortex was than ablated. After the initial paralysis began to dissipate, the animals performed the correct sequence of responses necessary to obtain the reward. Their movements were clumsy and awkward, but nonetheless correct. The lesion did not interfere with the learned behavior sequence, only with the skilled execution of the necessary movements.

Cerebellum

This structure, one of the oldest in the history of the vertebrate nervous system, is well developed in reptiles and very well elaborated in birds. Its general functions are clearly motor in nature, although its detailed mechanisms of action are only now beginning to be understood. The overall structure of the cerebellum is analogous somewhat to the cerebrum in that the cellular layers form a cortex covering the white matter and several deep nuclei. Typically, the cerebellum is highly convoluted in appearance, with considerable areas of cerebellar cortex buried in fissures. The general location of the cerebellum is dorsal to the brain stem and posterior to the cerebrum (Fig. 7.2). In primates it is almost completely covered over by the occipital lobes of the cerebral hemispheres.

Input to the cerebellum includes all varieties of sensory information. There is a detailed somatotopic organization of somatic-sensory projection on the surface of the cerebellum, just as on the cerebral cortex. In addition, strong input from spindle organs and other muscle receptors provides detailed information to the cerebellum about the state of contraction of the muscles. The major outputs of the cerebellum relay through a variety of brain structures concerned with the control of movement. Of particular importance are detailed reciprocal interconnections between the cerebellum and the sensory-motor areas of the cerebral cortex.

An interesting discovery has changed many ideas held previously about the functional organization of the cerebellum. You will recall that all output from the cerebellar *cortex* occurs via the axons of the Purkinje cells, large neurons in the cerebellar cortex (Fig. 7.15). Purkinje cell axons go mostly to the cerebellar subcortical nuclei, with a portion going to the vestibular nuclei. It has been demonstrated that *all Purkinje cells are inhibitory* (Eccles, Ito, and Szentágothai, 1967). All Purkinje cell axons exert inhibitory action on all cells upon which they terminate. More specifically, they induce postsynaptic inhibition on all cells they influence. Further, there is increasing evidence that the chemical inhibitory transmitter substance released by the axon terminals of Purkinje cells is gamma amino butyric acid (GABA), a simple amino acid.

It may seem somewhat puzzling that the Purkinje cells are exclusively inhibitory. Since Purkinje cells are the only output from the cerebellar

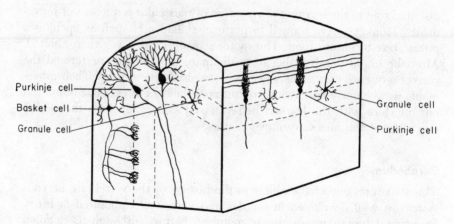

Figure 7.15 Histological organization of the cerebellar cortex. All output fibers from the cerebellum are Purkinje cell axons. (From Ranson, S. W., and Clark, S. L. *The Anatomy of the Nervous System.* 10th Ed. Philadelphia: W. B. Saunders Co., 1959.)

Motor control and
sensory-motor
integration

cortex, the cerebellum becomes a large mass of neural tissue whose only function is to inhibit! Actually, this is not quite the case. The major outputs from the cerebellum itself come from the cells in the subcortical cerebellar nuclei. These cells normally exhibit high levels of activity. The Purkinje cells from the cerebellar cortex for the most part terminate on these cells of the subcortical cerebellar nuclei. Consequently, the inhibitory actions of the Purkinje cell axons can serve to modulate and tune temporal patterns of activity in the cells of the subcortical cerebellar nuclei. The cerebellar cortex thus becomes a system that exerts its influence by continuously modulating or damping down the ongoing activity of the subcortical cells that act on the motor systems of the brain.

Damage to all or to portions of the cerebellar cortex can produce a variety of deficiencies in motor behavior. In man, cerebellar damage yields abnormalities in the force, rate, direction, and steadiness of rapid and volitional movements. A simple movement such as touching an outstretched finger is slow to develop, overshoots the mark, and exhibits marked tremor. This tremor, incidentally, is called "intentional" in that it occurs during movement but not when the limb is at rest.

It has been suggested that the cerebellum may play a role in the learning of complex skilled movements (Eccles, Ito, and Szentágothai, 1967).. This idea is reminiscent of the so-called *functional autonomy* of habits. A well learned habit, particularly a motor skill, becomes independent of deliberate effort. When first learning a complex motor skill, such as golf or tennis, you concentrate on every movement with deliberate attention and effort. However, after the skill is thoroughly learned you will do well *not* to concentrate on individual movements. The surest way to "blow" a well practiced golf shot is to concentrate on any or all individual movements. The movements that are inherent to a well learned skill are best allowed to occur independently or autonomously while you concentrate on the more general task of making the ball go where it should. Common sense suggests that different neuronal systems may be involved in initial learning of a complex task and control of later skilled performance of the task. Though there is no substantiating evidence yet, perhaps the cerebellum is in control of the later skilled performance. However, it must be emphasized that there is no basis for either support or denial of such a theory.

Basal ganglia

The functions of the basal ganglia in mammals are relatively obscure. They seem to have something to do with the control of movements. Anatomically, the term *basal ganglia* usually refers to the *caudate nucleus*, the *putamen,* and the *globus pallidus*, three large nuclear masses embedded in the subcortical white matter of the cerebral hemisphere (Fig. 7.2). One particular response to electrical stimulation of the caudate nucleus, the *arrest reaction*, has been described in numerous experiments (e.g., Mettler et al., 1939). The movements the animal makes at the time of stimulation cease and the animal holds his position, much like a still picture in a movie. Head turning and "searching" responses, and more long-lasting generalized inactivity have also been reported to follow caudate stimulation (Akert and Andersson, 1951).

Recent studies by N. A. Buchwald and associates (Buchwald and Hull, 1967) have clarified the nature of this reaction. The effect is seen with low-frequency stimulation and is observed most clearly when the animal is in the process of performing some learned behavioral response. If a cat has been trained to press a lever for a milk reward, caudate stimulation slows or stops the lever-pressing response but the animal remains behaviorally alert and if milk is made available will drink it during stimulation. The possibility has been raised (Laursen, 1963) that the caudate arrest reaction is secondary to current spread to the internal capsule that lies adjacent to the caudate nucleus (the internal capsule contains fibers coming from and going to the cerebral cortex). However, Buchwald has shown that the effects of caudate and internal capsule stimulation are quite different, although they may both stop a cat from performing a learned lever press for milk. Caudate stimulation, as we have indicated, merely causes the animal to stop responding and produces no gross motor activity. Stimulation of the internal capsule, on the other hand, produces awkward paw movements and tremor (shaking movements) in time with the low-frequency stimulus. In other words, the internal capsule stimulation directly interferes with the ongoing behavior by producing incompatible movements, whereas the caudate stimulus apparently has a much more subtle effect on the initiation of movement.

Several clinical syndromes occur in man following damage to basal ganglia, the best known being Parkinson's disease. This condition is characterized by a resting tremor and some degree of rigidity. It appears to be due to lesions in the basal ganglia and substantia nigra. *Athetoid* movements (slow twisting motions of hand or foot) and *choreiform movements* (quick, jerky motions) are associated with lesions of the caudate and putamen. These conditions are difficult to reproduce in animals, and the reasons why damage to the basal ganglia should produce them in man seem rather obscure (Ruch, 1960). One type of clinical disorder in man that results from damage to the basal ganglia appears to resemble the arrest of movement from electrical stimulation of the caudate nucleus found in animals, noted above. Mettler (1967) has termed this syndrome *motor disregard*. Thus some patients with Parkinsonism show a disinclination to move even though there is no discomfort or weakness associated with movement.

Descending reticular formation

In 1946 Magoun and Rhines reported that both inhibitory and facilitatory effects on reflex contractions of skeletal muscles could be obtained by stimulation of the reticular formation. They inserted stimulation electrodes in the brain stem reticular formation in anesthetized animals and tested the effects of repeated electrical stimulation of the reticular formation on muscle responses evoked by a variety of other means: stretch reflex to muscle tap, flexion reflex to pinch of the foot, responses to electrical stimulation of the motor area of the cerebral cortex. The inhibitory region, in the ventro-medial portion of the medulla, inhibited such responses as the knee jerk and the flexion reflex. The region having facilitatory effects on these responses is positioned more laterally and extended up to the midbrain.

Subsequent work has shown that these two separate areas are not purely excitatory or purely inhibitory. Both effects can be obtained from both areas. Sprague and Chambers (1954), for example, using normal awake animals with chronically implanted recording electrodes, found some intriguing sequences of "integrated" behavior of the whole animal to stimulation of the reticular formation. The entire postural substratum of "going to sleep" was produced in one experiment—the animal circled, curled up, and assumed the prone sleeping position. Their finding of reciprocal control of muscle actions is reasonable, of course, in terms of reciprocal innervation; a stimulus which inhibits an extensor muscle, for example, usually excites a flexor muscle. However, lesion studies indicate that overall inhibitory effects may predominate in the caudal region and facilitatory effects in more rostral areas (Lindsley, Schreiner, and Magoun, 1949; Schreiner, Lindsley, and Magoun, 1949).

The elegant experiments of Granit and his colleagues (see particularly Granit and Kaada, 1952) have shown that some influences on muscle activity of the descending reticular system are mediated primarily by the gamma motoneuron system rather than by direct effects upon the alpha motoneurons. These most important findings help in understanding how motor systems can exert subtle influences on the tendency of an organism to respond. Remember that activation of the gamma motoneurons does not directly cause muscle contractions, at least not of the extrafusal fibers that exert muscle tension. Instead such activation causes contraction of the intrafusal fibers that stimulate the spindle receptors, which in turn activate the sensory fibers that convey information about the state of muscle contraction to the nervous system, particularly to the alpha motoneurons (see Fig. 7.10). Thus the tendency or probability that the alpha motoneurons will respond and hence produce actual muscle contractions can be increased or decreased by activation or inhibition of the gamma motoneurons, without producing any observable movements. In engineering terms, these various motor systems can change the bias or tendency toward a given type of movement by influencing the gamma motoneurons without actually producing the response. We all have experienced occasions upon which we have an increased tendency or readiness to respond, even though we do not actually respond. The most obvious case is in the short period of time between "get ready" and "go" at the start of a race. At a much more subtle level, however, humans continually increase or decrease tendencies to make a host of different responses, many of which are not actually made.

The various extrapyramidal motor systems have connections with the brain stem reticular formation. It is in part through these connections in the inhibitory and facilitatory descending reticular systems that many extrapyramidal pathways exert their effects on motoneurons. Specifically, such functional connections have been shown for the basal ganglia, for extrapyramidal cortical systems, cerebellum, and the vestibular nuclei. In a very real sense, the descending reticular system appears to form a "final common path" for extrapyramidal influences on movement.

Interrelations of motor systems

It is important to emphasize again that all motor effects ultimately converge on the alpha motoneurons of the spinal cord and brain stem which directly control the activity of muscles. Elucidation of the role played by the gamma motoneurons is an extremely important recent development. Many of the extrapyramidal systems exert their effects on alpha motoneurons indirectly through the gamma system (gamma motoneurons, muscle spindles, and returning muscle afferent fibers which synapse on alpha motoneurons). Such indirect routes permit higher regions of the brain to control the tendency to respond without actually producing muscle contraction or relaxation. This increases enormously the possibilities for subtle control of behavioral response probability.

We have been unable to trace motor systems up to the structures or functional systems that initiate and program movement. The motor-sensory cortex may be the highest system yet known—however, neither are movements begun there nor is the programming of sequences of movements handled there. Complex integrated and skilled movements require the motor-sensory cortex but electrical activation of this cortex cannot produce them. Still higher and as yet unknown systems must be involved to explain how movements begin and how the sequences of movements occur that result in integrated behavioral responding. The critical clues to this very puzzling and unsatisfactory state of ignorance may lie in the processes and phenomena that intervene between sensation and responding—a field of study often termed *perception,* which is the subject of the next section.

PERCEPTION AND SENSORY-MOTOR INTEGRATION

A fundamental problem in psychology concerns how we develop our complex integrated perceptions, awareness and experience of the external world. Readers who are familiar with philosophy will recognize this as one of the "great debates" throughout the history of human thought. The basic issue is not at all complicated. Do humans see the world as they do because they have learned to see it through experience, or is perception of the world built into people? These two simple concepts have somewhat dignified names: *empiricism* holds that people learn to perceive through experience, and *nativism* asserts that human perception of the world is native or innate, that is, it is wired into us, presumably into our brains. Both points of view are of ancient origins. Nativism can be traced back at least to Plato and was championed more recently by such philosophers as Descartes and Kant. Empiricism was developed in modern form by the British empiricists, Locke, Hume, and Bishop Berkeley.

Berkeley and Kant may be taken as examples. Bishop Berkeley argued that the newborn human brain was a *tabula rasa,* a blank tablet. Visual perception developed through association of simple visual stimuli like dots, colors, and lines with each other and with other experiences. A particular arrangement of simple stimuli came to be seen and felt as, and called, a chair. Kant, a Germanic "transcendental" philosopher, modified Descartes' earlier and more rigid nativist view that the brain is completely prewired. Kant proposed that the brain had certain innate forms and rules built into its basic organization. Details are not, but notions or "ideas" were. Human behavior was determined by innate "categorical imperatives." He believed our perception of the world was at least in part determined by the nature of the brain, rather than the brain learning to perceive the world as it is. To put the issue still another way, do we learn to see the world as it "really" is or do we instead see what our brains are organized to see?

276

Motor control and sensory-motor integration

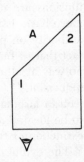

Figure 7.16 The effects of context on apparent size. The room in B is actually distorted; looked at from above, it appears as in A. To monocular vision, the room in B appears to be rectangular and our familiarity with the sizes of the two men is insufficient to overcome our assumption of rectangularity. If the room were actually rectangular, the view would be that shown in C. (Redrawn from Hochberg, J. *Perception*. Englewood Cliffs, NJ: Prentice-Hall, 1964.)

This argument may not seem a very burning issue to the modern reader, but it does make a difference not only to psychology but to all sciences. The only access the sciences have to knowledge is through the sensory perceptions of scientists. If we could not agree on how to read rulers and dials, if our perceptions differed too much, there would be no science. Both nativism and empiricism have been supported eloquently in arguments by their various proponents. This issue cannot be settled by armchair argument, only by experimentation.

Most readers have probably seen examples of visual *illusions*—trick distortions of perception. An impressive example of the deception of perspective is the distended room (Fig. 7.16). A small child looks larger than a grown man. In fact he is merely closer, but the lines of the room disguise the fact. An example familiar to everyone is the motion in motion pictures. There is no actual motion on the screen, but rather a rapid series of still projections. Illusions are interesting and entertaining, and illustrate that things are not always what they seem. The motion picture industry exists only because of the illusion of apparent motion. However, illusions are not crucially important for an understanding of the much more basic issue of how normal perception develops. Indeed, a modern authority on perception and illusions, Julian Hochberg, has stressed the fact that so far as illusions of perception and distance vision go, "there is no way at all of fooling an observer, once we let him determine his own *movements*" (italics mine). In the real world of three-dimensional objects, a large and irresolvable discrepancy between where objects appear to be located and where they are located would have led long ago to the extinction of the human species.

The evolutionary argument cannot be used to support either empiricism or nativism. We could have evolved to learn to see the world as it is or evolved brain structures that provide an adaptive relationship between our wired-in perceptions and the real world. The psychophysical relation between the intensity of stimuli and our experience of intensity discussed in Chapter 6 is an example of the latter. Experienced intensity increases much more slowly than physical intensity for most types of stimuli. They are related by the power law, apparently a very adaptive relationship. It makes very good sense. We can experience a much wider range of stimulus intensities, from very weak to very strong, because our sensory systems condense the range of intensities into a much narrower range of experienced intensities.

Studies on simpler organisms indicate that much of perception or sensory-motor integration may be inborn. *Fixed action patterns*, the rigidly stereotyped sequence of responses to specific releaser stimuli, are clearly genetic and predetermined. A well known example is prey retrieval by the digger wasp. When the prey insect has been paralyzed by stinging, the wasp deposits it near the nest which is a chamber in the ground covered by a trap door. The wasp then opens the trap door and drags the prey in. If the prey is moved away from the nest while the wasp is opening the trap door, the wasp will retrieve the prey to the original location, go to the trap door, and go through the motions of opening it and go back for the prey. If the prey is again moved away, the sequence is repeated and will continue indefinitely if the prey is moved away each time. The sequence of behavioral events is rigidly predetermined and released to run through its course by appropriate stimuli (i.e., prey) much like the unreeling of a tape recording.

In birds, many aspects of behavior are of this sort although the appropriate conditions seem more complex, involving such things as hormonal levels, period in the breeding cycle, amount of daylight, and so on. A particularly clear example of inborn perception in birds is the food pecking of newborn chicks (Fantz, 1957). As soon as the chicks hatched they were shown a number of small objects of different shapes, each enclosed in a clear plastic casing to prevent odor cues. The chicks pecked much more often at small spheres, the objects most closely resembling the chicks' normal food, than they did at pyramids or other shapes of similar

Motor control and
sensory-motor
integration

size. In fact newborn chicks with no previous visual experience have an innate ability to perceive shape, three-dimensionality, and size. They select those objects most likely to be edible: round, three-dimensional shapes the size of grain or seeds.

To what extent can this innate tendency or abstract capacity of newly hatched chicks to peck at grain-like objects be modified by early experience? Hess (1956) fitted prisms to one-day-old chicks that had spent their first day in darkness with no visual stimuli. The prism displaced the apparent location of objects 7 degrees to the side. The prism chicks never learned to compensate; they continued to peck 7 degrees off target. As we will see below, man and monkey can learn very rapidly to compensate for such visual distortions. Zoologists have coined the term *precocial* for birds like chickens that are independent and self-supporting immediately after hatching. Non-precocial birds like robins require varying periods of parental care and feeding after hatching. Hailman (1969) studied the development of the pecking response in Laughing Gull chicks; they are partially precocial but require a period of days to become independent of the parent and are born with a tendency to peck at the red-dotted bill of the parent—the "begging" response. Tinbergen, one of the pioneers of ethology (see Chapter 1), argued that these gull chicks were born with an innate perception of their parent—the parent was the releasing stimulus. Hailman showed that the innate releasing stimulus was, in fact, the red patch on the parent's bill. From the initial innate response to this stimulus, the chicks gradually learned to identify the parent. Even in rigid fixed action patterns of precocial birds, there is some learning of "innate" responses.

Of greater significance is the extent to which the perceptions of higher organisms, particularly primates and man, may be inborn. Pioneering work by Austin Riesen (1950), now at the University of California at Riverside, demonstrated that if infant monkeys are raised for even a few weeks in the dark, they subsequently have considerable difficulties with visual perception. In particular, they have trouble learning form discriminations, e.g., difference between a triangle and a square. The difficulty does not arise simply because of being in the dark, which might result in permanent damage to the light-sensitive chemicals in the rods and cones of the eye. The same loss of pattern vision occurs if the animals are raised with translucent screens (e.g., ping-pong ball halves) over their eyes so they receive diffuse light but not patterned stimuli. The degree of loss of pattern vision depends upon the length of time the monkey is kept in the dark (Fantz, 1961). If dark-reared for 11 weeks or longer, infant monkeys bump into objects, fall off tables, and generally act blind. Such monkeys require many weeks in the normal visual environment to learn to see again. However, if the animals are dark-reared for much shorter periods, they seem to recover even pattern vision rather quickly. Although these results seem to favor the idea that perception is learned, the interpretation is not that clear. If all that is required is experience with pattern vision, the same period of visual experience should be required regardless of the length of time in the dark; this is not the case. If, on the other hand, pattern vision developed independently of visual experience, then dark-rearing should have no effect; this also is not true. We will reconsider this issue below.

There are fascinating accounts of persons who have been born blind (with congenital cataracts), grown to adulthood without visual experience, and then had their sight restored by surgery (see Hebb, 1949). Such a patient finds visual experience a bewildering confusion of stimuli. He can immediately recognize and distinguish figures and ground—an object is seen as distinct from the background. However, he cannot distinguish a triangle from a square without *touching it* and requires several weeks of training to correctly name such simple objects as squares, triangles, and circles when presented visually. Interestingly, colors easily can be distinguished from one another the day the bandages are removed but training is required to name the colors correctly. Color and figure-ground might seem to be the only wired-in components of visual perception.

All these findings seem to be consistent with the idea that humans learn to perceive the world. However, studies by Hubel and Wiesel suggested a quite different interpretation. They determined the characteristics of single neurons in the visual cortex of the newborn animal and found the same types of edge and line coding cells present at birth as in the adult animal (Chapter 6). Further, they found that if an animal is raised for a period with one eye covered, cells in the cortex that were thus deprived of normal visual experience lost the ability to code complex forms. Interestingly, the deficit is worse after one eye is covered than with both eyes covered, that is, total darkness (Wiesel and Hubel, 1965; Ganz et al., 1968). It seems that discordant input is worse than no input. It appears that some aspects of form perception may be present in the brain at birth, but if the system is not normally activated by form stimuli during growth and development after birth, form coding is impaired. These findings do not imply that there is no perceptual learning after birth, but they do demonstrate that significant aspects of perception may be built into the brain at birth.

The entire issue of the role of experience in the development of visual perception has been opened wide again in some recent and dramatic studies. Hirsch and Spinelli (1970, 1971) employed a novel technique to rear kittens under conditions of controlled visual experience. The kittens were raised from birth with one eye exposed only to three vertical lines and the other eye viewing only three horizontal lines. The stimuli were presented in a mask which the kittens wore for eight hours every day in a lighted environment until they were 12 weeks old. During the remaining 16 hours of each day the animals were kept in a totally dark room. Thus, the only visual experience the animals received was that provided by the

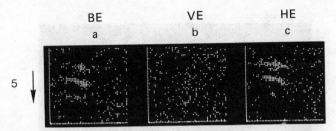

BE   VE   HE
a   b   c

5

Figure 7.17 Cortical unit with a horizontally oriented, elongated receptive field. In column BE the unit was mapped with both eyes open; in column VE the unit was mapped with the eye exposed to vertical lines and in column HE the unit was mapped with the eye exposed to horizontal lines. Note that the receptive field is activated by one eye only—the eye exposed to the three horizontal lines. Thus, both the orientation of and the number of lines comprising the receptive field are the same as the orientation and the number of lines to which the dominant eye was exposed during the rearing period. (From Hirsch, H. V. B., and Spinelli, D. N. Modification of the distribution of receptive field orientation in cats by selective visual exposure during development. *Exp. Brain Res.* **13**, 1971, pp. 509–527.)

Perception and
sensory-motor
integration

stimuli in the mask. At the conclusion of the rearing period visual receptive fields of single neurons in visual cortex were plotted using a special scanning technique developed by Spinelli (1967). The response of the cell to each position of a small black target moving across a large screen was recorded and analyzed. All locations in the visual field where the neuron's total activity exceeded a predetermined value were plotted by the computer, revealing receptive fields like those shown in Figure 7.17.

The receptive fields recorded from cells in the visual cortex of these kittens were oriented either horizontally or vertically, which is in sharp contrast to the full complement of receptive field orientations (i.e., in all directions) found in normal cats. Other units had diffuse, unresponsive receptive fields. Moreover, units with vertically oriented fields were activated only by the eye which had been exposed to vertical lines while cells with horizontally oriented fields could be activated only by the eye which had viewed the horizontal lines (Fig. 7.17). Normally, 80 to 90 per cent of the neurons in the visual cortex of the cat can be activated by both eyes. Six cats from the above group were revived and allowed normal binocular viewing. Following exposure to a normal environment for up to 19 months it was found that, indeed, there was an enormous increase in the percentage of those classes of receptive fields that were either absent or very weak following the selective visual experience (Spinelli, Hirsch, Phelps, and Metzler, 1972). Moreover, these receptive fields that were acquired during binocular viewing could generally be binocularly activated. However, those units whose response characteristics were found to mimic the stimuli viewed during development were almost completely unaffected by normal binocular experience; that is, they could

BE   VE   HE

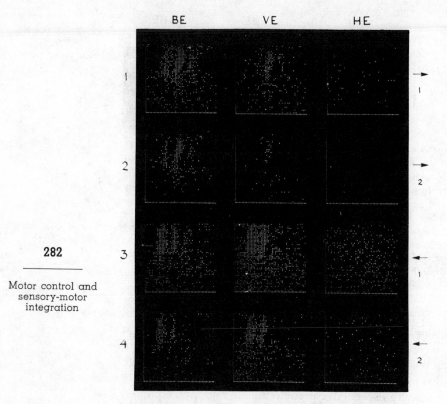

Motor control and
sensory-motor
integration

Figure 7.18. Cortical units with receptive fields that strongly mimic the three bars viewed during development. Conventions are as given in Figure 7.17. Note the presence of three parallel vertical bars, activated only by the eye which was exposed to the three vertical bars during the rearing period. (From Spinelli, D. N. et al. Visual experience as a determinant of the response characteristics of cortical receptive fields in cats. *Exp. Brain Res.* **15**, 1972, pp. 289–304.)

only be activated monocularly and had the orientation appropriate for the stimuli viewed by the eye from which they could be mapped. Most impressive are a few units whose receptive field shape is almost a carbon copy of the pattern viewed during development (Fig. 7.18). The results of these experiments provide evidence that visual experience may have a pronounced and lasting effect on the functional connectivity of cells in the visual cortex. Blakemore and Cooper (1970) found similar results using rather different techniques—binocular viewing by kittens of revolving drums containing either horizontal or vertical stripes.

It thus appears that visual field properties of neurons in visual cortex are to some degree prewired in the brain and to some degree modified and formed by critical early experience of the visual world. Studies noted above in which infant monkeys were kept in the dark for varying periods

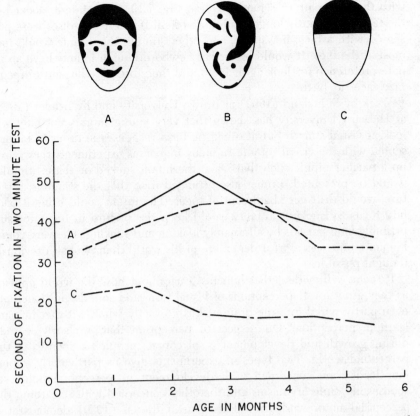

Figure 7.19 Amount of time human infants spent looking at a drawing of a normal face (A), a scrambled face (B), and an oval drawing (C). The infants' eye fixations were measured in two-minute test periods at various ages from two weeks to about six months. (Adapted from Fantz, R. L. The origin of form perception. Copyright © 1961 by Scientific American, Inc. All rights reserved.)

can be interpreted in two ways. Thus the longer the animal is kept in the dark, the more the pattern-vision networks in the brain could deteriorate. Consequently, if animals are dark-reared beyond some critical period, it will require a great deal of time and training to re-establish these complex pattern-vision networks. Similar considerations apply to the human patients whose sight was restored as adults. Indeed in many instances their visual performance never reached normal levels. Alternatively, it may be that the results are at least in part due to inability to form correct visual fields because of a lack of critical experience. Some combination of these factors is likely to be closest to the truth.

The work of Fantz on the perceptions of very young human infants provides some evidence for prewiring in man. Fantz and his associates simply measured the period of time a very young infant, e.g., four days after birth, would look at a face-like object vs. the same sized object with the face pattern scrambled (see Fig. 7.19). The infants looked at the face significantly longer and more often! If a series of discs were presented with a face, newsprint, and other stimuli, the infants would look most at the face. It would seem that newborn human infants have an innate preference for looking at faces and therefore may be said to recognize faces at birth.

Work by Siqueland (1968) at Brown University and by Bruner (1968) at Harvard University has shown that very young infants not only will look at visual stimuli but also will perform responses in order to be presented with the visual stimuli. In many ingenious experiments they wired up a pacifier nipple such that when the infant sucked on it the stimulus would be presented. Bruner also arranged it so that the stimulus, a picture, would drift very badly out of focus. The infant could bring it back into focus by sucking. Infants would keep the picture in focus for surprisingly long periods by alternately looking and sucking. The very young human infant sees a great deal more of his world than we had previously thought possible.

It seems self-evident that humans learn about how the world appears as they grow up. If perceptions of visual form and sounds and touch are even partly wired into the brain at birth, exactly what is it that humans learn in perception? One aspect of perception that is clearly learned during growth and development is, of course, people's responses to the perceptual world. Two types of experiments give us particularly important leads, one concerned with development of perceptual-motor responses in young organisms and the other concerned with relearning the perceptual-motor world by adults. Austin Riesen (1950) demonstrated that if kittens are raised in a normal visual world but restrained from walking, they are subsequently very poor at visual discriminations. There are at least two possible explanations for this—either they received substantially less visual stimulation because they did not move about or the normal movements of the growing kitten are somehow essential for the normal development of visual perception. To put it another way, the learning is either predominantly sensory or predominantly motor.

Held and Hein, at Massachusetts Institute of Technology, performed a series of experiments indicating that the perceptual learning appears to be predominantly motor. The experiment is illustrated in Figure 7.20. Two litter-mate kittens were given identical visual experience with the striped pattern on the wall. The active kitten could move about normally. As he moved, the passive kitten, restrained in a gondola chair, was moved about in exactly the same way. Both kittens could move their heads freely. Ten pairs of kittens were run in the experiment. All were raised in the dark until ten weeks of age and then given three hours each day in the lighted training apparatus. When not in the apparatus they were kept with their mother and litter mates in the dark. Thus the passive kittens could move about normally except when they were given visual stimula-

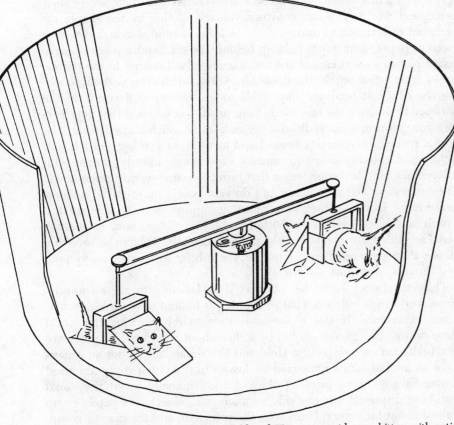

Figure 7.20 Arrangement used by Held and Hein to provide one kitten with active perception and the other with passive perception.

tion. The results were striking. After ten days' experience in the apparatus, the active kittens displayed normal visual behavior in a lighted test environment but the passive kittens behaved as though they were blind! Several days of normal experience in a lighted environment were necessary before the passive kittens obtained normal visual-guided behavior. Interpretation of this experiment should emphasize that the "passive" kittens were not simply passive, they suffered rather severe restraint and the attendant frustration from being unable to move. However, the experiment does suggest that perceptual learning is much more on the motor or response side of the organism than on the sensory or stimulus side. This, of course, is consistent with our earlier suggestion that the sensory-perceptual aspects of our experiential world may to some degree be prewired in the brain. What must be learned is to respond appropriately to a partly preformed world.

It appears that adult humans can learn very well to "reorganize" their perceptual world. You can convince yourself of this by the simple experiment of learning to mirror-draw. A large double star is drawn on a piece of paper, a mirror is held up behind the star, and a piece of cardboard placed so you cannot see the star directly. Looking in the mirror, try to draw a line within the double lines around the star without touching the edges. It is almost impossible to do. However, if you have the patience to practice the task for an hour or so, you will find that your performance improves markedly and the task seems much more natural. The mirror reverses movements toward and away from you but not left and right. Similar, but much more extreme, experiments have been done with subjects wearing inverting lenses that turn the visual world upside down. The subjects at first are clumsy and do very poorly on even the simplest motor tasks. However, they show amazing improvement. By the end of a month, a subject has been reported to bicycle, fence, and, in general, perform skilled visual-motor tasks almost normally. When the inverting glasses then are permanently removed, the subject again shows very poor performance and must relearn.

This experiment might be interpreted as learning to see an upside-down world right-side up. That is, learning is limited to reorganization of visual experience. If this is the case, then merely viewing the world through inverting glasses should be sufficient—it would not be necessary to actually perform responses. Held and Freedman carried out an experiment on human adults somewhat analogous to the kitten study discussed above. Subjects wore prisms (which did not actually invert the visual world but displaced it to one side, an analogous effect). The active group walked about for several hours with the prisms on and the passive group, also wearing prisms, were wheeled over the same route in wheel chairs. The subjects then were tested on a simple visual-motor task involving accurate localization of a visual target. The results were striking; as indicated in Figure 7.21, the active group showed progressive and marked improvement on the task but the passive group showed no improvement, even though both groups had the same visual experience of distortion.

We noted above that newly hatched chicks cannot achieve visual reorganization. Adult frogs are similarly "nonplastic." Roger Sperry (1956), at the California Institute of Technology, showed that if the eyes of a frog are rotated 180° (so that what looks up is down, and what looks down is up), the frog cannot learn to respond correctly. As shown in Figure 7.22, the frog strikes down with his tongue at a fly that is up, even after hundreds of trials and even if there is a bed of pins that damages the tongue when it strikes down. Plasticity of sensory-motor integration is limited to higher animals.

The consistent theme in studies of perceptual development and perceptual reorganization in higher animals is: *movement is crucial.* In order to develop normal perceptions of the world humans must respond to the

Figure 7.21 The same idea as in Figure 7.20. A human wearing prism goggles either moves freely or is moved about to gain active or passive experience.

world as infants. To learn to compensate for the distortions introduced by prisms, humans must behave actively. Perception is sensory-motor integration—the development of appropriate responses to sensory input. As Held has emphasized, sensory experience, per se, is not enough. Feedback about the world around us must be obtained by responding in and to that world. Feedback comparison of what humans see, feel, and do is the only way they can achieve accurate perception and integrated behavioral responding. Indeed, the study of Held and Freedman essentially predicted the problems encountered by the astronauts when they first lived in zero gravity. Normal feedback relations were altered suddenly and they had to learn new sensory-motor integrations.

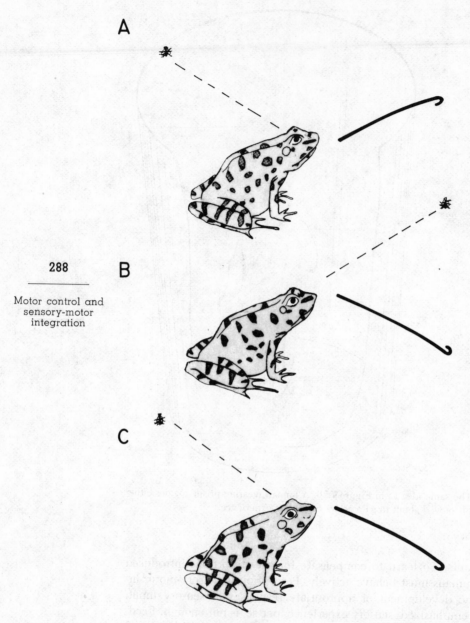

B

C

Figure 7.22 Frog with eyeballs rotated strikes down when fly is up.

Human experience of the world is due both to the prewired organization of their sensory systems and to their learned behavior. Neurons in
the motor-sensory area of the cerebral cortex, an area of the brain very
much on the behavioral response output side, receive detailed sensory
information, even about visual stimuli. Movement is necessary for normal

perceptual development. However, the perception of the world that normally develops seems to follow the architecture laid down in the brain. On balance, the truth seems to be somewhat closer to nativism than empiricism. The author is inclined to agree with Robert McCleary's summary of the issue:

Across a variety of disciplines, there are still several lifetimes of work for those interested in the question of how the innate microstructure of the visual system is adaptively modified through experience to produce the perceptually sophisticated adult. It now seems that genetically determined neural networks are responsible for much more visual capacity than once was thought possible, even though we are not at all clear on how they finally manage to do their job. At the same time, visual experience has certain specifiable responsibilities. It sharpens the tuning of innately provided pattern preferences and helps to maintain the functional integrity of pattern-sensitive neural circuits. It is very clear, moreover, that normal visual experience helps promote the proper development of spatially accurate visuomotor abilities. We now know, as well, that the ability to respond simultaneously to several complex visual variables also improves with age. So who was right, Descartes or Berkeley? My own preference is for Kant.

(Robert McCleary, 1970, page 141)

Summary

A great variety of sensory information continually directs our movements. Much of this sensory information is the result of movement and is fed back to the brain from sensory receptors. Biofeedback, or the sensory control of movement, plays a critical role in all movements. There appear to be higher order biofeedback systems within the brain which also help to guide movements. Sensory-motor integration occurs at all levels from the spinal cord to the motor-sensory cortex. The smooth and continuous behavior characteristic of higher animals results from this interplay of muscle actions and sensory biofeedback.

Most muscle responses are controlled by motoneurons of the spinal cord and cranial nerve nuclei. All motor systems ultimately act on these motoneurons. Direct synaptic action on the motoneurons is either excitatory or inhibitory in nature. The net balance of excitation and inhibition which exists on the motoneurons of the spinal cord and brain stem completely determines the nature and extent of behavioral responding at any given moment.

There are seven principal motor regions which are highly integrated. The basic system is that of the spinal reflex pathways. The vestibular nuclei and an old part of the cerebellum function to maintain balance.

Postural adjustments in relation to auditory and visual stimuli are mediated by a pathway from the midbrain tectum. Various regions of the descending reticular formation exert excitatory and inhibitory influences upon motoneurons controlling muscles related to postural adjustments. The cerebellum maintains descending influences on the brain stem motor systems and also acts on the motor area of the cerebral cortex. The extrapyramidal motor system is associated with generalized arrest of movement, and with the smoothness and continuity of limb movements. The pyramidal tract is the major descending pathway from the motor-sensory regions of the cerebral cortex.

Of the three general types of muscle tissue, smooth and cardiac muscle are controlled by the autonomic portion of the nervous system. Striated muscle, which consists of extrafusal and intrafusal fibers, is controlled by the somatic portion of the nervous system.

There are two common types of limb muscle connections. When an extensor muscle contracts, there is an extension of the limb. When a flexor muscle contracts, there is a contraction of the limb. The reciprocal control of muscle actions is strongly evident as each muscle or set of muscles which acts in one manner is balanced by another set which acts in the opposite manner.

Muscle fatigue is a neuronal phenomenon. Muscle fibers actually do not fatigue under conditions of normal health and use.

The motor unit is the basic unit of action of the neuromuscular system. Humans can easily learn to exert conscious control over the activity of single motor units.

There are two basic aspects of the sensory control of reflex activity. First, the spindle organs and tendons transmit relatively complete information on the state of muscles to the CNS. Secondly, gamma motoneurons exert motor control on the sensory receptors in muscles. They modify the degree of activity of certain sensory receptors in spindle organs of the muscles.

There are two types of individual muscle bundles. Regular muscle bundles, composed of extrafusal fibers, are innervated by alpha motoneurons. Spindle organs, which are contained in intrafusal fibers, are connected in parallel to regular muscle bundles or to tendons. The intrafusal fibers influence the activity of the spindle organ receptors. Golgi tendon organs, the other type of muscle receptors, are in series with muscle bundles. These receptors have a high discharge threshold and are not activated if a moderate resting tension is present in a muscle. Golgi fibers signal changes in muscle tension, and spindle organs signal the degree, direction, and rate of change.

Motor-sensory cortex appears to control complex integrated movements. In many respects, primary motor cortex is a mirror image of somatic-sensory-motor cortex. Primary motor-sensory cortex controls muscles on the contralateral side of the body. Muscles as well as movements may be represented in motor-sensory cortex. It also appears that motor-sensory cortex superimposes organization upon the control of movements.

Basically, very little is known about the nature and organization of the higher order central control systems which act upon motor-sensory cortex. Many neurons in motor-sensory cortex have detailed somatic-sensory receptive fields so that the projection of sensory information to motor-sensory cortex offers many opportunities for sensory-motor integration in the control of behavior. Besides somatic information, other sensory modalities also project to motor-sensory cortex.

The two major descending systems from the cerebral cortex which mediate cortical control over movement are the pyramidal tract and the cortical extrapyramidal system. The pyramidal tract is composed of fibers which pass through the pyramids. Most of these fiber tracts cross at the decussation of the pyramids. A complex feedback organization exists between the pyramidal tract and the cerebral cortex. Many pyramidal tract fibers project to various brain regions as the tract descends from the cerebral cortex to the spinal cord. These fibers serve as feedback loops which provide information to lower brain regions about the actions of the pyramidal tract. The lower brain regions also influence motor-sensory cortex and the pyramidal tract.

The pyramidal tract is found only in mammals and is most fully elaborated in primates. In primates, there is a substantial proportion of direct monosynaptic connections of pyramidal tract fibers to spinal motoneurons. PT neurons (cells of origin of pyramidal tract fibers), such as flexor- and extensor-type PT cells, appear to function in the performance of highly skilled movements. While the pyramidal tract appears to play a critical role in the performance of skilled movements, the possible role motor-sensory cortex plays in learning or retention of particular sequences of movements is unknown.

The general functions of the cerebellum are motor in nature. The input to the cerebellum consists of a variety of sensory information. On the surface of the cerebellum there is a detailed somatotopic organization of somatic-sensory projection. Detailed information about the state of contraction of muscles is provided to the cerebellum via input from spindle organs and other muscle receptors. There are also detailed reciprocal interconnections between the cerebellum and sensory-motor areas of the cerebral cortex.

The Purkinje cells are important structures in the functioning of the cerebellum. They act in an inhibitory manner and are the only output of the cerebellar cortex. Most Purkinje cells terminate on cells of subcortical cerebellar nuclei which exhibit high levels of activity. Therefore, the inhibitory actions of Purkinje cell axons on these nuclei serve to modulate their temporal patterns of activity. The cerebellar cortex exerts its influence by constantly modulating the ongoing activity of subcortical cells which act on the motor systems of the brain.

The basal ganglia are composed of the caudate nucleus, putamen, and globus pallidus. Their functions are related to movement control, but more specific knowledge about their functioning is unknown. Parkinson's disease usually results from damage to the basal ganglia and is manifested by progressive deterioration of movement control.

The descending reticular formation is another control system related to movement. In general, it appears that inhibitory effects predominate in the caudal region and facilitatory effects in more rostral areas of the descending reticular formation. Some influences of the descending reticular system in muscle activity are mediated primarily by the alpha motoneuron system. The extrapyramidal motor systems connect with the brain stem reticular formation.

All these systems related to motor control are tightly interrelated. All motor effects ultimately converge on the alpha motoneurons of the spinal cord and brain stem where muscular activity is directly controlled. The extrapyramidal motor system affects alpha motoneurons indirectly, at least in part, through the gamma system. These indirect effects allow higher brain regions to control the tendency to respond without actually producing muscular contraction or relaxation.

Nativism and empiricism are two views of how our perceptions and experiences of the world develop. It appears that some aspects of form perception may be present in the brain at birth, but if the system is not activated normally by form stimuli during growth and development, form coding is greatly impaired. Studies examining perceptual development have demonstrated that significant aspects of perception may be "wired" into the brain at birth. Even very complex perception may be wired into the brain. Obviously, human responses to the perceptual world are learned phenomena. Perceptual learning seems to be closely related to motor aspects. In order to develop normal perceptions of the world, movement and active responding are essential. Perception can be considered as sensory-motor integration or the development of appropriate responding to sensory input. Human experience of the world is a result both of prewired organization of sensory systems and of learned behaviors.

8

Motivation

8

The ubiquity of the concept of motivation, in one guise or another, is
... surprising when we consider that its meaning is often scandalously
vague ... It will be sufficient to note that, depending upon the particular writer consulted, motivation can be conscious or unconscious; it
can be the same as, or different from, drive; it may or may not
guide behavior; and all motives can be either learned or instinctive.
Moreover, arguments can be found to support the view that motivation
is both crucial to behavior and a useless concept, that it is simply the
energy that moves the body, or that it is identical with the neural discharges of specific central nervous-system structures. We thus find
ourselves in the position of trying to deal with an allegedly vital factor
in the face of violent disagreements as to its origins, its essential nature,
and its particular roles as a behavior determinant.

(Judson Brown, 1961, page 24)

Like so many concepts in psychology, for example, intelligence, personality, cognition, the terms *emotion* and *motivation* refer not so much to processes as to problems. The use of these terms reflects our preliminary attempts to group together behaviors which, while diverse in many respects, appear to share certain striking characteristics. The behaviors that we call "motivated" are frequently described as "goal-directed" and "purposive." They do not seem to happen either at random or in an automatic, reflexive fashion but appear to be guided by their consequences, related to some goal, and carried out in such a manner as to satisfy the present or future needs of the individual or the species.

Perhaps the central problem of motivation is the fact of variations in responsiveness to stimuli. Food may be continuously available to an animal but it does not always respond to food by eating. Males and females may be within easy reach of each other but they do not behave sexually continuously. A rat placed in a maze may amble through a few alleys and then settle down in a corner to rest. The same rat placed in the same maze may, under other circumstances, run rapidly through the maze without entering a single blind alley. A group of children seated in a classroom are exposed to the same stimuli, but some of the children are alert and responsive, while others remain, in the teacher's phrase, "unmotivated." A passer-by witnessing a mugging in progress may turn completely away in fear, may call for help, or may attack the criminal. All these examples indicate that the same set of stimulus factors may elicit very different types of behaviors in the same individual.

Motivation has been a central problem for psychology precisely because "motivational" phenomena testify to a limitation of the stimulus control of behavior. In the case of reflexes, given the proper stimulus, the response is highly predictable, and an S-R (stimulus-response) paradigm is applicable. In the case of hunger, sex, emotion, reinforcement, etc., the paradigm S-O-R (stimulus-*organism*-response) seems more appropriate. The response to a given external stimulus depends not only upon that stimulus but upon the internal state of the organism.

Because such internal states are not always easily accessible to experimental analysis, psychologists have postulated a variety of hypothetical processes (needs, drives, motives) to explain the initiation, maintenance and termination of specific behaviors. The statement that food depriva-

Written in collaboration with Dr. Timothy J. Teyler, Department of Psychology and Social Relations, Harvard University and Dr. H. Philip Zeigler, Department of Animal Behavior, The American Museum of Natural History.

tion produces a "need" for food which in turn leads to a strong hunger "drive" that results in eating seems clear enough. However, descriptions of complex human behavior in these terms are not so clear. What underlying need produces the behavior which characterizes the life-of-the-party type, the president of a corporation, the drug addict, the saint, or the criminal? Little is known about the biology of complex human motives, although we have considerable information on the sources of the simpler and more "biological" types of behavior such as eating, drinking, and sexual behavior.

In relatively simple motivating situations, the strength of drive can be inferred in two ways—by depriving the organism of something needed like food or water, and by measuring the amount and kind of behaviors the animal will produce to obtain the needed substance. These approaches work relatively well where simple needs like hunger and thirst can be manipulated. However, more complex "needs" are not so easily handled. Even as elementary a "drive" as sex is difficult to infer from the amount of deprivation. Strength of sexual drive depends on such factors as cyclic blood levels of hormones, species-specific behavior patterns, learned stimuli, and other circumstances. Actually, even hunger is not a simple function of deprivation. Persons who have fasted for long periods report that all hunger or desire for food ceases after a few days without food.

A simple and natural distinction is made between basic tissue needs, often termed *primary needs,* and derived or other sources of need. Every living cell in the body of a mammal must be maintained within a particular temperature range and must maintain a particular chemical environment. Every cell must obtain oxygen, water, energy, and certain basic chemical substances and must eliminate carbon dioxide and other waste chemicals. Consequently, all mammals must somehow regulate their chemical environment (e.g., in terms of acid-base balance), breathe, maintain a constant body temperature, drink water, and eat. Under normal circumstances, the "needs" to maintain chemical balance and breathe have little obvious influence on the behavior of higher animals and humans. In fact, even the needs for warmth, food, and water have little impact on the behavior of most people, at least in our relatively wealthy civilization. However, in the natural state, much of the behavior of higher animals is devoted to obtaining food and water.

Derived needs can have an enormous influence on behavior. This is particularly evident in the case of human social behavior. Actually *derived,* although widely used, is not a good term. It implies that more complex needs somehow develop from primary needs like hunger and thirst. There is no compelling evidence that any complex human motives are derived from primary needs. Further, quite "unnatural" needs may become primary. Addiction provides a good example. The heroin addict seems to develop a primary tissue need for heroin, as evidenced by the severe physiological withdrawal symptoms. This abnormal tissue need in no way develops from normal primary tissue needs. It may be, incidentally, that genuinely successful treatment of addiction will come only when we understand the brain mechanisms that underlie need and motivation.

Another concept important for an understanding of motivation is reward or reinforcement. The generally accepted operational definition of reinforcement in psychology relates to the probability of response. A positive reinforcement or reward increases the probability of response if it is associated with the response. A negative reinforcement or punishment decreases the likelihood of an associated response. The more subjective aspect of reward is also emphasized by many psychologists—a reward is something the organism likes. This latter definition is circular by itself and ultimately must relate to behavioral response probability, but is a current and sometimes important usage. Animals with lesions in a region of the hypothalamus (ventromedial area) will eat voraciously and become extremely obese if, and only if, they are given certain preferred foods they particularly like.

The general concept of drive is often abused, or at least misused. To say simply that a person "eats because he has a hunger drive" is of course circular. How do you know he has a hunger drive? Because he eats. External or independent definitions of motivated state or drive must be used (Brown, 1961).

PHYSIOLOGICAL PSYCHOLOGY AND THE CONCEPT OF MOTIVATION

The study of behavior has been complicated by endless arguments over the meaning of such terms as motivation and drive. The reader is referred to treatments of the topic by writers such as Bolles (1968), Brown (1961), and Hinde (1970). Motivation, a very broad term, generally refers to the causes of behavior. Actually, a complete analysis of all the "motivating" factors that enter into a single bit of behavior, particularly complex human behavior, would use almost the entire field of psychology since it would involve complete analysis of all biological, experiential, and behavioral factors that underlie the behavior. In physiological psychology the term motivation is generally used in a more restricted sense to refer to the causes of particular forms of behavior such as temperature regulation, eating, drinking, sexual behavior, self-reinforcement and emotional behavior. The term *drive*, on the other hand, is not a chapter heading but a theoretical construct. Drive is used in an explanatory sense to account for the variations in responsiveness characteristic of such *motivated* behaviors. As such, the term is useful, particularly in the early stages of experimental analysis of mechanisms underlying specific types of behavior. However, as techniques for the measurement or manipulation of physiological factors come into wider use, the term *drive* may gradually lose some of its utility. As one critic of the drive concept put it,

However willing the drive theorist may be to rally physiological data to his aid, his looking inside the nervous system for drives, defined in terms of behaviour, is a logical mistake; and discussion about where drives originate is based on a misconception. Although the drive theorist will not find any drives inside the organism, he will find physiological correlates. He may find, for instance, that changes in the frequency of copulation per day are correlated with androgen levels, and hope to find that minute-to-minute fluctuations in sexual behaviour are correlated with other physiological changes. But as the analysis proceeds he will inevitably find that he is not talking about drives any more: the drive, so useful at an earlier stage, has just ceased to be relevant.

(Hinde, 1970, pages 201–202)

Dethier's elegant analysis of feeding behavior in the fly illustrates the way in which a drive concept can appear to become superfluous as an analysis of physiological mechanisms underlying a given behavior is successfully carried out. The feeding behavior of this simple organism is initiated when taste receptors on the fly's tarsi (feet) encounter sweet substances. These chemosensory stimuli elicit extension of the fly's proboscis and feeding on the substance which then enters the gut region. Nerve impulses, responding to stimuli in the gut, become increasingly frequent as the gut is filled, thereby inhibiting proboscis extension and gradually turning off feeding. If the nerves from the gut are cut, this inhibition is removed and the fly continues to feed until it bursts. Dethier concludes:

Hunger can be equated with absence of stimulating fluid in the foregut, i.e., absence of inhibitory impulses carried by the recurrent nerve. At the moment there is no conclusive evidence of hunger "drive" in the sense of positive input from external or internal receptors or from endogenous centers within the central nervous system.

(Dethier, V. G., Bodenstein, D. (1958), Hunger in the blowfly,
Z. Tierpsychol. 15, pages 129–140)

In addition to its implications for the utility of the drive concept, Dethier's work illustrates some characteristics of motivational mechanisms that may have implications for the analysis of behavior in more complex organisms. First, note that the initiation of proboscis extension is a joint function of two factors, (1) the sweetness of the substance encountered by the tarsi, and (2) the amount of food present in the fly's gut. Second, feeding behavior, although correlated with the metabolic needs of the animal is not controlled directly by these needs. Thus if a starved fly is fed a certain very sweet but totally nonnutritive sugar, it will refuse sugars which are less sweet and actually starve to death in their presence. That is, the major determinant of what substance the fly eats is the amount of sensory stimulation it provides and not its nutritive value for the fly. In nature these two characteristics are almost always perfectly correlated, so that a mechanism based on sweetness will result in adaptive behavior even though the fly does not respond to any internal need when it starts to feed.

As we shall see, similar considerations may govern certain aspects of feeding behavior even in higher organisms. However, the greatest value of work such as Dethier's is that it illustrates for the student that the appearance of "purposiveness" characteristic of "motivated" behaviors need not involve purpose or foresight on the part of an organism, but may emerge from the interaction of internal and external factors which are amenable to physiological and behavioral analysis.

A note of caution must be added at this point. The approach illustrated by Dethier's analysis of motivated behavior in a simple animal is the hope of physiological psychologists and behavioral biologists but not yet a reality, particularly for more complicated animals. Indeed, as psychologists who favor the concept of drive are quick to point out, Dethier's analysis fails in one important respect: a hungry fly is much more active than a full fly. This activity actually can be used as an independent measure of drive. Dethier's analysis provides no explanation for this aspect of the fly's behavior. We may assume that relatively simple chemical and neural factors can account for the increased activity with hunger, but this is an assumption and not a demonstrated fact. It can be argued that even when we do understand the physiological mechanisms, a concept like drive still will be useful to describe the interrelationships between activity level and feeding behavior.

In this chapter we will try to illustrate the application of physiological and behavioral analyses to the study of the mechanisms that underlie temperature regulation, eating, drinking and self-reinforcement. The next chapter will deal with the analysis of sexual and emotional behaviors.

Brain mechanisms and motivation: the hypothalamus

While all behaviors involve the interaction of many regions of the brain, one region—the hypothalamus—has long been known to be of critical importance in the control of eating, drinking, sexual and emotional behaviors.

A brief summary of the anatomy of the hypothalamus and related limbic pathways is therefore necessary. The general location of the hypothalamus in the primate brain is indicated in Figure 8.1. Although small, it contains a number of different cellular groupings or nuclei in a rather complex array. The hypothalamus occupies a position of transition between midbrain and diencephalon (thalamic region) and is physically at the base of the cerebrum, lying above the crossing (chiasm) of the optic tracts. It is physically adjacent to the pituitary gland, the master control gland of the endocrine system (Fig. 8.1). The hypothalamic-

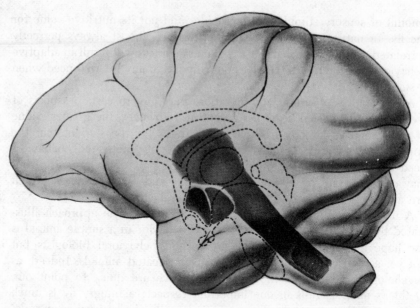

Figure 8.1 Schematic of the monkey's brain showing the general location of the hypothalamus in relation to the reticular formation. Both lie in the depths of the brain. The anterior and posterior portions of the hypothalamus are shown as two separate pie-shaped wedges (hatched) lying just below the rostral portion of the tube-shaped reticular formation (long vertical hatches). (From Livingston, R. B. Some brain stem mechanisms relating to psychosomatic functions. *Psychosom. Med.* **17**, 1955, pp. 347–354.)

pituitary endocrine relations will be treated further in the next chapter when we discuss hormones and behavior. The fourteen major nuclei, labelled in three major zones (a region adjoining the ventricle, a lateral region, and a medial zone), are schematized in Figure 8.2. For our purposes the critical regions are the anterior hypothalamus (the anterior extension of the lateral region), the lateral hypothalamus, and the lower portion of the medial region, the ventromedial hypothalamus (Fig. 8.2). The connections of the hypothalamus are enormously complex; we cannot even begin to detail them here. However, a few simple generalizations will be sufficient for our purposes. First, while there appear to be no very direct sensory projections to the hypothalamus, many sensory systems (e.g., gustatory, somatosensory, and olfactory) pass through the region en route to thalamic relay nuclei. Second, major projections of the hypothalamus to and from lower regions of the brain appear to relay through the "limbic" region of the midbrain, the most anterior region of the brain stem reticular formation in the midbrain tegmentum. Third, its interconnections with higher brain regions are primarily with the so-called limbic forebrain structures—the hippocampus, septal area and amygdala, and the medial region of the thalamus and the frontal region of the cerebral cortex. A few of the most important pathways interconnecting these structures with the hypothalamus are shown in Figure 8.3.

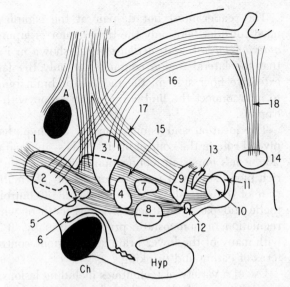

Figure 8.2 Diagram showing the relative positions of the hypothalamic nuclei in a typical mammalian brain and their relation to the fornix (17), stria habenularis (16), and fasciculus retroflexus of habenulo-peduncular tract (18). A, anterior commissure; Ch, optic chiasm; Hyp, hypophysis (pituitary); 1, lateral preoptic nucleus (permeated by the medial forebrain bundle); 2, medial preoptic nucleus; 3, paraventricular nucleus; 4, anterior hypothalamic area; 5, suprachiasmatic nucleus; 11, lateral mammillary nucleus; 12, premammillary nucleus; 13, supramammillary nucleus; 14, interpeduncular nucleus (a mesencephalic element in which the habenulo-peduncular tract terminates); 15, lateral hypothalamic nucleus (permeated by the medial forebrain bundle). These many nuclei can be grouped in three general clusters which have some functional meaning: anterior (e.g., 1, 2, 4); lateral (e.g., 15); medial-ventral (e.g., 7). (From Clark, W. E. Le Gros *The Hypothalamus.* London: Oliver and Boyd, 1938.)

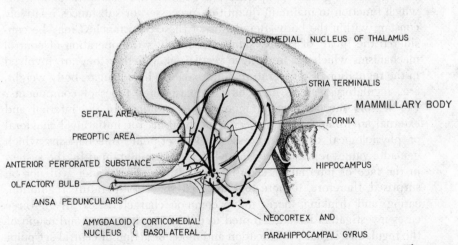

Figure 8.3 Schematic drawing of some major connections of the limbic system. The hypothalamic nuclei of Figure 8.2 range from the preoptic area to the mammillary body. (Redrawn from Noback, C. R. *The Human Nervous System.* New York: McGraw-Hill, 1967.)

The reader must not despair at the complexity of the system. We need consider here only the three major groupings of the hypothalamus, *anterior*, *lateral*, and *medial-ventral*, shown in Figure 8.2. Keep in mind that the lateral region contains not only the lateral nuclei but has an extensive fiber system, the medial forebrain bundle, passing through it to interconnect the limbic midbrain region with the septum and hippocampus.

The location and connections of the hypothalamus have given it a pivotal role in the control of the body's "internal economy." On the input side, it has important connections with forebrain regions and through its rich blood supply it receives important information about the metabolic state of the animal. On the output side, it controls the activity of sympathetic and parasympathetic systems, both of which are involved in the regulation of homeostatic processes. Finally, it has neural connections with many of the lower brain stem regions controlling the response patterns of eating and drinking.

Use of a variety of techniques including lesions, local cooling and heating, injections of chemicals and hormones, electrical stimulation and recording has shown that specific regions of the hypothalamus are involved in the neural control of temperature regulation, eating, drinking, sexual behavior, anger, fear, etc. It appears to contain critical links between the sensory systems initiating and directing such behaviors and the effector systems which control the movement patterns involved.

Motivational analysis of regulatory processes

Eating, drinking, and temperature regulation are examples of systems which function to maintain quantities, processes, or substances relatively constant within the body. Regulation of these "constancies" may be considered the "goal" of such systems and involves the operation of control mechanisms which act to achieve regulation. Whether they are involved in the regulation of temperature, fluid balance, blood sugar, body weight, etc., regulatory systems must have at least three types of components: (1) sensory mechanisms for monitoring conditions in the internal and external environment; (2) effector mechanisms for initiating behavioral or physiological control processes; (3) "set-point" mechanisms which generate values representing the balance to be maintained by the system in the face of internal or external fluctuations. The reader will not be surprised, therefore, to note that the analysis of temperature regulation, eating, and drinking shares many common characteristics. In all three cases investigators have attempted to determine the nature and origin of the regulatory signals, the location and mode of action of central set-point mechanisms and the relation of sensory and central mechanisms to the effector systems mediating the regulatory behaviors. However, because it is possible to come closer to specifying the control mechanisms for temperature than for eating or drinking we begin with an analysis of temperature regulation as a relatively simple model of a regulatory system.

TEMPERATURE CONTROL—A SELF-REGULATING SYSTEM

Temperature control in warm-blooded animals (*endotherms*) comes close to being a self-regulating system. Humans automatically maintain a constant body temperature of 37°C in the face of reasonably large fluctuations in the environmental temperature. As every reader knows, however, this works only up to a point. If the environment becomes too hot or too cold, the human internal regulating system cannot handle it and we either escape to a more moderate environment or die. This purely behavioral aspect of temperature control is characteristic of all warm-blooded animals—they seek the ecological niche best suited for them in temperature range. On the other hand, the occurrence of evolutionary adaptations permits some endotherms to exist in environments that would be lethally hot or cold for others. In fact, behavioral and evolutionary adaptation to temperature continually interact with environmental climate. Even within humans there are examples that may be at least partly genetic; the Australian aborigines appear able, without clothing, to tolerate lower temperatures than other races of man.

Behavioral and genetic adaptation to climate are the aspects of temperature control that are not self-regulating in any direct way. Even this simple form of homeostatic control, temperature regulation, is open-ended. Animals need not rely entirely on internal self-regulation of temperature; they also can develop special behavior patterns, or migrate to a better climate, or even evolve adaptations to an unfriendly climate.

The internal mechanisms of temperature control in endotherms are remarkably sensitive and efficient. Such mechanisms provide a particularly clear example of self-regulation or *homeostasis*. This term refers to any process that, in response to alteration of a given condition, initiates other reactions and processes that tend to re-establish the initial condition. The most common nonbiological example of a homeostatic control system is the thermostat in a home. The thermostat senses the temperature; when it rises above the "set-point" (say it has been set at 70°F) the furnace is turned off. When the temperature falls below 70°F, the thermostat turns the furnace on. Walter Cannon, an American physiologist, first coined the term homeostasis (in 1932) and emphasized that animals are homeostats—they always strive to maintain constancy in the form of an optimal internal environment.

Internal temperature regulation in mammals works very much like the thermostat on a furnace/air-conditioner system. Sensors in the skin and in the brain detect the temperature of the environment. When temperature drops much below 37°C, a variety of furnace reactions occur in a mammal, such as shivering and increased metabolism. When external temperature rises much above 37°C, a variety of air-conditioning reactions occur, like sweating and panting. It now seems quite certain that the thermostat exists in a particular region of the hypothalamus in the brain (see discussion below and Fig. 8.2). The set-point of the hypothalamic thermostat is 37°C and the temperature it senses is the temperature of the circulating blood. Apparently it can detect changes of considerably less than 1°C and initiate appropriate reactions. The thermostat is, of course, a group of neurons whose rate of discharge of spikes is proportional to blood temperature. These temperature detector neurons presumably act on other neurons to activate the various warming and cooling reactions (Hammel, 1968).

Surprisingly, the importance of the temperature sensors in the skin is not yet clear in humans. Much of the initial discomfort felt when a person steps into very cold air or water is presumed to be due to skin sensors. However, if we can judge from animal studies, the reactions, responses, and perhaps even the experiences necessary to combat cold do not occur if the hypothalamic thermostat is destroyed. Spinal humans—accident victims with complete transsection of the spinal cord—do show some primitive degree of temperature control, for example, some sweating by local spinal reflexes, but it is not adequate to regulate body temperature.

The thermostatic control system for temperature regulation is diagrammed in Figure 8.4A. Afferent information from skin temperature receptors and, more importantly, the direct blood temperature receptors in the hypothalamus determine the activity of the hypothalamic thermostat. This, in turn, initiates appropriate reactions. The major mechanisms for warming include increased muscular tone and activity, increased metabolism of stored energy in the body accomplished via hormonal controls from the hypothalamus, pituitary and endocrine glands (see Chapter 9), shivering, and peripheral vasoconstriction—the veins in

Figure 8.4 A, Diagrammatic view of a general thermostatic control system for temperature regulation. See text for explanation. (From Myers, R. D. Temperature regulation: Neurochemical systems in the hypothalamus. In Haymaker, W., Anderson, E. and Nauta, W. J. H. (eds.). *The Hypothalamus.* Springfield, Ill.: Charles C. Thomas, 1969, pp. 506–523. Courtesy of Charles C. Thomas, Publisher.) B, A schematic model of the hypothalamic control systems for temperature in the infrahuman primate. The temperature of the blood, a pyrogen, or certain drugs such as anesthetics impinge upon 5-HT- or norepinephrine (NE)-containing cells of the anterior thermostat. For body warming, 5-HT is released in order to stimulate a cholinergic heat production pathway which passes through the posterior hypothalamus. In the posterior area, the set-point is maintained by an inherent ratio in the concentrations of sodium and calcium ions. Also in the region are the efferent cholinergic synapses for heat production and heat loss which are found again in the mesencephalon. Ascending monoaminergic nerve fibers follow a mesencephalic trajectory to the rostral hypothalamus. These fibers probably end on the cold and warm sensitive neurons, which are those sensitive to 5-HT and norepinephrine. Thermal input from peripheral receptors may be carried by these fiber systems. (From Myers, R. D. Hypothalamic mechanisms of pyrogen action in the cat and monkey. In Wolstenholme, G. E. W., and Birch, J. (eds.). *Ciba Foundation Symposium on Pyrogens and Fever.* London: Churchill, 1971a, pp. 131–153.)

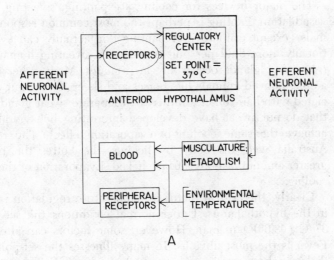

A

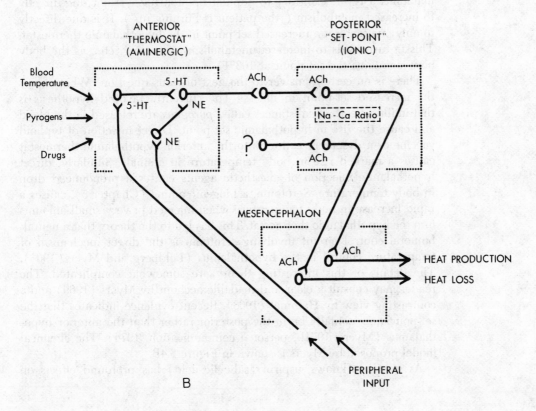

TEMPERATURE CONTROL MODEL: PRIMATE HYPOTHALAMUS

B

the arms, legs, and head constrict so less heat is lost from circulating blood.

The major devices for cooling are panting, sweating, and peripheral vasodilation. Panting is perhaps the most common response among mammals (except primates). A panting dog actually can evaporate proportionally more fluid per unit time than a sweating human. The so-called *true* sweat glands occur only in primates. Many other animals, for example, hooved animals like horses and sheep, sweat but use glands associated with hair follicles rather than separate sweat glands. Some animals that do not sweat have developed interesting behavioral adaptations to achieve the same cooling-by-evaporation effect. The red kangaroo of Australia wets his body by licking—the hotter the temperature the greater amount of body surface licked. Evaporation of the saliva provides cooling.

Clearly, the critical factor in temperature regulation is the thermostat in the hypothalamus. Under normal conditions the set-point is always 37°C (98.6°F) in man. However, some factors can alter this set-point. Fever is the most obvious. In many illnesses the set-point of the hypothalamic thermostat is raised as high as 5° or 6°F. The entire temperature control system of the brain and body continues to function in a completely normal manner. However it now functions to maintain body temperature at, say, 103°F, rather than 98.6°F. Consequently the patient maintains a fever. Contrary to popular opinion fever is not due directly to increased metabolism ("the patient is burning up"). It is due directly to only one factor, an increased set-point in the hypothalamic thermostat. This in turn leads to increased metabolisms, shivering, etc., as the body now maintains the set-point at 103°F.

There is no certain answer to the next obvious question: What causes the increased set-point in illness? The currently favored hypothesis is that in illness certain substances called *pyrogens* are released in the blood and cause the rise in hypothalamic set-point. Direct injection of typhoid vaccine or a dysentery extract into the anterior hypothalamic thermostat causes a marked rise in body temperature in animals. Similarly, direct hypothalamic injection of anesthetic agents causes a pronounced drop in body temperature. Serotonin, a biogenic amine (Chapter 5), causes a rapid increase in body temperature when injected in very small amounts into the hypothalamic thermostat. This has led to the theory that a neural-humoral control circuit involving serotonin is the direct mechanism of temperature control in the hypothalamus (Feldberg and Myers, 1963). The details of this interesting theory are somewhat complicated. The reader may consult a clear and readable account by Myers (1969) and a contrasting view by Hammel (1968). Recent evidence indicates that the set-point may actually be in the posterior rather than the anterior hypothalamus (Myers, 1971b; personal communication, 1974). The chemical model proposed by Myers is shown in Figure 8.4B.

As everyone knows, aspirin (salicylic acid) has profound effects on fever. Aspirin seems to act directly on the hypothalamic thermostat. It reduces the fever set-point from, say, 103°F to the normal level of 98.6°F. This of course is the reason why copious sweating occurs when fever is broken by aspirin. The set-point, shifted down to normal, leaves the body suddenly 5°F too hot. The body must immediately cool down to normal and can do so only by massive sweating, even if the external environment is cool. This mechanism of action of aspirin also explains why aspirin has no effect on transitory increases in body temperature that result from vigorous exercise. The hypothalamic thermostat set-point remains normal at 98.6°F and is not altered by aspirin.

It is easy to build electromechanical analogs of the mammalian temperature control system. A heater/air-conditioner system with a thermostat is the simplest but it is not interesting—it is not a realistic model for temperature regulation in animals. A better model would be a portable version on wheels that not only warmed or cooled itself but also sought out optimal air temperature. The fact that such a device would be relatively easy to build has led to theoretical modeling of temperature regulation as a self-controlling control system in engineering terms (see Hardy, 1963; Hammel, 1968).

As noted above, even a mechanism as simple as temperature regulation is not a completely self-regulating system—it is open-ended because of the behavioral and evolutionary options available to animals. Indeed, many historians view climate, particularly drastic changes in climate, as a major determining factor in the development of human behavior and society. Modern Homo sapiens evolved during a long and violent series of ice ages that pushed early humans back and forth across the face of Europe and Asia. Human evolution, and the development of many aspects of society and culture may be, to a significant degree, a response to environmental temperature. Similarly, many specialized behavior patterns in mammals are related to climate and temperature. None of these can be understood or predicted by viewing temperature regulation merely as a self-regulating system whose mechanisms are relatively simple. Even in the case of temperature control, more generalized concepts like motivation may help to provide a fully convincing account of how we do in fact control temperature.

HUNGER AND THIRST

It is an often tiresome truism that important aspects of behavior have many causes and correlates. Clearly, this is true in the case of eating and drinking. As an exercise, the reader might try to list all the things that influence his or her own hunger and eating behavior. Obvious factors include time since last meal, time of day (even if you skip lunch you will probably not feel hungry in mid-afternoon), fluid intake, occurrence of stomach contractions, conversations about food, emotional state, . . . The list could be extended almost indefinitely. However, it is clear that some causal factors are more important than others. Only the most important factors known to control eating and drinking will be considered here. The reader is asked to remember that the role of many other factors has yet to be experimentally analyzed.

The relation between hunger and thirst

In most laboratory mammals, as in man, eating and drinking are closely related to each other. In many mammals eating and drinking tend to be associated in time so that the animal drinks just before or after eating a dry food. Depriving an animal of water results in a greatly reduced food intake, and deprivation of food reduces the animal's water intake. However, despite these relationships, there are fundamental differences between eating and drinking behavior which suggest that the factors that regulate hunger are more complex than those that control thirst. Obesity presents a striking example of these differences in complexity: many people are too fat but we never hear of someone being too wet. Regulation of fluid intake (at least *water* intake) poses no problem at all for healthy individuals; regulation of caloric intake is a constant problem. Among the many reasons for this difference, perhaps the simplest is that water regulation is much more tightly controlled by the body. It is not possible (except for the camel) to store much extra water. Food energy, as in the case of chronic overeating, can be stored to four or five times our normal body weight. The time constants for food and water needs are quite different. A healthy person can survive only a few days without water but can last two or three months without food. The following quotation illustrates these distinctions:

Appetite comes with eating ... and thirst departs with drinking. Is there a remedy for thirst? It is the opposite of that for a dog bite. Always run after the dog and he'll never bite you; always drink before a thirst and it'll never come to you.

(The drunkard's conversation, in **The Histories of Gargantua and Pantagruel,** François Rabelais; cited in Fitzsimons, 1971, page 193.)

Peripheral factors in thirst and drinking

The brain is the obvious necessary link between tissue need for water and the reduction of this need by drinking. Drinking behavior is a complex *voluntary* act generated by the brain. Two biological mechanisms control body fluid levels: one mechanism detects body water need and communicates it to the brain; the other mechanism is comprised of the brain systems linking detection of water need to drinking behavior. It will come as no great surprise to the reader that, after sixty years of research, experts in the field now believe the fundamental reason higher animals drink water is because they become thirsty. The experience of thirst is the immediate cause of drinking behavior. The issue in terms of peripheral mechanisms thus becomes how the body translates tissue needs for water into brain activity that results in the initiation of drinking and, perhaps, in the experience of thirst. The simplest possible way to do this would be for the body to manufacture a "thirst substance," such that when tissues need water the substance is released into the blood to act on "thirst receptors" in the brain. This is apparently exactly what happens!

Walter Cannon, mentioned earlier, emphasized some years ago that a dry mouth is the immediate cause of drinking. When the organism becomes dehydrated, the salivary glands dry out because of lowered water content in the blood; this leads to dry mouth, the experience of thirst, and drinking. However, if water is introduced directly into the stomach of a thirsty animal, he rapidly will cease drinking behavior. Further, removal of the salivary glands, leading to chronic dry mouth, does not result in increased drinking behavior. Consequently, dry mouth, although it unquestionably plays some role in modulating drinking behavior, is neither a necessary nor a sufficient mechanism to explain drinking.

In adaptive terms, it is critical for survival that animals have the ability to gauge and maintain their water content, which amounts to about 75 per cent of total body weight. Even a relatively small loss of fluid can result in death. Under normal circumstances, water loss develops gradually in the absence of drinking. However, injury that results in substantial blood loss produces considerable fluid loss. Indeed, an immediate effect of external hemorrhaging (bleeding) is intense thirst.

It is clear that physiological mechanisms must exist to measure and regulate fluid content of the body. Body fluid is maintained in two "compartments": cellular (inside cells) and extracellular (outside cells)—see Figure 8.5. The extracellular compartment, in turn, is composed of vascular (blood) and nonvascular (interstitial tissues and lymph fluid) com-

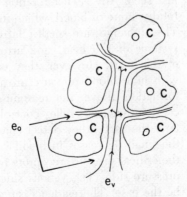

Figure 8.5 Schematic drawing of extracellular and intracellular (c) fluid compartments. The extracellular space includes blood vessels (e_v) (vasculature) and spaces outside cells (e_o). Fluids pass from blood vessel to regions around cells, cross cell membranes into cells, and return from cells to blood vessels.

partments. The salt concentration in all body fluids, both inside and outside cells, must remain constant at about 0.9 per cent—equivalent to about one teaspoon of salt dissolved in a glass of water. If, for some reason, the salt concentration increases in some cells, water crosses the cell walls into the cells until the salt concentration is reduced to normal; this produces an actual physical swelling of the cells. If the salt level of the blood goes up, due to eating salt or injecting concentrated salt solution into the blood stream, water comes from cells to dilute the blood concentration of salt to normal; this produces shrinkage of cells.

Fluid levels in both compartments play important roles in drinking behavior. The weight of evidence favors extracellular fluid volume as the more critical factor. If hypertonic saline (more than normally concentrated salt solution in body tissues) is injected in the blood stream of dogs, water moves out of cells to reduce the concentration of salt in the blood. The cells themselves thus become dehydrated. However, some dogs drink little or no water after such treatment. No dogs drink enough water to restore normal cellular water volume. Perhaps most important, water deprivation in normal animals is always a powerful stimulus for drinking behavior, even though the effect of moderate water deprivation on intracellular water volume is miniscule (Adolph, Barker, and Hoy, 1954). Consequently the major source of control must relate to extracellular fluid volume. In severe dehydration, reduced cellular content of water can become a powerful stimulus for thirst. The mechanism appears to be a direct activation of "thirst receptors" in specialized cells of the hypothalamus due to reduced water (Fitzsimons, 1971). However, under normal conditions of mild deprivation this does not appear as important as extracellular fluid volume.

Given that the major body factor in regulating drinking resides in the blood, what is the mechanism? Changes in salt concentration of blood or cells result in changes in the water content of the blood, as we have just seen. Any such alteration in water content leads to change in the total volume of blood, which in turn leads to a change in blood pressure. These changes are small relative to the major blood pressure regulating systems of the heart and arteries that control the normal functioning of the heart. However, they can be significant—for this reason people with high blood pressure are placed on a salt-free diet. (From the information above, the reasoning should be obvious.) The pressure receptors that exert reflex control on the heart are in the arteries, particularly the aorta; they detect changes much greater than those involved in the small decreases in blood volume that produce thirst. Consequently, the critical pressure receptors for drinking behavior should be in the low pressure side (i.e., venous side) of the vascular system. This seems to be the case. The evidence suggests that pressure receptors in the veins mediate thirst. Thus, tying off major veins such as the vena cava in the abdomen of the rat produces decreased venous pressure and prolonged drinking.

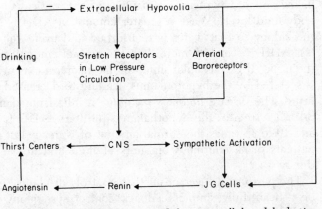

Figure 8.6 Possible mechanism for drinking caused by extracellular dehydration (hypovolia). This deficit results in a change in sensory information from stretch receptors and, in more severe instances, also results in changes in arterial baroreceptors. This information is conveyed to the CNS. Renin and angiotensin from the kidney act on the hypothalamic receptors. JG cells (*juxtaglomerular* cells) in the kidney. (From Fitzsimons, J. T. The renin-angiotensin system in the control of drinking. In Martini, L., Motta, M., and Fraschini, F. (eds.) *The Hypothalamus*. New York: Academic Press, 1970, pp. 195–212.)

The information from venous pressure receptors is transmitted to the brain and can serve as a direct system for producing thirst, but it is considerably less important than another mechanism. If you were designing an animal, you would have to include a device to eliminate water and soluble waste products from the blood. It would be most efficient to include regulation of fluid intake in this device. The "device" is, of course, the kidney. Evidence now indicates that reduced venous pressure leads to release by the kidney of a substance called *renin*. The release is triggered both in the kidney itself and by reflex control from the venous pressure receptors which relay back to the kidney via the sympathetic nervous system. Renin itself acts as an enzyme on one of the normal plasma proteins contained in the blood, a substance called *angiotensinogen*. It converts this substance to *angiotensin II*, the body thirst substance. Angiotensin II is believed to act directly on receptors in the hypothalamic region of the brain to produce the sensation of thirst, and hence drinking behavior. These mechanisms are summarized in the diagram of Figure 8.6.

Evidence is now accumulating that the angiotensin II may be the adequate stimulus for the "thirst receptor" cells in the hypothalamus. A variety of substances including saline and acetylcholine can produce drinking when injected directly into the hypothalamus. However, angiotensin II is the most effective at the lowest doses and has the most prolonged action.

Finally, the antidiuretic hormone (ADH) released by neurons from the anterior hypothalamus via the posterior pituitary gland (discussed below and in Chapter 9) also plays a very critical role in regulation of body fluid levels. When a greater amount of ADH is released it acts on the kidney so that water is reabsorbed and urine volume is reduced. If less ADH is secreted, more than the normal amount of water is lost into the urine. If extracellular fluid volume decreases, as in thirst, more ADH is secreted by the hypothalamus, leading to decreased water loss via the urine. The disease *diabetes insipidus* results from damage to the ADH release system of the hypothalamus-pituitary. ADH is no longer present and 10 to 15 times the normal amount of water is lost in the urine. Such patients drink enormous amounts of fluid and are almost continuously thirsty.

The peripheral mechanism that controls drinking behavior appears to be a beautifully simple feedback control system involving the kidney, itself the major fluid-regulating organ of the body. A dramatic example showing how critical the kidney is to the regulation of thirst has been provided in the human clinical literature (Brown et al., 1969). A patient had a malignancy of the kidney that resulted in a marked overproduction of renin. His thirst was continuous and severe, so much so that in addition to water given him for drinking, he concealed and drank all water provided to him for shaving and bathing! Following removal of his kidneys, his thirst immediately returned to normal.

Hunger: peripheral mechanisms of regulation and control

Food intake control is related to at least two types of regulatory processes; those involved in the organism's energy balance and those having to do with body weight. In both cases the regulation is quite precise. Animals adjust daily caloric intake to meet their energy requirements. Indeed, if a rat's diet is diluted with a nonnutritive substance it will increase its ingestion proportionately so as to maintain a fairly constant caloric intake. Similarly, the body weight of normal animals, including man, is regulated within a relatively narrow range over extended periods of time. This regulation is so precise that it is possible to write equations relating food intake to body weight for many mammalian species.

The existence of such regulations suggests that the feeding system has some means of monitoring energy and body weight levels and relating this information to the control of intake. While very limited stores of energy are available within the animal itself, through the breakdown of blood sugar and fat, the major sources of energy for any animal lie in its external environment. The replacement of this energy thus requires complex and extensive behavioral interactions with the environment in which the animal's sensory systems may be expected to play a major role.

In analysis of the mechanisms which lead to the initiation and termination of eating, at least three classes of factors must be considered: oral, gastric, and metabolic. The first two classes are neurosensory and originate in the oropharyngeal (mouth and throat) region and alimentary canal (stomach and gut), respectively. Metabolic signals are related to the body's metabolic processes, particularly the regulation of energy balances and body weight levels.

Gastric factors. Because digestion is related to the organism's nutritive and energy requirements and because of the obvious association of stomach sensations and the experience of hunger, gastric factors often are assumed to play a critical role in turning on and turning off hunger. Frequently it is assumed that we start to eat because our stomach is empty and stop when our stomach is filled with substances that meet our nutritional or energy requirements. A moment's thought should indicate that the situation must be more complicated than that. Except at breakfast we rarely come to eat with an empty stomach. Conversely, there are many occasions, such as Thanksgiving, when, having "eaten our fill" we still manage to be hungry for more—especially if dessert is to follow. On the other hand, since the organism stops eating long before any significant amount of food has been digested the satisfaction of nutritional or energy requirements can have little to do with the termination of any individual meal. Thus at least some of the signals involved in turning off eating must be related to gastric factors. In view of these facts, it is necessary to separate the role of gastric factors in the initiation of eating from their role in the termination of eating.

The most impressive evidence on the first point comes from studies which involve either the removal of the stomach or the cutting of nerve pathways carrying signals from the gastric region to the brain. Such studies have shown that denervation or removal of the stomach in animals or human ulcer patients does not abolish hunger. The patient may eat more frequently and take smaller meals but he gets hungry and starts eating even without his stomach.

Evidence on the second point comes from experiments which involve placing food or other substances directly into the stomach and then studying the effects of such *preloading* upon subsequent eating. Such experiments have been carried out in both animals and humans and in all cases preloading does produce a significant reduction in the subsequent intake. Furthermore, this reduction can take place within a very short time after preloading, long before digestion can have taken place, so that the metabolic or nutritional effects of food cannot be the sources of signals turning off feeding. Analysis of such experiments indicates that both the osmotic pressures of the substances and their mechanical distention effects can inhibit subsequent eating by producing stimuli which are relayed to the central nervous system. In summary the gastric factors appear to be of little significance in the initiation of feeding but are important in its termination.

Oral factors. As noted above, the nutritional value of a substance cannot become manifest until long after the food is ingested. Thus while food intake must be related in some way to the organism's bodily needs the relation may be very indirect. The most obvious source of the signals eliciting feeding behavior are, of course, stimuli that come from the food itself.

It will be recalled that feeding behavior in the fly is "turned on" by such signals and that the power of stimuli is such that the fly ingests sweet substances which have no nutritive value and may even be nutritionally detrimental. A similar situation is found in the feeding behavior of higher animals including man. Even a rat will eat more of a given diet if it is presented in several distinct portions each of which is distinctively flavored. The more variety in the stimuli, the more eating is prolonged.

It has been noted by nutrition specialists that in a culture such as ours, where a variety of food substances is available, humans tend to eat for palatability rather than for nutrition. That is, the sights, smells, and tastes of foods play a central role in determining our eating habits. The enormous consumption of soft drinks, salty snacks, and gourmet foods, many of which are nutritionally valueless or tend to produce obesity, is based almost entirely on palatability. Moreover, most striking is the fact that consumption of such foods seems to be almost compulsive or obligatory. Soft drinks taste good but leave us wanting more while, in the words of a famous potato-chip advertisement, "it's impossible to eat only one." It is almost as impossible to forego a sweet dessert, even after a heavy Thanksgiving meal.

Such observations suggest that stimuli coming from food can, even in the absence of any nutritional consequences, elicit and maintain a state of hunger; that is, that they can serve as *incentives* for such behavior. The potency of such incentives can be seen from experiments showing that rats learn a variety of tasks when the only reinforcement is a few drops of weak sugar solution. Similar results can be obtained using saccharine, a sweet tasting but nonnutritive substance. Such data suggest that the stimulus properties of food make an important contribution to the control of hunger, which is another way of saying that "appetite comes with eating."

Just how important this contribution can be is shown by an ingenious series of experiments employing a technique which makes possible the elimination of oral sensations while at the same time permitting food to reach the stomach. The technique was developed by Teitelbaum and Epstein (1962) and is illustrated in Figure 8.7. Rats are implanted with a nasopharyngeal gastric tube leading from a source of liquid food to the stomach. They are then trained to deliver the food to their own stomachs by pressing a lever. Under these conditions they do manage to regulate food intake to the extent necessary to maintain body weight. However,

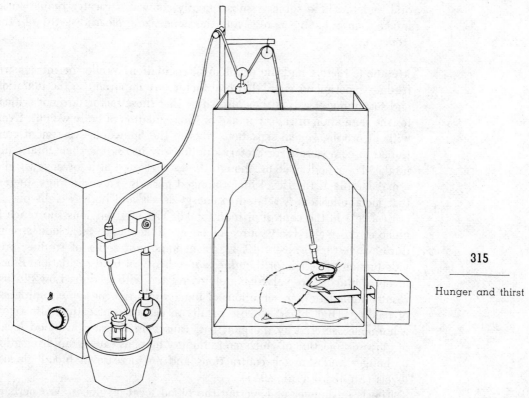

Figure 8.7 Schematic of the apparatus for intragastric self-injection by the rat. The rat presses the bar in order to activate the pipetting machine, thus delivering a liquid diet from the reservoir through the chronic gastric tube directly into its own stomach. The course of the nasopharyngeal gastric tube is also shown. (Modified from Epstein, A. N., and Teitelbaum, P. Regulation of food intake in the absence of taste, smell, and other oropharyngeal sensations. *J. Comp. Physiol. Psychol.* **55**, 1962, pp. 753–759. Copyright 1962 by the American Psychological Association. Reprinted by permission.)

Snowdon (1969) has shown that when rats are transferred from oral to intragastric feeding, bar-pressing for food disappeared and could only be restored by using an oral supplement and gradually retraining the rats to bar-press for intragastric food. Once trained to feed intragastrically, they ate only 75 per cent of their oral nutrient intakes, keeping their body weight stable but not showing the normal weight increases of rats that were fed orally. In addition, bar-pressing for intragastric food was brief and not sustained and intragastric meals were smaller than those eaten orally. It would seem that oral factors are of significant importance in initiating and sustaining feeding at *optimal* levels.

Oral factors have also been shown to be involved in the termination of eating. Preloading experiments have been carried out in which the animals are allowed to eat their preload so that the food passes through the oral region. These subjects subsequently showed a greater reduction in intake than did subjects receiving the same size preload directly into the stomach.

Metabolic factors and the problem of regulation. While the intragastric feeding experiments show that oral factors are important in the initiation and sustaining of eating they also show that these factors are not critical for the regulation of caloric intake or the regulation of body weight. Even without oropharyngeal sensations, rats in the Snowdon experiment continued to compensate for dietary dilutions by increasing their total daily intake. Their body weight, though it was regulated at a lower level, did remain stable at that level for prolonged periods. These findings suggest that metabolic factors related to energy levels and body weight play a critical role in the control of food intake. The most obvious substance is glucose, the major food source of energy that enters the blood stream during digestion. Mayer (1953), in an important series of studies, provided much evidence for the *glucostatic* theory of food regulation. Blood levels of glucose are very definitely correlated with feeding. Low glucose results immediately in sensations of hunger and the consequent initiation of feeding. High blood glucose results in cessation of eating. Glucogen, a hormone secreted by the pancreas, causes an increase in blood levels of glucose. Injection of glucogen in hungry humans causes rapid cessation of hunger and stomach contractions and an increase in blood glucose levels (Stunkard et al., 1955).

Effects on hunger of lowering the blood level of glucose are perhaps even more convincing. Injection of insulin, another hormone normally secreted by the pancreas, causes a decrease in blood glucose levels. (Most readers probably know that in a person with diabetes the pancreas does not produce enough insulin and blood sugar can rise to dangerous levels, hence the need for insulin.) Injection of insulin in normal animals causes an increase in eating.

Actually, it is a little more complicated than simply the blood levels of glucose. The critical factor is the rate of utilization of glucose by tissues, particularly brain tissue in the hypothalamus. A dramatic demonstration of this is the effect of injecting *2-deoxy-D-glucose*, a substance that reduces cellular availability of glucose to zero. Animals show dramatic and prolonged overeating, called *hyperphagia*. On the basis of such data as these it has been suggested that there are glucoreceptors in the hypothalamus and other brain areas. While the evidence on this point is not yet totally compelling, the participation of glucose in the control of feeding is generally accepted.

To summarize, all authorities seem to agree that *lowered* blood glucose level and hence lowered brain tissue *utilization* of glucose is a very powerful direct stimulus to certain regions of the hypothalamus that produce the sensation of hunger and the initiation of feeding. This effect is the basis for the recommendation to dieters that they eat a candy bar an hour before dinner. The blood sugar will be elevated at dinner time and hunger will be reduced. However, authorities are less agreed on the satiating effects of increased blood sugar utilization. The evidence is certainly less clear. Direct injection of glucose into the appropriate region of the hypothalamus does not stop hungry rats from eating. This may explain why the candy-bar-before-dinner diet doesn't work very well. The actions of glucose and other chemicals on neural activity in the hypothalamus will be discussed further below. The only point of importance here is that increased blood level of glucose is less reliable in stopping feeding than a decreased level is in starting it.

The fat-level hypothesis is beginning to gain ground as the mechanism for cessation of feeding. Kennedy (1953) pointed out that normal animals tend to maintain a constant fat level. Older animals stabilize at a higher level of body fat than young animals but they do not become obese. Most middle-aged humans develop "middle-aged spread" but do not become grossly fat. Food intake actually is reduced in middle age at a point where a relatively small and constant overweight level is maintained. These arguments can hardly be called convincing. More direct evidence has been obtained by LeMagnen (1969), who showed that onset of feeding in rats corresponds to maximal blood levels of fatty acids available for energy (lipolysis). At the end of the meal glucose is being used and lipolysis reaches a low point. The issue of glucose level vs. fat level in cessation of eating remains to be determined, but there is no question that blood levels of these and possibly other substances, and more particularly the rates of brain tissue utilization, are the critical determinants of both the onset and cessation of hunger and feeding.

Before concluding, it should be noted that the relation between orosensory factors and caloric regulation may be somewhat different in food-deprived than in nondeprived animals. Experiments by Jacobs and Sharma (1969) indicate that the normal rat under *ad libitum* (freely accessible) food availability controls his total food intake much more on the basis of number of calories eaten than in terms of taste. However, the voraciously hungry food-deprived rat will eat voraciously only if the food tastes good. The starved rat's food intake is much more dependent on the taste of the food. This paradox is important as it relates to the effects of brain lesions on feeding behavior, discussed below.

Brain mechanisms of eating and drinking

The hypothalamus is a critical brain region for the control of eating and drinking behaviors. It is not the only region involved but it appears to form a critical *nexus* or link between higher brain regions, such as the thalamus, limbic system and cerebral cortex, and lower regions of the midbrain and hindbrain. The coordinated reflex behaviors involved in eating and drinking—licking, chewing, swallowing—are mediated by nuclei in these lower regions. Rats without the hypothalamus or higher brain regions show well coordinated consummatory behavior. Indeed, they eat equally of food, pencils, or any objects placed in the mouth. However, they never engage in food-seeking behavior.

A rather clear picture is now emerging of at least some aspects of hypothalamic function in eating and drinking. This picture is based upon the analysis of lesion effects on three critical regions of the hypothalamus: the anterior, the lateral, and the ventromedial regions. Lesions of these regions produce specific syndromes, that is, groups of deficits in ingestive behavior, which suggest that they are critically involved in the initiation, direction, and termination of eating and drinking.

Hypothalamic mechanisms in drinking and fluid balance

Recent evidence indicates that there are two separate regions of the hypothalamus (see below and Fig. 8.2) that contain the receptors for the detection of intracellular fluid level (lateral region) and extracellular fluid level (anterior region) (Wayner and Carey, 1973). Both are important in regulating fluid intake, although as indicated above, extracellular level detection is more sensitive under mild conditions of fluid deprivation. Further, there remain some potentially troublesome problems with the angiotensin II story. It is not yet clearly established how effectively it can cross the blood-brain "barrier" from the blood stream to the brain, particularly to the hypothalamus. Finally, there is evidence that the brain itself, may produce angiotensin (Wayner and Carey, 1973). In any event, the main outline of the story we have given here is generally accepted. Extracellular fluid level monitoring is the more sensitive detection system. A major role is played by the kidney, which releases angiotensin II to act on receptors in the anterior hypothalamus. Activation of these receptors leads, in turn, to activation of the brain systems that result in the sensation of thirst and drinking behavior.

The role of anterior hypothalamus in drinking and thirst seems quite clear. Andersson (1953) first showed that injections of small amounts of concentrated salt solution into the anterior preoptic area in goats produced drinking. The effect was powerful but not completely selective. More recent work indicates that concentrated saline injection in the lateral hypothalamus also can produce drinking. In 1960, Grossman published a dramatic and important effect of implantation of small amounts of a substance called *carbachol*, which imitates the actions of the neural transmitter acetylcholine (ACh) but is not inactivated by the enzymes that normally inactivate ACh. When carbachol is placed in the hypothalamus of the otherwise intact rat, drinking behavior occurs. Grossman also found that, if another neural transmitter called norepinephrine is injected into the hypothalamus, eating behavior occurred. These transmitter effects were specific—acetylcholine-like substances elicited only drinking and norepinephrine evoked only eating.

Until quite recently it was believed that the eating and drinking regions of the hypothalamus could not be separated anatomically. The evidence is now clear that the anterior preoptic area is selective for drinking. Although drinking is elicited by injecting saline in regions other than anterior hypothalamus, drinking elicited by cell dehydration can be stopped by injections of plain water only in the anterior area. Finally, the very recent data on angiotensin II indicate that it is effective in eliciting drinking only in the anterior hypothalamus at very low doses (5 nanograms or 5/1,000,000,000 of a gram).

The very specific actions of the thirst hormone, angiotensin II, must be contrasted with the more general actions of ACh-like drugs. Acetylcholine is a presumed neural transmitter and would be expected to act wherever ACh synapses exist. Indeed, it has been clearly demonstrated by Fisher and Coury (1962) that injection of carbachol in most of the forebrain limbic structures (Fig. 8.3) induces drinking. These observations give rise to the idea that a chemical drinking circuit exists in the brain. Some regions, for example, the hypothalamus, are more effective in eliciting drinking per se. Other limbic structures tend to modulate drinking rather than invariably elicit it (see Russell, 1966; Grossman, 1967).

Injection of carbachol in the amygdala (Fig. 8.3) elicits drinking in rats that have been deprived of water but has no effect if the animal is not thirsty. In sharp contrast, application of effective substances to the anterior hypothalamus produces drinking in rats that are not thirsty.

The ventromedial feeding center and the "fat rat" syndrome

In a classical experiment, Hetherington and Ranson (1940) showed that destruction of the ventromedial region of the hypothalamus produces the hyperphagic syndrome—the animals eat voraciously until they become very obese and exhibit irritability and viciousness (Fig. 8.8). Eventually these hyperphagic animals decrease their food intake to almost normal levels and maintain body weight at about two to three times normal levels.

An interesting fact about the hyperphagic rat concerns the role of palatability, the taste and smell of food. Teitelbaum (1955) showed that even though the hyperphagic animals eat much more of their regular laboratory diet than normals, they are very finicky eaters. If the diet of a normal rat is adulterated with cellulose, which adds to the bulk but not to the nutritional value of food, the animal increases intake to obtain the correct amount of nutrition. The hyperphagic rat does not. Further, hyperphagic rats prefer a diet containing dextrose, independent of nutritional value, in contrast to the normal rat. As you may recall this increased concern with the taste of foods is characteristic also of the very hungry food-deprived normal rat.

Electrical stimulation and recording studies of the ventromedial hypothalamus give results consistent with lesion-produced hyperphagia. Stim-

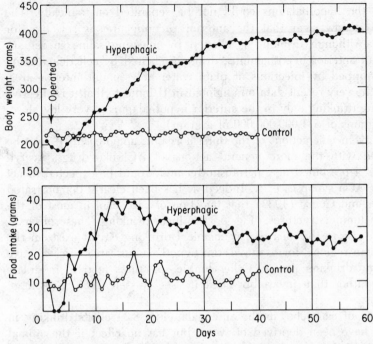

Figure 8.8 Development of hyperphagia in rats following lesions of the ventromedial hypothalamus. Note that food intake increases markedly at first and then levels off, but that body weight increases more slowly and for a longer period of time. (From Teitelbaum, P. Disturbances of feeding and drinking behavior after hypothalamic lesions. From Jones, M. R. (ed.). *Nebraska Symposium on Motivation.* Lincoln: Univ. of Nebraska Press, © 1961, pp. 39–65. Reprinted by permission.)

ulation through implanted electrodes inhibits eating in hungry rats (Margules and Olds, 1962; Hoebel and Teitelbaum, 1962). Further, the electrical activity of this region of the hypothalamus is increased by factors, such as increased blood glucose, that normally stop eating.

All these observations suggested that the ventromedial hypothalamus (VMH) acts as a "satiety" center. It turns off hunger and feeding behavior when sufficient nutrients have been consumed. However, more recent work indicates that the VMH is not a satiety *center,* but a region of passage for many fiber tracts involved in the termination of feeding. Early work by Graff and Stellar (1962) suggested that it might be possible to separate these VMH regions responsible for finickiness from those related to overeating. Hoebel and his colleagues have confirmed the dissociation of finickiness and obesity using both chemical and electrolytic lesion techniques (Ahlskog and Hoebel, 1973). More recently both Hoebel and Gold (1973) have shown that lesions restricted to the VMH nucleus itself had no effects on eating but larger lesions which overlapped adjacent areas produced overeating proportional to the extent of the overlap . . . "the largest lesions typically producing the fattest rats"

(Gold, p. 488). Both Hoebel and Gold suggest that the effects on feeding seen after VMH lesions are the result of damage to fibers of neurochemical systems passing through the region which are involved in the regulation of adrenergic transmission in the forebrain. We noted earlier that such chemical circuits may be involved in the control of eating.

The neurochemical systems involved appear to originate in brain stem areas which themselves receive inputs from oropharyngeal and alimentary regions. It thus appears that VMH lesions have disrupted neuronal circuits involved in the monitoring of signals which can tell the animal about the passage of food through the mouth and indicate its presence in the stomach and gut. As noted earlier, sensory inputs from both these regions must be involved in the termination of feeding.

The lateral hypothalamic area and the "thin rat" syndrome

Lesions of the lateral hypothalamic area in the rat produce a syndrome whose most striking feature is disruption of eating (aphagia) and drinking (adipsia) so severe that the animals will starve to death if not tube-fed. The discovery of this effect by Anand and Brobeck (1951) suggested that the LH region might contain a "center" for the initiation of eating and drinking which complimented the supposed satiety "center" in the VMH. Epstein and Teitelbaum and their colleagues (see Epstein, 1971; Teitelbaum, 1971) have carefully studied the recovery of eating and drinking after lateral hypothalamic lesions and have provided the most complete description of this LH syndrome (Fig. 8.9).

Recovery takes place in several stages. In Stage I (aphagia, adipsia) the animals neither eat nor drink for several days and must be fed by stomach tube. In Stage II the rat eats very palatable tasty foods (e.g., chocolate, sweet milk and cookie mixture, etc.) but does not eat dry food or water. In this sense, LH animals are also finicky eaters. In Stage III they take a liquid diet but do not drink water. A variety of tests show they are treating the liquid diet as food, not water. If given sweetened water, they drink it and gradually may be weaned to a dry food diet. As noted earlier, rats that are not drinking will not eat so the absence of eating in Stage III reflects the dehydration effects of not drinking. Finally in Stage IV, animals ingest enough water and dry food to maintain stable weights. Although they appear to have recovered, they still have subtle deficits in the control mechanisms for hunger and thirst. First, while they drink in association with eating dry food they do not respond to the kinds of situations that elicit drinking in normal rats (water deprivation, dehydration, decreases in blood volume, etc.). Thus they appear to have a permanent thirst deficit. Second, they do not respond to decreases in intracellular glucose utilization (glucoprivation) such as are produced by injections of insulin. In normal animals such injections produce an increase in food intake but the recovered LH, although he

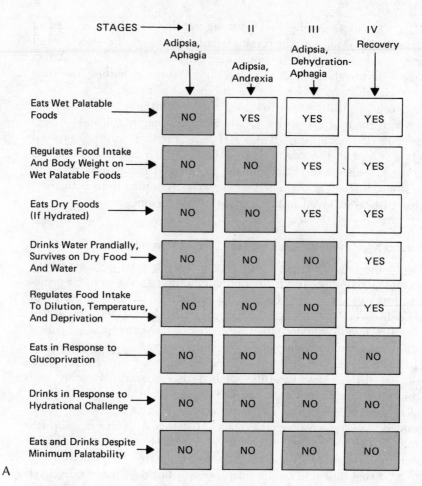

322

Motivation

A

Figure 8.9 A, The stages of recovery of the lateral hypothalamic syndrome expanded from Teitelbaum and Epstein (1962) to show the complexity of Stage IV. (Epstein, A. N. The lateral hypothalamic syndrome: its implications for the physiological psychology of hunger and thirst. From Stellar, E., and Sprague, J. M. (eds.) *Progress in Physiological Psychology* 4, New York: Academic Press, 1971.) B, The production of both aphagia and adipsia by lateral hypothalamic lesions. Note the recovery of eating of palatable foods on day 16, the recovery of drinking on day 21, and the greatly delayed return to ordinary, dry food. The animal was kept alive by tube feeding during Stages I and II of the syndrome. (Teitelbaum, P., and Stellar, E. Recovery from the failure to eat produced by hypothalamic lesions. *Science* 120, 1954, pp. 894–895. Copyright 1954 by the American Association for the Advancement of Science.)

shows an appropriate response to food deprivation, does not show a normal response to glucoprivation.

There is one additional characteristic of the LH animals which is of interest from the point of view of regulation. Normal animals food-deprived for a number of days and then given access to food will eat

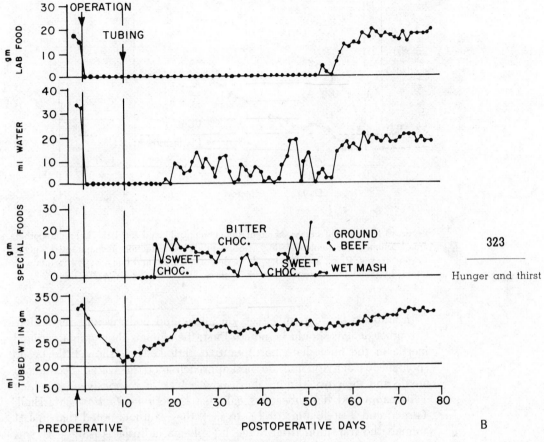

Figure 8.9 (continued)

enough over the next few days to compensate for the weight lost during food deprivation. LH animals, even after they have recovered the capacity to eat, do not compensate for weight lost during the postoperative periods of aphagia and go on maintaining their weight at levels substantially below preoperative values (Fig. 8.10). Moreover, animals food-deprived to a new, lower weight prior to LH lesions do not show the typical period of aphagia and may even overeat in the postoperative period until they reach a stable, but lower, body weight. Powley and Keesey (1970) have therefore suggested that LH lesions affect brain mechanisms involved in the regulation of body weight set-point; that is, the mechanisms involved in determining the constant weight value which is being regulated by the animal's food intake. In this interpretation, the lesion produces a lowered set-point as the rat reduces its input to maintain this lowered set-point.

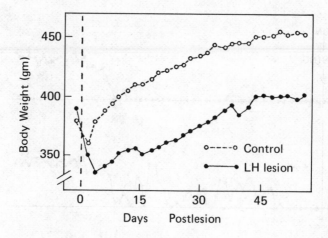

Figure 8.10 Weight curves of eight intact (control) and ten LH (lateral hypothalamic)-lesioned rats demonstrating a lesion-produced reduction in maintained weight. (From Keesey, R. E., and Powley, T. L. Self-stimulation and body weight in rats with lateral hypothalamic lesions. *Amer. J. Physiol.* **224**, 1973, pp. 970–978.)

In addition to clear-cut effects on intake and body weight regulation, two other deficits should be noted. First, the animals show a motivational inertia in the immediate postoperative period. They show little or no spontaneous activity and do not approach food or water. Second, to tactile and olfactory stimuli they show a lack of responsiveness, which Teitelbaum and his colleagues called a sensory *inattention* (Marshall, Turner, and Teitelbaum, 1971). In fact, these authors noted that in LH animals the transition from Stage I (aphagia, adipsia) to Stage II was preceded by or coincided with the recovery of head orientation responses to olfactory and trigeminal (snout) stimuli. Finally, many investigators have reported that LH rats show a great deal of food spillage, suggesting some disruption of the sensorimotor control of the consummatory response of eating.

It is easy to see why the characteristics of the LH syndrome led many early investigators to suggest that the LH region contained a *center* for the initiation of eating and drinking. Moreover, other types of evidence appeared to support this hypothesis. Studies by Andersson and his associates demonstrated that electrical stimulation of the LH region could produce both eating and drinking behavior even in animals that had previously eaten or drunk their fill (Andersson and Wyrwicka, 1957). Similarly, implantation of small amounts of norepinephrine in this region could produce feeding behavior (Khavari and Russell, 1966). There was also some evidence that single-neuron activity in the LH region was related to the level of blood glucose. Taken together, the data on the LH and VMH syndromes strongly suggested that eating and drinking were turned on and off by two opposed centers, one in the VMH and one in the LH region. As we have already noted, such a view is an oversimplification of a much more complex situation.

The lateral hypothalamic syndrome: a re-examination

The characteristic lesion which produces the LH syndrome, described above, is a very large one, involving not only the lateral hypothalamic nucleus itself but also the medial forebrain bundle, the internal capsule, the zona incerta, and a number of other adjacent regions. Moreover, it has been possible to produce many aspects of the LH syndrome by lesions, outside the lateral hypothalamus, involving a variety of brain stem structures. These facts have led some workers to suggest that the LH syndrome does not reflect damage to a center but, as with the VMH syndrome, results from damage to a variety of different neural systems involved in the initiation of eating and drinking. Recent work has focused on dissociating the various components of the syndrome and trying to relate each of them to specific brain structures.

Drinking behavior and the LH syndrome

Because of the association of adipsia and aphagia in the LH syndrome it was assumed originally that the LH region contained centers for both eating and drinking. However, Epstein has recently suggested that the effects upon drinking seen after LH lesions are due to the interruption of pathways from the anterior preoptic areas which, as we have seen, are involved in the regulation of body water. Moreover, as we shall see below, at least some of the effects of LH lesions upon drinking behavior are due to the interruption of afferent systems from the oropharyngeal region which pass through the lateral hypothalamic area en route to the thalamic relay nuclei (Chapter 6).

Caloric regulation and the LH syndrome

It was noted above that one of the permanent deficits of LH rats was an absence of appropriate eating responses to the lowered glucose level produced by insulin injections. In an important recent paper, Blass and Kraly (1974) showed that lesions of the medial forebrain bundle (MFB) can produce the glucoprivation deficit without producing any of the other aspects of the LH syndrome. Rats with MFB lesions did not respond to glucoprivation, but were able to regulate their food and water intake in response to deprivation, temperature changes, and caloric dilution, and showed no signs of finickiness. These results have two implications for our understanding of the neural control of feeding. First, they indicate that structures outside the LH area itself are critical for the control of food intake in response to glucoprivation. More important, the existence of normal intake and weight regulation in the absence of a glucoprivation response strongly suggests that glucostatic mechanisms are much less important in the control of eating than was previously thought.

Central oropharyngeal inputs and the LH syndrome

As noted earlier, there is considerable evidence that peripheral inputs from the oral region are important in initiating, directing, and sustaining ingestive behavior in invertebrates and vertebrates, including man. Until recently, however, few investigators had considered the role of central orosensory mechanisms (i.e., afferent pathways and nuclei for smell, taste, and touch) in the control of such behavior. You may recall that one characteristic of rats in the early stages of the LH syndrome is absence of responsiveness to the types of olfactory and tactile stimuli that might be expected to arouse and direct feeding behavior. Recent work on the orosensory control of eating and drinking in both birds and mammals has clarified the implications of this finding for an understanding of the LH syndrome. Moreover, it has been suggested that central orosensory mechanisms may play a critical role in the control of weight regulation, body water, and ingestive behavior.

The trigeminal system and ingestive behavior in pigeon and rat

In an extensive program of research on the feeding behavior of the pigeon, Zeigler (1974) has shown that the trigeminal system plays a critical role in the neural control of eating in this species. His studies are based on the anatomical findings of Karten who has shown that the organization of sensory systems in the avian brain parallels that of the mammalian brain in many respects (Nauta and Karten, 1970). The trigeminal system is extremely well developed in many vertebrate species and carries somatosensory input from the oral region, for example, the beak of birds and the snout region of rodents, carnivores, etc.

Zeigler and Karten (1973) have found that lesions of central trigeminal pathways and nuclei disrupt both the pigeon's responsiveness to food and the sensory control of its feeding behavior. The *trigeminal syndrome* in the pigeon includes a period of aphagia, considerable food spillage, and a prolonged reduction in body weight. These characteristics are similar to those seen after LH lesions in the rat but no such effects were seen after LH lesions in the pigeon. Moreover, Zeigler (1973) has found that even a peripheral section of trigeminal sensory nerves (deafferentation) produces a profound disruption of feeding. Indeed, the prolonged reduction in intake and body weight of the deafferented pigeon is reminiscent of the effects seen in rats deprived of oral sensations while barpressing for food delivered directly into the stomach (p. 315, Fig. 8.7).

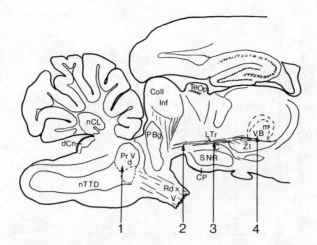

Figure 8.11 Sagittal section through the rat brain illustrating the trajectory of the trigeminal lemniscus at several levels, from its origin, in the principal sensory trigeminal nucleus (level 1). After leaving the nucleus the lemniscus decussates at the level of the interpeduncular nucleus (level 2) and continues through the mesencephalon, lying immediately dorsal to the medial portion of the substantia nigra at the level of the ventral tegmentum (level 3). At the diencephalic level it gives off collaterals to the posterior thalamic region and zona incerta before terminating in the medial portion of the ventrobasal complex of the thalamus (level 4). Redrawn from data in Smith, 1973. (From Zeigler, H. P., and Karten, H. J. Central trigeminal structures and the lateral hypothalamic syndrome in the rat. *Science* **186**, 1974, pp. 636–637. Copyright 1974 by the American Association for the Advancement of Science.)

In a recent study on the rat, Zeigler and Karten (1974) pointed out that the characteristic LH lesion invariably damages central trigeminal pathways. In order to separate trigeminal and lateral hypothalamic effects upon eating, they placed lesions of the trigeminal pathways at several loci outside the hypothalamus (Levels 2, 3, 4, Fig. 8.11). They found that such lesions produce many of the characteristics of the LH syndrome: aphagia, adipsia, finickiness, food spillage, and inattention to tactile stimuli in the snout region (Fig. 8.12). To complete the analogy with the pigeon work, Zeigler (1974) developed a technique for trigeminal deafferentation in the rat and found that this procedure also produced deficits in eating and drinking.

Further research undoubtedly will reveal differences between the LH syndrome and the trigeminal syndrome in the rat. Such analyses will be important in determining the specific role of trigeminal structures in the control of eating and drinking. However, the studies of Zeigler and Karten have helped to focus attention on the possible role of central orosensory mechanisms in the control of ingestive behavior. Work by Emmers (1973) and Wolf and DiCara (1974) have shown that effects upon drinking and sodium appetite, similar to those reported after LH lesions, can also be produced by damage to the thalamic taste nucleus and other gustatory

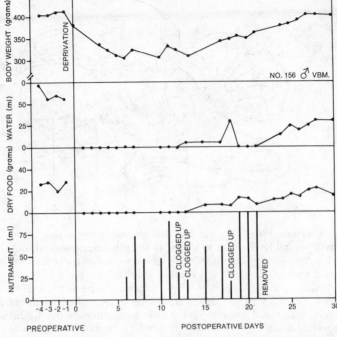

Figure 8.12 Effects of lesion of the trigeminal system upon eating and drinking in the rat. The lesion was placed at the thalamic level (level 4 in Fig. 8.11) and completely spared the lateral hypothalamic area and the medial forebrain bundle. The rat was adipsic and aphagic for five days and then began to ingest a chocolate-flavored liquid diet. It did not begin to regulate its weight on dry food and water for almost three weeks postoperatively. (From Zeigler, H. P., and Karten, H. J. Central trigeminal structures and the lateral hypothalamic syndrome in the rat. *Science* **186**, 1974, pp. 636–637. Copyright 1974 by the American Association for the Advancement of Science.)

structures located in close proximity to trigeminal pathways. (Norgren and Leonard, 1973). It appears that many important components of the LH syndrome may be attributable to incidental damage of central sensory pathways carrying information from the oral region to the brain.

Conclusions: from hypothalamic syndromes to brain mechanisms

The early finding that lesions of hypothalamic regions could disrupt eating and drinking was significant for two reasons. First, it suggested specific brain regions that might be involved in the control of these behaviors and led to careful analyses of the effects of lesions of these regions. Second, such analyses made it clear that the original concepts of hunger and thirst as unitary phenomena were oversimplifications. Further research may make it possible to dissociate specific neurobehavioral mecha-

Figure 8.13 A fat rat and a fat human contemplating one another. The symptoms shown by hypothalamically lesioned fat rats and "normal" fat humans are strikingly parallel.

nisms that underlie eating and drinking behavior and to identify the neural substrates of these mechanisms.

HUMAN OBESITY

"Inside every fat man there is a thin man crying to get out."

It is generally agreed that obesity, whether in rats or humans, is due to overeating; however, little is known about why overeating occurs in some people and not in others. In a delightful article on "some extraordinary facts about obese humans and rats," Stanley Schachter (1971) has attempted to relate work on feeding mechanisms in rats to the phenomenon of obesity in humans. Schachter is a social psychologist interested in the interaction of physiological determinants and emotional states in humans (Chapter 9). His interest in the problem of obesity was stimulated by the work of the psychiatrist Albert Stunkard on the relation between obesity and gastric motility (stomach contractions) in man.

Table 8.1 Effect of taste on eating

Subjects	Ounces consumed	
	Good taste	Bad taste
Normal	10.6	6.4
Obese	13.9	2.6

From Decke, E. Cited in Schachter, S. **Emotion, Obesity and Crime.** New York: Academic Press, 1971.

Stunkard's experiment is a model of simplicity. His subjects reported for duty at nine o'clock in the morning without breakfast and swallowed a gastric balloon, a device used to measure stomach contractions. Monitored continuously for a period of four hours, every fifteen minutes the subjects were asked if they felt hungry and they answered simply Yes or No. The degree of correspondence between the verbal report "Yes" and the presence or absence of stomach contractions was compared for a group of normal-sized subjects and a group of obese subjects. The normal-sized subjects showed a high degree of correspondence between the presence of stomach contractions and the report "Yes," and similarly, a high degree of correspondence between the absence of stomach contractions and the report "No." The obese subjects, on the other hand, showed a very low correspondence between stomach contractions and verbal report. In short, the verbal behavior of the obese subjects was influenced relatively little by their own physiological condition.

Schachter and his associates further developed the Stunkard hypothesis by making the simple assumption that obese subjects are more influenced by external cues and less by internal cues than normal subjects. Decke (1971) tested this hypothesis utilizing the taste of food as an external cue. Good taste should stimulate obese subjects more than normals and bad taste should have the reverse effect. Decke provided her subjects with either a normal vanilla milkshake or a vanilla milkshake adulterated with quinine so that it tasted terrible. The results are shown in Table 8.1. Normal subjects, as expected, consumed somewhat less of the bad-tasting milkshake. Obese subjects consumed more of the good-tasting milkshake but a great deal less of the bad-tasting concoction. The reader will recognize the striking similarity of this finding to comparable studies described above on rats with lesions of the ventromedial hypothalamus. These rats, while normally consuming more than unoperated controls, show dramatic decline in food consumption if food is adulterated with quinine or other bad-tasting substances. Ventromedially lesioned rats eat less bad-tasting food than do normal rats but they eat more good-tasting food.

Table 8.2 Eating habits

Variable	Animals		Humans	
	Batting average	Mean F/N	Mean F/N	Batting average
Amount of food eaten ad lib	9/9	1.19	1.16	2/3
Number of meals per day	4/4	.85	.92	3/3
Amount eaten per meal	2/2	1.34	1.29	5/5
Speed of eating	1/1	1.28	1.26	1/1

Note: F/N = fat to normal ratio.

From Schachter, S. Some extraordinary facts about obese humans and rats. **American Psychologist 26,** 1971, pp. 129–144. Copyright 1971 by the American Psychological Association. Reprinted by permission.

Schachter went on to explore a number of parallels between obese humans and ventromedially lesioned rats. He surveyed the lesion literature completely and computed an index comparing fat to normal animal behavior and fat to normal human behavior. Results of this survey are shown in Table 8.2. The correspondences are almost incredible. With good food the fat to normal ratio (F/N) for animals is 1.45, for humans 1.42. The same kind of correspondences exist for bad food eaten, amount of food eaten ad lib, number of meals per day, the amount eaten per meal, and speed of eating. Schachter constructed additional parallel experiments for humans, comparing normal and obese humans on measures that were available from rat literature but not in humans. One of the most striking facts about ventromedially lesioned obese rats is that although they eat more than normals under normal conditions, they will not work as hard for food. They will eat only if food is available. If they must press a lever, as shown by Teitelbaum (1957), they work far less and eat far less than normal rats. Schachter's experiment involved testing the subject, normal or fat, at a desk which contained a large bag of almonds. There were two conditions in the experiment; in one, the nuts had shells, and in the other, the nuts had no shells. The results are shown in Table 8.3. Schachter described these experiments and a comparable series done on Chinese and Japanese restaurants in the following passage:

... Table [8.3] presents for normal subjects the numbers who do and do not eat nuts in the two conditions. As you can see, shells or no shells has virtually no impact on normal subjects. Fifty-five percent of normals eat nuts without shells, and 50% eat nuts with shells. I am a little self-conscious about the data for obese subjects, for it looks as if I were too stupid to know how to fake data. I know how to fake data, and were I to do so, the bottom half of Table [8.3] certainly

Table 8.3 **Effects of work on the eating behavior of normal and fat subjects**

Subjects	Nuts have	Number who	
		Eat	Don't eat
Normal	Shells	10	10
	No shells	11	9
Fat	Shells	1	19
	No shells	19	1

From Schachter, S. Some extraordinary facts about obese humans and rats. **American Psychologist 26,** 1971, pp. 129–144. Copyright 1971 by the American Psychological Association. Reprinted by permission.

would not look the way it does. When the nuts have no shells, 19 of 20 fat subjects eat nuts. When the nuts have shells on them, 1 out of 20 fat subjects eats. Obviously, the parallel to Miller's and to Teitelbaum's rats is perfect. When the food is easy to get at, fat subjects, rats or human, eat more than normals; when the food is hard to get at, fat subjects eat less than normals.

Incidentally, as a casual corollary of these and other findings, one could expect that, given acceptable food, fat eaters would be more likely than normals to choose the easiest way of eating. In order to check on this, Lucy Friedman, Joel Handler, and I went to a large number of Chinese and Japanese restaurants, categorized each patron as he entered the restaurant as obese or normal, and then simply noted whether he ate with chopsticks or with silverware. Among Occidentals, for whom chopsticks can be an ordeal, we found that almost five times the proportion of normal eaters ate with chopsticks as did obese eaters —22.4% of normals and 4.7% of the obese ate with chopsticks.

(Stanley Schachter, 1971, page 135)

To date, Schachter and his associates have found twelve nonobvious facts or variables in which the behavior of ventromedially lesioned rats identically parallels the behavior of obese humans. So far, they have found no instance of a lack of correspondence.

A series of studies by Rodin, one of Schachter's students, demonstrates that obese subjects are much more influenced by distraction in their performance of routine tasks. This follows if one assumes that the greater influence of external cues on the obese subject is due to the fact that the subject is more "stimulus-bound," that his behavior is more under the control of external stimuli than a normal person. She had the subjects proofread and scored performance while presenting varying degrees of distracting stimuli during the course of proofreading. The results are

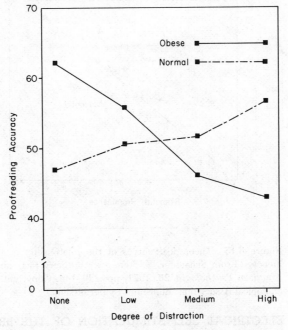

Figure 8.14 The effects of distraction on performance. As shown here, the obese humans are better at proofreading than normals when undistracted. When distracted, their performance deteriorates. (From Rodin, J. Effects of distraction on performance of obese and normal subjects. Unpublished doctoral dissertation. New York: Columbia University, 1970.)

given in Figure 8.14. Note that obese subjects do better than normal subjects when there is no distraction but they do significantly poorer than normals when there is a high degree of distraction. Schachter summarizes his hypothesis in a theoretical diagram, Figure 8.15. Obese subjects are more stimulus-bound and more reactive. Hence as stimulus prominence increases, the degree of reactivity of the obese subjects increases. At low levels of stimulus prominence, obese subjects would be less active or reactive than normals, but at high levels they would be more so. In a simple test of this hypothesis, Ross (1969) seated normal and obese subjects at a table with a large tin of shelled cashew nuts, either brightly lighted, or dimly lighted in the background. As expected, fats ate many more nuts than normals in bright light, but fewer than normals in dim light.

Schachter's studies are of great importance to those interested in mechanisms of feeding behavior because of their emphasis on the role of differential reactivity to internal and external stimuli. Such an approach is in keeping with the renewed interest in peripheral and central sensory factors discussed in relation to the VMH and LH syndrome.

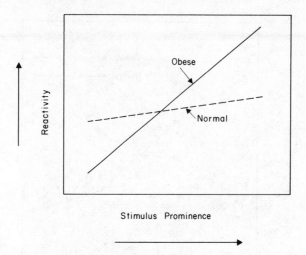

Motivation

Figure 8.15 Theoretical curves of the relationship of reactivity to stimulus prominence. (From Schachter, S. Some extraordinary facts about obese humans and rats. *American Psychologist* **26**, 1971, pp. 129–144. Copyright 1971 by the American Psychological Association. Reprinted by permission.)

ELECTRICAL SELF-STIMULATION OF THE BRAIN

The finding by James Olds, in 1953, that an animal will actively seek to deliver a weak electric shock to its own brain is perhaps the most important discovery yet made about the physiological substrates of behavior. Olds' description of how the discovery was made conveys some of the excitement he must have felt and illustrates how a very gifted scientist quickly "zeroed in" on an almost accidental observation.

With the help of Hess's technique for probing the brain and Skinner's for measuring motivation, we have been engaged in a series of experiments which began three years ago under the guidance of the psychologist D. O. Hebb at McGill University. At the beginning we planned to explore particularly the mid-brain reticular system—the sleep-control area that had been investigated by Magoun.

Just before we began our own work, H. R. Delgado, W. W. Roberts and N. E. Miller at Yale University had undertaken a similar study. They had located an area in the lower part of the mid-line system where stimulation caused the animal to avoid the behavior that provoked the electrical stimulus. We wished to investigate positive as well as negative effects—that is, to learn whether stimulation of some areas might be sought rather than avoided by the animal.

We were not at first concerned to hit very specific points in the brain, and in fact in our early tests the electrodes did not always go to the particular areas in the mid-line system at which they were aimed. Our lack of aim turned out to be a fortunate happening for us.

In one animal the electrode missed its target and landed not in the mid-brain recticular system but in a nerve pathway from the rhinencephalon. This led to an unexpected discovery.

In the test experiment we were using, the animal was placed in a large box with corners labeled A, B, C and D. Whenever the animal went to corner A, its brain was given a mild electric shock by the experimenter. When the test was performed on the animal with the electrode in the rhinencephalic nerve, it kept returning to corner A. After several such returns on the first day, it finally went to a different place and fell asleep. The next day, however, it seemed even more interested in corner A.

At this point we assumed that the stimulus must provoke curiosity; we did not yet think of it as a reward. Further experimentation on the same animal soon indicated, to our surprise, that its response to the stimulus was more than curiosity. On the second day, after the animal had acquired the habit of returning to corner A to be stimulated, we began trying to draw it away to corner B, giving it an electric shock whenever it took a step in that direction. Within a matter of five minutes the animal was in corner B. After this, the animal could be directed to almost any spot in the box at the will of the experimenter. Every step in the right direction was paid with a small shock; on arrival at the appointed place the animal received a longer series of shocks.

Next the animal was put on a T-shaped platform and stimulated if it turned right at the crossing of the T but not if it turned left. It soon learned to turn right every time. At this point we reversed the procedure, and the animal had to turn left in order to get a shock. With some guidance from the experimenter it eventually switched from the right to the left. We followed up with a test of the animal's response when it was hungry. Food was withheld for 24 hours. Then the animal was placed in a T both arms of which were baited with mash. The animal would receive the electric stimulus at a point halfway down the right arm. It learned to go there, and it always stopped at this point, never going on to the food at all!

After confirming this powerful effect of stimulation of brain areas by experiments with a series of animals, we set out to map the places in the brain where such an effect could be obtained. We wanted to measure the strength of the effect in each place. Here Skinner's technique provided the means. By putting the animal in the "do-it-yourself" situation (i.e., pressing a lever to stimulate its own brain) we could translate the animal's strength of "desire" into response frequency, which can be seen and measured.

The first animal in the Skinner box ended all doubts in our minds that electric stimulation applied to some parts of the brain could indeed provide reward for behavior. The test displayed the phenomenon

Electrical self-stimulation of the brain

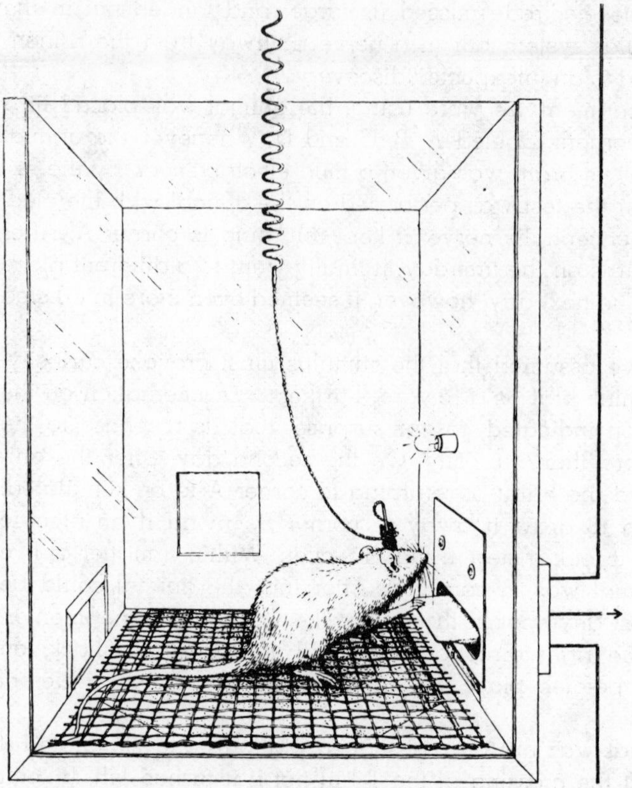

Figure 8.16 Experimental arrangement for intracranial self-stimulation. When the rat presses the lever it triggers an electrical stimulus to its brain and simultaneously records action via wire at left. (From Olds, J. Pleasure centers in the brain. Copyright © 1956 by Scientific American, Inc. All rights reserved.)

in bold relief where anyone who wanted to look could see it. Left to itself in the apparatus, the animal (after about two to five minutes of learning) stimulated its own brain regularly about once every five seconds, taking a stimulus of a second or so every time. After 30 minutes the experimenter turned off the current, so that the animal's pressing of the lever no longer stimulated the brain. Under these conditions the animal pressed it about seven times then went to sleep. We found that the test was repeatable as often as we cared to apply it. When the current was turned on and the animal was given one shock as an **hors d'oeuvre** it would begin stimulating its brain again. When the electricity was turned off, it would try a few times and then go to sleep.

(From Pleasure centers in the brain, James Olds, pages 107–108. Copyright © 1956 by Scientific American, Inc. All rights reserved.)

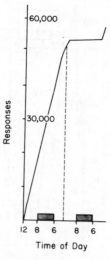

Figure 8.17 Graph of continuous self-stimulation for a 48-hour period. Cumulative response totals are plotted along the ordinate, hours along the abscissa. The experiment began at noon; cross-hatching indicates darkness from 8 p.m. to 6 a.m. The animal (with an electrode implanted in the anterior medial hypothalamus) stimulated itself at a rate of more than 2000 responses an hour for 26 hours, then slept, and then resumed self-stimulation at the same rate. (From Olds, J. Self-stimulation of the brain. *Science* **127**, 1958, pp. 315–324. Copyright 1958 by the American Association for the Advancement of Science.)

The general experimental arrangement for electrical self-stimulation is shown in Figure 8.16. When the animal presses the lever, a weak shock of specified characteristics is delivered through the implanted electrode to the desired region of the brain. An example of the high rate of self-stimulation generated by a rat with an electrode in a "hot" spot is shown in Figure 8.17. Animals will press at rates up to 5000 times per hour (more than once per second) under appropriate circumstances! The lever-press method of measuring the reward value of various brain regions has been criticized and various alternatives suggested, such as amount of time standing on a platform that results in brain shocks vs. a neutral platform (Valenstein and Meyers, 1964). Nonetheless, lever-press provides a simple, clear-cut, and easily quantifiable measure.

In the initial studies by Olds, and Olds and Milner (1954), the septal region appeared to be the region of greatest reward value. Olds (1962) subsequently completed a very extensive mapping study of reward value of various regions of the brain. Many brain regions are neutral—the animal presses at the same low rate with and without stimulation; and some are negative—after a few presses the animal will not continue and may even avoid the lever, presumably reflecting a painful experience. The mapping study indicated that the general region of the medial fore-

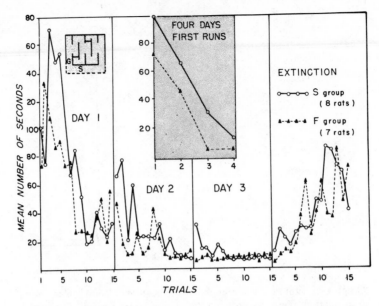

Figure 8.18 Maze experiment. At the upper left is a maze. The animal runs from the start position (S) through the maze to the goal position (G). At G it finds a pedal, steps on it, and stimulates its brain. After the stimulation, the pedal is swung back, and the goal box becomes the start box as the animal runs the maze again. The graphs show a comparison of a group running for food as the reward (broken line) with another group running for electric shock as the reward (solid line). Both groups were 24-hours-hungry. The shock-reward group ran as fast as the food-reward group, at the end of the test, and learned almost as fast. The marked day-to-day improvement shown in the first runs of the four days is especially important. The animals of the shock-group averaged over 100 seconds on the first run the first day. They took about 50 seconds on the first run the second day, 30 seconds on the first run the third day, and 12 seconds on the fourth day. This indicates that an animal runs directly to its goal on the first run of the day, having had no pretaste of the electric stimulus to whet its desire. (From Olds, J. Self-stimulation of the brain. *Science* **127**, 1958, pp. 315–324. Copyright 1958 by the American Association for the Advancement of Science.)

brain bundle and lateral hypothalamus was the most reliable hot spot (Fig. 8.2). Other portions of the limbic forebrain generally have reward value but less reliably and of lesser magnitude.

An enormous amount of research has been done on the phenomenon of electrical self-stimulation of the brain. Olds' basic observations and his general operational interpretation of high self-stimulation rates as indicants of positive reinforcement have been attacked on almost every conceivable ground. It is not necessary to review this vast literature here. Much of it, particularly the various criticisms, have not been overly important. In general, the best and most valuable work on the phenomenon over the years since its discovery has been done by Olds and his associates. Only a few of the basic points are emphasized here. A major objection has been that self-stimulation is analogous to a "forced-motor" seizure

—once started the animal can't stop—and may not have reinforcement value. Olds (1956) demonstrated that rats will learn mazes to obtain electrical brain stimulation in a manner essentially identical to hungry rats learning the same maze for food reward (Fig. 8.18).

Another point of major concern to many is the fact that extinction of self-stimulation behavior can be very rapid. Once the shock is turned off, the animal may continue pressing for only a short time. This contrasts somewhat with rats trained to press for food or water. When delivery of food or water ceases animals typically continue pressing for some time. Deutsch (1960), for example, developed an alternative theory in terms of a short term *intrinsic decay* process. An ingenious experiment by Gibson and associates (1965) rather neatly dispels this objection. Two groups of rats were trained to lick water—one group received brain stimulation reward for licking and the other group received sugar water. For extinction, the brain stimulus and the sugar water were turned off. Both groups extinguished rapidly at the same rate. The main point seems to be that the brain stimulus, like sugar water, is highly discriminable and occurs at the same time as the response. When brain stimulus and sugar water are removed, it is immediately obvious to the animal. In the ordinary lever-press food-or-water reward situation there is a substantial delay in delivery of reinforcement and a spatial separation between the response (lever press) and the reward. Gibson and his colleagues demonstrated this for self-stimulation by training groups to press a lever in order to deliver a water dipper which, when licked, gave brain stimulation or sugar water. Extinction rates of these groups were both normal and much slower than the animals given direct reward for licking.

To summarize, positive electrical self-stimulation of the brain is a very powerful effect, particularly when delivered in the general region of the medial forebrain bundle–lateral hypothalamus. It does not appear to differ in basic properties from other types of reward or reinforcement.

Brain stimulation vs. natural reward

Undoubtedly, the reader has noticed that the region of the brain giving the highest rates of electrical self-stimulation is the "feeding center," the lateral hypothalamus. In 1962 Margules and Olds, and Hoebel and Teitelbaum, independently reported that both feeding behavior and self-stimulation could be obtained from the same electrodes implanted in the lateral hypothalamus. You will recall that satiated animals eat when stimulated in the lateral hypotahalmus. Olds and Margules implanted electrodes in the region of the lateral hypothalamus in 50 animals. Twenty-eight of the animals showed stimulus-bound eating behavior. All these animals demonstrated self-stimulation. Only four of the 18 non-feeding rats showed self-stimulation—a very convincing demonstration.

In other studies it has been shown that some sites producing seminal emission are self-stimulating and that drinking behavior sites can also be self-stimulating. Further, rats with lateral hypothalamus electrodes will self-stimulate more when hungry than when satiated. Olds reported early (1958) that rats, in fact, prefer self-stimulation to other forms of reward. Routtenberg and Lindy (1965) provided a dramatic example of this. Previously starved rats with lateral hypothalamus electrodes were given one hour each day during which they could choose between food and electrical self-stimulation. Many animals chose electrical reward over food, even to the point of dying of starvation.

These results, indicating that the brain sites for best self-stimulation and for natural reward, particularly feeding, are the same, would seem at first glance to be very satisfying. The electrical brain stimulus appears to mimic natural rewards—eating most strongly but also drinking and copulation. Actually the fact that the hottest spot for self-stimulation is in the lateral hypothalamus is a paradox. The lateral hypothalamus is the region whose neurons are activated by *low* blood glucose. Stimulation or activation of this region makes the organism feel hungry and eat, not feel satisfied and stop eating. To be consistent, the most effective brain region for self-stimulation ought to be the ventromedial hypothalamus, the hypothetical satiety center. However, electrical stimulation in the ventromedial nucleus yields uncertain and mixed results—sometimes negative and sometimes positive, but never as strongly positive as the lateral hypothalamus. We will return to this paradox after a brief look at the kinds of behaviors directly elicited from stimulation of the lateral hypothalalmic region.

The general technique of eliciting behavior patterns from brain stimulation was developed first by Hess, working in Switzerland. He demonstrated that in cats electrical brain stimulation in the general region of the hypothalamus could elicit a variety of *emotional* or motivated behaviors, ranging from eating and sleep to hissing, biting, and full-blown rage. The work of Hess will be treated further in Chapter 9. Behaviors evoked by hypothalamic stimulation often are described as *stimulus-bound*. The animal performs a particular sequence of responses such as eating or attack very mechanically, like a puppet on a string. It is as though he were forced to perform the sequence of responses without his heart in the action. This characteristic, evident to those who have seen such animals but difficult to describe, led to the term *sham rage*. With stimulation in certain regions, the animal exhibits all the autonomic behavioral signs of rage but can be safely petted during the rage. An interesting series of experiments showing the wide range of "natural" behaviors that can be evoked in the chicken by brain stimulation has been presented by von Holst and von Saint Paul (1962). These stereotyped behavior patterns occur mechanically and completely out of context with the bird's ongoing normal behavior, yet each elicited pattern is quite normal by itself.

We described above the experiment by Margules and Olds where stimulus-bound eating was evoked in rats by electrical stimulation of the lateral hypothalamic self-reward region. Eliot Valenstein and colleagues have studied these stimulus-bound behaviors to electrical stimulation of the hypothalamus in great detail (Valenstein, Cox, and Kakolewski, 1970). They arranged the experimental situation in such a way that the brain-stimulated rat could choose his own brand of "kick." Food, water, a piece of wood to gnaw, and a receptive female might all be present in the test cage. When weak shocks were delivered in the lateral hypothalamus a particular form of behavior often occurred. Feeding and drinking were most common, followed by gnawing and copulation. When a given behavior was being elicited the experimenters very cleverly removed the behavioral object. If stimulation elicited feeding, they removed the food and then restimulated. The animals characteristically shifted to some other behavior—perhaps drinking, gnawing, or digging. In short, there was some plasticity in the evoked behavior, depending on what stimulus objects were presented. If the preferred stimulus object was left in the cage, they often observed a fatigue or habituation effect. After the animal had repeatedly exhibited feeding, he might shift over to gnawing or drinking. However, Valenstein cautions against overgeneralizing the plasticity of response to brain stimulation. A given electrode site tended to elicit a given behavior; alternative behaviors only appear when the preferred stimulus is absent or the response is habituated.

Valenstein's work suggests a possible explanation of the contradictory findings that the best locus of eliciting self-stimulation is the best locus for feeding. Most studies of brain-elicited feeding provided only food to the rat. He might actually have preferred to do many other things but the only stimulus-satisfaction object was food. This would weaken the paradox but an unsatisfactory contradiction remains. Why is the lateral hypothalamus, which from Valenstein's work can generate many kinds of motivated behavior, the best self-stimulation site?

A more recent and very important paper by Olds and associates (Olds, Allan, and Briese, 1971) appears to resolve the paradox and to have significant implications for the general understanding of motivation. The study involved a detailed mapping of the kinds of behavior—feeding, drinking, and electrical self-stimulation—that could be elicited in the general region of the hypothalamus. The major technical innovation was use of a very small electrode, a *microelectrode,* and weak currents so that a given stimulus activated only a tiny region of brain tissue. Results, although complicated in detail, produce a clear overall picture. Stimulation of the anterior region of the hypothalamus yields only drinking. Eating alone was obtained from stimulation of the middle lateral region of the hypothalamus (as we have noted in other studies above) *but only in the upper or more dorsal portion.* Electrical self-stimulation alone was obtained from the fairly wide lateral region occupied by the medial forebrain bundle. Stimulation of the ventromedial nucleus (the satiety center) tended to inhibit or disrupt eating and did not elicit self-stimulation. Finally, stimulation in the middle lateral region of the hypothalamus, somewhat below the eating area, regularly produced mixed effects— sometimes eating, sometimes drinking, and sometimes self-stimulation in a fashion identical to that described by Valenstein and associates.

This study by Olds suggests that the hunger center in the lateral hypothalamus is separate and distinct from the self-stimulation zone. They just happen to be close together anatomically. Stimulation with larger electrodes would activate both regions indiscriminately. Consequently, the paradox is resolved. "Feeling hungry" is not rewarding; the hunger center is simply close to the reward system. Furthermore, "feeling full" by stimulating the ventromedial hypothalamic satiety region, is disruptive to feeding behavior, as it ought to be, and more important it is not by itself rewarding.

MOTIVATION AND REWARD

A picture of hypothalamic function in motivation and reward begins to emerge from these observations, a picture that does not agree with traditional behavioral or biological theories of motivation. Oddly enough though, it seems to correspond more to our own simple experience and to common-sense views of motivation and reward.

There are two major extreme theoretical positions concerning motivation and reward or reinforcement. One, which we label the *mechanism theory*, is prevalent among behaviorally oriented biologists. Basically, they believe there is no such thing as general motivation or drive. Any given stimulus situation elicits an appropriate response; for example, the internal stimuli from hunger elicit specific food-seeking and consuming responses. An example is Dethier's elegant analysis of hunger in the blowfly (see above). The feeding behavior of this simple organism can be analyzed in direct mechanical terms.

Scientists who adopt the mechanism theory generalize this kind of analysis to the motivated behavior of higher animals. Such an approach is appealing in its simplicity. It is not necessary to deal with more complex issues and concepts such as hunger or drive and motivation. At the other extreme is drive reduction theory, stemming from Hull's concepts of habit and drive. As we noted at the beginning of the chapter, this point of view has been treated comprehensively by Judson Brown (1961). The basic idea is that motivation has general properties. A hungry organism is in a higher general drive state than a satiated animal. Increase in general arousal and activity would reflect this higher drive level. The increased drive is not simply food-seeking behavior but is, instead, general. Hunger, thirst, sexual need, and other needs can contribute to the level of generalized drive. When these needs are satisfied the drive state is reduced. Drive reduction is held to be rewarding or reinforcing. In fact, reward or reinforcement is held to be solely the result of drive reduction. Since in Hull's view learning new behaviors occurs solely as a result of reinforcement, drive and its reduction becomes the primary factor not only in generating behavior but also in shaping and modifying behavior.

Olds' discovery of electrical self-stimulation posed fundamental problems for both mechanistic and drive reduction theories. Shocking the medial forebrain bundle clearly is the most rewarding act of an animal— he does it in preference to reducing hunger and thirst drives and increases the probability of doing it immediately to very high levels. Self-stimulation is not part of any mechanistic system involved in feeding, drinking, or other activities. It is also not drive-reducing. Self-stimulation satisfies no known need and cannot be conceived easily as reducing drive. It is a strong positive effect of direct brain stimulation, not a negative effect of reducing drive stimuli.

All studies on electrical stimulation of the ventromedial satiety center agree that it stops an animal from eating; they also agree that it is not particularly rewarding or reinforcing to the animal. Yet the mechanism of drive reduction for hunger seems to involve activation of this region.

It is undisputed that food is rewarding to a hungry animal or man. It is also drive-reducing. The two effects may be separate. Hunger drive reduction by eating would correspond to a full stomach, an increased blood sugar, increased activation of the ventromedial hypothalamus, and satiation. The good taste of the food also would provide reward. The two factors, taste reward and drive reduction, normally always would occur together. A full animal is unlikely to eat. However, electrical brain stimulation can uncouple the two kinds of effects. Stimulation of ventromedial hypothalamus mimics satiation and stops eating—it is drive-reducing—but is not rewarding. Stimulation of the *dorsal* part of the lateral hypothalamus elicits hunger and causes eating but is not rewarding also. Stimulation of the medial forebrain bundle is rewarding but neither elicits nor reduces drives like hunger and thirst.

Under normal conditions eating food reduces hunger drive and provides reward. If reward is dependent on positive factors as well as on the negative feature of drive reduction, then the taste, or rather palatability, of foods ought to be a critical determinant of behavior, particularly in terms of immediate effects on eating. This is indeed the case. You will remember that a food-deprived hungry animal is more sensitive to the palatability of foods than others. The classical hyperphagic rat with damage to the ventromedial hypothalamus is far more sensitive than the normal rat to the palatability of food. He is hyperphagic only for good food. Similarly the aphagic animal with lateral hypothalamic damage is abnormally sensitive to the palatability of food. Finally, fat humans are also much more influenced by food palatability than normals. If there is any one variable that is common to all abnormalities of feeding behavior it is the influence of taste, or palatability. Taste, as noted above, is largely composed of olfactory cues and the only relatively direct sensory input to the hypothalamus is olfactory. In fact, the entire limbic forebrain system (Fig. 8.3) evolved from the elementary olfactory forebrain of primitive vertebrates. Much of the limbic forebrain was once thought to be olfactory in function and was called the *rhinencephalon* (nose brain). Except for very limited regions the limbic forebrain is now known not to have any direct olfactory function; however, it evolved from a system that was olfactory in function. Although the olfactory system in humans is tiny and almost rudimentary, consider the powerful influence of odors on your experience and behavior, not only in terms of eating but also sexual activity, emotional reactions, and even memories. The brain system that mediates the overridingly powerful effect of rewarding electrical self-stimulation is this limbic brain system that evolved from a primitive olfactory forebrain. As Olds has stated, this system appears to mediate reward and reinforcement independent of any particular drives or needs such as hunger and thirst, and in a direct positive manner rather than in terms of need reduction.

Ignoring extreme environmental conditions, all an individual animal in the natural state must do to survive is to maintain a reasonable temperature and obtain food and water. Nature was faced with the problem of designing organisms that can do this successfully. Perhaps the easiest solution was to build a relatively simple set of reflexes utilizing few neurons that would work in a machine-like manner under appropriate conditions. Feeding of the blowfly exemplifies this approach. Another extreme approach was the design of an organism that experiences need and drive and generalized pleasure or reward but with less rigid reflex machinery. Evolution of higher vertebrates appears to have gone in this direction. Many more neurons are needed for such an animal. He must modify his behavior and learn from experience in order to satisfy need and obtain reward. Of course, higher organisms also must have the reflex machinery necessary to chew, eat, and drink.

The hypothalamus appears to be the critical link or nexus between the brain stem regions that control reflex mechanisms of motivated behavior and the higher brain regions that mediate the expressions of motivation —hunger, thirst, sex, and other needs. The limbic forebrain system, particularly the medial forebrain bundle region, appears to have developed from an olfactory brain into a general system mediating pleasure and reward. To overstate this position even more, the hypothalamus is the link between the biological machinery of motivated behavior and the subjective experience of needs and pleasure mediated by higher brain regions. The critical factor is development of the limbic system to mediate general drive or need and pleasure or reward independent of particular needs and stimuli.

Fragmentary human data on electrical self-stimulation of the brain support this general view. Stimulation of certain limbic brain structures in humans, as in other animals, leads to compulsive self-stimulation. Subjective reports indicate an almost complete absence of specific sensations or experiences associated with electrical self-stimulation. Patients are vague and confused about what they experience or why they like it but very clear that they *want it*. The development of brain systems for generalized need or drive would seem to offer a possible explanation for the very powerful drug addictions that develop in humans and other higher animals. Heroin is an artificial substance that satisfies no known need. Yet the addict develops such a strong need or craving for it that, like the self-stimulating rat, he will starve to death if necessary to "consume" it. It may be that addicting drugs have particular actions on the hypothalamus and limbic brain structures that serve to mediate general need. In short, higher animals are by nature driven. The ecological dominance of mammals may be the result not only of more brain cells but also of a specialized brain system that can drive them to behave even when particular tissue needs are not strong.

Summary

The term *motivation* is generally utilized to refer to presumed or inferred mechanisms underlying specific behavioral activities, such as eating or drinking. The term *drive* has been used to describe motivated behavior in two different ways. It is used to refer to specific sources of motivated behavior, such as hunger or thirst, and with reference to a more generalized drive state which is independent of particular sources of drive.

One of the simplest aspects of motivated behavior is temperature regulation. In endotherms ("warm-blooded" animals), temperature control comes close to being a self-regulating system. However, in extreme environments where the internal regulating system is ineffective, humans will die unless they move to a more moderate environment. One characteristic of all endotherms is their ability to locate an ecological niche most suited to their environmental temperature range. Behavioral patterns and evolutionary adaptations provide other means by which animals may accommodate to their environmental temperature range.

In endotherms, the homeostatic mechanism for internal temperature regulation functions like the thermostat on a furnace/air-conditioner system. This mechanism is located in the anterior hypothalamus and senses the temperature of circulating blood. The rate of discharge of temperature detector neurons is proportional to blood temperature. By means of the action of these neurons upon other neurons, the needed warming and cooling reactions are activated. Afferent information from skin temperature receptors in the hypothalamus determines the activity of the hypothalamic thermostat.

Fever results from an increase in the set-point of the hypothalamic thermostat. One current hypothesis about the cause of the increased set-point is that "pyrogens" from bacteria and other disease factors are released into the blood and act directly on the hypothalamic set-point neurons. Aspirin apparently reduces fever by decreasing the hypothalamic set-point to its normal level.

There are two aspects to the biological mechanisms controlling body fluid levels. One is concerned with the manner in which body water need is detected and communicated to the brain. The other involves the brain systems which link detection of water need to drinking behavior. The immediate cause of drinking behavior is the experience of thirst. It appears that the body manufactures a "thirst substance" which is released into the blood when tissues need water and then acts upon "thirst receptors" in the brain.

Although extracellular fluid volume is the more critical factor, the fluid levels in both cellular and extracellular compartments play significant roles in drinking behavior. Under normal conditions of mild deprivation, extracellular fluid volume is more important than cellular water content. In severe dehydration, reduced cellular content of water can become a powerful stimulus for thirst. The mechanism appears to be a direct activation of thirst receptors in specialized cells of the hypothalamus.

The major body factor involved in the regulation of drinking behavior concerns changes in salt concentration of blood or cells. This results in changes in the water content of blood which lead to a change in the total volume of blood. Blood pressure changes result from the above changes. The critical pressure receptors for drinking behavior are located in the venous side of the vascular system. The majority of evidence suggests that pressure receptors in veins mediate thirst.

Reduced venous pressure results in the release of renin by the kidneys. The release of renin is triggered in the kidney and also by reflex control from venous pressure receptors which relay back to the kidney via the sympathetic nervous system. Renin serves as an enzyme acting on angiotensinogen and converts this substance to angiotensin II. Angiotensin II is believed to act directly on the receptors in the hypothalamic region to produce the sensation of thirst and hence drinking behavior.

The antidiuretic hormone (ADH) also plays a role in the regulation of body fluid levels. ADH is released by neurons from the anterior hypothalamus via the posterior pituitary. When an increased amount of ADH is released, it acts on the kidney so that water is reabsorbed and urine volume reduced. If a decreased amount of ADH is secreted, a greater than normal amount of water is lost in urine.

There are two separate regions of the hypothalamus which contain receptors for the detection of intracellular fluid level (lateral region) and extracellular fluid level (anterior region). Both regions are important in the regulation of fluid intake. The extracellular fluid level monitoring is the more sensitive detection system. The kidneys play a crucial role by releasing angiotensin II which acts upon anterior hypothalamic receptors. Activation of these receptors leads to activation of the brain systems which result in thirst and drinking behavior.

There appear to be two brain "centers" in the hypothalamus related to eating behavior, one which initiates feeding and one which terminates it. While smell and taste play a critical role in food selection, the blood levels of particular nutrients and hormones are more important in actual eating. Oral and gastric factors are important in the modulation of feeding behavior. The glucostatic theory of food regulation has shown that blood levels of glucose are correlated with feeding. The critical factor is the *rate of utilization* of glucose by tissues, especially hypothalamic tissue.

Evidence suggests that glucose receptors do exist in the brain. Lowered blood glucose level and the resultant lowered brain tissue utilization of glucose is a direct stimulus to regions of the hypothalamus which produces the sensation of hunger. Increased blood levels of glucose are less reliable in terminating feeding than decreased levels are in initiating it. The critical determinants of the onset and offset of feeding and hunger are the blood levels of glucose and perhaps other substances, and the rates of brain tissue utilization of glucose.

The hypothalamus is the critical region for sensations of hunger and thirst, and for feeding and drinking behaviors. While brain regions higher than the hypothalamus are presumed to be necessary for the sensations of hunger and thirst, the hypothalamus forms the critical link in these sensations. The crucial regions of the hypothalamus are the anterior, lateral (composed of lateral nuclei and the medial forebrain bundle), and ventromedial areas. Lesion studies have shown that adipsia (absence of drinking) results from destruction of the anterior portion of the lateral region of the hypothalamus. When the ventromedial hypothalamus is destroyed, the hyperphagic (increased eating) syndrome is evident. Both aphagia (absence of eating) and adipsia result from destruction of lateral hypothalamus.

The anterior hypothalamus plays a significant role in drinking behavior. The anterior preoptic area of the hypothalamus is selective for drinking. It appears that some regions, for example, the hypothalamus, are more effective in eliciting drinking per se, while other limbic structures tend to modulate drinking. Evidence relating to the hyperphagic syndrome suggests that the ventromedial hypothalamus acts as a "satiety center," turning off hunger and feeding behavior when sufficient nutrients have been consumed.

The lateral hypothalamus (LH) appears to be the activating center for the initiation of eating and drinking behaviors. Lesions of the lateral hypothalamus produce animals with a permanent deficit in eating behavior. They also exhibit motivational inertia. Recent evidence suggests that a significant part of the LH syndrome may be due to interference with sensory pathways relating to eating.

The eating behavior of obese humans is less influenced by their internal physiological state than that of normal subjects and more strongly influenced by external cues. There are also striking parallels between obese humans and ventromedially lesioned rats. For both fat humans and fat rats, when food is easily obtainable, they eat more than normals; when it is necessary to work to get the food, they both eat significantly less than normals. Obese humans are more influenced by distraction in the performance of routine tasks. With damage to the ventromedial hypothalamus, humans manifest the same hyperemotionality as do rats with this type of lesion.

The phenomenon of electrical self-stimulation of the brain poses problems for hypotheses about motivation and reward. Animals will actively seek to deliver weak electric shocks to their own brains. This self-stimulation acts as a reward for the animal. The general region of the medial forebrain bundle and lateral hypothalamus have the greatest reward value with self-stimulation. Electrical self-stimulation does not appear to differ in its basic properties from other types of reward or reinforcement. Studies examining the effects of stimulation in various regions of the hypothalamus have shown that the hunger center appears to be separate and distinct from the self-stimulation region occupied by the medial forebrain bundle.

There are two major theoretical positions concerning motivation and reward. The view of the ethologists is the "mechanism" theory which argues that there is no such thing as general motivation or drive. A given stimulus situation elicits specific food seeking and consuming responses. This approach, however, cannot be generalized to the motivated behavior of higher animals. The drive reduction theory states that motivation has general properties and that various needs contribute to the generalized drive level. Reward and reinforcement are viewed as solely the result of drive reduction. The greatest problem with the drive reduction theory is its dependency upon drive reduction as the only mechanism of reward or reinforcement. Electrical self-stimulation poses a basic problem for both positions as it is neither drive "reducing" nor part of any specific mechanism.

9

Sexual and emotional behavior

9

SEXUAL BEHAVIOR

Eating and drinking, together with self-regulating mechanisms like temperature control, are the principal motivated behaviors necessary to ensure survival of an individual animal under benign environmental conditions. Hence these activities are of overriding importance to the individual. However, the survival of the individual is of little or no biological importance; all that counts is survival of the species. Among higher animals the species survives only as a result of successful sexual behavior. Sex satisfies no survival needs for the individual and is not necessary for biological (as opposed to personal) well-being. In this sense it is not a tissue need. Nevertheless, there are some obvious similarities between sexual behavior and ingestive behaviors in terms of their mechanisms of control.

First, as with eating and drinking, stimuli play an important role in eliciting and directing sexual behavior. Stimuli may be interpreted as signals announcing "to whom it may concern" that a sexually receptive member of the species is in the vicinity. The courtship calls of male frogs and birds, the odor trails of deer, cats, and dogs, the fluttering behavior of butterflies, the cosmetics used by humans—all serve to attract potential sexual partners. Frequently, behavior patterns themselves may function as important sexual signals, serving both to identify the animal as sexually receptive and to increase its attractiveness to the potential mate. Such courtship displays in animals may be very elaborate and their superficial similarity to human courtship behavior has often been noted. Second, it is clear that neural mechanisms play a critical role in organizing the motor patterns which constitute sexual behavior in response to such external stimuli. Finally, the presence of a sexual object, though it can elicit sexual behavior, does not invariably do so—animals display variations in sexual responsiveness which may be either short term or very long term. In the case of the female, these variations are often cyclical or periodic. Such *oestrus* cycles are correlated with the production of an egg (ovulation) by the female at regular intervals. In the case of the male, sexual excitement may appear to build up rapidly and then decline following the completion of the sexual act.

The cyclicity of sexual behavior in females and the relations between the long-term development of the reproductive systems and the occur-

Written in collaboration with Dr. Timothy J. Teyler, Department of Psychology and Social Relations, Harvard University and Dr. H. Philip Zeigler, Department of Animal Behavior, The American Museum of Natural History.

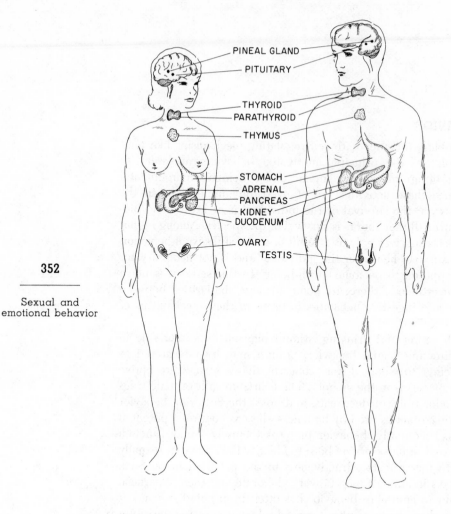

Figure 9.1 The major endocrine glands.

rence of sexual behavior in both sexes led early investigators to assume that the critical physiological factors underlying sexual behavior must be chemical substances. It was assumed that such substances were accumulated and released in the body and that the buildup and decline of the substances accounted for the arousal and decline of sexual responsiveness. With the discovery of the endocrine system, it appeared at first that the action of hormones could account completely for the known facts of sexual behavior. The relation between hormones and sexual behavior has not proved to be as simple as was first assumed. However, rather close parallels can be drawn between the mechanisms of control of eating and drinking via blood levels of chemicals acting on hypothalamus and pituitary and the mechanisms of hormonal control of sexual behavior.

The endocrine system and hormonal mechanisms

The body has two types of glands. The *endocrine* glands secrete chemicals into the blood stream to be carried to all parts of the body. They also are called ductless glands because they secrete directly into the blood rather than into specialized ducts. The other type of glands are the *exocrine* or duct glands, which include sweat, tear, salivary, pancreatic, and other glands whose products pass out through special ducts and do not enter the blood stream.

The endocrine system includes one master gland, the pituitary gland or hypophysis, which is located at the base of the brain and is physically continuous with the hypothalamus (see Fig. 9.1). There are several target endocrine glands in the body, the major ones being the *gonads*, concerned with sex, the *adrenal*, concerned with stress, emotionality, and the autonomic nervous system, and the *thyroid* and *thymus*, involved in regulation of growth and metabolism. We will be concerned primarily with the gonads in this section and with the adrenal gland later when emotionality is discussed.

Detailed discussions of the endocrine system are apt to be confusing to the student new to the subject, probably because so many different chemical substances are involved. A brief review of the pituitary gland itself is helpful at this point. The pituitary is really two quite different glands. Both are under direct control of the hypothalamus but the methods of control are quite different, often a source of confusion (Fig. 9.2). The posterior pituitary is called the *neurohypophysis*—it receives a massive supply of nerve fibers from two regions of the hypothalamus. One of the regions is the supraoptic nucleus, the area of the hypothalamus concerned with thirst and drinking behavior. The other area is the paraventricular nuclei. These two regions of the hypothalamus have nerve cell bodies that send their axons down into the neurohypophysis. The hormones released by the neurohypophysis are manufactured by the nerve cell bodies in the hypothalamus, transported down the axons to the neurohypophysis, and held there to be released into the blood. The neurohypophysis or posterior pituitary gland does not manufacture its own hormones but instead serves as a store and release point for hormones manufactured in the hypothalamus. These hormones, oxytocin and ADH (vasopressin), regulate water secretion by the kidney, and contractions of the uterus and secretion of milk in the pregnant female at the appropriate times.

The anterior pituitary gland or *adenohypophysis* is controlled by the hypothalamus in quite a different way. It contains no nerve cells from the hypothalamus. Instead it has a very rich blood supply via blood vessels that come directly from the hypothalamus. A region of the hypothalamus called the *median eminence* is the immediate source of the blood supply to the adenohypophysis (Fig. 9.2). Indeed, the median eminence has been referred to as a gland. It is now known that nerve

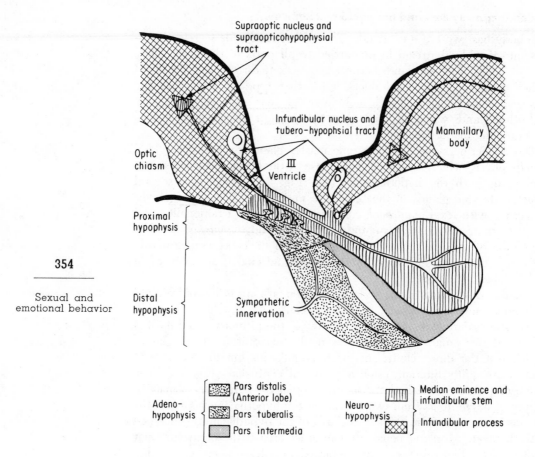

Figure 9.2 Interrelationships of hypothalamus and pituitary gland (see text). (From Reichlin, S. Neuroendocrinology. Reprinted, by permission, from *The New England Journal of Medicine* **269**, 1963, pp. 1182–1191.)

cells in the median eminence region of the hypothalamus secrete hormones into the blood supply to the adenohypophysis. There they act on gland cells of the adenohypophysis to stimulate release of the major pituitary hormones. The hormones released by the hypothalamus are listed in Table 9.1.

The major hormones released in turn by the adenohypophysis are listed in Table 9.1. Except for the growth hormone that acts on all cells, each pituitary hormone influences a particular target organ to release its own hormones.

The functions of hormonal feedback regulatory mechanisms are clear examples of the general principle of *homeostasis* or self-regulation (see discussion of temperature regulation in Chapter 8). Most aspects of homeostatic self-regulation in humans are accomplished without awareness, primarily by the autonomic nervous system and endocrine system.

Table 9.1 Summary of the major hormones and their immediate controls.

Gland	Hormone	Secretion directly controlled by
Anterior pituitary	Growth hormone	Hypothalamic GH-releasing factor
	Thyroid-stimulating hormone	Hypothalamic TSH-releasing factor and thyroxine
	ACTH	Hypothalamic ACTH-releasing factor and cortisol
	Gonadotrophic hormones: FSH, LH	Hypothalamic FSH and LH-releasing factors and Female: estrogen and progesterone Male: testosterone
	Prolactin	Hypothalamic prolactin-inhibiting factor
Thyroid	Thyroxine	TSH
Adrenal cortex	Cortisol	ACTH
	Aldosterone	Angiotensin and plasma K^+ concentration
Gonads		
Female: ovaries	Estrogen and progesterone	FSH and LH
Male: testes	Testosterone	LH
Posterior pituitary	Oxytocin and antidiuretic hormone (ADH, vasopressin)	Action potentials in hypothalamic secretory neurons
Adrenal medulla	Epinephrine	Preganglionic sympathetic nerves
Parathyroids	Parathormone	Plasma calcium concentration
Pancreas	Insulin and glucagon	Plasma glucose concentration
Kidneys	Renin-angiotensin and erythropoietin	

From Vander, A. J. et al., **Human Physiology: The Mechanisms of Body Function.** New York: McGraw-Hill, 1970.

A simple example is the release of ACTH by the adenohypophysis. When an organism is subject to physical stress, unknown brain mechanisms cause the hypothalamus to release the corticotropin-releasing factor (CRF). The CRF acts on the adenohypophysis to release ACTH. It acts on the adrenal cortex (a part of the adrenal gland; see Fig. 9.1) to release the adrenal cortical hormones, the so-called *adrenocorticosteroids*. These substances do a variety of things, such as improve appetite and gastrointestinal function, increase blood pressure and temperature, and help the adrenal cortex respond to stress. When blood levels of these

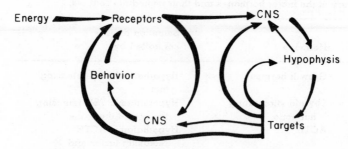

Figure 9.3 The basic feedback organization of the endocrine system (CNS is the central nervous system; hypophysis is the pituitary gland; targets are the other endocrine glands). (Whalen, R. E. Hormones and behavior. From Whalen, R. E. (ed.). *Hormones and Behavior.* Princeton: Van Nostrand, © 1967. Reprinted by permission of D. Van Nostrand Company.)

adrenocortical hormones increase, hypothalamic release of CRF is decreased and hence pituitary release of ACTH is reduced.

The endocrine system works fundamentally as a feedback system. The outputs of the pituitary gland cause effects which, in turn, regulate the output of the pituitary gland. Behavioral variables and peripheral stimuli also regulate the outputs of the pituitary; the ultimate actions of the pituitary, in turn, regulate behavior. Whalen (1967) summarizes these relationships very nicely in the diagram of Figure 9.3.

Hormones and reproductive physiology

The hormones responsible for changes in sexual morphology and behavior in the female are *progesterone* and a group of related substances known collectively as *estrogen*. The corresponding group of hormones in the male is termed *androgen*. These hormones are manufactured and released by the ovary and testis, respectively, given appropriate levels of pituitary gonadotrophic hormone. The female ovary has a dual role of producing eggs and secreting hormones. These gonadal hormones (estrogens) regulate the activity of the female reproductive system and control secondary sex characteristics.

The adenohypophysis secretes the gonadotrophic hormones, FSH (follicle stimulating hormone) and LH (lutenizing hormone) cyclically during the reproductive span of the female (roughly one-third of the life span). It is important to note that the adenohypophysial gonadotrophins, FSH and LH, are secreted in the male as well as in the female, and have as their target gland the testes. The third pituitary gonadotrophic hormone, prolactin, is concerned with the secretion of milk in the mammilary glands of post-partum females.

The estrous cycle of the female depends upon the interrelated activity of the brain, pituitary, and ovaries. The normal cycle consists of the maturation of the ovarian follicle, ovulation, and preparation for the implantation of the fertilized ovum. If fertilization does not occur the preparatory tissue changes are sloughed off and the process repeats itself. At the beginning of a cycle pituitary FSH stimulates the maturation of the ovarian follicle; FSH in combination with LH promotes the rapid growth of the follicle and secretion of gonadal estrogen. When blood estrogen levels approach a critical level the pituitary reduces the output of FSH, another example of a negative feedback system. The high level of blood estrogen also causes an increase in pituitary LH secretion which in turn produces ovulation. At this time pituitary prolactin output increases to facilitate *corpus luteum* formation. The corpus luteum is a "temporary endocrine gland," formed in the ovary, which secretes estrogen and progesterone. Progesterone acts upon the reproductive system to prepare it for the implantation of a fertilized egg and to maintain gestation and lactation. In the absence of a fertilized ovum the corpus luteum degenerates, along with the hormones it produces, and the cycle repeats. The recycling occurs because the level of circulating estrogen inhibiting pituitary FSH production is decreased.

The mechanism by which the corpus luteum is preserved after conception has occurred is not known. Nevertheless the estrogen and progesterone are maintained at levels which prevent sloughing off of the preparatory tissue and inhibit normal cyclical estrous activity. (Birth control pills usually contain both estrogen and progesterone.) During the term of pregnancy several changes occur to ensure the maintenance of the fetus and the adaptive responses on the part of the mother to the presence of this growing "foreign body."

The testes of the male have the dual role of sperm formation and hormone secretion. The production of sperm is dependent primarily upon androgen secretion by the testes, which in turn depends upon gonadotrophic hormones from the adenohypophysis. Both FSH and LH are necessary for spermatogenesis and androgen secretion. The testicular androgens, the chief among them being testosterone, are, like the estrogens, steroid compounds. The male usually does not exhibit cyclical variations in the amount of gonadotrophic hormone secretion. In both males and females the gonadal hormones are essential for the full elaboration of the reproductive system, including genitalia and secondary sex characteristics (body fat stores, distribution of body hair).

Hormones and sexual behavior

The evidence that links the sex hormones to sexual behavior is of several types. First, experiments have been done in which the gonads of an animal were removed and the effects upon its sexual responsiveness were studied. Removal of the ovaries (ovariectomy) in many mammalian species abolishes the estrous cycle and sexual receptivity in females. Removal of the testes in many lower animals either abolishes sexual behavior immediately or produces a gradual decline in sexual activity.

Second, studies have been done that involve the injection of hormones into animals not yet mature (prepuberal) or into mature animals from which gonads have been removed. The results of such studies are rather complex and may be summarized as follows:

1. Injection of sex hormones into immature animals can elicit sexual behavior which is typical of the sexually mature adult.
2. Hormones injected into castrated or ovariectomized animals can produce a return to preoperative levels of sexual activity.
3. In seasonal breeders, or animals that copulate only during cyclical periods of heat, sexual behavior can be elicited when the animal is not in heat by injecting the appropriate sex hormones.
4. Injections of the hormones of one sex may elicit sexual behavior typical of that sex when injected into an animal of the opposite sex. (A female rat given massive doses of male hormones may show some parts of the male sexual behavior pattern and vice versa.)

These data seem to suggest a potential for bisexuality in the reproductive system. This will be discussed further below with respect to the mechanisms of sexual differentiation.

All this evidence points to an important contribution of hormones to the control of sexual behavior but this control by no means is simple. For example, there is no straightforward quantitative relationship between the amount of hormone and the amount or intensity of sexual behavior. In the castrated rat, cat, or dog, an increase in the amount of injected male hormone beyond the level that restores sexual behavior does not increase sexual activity. Regardless of the dosage increase, the animal will not exceed his preoperative level of sexual activity. Moreover, the decline of sexual behavior after copulation in a male animal is not due to any change in the level of hormones in the blood; that is, the sex hormone is not "used up" during copulation. Conversely, there is no good evidence that the amount or direction of sexual behavior in man is related in any simple way to the amount of circulating hormone. Homosexuality, for example, does not appear to be related in any apparent way to the presence of abnormal levels of female hormones in males, or vice versa. Some attempts have been made to treat male homosexuals with large doses of male sex hormone, but while sometimes this reportedly results in an intensification of sexual behavior, it is homosexual, not heterosexual, behavior that increases.

These observations suggest that the hormonal control of sexual behavior even in lower animals such as the rat is complex and indirect, and that a variety of other factors also are involved. Further, as the evolutionary scale from lower to higher animals is considered, we find that sexual behavior becomes increasingly independent of hormonal factors.

This process of "emancipation," as one author calls it, is manifest in several ways. In subprimate forms, and even in some of the primitive monkeys, the female does not accept the male at any time except during estrous (i.e., around the time of ovulation). In the higher primates, the female, although most receptive during the period of ovulation, will accept the male throughout the entire estrous cycle. This "emancipation" is seen most clearly in the human female. Although some women do experience peaks of sexual desire which are correlated with certain phases of their menstrual cycle, the sexual responsiveness of the human female is effectively independent of hormonal control. Moreover, ovariectomy (for medical reasons) is sometimes performed on women, and studies of such women indicate that a high percentage of them experience normal sexual desire and engage successfully in sexual relations. Also, the maintenance of high levels of sexual responsiveness is frequently reported in women who have undergone menopause.

The situation for the male is similar. Although castration of lower animals such as rats or guinea pigs produces a fairly rapid decline and eventual cessation of sexual behavior, this is not true in the case of higher animals. The cat and dog may continue to show vigorous sexual behavior for as long as two years following castration. Indeed, one study showed that the more sexual experience a cat was allowed preoperatively, the longer his sexual behavior was maintained after castration. In adult human males whose testes have been removed for medical reasons, there are enormous individual differences in the effects of castration upon sexual behavior. Although some patients report a gradual decline in capacity and responsiveness, others appear to continue to function normally for many, many years. Such data indicate that in the course of evolution sexual behavior has come increasingly under the control of psychological, rather than simple biological, factors. It is generally assumed that the many correlations between hormones and sexual behavior reviewed above reflect hormonal effects upon the brain mechanisms underlying sexual behavior.

Hypothalamic mechanisms and sexual behavior

Analysis of the neural mechanisms involved in sexual behaviors indicates that the hypothalamus plays a critical role in the relation between hormones and such behavior. In female cats with brain transections the characteristic integrated estrous behavior pattern is seen only if the hypothalamus and lower brain structures are intact. In male cats, erection and ejaculation can be elicited as reflexes after complete transection of the spinal cord in the lumbar region. Nevertheless, the hypothalamus is essential for the maintenance of normal sexual activity in the intact male.

Because of its proximity to and connections with the pituitary gland, experimental manipulations of the hypothalamus may produce their effects upon sexual behavior either through neural mechanisms, endocrine mechanisms, or the interaction of both systems. However, a considerable body of evidence suggests that specific hypothalamic regions are involved in the integration of neuroendocrine processes underlying sexual behavior. Lesions of hypothalamic sites can abolish sexual behavior in several mammalian species while electrical stimulation of the hypothalamus can elicit sexual behavior in male monkeys (MacLean and Ploog, 1962) and in male rats (Vaughn and Fisher, 1962). Penile erection is continuous during stimulation; one animal in the Vaughn and Fisher study was reported to have 20 ejaculations in one hour of stimulation (!). The most impressive evidence comes from studies that involve the implantation of tiny amounts of sex hormones directly into the hypothalamus. By the use of such techniques sexual behavior has been elicited in female cats (Harris and Michael, 1964) and male rats (Davidson, 1966). Moreover, use of radioactively labeled hormones as tracers has shown that hypothalamic (and other) regions implicated in the control of sexual behavior overlap with sites whose cells show high levels of estrogen uptake (Pfaff et al., 1974). It thus appears that hormonal effects upon sexual behavior are mediated by the action of hormones upon brain structures involved in the neural control of such behavior.

Sexual differentiation: neuroendocrine control of masculinity and femininity

The fundamental requirement for sexual behavior in any animal is sexual differentiation into male and female. However, a moment's thought reveals that there are many possible criteria for distinguishing between male and female. Indeed, John Money, some of whose work is reviewed below, has suggested that there are at least seven such criteria:

1. Genetic sex, revealed by the presence of XX or XY chromosomes.
2. Gonadal sex, indicated by the presence of ovaries or testes.
3. Hormonal sex, which is indicated usually by secondary sex characteristics such as breasts, body hair distribution, etc., and which reflects the balance of androgens and estrogens.
4. Genital morphology, that is, the presence of a penis and scrotum in males and a vagina and clitoris in females.
5. Internal accessory reproductive structures, which in males includes the seminal vesicles and in females the uterus.
6. Sex of assignment and rearing, that is, the designation of an infant at birth as a boy or a girl. The act of assignment may have profound consequences for the observed differences between males and females as we shall see below.

7. Psychological sex. Money has used the terms *gender identity* to express the fact that individuals tend to see themselves privately as male, female, or ambivalent to some degree, and *gender role* for those behaviors which express to others the nature of one's gender identity.

Normally, these characteristics tend to be highly correlated with each other; if an individual is genetically male (has XY chromosomes) he will be male in all other respects, including experiential and behavioral characteristics. For this reason it is easy to think of the genetic factors as directly determining the differences between males and females; that is, as Freud put it, "anatomy is destiny." Sometimes, however, these correlations are imperfect and individuals who are male in some respects are female with respect to other criteria. The study of such individuals has helped to clarify the nature of normal sexual differentiation. Such studies indicate that the process is extremely complex and involves interactions between genetic, neuroendocrine, and environmental factors, and that sex hormones play a critical role in psychosexual differentiation. Before such studies are discussed fully, it is necessary to outline briefly the nature of sexual differentiation during embryonic development.

Figure 9.4 indicates the process of genital differentiation in the human embryo. Initially the embryo contains the substrate for the later development of either male or female characteristics. Sexual differentiation at this stage consists of the regression and atrophy of one set of sexual structures and the growth and differentiation of the other set. This process is under the control of the primitive sex gland (gonad). The first step in sexual determination, then, is the differentiation of the primitive gland into either a male sex gland (testis) or a female sex gland (ovary). It is this process of gonadal differentiation which appears to be under genetic control. Once this differentiation has taken place the sex gland itself controls the differentiation of the other sexual structures.

Hormonal processes and the development of neuroendocrine mechanisms

In view of the demonstrated effects of sex hormones upon the behavior of adult animals it seemed reasonable to assume that hormones might play some role in the differentiation of sexual structures during development. Several experimental techniques used to explore this possibility are: (1) *Transplantation* experiments, in which sex glands of newborn animals are replaced by those of the opposite sex, that is, ovaries implanted into males and testes into females. (2) *Castration* experiments involve removal of the sex glands (either ovaries or testes) at different stages of development. (3) *Injection* experiments, as their name implies, involve injection of either estrogens or androgens during development.

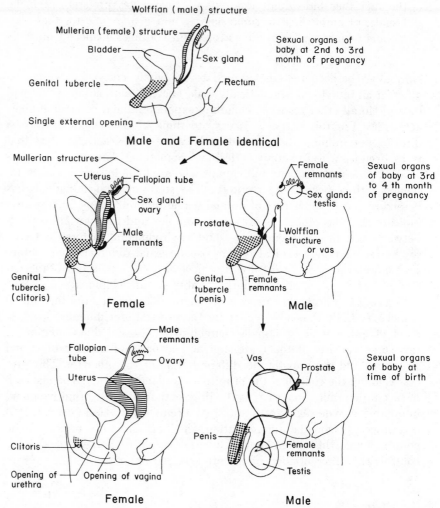

A

Wolffian (male) structure

Mullerian (female) structure

Bladder

Sex gland

Genital tubercle

Rectum

Single external opening

Sexual organs of baby at 2nd to 3rd month of pregnancy

Male and Female identical

Mullerian structures

Uterus — Fallopian tube

Sex gland: ovary

Male remnants

Genital tubercle (clitoris)

Female

Female remnants

Sex gland: testis

Prostate

Wolffian structure or vas

Genital tubercle (penis)

Female remnants

Male

Sexual organs of baby at 3rd to 4th month of pregnancy

Male remnants

Fallopian tube

Ovary

Uterus

Vas

Prostate

Clitoris

Penis

Opening of urethra

Opening of vagina

Female remnants

Testis

Female

Male

Sexual organs of baby at time of birth

Figure 9.4 A, Internal genital differentiation in the human fetus. B, External genital differentiation in the human fetus. (Redrawn from Money, J. Psychosexual differentiation. From Money, J. (ed.). *Sex Research: New Developments.* New York: Holt, Rinehart and Winston, Inc., © 1965. Reprinted by permission of Holt, Rinehart and Winston, Inc.)

The results of such experiments demonstrate clearly that sexual differentiation is under hormonal control. Thus genetically male rats, if castrated before day 10, as adults display the female behavior of squatting in the presence of a normal male (Grady et al., 1965). Administration of testosterone (male hormone) to five-day-old genetically female rats permanently impaired the regulation of the periodic sexual cycle of the

B

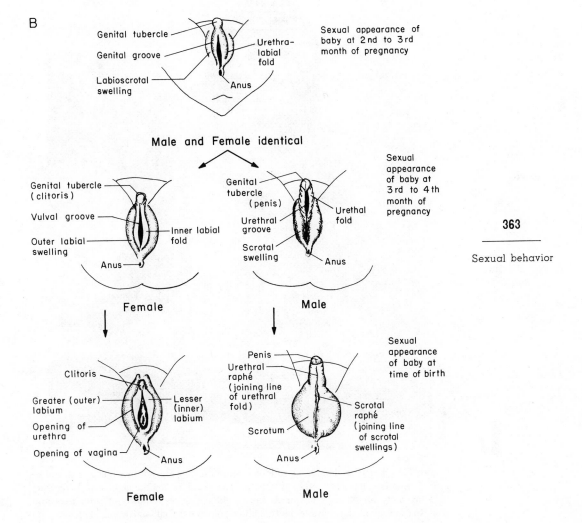

Genital tubercle

Genital groove

Labioscrotal swelling

Urethra-labial fold

Anus

Sexual appearance of baby at 2nd to 3rd month of pregnancy

Male and Female identical

Genital tubercle (clitoris)

Vulval groove

Outer labial swelling

Inner labial fold

Anus

Female

Genital tubercle (penis)

Urethral groove

Scrotal swelling

Urethal fold

Anus

Male

Sexual appearance of baby at 3rd to 4th month of pregnancy

Clitoris

Greater (outer) labium

Opening of urethra

Opening of vagina

Lesser (inner) labium

Anus

Female

Penis

Urethral raphé (joining line of urethral fold)

Scrotum

Anus

Scrotal raphé (joining line of scrotal swellings)

Male

Sexual appearance of baby at time of birth

adult and made them sexually unresponsive to males. Young, Goy, and Phoenix (1964) gave a particularly striking demonstration of the predetermining effects of early hormone treatment by injecting testosterone into the mother of a genetically female fetus from day 42 to day 122 of the 166 day gestation period. The result was a female *pseudohermaphrodite* infant (Fig. 9.5). The animal was a genetic female, but had a prominent

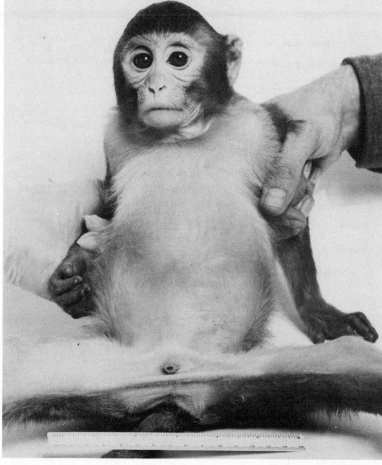

Figure 9.5 Yorty, a female pseudohermaphrodite produced by injecting testosterone propionate into its mother during pregnancy. The treatment involved injection of 5 mg daily for 80 days beginning on the 42nd day of gestation. A prominent and well formed phallus is visible in the photo. Yorty's social and sexual behavior are completely masculine. (Courtesy R. W. Goy.)

and well formed phallus though no testis. On behavioral measures of dominance and aggression that clearly separate normal male and female monkeys the female pseudohermaphrodite behaved like a male (Fig. 9.6). Thus hormonal processes during development not only involve the differentiation of the monkey's adult sexual behavior but also the differentiation of other nonsexual behaviors which are sexually differentiated in the normal monkey.

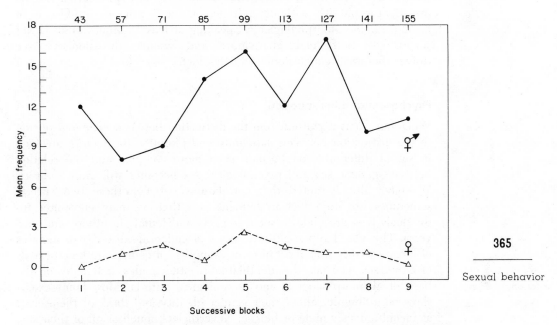

Average age (days)

Figure 9.6 Display of facial threat by pseudohermaphroditic female (solid line) and normal female (broken line) monkeys plotted relative to age. The abscissa is scaled in successive blocks of five trials. (Redrawn from Young, W. C., Goy, R. W., and Phoenix, C. H. Hormones and sexual behavior. *Science* **143**, 1964, pp. 212–218. Copyright 1964 by the American Association for the Advancement of Science.)

It was noted above that rats, castrated or androgenized during development, do not, as adults, respond to hormone injections with the sexual behaviors appropriate to their genetic sex. Moreover, the injection of androgen, *if it takes place during a critical developmental period,* can abolish the normal development of the hypothalamic-pituitary mechanisms responsible for the cyclicity of reproductive function in the female. These two facts imply that hormonal processes not only affect the differentiation of the internal and external reproductive structures but are involved in the development and differentiation of brain mechanisms controlling reproductive cycles and sexual behavior in both males and females.

One additional implication of such studies is that the process of sexual differentiation involves the suppression of the development of the female's neurobehavioral system rather than the enhancement of the male's. That is, in the absence of the male gonadal hormones, sexual differentiation proceeds according to a female ground plan. It seems that in the mammal the basic, genotypically determined sexual disposition (phenotype) is female. For differentiation to proceed according to the male pattern the presence of male gonads and hormones is essential. As one investigator put it, "without androgen, nature's primary impulse is to make a female—morphologically speaking at least" (Money, 1965). Not surprisingly, both "male chauvinists" and "women liberationists" have drawn rhetorical conclusions from this fact.

Psychosexual differentiation

When our focus is shifted from the distinction between *male and female* to the distinction between *masculine and feminine* the factors involved in sexual differentiation become even more complex and the relation between genetic sex and psychological sex becomes still more indirect. We have already noted that correlations between these two criteria sometimes are imperfect in humans and that we may encounter individuals who are male in some respects and female in others, and vice versa. This may happen either in cases of endocrine disorder or in cases of homosexuality. The most obvious examples, of course, are homosexuals of either sex who may be identifiable as either males or females on the basis of all morphological and physiological criteria. Most homosexuals show no ambiguity about their gender identity and think of themselves as unambiguously male or female. Nevertheless, much or all of their sexual behavior is directed at individuals of the same sex. The origins of such behavior and its implications for both the individual and society currently are being widely debated, and the notion that homosexuality reflects a behavior pathology has been rejected by many members of the psychiatric profession. It is, however, indicative of the complex processes that underlie sexual differentiation in humans.

More instructive with respect to our understanding of these processes are cases of human *hermaphroditism*. This is defined as *a condition of prenatal origin in which embryonic and/or fetal differentiation of the reproductive system fails to reach completion as either entirely female or entirely male*. The condition may arise as a result of a malfunctioning endocrine system during development or the pathological presence of androgens during pregnancy. In such cases a genetic female may be androgenized and at birth look like a boy with undescended testes; a genetic male may at birth appear genitally indistinguishable from a normal female. Like other infants, such individuals are assigned a sex on the basis of the appearance of the external genitalia and are reared as a member of the assigned sex.

Money has recently summarized a large body of data which indicates that the most important factor in determining the gender identity and psychosexual development of such individuals is the postnatal act of assigning the child a given sex and rearing him as a member of that sex. Such children took the assigned gender role even though it contradicted

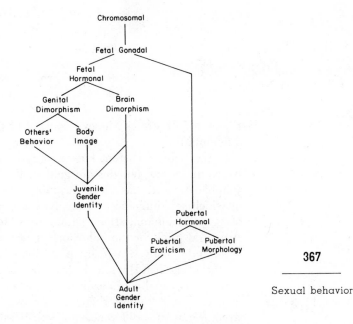

Figure 9.7 Illustration of the sequential and interactional components of gender-identity differentiation. (From Money, J., and Ehrhardt, A. A., *Man and Woman, Boy and Girl*. Baltimore: Johns Hopkins Press, © 1972.)

either their genetic, gonadal, or genital sex. Contradictions between genital sex and sex of assignment produced the most difficult problems of adjustment and in such cases cosmetic surgery is of great assistance. This is not surprising since the external genitalia are the most important signs of gender, not merely to the parents but to the individual.

To summarize, then, genetic factors in humans may account directly for the differentiation of the gonad into testes and ovaries but further differentiation takes place under the control of hormonal factors. These, in turn, account for the development of sex-differentiated internal reproductive systems and external genitalia. The external genitalia, in turn, become the basis for the assignment of the infant to one or the other sex and this assignment in turn initiates a host of sex-differentiated experiences. As Money and Ehrhardt point out,

Parents wait for nine months to see whether the mother gives birth to a boy or girl . . . It simply never occurs to them that they are also waiting for the first cue as to how to behave toward the new baby. Yet as soon as the shape of the external genitals is perceived it sets in motion a chain of communication: It's a daughter! It's a son! This communication itself sets in motion a chain of sexually dimorphic responses, beginning with pink and blue, pronominal use, and name choice, that will be transmitted from person to person to encompass all persons the baby ever encounters, day by day, year in and year out, from birth to death.

(Money and Ehrhardt, **Man and Woman, Boy and Girl,**
Johns Hopkins Press, 1972, page 12)

Figure 9.7 illustrates Money's concept of the processes underlying sexual differentiation.

In the light of current knowledge, the notion that the differences between males and females are genetically determined is an obvious oversimplification. It has clear meaning when applied to those organisms in which sex differences in behavior are a relatively direct consequence of genetic differentiation. Drone bees, for example, do not have any structural basis for the behaviors of brood tending, foraging, or feeding other individuals which are performed by workers. The human male, on the other hand, while he cannot menstruate, gestate, or lactate, is structurally capable of performing most of the functions popularly termed female. Thus, although there is a consistent relationship between genetic structure and sex differences in both bees and humans, the relationships are the outcome of very different developmental processes.

EMOTIONAL BEHAVIOR

Emotion and *emotionality* are deceptively simple terms. We use words to describe emotions quite easily; indeed there are hundreds of such emotionally descriptive words in the English language. We employ such words with the distinct impression that we are communicating to others, that our statements about emotion have relatively clear meaning. If you observe an enraged person attacking another person you infer that the aggressor exhibits and experiences the emotion of anger or rage. For that matter, you infer the same thing about an enraged dog attacking a person, even though you cannot ask the dog to describe his feelings. Extreme clear-cut emotional situations of this sort do not present as great difficulties as do the more subtle characterizations of emotion.

Three rather clearly separable aspects of emotion may be distinguished. One is the *experiential* aspect: What do we feel? What are our subjective experiences of emotions and emotional state? It is easy to label extreme emotions like rage, fear, and ecstasy, but quite difficult to make fine distinctions in the absence of strong emotions. Describe your own emotional state as you read these words. You probably are not experiencing any clearly defined emotions at this moment. We convey our experiences in words—much effort has been expended in having subjects rate the emotional meaning or tone of words without very clear results. Nonetheless, we can convey something of what we feel in words, largely because we assume most people experience similar emotions under similar conditions.

The next aspect of emotion is that of motor behavior. We describe the general behavior, or some conveniently measurable aspect of that behavior, and label it. A monkey confronted with a strange object may flee in fear, attack in rage, or behave in a manner that shows combined fear and rage. Fear and aggression are easy emotional behaviors to define and study in animals as well as humans.

Tinbergen has categorized the "facial expressions" exhibited by the gull into recurring patterns that are directly related to environmental stimuli, and has suggested that these behavioral states are the avian counterpart of human emotions. Konrad Lorenz (1966) has done the same kind of analysis with the dog. Observation of facial expressions may permit some description of the emotional behavior and inferred experience of an animal. Here emotion is defined in terms of the situation in which the behavior occurs. Such an idea is of doubtful legitimacy. We infer emotions from a knowledge of the stimulus situation and the resultant behavior, and probably "anthropomorphize"—imagine the animal experiences the same feelings as humans. Studies done in man (Schlosberg, 1954) indicate that such a great degree of variability exists between different subjects' facial responses to a given situation that any reliable labeling of emotional behavior is difficult.

Finally, another aspect of emotion concerns the physiology of emotion. When people are very fearful they may cry, have an increased rate of heartbeat, a dry mouth, and sweating hands. These responses are under the direct control of the autonomic nervous system which, in turn, is under the control of higher brain regions.

Varieties of emotional behavior

Many attempts have been made to summarize the *dimensions* of emotional behavior and experience; an example is given in Figure 9.8 modified from Schlosberg (1954). Such charts should not be taken to have fundamental meaning for the nature of emotion—they have some heuristic value and provide a convenient set of labels. In Figure 9.8 the graphical position of an emotional response and/or experience depends on whether it is avoidance-neutral-approach and upon its intensity.

In order to respond to a stimulus, emotionally or otherwise, one must first attend to it. The novelty of a stimulus is a powerful factor in determining the degree of orienting (Thompson, 1967). Berlyne (1958), for example, reported that human infants attended longer to complex than to simple stimuli. Sokolov (1963a) characterized the human orienting response as a complex of physiological changes in such indices as heart rate, respiration, and galvanic skin response (GSR). The orienting re-

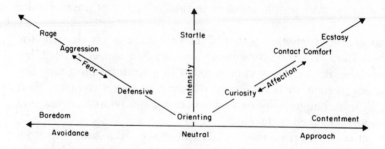

Figure 9.8 An attempt to indicate the *dimensions* of emotionality. The two underlying dimensions in this conception are degree of approach or avoidance (ordinate) and intensity of response (abscissa). (Modified from Schlosberg, H. Three dimensions of emotion. *Psychol. Review* **61**, 1954, pp. 81–88. Copyright 1954 by the American Psychological Association. Reprinted by permission.)

370

Sexual and
emotional behavior

sponse presumably carries little emotional loading, being neither approach nor avoidance, but rather a neutral "what is it?" response. In cases where the stimulus is intense or the organism is in an aroused state the magnitude of the orienting response may be greatly augmented. We speak of this as a *startle response*. A familiar example of the startle response is a person "jumping" to a sudden loud noise that is unexpected. This response is dependent not only on stimulus intensity but also context. A similar noise in another setting would not elicit the startle response.

Fear and aggression usually are included together under the term *agonistic* behavior. They have obvious survival value. A case can be made that at least some aspects of fear represent a primary need. Pain is an inevitable correlate of tissue damage. Aversive stimuli that inflict pain always lead to avoidance and escape responses under normal circumstances. The reduction of aversive stimulation is clearly reinforcing. Shock avoidance perhaps is even more effective in training animals than is food reward. Physiological mechanisms underlying fear and aggression include significant hormonal controls. However, the autonomic nervous system, the peripheral portion of the nervous system that controls behavioral expression of emotion such as crying, sweating, cardiovascular and gastrointestinal changes, is most directly involved in emotional behavior. Agonistic behavior can be considered as on the short-term end of a time continuum of emotionality; the more long-term aspects can be included under the general category of stress.

The emotional responses of boredom and contentment, opposite in hedonistic (i.e., experienced feeling) quality, are similar in that they are nearly devoid of overt behavior. As can be seen from Figure 9.8, both are at the bottom of the intensity scale, although at opposite ends of the approach-avoidance scale. Beginning at "orienting" in Figure 9.8 and proceeding diagonally leftward, we encounter various degrees and strengths of fear responses. Fear responses are avoidance responses; these involve escape from danger or perceived danger. Most animals, except perhaps man, seem to prefer to flee rather than fight when in danger. Rage and attack occur more often when the road of escape is blocked.

The perception of danger is an important factor in the elicitation of agonistic behavior. Donald Hebb (1946) exposed chimpanzees and categorized their responses to strange and foreign objects. Two very fearful objects were a model of a human face and an ape head. The animals feared objects that looked or behaved differently than would be expected from past learning. Studies of human infants indicate that in addition to fears based on past learning, some stimuli such as loud noises elicit fear responses without any prior exposure to the stimuli.

The right diagonal of Figure 9.8 lists various degrees and strengths of approach responses. The kinds of stimuli leading to approach responses are as numerous as but less well understood than those leading to avoidance responses. Aside from certain *critical period* phenomena (such as imprinting, see below), most approach responses seem to depend on a learned positive relationship with an object. Unfortunately, there has been little research done on affectionate behavior and love in men or animals. The most extensive studies, those by Harry Harlow and associates, will be reviewed in the next section.

This simplified description of emotional behavior and experience is in no way meant to be complete, extensive, or "real." Rather, it merely provides a descriptive framework for discussion.

Affectional behavior

One arena in which much of the affectional behavior of an organism occurs is that of the primary social group or family. Konrad Lorenz (1952) first described the existence of limited periods of an animal's life during which the young animals would follow almost any moving object. The time interval is termed the *critical period*, the process is termed *imprinting*. Imprinting occurs only during the critical period, which, for the *precocial* (able to fend for themselves at hatching) birds in whom it was first observed, is between 10 and 25 hours after birth. It was initially thought that once a bird imprinted on an object, it would follow the imprinted object from that moment on, and that imprinting would be impervious to disruption. It is now known that the behavior toward imprinted objects can be modified. We await the demonstration of imprinting in other than precocial birds. These reservations are not meant to diminish the importance of this discovery of a mechanism in precocial birds that solidifies the primary social group. In the wild, the imprinting object the newborn chick sees is usually one of its parents.

The question of the development of the primary social bond has also been studied in mammals. J. P. Scott (1968) argues that imprinting is merely the avian form of the critical period for primary socialization. He assumes that all animals in which the phenomenon has been studied are similar in that they can form social attachments rapidly during this critical period. Scott has done most of his work, which is a combination of ethological observation and laboratory experimentation, with young puppies. He finds that in contrast to the several-hour critical period in birds, the puppy critical period for primary socialization, as most dog owners know, lasts several weeks. One feature stressed by Scott is that the primary social bond may be either an elaboration of an innate behavior pattern that unfolds with maturation, or it may be learned as a result of rewarding interactions with other organisms in the immediate vicinity, or, most likely, it may be some combination of these factors.

The problem of the origins of the primary social bond in primates has been analyzed in brilliant studies by Harry Harlow and associates at Wisconsin. Infant rhesus monkeys were chosen for these studies, primarily because their development closely parallels that of humans; see

Figure 9.9 Cloth and wire surrogate mothers. Both provided food but only the cloth mother provided contact comfort. (Harlow, H. F., McGaugh, J. L., and Thompson, R. F. *Psychology.* San Francisco: Albion, 1971.)

Harlow (1973) for a recent and very readable review of this work. In the basic experiment infant monkeys were reared in cages that contained two surrogate mothers. One surrogate was constructed of wire mesh and the other of terry cloth; both had wooden heads. Either surrogate mother could be provided with a nursing nipple for the infant. One group of infants received milk from the wire mother, another group from the cloth mother (Fig. 9.9). The response measure was taken simply as the amount of time the infants spent with each of the surrogate mothers. The results showed that both groups of infant monkeys preferred to spend their time with the cloth mothers, regardless of which mother provided food.

Two important conclusions can be drawn from Harlow's study. First, feeding does not of itself determine the recipient of the primary social bond, as was thought earlier. The social bond of affection is not derived from reduction of primary needs like hunger. Second, the young monkeys preferred the mother to which they could cling, the cloth mother, and would do so for hours on end. Thus, there exists an innate tendency to cling or grasp an object resembling a natural mother. This grasping has been termed *contact comfort*. The role of physical contact in young humans is also of major importance, and is one reason why breast feeding often is recommended rather than bottle feeding.

These results attest the importance—possibly the overwhelming importance—of bodily contact and the immediate comfort it supplies in forming the infant's attachment for its mother. All our experience, in fact, indicates that our cloth-covered mother surrogate is an eminently satisfactory mother. She is available 24 hours a day to satisfy her infant's overwhelming compulsion to seek bodily contact; she possesses infinite patience, never scolding her baby or biting it in anger. In these respects we regard her as superior to a living monkey mother, though monkey fathers would probably not endorse this option.

(From "Love in infant monkeys" by H. F. Harlow, 1959a, page 70. Copyright © 1959 by Scientific American, Inc. All rights reserved.)

Maternal deprivation and the disruption of affectional behavior

By contrast with the monkeys reared with surrogate mothers, infant monkeys reared in bare wire cages with no companions showed obvious behavioral abnormalities very early in their development. They displayed the kinds of stereotyped rocking and self-clutching movements characteristic of disturbed (autistic) children. Subsequently, they were apathetic and indifferent to external stimulation, sat and stared aimlessly into space for prolonged periods, and froze in terror at the sight of another infant. None of these behaviors were seen in the surrogate-reared infants.

As the months went by, however, it became clear that the initial optimistic description of the effectiveness of the surrogate mother required revision. When these monkeys grew old enough to breed, they were brought together and the investigators waited hopefully for the usual results. But the results were far from usual, because there appeared to have been a complete breakdown of sexual behavior on the part of the surrogate-reared monkeys. Harlow describes the subsequent events, when lab-reared monkeys were placed with sexually mature, normally reared monkeys:

> When the laboratory-bred females were smaller than the sophisticated males, the girls would back away and sit down facing the males, looking appealingly at these would-be consorts. Their hearts were in the right place, but nothing else was. When the females were larger than the males, we can only hope that they misunderstood the males' intentions, for after a brief period of courtship, they would attack and maul the ill-fated male. . . . They [the males] approached the females with a blind enthusiasm, but it was a misdirected enthusiasm. Frequently the males would grasp the females by the side of the body and thrust laterally, leaving them working at cross purposes with reality.
>
> (Harlow, 1962, page 7)

When the females were finally mated, they failed to take proper care of their own infants. In many cases the infants had to be removed to prevent their death, either by the mother's neglect or her physical abuse.

Subsequently, Harlow and his associates have used various modifications of the technique of rearing monkeys in social isolation to produce syndromes of behavioral depression, to study the role of biochemical factors in such a disorder, and to develop techniques for behavioral rehabilitation of the disturbed monkeys. Such research is of obvious importance both for the study of the normal mechanisms of development of affectional behavior and for our understanding of the origins of pathological behavior in the higher primates, including man.

VISCERAL FACTORS IN EMOTIONAL BEHAVIOR

In this section we will review briefly attempts to deal with the physiology of emotion. Typically these attempts involve peripheral measures, such as heart rate, sweating of the palms, and salivation, that are under primary control of the autonomic portion of the nervous system.

The autonomic nervous system and emotion

The autonomic nervous system is primarily responsible for the maintenance of an optimal internal environment for the body. The system is

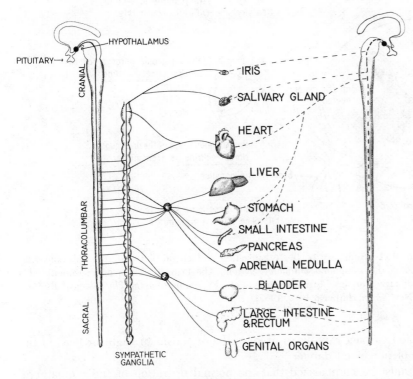

A   B
SYMPATHETIC   PARASYMPATHETIC

PITUITARY→
HYPOTHALAMUS

CRANIAL

IRIS

SALIVARY GLAND

HEART

LIVER

THORACOLUMBAR

STOMACH
SMALL INTESTINE
PANCREAS
ADRENAL MEDULLA

SACRAL

BLADDER

LARGE INTESTINE
&RECTUM

GENITAL ORGANS

SYMPATHETIC
GANGLIA

Figure 9.10 Organization of the sympathetic (A) and parasympathetic (B) divisions of the autonomic nervous system. The sympathetic nerves relay through ganglia at some distance from target organs. The parasympathetic nerves relay on small ganglia at the target organs. (See Fig. 9.11.)

generally involuntary and acts on the smooth muscle of the gastrointestinal tract, the cardiac muscle, exocrine glands, and some endocrine glands. The autonomic nervous system consists of two divisions, the sympathetic and the parasympathetic (Fig. 9.10). The sympathetic division of the autonomic nervous system acts as an arousal mechanism for the whole body and can prepare for vigorous action. It is important to note that the individual need not actually engage in vigorous activity to produce sympathetic effects. The mere thought of a fight activates the sympathetic division. The effect of this thought would be to increase heart rate and respiratory depth, halt gastrointestinal activity, release glucose stores, shunt blood away from viscera and skin into the muscles, and start sweat glands operating. Undoubtedly the reader has experienced some, if not all, of these symptoms at times other than when they were unaccompanied by vigorous activity. In short, the sympathetic

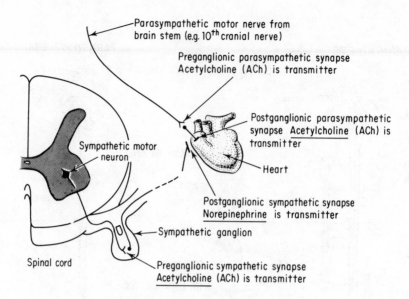

Parasympathetic motor nerve from brain stem (e.g. 10th cranial nerve)

Preganglionic parasympathetic synapse Acetylcholine (ACh) is transmitter

Postganglionic parasympathetic synapse Acetylcholine (ACh) is transmitter

Sympathetic motor neuron

Heart

Postganglionic sympathetic synapse Norepinephrine is transmitter

Sympathetic ganglion

Spinal cord

Preganglionic sympathetic synapse Acetylcholine (ACh) is transmitter

Figure 9.11 Summary of the organization and chemical transmitter substances involved in the peripheral autonomic system. The heart is shown as an example of a typical target organ. (From Thompson, R. F. *Foundations of Physiological Psychology.* New York: Harper & Row, 1967.)

division can act rapidly to prepare the organism to "fight or flee" in the face of perceived danger.

It must be emphasized that the normal operation of the sympathetic and the parasympathetic divisions is to regulate and balance bodily functions and that response to sudden stress is an extreme and less common operation. The parasympathetic division of the autonomic nervous system acts somewhat more directly on the organ level than does the sympathetic. Functionally, the parasympathetic division is concerned with the recuperative, restorative, nutritive functions of the body at rest. Activities such as digestion and tissue maintenance occur under the control of the parasympathetic. Activation of the parasympathetic division tends to produce effects opposite to those of the sympathetic division. Most organs of the viscera have dual antagonistic innervation, which means that they are supplied with both sympathetic and parasympathetic nerves (Fig. 9.11). In the case of the heart this means that increased sympathetic activity results in a faster than normal heart rate while increased parasympathetic activity would result in lowering the heart rate. The autonomic nervous system typically maintains a tonic level of output over both divisions, termed *tone*. Because of tone, the heart rate can be increased either by an increase in sympathetic input or by a decrease in parasympathetic input, since it is the algebraic sum of the inputs that determines the organ response.

The autonomic nervous system is under the direct control of various nuclei in the brain stem. These in turn are influenced by the hypothalamus and certain of the limbic forebrain structures. The autonomic nervous system is the peripheral *motor* system for the brain structures most directly involved in the mediation of emotional and motivational aspects of behavior.

Autonomic measures of emotionality

A change in skin resistance, due to changes in sweat gland activity, has been termed the galvanic skin response (GSR). Those working in the field now prefer to call it the *EDR* or *electrodermal response* (Grings, 1974). Sweat glands are innervated by the sympathetic division of the autonomic nervous system, which is active in stressful, threatening situations. It is normally considered to not be under voluntary control; thus it has been used in lie detector systems. As an example of work of this nature, Weller and Bell (1965) studied the EDR in several day-old human neonates and found a high correlation between degree of arousal, as measured by amount of crying and movement, and variations in the EDR. It is not a perfect reflection of emotional activity, however, as the EDR occurs to environmental and bodily events, such as temperature, physical activity, and mental concentration, as well as to emotional states. It is often difficult to separate these factors.

Changes in blood pressure are thought by some to provide valuable information regarding emotional states. Most peripheral cardiovascular neural control is supplied by the sympathetic branch of the autonomic nervous system, which functions to provide sufficient blood supply to the skeletal muscles during activity. Since much emotional behavior requires activity, blood pressure increases often reflect this underlying emotionality. By the same means the *heart rate* also increases during certain kinds of emotional states (those preparatory to action).

Hess and Polt (1960) studied the *pupil size* of the human eye as a function of exposure to affection-arousing stimuli. Pupil size is a measure of arousal not under volitional control. The stimuli were projected slides of sexual and neutral objects: baby, nude male, nude female, landscape, woman holding baby. The pupil of the male subjects increased sharply only when viewing a nude female. The pupil of the female subjects increased to the sight of the baby, woman with baby, and nude male. They also dilated slightly to the nude female and constricted some to the landscape. That pupil size is a crude reflection of emotionality or arousal has been known for many years by good salesmen, who gauge the buyer's reaction by this means.

Other physiological responses that have been implicated in various emotional states include increasing depth of respiration, increased rate of eye blinking, decreased intestinal motility, muscle tension increases,

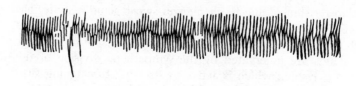

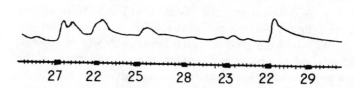

27   22   25   28   23   22   29

Figure 9.12 Countermeasure is illustrated by a record from Kubis' series. The subject lied about number 27. He simulated lying about number 22 by tensing his toes. The respiratory trace (top) shows that he held his breath as he undertook the first countermeasure. He was able to produce sizable reactions in the cardiac (middle) and skin-resistance (bottom) traces. (Courtesy, Joseph F. Kubis.)

decreased peripheral blood flow, changes in salivary fluid composition. Unfortunately, all the above physiological reactions can be recorded in almost *any* intense emotional state as well as in several other nonemotional conditions. The problem that confronts most physiological measures of emotionality is that while some are reliable indicators of a generalized arousal, the fine differentiation between specific emotions becomes tenuous at best. This issue has been analyzed in detail by the Laceys at Fels Research Institute in Ohio. Their work will be reviewed in the next chapter when we deal with the subject of "arousal." The answer to the question "Does each emotional state have a physiological pattern unique to it?" must remain open, due to the difficulty in defining the various emotions, the complexity and interrelatedness of the physiological responses involved, and, as we shall see later, the effect of the environmental context on the expression of emotion (Schachter and Singer, 1962).

We will discuss the autonomic indices of arousal and the orienting reflex at greater length in the next chapter. Autonomic responses are the measures used in the lie detector. In view of the complexities of human autonomic responses it is surprising that the lie detector can even be used. The lie detector is merely a polygraph recording of a subject's heart rate, blood pressure, and the like, made while he answers questions. An example of a lie detector polygraph is shown in Figure 9.12. Note that when the subject lied he exhibited marked autonomic responses which he attempted to cover up in subsequent responding. A common technique for beating the lie detector is to think very unpleasant or anxiety-producing thoughts so that autonomic arousal is relatively continuous. Surprisingly, there is little careful published work on validation of the lie detector.

Conditioning of autonomic responses

The autonomic nervous system exerts primary control of heart rate, blood pressure, and peripheral vascular circulation. It is generally assumed that these systems are not under volitional control. Yet we are confronted by data suggesting that certain individuals, Indian mystics for example, can stop the bleeding from a wound, or walk on a bed of hot coals, or "stop" their hearts. Neal Miller, Leo DiCara, and their associates at Rockefeller University (1969) challenged the traditional notion that we cannot volitionally control the autonomic nervous system.

Miller and his colleagues reported successful instrumental conditioning of salivary increases and decreases, heart rate accelerations and decelerations, intestinal motility and relaxation, changes in renal blood flow, and increases and decreases in blood flow in one ear of the rat, the other ear remaining unchanged. The procedure of instrumental conditioning is analogous to the manner in which you teach a dog a trick. Usually you prod, coax, push, and pull at a dog until he does something close to what you try to teach him; then you *reward* him. The reward reinforces the last response to occur, which is the desired behavior, and increases the probability that the dog will perform the behavior again. Gradually, you bring the dog's behavior nearer to the goal by rewarding only those responses that are closer and closer to the desired behavior. In other words, you elicit the behavior, then reinforce it. One of the problems in training autonomic responses is to find the appropriate reward. Miller and associates primarily worked with chemically paralyzed animals so the obvious rewards of eating and drinking were of no use. They chose to use electrical stimulation of the lateral hypothalamus region of the brain—the rewarding self-stimulation region of the medial forebrain bundle (Chapter 8)—as the reward. For example, to decrease blood flow in the left ear of the paralyzed rat, Miller delivered the rewarding brain stimulation when, due to normal variations, the blood flow in the left ear decreased slightly. Gradually, Miller was able to reduce the blood flow by a considerable amount by withholding the re-

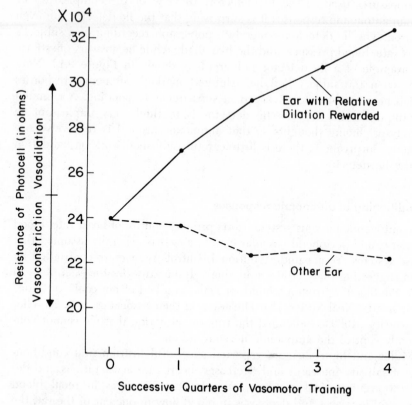

Figure 9.13 Differential instrumental conditioning of blood flow in the two ears of a paralyzed rat. Reward (hypothalamus stimulation) was given only for changes in flow (dilatation) in one ear. (From Miller, N. E. Learning of visceral and glandular responses. *Science* **163**, 1969, pp. 434–445. Copyright 1969 by the American Association for the Advancement of Science.)

ward until a large drop occurred (Fig. 9.13). The animals were paralyzed to remove any influence of muscular activity, which can directly mediate many of these changes.

An interesting problem has developed with these experiments. It has been difficult to replicate the original effects in more recent studies (Miller, personal communication, 1973). These negative replications have also been done in Miller's laboratory. Thus the obvious explanation of unknown factors that differ in different laboratories does not hold. As many scientists will testify, failure to replicate a newly discovered phenomenon of some degree of complexity is not uncommon. As experimental procedures and techniques are refined and improved, the phenomenon becomes more elusive. We must now await more definitive replications of this important phenomenon of instrumental conditioning of autonomic responses (in paralyzed animals).

In any case, it is important to remember that there are many sources of evidence, from both American and Russian laboratories that demonstrate unequivocally the conditioning of glandular and visceral responses to external stimuli. The implications of this fact for the understanding of psychosomatic disorders are indicated in the following statement by Miller.

... Suppose a child is terror stricken at the thought of going to school in the morning because he is completely unprepared for an important examination. The strong fear elicits a variety of fluctuating autonomic symptoms, such as a queasy stomach at one time and pallor and faintness at another; at this point his mother, who is particularly concerned about cardiovascular symptoms, says, "You are sick and must stay home." The child feels a great relief from fear, and this reward should reinforce the cardiovascular responses producing pallor and faintness. If such experiences are repeated frequently enough, the child, theoretically, should learn to respond with that kind of symptom. Similarly, another child whose mother ignored the vasomotor responses but was particularly concerned by signs of gastric distress would learn the latter type of symptom. I want to emphasize, however, that we need careful clinical studies to determine how frequently, if at all, the social conditions sufficient for such theoretically possible learning of visceral symptoms actually occur. Since a given instrumental response can be reinforced by a considerable variety of rewards, and by one reward on one occasion and a different reward on another, the fact that glandular and visceral responses can be instrumentally learned opens up many new theoretical possibilities for the reinforcement of psychosomatic symptoms.

(Miller, N. E. Learning of visceral and glandular responses. **Science 163**, 1969, pp. 434–445. Copyright 1969 by the American Association for the Advancement of Science.)

Stress and the adrenal system

Many bodily changes that accompany short-term emotional reactions also occur over a much longer time scale. Here we refer to a variety of stimuli and situations, termed *stressful*, that require the body to mobilize its reserves to cope with the stress. We emphasize chronic, long-lasting stresses as they are most familiar to us. You should keep in mind that while it may require an electric shock or confining cage to produce a stress response in a laboratory animal, a stress response can be triggered in a human by the fear of an upcoming examination, daily bickering with a spouse, or the thwarted desire to beat your neighbor in the game of bridge. Obviously these are not physical stresses like electric shock or confinement; rather they are psychological stresses. However, they can be as powerful and devastating as the most severe physical stress. Psychological stress is not limited to man; it can be produced in many animals under appropriate conditions.

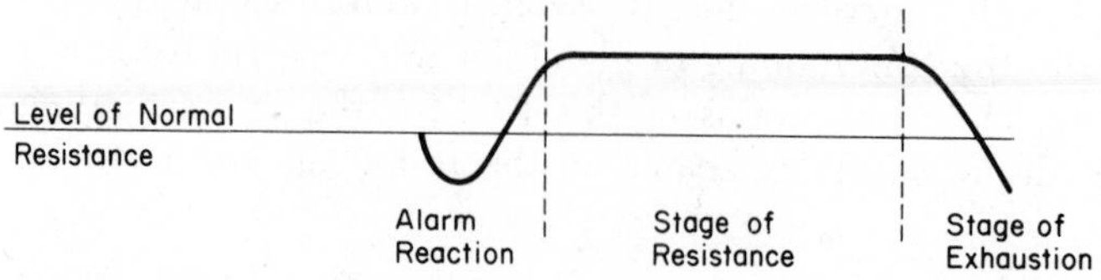

Figure 9.14 The hypothetical general adaptation syndrome of response to stress. (Modified from Selye, H. *The Stress of Life*. New York: McGraw-Hill, 1956.)

Hans Selye (1950, 1955, 1974) has studied extensively the response to chronic stress, and has termed the stereotyped stress response the *general adaptation syndrome* (Fig. 9.14). The first stage of the triphasic response is termed the *alarm reaction*. This stage typically consists of the bodily changes that occur with emotional responses, which we have reviewed. Given a prolonged stress the organism enters the second stage, *resistance to stress*. During this stage a human recovers from the emotional alarm reaction and attempts to cope with the situation. Physiologically, the sympathetic output decreases, the endocrine glands resume a lower, more normal rate of secretion, and the organism gives every appearance of adapting successfully to the stress. This is deceptive, for this endurance seems to consume whatever resources are available and if the stress continues the organism reaches the terminal stage, *exhaustion*. Rarely do psychological stresses result in exhaustion. Stresses of disease, exposure, or injury can often result in exhaustion. The symptoms and signs of the first stage reappear and the organism dies unless treated.

The adrenal gland plays a major role in the stress syndrome (Fig. 9.15). It is really composed of two glands, the adrenal cortex and the adrenal medulla. The adrenal medulla is regulated directly by sympathetic innervation which, when active, causes the adrenal medulla to secrete large amounts of epinephrine and norepinephrine into the blood. This acts to release energy stores and increase metabolism and provides an efficient mechanism for distributing the energizing effect of sympathetic activity throughout the body.

The adrenal cortex is necessary for life. Its proper functioning depends on adrenocorticotrophic hormone (ACTH) from the pituitary. The adrenal cortex manufactures over 40 hormones. These compounds, structurally related to cholesterol, are known as adrenocortical steroids. The functions of the steroids are best described by the changes which occur in the adrenalectomized animal. The animal suffers from loss of appetite, gastrointestinal disturbances, reduced blood pressure and body temperature, kidney failure, and if not treated will die. When subjected to physical or psychological stress the pituitary secretes more ACTH, resulting in more circulating steroids, which then "turn off" the pituitary ACTH (Selye, 1950). As an elaboration of this stress response it has been discovered that by exposing young animals to mild stresses (handling or

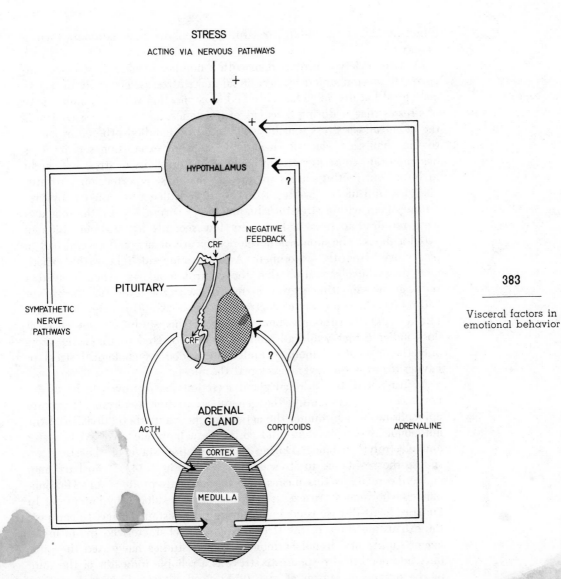

STRESS
ACTING VIA NERVOUS PATHWAYS

+

HYPOTHALAMUS

+

−

?

CRF

NEGATIVE
FEEDBACK

PITUITARY

SYMPATHETIC
NERVE
PATHWAYS

CRF

−

?

ADRENAL
GLAND

ACTH

CORTICOIDS

ADRENALINE

CORTEX

MEDULLA

Figure 9.15 Schematic diagram of interrelations of pituitary-adrenal system. (From Clegg, P. C., and Clegg, A. G. *Hormones, Cells and Organisms*. London: Heinemann, 1969.)

weak electric shock) they become more resistant to the deleterious effects of stress as adults. In general, they are stronger, larger, and more adapted to survival than their littermates who were not stressed as infants (Levine, 1960). They also have larger adrenal glands. This seems to indicate that it is beneficial, rather than harmful, to expose developing organisms to mild environmental stresses and further suggests that by protecting infant humans from mildly stressful situations we may be doing them a disservice.

Modern society confronts man with a number of chronic stresses concurrently, accompanied by occasional acute stresses, generally of a psychological nature. Selye has observed in connection with this multiplicity of stresses that, if during the stage of resistance, a second stress confronts the organism—a stress that by itself could be handled—the entire adaptive mechanism breaks down and the stage of exhaustion sets in. This has important consequences for medicine. Multiplicity of stress is thought to be a contributing factor in diseases such as hypertension, arthritis, allergies, and ulcers. Brady (1958) produced ulcers in monkeys by presenting them with a stressful situation. Over several weeks, the monkeys were required to press a bar every few seconds for six-hour shifts to avoid a shock. The monkeys developed severe ulcers, and several had to be removed from the experiment. An interesting sidelight of this experiment was the observation that the control monkeys, who received a shock at the same time as did the monkey with the lever, but themselves had no lever and no way of controlling the shock, did not develop ulcers (Brady, 1958). Although some aspects of this study are not clear, it does indicate that while all animals were subjected to the same stress only the "executive" monkey under the added psychological stress of having to press the lever developed the ulcers.

As just noted, two adrenal gland secretions have proven to be of importance in understanding the general adaptation syndrome. They are epinephrine, which mimics the actions of the sympathetic division of the autonomic nervous system, and cortisone, a hormone involved in water and electrolyte balance. During the adaptation stage of the stress response the resistance to stress is increased (Fig. 9.14). Translated into endocrine relations this means that the adrenals produce an overabundance of hormones. An excess of epinephrine results in hypertension. In humans, heart disease is common during the resistance stage. In contrast, the exhaustion stage of the stress response is characterized by an insufficient supply of adrenal hormones. Animal studies have used the pituitary adrenocortical response to stress as a reliable indicator of the state of the organism. Mason et al. (1957) used plasma 17-hydroxycorticosteroid levels as an index of ACTH secretion and found that the level of plasma steroids was high for monkeys receiving avoidance training, where the animal's response controlled the receipt of electric shock. However, the plasma levels were equally high for a group that had no control over the shocks they received.

The procedure of presenting signaled shocks has been widely used in the study of fear responses in animals. A painful or aversive stimulus is paired with a neutral one such that with repeated pairings the animal responds to the neutral stimulus with a fear response. This is a *conditioned emotional response* (CER), a learned fear. Often the CER procedure is superimposed on some other learning task to observe the disrupting effects of emotionality on the task. This acquired fear can now serve to motivate other behaviors. In a study by Miller (1948), rats in a white box were given a series of strong shocks. The animals subsequently learned to turn a wheel or press a lever to escape from the white box with no shock present. The animals were presumably motivated only by their acquired fear of the white box. Learned behaviors have a tendency to generalize. Once a fear has been associated with one stimulus it will generalize to other stimuli, as demonstrated in the classical experiment by Watson and Rayner (1920), who exposed an 11-month old child to a white rat and at the same time sounded a loud noise. The child had no fear of the rat but disliked the noise. After repeated pairings the child developed a CER to the rat and this fear response generalized to a number of other white, furry objects—a rabbit, a beard, etc. This generalization of conditioned fear provides a mechanism whereby stressful stimuli can become generalized to wide classes of seemingly innocuous stimuli.

Studies by Seymour Levine at Stanford University indicate that ACTH and the hormones from the adrenal cortex can have wide-ranging and profound effects on behavior. The brain-pituitary-adrenal system was schematized in Figure 9.15. Recall from our earlier discussion of the endocrine system that the hypothalamus secretes a substance called the corticotropin releasing factor (CRF) into blood vessels that carry it directly to the anterior pituitary (adenohypophysis), which in turn releases ACTH. Apparently, ACTH has both general actions on tissues of body and brain and also acts specifically on the adrenal center to stimulate release of corticosteroid hormones, particularly hydrocortisone in humans.

Levine, Brush, and others have shown that variation in ACTH level has dramatic effects on extinction of learned avoidance responses, learning of passive avoidance and in habituation of startle responses to intense sounds. Injection of ACTH has rather complicated effects—the result is not necessarily simply an increase in blood ACTH level. Of course there is an immediate increase in ACTH, which leads to increased production of adrenal corticosteroids, which leads to decreased hypothalamic production of CRF and a *decrease* in pituitary release of ACTH. An experiment by David deWied (1969) illustrates this. Rats were trained in a shuttle box to run to avoid shock when a light and a tone came on. After learning, the rats were placed on extinction—that is, given the light and tone but no shock. Normal animals showed a rapid decrease or extinction in response (Fig. 9.16). However when the adrenal glands were removed, resulting of course in complete absence of adrenal corticosteroids and an increased ACTH, the animals did not extinguish. To determine whether this was due simply to no corticosteroids or to more ACTH, deWied removed the pituitary as well as the adrenal glands in

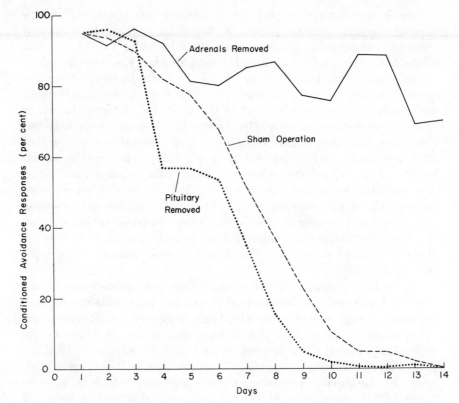

Figure 9.16 Extinction of the avoidance response was studied by David de Wied of the University of Utrecht. Removal of the adrenal gland inhibited extinction (*solid line*); the rats responded to the conditioned stimulus in the absence of shock, presumably because adrenal hormones were not available to restrict ACTH output. When the pituitary was removed, the rate of extinction (*dotted line*) was about the same in rats given only a sham operation (*broken line*). (Adapted from Levine, S. Stress and behavior. Copyright © 1971 by Scientific American, Inc. All rights reserved.)

other animals. This resulted in normal extinction behavior (Fig. 9.16). Consequently the critical variable seemed to be increased ACTH.

Levine has obtained a striking effect of ACTH on habituation. Rats were tested in a little jump box which measures the degree of startle response to a loud sound. Normal rats show habituation of startle as the sound is repeated—they respond progressively less to the sound. Levine implanted a crystal of adrenal corticosteroid hormone (hydrocortisone) in the hypothalamus of each in a group of rats. This led to marked decrease in ACTH by suppressing hypothalamic release of CRF. These animals showed much more rapid and pronounced habituation than normals. Levine and Brush (1967) also showed close relations between blood levels of adrenal corticosteroid hormones and the development of learned avoidance behavior. These experiments seem to indicate that

ACTH, and perhaps the adrenal cortical hormones as well, directly act on brain systems involved in learning, particularly in extinction and habituation of responses. At this writing, we have no idea how or where these actions occur.

At the beginning of our discussion of emotionality we said that the substances produced by the adrenal *medulla*, epinephrine and norepinephrine, produce and mimic the peripheral sensations of emotion—heart pounding, face flushing, hands trembling. Epinephrine and norepinephrine are released in copious amounts by the adrenal medulla under situations of stress or emotion. These two substances are members of a group of compounds called the *biogenic amines,* which have characteristic chemical structures and are biologically active. The best known are *norepinephrine, epinephrine* (made from norepinephrine in the adrenal medulla), *dopamine,* and *serotonin.* These substances are found also in certain regions of the brain and may function as synaptic transmitters. They do not simply enter the brain from the blood stream; they are made in the brain as well. Norepinephrine, for example, cannot cross the blood-brain barrier; hence the norepinephrine released from the adrenal medulla into the blood cannot enter the brain, so brain norepinephrine must be manufactured in the brain.

Recent interest has focused on the role of these biogenic amines in emotion, particularly the general emotional level or emotionality of people. A variety of drugs have been developed to treat the extremes of emotional reactivity, particularly the pathological conditions of depression and mania. Drugs that have proven effective in treating depression and mania also have potent effects on the brain levels of the biogenic amines. These observations led Schildkraut and Kety (1967) to develop a brain biogenic amine theory of emotions (see Chapter 5). In particular, it appears that brain levels of norepinephrine are critical. A decrease in brain norepinephrine is associated with depression and an increase is associated with excitement, euphoria, and mania.

BRAIN MECHANISMS AND AGONISTIC BEHAVIOR

It is obvious that the brain is involved in emotionality, just as it is involved in every behavior or feeling. In this section we shall examine some of the known brain contributions to emotionality, with emphasis placed on rage and aggression.

The limbic system is the forebrain system that has been most implicated in emotional behavior. The first indication of limbic involvement came as a result of a bilateral removal of limbic structures in the temporal lobes in monkeys. Klüver and Bucy (1937) noted that following recovery from surgery the behavior of the monkeys was drastically altered. The animals exhibited increased oral behavior (putting various objects into the mouth), increased sexual behavior (the animals attempted to mate not only with monkeys but with animals of other species), and loss of fear and aggressiveness.

The limbic system and the circuit of Papez

James W. Papez in a famous paper (1937) proposed a reverberating circuit among structures of the limbic regions of the brain as the neural basis of emotion. This has come to be known as the *circuit of Papez*. The limbic structures and their interrelations are difficult to describe for two reasons: The physical geometry of the structures, buried deep in the forebrain, are hard to visualize, and the anatomical interconnections are complex, to say the least. Research by Walle Nauta and associates at Massachusetts Institute of Technology clarified the anatomical interrelations.

The general region of the brain that includes the limbic system is shown in Figure 9.17, a view of the midline or medial surface of the right hemisphere of the human brain. The limbic system includes structures around the core of the medial region of the brain and extends down and around to the right (facing the same way as the brain in Figure 9.17) into the temporal lobe. In evolution the limbic system was the earliest form of forebrain to develop. Essentially the entire forebrain of the crocodile is limbic brain. No inferences about function are meant by this example. In addition to being vicious, the crocodile is an intact, functioning organism responsive to sensory stimulation, that engages in a variety of behaviors, including the "four Fs"—feeding, fleeing, fighting, and reproductive behavior.

In relatively primitive beasts like the crocodile, much of the limbic forebrain has to do with olfaction—the complex analysis of odors, their intensity, quality, and direction. The limbic forebrain first evolved to provide sophisticated analysis of olfactory stimuli. It was also concerned with appropriate responses to odors—approach, attack, mating, fleeing. In the course of evolution, much of the specific olfactory function of the limbic system seems to have been lost. Among higher animals, only a portion of the amygdala has direct projections from the olfactory system. There are some secondary connections from the "olfactory" amygdala to the hypothalamus and septal area (Fig. 9.18). However, most structures of the limbic system, including the hippocampus, a large portion of amygdala, and the cingulate gyrus seem to have nothing to do with olfaction.

The structures of the limbic system and some of their major interconnections are shown in Figures 9.18, 9.19, and 9.20. The amygdala, Figure 9.18, projects to the septal area, hypothalamus, dorsomedial nucleus of the thalamus (which in turn projects to prefrontal regions of

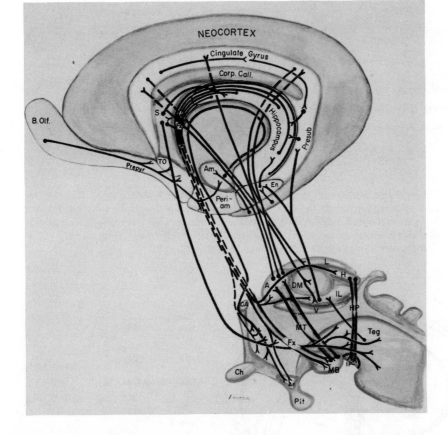
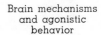

Figure 9.17 Schematic of the principal anatomical relationships between the allocortex, the juxta-allocortex, and the several subcortical structures considered in the present treatment of the limbic system. The brain-stem portions of the system are schematically displaced from the hilus of the hemisphere and represented in the lower half of the illustration in order to facilitate visualization of the numerous anatomical interconnections involving these structures. Abbreviations: A, anterior nucleus of the thalamus; Am, amygdaloid complex; Ar, arcuate nucleus; B. Olf., olfactory bulb; CA, anterior commissure; Ch, optic chiasm; Corp. Call., corpus callosum; DM, medial dorsal nucleus of the thalamus; En, entorhinal area; Fx, fornix; H, habenular complex; HP, habenulo-interpeduncular tract; IL, intralaminar thalamic nuclei; IP, interpeduncular nucleus; L, lateral thalamic nucleus; MB, mammillary body; MT, mammillothalamic tract; Periam, periamygdaloid cortex; Pit, pituitary; Prepyr, prepyriform cortex; Presub, presubiculum; S, septal region; Teg, midbrain tegmentum; TO, olfactory tubercle; V, ventral nucleus of the thalamus. (Brady, J. V. Motivational-emotional self-stimulation. From Sheer, D. E. (ed.) *Electrical Stimulation of the Brain.* Austin: Univ. of Texas Press, 1961, pp. 413–430.)

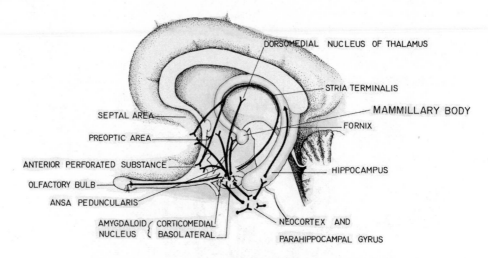

Figure 9.18 Schema of some interconnections of the limbic system. The amygdaloid nucleus projects via the stria terminalis and ansa peduncularis to the septal area, anterior perforated substance, hypothalamus, contralateral amygdaloid nucleus, dorsomedial nucleus of thalamus, and cerebral cortex. (Redrawn from Noback, C. R. *The Human Nervous System.* New York: McGraw-Hill, 1967.)

Sexual and
emotional behavior

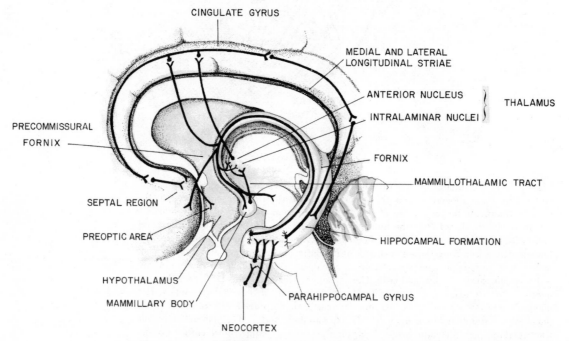

Figure 9.19 The *circuit of Papez* includes hippocampus to mammillary body via the fornix; mammillary body to anterior nucleus of thalamus via mammillothalamic tract; anterior nucleus to cingulate gyrus; and cingulate gyrus via several neurons back to the hippocampus. (Redrawn from Noback, C. R. *The Human Nervous System.* New York: McGraw-Hill, 1967.)

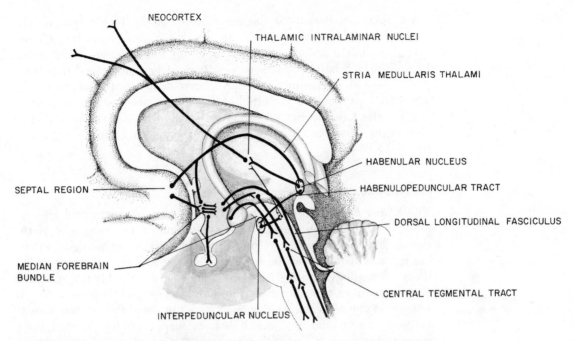

NEOCORTEX

THALAMIC INTRALAMINAR NUCLEI

STRIA MEDULLARIS THALAMI

HABENULAR NUCLEUS

HABENULOPEDUNCULAR TRACT

SEPTAL REGION

DORSAL LONGITUDINAL FASCICULUS

MEDIAN FOREBRAIN BUNDLE

CENTRAL TEGMENTAL TRACT

INTERPEDUNCULAR NUCLEUS

Figure 9.20 The medial forebrain bundle is a multineuronal pathway extending from the septal region through the lateral hypothalamus to the brain stem tegmentum. Note the pathway system of septal region and preoptic area to habenular nucleus via stria medullaris thalami; habenular nucleus to midbrain tegmentum and the interpeduncular nucleus via the habenulopeduncular tract. The interpeduncular nucleus projects to the brain stem tegmentum and its reticular systems. (Redrawn from Noback, C. R. *The Human Nervous System*. New York: McGraw-Hill, 1967.)

the cerebral cortex), and to an old region of neocortex on the bottom or base of the temporal lobe. The circuit of Papez is shown in Figure 9.19. The hippocampus projects to the mammillary body (a part of the hypothalamus) via a fiber tract called the *fornix*. The mammillary body projects to the anterior nucleus of the thalamus, which in turn projects to the cingulate gyrus of the cerebral cortex. The cingulate gyrus in turn projects through several neurons back to the hippocampus. This circuit of Papez is thus an anatomical reverberating circuit in which the hippocampus, itself a very complex neuronal structure, seems to play a critical role. In addition, the region of basal temporal neocortex receiving projections from the amygdala itself projects to the hippocampus (Fig. 9.18).

Still additional interconnections are shown in Figure 9.20. The medial forebrain bundle region, important in electrical self-stimulation of the brain (Chapter 8), is a multineuronal pathway extending from the septal region through the lateral hypothalamus to the brain stem (Fig. 9.20). Other connections involving midbrain and habenular nucleus project to the medial thalamus (thalamic intralaminar nuclei) and from here to several regions of the neocortex, particularly *association* and *motor* regions.

You must not despair at the complexities of the limbic system. The major point to remember is that all the limbic structures are interconnected. Neuronal activity can move from any one structure to any other by crossing a relatively few synapses. It must be emphasized that these pathways and interconnections have been demonstrated anatomically. The functional roles of circuits like the circuit of Papez in motivation and emotion are theories and inferences based on the anatomical data and on the effects of either destroying or stimulating various regions of the limbic system.

Limbic system and aggressive behavior

The *Klüver-Bucy syndrome* which was first seen after temporal lobe removal can also be produced with lesions limited to a segment of the limbic lobe, the *amygdala* (Fig. 9.18). The results of amygdalectomy are not completely clear, however, for taming and placidity are not always seen following surgery. Bard and Mountcastle (1947) observed that removal of the amygdala resulted in rage and hyposexuality. It seems that amygdalectomized animals have lost the ability to discriminate between stimuli and as a result behave inappropriately toward these stimuli. It is possible that following limbic lesion an animal must relearn the discriminations he has lost, and will become tame or aggressive depending upon that relearning.

In an interesting study by Downer (1962), the corpus callosum of a rhesus monkey was sectioned so each eye projected only to its own hemisphere of cortex (see Chapter 3). The right amygdala was then removed. After recovery, when the animal was approached from the right it was completely tame and docile. However, when approached from the left it exhibited the normal aggression and fear characteristic of the species.

The amygdala is also involved in the social behavior of monkeys. The rhesus monkey has developed a dominance hierarchy wherein each animal has a position on the hierarchy. Rosvold, Mirsky, and Pribram (1954) removed the amygdala in the most dominant monkey in a group. When placed back into the group the operated monkey rapidly lost his seniority and dropped to the bottom of the hierarchy. That this loss in dominance was due to a loss of learned discriminations between social stimuli and therefore a lack of responsiveness that allowed other animals to socially dominate was demonstrated in an experiment by Mirsky (see Pribram, 1962). After surgery, the amygdala lesioned dominant adults were placed in cages with easily dominated juveniles. This was done to allow the lesioned adult to relearn the discriminative associations involving dominance in a nonthreatening environment. Once done the lesioned animals were reintroduced into the adult group. The operated animals did not show a drop in social dominance (Fig. 9.21). Thus, while alternative

Sexual and
emotional behavior

Figure 9.21 A, Dominance hierarchy of a colony of eight preadolescent male rhesus monkeys before any surgical intervention. B, Same as A after bilateral amygdalectomy had been performed on Dave. Note his drop to the bottom of the hierarchy. C, Same as A and B, except that both Dave and Zeke have received bilateral amygdalectomies. D, Final social hierarchy after Dave, Zeke, and Riva have all had bilateral amygdalectomies. Minimal differences in extent of locus of the resections do not correlate with differences in the behavioral results. Herby's nonaggressive "personality" in the second position of the hierarchy accounts for the disparate effects of similar lesions. (From Pribram, K. H. Interrelations of psychology and the neurological disciplines. In Koch, S. (ed.). *Psychology: A Study of a Science* 4. New York: McGraw-Hill, 1962, pp. 119–157.)

interpretations exist, it seems clear that the limbic system, particularly the amygdala, is involved in a variety of emotional aspects of behavior.

Bard (1928) performed a number of studies on effects on emotionality of lesions of various brain structures. With all tissue above the hypothalamus removed it is possible to elicit rage behavior in a cat. With the hypothalamus removed, only isolated bits of the rage behavior remained. It appears that an essential substrate for aggression is the lateral hypothalamus. If it is destroyed, aggression is eliminated. If it is stimulated, electrically or chemically, animals will show directed attack.

The relationship of the hypothalamus to the amygdala seems to be important in the elaboration of aggressive behavior. The amygdala is not a simple structure but consists of three subdivisions: *anterior, corticomedial,* and *basolateral.* The anterior group is related to olfactory input, and may possibly be important for aggressive behavior in lower vertebrates. Killer rats will distinguish between rat pups and mice in their aggressive behavior, but will fail to do so if the olfactory bulbs are removed. The corticomedial group of the amygdala is connected to ventrolateral and medial hypothalamus. The basolateral amygdala connects to the lateral hypothalamus, providing an anatomical pathway between these two structures implicated in emotional behavior.

Stimulating or lesioning the proper divisions of the amygdala elicits a specific response that either facilitates or inhibits aggressive behavior. The facilitatory center for aggression apparently exerts a greater influence than the inhibitory center since the result of total amygdala lesions is usually a cessation of aggression and increased tameness. Involvement of both amygdala and hypothalamus in aggressive behavior was suggested by the work of Kaada et al. (1954). They observed aggressive behavioral responses following stimulation of amygdala basolateral nuclei. Since sectioning of the pathway connecting the basolateral group to the lateral hypothalamus abolishes the aggressive effect of amygdala stimulation, and since destruction of the lateral hypothalamus prevents aggressive behavior via amygdala stimulation, this would suggest that the hypothalamus is necessary for the elaboration of aggressive behavior. If the amygdala is destroyed, and the fiber tract going to the lateral hypothalamus is stimulated, the result is aggressive behavior. It thus appears that the basolateral amygdala has excitatory influences upon hypothalamic structures involved in aggression.

Lesions of the corticomedial nuclei of the amygdala result in increased aggressive behavior (Ursin, 1965). Sections of the fiber tract from the corticomedial amygdala group to the ventromedial and medial hypothalamus result in the same increase in aggressive behavior. It is possible that the corticomedial group acts as the "flight" zone and has inhibitory influences on the hypothalamus. The above observations suggest that the amygdala may play a role in the control of aggressive behavior and that the hypothalamus may be critical as an integrating structure.

The septum (Fig. 9.18) is another portion of the limbic system involved in aggressive behavior. Studies have shown rather consistently that septal lesions produce wild and ferocious animals. This behavior declines with time. However, if the amygdala is lesioned following a septal lesion the aggressive behavior is immediately abolished (King and Myers, 1958). The septum may inhibit aggressive centers in the hypothalamus which are released after lesioning. This is speculative as the mechanisms involved in septal lesions are poorly understood.

It appears that both excitatory and inhibitory influences, particularly from the amygdala and septum, are projected upon the hypothalamus which, in turn, integrates and directs the response of the organism. There are, however, conflicting reports on many aspects of limbic forebrain functions in aggression.

Hypothalamic stimulation and the attack response

A critical brain region for rage behavior is the hypothalamus. This was first shown in 1927 in pioneering work by Hess in Switzerland. Hess developed the technique of implanting stimulating electrodes in the brain and then observing an animal's behavior when stimulated. In a long and important series of studies he found that stimulation in the general region of the hypothalamus could produce full-blown rage in the cat. This rage was very similar to that a normal cat would show under appropriate conditions—hissing, hair raised on back, claws out—and often grew into a directed attack. Hess and Akert emphasized that the experimenter could even be the object of the attack: "a slight move on the part of an observer is sufficient to make him the object of a brisk and well directed assault. The sharp teeth and claws are effectively utilized in this attack." (1955, p. 127).

In quite independent early work the American psychiatrist Jules Masserman obtained a rage phenomenon, which he termed *sham rage,* from stimulation of the hypothalamus. The cat showed signs of rage—hair raised, claws out, hissing—but did not attack. Instead he allowed the experimenter to pet him, lapped milk, and even purred during stimulation-induced sham rage. Masserman argued that the electrodes activated some of the motor mechanisms involved in rage, hence the term sham rage; the cat didn't really "feel" angry.

John Flynn at Yale University began a long series of basic experiments on brain mechanisms of rage, in part to resolve the apparent conflict between the results of Hess and Masserman. Further, he felt that stimulus-bound elicited rage and attack provided a most important model for the study of aggression. Currently his work is the most important being done on brain mechanisms of aggression. Flynn emphasized attack, rather than rage per se, using rats, either normal, anesthetized, or stuffed, and a variety of other stimulus objects in the test cage.

It appears that the different kinds of rage behavior described by Hess and Masserman were due to stimulation of different regions of the brain. Flynn has observed that Masserman's syndrome of sham rage without attack can be elicited regularly by stimulation of the central grey—a region close to the hypothalamus but not a part of the hypothalamus. However, stimulation of the hypothalamus, particularly the more lateral portions, elicits directed rage and attack, as described by Hess. Flynn

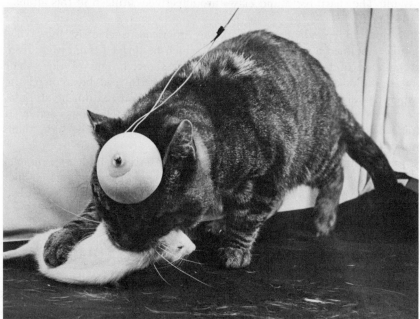

Figure 9.22 Two types of agonistic behavior elicited in a cat by stimulation of closely adjacent points in the hypothalamus. *Above*, rage and attack behavior; *below*, quiet biting predation attack. (Flynn, J. P. The neural basis of aggression in cats. From Glass, D. C. (ed.). *Neurophysiology and Emotion.* New York: Rockefeller Univ. Press and Russell Sage Foundation, © 1967.)

has found two quite different forms of directed attack—*affective attack* where the animal shows full-blown rage and attacks, and *quiet biting attack*, where the cat quietly stalks the rat, pounces and kills. The latter seems to resemble the normal predation of the cat. Flynn graphically describes the two forms of attack (see Figure 9.22).

Affective attack is characterized by a pattern of pronounced sympathetic arousal commonly regarded as indicative of feline rage. The response invariably begins with behavioral alerting and dilation of the pupils. At lower stimulus intensities, alerting constitutes the extent of the response, even if one stimulates for as long as 2 min.

As one increases the stimulus intensity up to attack threshold, in addition to the initial alerting, piloerection becomes prominent, especially along the midline of the back. The tail becomes bushy and fluffed out. Occasionally the ears go back. Hissing occurs alternately with low growls. Urination often occurs on the first trial of a session. If sitting, the animal leaps to its feet and begins to move with head low to the ground, back arched, claws unsheathed, hissing and/or snarling, sometimes salivating profusely, and breathing deeply. The cat either comes up to the rat directly or circles to the rear of the cage and then approaches the rat. The cat stands poised, appearing to watch the rat intensely, while the affective aspect of the reaction becomes still more pronounced. After a second or two, the cat raises a paw with claws unsheathed and then strikes with its paws in a series of swift, accurate blows. Any sudden movement of the rat serves to trigger the attack, but attack will occur even if the rat remains motionless. In some instances, the cat, instead of delivering discrete blows with a single paw, springs at the rat with a high-pitched scream and pounces, tearing at the rat with its claws. If the stimulus is continued, the cat will savagely bite the rat, although the initial part of the attack is clearly with its claws.

The second form of attack pattern **[Quiet Biting Attack]** reminds observers of an animal stalking a prey. At lower intensities, the alerting response, accompanied by mydriasis, is quite sudden and discrete. The cat often leaps to its feet almost with the onset of the stimulus and attentively looks about from side to side. If the stimulus is continued, it will walk about the cage but will ignore the rat. At higher stimulus intensities, above attack threshold, the cat moves swiftly with its nose low to the ground and hair slightly on end.

Sometimes the cat's nose twitches slightly, as if it were sniffing. The cat usually goes directly to the rat and bites viciously at its head and neck. The cat uses its paws primarily to knock the rat on its back in order to get at its throat. The paws are used neither to deliver discrete blows nor to rake the rat with the claws. Although the cat will sometimes bite the rat's stomach or back first, biting is ultimately aimed at the head and neck. On some trials, the cat circles around the observation box a few times, ignoring the rat or sniffing at it in passing. In the course of circling, the cat will suddenly pounce on the rat and savagely tear at it with its mouth. This circling behavior does not constitute a stereotyped motor response, in that it does not occur regularly nor is it always in the same directions for a given animal, although there is a tendency for it to be the side contralateral to the one stimulated.

The stalking attack is characterized, especially at low stimulus intensities, by only minimal signs presumed indicative of feline rage. Piloerection is present down the midline. The animals never growl, emit high-pitched screams, or salivate profusely. The cat's movement around the cage, however, is quicker and more persistent. Although this prowling or stalking behavior is never as dramatic as the presumably "enraged" attack, it is, in reality, more effective and deadly, as far as the rat is concerned.

(Flynn et al., 1967, pages 138–139)

Occasionally, mixed behaviors can occur with some elements of both affective and quiet attack, particularly with stimulation of the hypothalamus. However, it does appear that exact anatomical locus of the electrode is the primary determinant of the type of attack. Somewhat different regions of the hypothalamus mediate the two forms of behavior.

In the natural state, animals must often choose between fight and flight. The situational and physiological conditions for attack and flight are not too different. Similarly, flight behavior has often been reported as associated with rage elicited by hypothalamic stimulation. One possible interpretation of rage is simply that the stimulus hurts. Several investigators have succeeded in dissociating fight and flight. Fonberg (1967) elicited several types of rage responses to hypothalamic stimulation in dogs, presumably depending on electrode location. Animals that showed a predominant fear reaction—whining and biting not at the experimenter but at restraint straps—could easily be considered to raise a paw to avoid stimulation. They learned to avoid the stimulus as they would any unpleasant or painful stimulus. Animals showing directed rage, on the other hand, bit the experimenter or anything else within reach and could not be conditioned to avoid the brain stimulus—they behaved as though it was not unpleasant or painful. Flynn has been able to dissociate flight and rage quite clearly in his studies on cats. Different hypothalamic regions appear to be involved.

In other studies, Flynn explored the functions of limbic forebrain structures such as amygdala and hippocampus in the directed-rage behavior. In general, these structures seem to modulate rather than initiate attack. In other work, Flynn and associates have shown that hypothalamic stimulation effective in eliciting directed attack also has marked effects on sensory motor reflexes involved in striking with the paw and biting, and on the receptive fields of neurons in the visual cortex (vision is the primary sensory modality used by the cat in directing attack).

In current work, Flynn and his colleagues have undertaken a combined anatomical and physiological mapping of the attack system in the brain. In animals where hypothalamic stimulation reliably produced quiet biting attack, small lesions were made at the electrode sites and the pathway of neurons projecting from the region mapped; silver stains were used to identify the degenerating nerve fiber terminals. The pathway followed the medial forebrain bundle posteriorly and terminated in a restricted region of the midbrain tegmentum (Chi and Flynn, 1971). Electrical stimulation on other animals in this region of the midbrain also produced quiet biting attack (Bandler, Chi, and Flynn, 1972). Interestingly, the attack was not accompanied by signs of autonomic arousal (hissing, laying ears back), other than pupillary dilation and some raising of hair on the back as seen in the normal stalking cat. Other data indicated that this was not simply a midbrain eating region—animals would ignore a bowl of food in order to attack an anesthetized rat. Thus this midbrain region seems to be part of a quiet biting attack system that can be separated from the more emotional affective rage attack syndrome.

Human violence and psychosurgery

Psychosurgery to control emotional disorders is the subject of much emotional discussion today. The term *psychosurgery* refers to the use of neurosurgical procedures to treat disorders that are primarily behavioral, at least insofar as symptoms are concerned. Such procedures have been used not only to control extreme violence but also for cases of severe terminal cancer pain, severely debilitating compulsions—the patient whose hands are raw and bleeding because he washes them several hundred times a day—for extreme fear and anxiety that completely incapacitate a person, and for severe psychosis. The problems surrounding the use of psychosurgery do not admit to easy solutions; not only are there scientific and medical problems but also moral and ethical problems. It must be emphasized that our discussion here does not apply to standard neurosurgical procedures, for example, removal of brain tumors, treatment of head injuries, etc., but only to the brain surgery to treat disorders that are first manifested by behavior.

The first modern use of psychosurgery (trephining the skull to let out devils was an ancient use) is instructive. Moniz, a Portuguese neurosurgeon, attended a scientific conference in 1935. He heard a paper by an American scientist, Jacobsen, who reported on the effects of removing the prefrontal cortex of monkeys. Jacobsen noted that his previously aggressive and hostile animals became tame and gentle following the operation. On the basis of this evidence, Moniz developed the procedure of frontal lobotomy in humans and was later awarded the Nobel prize for his "achievement." However, what Moniz apparently failed to hear in Jacobsen's talk was the main point of the research: namely that following surgery, the monkeys had severe difficulty in solving tasks involving temporal memory—the so-called *delayed response problem*, in which the animal must remember which of two or more food wells was baited. Much of the subsequent history of psychosurgery has this unfortunate character. Neurosurgeons jump to completely unwarranted scientific conclusions on the basis of inadequate animal experiments, and apply their conclusions to the human brain. This is not meant to be a blanket condemnation of psychosurgery, only a plea for better science.

Among the most extensive experimental studies of human psychosurgery was the Columbia Greystone Project (Mettler, 1952), in which a series of lesions of the prefrontal cortex of systematically varied size were made on a group of "volunteer" psychiatric patients. Although one may question their morality, these studies were rather well done from a scientific viewpoint but the results were disappointing. First, the beneficial effects of surgery on psychosis were quite variable. Second, there were no clear effects on psychological test performance. No change occurred in IQ or in any other abilities or personality measures. However, in many cases the relatives of the patients reported marked changes in the patients' personalities. The most common impression was that a patient was only a "hollow shell" of his former self. This is a very real and significant effect, even though it was not detected in the psychological tests.

Studies like the Columbia Greystone Project have led to virtual abandonment of prefrontal lobotomy for treatment of psychosis or severe neurosis. However, the procedure still has an important use in terminal pain. For reasons not known, after frontal lobotomy severe chronic pain, as in cancer, no longer seems to bother the patient, at least in many instances. The frontal cortex does have fairly direct connections with the limbic system; the amygdaloid nucleus projects to the dorsomedial nucleus of the thalamus, which in turn projects to the frontal cortex. Whether this limbic input is relevant to altered pain perception or to the changes in personality that often accompany frontal lobotomy remains to be determined. The functions of the frontal cortex and other association areas of the brain will be considered further in Chapter 12.

Psychosurgery to control extreme violence, particularly episodic violence that resembles epilepsy, has focused on the limbic system. Favored targets for lesions are the cingulate gyrus—by placing a lesion here the circuit of Papez can be interrupted without extensive damage to other brain tissue—and the amygdala. We reviewed some of the animal studies on effects of destruction of the amygdala above. The consensus of animal studies does seem to be that destruction of the amygdala tends to reduce aggressive behavior. However, the mechanisms remain unknown and there are many puzzling and contradictory findings.

A most interesting and careful series of clinical-surgical studies on humans have been done by Vernon Mark, Frank Ervin, and their associates at the Massachusetts General Hospital. A readable and interesting account of their work in nontechnical terms is given in the book, *Violence and the Brain* (Harper and Row, 1970), where Mark and Ervin focused on the amygdala. They developed their procedures in several stages on a series of patients. First, recording electrodes were implanted in deep structures like the amygdala to detect abnormal epileptic brain-wave activity. Then, using remote stimulation techniques, they electrically stimulated these regions. Finally lesions of the amygdala were made. The patients selected had episodic "attacks" of extreme and uncontrollable violence which resembled in many ways the clinical epileptic condition of temporal lobe epilepsy. The case history of one of Mark's and Ervin's patients, Julia S., is abstracted here:

In Julia's case, the relationship between brain disease and violent behavior was very clear. Her history of brain disease went back to the time when, before the age of 2, she had a severe attack of encephalitis following mumps. When she was 10, she began to have epileptic seizures; occasionally these attacks were grand mal seizures. Most of the time, they consisted of brief lapses of consciousness, staring, lip smacking, and chewing. Often after such a seizure she would be overcome by panic and run off as fast as she could without caring about destination. Her behavior between seizures was marked by severe temper tantrums followed by extreme remorse. Four of these depressions ended in serious suicide attempts. . .

On twelve occasions, Julia had seriously assaulted other people without any apparent provocation. By far the most serious attack had occurred when she was 18. She was at a movie with her parents when she felt a wave of terror pass over her body. She told her father she was going to have another one of her "racing spells" and agreed to wait for her parents in the ladies lounge. As she went to it, she automatically took a small knife out of her handbag. She had gotten into the habit of carrying this knife for protection because her "racing spells" often took her into dangerous neighborhoods where she would come out of her fuguelike state to find herself helpless, alone and confused. When she got to the lounge, she looked in the mirror and perceived the left side of her face and trunk (including the left arm) as shriveled, disfigured, and "evil." At the same time, she noticed a drawing sensation in her face and hands. Just then another girl entered the lounge and inadvertently bumped against Julia's left arm and hand. Julia, in a panic, struck quickly with her knife, penetrating the other girl's heart and then screamed loudly. Fortunately, help arrived in time to save the life of her victim. . .

The neurological examination made in our hospital showed Julia's ability to assimilate newly learned material was impaired, and, because of her shock treatments, she had a severe deficiency in both recent and remote memory. A brain wave examination disclosed a typical epileptic seizure pattern with spikes in both temporal regions, in addition to widespread abnormality over the rest of the brain. . .

Electrodes were placed stereotactically into both temporal lobes, and after she had recovered from the surgical procedure, we recorded epileptic electrical activity from both amygdalas. Electrical stimulation of either amygdala produced symptoms characteristic of the beginning of her seizures. These symptoms were more easily elicited by stimulating her left amygdala, and therefore, a destructive lesion was made in the left temporal lobe in the region of the amygdala and all electrodes were withdrawn. However, her symptoms and seizures persisted and changed to include signs that indicated a small portion of her brain was firing abnormally, and that this area was related to the movement of her left arm (the one that was brushed against by the girl she stabbed). As the motor tract crosses over from one side of the brain to the opposite side of the body, this suggested that her persistent seizures and attack behavior were initiated in her right temporal lobe. Therefore, we again placed electrodes in her right amygdala. . .

The following records were made from this patient in a hospital room. . . Both Julia and her parents knew that sometime during the day her brain was going to be recorded from and stimulated, but they had no idea when we were going to do it. Before we had done any stimulating, but while we were recording, the electrical activity recorded from the leads in Julia's amygdaloid nucleus showed a typical epileptic seizure pattern . . . The behavior that accompanied this change in Julia's brain waves involved her getting up and running over to the wall of her bedroom. Once there, she narrowed her eyes, bared her teeth, and clenched her fists—that is, she exhibited all the signs of being on the verge of making a physical attack . . .

(Vernon Mark and Frank Ervin, **Violence and the Brain,**
Harper & Row, 1970, abridged from pages 97–99.
Copyright © 1970 by Harper & Row, Publishers, Inc.
By permission of Harper & Row, Publishers, Inc.)

Following these observations, a destructive lesion was made in Julia's right amygdala. She had only two mild rage episodes in the first postoperative year and none in the second. The investigators are properly cautious in noting that two years follow-up is not sufficient to make a final evaluation of this case. Julia still had generalized brain disease and epileptic seizures following the procedure. However, her episodes of extreme violence were clearly reduced.

Although it is possible to criticize aspects of their work on both scientific and ethical grounds, these clinical studies by Mark and Ervin are well done. Considerable animal experimentation implicates the amygdala in aggressive behavior. Prior to making lesions, electrical activity of the amygdala was first recorded to determine if abnormal activity was present. The behavior of the patients resembled the clinical diagnosis of temporal lobe epilepsy. Finally, they were extremely violent and dangerous to other humans.

It should be pointed out, however, that cases with such an obvious relation between a brain disorder and a behavioral pathology involving violent attacks are extremely rare. Most individuals who show disturbed patterns of brain-wave activity, as in the case of psychomotor epilepsy, show no higher incidence of violent behavior than the general public. Conversely, many individuals arrested each year for violent crimes show no obvious abnormalities in their brain-wave patterns. The relation between brain function and behavior is extremely complex; even where more impressive correlations are seen, these are not necessarily causes. The reader is urged to consult a very readable and important discussion of these issues in the recent book *Brain Control* by Eliot Valenstein (1973).

Biology, psychosurgery, and human aggression

Is extreme human violence primarily a biological phenomenon? Several types of abnormalities clearly suggest an affirmative answer. The *XYY* syndrome—the tall, retarded violent male criminal with an extra Y chromosome (Chapter 2)—suggests that the Y chromosome disposes to violence. The temporal lobe epilepsy patients of Mark and Ervin provide support. Interestingly, in a study they conducted on a sample of violent criminals in a penitentiary, half the subjects showed signs of abnormal brain activity. However, the *XYY* syndrome and temporal lobe epilepsy are abnormal conditions. By no means is it clear that all, or even a majority, of violent criminals have gross genetic or brain abnormalities. The ethologist Konrad Lorenz in his book *On Aggression* (1966) argues that violent aggression is the natural, animal inheritance of man. His evidence and arguments are not compelling, at least to this writer. The fact that the incidence of crimes of violence varies so widely between countries—contrast the high crime rate in the United States with the very low rate in Scandinavian countries—would seem to argue for the contribution of social and cultural factors. One conclusion is absolutely clear. We need far more research and study on both the biological and environmental factors that underlie human violence.

TOWARDS A PSYCHOPHYSIOLOGY OF EMOTION

As we pointed out at the start of our discussion, emotion usually involves at least three distinct aspects: visceral, experiential, and behavioral. The study of emotion would be much simpler if the three aspects were always correlated. In many cases, such as times when we are very frightened and our heart pounds and we run away, these aspects are correlated. However, in less intense situations, experience, behavior, and visceral physiology may not all be consistent with one another. For example, experientially and behaviorally we find it easy to distinguish between an emotional state of fear and one of anger, but it is not so easy to find clear differences in the visceral activity which is correlated with these states. Because these aspects are not always correlated, the causal relationships between them are not always clear. The main task of a theory of emotion would be to account for the way in which these aspects are related to produce the integrated process which we call emotion. While no satisfactory theory of emotion currently exists, recent work suggests directions for further research on this problem.

In the earliest attempt at such a theory—that of James and Lange—the major emphasis was on the role of visceral factors which were viewed as playing a major role in mediating both experiential and behavioral effects. That is, we feel afraid because we run, rather than running away because we feel afraid. The sight of a frightening object, such as a bear, produces both visceral activation and the behavior of running, and our experience of fear is a consequence rather than a cause of the other two factors. As James put it, "our feeling of the (bodily) changes is the emotion."

In 1929 the physiologist Walter B. Cannon criticized the adequacy of the theory by noting that emotional behavior is present even after the viscera have been surgically separated from the central nervous system. He also noted that visceral changes are much slower than would be expected from experiential evidence and that there is no clear distinction between the visceral changes which accompany different, clearly defined emotional states. Cannon suggested that the essential mechanisms underlying emotion involved central brain mechanisms rather than peripheral visceral factors. Cannon and Bard suggested that emotional behavior depended on neural mechanisms located in the hypothalamus and lower brain regions and involved the interaction of these regions with cortical regions.

As we have already seen, there is considerable evidence that both sets of factors must be taken into account in any theory of emotion. It is equally clear that stimulus factors must play a critical role. The real problem is to clarify the way in which the various sets of factors interact in producing emotional behavior.

In 1924 Marañon had the ingenious idea of injecting Adrenalin into subjects and asking them to report their feelings. Since Adrenalin activates the sympathetic nervous system in a manner which mimics its effects during emotional behavior it was expected that subjects would experience emotion. To Marañon's surprise most of the subjects simply reported their physical symptoms with no emotional overtones. In the few cases where it was possible to obtain an emotional reaction it was necessary to superimpose on the injection an emotional stimulus, such as asking subjects to think of sick children or dead parents. The combination of Adrenalin and such a stimulus produced, in a very few cases, what seemed like a genuine emotion.

More recently, Schachter and colleagues carried out a more elaborate version of the adrenaline injection study to explore the relation between complex perceptual (cognitive) factors and visceral factors in emotion. The substance norepinephrine (also called noradrenalin) is released by the medullary portion of the adrenal glands under conditions of fear or stress and produces a variety of autonomic peripheral effects—heart pounding, face warm and flushing, hands shaking. The same symptoms can be induced by injecting norepinephrine (or a very similar compound, epinephrine) even when the person has not been exhibiting emotion. Schachter reasoned that subjects could be made to have a variety of emotional experiences after injection, depending on what they expected or thought they were supposed to feel.

All subjects were told they would receive injections of a drug called Suproxin (a fictional name) to improve performance on certain visual skill tests. Half the subjects were actually given a placebo (saline) and half were given epinephrine. Different groups of subjects received two types of instructions, informative, or uninformative:

Informed subjects. Before receiving the injections, such subjects were told, "I should also tell you that some of our subjects have experienced side effects from the Suproxin. These side effects will only last for 15 or 20 minutes. Probably your hands will start to shake, your heart will start to pound, and your face may get warm and flushed."

These subjects, then, are told precisely what they will feel and why they will feel it. For such subjects, the evaluative needs are low. They have an exact explanation for their bodily feelings, and cognitive or situational factors should have no effects on how the subject labels his feelings.

Uninformed subjects. Such subjects are told that the injection will have no side effects at all. These subjects, then, will experience a state of sympathetic arousal, but the experimenter has given them no explanation for why they feel as they do. Evaluative needs then should be high, and cognitive-situational factors should have maximal effect on the way such a subject labels his bodily state.

Finally, in order to expose subjects to situations from which they might derive explanatory cognitions relevant to their bodily state, they were placed in one of two situations immediately after injection:

Euphoria. A subject was placed alone in a room with a stooge who had been introduced as a fellow subject and who, following a completely standardized routine, acted in a euphoric-manic fashion, doing such things as flying paper airplanes, hula-hooping, and the like, all the while keeping up a standard patter and occasionally attempting to induce the subject to join in.

Anger. A subject was asked to fill out a long, infuriatingly personal questionnaire that asked such questions as: "With how many men (other than your father) has your mother had extramarital relationships? 4 and under_____: 5–9_____: 10 and over_____."

Filling in the questionnaire alongside the subject was a stooge, again presumably a fellow subject, who openly grew more and more irritated at the questionnaire and who finally ripped the thing up in a rage, slammed it to the floor while biting out, "I'm not wasting any more time; I'm getting my books and leaving," and stamped out of the room.

In both situations, an observer, watching through a one-way mirror, systematically recorded the behavior of the subject in order to provide indexes of the extent to which the subject joined in the stooge's mood. Once these rigged situations had run their course, the experimenter returned and, with a plausible pretext, asked the subject to fill out a series of standardized scales to measure the intensity of anger or euphoria.

(Schachter, S. Cognitive effects on bodily functioning: studies of obesity and eating. In Glass, D. C. (ed.) **Neurophysiology and Emotion.** New York: Rockefeller University Press, 1967, pages 121–123.)

Results were as expected. Uninformed epinephrine subjects experienced and exhibited exactly the kind of emotion the stooge was portraying—euphoria or anger. Informed subjects and placebo subjects did not. In other experiments the same effects were replicated for various other emotional situations including amusement and fear. In all cases the uninformed epinephrine subjects interpreted their own bodily sensations (pounding heart, flushed face) in terms of the appropriate emotional feeling for the situation. It is important that the informed epinephrine subjects did not report any emotional experience whatever. They knew they would have the bodily sensations produced by the drug. Even though the behavioral situation and the physiology were the same, they did not experience emotion.

Conclusions

In an interesting attempt at a synthesis of various approaches to emotion, George Mandler has suggested that the reason people tend to group the different emotional states is that they all have in common a general visceral arousal of greater or lesser intensity. Psychologists have responded in the same way but they have gradually become aware of the fact that the term *emotion*, like the term *motivation*, reflects a preliminary grouping of diverse behaviors which appear to have certain things in common. Mandler's conclusion is instructive:

The particular combination of environmental events, physiological response, and prior experience that determines emotional behavior is often specific to that behavior, but it is unlikely that any special laws will have to be invoked for a peculiarly "emotional" explanation. At the same time it is too early to specify the laws that operate within the confines of emotional behavior. The major laws governing behavior—and thus emotional behavior—are still to be pronounced to the satisfaction of most psychologists. But the layman will be disappointed if he expects to find any special emotional "things" in those laws.
(Mandler, 1962, page 338)

Summary

Sex is analogous in some ways to eating and drinking: peripheral stimuli play an important role in eliciting and directing sexual behavior, neuronal mechanisms play a critical role in initiating and organizing the motor aspects of sexual behavior, and internal state is critical—the presence of a sexual object does not always elicit sexual behavior. Unlike eating and drinking, sexual behavior is not necessary for the biological well-being (as opposed to personal well-being) of the individual. However, it is obviously of critical importance for the survival of the species.

The endocrine system, which acts basically as a complex feedback system, is the mechanism of control of sexual behavior. The pituitary, one of the major structures in the endocrine system, acts upon various target organs throughout the body. The neurohypophysis receives nerve fibers from the supraoptic nucleus and the paraventricular nuclei. Oxytocin and ADH, hormones released by the neurohypophysis, are actually produced in the hypothalamus, and are transported to the neurohypophysis for storage until they are released into the blood stream. While the adenohypophysis contains no nerve cells from the hypothalamus, it receives a blood supply from the median eminence of the hypothalamus. Nerve cells located in the median eminence secrete hormones into the blood supply which act on the gland cells of the adenohypophysis to stimulate release of the major pituitary hormones.

Particular hormones in the male and female, androgen, and estrogen and progesterone, respectively, are responsible for changes in sexual morphology and behavior. These hormones are manufactured and released by the ovary and testis with appropriate levels of the pituitary gonadotrophic hormones. The female estrous cycle is dependent upon the interrelated activity of the brain, pituitary, and ovaries. FSH and LH are both vital for functioning of the testes and ovaries.

The hypothalamus plays an integral role in the control of sexual behavior. Neural actions on the control of sexual behavior involve hypothalamic-pituitary reactions. Studies of the effects of lesions of the pituitary and anterior hypothalamus have shown that while lesions of either structure abolish sexual behavior, hormone therapy can restore sexual behavior only after lesions of the pituitary. Electrical and chemical stimulation studies of the anterior hypothalamus have confirmed the results of lesion studies and indicate that hypothalamic regions are essential for normal sexual activity in both males and females.

The effects of gonadectomy upon sexual behavior are highly dependent upon species, age, and amount of prior sexual experience of the animal. Studies involving hormonal injection into infant animals (rodents) have shown that sexual behavior or morphology may be altered only when the animals are very young, until the circulating levels of androgens or estrogens are fully established. Hormonal injection after this critical period of growth and tissue differentiation has little effect upon either morphology or behavior. These gonadal hormones also cause morphological differentiation and specialization of neural tissue in the infant.

The hypothalamus is a critical region for sexual behavior. The various hormonal systems serve a dual function: they must establish the necessary physical substrate for conception (sperm formation and ovulation), and they must generate receptive sexual behavior. In addition to the role of these hormonal systems upon behavior and the target organs, the hormones also act back on the brain to regulate hypothalamic-pituitary functions.

Human sexual differentiation into male and female is of course largely determined by genetic, neuronal, and hormonal factors. However, the assignment of sex to an infant by parents may have profound effects on the development of sexual behavior and even on biological sex characteristics. Psychosexual differentiation is critically dependent upon the attitude of the parents toward the infant.

Three levels of meaning for emotion may be distinguished, those of experience, behavior, and physiology. Physiological responses to emotion are under the control of the autonomic nervous system which, in turn, is controlled by the hypothalamus, limbic forebrain, and certain brain stem regions. Experience, behavior, and physiology are not always consistent phenomena. One of the major problems in developing theories of emotion is to establish close correlations among these three levels of emotion.

A number of different types of behavioral studies of emotionality have been conducted. While ethological studies have clarified the processes of emotional behavior sequences and the stimuli controlling these sequences in animals, the problem with the ethological studies is that the emotions described have been inferred from knowledge of the stimulus situation and the resultant behavior. In animal behavior studies of conflict situations where two antagonistic behavioral tendencies interact, "displacement" behaviors have been observed. These behaviors are found only when two conflicting tendencies co-exist and presumably represent the interaction of these incompatible emotions.

It is believed that many aspects of emotional responses are innate and that the neural pathways underlying these responses are genetically determined. Imprinting in precocial birds is one mechanism by which the primary social group (the family) is solidified. Work with primates has shown that feeding itself does not determine the recipient of the primary social bond, and that contact comfort is an innate tendency among primates.

Peripheral measures of emotionality, such as heart rate and sweating of the palms, are controlled by the autonomic nervous system. By means of its sympathetic and parasympathetic divisions, the autonomic nervous system functions to maintain an optimal internal environment. The autonomic nervous system is directly controlled by nuclei in the brain stem which in turn are influenced by the hypothalamus and limbic forebrain structures. The difficulty associated with most autonomic measures of emotionality is that they can be recorded in nearly any intense emotional state and in some nonemotional situations.

The limbic system is the forebrain system most frequently implicated in emotional behavior. In terms of evolution, the limbic system was the earliest form of forebrain to develop. While much of limbic forebrain in relatively primitive animals deals with olfaction, most of this function has been lost through evolution. The circuit of Papez, an anatomical reverberating circuit, has been proposed as the neural basis of emotion. The hippocampus appears to play a critical role in this circuit. Essentially all of the limbic system is interconnected via the circuit of Papez. While the circuit of Papez has been neuroanatomically demonstrated, the functional role of the circuit has not been completely verified.

The limbic system, particularly the amygdala, is involved in a variety of emotional aspects of behavior. Lesions of the amygdala seem to not only reduce aggressive behavior, but also to be related to the social behavior (dominance hierarchy) of monkeys. The lateral hypothalamus appears to be an essential substrate for aggression. The relationship of the hypothalamus to the amygdala is important in the elaboration of aggressive behavior, with the basolateral amygdala influencing the lateral hypothalamus in an excitatory fashion. A number of experiments suggest that the amygdala may play a role in the control of aggressive behavior and the hypothalamus may serve as an integrating structure. It now appears that excitatory and inhibitory influences from the amygdala and septum are projected upon the hypothalamus which then integrates the organism's response.

The critical brain region for rage behavior is also the hypothalamus. The behavioral differences manifested in rage and sham rage appear to be due to stimulation of different brain regions. Sham rage occurs with stimulation of the central gray while directed rage and attack is evidenced with lateral hypothalamic stimulation. The exact anatomical location of the electrode appears to be a major determinant of the form attack takes, whether it is stalking attack or affective attack.

Brain surgery has been used to treat apparent behavioral disorders for many years. Prefrontal lobotomy was used in the treatment of psychoses for many years, but has been abandoned generally due to the inconsistency of its beneficial effects and its deleterious effects on personality. Recently, psychosurgery has been utilized with humans with severe behavioral disorders, such as Julia, with some degree of success. The moral and ethical problems, notwithstanding the medical problems, demand that caution be exercised in the use of psychosurgery. However, the problems with violence in the United States also suggest that methods of dealing with violence and aggression, such as psychosurgery, be given due consideration.

Longer term emotional reactions, such as stress, require the body to activate its reserves in order to handle the stress. Psychological stress is evident in both man and other animals. The stereotyped response to chronic stress has been termed the general adaptation syndrome. While an individual can usually cope with one stressful situation at a time, multiplicity of stress often creates a situation with which an animal cannot cope and may lead to a breakdown in the adaptive mechanism to stress.

The adrenal glands play a major role in the stress syndrome. Epinephrine and cortisone are two adrenal gland secretions important in the general adaptation syndrome. During the adaptation stage of the stress response, the adrenal glands produce an excess of hormones, with an excess of epinephrine resulting in hypertension. The exhaustion stage of the adaptation syndrome is characterized by an insufficient supply of adrenal hormones. ACTH and the adrenal cortical hormones have profound effects upon behavior. Variation in ACTH level has striking effects on the extinction of learned avoidance responses, learning of passive avoidance, and in the habituation of startle responses to intense sounds. Numerous studies implicate ACTH and perhaps other adrenal cortical hormones as having direct actions on brain systems involved in learning, particularly in the habituation and extinction of responses.

10

Sleep, dreaming,
arousal, and attention

10

All men sleep. Between the darkness out of which we are born and that in which we end, there is a tide of darkness that ebbs and flows each day of our lives. A third of life is spent in sleep, that profoundly mysterious sovereign to which we irresistibly submit, lying almost immobile for hours, removed from the waking world. It is surprising that men succumb to this daily plunge from consciousness with so little curiosity. During the brief span of life each person tries to find out who he is, taking pride in the acts and thoughts that are peculiarly his own and seeking command over his inner forces. The search for identity is never finished, nor the self-command complete, and at the end of a lifetime a man is still more of a stranger to himself than he thinks. He has led two lives, but has known only one of them. By age seventy he has been almost a total stranger to the twenty years of his sleep.

(Reprinted by permission of Coward, McCann & Geoghegan, Inc. from Sleep by Gay Gaer Luce and Julius Segal, page 13. Copyright © 1966 by Gay Gaer Luce and Julius Segal.)

Sleep and waking are a rhythmic pattern that recur every 24 hours in normal humans. Such biological rhythms are called *circadian* (from the Latin for *about a day*). The classical studies of Conrad Richter on activity rhythms in rats demonstrated that the 24-hour activity cycle persisted indefinitely in the absence of dark-light changes and after destruction of almost any area of the brain except the hypothalamus. The circadian clock appears to be located in or near the hypothalamus. The biological utility of alternating periods of activity and inactivity seems clear enough. Many predators and some prey animals are active at night. Primates and other animals that tend to rely on vision to guide their behavior are active in the daytime and quiet at night.

Sleep, obviously, tends to occur during the periods of inactivity. It is an arbitrary matter whether one sleeps by night or by day. However, as jet travelers know, it is difficult and tiring to shift the day-night cycle by several hours. Indeed, it seems to require at least a week to adapt to such a shift. Actually it takes much longer for the 24-hour body temperature cycle—which is lower at night than during the day—to shift completely.

One of the most common ideas about sleep is that it provides necessary rest for the body. In a general way this is obviously true—animals eventually die, and humans become psychotic, if kept awake for sufficiently long periods of time. However, there is as yet no evidence to indicate why this should be so. There is little significant change in energy consumption by the body between quiet waking and sleep. We have yet to discover any metabolic poisons or toxins that require the occurrence of sleep to be dissipated. In short, the reasons for sleep to occur at all and to seem necessary remain a complete mystery.

SLEEP AND DREAMING

Sleep researchers are becoming increasingly convinced that all mammals live in three quite different states: waking, sleep, and deep sleep. Aserinsky and Kleitman discovered deep sleep in 1953. Prior to that time scientists and laymen agreed that there were only the two normal biological states of waking and sleep. Generally, dreaming was believed to occur only very briefly at the moment of awakening. *State* implies a set of criteria or measures that occur together in a reliable pattern qualitatively different from those of another state. It can be argued that the transition from drowsy waking to light sleep is gradual and one of degree. The properties of normal waking and sleep are sufficiently distinct, however, to justify the use of *state*.

Sleep

Aserinsky and Kleitman recorded EEG and eye movements during an entire night's sleep, initially in infants and then in adult humans. They discovered that rapid jerky eye movements occurred periodically during sleep. A most uncharacteristic EEG pattern seemed to occur together with the periods of eye movement. Prior to this time students of electro-encephalography had developed a rather neat and tidy progression of EEG patterns from waking through several stages of sleep. These are shown in Figure 10.1. The waking pattern can show either alpha or low-voltage fast waves. Alpha predominates if the subject is awake but resting quietly with eyes closed. If the subject is alert with eyes open low-voltage fast waves predominate. Alpha, remember, is characterized as large 8- to 12-per-second waves. The general methods of recording EEGs in humans and some characteristic patterns were discussed earlier in Chapter 4. Metal disc electrodes are placed on the surface of the scalp, usually over the back (occipital) and upper sides (parietal) of the head. The electrical activity so recorded is believed to be generated by the graded synaptic potentials of millions of neurons in the cerebral cortex active with varying degrees of synchronization (refer to the discussion in Chapter 4).

As the subject passes from waking to the lightest stage of sleep—stage 1—alpha tends to decrease and rather low-voltage, 4- to 6-cycle-per-second activity begins to occur. Stage 2 is marked by the appearance of so-called *sleep spindles* at 13 to 15 cycles per second. Stage 3 is characterized by the appearance of the large slow delta waves at 1 to 4 cycles per second. In stage 4, delta waves dominate the EEG. This seemed a very satisfactory description of the EEG stages of sleep. Stage 4, with its prominent delta, was quite similar to the EEG of patients in coma, and it became progressively more difficult to awaken a person as they passed from stage 1 to stage 4.

In their study, Aserinsky and Kleitman discovered, to their surprise, that when periods of eye movements began the EEG shifted abruptly and directly from the stage it was recording (2, 3, or 4) to a pattern resembling stage 1 or alert waking, the characteristic low-voltage fast-arousal EEG. The EEG pattern remained in this stage while eye movements continued. This could be interpreted as the subject beginning to wake up. However it was harder to wake the subject up from this atypical stage 1 sleep than from the presumably deepest stage 4. Further, the

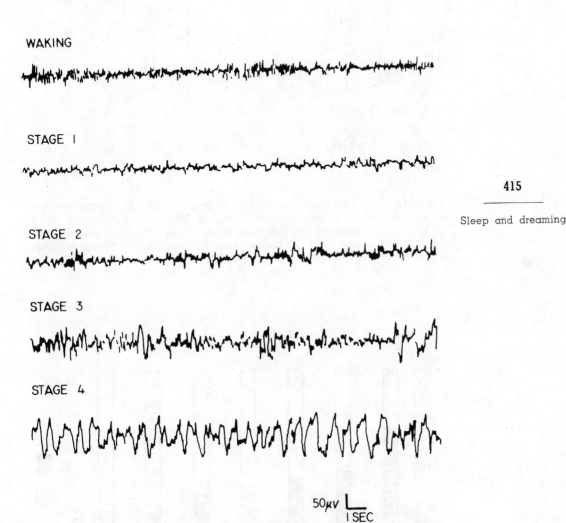

WAKING ALERT AND D (DEEP)SLEEP

WAKING

STAGE 1

STAGE 2

STAGE 3

STAGE 4

50μV

1 SEC

Figure 10.1 The EEG stages of sleep in the adult human recorded monopolarly from the scalp overlying the parietal area of the cerebral cortex. The top tracing shows alert waking and D (deep or desynchronized) sleep. The tracing labeled "Waking" is awake restful with eyes closed and exhibits prominent alpha. Stages 1 through 4 show the gradual development of S (slow-wave) sleep. Note the prominent slow delta waves in Stage 4. When D sleep develops, the EEG suddenly shifts to the arousal pattern of the top tracing. (All but top tracing redrawn from Hartmann, E. *The Biology of Dreaming*. Springfield, Ill.: Charles C. Thomas, 1967.)

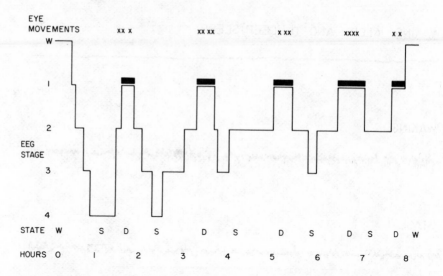

Figure 10.2 A young adult's typical night of sleep. The diagram actually represents a mean derived from many all-night recordings. The heavy lines indicate the D periods with characteristic desynchronized or alert EEG (Fig. 10.1) and rapid conjugate eye movements (REM). (Redrawn from Hartmann, E. *The Biology of Dreaming*. Springfield, Ill.: Charles C. Thomas, 1967.)

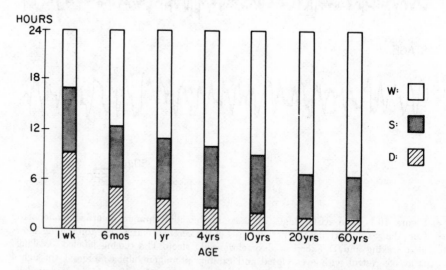

Figure 10.3 The development of proportion of time spent in W (waking), S, and D states in humans as a function of age. (Redrawn from Hartmann, E. *The Biology of Dreaming*. Springfield, Ill.: Charles C. Thomas, 1967.)

subjects almost invariably reported that they had been dreaming. This stage of sleep has been termed deep sleep, paradoxical sleep (because it is a paradox because the EEG is that of an awake subject), dreaming sleep, rapid eye movement (REM) sleep, and many other names. Here we call it simply D sleep; generally, a stronger stimulus is required to awaken the subject from D sleep than is true for the other stages. The reader may think of "D" standing for *deep* or *dreaming*. Non-D sleep will be termed S sleep, standing for *slow*-wave (in the EEG) sleep.

The characteristic pattern of a night's sleep for a normal adult is shown in Figure 10.2. There are typically five or six periods of D sleep during the night that alternate with S sleep. D sleep occupies perhaps one-quarter of the sleep time of an adult. Interestingly, D sleep seems to occur at least half the time in infants. The proportions of time spent in waking (W), S sleep, and D sleep for humans of different ages are shown in Figure 10.3.

The D sleep state has a number of characteristic signs in addition to the arousal EEG pattern and eye movements. Heart rate is slow and steady in S sleep, ranging between 50 and 60 beats per minute. In D sleep it becomes highly irregular, ranging from 45 to 100 beats per minute. The heartbeat is characteristic of a vigorous active waking state during which the subject periodically engages in strenuous or exciting activity, even though the subject lies very quietly and relaxed. Blood pressure is similarly highly variable during sleep, in contrast to a relatively low stable level during S sleep. Respiration is very slow and regular in S sleep but highly variable and irregular in D sleep.

Perhaps the clearest symptoms of D sleep are the changes in the muscular system. Most prominent are the eye movements. They are conjugate (eyes together) rapid shifts lasting from 100 to 200 milliseconds and occur in bursts rather than continuously. The body musculature shows a general and marked reduction in tone—the neck muscles relax so completely that the head "flops" if not supported. In spite of the lowered musculature there are characteristic jerks and twitches of the face, laryngeal muscles, hands, and feet during D sleep. The temptation to relate these movements to dream content is almost irresistible but the evidence is not yet clear. A somewhat unexpected characteristic of D sleep in man is the occurrence of penile erection. Partial to complete erection occurs throughout each D period, but not during S sleep. Contrary to popular opinion, D sleep erection is not necessarily correlated in any way with sexual dream content, and occurs during D sleep in human infants as well as adults.

Perhaps the most striking fact about D sleep is that it occurs in all mammals and even to a small extent in birds. Table 10.1 summarizes the little that is known about the occurrence of the three states of waking, S sleep, and D sleep in various phyla. Of course, no information is available on dreaming in nonhuman animals. However, to anyone who has

Table 10.1 D-time, length of D-periods, and sleep-dream cycle length in various mammalian species (young adult mammals)

Species	D-time as a percentage of total sleep	Average length of a D-period (minutes)	Average cycle length (minutes)
Mouse	...*	...	3–4
Rat	15–20	4–7	7–13
Rabbit	1–3	...	24
Opossum	22–44	5	17
Cat	20–60	10	20–40
Sheep	2–3	...	...
Monkey	11–25	4–10	40–60
Man	20–24	14	80–90
Elephant	...	...	120

*...indicates no information.

From Hartmann, E. **The Biology of Dreaming.** Springfield, Ill.: Charles C. Thomas, 1967.

watched a young dog in D sleep showing coordinated twitches of the four paws, with soft growling and whining, and tongue movement, the inference that the animal is dreaming of a good chase is most compelling. The various physiological criteria of D sleep noted above for man are also generally true of other mammals, particularly the rapid eye movements, marked relaxation of neck and body musculature, and irregular twitching of extremities.

Dreaming

The obvious question of greatest interest concerning the D state is whether, in fact, it represents dreaming. In general, this does seem to be true, if one can believe the subjective reports of subjects awakened from sleep. Hartmann summarizes results of 12 studies, for which subjects were awakened during D sleep and S sleep and asked whether they were dreaming. On the average, dreams were reported on about 80 per cent of the awakenings from D sleep and on about 20 per cent of the awakenings from S sleep. Figures in the different studies varied a good deal with the experimenter's definition of dreaming. Given the difficulty and unreliability of subjective memory of dreaming, these statistics are not too bad.

An even more difficult issue for study is the possible relation between the physiological events of the D state and the events of the dream. In a most interesting and careful study by Roffwarg and associates, a few highly verbal intelligent subjects were awakened from D periods and asked to describe precisely what they had been looking at for the last few seconds before awakening. Judges unfamiliar with the actual eye movement records tried to predict how the subject's eyes would have moved if he had in fact been looking at the scenes he described. There was a very close correspondence between the actual recorded eye movements and the judges' predictions of eye movements. Interestingly, the correspondence occurred in *real time*. The time sequencing of eye movements recorded and reported for the last few seconds of dreaming before awakening occupied the same length of time as they would have done in normal waking viewing. This suggests that the duration of events in dreaming is about the same as their corresponding duration in an awake state. A great many careful studies of this type are needed before we can infer that the physiological concomitants of D sleep correspond to dream events. The fact that rapid eye movements usually occur in bursts during D sleep would seem to argue against this correspondence in general.

The actual content of dreams is a continuing source of fascination. Of course, the study of dream content is always complicated by the fact that we must rely on the person's recollection of what he dreamed about; memories of dreams are notoriously poor—very significantly poorer than our memory of waking events and experience. In a sense, this is fortunate; otherwise we might tend to confuse the two. All readers probably are familiar with Freud's attempts at dream interpretations. His efforts perhaps reflect more on his very considerable intelligence and ingenuity than on the meaning of dreams. There was no normative data available then on the common properties of dreams. Calvin Hall, at the University of California at Santa Cruz, is the leading authority on dream content. He has collected many thousands of dream descriptions from people, and summarizes his findings as follows:

We come now to actions or behavior: What do people do in their dreams? We classified 2,668 actions in 1,000 dreams. By far the largest proportion (34 per cent) fall into the category of movement—walking, running, riding or some other gross change in bodily position. We found that, contrary to popular belief, falling or floating in dreams is not very common. After movement, the next most common activities were talking (11 per cent), sitting (7 per cent), watching (7 per cent), socializing (6 per cent), playing (5 per cent), manual work (4 per cent), thinking (4 per cent), striving (4 per cent), quarreling or fighting (3 per cent) and acquiring (3 per cent). From this it can be seen that passive or quiet activities occupy a large part of dreams, while manual activities are surprisingly infrequent. Such common waking occupations as typing, sewing, ironing, and fixing things are not represented in these thousand dreams at all; cooking, cleaning house, making beds and washing dishes occur only once each. But strenuous recreational activities, such as swimming, diving, playing a game and dancing, are fairly frequent. In short, dreamers go places more than they do things; they play more than they work; their activities are more passive than active.

The major theories about dreaming are those of Sigmund Freud and Calvin Hall. As most readers know, Freud emphasized the notion of complex unconscious mental processes that are released in the dream state. The motive force that produces the dream experience originates in the basic instincts, drives, and conflicts that lie deep in the human personality. These are primarily sexual and aggressive in character and are too unpleasant to be revealed even in the dream state. Freud terms these hypothesized underlying processes the *latent* content. They are transformed into an apparent content, the reported memories of dreams, that is more acceptable to the dreamer. The obvious scientific problem in testing Freud's theory of dreaming is that things are not what they seem. Usually, our memories of dreams are poor enough. How much more difficult it is to decide what the real underlying meaning is, when it does not even bear a simple relationship to the dreamer's fragmentary recollections. Patients undergoing psychoanalysis become very adept at reporting details of dreams, particularly those that please the analyst. Such data are without value.

Calvin Hall has developed a much simpler and more direct theory of dream content. Thought processes in sleep and dreaming are less complicated than in normal waking. Yet Freud's theory holds them to be, if anything, more complex (see Murray, 1965, for a clear discussion of this issue). Hall assumes that dreaming is reduced and simplified thinking. Dream content is a succession of scenes or images. It tends to be primarily visual, often in color, with some auditory and tactile sensations as well. Dreaming resembles a motion picture where the dreamer is both a viewer and a participant. In Hall's view, this is simple thinking. In the normal waking thought processes of adults, stimuli, sensations, and ideas are transformed primarily into verbal and linguistic processes; we tend to think in words. In dreaming, moreover, thoughts and even sensations are transformed into visual images. Concepts become pictures, perhaps the simplest form of thinking or cognition. Pictorial thinking is common among children and mentally ill people.

As Murray (1965) notes, the development of thought processes in children described by Piaget provide support for Calvin Hall's theory of dream content:

Very young children confuse dreams with perceptual reality; they think a person or thing is actually in the room. At around school age, the child no longer believes the dream to be real, but thinks of it as external to himself—a projected image. A few years later, the child understands the dream as an internal image—it may be described as a picture or a thought, with some confusion between the two.

(Murray, 1965, page 83)

Hall's extensive research indicates that the major themes in dream content relate to a person's most important or stressful problems, such as competition for love in the family, sex, life and death, rage and aggression, and morality. At least in terms of the major themes in dreaming, Hall and Freud are in agreement.

We are still a long way from a physiological analysis of dream content. It is possible to specify, with some reliability from physiological measures, when a sleeping person is dreaming. However, what he or she dreams about is still largely unknown. The intriguing studies of Roffwarg and associates, noted above, indicated some success in predicting types of visual dream images by analyzing eye movements just prior to waking. It is not beyond the realm of possibility that as we learn more about the analysis and interpretation of muscular activity and the EEG, we may someday have objective physiological measures that relate to the content of dreams.

Sleep deprivation

Every reader is familiar with the effects of mild sleep deprivation. It can be difficult to get up early in the morning after a late night, and periods of drowsiness occur during the day. Those of you who have had less than the normal night's sleep for a period of days know that you tend to become less efficient, have difficulty concentrating, and may become irritable.

The author served as a subject in a sleep-deprivation study when he was a graduate student. We were kept awake continuously from Friday morning until Sunday night, a period of about 60 hours, and given a battery of perceptual-motor performance tests every two hours or so. It becomes exceedingly difficult to remain awake, particularly in the early morning hours when the 24-hour temperature cycle is at its low point. Your eyes begin to sting and you experience brief periods of "sleeping on your feet." After about 48 hours very mild perceptual distortions, illusions, and even hallucinations occur. The most noticeable distortions are apparent movements at the periphery of vision. Interestingly, there is no consistent decrease in performance of skilled or perceptual tasks. Your performance becomes more erratic, but even after long periods of sleep deprivation it is possible to rally yourself to perform well, at least for brief periods. Following deprivation, a single long night's sleep is sufficient for complete recovery.

One of the most carefully studied cases of sleep deprivation was provided by Peter Tripp, a New York disc jockey, who stayed awake for 200 hours. Luce and Segal describe his marathon graphically:

In 1959, New York City beheld one of the most disturbing ordeals a man can undergo. Day and night, while the public gathered in a spirit of carnival curiosity around a Times Square recruiting booth, a well-known disc jockey was staying awake for 200 hours to benefit the Polio Fund of the National Foundation. He looked weary, but no radio listener or casual onlooker could have imagined the truth of his experience. It resembled a medieval torture. . . . When Peter Tripp decided to forgo sleep for over eight days, scientists tried to dissuade him from a courageous but risky undertaking. Tripp was determined. He set up broadcasting headquarters in a glass-walled Army recruiting booth in Times Square. Across the street in the Hotel Astor a suite was converted into a psychological laboratory. An impressive crew of psychologists, psychiatrists and medical specialists offered to participate under the direction of Louis Jolyon West, of Oklahoma, and Harold L. Williams, then of Walter Reed. A preliminary checkup and some baseline tests were made to establish Tripp's normal functions. Then a regular daily routine involved medical and psychological tests, including tests of mental ability. EEG recordings were to be made at Columbia University each day, and blood samples and urine collected and analyzed. For more than eight days Tripp was never away from the watchful care of doctors and nurses. He broadcast his regular program and a dozen spot comments on his progress from the booth, and every few hours he was escorted to the Hotel Astor Laboratory where he could also clean up and change clothes. If there was any known safeguard to be obtained under the circumstances, Peter Tripp had it.

Almost from the first the overpowering force of sleepiness hit him. Constant company, walks, tests, broadcasts helped, but after about five days he needed a stimulant to keep going. Although his health was good and he stayed on a high-protein athletic diet, he soon remarked that he felt like "the last pill in the bottle." After little more than two days as he changed shoes in the hotel he pointed out to West a very interesting sight. There were cobwebs in his shoes—to his eyes, at least. West had warned him that he would have visual illusions. Specks on the table began to look like bugs. He thought he saw a rabbit in the booth. He was beginning to have trouble remembering ·things.

By 100 hours, only halfway, he had reached an inexorable turning point. Now he could perform only one or two of the daily battery of tests. Tests requiring attention or minimal mental agility had become unbearable to him and the psychologists testing him. As one later recalled, "Here was a competent New York disc jockey trying vainly to find his way through the alphabet." By 170 hours the tests were torture. A simple algebraic problem that Tripp had earlier solved with ease took such superhuman effort that he was frightened, and his agonized attempts to perform were painful to watch.

Loss of concentration and mental agility were not the worst, however. By 110 hours there were signs of delirium. As one of the doctors recalled, "We didn't know much about it at the time because he couldn't tell us." From his later statements, his curious utterances and behavior at the time, it became clear. Tripp's visual world had grown grotesque. A doctor walked into the recruiting booth in a tweed suit that Tripp saw as a suit of furry worms. A nurse appeared to drip saliva. A scientist's tie kept jumping. This was frightening, hard to explain, and sometimes Tripp grew angry wondering if this were a bona fide experiment or a masquerade. Around 120 hours, he opened a bureau drawer in the hotel and rushed out calling for help. It seemed to be spurting flames. Tripp thought the blaze had been set deliberately to test him. In order to explain to himself these hallucinations—which appeared quite real—he concocted rationalizations resembling the delusions of psychotic patients.

By about 150 hours he became disoriented, not realizing where he was, and wondering who he was. He developed a habit of glancing oddly at the large clock on the wall of the booth. As the doctors later found, the clock bore the features of an actor he knew, made up like Dracula for a television show. He began to wonder whether he were Peter Tripp or the actor whose face he saw on the clock. Still his teen-age admirers, radio audience, and onlookers would not have guessed his torment. Sometimes he would back up against a wall and let nobody walk behind him. Yet from 5 to 8 P.M. all his forces were mysteriously summoned, and he efficiently organized his commercials and records and managed a vigorous patter for three hours. Although he had passed the breaking point, he never made careless indiscretions, profanities, or the kind of impulsive utterances he made when off the air. His broadcast time occurred at the peak of his diurnal temperature cycle. It was later, when his temperature was low, that he showed the worst symptoms. Although he managed to act awake continuously, his brain waves were like those of deep sleep.

On the final morning of the final day a famous neurologist arrived to examine him. The doctor carried an umbrella, although it was a bright day, and had a somewhat archaic manner of dress. To Tripp he must have appeared funereal. He always insisted that patients undress and lie down on the examining table. Tripp complied, but as he gazed up at the doctor he came to the morbid conclusion that the man was actually an undertaker, there for the purpose of burying him alive. With this gruesome insight, Tripp leapt for the door with several doctors in pursuit. Nightmare hallucination had merged with reality, and the only explanation seemed to be that the doctors had formed a sadistic conspiracy in which he was the victim.

With some persuasion, Tripp managed to get through the day, give his final broadcast, and then, following an hour of tests, he sank into sleep for 13 hours. When he awakened, the terrors, ghoulish illusions, and mental agony had vanished. He no longer saw a visual world where objects changed size, specks turned into bugs, and clocks bore human faces. Now it was no effort to remember a joke and solve simple problems. In 13 hours that unspeakable purgatory had vanished, although a slight depression lingered for three months. The strain and publicity had probably contributed to the ordeal, but it had been a valuable one for research.

(Reprinted by permission of Coward, McCann & Geoghegan, Inc. from **Sleep** by Gay Gaer Luce and Julius Segal, pages 82, 90–93. Copyright © 1966 by Gay Gaer Luce and Julius Segal.)

Peter Tripp's experiences and symptoms are characteristic of all persons who have stayed awake for long periods. Animals die if kept awake too long. Although there are no modern documented cases of death from sleeplessness, medieval historians report instances of execution being done simply by forcing the victim to remain awake. As most readers know, forced wakefulness is an essential element of brainwashing in modern police states. After a certain point is reached, the victim genuinely cannot distinguish dreaming from reality and may be convinced he is dreaming when he signs a "confession."

In sum, the effects of sleep deprivation are devastating, both in terms of behavior and experience, and in terms of physiology. It requires very severe stress to produce death in a healthy animal.

A more subtle kind of interference with sleep involves depriving subjects of D sleep. Dement was the first to do this experiment. During all-night recordings of EEG and eye movements, subjects were awakened each time D sleep developed. After a few-day recovery periods, subjects were then awakened the same number of times from S sleep. The most clear-cut finding was that following D sleep deprivation, the subjects spent a significantly higher per cent of time in D sleep during recovery nights. Subjects in Dement's original experiments appeared also to become increasingly irritable after D sleep deprivation but this effect has not been obtained consistently by other investigators. The increase in D sleep following D sleep deprivation has also been obtained quite clearly in cats (Siegel and Gordon, 1965). It is almost as though the organism requires a given amount of D sleep each night. Reasons for this at present are unknown.

Why is sleep necessary? The effects of prolonged deprivation are psychosis and ultimate death. Even deprivation of D sleep has noticeable consequences. Giuseppi Moruzzi, head of the Physiological Institute of the University of Pisa in Italy, and one of the pioneers in the study of the neural basis of sleep, summarizes the problem in the following passage:

We are now rather well informed on the neural mechanisms which lead to sleep or to arousal, but we know surprisingly little about the fundamental problem which was raised by Professor Hess. It can be stated very simply and with only one sentence: why do we sleep? . . . Let us start with Von Economo's old distinction between sleep of the body and sleep of the brain. All the manifestations of sleep of the body, interesting as they undoubtedly are, seem to be rather peripheral with respect to the main problem. Muscular relaxation? It is absent in the forelimb and in the neck of oxen. Eye closure? It is extremely rare in oxen, and short-lasting manifestations of lagophthalmos have been described even in man. Abolition of the righting reflexes? They are present in birds, which can sleep while perching. We may end with a very simple consideration. When we lie sleepless in bed, we are fully aware that the main aim of sleep is not to give a period of rest to our body.

Hence, sleep of the brain should receive all of our attention. But for several centers of the encephalon there is no need of sleep, at least if we define sleep as a long period of inactivity, or of decreased activity. The validity of this definition can be undoubtedly accepted for the neural structures underlying the processes of consciousness. However, the vasomotor center, the vagal cardioinhibitory center, the respiratory center do not sleep, although their activity may be modified by sleep or arousal. It has been tacitly accepted that these were really not exceptions to the rule, since sleep would concern only the brain. Obviously all the structures which are essential for life should not be expected to interrupt their activity during sleep . . . neocortical neurons may be as active, indeed occasionally even more active, during synchronized sleep as during relaxed wakefulness.

(Giuseppi Moruzzi, 1965, page 241)

We will return to the topic of sleep at the end of this chapter when we examine the brain mechanisms that are involved in sleep.

AROUSAL

The general concept of arousal encounters the same kind of definition problem that is true of emotion. Of the many different possible measures of arousal, few are in agreement. The measures most widely used in defining arousal are the EEG, peripheral autonomic responses such as heart rate, blood pressure, and palmar (skin on palm of hand) conduc-

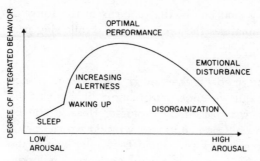

Figure 10.4 Hypothetical relation between the degree of "integrated behavior"—the effective level of function or performance—and the level of arousal. Note the inverted U shape. (Based on Hebb, D. O. *A Textbook of Psychology.* 2d Ed. Philadelphia: W. B. Saunders, 1966.)

tance (EDR, earlier termed the GSR), and general behavior. Subjective report of experience of arousal has not been a very widely used or useful measure.

The pioneering work of Donald Lindsley at the University of California at Los Angeles laid the foundation for the concept of arousal. Together with Magoun and others, Lindsley emphasized that the low-voltage fast-EEG characteristic of the alert waking state (Fig. 10.1) was a brain index of arousal. The writings of Malmo (1959), Duffy (1962), and Hebb (1949) contributed to our concept of general behavioral arousal. The diagram of Figure 10.4, taken from Hebb, shows the hypothetical relation between state of arousal and degree of successful or integrated behavior. A simple experiment illustrates this inverted U function. A person is asked to perform a simple task like mental arithmetic while squeezing a spring-handle device that measures strength of squeeze. If the subject squeezes very weakly there is little effect on mental arithmetic performance. If he squeezes moderately, his performance on the task improves. However, if he squeezes very hard, his performance on mental arithmetic deteriorates. In an experiment of this sort, level of arousal is inferred from strength of squeeze.

Berlyne (1966) has described a variety of experiments in which arousal level of human subjects was systematically varied. He used elementary and relatively nonthreatening "conflict" situations which consistently caused increased arousal, as measured by palmar conductance and the EEG. As an example, if the subject were trained to respond by pushing a lever one way for a light on the right and the opposite way for a light on the left, both lights would occasionally be turned on to produce conflict. Berlyne has also shown that, other things equal, more complex visual stimuli produce more arousal than simpler stimuli.

The other end of the waking arousal continuum is represented by sensory deprivation. In a famous series of experiments at McGill University

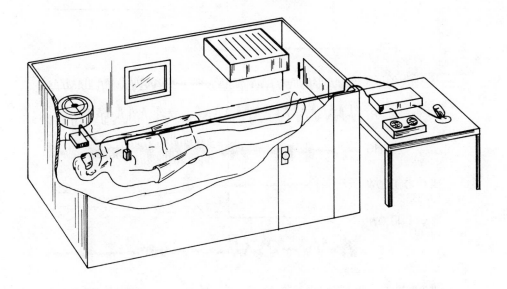

Figure 10.5 Experimental arrangement to study effects of stimulus deprivation in humans. Experimental cubicle constructed at McGill University to study the effects of perceptual isolation is at the right in this semi-schematic drawing from above. The subject lies on a bed 24 hours a day, with time out for meals and going to the bathroom. The room is always lighted. The visual perception of the subject is restricted by a translucent plastic visor; his auditory perception, by a U-shaped pillow covering his ears and by the noise of an air conditioner and a fan (ceiling of cubicle). In the experiment depicted here a flat pillow is used to leave room for the wires attached to the subject's scalp, which are connected to an electroencephalograph in an adjacent room. The subject's sense of touch is restricted by cotton gloves and long cardboard cuffs. The experimenter and the subject can communicate by means of a system of microphones and loudspeakers.

under the direction of Donald O. Hebb, volunteer subjects were placed in extreme sensory deprivation conditions for a period of days (see Heron, 1957). They lay on a soft mattress in a light- and sound-proof chamber with their hands and arms bound in soft cotton and cardboard cuffs (see Fig. 10.5). A variety of performance tests given to the subjects before and after sensory deprivation demonstrated consistent impairments in performance. Furthermore, the EEG showed consistent changes in the direction of more S sleep EEG tracings during waking. Many of the subjects also reported bizarre delusions and hallucinations. John Lilly has described an even more effective method of sensory deprivation by total immersion in water maintained at body temperature. Hallucinations apparently occur quite regularly in this extreme condition of reduction of normal sensory input.

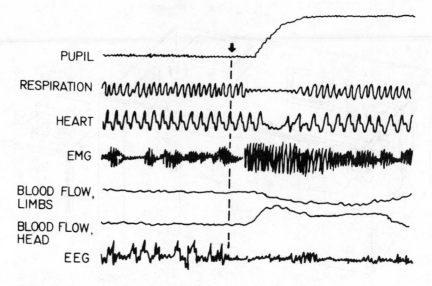

PUPIL

RESPIRATION

HEART

EMG

BLOOD FLOW,
LIMBS

BLOOD FLOW,
HEAD

EEG

Figure 10.6 The orienting reflex. When a sudden, novel, or significant stimulus is presented to a human subject (arrow), the pupil dilates, respiration is temporarily arrested, the heartbeat slows temporarily, muscle tone (EMG) increases, blood flow in the limbs decreases but blood flow in the head increases, the EEG shifts to a low-voltage fast-arousal pattern, and the subject turns his head toward the source of stimulation. (Redrawn from Harlow, H. F., McGaugh, J. L., and Thompson, R. F. *Psychology.* San Francisco: Albion, 1971; after Sokolov, 1963b.)

Arousal, of course, is an inferred or hypothetical construct. Measures such as EEG arousal cannot be taken as direct measures of hypothetical general arousal but rather as possible indicants. The current approach to the problem of defining arousal is to use a set of measures—EEG, autonomic, and behavioral—to characterize the syndrome of arousal and determine the degree of arousal from the magnitudes of these various measures.

Many attempts have been made to specify consistent patterns or syndromes of the physiological responses of arousal to various stressful or emotional situations. Perhaps the best known is the orienting response, referred to earlier. This was first defined by Pavlov (1927) and characterized in detail by the contemporary Soviet scientist Sokolov (1963b). As indicated in Figure 10.6, the normal human response to sudden presentation of a novel, but not too intense, stimulus is said to consist of a relatively clear pattern of physiological changes. These changes include pupil dilation, temporary arrest of breathing, brief slowing of heart rate, increased muscle tone, decreased blood flow in limbs but increased flow in head, and the EEG arousal pattern. Upon repetition of the stimulus, these response patterns rapidly diminish or habituate. If the stimulus is more intense or threatening, a different pattern termed the *defensive syndrome* occurs. The orienting and defensive syndromes permit some characterization of arousal and differentiation of degree of arousal.

Several lines of evidence indicate that the constellation of responses characterizing orienting or arousal can be dissociated by various means. One of the simplest ways to produce a dissociation between EEG activity and behavior is to administer atropine. Following moderate doses (15 mg/kg) the EEG becomes strongly synchronized, showing the typical spindling and slow waves of sleep, even though the animal remains behaviorally awake. In fact, strong sensory stimulation cannot produce EEG arousal after atropine administration. Bradley and his associates (1964) completed a rather careful evaluation of the behavioral state of atropinized rats. They measured the EEG to insure that the atropine-induced EEG synchrony was present in all cases. Three separate behavioral experiments were done: Shock avoidance responses to a bell, differential responding to a bell versus the buzzer, and maze learning. In all cases there were no differences between animals given atropine and control animals given saline, even though the atropine groups showed total EEG synchrony during the experiments and the saline groups did not. Thus the marked EEG synchrony produced by atropine appears to have no influence whatever on performance in these three behavioral situations.

Indices of arousal can also be dissociated by various types of behavioral tasks. John Lacey at Fels Research Institute has done the most extensive and careful studies of autonomic responses in man. The picture is considerably less clear than our summary description of the orienting response would seem to imply. In response to a cold pressor test (foot immersed in ice water for a period of many seconds), some subjects showed changes in palmar conductance (sweating activity in palm of hand) but no heart rate change. Others showed increases in both palmar sweating and heart rate. On the other hand, when male college students are shown pictures of nude females, heart rate decreases as palmar sweating increases. In a long-term four-year study of individual patterns of response in children, Lacey and Lacey (1962) report a high correlation (+0.80) over time for given individuals in blood pressure response to cold pressor, a somewhat lower correlation for heart rate and a correlation of only +0.50 for palmar conductance. In an extensive series of studies Lacey (see Lacey et al., 1963) compared responses of subjects to "stressors" ranging from merely watching a flashing light to mental arithmetic and problem-solving. Heart rate and blood pressure showed consistent patterns—a decrease in heart rate with little change in blood pressure for simply observing stimuli but a massive increase in heart rate and blood pressure for mental problem-solving. Palmar conductance and respiration showed changes but did not differentiate between the two situations. The heart and blood pressure responses to simple stimuli resemble the orienting reaction of Sokolov (Fig. 10.6) but the reactions to internal problem-solving are quite different.

These studies do not mean that we must dispense with the concept of arousal. After all, drugs are artificial. The qualifications emphasized by Lacey are much more important. The detailed studies he and others are doing on the influence of task and situational variables on the different measures of arousal ultimately will provide a much clearer picture of the complexities of autonomic and behavioral responses of man to hypothetical arousal. Most workers now agree that at least for nonhuman animals, arousal can be defined by a complex of measures, EEG, autonomic, and behavioral, that normally, taken together, form the arousal syndrome.

Attention

In a general sense, arousal is normally a concomitant of *attention*. An attentive person or animal almost always exhibits behavioral and physiological signs of arousal. The EEG of an "attentive" higher organism is probably always of the low-voltage fast-arousal type. Attention means more than this: It usually refers to selective response—response to one aspect of the environment rather than another. Nonetheless, attention may be considered legitimately within the general rubric of arousal or alerting; it is a special form of alerting wherein the subject responds more to one stimulus than another.

Perhaps the most difficult aspect of research on the neural basis of attention is a satisfactory definition of *attention*. Like so many terms in psychology, this word has been borrowed from everyday language and carries with it a good bit of surplus meaning. Ordinary usage of the word *attention* seems to imply some kind of active arousal, *focusing of the mind* or *concentration of awareness*. Clearly, such definitions are unsatisfactory from a behavioral point of view. It is not difficult to give an operational definition in any particular situation for attention, as when an animal attends to a stimulus by pointing his receptors toward it (a cat looking at a rat). In experiments on humans, attention is often defined by the verbal instructions given to the subject. He might be told to "listen to the tone," or "ignore the tone," or he may be required to count the number of tones, and so on. The difficulty comes when we try to use *attention* as the *explanation* for behavior. In a simple example, suppose an animal were given a sound and did not respond to it. To say that the animal did not respond because it did not attend to the stimulus is misleading—perhaps the sound was not heard or the animal was trained not to respond to the sound. The confusion over the use of the word *attention* comes when it is used to explain selective responses to stimuli.

It is obvious that we neither respond to nor remember all of the wide range of stimuli that continuously bombard our receptors. Attention thus implies selective response. This has been termed the cocktail-party phenomenon: You may stand in a crowded noisy room and not listen to the boring conversation of the person talking directly to you; rather, you hear a more interesting discussion some distance away (Cherry, 1953). The British psychologist Broadbent developed the most comprehensive analysis of selective listening or selective attention. He proposed that the brain somehow contains selective filters that can tune out one message in order to listen to another. In Broadbent's classical experiment, two quite different messages were put into the two ears of a subject, via earphones, and the subject instructed to listen only to one ear. When tested for retention the subject can reproduce much more information for the listened-to ear than the ignored ear. However, subjects do retain information they consider important to them if it is given to the unattended ear. Anne Treisman (1964) proved this in a most important study. Consequently the information entering the ignored ear must reach a point in the brain where evaluation can be made in relation to the subject's memory store and general judgment of what is important or significant. This analysis leads to the conclusion that the location of the brain processes responsible for attention, defined as stimulus selection, must be beyond the primary sensory systems. Raw sensory input must be analyzed and coded into the language of the brain before it can be evaluated for remembering or forgetting.

Note that we move farther and farther away from the notion that attention is some form of selective arousal filter on the sensory information channels (in physiological terms, the primary sensory pathways). Recent data from human studies of learning and performance suggest that it may not be possible to separate attention from long-term memory storage. What is stored and later retrieved from permanent memory is what has been attended to. The question then becomes: Why are some items stored in memory and others not? It is still a question of selection but quite possibly it is a much simpler question to answer.

We examined the relations between EEG arousal and behavioral state above. An observation was made in early studies involving electrical stimulation of the reticular formation when a normal resting or sleeping animal showing EEG spindling was stimulated. The EEG changed to the low-voltage fast-arousal pattern and the animal gave behavioral signs, such as lifting his head, opening his eyes, pricking up his ears, and looking about. This general observation has been reported in many studies. An experiment by Fuster, described later in the chapter (see pp. 442–443), illustrates that electrical stimulation of the reticular formation can lead to improved selective responding in monkeys.

A great many investigators have studied the relations between attention and sensory evoked responses recorded from various regions of the brain. Hernández-Peón, Scherrer, and Jouvet (1956) were the first to report that auditory evoked responses decreased in amplitude when a cat looked at a mouse, smelled fish, or received a forepaw shock. (In the original experiment, responses were recorded from the cochlear nucleus to click stimulation.) Similar depressions of auditory and visual cortical evoked responses were reported in subsequent studies when the animal was attending to another type of novel or distracting stimulus. Thus, the auditory evoked cortical response decreased when the animal looked at a mouse or smelled fish, and the visual evoked cortical response decreased in amplitude when the animal attended to a novel sound or odor (Hernández-Peón et al., 1957). On the basis of these intriguing findings, Hernández-Peón postulated that when the animal attended to a given stimulus, input to other sensory modalities was filtered out or attenuated by peripheral gating mechanisms so that the animal could remain maximally sensitive to input from the attention-evoking stimulus.

It might possibly be concluded from Hernández-Peón's hypothesis that evoked responses from stimulation of the same modality as the attention-arousing stimulus ought to increase in amplitude rather than decrease. Thus, if a cat subject to a repeated click is suddenly shown a mouse, click-evoked responses will decrease, but the visual responses evoked by a light flash ought to increase. Horn (1960) tested this possibility in a careful experiment, in which a light flash was given to cats at rest and cats watching a mouse. The amplitude of the recorded flash-evoked response decreased rather than increased when the animal looked at the mouse. These findings suggest that all modalities of primary cortical evoked responses may decrease in amplitude when an animal attends to any type of novel stimulus.

Measurement of nonspecific evoked cortical association responses has provided further evidence against the hypothesis that attention involves selective depression of irrelevant stimulus modalities and augmentation of activity in the relevant modality (Thompson and Shaw, 1965). Association evoked responses were recorded from the posterior middle suprasylvian gyrus of the normal unrestrained cat to click, light flash, and forepaw shock stimulation. The effects of novel stimuli of all three modalities (sight of a white rat; growling sounds; air jet directed on fur of back) on the evoked responses were measured. Each modality of novel stimulus caused marked and significant depression of cortical association responses evoked by *all* modalities of stimulation. There was no modality selective effect of novel stimuli, but rather a blanket depression of responses evoked by all types of stimuli. At the same time, there was a marked increase in ongoing single neuron activity during presentation of novel stimuli, as though the neurons were processing information of significance and were not available to respond to the repeated uninteresting probe stimuli (Fig. 10.7A). This uniform depression of evoked association activity by novel stimuli would seem to suggest a common central mode of action rather than peripheral gating at each type of receptor input. However, the latter possibility cannot be ruled out conclusively.

Unfortunately, these animal studies cannot be said to apply directly to stimulus selection. In the example cited there was a differential response

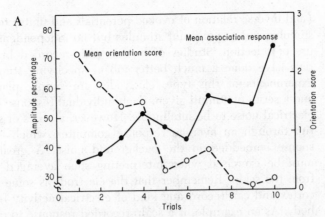

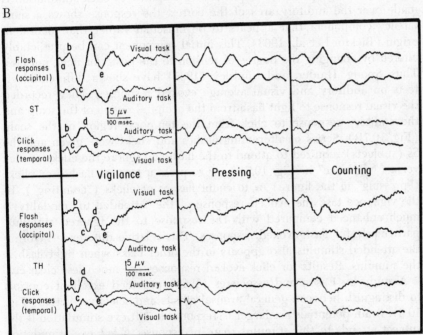

Figure 10.7 A, Inverse relationship of cortical association responses and behavioral orienting responses to a series of click stimuli. (From Thompson, R. F., and Shaw, J. A. Behavioral correlates of evoked activity recorded from association areas of the cerebral cortex. *J. Comp. Physiol. Psychol.* **60**, 1965, pp. 329–339. Copyright 1965 by the American Psychological Association. Reprinted by permission.) B, Computer-averaged cortical evoked potentials obtained from two subjects in response to flashes and clicks. The potentials were recorded from the occipital and temporal areas while the subjects performed visual and auditory tasks under three experimental conditions: vigilance, key-pressing, and counting. Flashes alternated with clicks throughout. Each trace is the averaged evoked response to 300 stimuli. Analysis time, 500 msec. Recordings: right occipital and temporal areas to left ear: negative upward. (From Spong, P., Haider, M., and Lindsley, D. B. Selective attentiveness and cortical evoked responses to visual and auditory stimuli. *Science* **148**, 1965, pp. 396–397. Copyright 1965 by the American Association for the Advancement of Science.)

(and inverse relation of evoked potentials and units) to a repeated probe stimulus and a significant stimulus but no independent behavioral measure of selection. Studies of human scalp-recorded brain-evoked potentials have done a much better job of specifying stimulus selection. In experiments of this type, electrodes are simply placed on the scalp and a series of stimuli given. Each individual response contains too much electrical noise to be intelligible. However, a series of such responses are run through an average response computer, which "develops" the response embedded in the background noise. A great deal of caution must be exercised when interpreting such averaged evoked responses from the scalp. Remember that the electrode is some distance from the cortex and can record any kind of electrical activity from the head and body. As an example, if a scalp-recorded response to click stimulation is made over the auditory area of the cortex, the response shows a short latency component that appears to be muscular rather than neural in origin (Bickford et al., 1963). This initial component can be predictably altered by changing the degree of tension to the posterior neck muscles. Thus, Spong, Haider, and Lindsley (1965) have shown differential effects on auditory and visual average evoked responses. They recorded the visual response to light flash from the occipital region of the scalp and the auditory response to click from the temporal region of the scalp (Fig. 10.7B). Series of alternating flashes and clicks were given and the Ss (subjects) required to attend to the flash and ignore the clicks or vice versa ("vigilance" in Fig. 10.7B), or to press a key for flashes or clicks ("pressing" in the figure) or to count flashes or clicks ("counting"). In the vigilance task the evoked response of the "attended to" modality is much enhanced compared with the response to the ignored stimulus, particularly for flash-evoked responses. This relative difference favoring the attended stimulus also appears in the other tasks when light flash is the stimulus. Results for click-evoked responses are much less clear-cut.

A study by Eason and associates (1969) provided excellent controls to distinguish between general arousal effects and selective factors (Fig. 10.8). Brain potentials are larger in response to left eye stimulation if the subject attends to this stimulus than in response to left eye stimulation when he is instructed to attend to right eye stimulation. In both cases he must count number of flashes correctly to avoid electric shock. Arousal level due to fear of shock is the same for both stimuli; all that differs is the instruction to the subject to attend to one rather than to the other.

In a recent comprehensive review of attentive processes, Norman Weinberger of the University of California at Irvine, concluded:

What is the fate of sensory information that is selected for or against [when an organism attends]? We do not know. It must be stressed that we have no certain CNS measures of information. We can record evoked potentials to [sensory] stimulation, and seek systematic changes

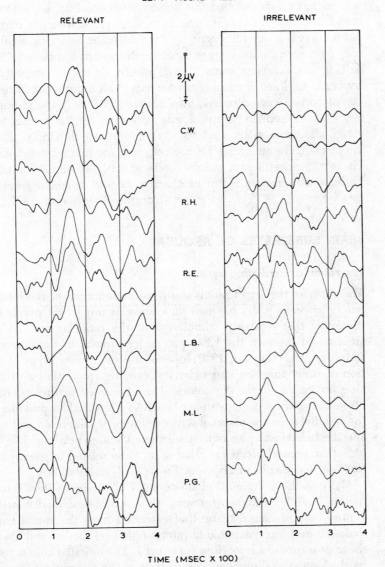

LEFT VISUAL FIELD

RELEVANT   IRRELEVANT

2 μV

C.W.

R.H.

R.E.

L.B.

M.L.

P.G.

0   1   2   3   4   0   1   2   3   4

TIME (MSEC X 100)

Arousal

Figure 10.8 Effects of attention on scalp-recorded brain potentials evoked by visual stimuli (light flash). Flashes are presented to the two eyes, but brain responses are recorded only for flashes given in the left visual field, and each tracing is the average of 100 individual responses. The evoked potentials in this left visual field are substantially larger if the subject is attending to the left flash—he is required to count to himself the number of left flashes to avoid an electric shock (relevant). When he is required to count to himself the number of flashes on the right in order to avoid shock, the brain potentials for the left flashes (irrelevant) are much smaller. (From Eason, R. G., Harter, M. R., and White, C. T. Effects of attention and arousal on visually evoked cortical potentials and reaction time in man. *Physiol. Behav.* 4, 1969, pp. 283–289.)

related to behavioral stimulus selection. Such changes, when they are found, indicate that something in a sensory pathway is changing. . . . But the evoked potential is not yet validated as an index of information, only as a convenient marker that something has happened. The Fehmi, Adkins, and Lindsley study [(1969) where, by use of temporal masking by flash, all later components of a visual stimulus evoked response in visual cortex were blocked, they showed that only the initial short latency visual evoked potential was necessary for the animal to perform visual discriminations successfully] suggested that only the minimal initial components of the EP are required for information transmission. These components are, in fact, the least labile of all EP components, so perhaps information is not blocked or altered in sensory systems.

(Norman Weinberger, 1971, page 185)

BRAIN SUBSTRATES OF AROUSAL

The reticular activating system

The study of the organization and possible functions of the *reticular activating system* (RAS) has had an enormous impact on psychology. The discovery that electrical stimulation of the reticular core of the brain stem could produce the EEG pattern of arousal in the cerebral cortex (Moruzzi and Magoun, 1949) opened up many new areas of investigation of brain function and behavior, ranging from studies of coma and sleep to analysis of the physiological and behavioral correlates of alerting, attention, and even motivation. The RAS appeared to provide the missing link between the classical sensory systems of the brain and many nonspecific behavioral phenomena subsumed under headings like *alertness, attention, arousal, sleep,* etc., that seem to be related to sensory activation but not necessarily to any specific type of stimulation.

Many of the anatomical characteristics of the brain stem reticular formation have been known for some time. Cajal described it in 1909 as a ventral core of neural tissue that extended from the spinal cord to the thalamus and was composed of intermingled cell bodies and fibers having the appearance of a *reticulum* (network). The reticular core is surrounded by the long ascending fibers and systems of the classical sensory pathways and the descending motor pathways. The general location of the reticular formation within the brain is sketched in Figure 10.9.

In an early paper, Allen (1932) noted that embryological and anatomical characteristics of the reticular formation indicated that it very likely serves general functions of inhibition, excitation, and integration of brain activity, a remarkable prediction in the light of subsequent research. Phylogenetically it is a very old system, developing in the embryo from cells that are "left over" after the sensory and motor systems of the brain stem are formed. In lower vertebrates it is relatively undifferentiated.

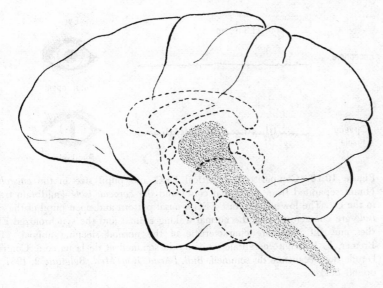

Figure 10.9 General location of the reticular formation (shaded area) lying within the brain stem and diencephalon. (From Thompson, R. F. *Foundations of Physiological Psychology.* New York: Harper & Row, 1967.)

Allen noted that it receives many axons from the principal sensory and motor pathways.

Physiological analysis of the RAS really began with Bremer's now classical observation in 1935 concerning the effects of transection of the brain stem on EEG sleep. If the brain stem of the cat is completely transected at the level of the midbrain, a rather special set of symptoms resembling normal sleep develop. Such an animal displays a permanently "sleeping" cortical EEG; high-voltage relatively slow (8-12/sec) sleep spindles appear continuously (see Fig. 10.10). Bremer termed this preparation the *cerveau isolé.* The level of brain section used in the cerveau isolé cuts off all afferent cranial nerve inputs to the brain except I and II (olfactory and visual), and interrupts all motor outputs of the brain except some control of eye movement.

Because most sensory input cannot reach the portion of the brain above the level of section, and this portion of the brain can no longer control muscle activity, most behavioral measures of the state of the brain (that is, whether it is asleep or awake) above the level of section are simply not possible. One sign of sleep in the normal cat that can be mediated by the isolated forebrain of the cerveau isolé is pupil diameter. The pupil of the normal sleeping cat is constricted to a narrow slit. The same is true of the pupil in the cerveau isolé cat (Fig. 10.10). Thus the cortical EEG pattern and the pupillary reflex of the cerveau isolé resemble those of the normal sleeping animal.

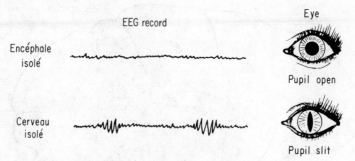

EEG record

Eye

Encéphale isolé

Pupil open

Cerveau isolé

Pupil slit

Figure 10.10 Comparison of cortical EEG and pupil size in the *encéphale isolé* (brain separated from the spinal cord) and the *cerveau isolé* (midbrain transected) in the cat. The low-voltage fast EEG arousal pattern and open pupil of the *encéphale isolé* are characteristic of the normal waking animal and the synchronized EEG spindles and slit pupil are characteristic of the normal sleeping animal. (Based on Bremer, F. L'activité cérébrale au cours du sommeil et de la narcose. Contribution à l'étude du mécanisme du sommeil. *Bull. l'Acad. Roy. Med. Belgique* **2**, 1937, 6e Série, pp. 68–86.)

If the normally sleeping cat or man is aroused or awakened, the sleep spindle pattern of the EEG suddenly disappears, and is replaced by a pattern of rapid, low-voltage activity. This latter EEG pattern is variously termed EEG arousal, EEG alerting, alpha blocking, desynchronization, low-voltage fast activity, etc. The EEG arousal pattern tends to persist as long as the organism is awake and alert. Bremer attempted to induce EEG arousal in the cerveau isolé by strong sensory stimulation of the available sensory inputs (olfactory and visual). He found that only a brief and feeble EEG arousal could be induced, even by very strong stimuli. The arousal effect did not outlast the arousing stimulus.

Bremer's discovery of the cerveau isolé was of great importance in terms of the then prominent view that sleep resulted from a withdrawal of sensory stimulation. Because the transection used in preparing the cerveau isolé removes most sensory input that normally goes to the brain, it is a natural assumption that the forebrain permanently sleeps because there is insufficient sensory input to arouse it. To test the relative importance of somatic-sensory stimulation from the body in controlling sleep, Bremer developed another preparation in which he transected the brain stem at the point at which the brain joins the spinal cord. Section of the CNS at this level eliminates sensory input from the body but preserves all inputs of the cranial nerves, including somatic-sensory input from the face and head via the fifth cranial nerve. This preparation, termed the *encéphale isolé* by Bremer, exhibited EEG and pupil signs comparable to those of the normal animal. When the EEG showed the sleep spindles and the pupils were slit, sensory stimulation induced long-lasting EEG arousal and dilation of the pupil (Fig. 10.10). In the absence of stimulation both EEG and pupil measures showed alternate

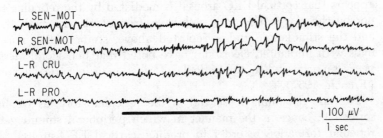

L SEN-MOT

R SEN-MOT

L-R CRU

L-R PRO

Figure 10.11 Cortical EEG arousal produced by rapid electrical stimulation of the brain stem reticular formation (horizontal bar). The four traces were recorded from different regions of the anterior portion of the cortex. (From Moruzzi, G., and Magoun, H. W. Brain stem reticular formation and activation of the EEG. *Electroencephalog. Clin. Neurophysiol.* **1**, 1949, pp. 455–473.)

periods of "waking" and "sleeping" similar to those of the normal cat. Consequently, elimination of sensory input from the body did not appear to be a crucial factor in the permanently "sleeping" EEG of the cerveau isolé.

The above interpretation of Bremer's experiments was prevalent until the publication, in 1949, of Moruzzi and Magoun's now famous study of reticular activation. They delivered electrical stimuli to the brain stem reticular formation of chloralose-anesthetized, or encéphale isolé, cats. Relatively high-frequency stimulation (100-300/sec) of the reticular formation produced immediate and often long-lasting EEG arousal. An example of this finding is shown in Figure 10.11. This stimulus (horizontal bar below the EEG records) was delivered while the EEG showed typical sleep spindles. There is an immediate transition to the low-voltage fast-activity characteristic of EEG arousal.

The results of Moruzzi's and Magoun's experiments immediately suggested a new explanation for Bremer's cerveau isolé experiment. The reticular formation rather than the classical sensory pathways might be the source of EEG arousal. Because both are transected in the cerveau isolé, the issue could be settled only by destroying the sensory pathways in isolation or the central reticular core of the brain stem in isolation. Lindsley, Bowden, and Magoun (1949) and Lindsley, Schreiner, Knowles, and Magoun (1950) performed these crucial experiments. They found that animals with lesions limited to the classical sensory pathways exhibited normal behavioral sleep-wake cycles with appropriate EEG activity—spindles during sleep and arousal when awakened and alert (Fig. 10.10). On the other hand, animals with reticular lesions tended to be stuporous after lesion and exhibited only a spindling EEG (Fig. 10.10). Short duration EEG arousal could be induced in these reticular lesioned animals by strong sensory stimulation but the arousal did not persist after the stimulus was removed. This is comparable to the short duration EEG arousal reported by Bremer for the cerveau isolé. It thus appears that cortical EEG arousal is mediated by the reticular core and not by the classical sensory pathways. Consistent with both the lesion and the stimulation studies reported above, studies using normal animals with implanted electrodes have noted that behavioral alerting appears to occur when the reticular formation is electrically stimulated (French, 1957).

The one remaining loose end in the reticular story, as we have described it, concerns the manner in which peripheral stimuli get to the reticular formation in order to produce cortical EEG arousal. Electrophysiological studies demonstrated that gross evoked responses could be recorded from the reticular formation to all modalities of peripheral sensory stimulation (French et al., 1952). In addition, it was shown that electrical stimulation in certain regions of the cortex produced EEG arousal in the reticular formation, suggesting the existence of reciprocal connections. The evoked response studies thus indicated that all manner of stimuli, including electrical stimulation of the cortex, could activate the reticular formation. Anatomical evidence is consistent with the view that the various classical sensory pathways send axon collaterals to the reticular core of the brain stem.

In terms of its behavioral implications, the most significant early experiment on the RAS was that by Lindsley, Schreiner, Knowles, and Magoun (1950), showing that lesions of the reticular formation produced permanently sleeping animals. Other experimenters have shown that this conclusion, while generally correct, must be tempered somewhat. Several studies indicate that animals can exhibit a considerable degree of recovery from lesions of the RAS if the damage is done in stages by several operations. Adametz (1959) obtained animals that showed sleep-wake cycles after two-stage lesions of the reticular formation. There is apparently a marked recovery of function if the damage is done first on one side, with time for recovery, and then on the other side. Nonetheless, in general, reticular lesions produce animals that are comatose and unresponsive.

Feldman and Waller (1962) prepared cats with extensive bilateral lesions in the midbrain reticular formation that spared the most medial portions and the periventricular grey. They reported that such lesions were followed not by somnolence, but rather by sluggish behavior. The animals fed themselves, attended to auditory and visual cues and showed alternation of sleep and wakefulness. The EEG records showed spontaneous shifts from slow high-voltage activity to fast low-voltage activity. This correlated only approximately with behavioral arousal. On the other hand, animals with extensive bilateral lesions of the *posterior hypothalamus* were unresponsive to sensory stimuli, exhibited virtually continuous somnolence, required tube-feeding, showed no spontaneous movements, and could not be behaviorally aroused. These latter findings are similar to the results of early experiments by Ranson (1939) showing that posterior hypothalamic lesions produce permanent somnolence or coma. Feldman and Waller made the important additional observation that the permanently somnolent hypothalamically lesioned animals showed cortical EEG arousal to reticular and peripheral stimuli that was not accompanied by behavioral arousal. You may remember from Chapter 8 that lesions of the lateral hypothalamus producing the aphagic rat also yield an animal that is very sluggish and unresponsive.

Sprague, Chambers, and Stellar (1961) completed an extensive analysis in the cat of the effects on behavior of destroying the classical sensory pathways of the midbrain. The animals were studied in a wide variety of both observational and learning situations utilizing all types of stimuli, for periods of up to two and one-half years following either unilateral or bilateral electrolytic lesions. In addition to destruction of the classical ascending sensory pathways, there is some invasion of the reticular formation, and extensive undercutting of the superior colliculus. After bilateral lesions the animals showed marked tactile, auditory, proprioceptive, nociceptive (pain response), gustatory, visual, and olfactory deficits. They were mute, exhibited no rage or aggression, showed little sexual behavior, and little response to normally aversive situations. Much of their waking activity consisted of "aimless, stereotyped wandering, and apparent visual and olfactory searching, hallucinatory in nature and very difficult to break into." In interpreting their results, the authors point out that the visual deficits (often amounting to virtual blindness on one side of the unilateral lesioned animal) are probably due to undercutting of the superior colliculus.

The olfactory deficits were unexpected. All other sensory deficits are, of course, to be expected. The most significant findings of the experiment concern the general debility of the animals, and the very striking changes in emotional behavior. As Sprague, Chambers, and Stellar point out, the absence of affect and lack of interest in sex shown by the animals resemble the behavior of the totally neodecorticate animal (Bard and Mountcastle, 1947). Indeed, these effects are much more marked than in animals in which only sensory receiving areas of the cortex are removed. Sprague et al. interpret their results in terms of a massive sensory deprivation of the neocortex, and draw parallels to the sensory deprivation literature.

Sprague, Chambers, and Stellar prepared two animals with reticular lesions; one with a limited lateral reticular lesion on each side, and one with an extensive bilateral lesion destroying all medial reticular formation. The limited lesion produced no observable effects. The more extensive lesion produced coma that lasted for about one month. Subsequently the animal slowly recovered most behavioral functions, but tended to remain drowsy unless stimulated. It was hyperexcitable in response to painful stimulation and performed poorly on learning tasks.

Several reasonably consistent syndromes appear to emerge from this reticular lesion literature. First, massive one-stage bilateral lesions of the midbrain reticular formation produce severe coma and death. If the lesion is made in several stages, the animal can be kept alive and exhibits considerable recovery of gross functions. Smaller one-stage bilateral lesions, particularly those sparing the most medial portion of the midbrain tegmentum, produce severe but transitory coma, with partial recovery of gross function and learning abilities occurring about a month after lesion. Similar lesions made in two stages result in little gross behavioral impairment. Still smaller lesions, even if made in one stage, appear to produce few symptoms. The coma and death resulting from large one-stage reticular lesion is not too surprising, incidentally. Fibers and cell nuclei concerned with a host of crucial physiological regulatory mechanisms (body temperature, respiration, metabolism, etc.) are embedded in the brain stem reticular formation and are likely to be damaged by massive lesions.

The considerable recovery of function shown with long-term postoperative care following relatively large reticular lesions, or after large lesions made in several stages, demonstrates that the bulk of the midbrain reticular core is not an *absolutely essential structure* for behavioral sleep and waking, learning ability, emotional reactivity, or even of gross aspects of attention behavior. However, the residual deficits of such animals suggest that the reticular core normally may play an important role in many of these functions.

It is difficult to assess the relative importance of the reticular formation and the classical sensory pathways for normal behavioral functions. Most large reticular lesions have also invaded the sensory pathways, and large sensory lesions tend to invade the reticular formation. The kinds of deficits, reported by Sprague et al. after destruction of the sensory pathways, are not unexpected. Indeed, prior to the discovery of the RAS most authorities probably would have predicted that they would occur. Attentive and affective behavior ought to be impaired if sensory input is virtually wiped out. As this is written, the RAS appears to play some role in these functions, but the exact nature of that role is somewhat obscure.

It was observed in early experiments that activation of the reticular formation, either by external stimuli or direct electrical stimulation, produced EEG arousal and behavioral arousal (Lindsley et al., 1950; French et al., 1953). Upon stimulation a normally sleeping animal will open his eyes, raise his head, and look about. These observations led to the well known hypothesis that behavioral alerting or attention is mediated or controlled by the RAS. Surprisingly enough, few attempts have been made to test this hypothesis experimentally.

Perhaps the most direct attempt to evaluate the behavioral role of the RAS in arousal and attention is an experiment done by Fuster (1958) in Lindsley's laboratories (see also Lindsley, 1958). Normal monkeys with stimulating electrodes implanted in the reticular formation were trained to discriminate between two objects. The objects were on a tray

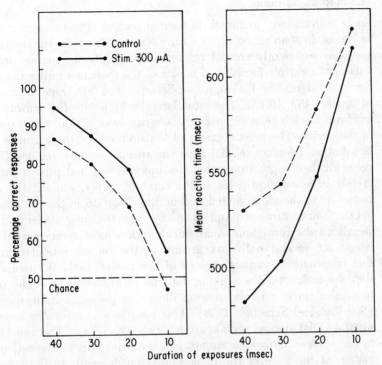

Figure 10.12 Performance of a monkey (per cent correct responses and reaction time) on an object discrimination task both during electrical stimulation of the reticular formation (solid lines) and in the absence of such stimulation (broken lines). (From Fuster, J. M. Effects of stimulation of brain stem on tachistoscopic perception. *Science* **127**, 1958, p. 150. Copyright 1958 by the American Association for the Advancement of Science.)

in front of the animal and were lighted only briefly by a tachistoscopic device. The monkey was required to reach through a trap door under the correct object (one object was always correct and the other incorrect) to obtain a reward. Both the number of correct responses and the latency of response were recorded, as functions of the duration of the tachistoscopic light. This procedure was repeated both with reticular stimulation and without reticular stimulation. The results on one animal are shown in Figure 10.12. If the RAS is stimulated during the discrimination the animal makes a significantly greater percentage of correct responses and also has a significantly shorter reaction time. If only reaction time were improved, it might be argued that the major effect of reticular stimulation was to increase muscle tone, perhaps via the descending reticular system. However, the significant improvement in correct choices demonstrated that something more is occurring, for example, increased arousal or even improved selective attention.

The medial thalamus

Some authors have included the medial portion of the thalamus as a part of the brain stem reticular activating system. However, the medial thalamus has sufficiently special properties to justify a separate treatment. First and most obviously, it is a part of the thalamus rather than part of the brain stem. The thalamus can be separated into three different types of nuclei (Fig. 10.13). The most lateral regions are the sensory specific extrinsic nuclei, relaying primary sensory information to sensory areas of the cortex. The second group of thalamic relays, the extrinsic association nuclei, lie more medial than the specific sensory regions. They receive all their input from other thalamic regions and project rather discretely to association fields of the cerebral cortex. Finally, the intrinsic nuclei lie in the most medial and midline location in the thalamus.

One major source of input to the intrinsic thalamic nuclei is the brain stem reticular formation. Anatomical studies have demonstrated the existence of several pathways arising in the bulbar reticular formation that terminate in various regions of the medial thalamic nuclei and in the hypothalamus. The striking diagram in Figure 10.14 of the ramifications of a single reticular neuron illustrates these ascending projections (Scheibel and Scheibel, 1958). This neuron was reconstructed from a sagittal Golgi stained section from a two-day-old rat. The cell body lies in the *nucleus reticularis magnocellulars*, a nucleus of the reticular formation at the level of the pons. One axon descends to the spinal cord and the other ascends to terminate in many regions of the intrinsic thalamic nuclei, and the other regions noted above.

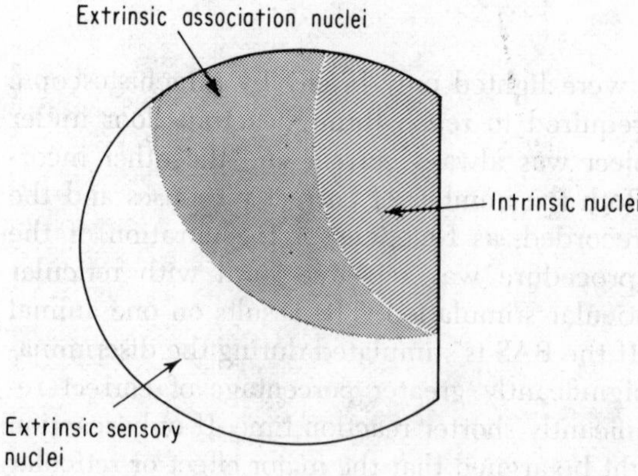

Figure 10.13 Schematic of a cross section through the left thalamus indicating the general locations of the three functionally differentiated types of thalamic nuclei. (From Thompson, R. F. *Foundations of Physiological Psychology.* New York: Harper & Row, 1967.)

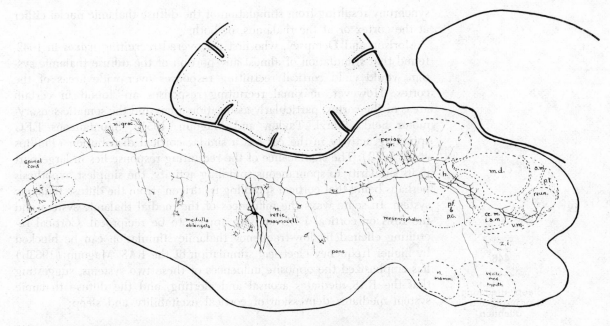

Figure 10.14 Drawing of sagittal Golgi section of a two-day-old rat, showing the axon branches of a *single* reticular cell. (From Scheibel, M. E., and Scheibel, A. B. Structural substrates for integrative patterns of the brain stem reticular core. In Jasper, H. H. (ed.). *Reticular Formation of the Brain.* Boston: Little, Brown & Co., 1958, pp. 31–55.)

Before considering the functional aspects of the medial thalamic system, the following brief overview gives the reasons why the medial thalamus often is included in the RAS. First and foremost, the medial thalamus appears to be the region of the brain that acts as a "pacemaker" to induce rhythmic spindling or alpha activity in the cerebral cortex. In a brain stem preparation where all of the reticular formation below the level of the medial thalamus is separated from the forebrain, the cortex exhibits continued EEG synchrony. Alternatively, destruction of the medial thalamic nuclei in an otherwise intact animal abolishes cortical EEG spindling. Repetitive electrical stimulation of the medial thalamic nuclei at rates of about 8-12/sec evokes large cortical waves, called *recruiting waves,* that closely resemble spontaneous spindle waves in the cat. Moruzzi and Magoun (1949) showed that high-frequency stimulation of the bulbar reticular formation abolished the recruiting waves produced by slow thalamic stimulation and abolished spontaneous cortical spindling. Further, stimulation of the diffuse thalamic nuclei on one side at 8-12/sec induces recruiting waves in the diffuse thalamic nuclei of the other hemisphere, and reticular activation also blocks these waves. In other words, reticular activation can act to block the EEG synchrony resulting from stimulation of the diffuse thalamic nuclei either at the cortex or at the thalamus, or both.

Morison and Dempsey, who first discovered *recruiting waves* in 1942, found that stimulation of almost any portion of the diffuse thalamic system would yield cortical recruiting responses over wide areas of the cortex. However, maximal recruiting responses are found in certain areas of the cortex, particularly association areas and the somatic-sensory-motor field (Starzl, Taylor, and Magoun, 1951). Spontaneous EEG spindling activity in the cat has a similar cortical distribution (Phillips et al., 1972). The significance of the recruiting response lies in large part in its similarity to spontaneous spindling activity, the simplest hypothesis perhaps being that cortical spindling is "driven" from the diffuse thalamic system. In some ways the influences of the medial thalamic system and the RAS on cortical EEG activity appear to be reciprocal. Cortical recruiting elicited by low-frequency thalamic stimulation can be blocked by higher frequency electrical stimulation of the RAS. Magoun (1963b) has emphasized the opposite influences of these two systems, suggesting that the RAS mediates arousal and alerting, and the diffuse thalamic system mediates depression of cortical excitability and sleep:

If the inferences drawn from these many conclusions are correct, it is now possible to identify a thalamo-cortical mechanism for internal inhibition, capable of modifying activity of the brain partially or globally, so that its sensory, motor, and higher nervous functions become reduced and cease. The consequences of the action of this mechanism are the opposite of those of the ascending reticular activation system for internal excitation [see Magoun, 1963a, p. 90]. The principle of reciprocal innervation proposed by Sherrington to account for spinal-reflex integration would additionally appear relevant to the manner in which these two higher antagonistic neural mechanisms determine the alternating patterns of brain activity manifest as wakefulness and light sleep.

(Magoun, 1963b, page 174)

Role of other brain structures in arousal

In our discussion of the reticular activating system above we emphasized its role in production and maintenance of EEG and behavioral arousal. Several other brain structures also play crucial roles in arousal. One of the simplest and most clear-cut measures of behavioral arousal in non-human animals is gross bodily activity.

If brain structures are summarized simply in terms of the extent to which damage produces marked increases in activity, termed *hyperactivity*, two structures are singled out—the frontal lobe of the cerebral cortex (Chapter 3) and the hippocampus, a portion of the limbic forebrain (Chapter 9). One of the classical syndromes of brain damage in primates is the marked and long-lasting hyperactivity following lesions of the frontal cortex (Ferrier, 1886; French, 1959). Interestingly, this hyperactivity is exhibited only in a lighted room and not in darkness (Gross, 1963; Isaac and DeVito, 1958). In lower mammals, hyperactivity did not seem a consistent characteristic of frontal damage. Campbell and Lynch (1969) showed that frontal rats, while seemingly not hyper-active under normal conditions, showed marked hyperactivity relative to normals if starved—which itself produces heightened activity. Other conditions such as amphetamine administration and period in the estrous cycle also show potentiation of hyperactivity in frontal rats. Thus frontal rats are much more active than normals under conditions that tend normally to increase activity and arousal.

The frontal lobe of the brain also plays a very important role in regulation of cortical EEG arousal. Skinner and Lindsley (1967) showed that damage in this region appeared to abolish spindles and slow waves in the cortex. Robertson and Lynch (1971) presented recent evidence that the role of frontal cortex in cortical EEG arousal tends to be that of a modulator—cortical spindle waves are much less likely to occur after frontal damage.

An important series of studies by Hugelin, Dell, Bonvallet and associates (Bonvallet et al., 1954) provides a clear demonstration of reciprocal relations between the RAS and frontal cortex. They measured not only EEG arousal but the entire syndrome of autonomic responses characteristic of arousal and were able to show that activation of the RAS causes cortical activation which, in turn, feeds back from frontal cortex to decrease activity of the RAS. Destruction of the frontal cortex would presumably interrupt this link and lead to hyperactivity. These data are in close accord with the neuroanatomical studies of the Scheibels (1967).

Damage to the hippocampus also produces marked effects on activity levels. In rats, hippocampal lesions increase nighttime activity and decrease amount of sleep (Kim et al., 1971). As indicated in our earlier discussion of the limbic forebrain system, the RAS and hippocampus are interrelated. Kimble (1968) summarized a great deal of evidence for the notion that reticular formation and hippocampus are linked in a loop much like the reticular-frontal cortex loop (Fig. 10.15). Both these systems pass through or near the hypothalamus, thus providing a possible explanation for the effects of hypothalamic lesions on activity level.

Lynch and Campbell (see Campbell et al., 1971) suggest that hippocampus and frontal cortex, although they may be involved in very different types of behavior, may exert similar final effects on arousal level. Behavioral measures utilized in studies of activity level are easily influenced by arousal levels, which hippocampus and frontal cortex influence either directly or indirectly.

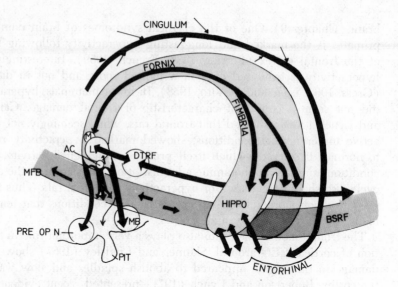

Sleep, dreaming,
arousal, and
attention

Figure 10.15 Schematic of some of the major connections of the hippocampus (HIPPO). M is the medial septal nuclei; L is the lateral septal nuclei; AC is the anterior commissure; MFB is the medial forebrain bundle; DTRF is the diffuse thalamic reticular formation; PRE OP N is the preoptic nucleus; MB are the mammillary bodies; PIT is the pituitary; BSRF is the brain stem reticular formation. (From Kimble, D. P. Hippocampus and internal inhibition. *Psychol. Bull.* **70,** 1968, pp. 285–295. Copyright 1968 by the American Psychological Association. Reprinted by permission.)

Altered arousal levels could easily account for the changes in performance levels, disruption of responses, or decreased rates of habituation frequently reported following hippocampal or frontal lesions. Studies indicate that in primates an optimal level of reticular unit activity exists for the performance of visual discrimination tasks. Other evidence suggests that changes in performance following frontal lesions are arousal-dependent, and that habituation is also arousal-dependent. In other words, brain lesions could effectively push the animal one way or the other on the arousal-performance curve shown in Figure 10.4.

BRAIN MECHANISMS OF SLEEP

Following the discovery of the RAS, a very simple initial picture of the mechanism of sleep developed. Activation of the RAS caused EEG arousal and waking. Activation of the medial thalamus, in turn, caused slow waves in the EEG and sleep. However, even then, studies from laboratories such as Moruzzi's (in Pisa, Italy) indicated that there were additional mechanisms in the brain stem. Then, the discovery of D sleep threw the picture into confusion again. Several general theories of the brain substrates of sleep have been developed more recently, the most influential being that of Jouvet. However, no theory is entirely satisfactory. Interestingly, we have a clearer view of the mechanism of D sleep than is true for S sleep, which has been recognized a much longer time.

Briefly we review here the properties of S sleep and D sleep, with emphasis on the cat. This unlucky species has been the favored experimental subject of the neurophysiologist, largely because of its availability and hardiness, but also now because most of what we know about brain mechanisms is based on studies of the feline brain. The pattern of autonomic, muscular, and EEG changes seen in the cat in S sleep and D sleep (Fig. 10.16) is essentially identical to the human pattern described earlier in the chapter. In S sleep, the heart rate slows; the EEG shows slow waves and spindles resembling human alpha or sleep spindles. Cats in S sleep more commonly show spindle than the very slow delta waves that humans exhibit in relatively deep S sleep. As in man, neck muscle tone is fairly high in the cat during S sleep and there are no eye movements.

D sleep was discovered in the cat by Jouvet and Michel in 1958 (Fig. 10.16). The EEG shifts to the arousal pattern of low-voltage fast activity. Rapid eye movements develop and occur in bursts, and the neck muscles relax greatly, just as in humans. There are small twitches of the paws, and heart rate and respiration become irregular. As in humans, the impression is strong that the D sleeping cat is dreaming.

In addition to the low-voltage fast activity in the EEG recorded from the cerebral cortex, there are two other brain signs of D sleep in cat. One is large waves at a slow rate of four to eight cycles per second in the hippocampus, the so-called *hippocampal theta waves*. These are to be expected; they also occur in the normal waking state when the cortical EEG shows the arousal pattern. In general, whenever the EEG of the cerebral cortex shows low-voltage fast activity, the hippocampus shows theta waves.

Another brain sign of D sleep in the cat is the occurrence of *PGO spikes* (see Fig. 10.16), large spike-like brain waves that occur in the pons, lateral geniculate body, and occipital cortex. These PGO (abbreviated from *P*ons, lateral *G*eniculate body, and *O*ccipital cortex) spikes occur in close correspondence with the bursts of REM. They are not electrical artifacts of the eye movements but rather genuine large synchronized neural responses that may reflect the brain substrates of the eye movements. They occur very slowly in the motor neuron nuclei in the brain stem that control movements of the eyes.

The earlier established roles of the RAS and medial thalamus remain approximately true. When the RAS is turned off, the medial thalamus drives the cerebral cortex in the slow-wave synchronized pattern of S sleep—the sleep spindles. When the RAS is turned on it overrides the medial thalamus and produces the cortical EEG arousal pattern of waking. The critical issues thus become: (1) the mechanisms for turning

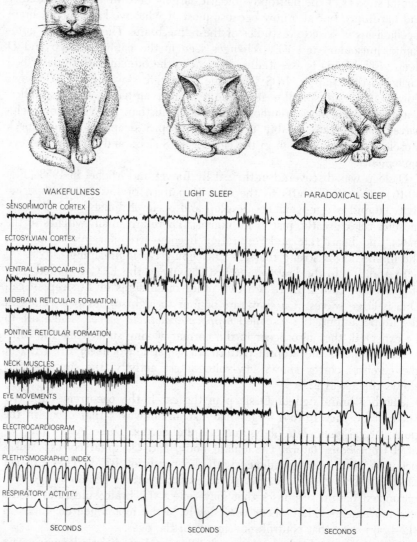

WAKEFULNESS	LIGHT SLEEP	PARADOXICAL SLEEP

SENSORIMOTOR CORTEX

ECTOSYLVIAN CORTEX

VENTRAL HIPPOCAMPUS

MIDBRAIN RETICULAR FORMATION

PONTINE RETICULAR FORMATION

NECK MUSCLES

EYE MOVEMENTS

ELECTROCARDIOGRAM

PLETHYSMOGRAPHIC INDEX

RESPIRATORY ACTIVITY

SECONDS   SECONDS   SECONDS

Figure 10.16 Characteristic rhythms associated with deep sleep in a cat (group of traces at right) are so much like those of wakefulness (left group) and so different from those of light sleep (middle group) that Jouvet has applied the term "paradoxical" to deep sleep. Normal cats spend about two-thirds of the time sleeping. They usually begin each sleep period with 25 minutes of light sleep, followed by six or seven minutes of paradoxical sleep. In the latter state, they are hard to wake and their muscles are relaxed. (From Jouvet, M. The states of sleep. Copyright © 1967 by Scientific American, Inc. All rights reserved.)

the RAS on and off, and (2) the mechanisms that yield D sleep, as opposed to simply waking the animal.

The S-sleep system

Studies by Jouvet and associates (see Jouvet, 1967) have implicated two regions of the lower brain stem in the control of S sleep and D sleep (see Fig. 10.17). Although there are many uncertainties in Jouvet's theory its simplicity is appealing. There is a region lying in the midline throughout the extent of the pons that seems to play a crucial role in the production of S sleep. Lesions in this region yield an animal that *does not show slow-wave or S sleep*. This region is tentatively identified by Jouvet as the *raphé system*. This system of neurons sends projections to the reticular activating system, hypothalamus, and limbic forebrain structures. Further, these cells appear to contain all the known serotonin in the brain. Serotonin (see Chapter 5) is a biogenic amine that may function as a specialized neuro-transmitter. The Swedish histochemistry group (Fuxe and Dahlström) has identified these serotonin neurons by a special fluorescent stain that has a characteristic yellow appearance under ultraviolet light when it reacts with *serotonin*. The basic idea, then, would be that activation of the raphé center inhibits the arousing action of the RAS and associated structures, allowing the medial thalamus to drive the cerebral cortex into the characteristic spindles and slow-wave pattern of S sleep. Destruction of the raphé system prevents inhibition of the RAS and results in an animal that is either waking or in D sleep. If this inhibitory system is, in fact, the raphé nuclei, then serotonin would presumably be the inhibitory neuro-transmitter.

Certain biochemical experiments provide evidence consistent with this view of the role of the raphé system. Morgane (1972), for example, showed that lesions of the raphé system in cats and treatment of other normal cats with a drug called PCPA (*p*-chlorophenylalanine) yielded an identical effect—they no longer showed S sleep but only D sleep and waking. Furthermore, they remained awake much more at the expense of S sleep. The significance of this effect of PCPA is that the drug blocks the synthesis of serotonin. It is a chemical means of inactivating the raphé system.

At this point we must insert a cautionary note about the interpretation of pharmacological studies, such as the PCPA experiment. A powerful drug like PCPA that blocks the synthesis of a presumably important neurochemical such as serotonin usually has other effects as well. Resnick (1972) has shown that PCPA also yields the condition known as PKU (see Chapter 2). PCPA interferes with normal metabolism of phenylalanine, an amino acid in protein foods, and yields the same kinds of toxic by-products that occur in those humans afflicted with the disease PKU. The effect of PKU is severe brain damage and feeble-mindedness. In short, PCPA is likely to have many other severe effects on brain function in addition to its action on the synthesis of serotonin.

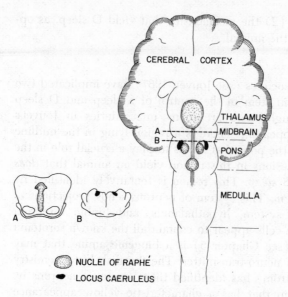

CEREBRAL CORTEX

THALAMUS
MIDBRAIN
PONS

MEDULLA

A   B

⊘ NUCLEI OF RAPHÉ
● LOCUS CAERULEUS

Sleep, dreaming,
arousal, and
attention

Figure 10.17 Several regions of brain stem of cat believed by Jouvet to be involved in control of S and D sleep.

Another interesting experimental observation seems to fit with the raphé picture. Some years ago Nauta (1946) reported that lesions in the anterior region of the hypothalamus in the preoptic area (see Chapter 8) yielded rats that remained awake for many days until they died. This result was puzzling for many years. It was more recently repeated in cats by McGinty and Sterman (1968). In fact, this preoptic region is connected to the raphé system by the medial forebrain bundle. In this sense, the raphé system is linked to the limbic system. Lesions to the anterior or preoptic region of the hypothalamus destroy an essential descending control projection to the raphé system.

One other region of the brain can produce inhibitory effects on the RAS similar to the effects of raphé stimulation. Clemente and his associates (1968) at the University of California at Los Angeles have localized a region of the frontal-orbital cortex that, when stimulated, produces S sleep. It is in the general frontal region that we described earlier as playing a critical role in modulating behavioral (and EEG) arousal and activity levels.

In summary, the raphé system in the upper brain stem is believed to act on the RAS to inhibit it and yield S sleep. The orbital frontal region of the cerebral cortex and the preoptic region of the hypothalamus have similar actions that might be explained by assuming they exert their influences via the raphé system. The raphé system is believed by some to exert its inhibition on the RAS by the neuro-transmitter serotonin (see Fig. 10.18).

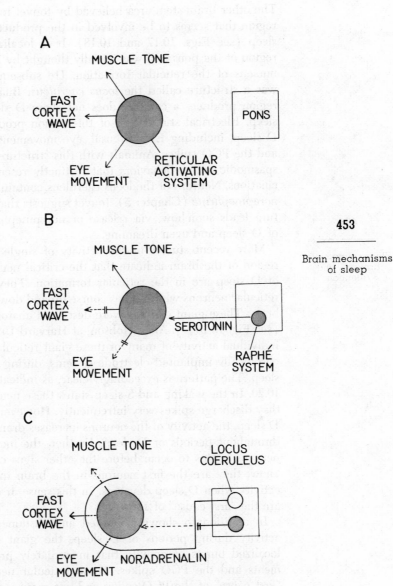

Figure 10.18 Working hypothesis, proposed by Jouvet to provide a bridge between the neurophysiology and the biochemistry of sleep, suggests that the normal state of wakefulness (A) is transformed into light sleep (B) when a secretion produced by the nuclei of raphé modifies many effects of the reticular activation system. Paradoxical sleep follows (C) when a second secretion, produced by the locus coeruleus, supplants the raphé secretion and produces effects that resemble normal wakefulness except for the loss of muscle tension. (Redrawn from Jouvet, M. The states of sleep. Copyright © 1967 by Scientific American, Inc. All rights reserved.)

The D-sleep system

The other brain stem area believed by Jouvet to be critical for sleep is a region that seems to be involved in the production of paradoxical or D sleep (see Figs. 10.17 and 10.18). It is localized in the lateral-dorsal region of the pons and was initially thought by Jouvet to be a particular nucleus of the reticular formation. He subsequently suggested that it was a structure called the *locus caeruleus*. Bilateral destruction of this region produces a cat that does not show D sleep, only waking and S sleep. Electrical stimulation of this region produces the phenomena of D sleep, including EEG arousal, eye movements, reduced muscle tone, and the PGO spikes. Animals with this structure destroyed often exhibit spasmodic active behaviors that distinctly resemble responses to hallucinations. Neurons of the locus caeruleus contain another biogenic amine, *norepinephrine* (Chapter 5). Jouvet suggests that activation of this structure leads somehow, via release of norepinephrine, to the phenomena of D sleep and even dreaming.

More recent studies of the activity of single neurons in this general region of the brain indicate that the critical neurons involved in control of D sleep are in the reticular formation. They are, in fact, the giant reticular neurons whose axons course up and down the greater part of the brain. These giant neurons were described anatomically by the Scheibels (see Fig. 10.14). J. Allen Hobson, at Harvard University, has studied the individual activity of many of these giant reticular neurons in cats, using chronically implanted electrode systems, during waking, S sleep, and D sleep. The pattern is exceedingly clear, as indicated in Figures 10.19 and 10.20. In the waking and S-sleep states these neurons are very inactive—they discharge spikes very infrequently. However as the animal goes into D sleep, the activity of the neurons increases dramatically and remains up throughout periods of D sleep. Further, the increased activity of these neurons begins to occur before the other signs of D sleep. So far as we know, they are the first neurons in the brain to show clear changes in activity when D sleep develops. In this sense, it can be argued that they are the "first cause" of D sleep.

In addition to showing marked and sustained or tonic increases in activity during periods of D sleep, the giant reticular neurons show localized bursts of activity that immediately precede rapid eye movements and the PGO spikes. These reticular neurons may also be the "first cause" of the PGO spikes and eye movements that occur in bursts during D sleep.

The eye movements and PGO spikes of D sleep occur in the normal pattern after removal of the cerebral cortex and other forebrain structures. This fact raises certain questions about the occurrence of dreaming during D sleep. Some authors have assumed that the rapid eye movements and associated PGO spikes are indications that the animal (or per-

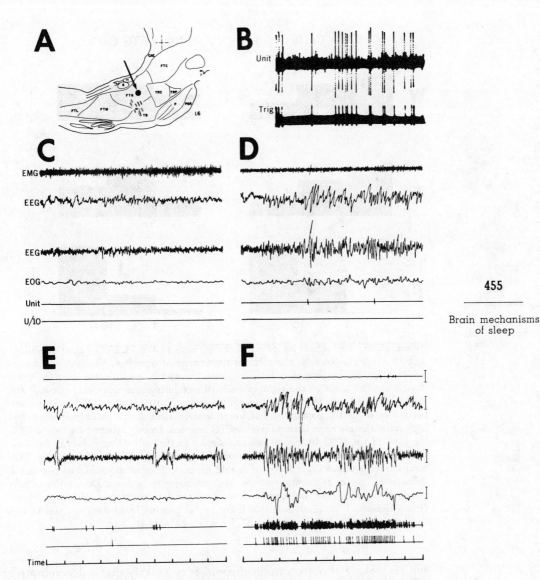

Figure 10.19 Polygraphic records of an FTG (giant reticular) neuron in several behavioral states. In A, the arrow indicates the histologically localized recording site. In B, 10 sec of extracellular microelectrode recording are shown together with pulses (triggered by the action potentials of the unit) that were used in computer data analysis. Parts C through F show the polygraph records of unit activity in each of four behavioral states. In C, waking, the unit is silent. In D, synchronized sleep, sporadic firing occurs. In E, desynchronized sleep without rapid eye movements (REM), firings are more abundant and tend to occur together with PGO wave activity in the EEG. In F, also desynchronized sleep, firings are most intense coincident with a burst of REMs and intense PGO wave activity. Note that unit activity begins to increase before the first eye movement and subsides gradually after the last eye movement. (From Hobson, J. A. et al. Selective firing by cat pontine brain stem neurons in desynchronized sleep. *J. Neurophysiol.* **37**, 1974, pp. 497–511.)

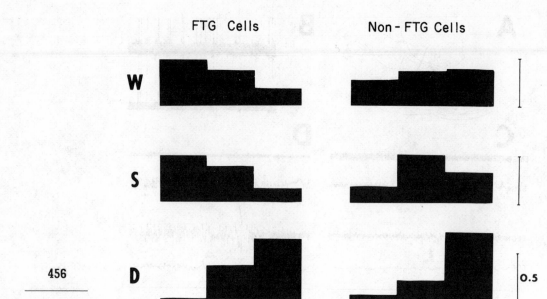

FTG Cells　　　　　**Non-FTG Cells**

W

S

D

0.5

1　　　10　　　　　　1　　　10

Figure 10.20　Histograms of mean discharge rates of the 74 FTG (giant reticular) and 56 non-FTG neurons. Each bin in the histogram represents the number of cells whose mean discharge rate is less than one, one to ten, and greater than ten (discharge/s). The scale to the right of each pair of histograms represents one-half the total number of cells in each anatomical subgroup. During waking (W), a large proportion of the FTG population has low discharge rates and a small proportion has high rates; the converse is true for non-FTG neurons. During synchronized sleep (S), the form of the FTG histogram remains similar to that of waking, whereas the non-FTG histogram shows a larger proportion of intermediate rates than in waking. This results from a concomitant increase in rate by central tegmental field nuerons and a decrease in rate by tegmental reticular and pontine gray neurons. During desynchronized sleep (D), both histograms show a preponderance of high discharge rates. (From Hobson, J. A. et al. Selective firing by cat pontine brain stem neurons in desynchronized sleep. *J. Neurophysiol.* **37**, 1974, pp. 497–511.)

son) is looking at objects in his dreams. It is unlikely that a decerebrated animal is experiencing anything, let alone dreams. PGO spikes and eye movements are initiated and controlled by brain stem mechanisms. It is still possible to assume that PGO spikes and rapid eye movements accompany dreaming in the normal animal, but perhaps less likely that these bursts of eye movements represent looking at dream objects.

As soon as the increase in the activity of these giant reticular neurons begins to develop, there is a corresponding decrease in the activity of neurons in the region of the locus caeruleus (l.c.) which lies just above the giant-celled reticular region. Locus caeruleus neurons shut off their activity during periods of D sleep. There is a striking reciprocal relationship between the activity of the giant reticular neurons and the neurons in the locus caeruleus. As D sleep develops, the giant reticular neurons begin to fire, which leads to further increases in reticular neuron activity, etc. (see Figs. 10.19 and 10.20). These patterns can most easily be explained if it is assumed that the two groups of neurons directly influence each other in a predominantly inhibitory fashion.

The most important neural systems involved in sleep and waking can be summarized very briefly as follows. In waking, the RAS is active and maintains the cerebral cortex in a state of EEG arousal and the animal awake. The state of S sleep develops when the raphé system becomes active, perhaps as a result of influences from the orbital frontal cortex and preoptic region of hypothalamus, and inhibits the RAS. This permits the medial thalamus to drive the cerebral cortex in the typical EEG pattern of S sleep. During S sleep, the giant reticular neurons periodically become active perhaps as a result of reciprocal connections with the neurons of the locus caeruleus. As the giant reticular neurons become very active, and the l.c. neurons inactive, a form of cortical EEG arousal, eye movements, PGO spikes, relaxation of neck muscles, and the other signs of D sleep occur. This brief description must be recognized as a current "state-of-the-field" summary and by no means a final or complete description of the sequence of brain events that leads to sleep, dreaming, and waking.

It is worth repeating again that we still do not know why sleep is necessary at all. Clearly it is necessary for all higher animals, but reasons for this remain undetected after nearly half a century of intensive research and inquiry.

Summary

Three biological states are characteristic of all mammals—waking, sleep, and deep sleep. Waking and sleep are examples of circadian rhythms; it is believed that the "circadian clock" is located near the hypothalamus. No evidence yet indicates why sleep is essential for continued functioning of humans or animals.

The EEG patterns of waking and sleep are quite distinct. The waking pattern is characterized by alpha or low-voltage fast waves. In stage 1, the lightest stage of sleep, alpha activity tends to increase and then decrease, and low-voltage 4–6 cps activity appears. Sleep spindles appear in stage 2, while large slow delta waves characterize stage 3. These delta waves predominate in stage 4. Studies of eye movements during sleep have shown that when periods of eye movements begin, the EEG pattern shifts immediately from whatever stage it is in to a pattern closely resembling stage 1. This pattern continues until the eye movements cease. This stage of sleep has been called *D sleep*, while non-D sleep is termed S or *slow-wave sleep*.

S sleep is characterized by a slow heart rate, slow waves and spindles in the EEG pattern resembling human alpha, and an absence of eye movements. The D-sleep stage is characterized by an arousal EEG pattern, eye movements, irregular heart rate, and highly variable blood pressure and respiration. Hippocampal theta waves and PGO spikes are also found in D sleep. The PGO spikes occur in close correspondence to bursts of rapid eye movements. It is possible that these spikes may reflect the brain substrates of the eye movements.

On the basis of subjective reports it would appear that the D state represents dreaming. In addition, a few studies suggest that physiological concomitants of D sleep correspond to dream events. Freud and Hall postulated the two major theories of dreaming. According to Freud, complex unconscious mental processes which are released in a dream state are transformed into an apparent content in dreaming. Hall's theory of dreaming is more direct and assumes that dreaming is reduced and simplified thinking; the dream content is a succession of images, primarily visual ones.

The effects of sleep deprivation are behaviorally and physiologically devastating. A very severe stress is normally required to produce death in a healthy animal. Sleep deprivation does kill healthy animals; it must be a very severe stress. We do not yet know why or how. D-sleep deprivation is a more subtle interference with sleep and experiments suggest that an organism may require a certain amount of D sleep each night.

Arousal is located on the opposite end of a continuum from sensory deprivation. The orienting response is one measure of the arousal syndrome. The reticular activating system (RAS) is thought to be one of the brain substrates of arousal. Electrical stimulation of the reticular core of the brain stem produces an EEG pattern of arousal in the cerebral cortex. The reticular formation, not the classical sensory pathways, is the source of EEG arousal. Evoked-response studies indicate that all types of stimuli, including electrical stimulation of the cortex, can activate the reticular formation.

The effects of transection of the brain stem on EEG sleep have helped to provide a better understanding of the mechanisms underlying sleep and wakefulness. In a *cerveau isolé* preparation (see pp. 437–438), a set of symptoms resembling normal sleep are apparent; animals display permanently "sleeping" cortical EEG patterns. The EEG arousal pattern cannot be easily induced in a cerveau isolé animal. The *encéphale isolé* preparation, in contrast, exhibits EEG and pupillary signs comparable to those of the normal animal. It is now known that the critical factor in the permanently "sleeping" EEG of the cerveau isolé animal is not the elimination of sensory input from the body, but rather the interruption of the RAS.

Recovery from reticular lesions demonstrates that most of the midbrain reticular formation is not essential for behavioral sleep and waking, and various other behaviors. The residual deficits suggest though that the reticular core may normally play an important role in many of these functions.

The medial thalamus also appears to be involved in sleep and waking by serving as a "pacemaker" to induce rhythmic spindling or alpha activity in the cerebral cortex. The reticular formation activation may act to block EEG synchrony resulting from stimulation of the diffuse thalamic nuclei either at the cortex, thalamus, or both.

The *recruiting response* closely resembles spontaneous spindle waves in cat. The significance of the recruiting response lies in its similarity to spontaneous spindle activity. The influences of the medial thalamic system and RAS upon cortical EEG activity appear to be reciprocal. Cortical recruiting elicited by low-frequency thalamic stimulation may be blocked by higher frequency electrical stimulation of the RAS. It has been suggested that the RAS mediates arousal and alerting, and that the diffuse thalamic system mediates depression of cortical excitability and sleep.

Other brain structures involved in arousal are the hippocampus and frontal lobes of the cerebral cortex. The frontal lobe regulates cortical EEG arousal by acting as a modulator. There are reciprocal relations between RAS and frontal cortex such that activation of RAS results in cortical activation which then feeds back to decrease activity of the RAS. Destruction of frontal cortex presumably interrupts this loop and leads to hyperactivity. It is believed that there is also a loop linking the RAS with hippocampus which resembles that between frontal cortex and RAS.

The initial view of the mechanism of sleep was simple and assumed that activation of RAS caused EEG arousal and waking, while activation of the medial thalamus resulted in slow waves in the EEG and sleep. This view of the mechanism of sleep is still basically valid. When the RAS is turned off, the slow-wave synchronized pattern of S sleep appears in the cerebral cortex via medial thalamic activity. When the RAS is activated, the medial thalamus is inhibited, and the cortical EEG arousal pattern of waking appears.

The raphé system appears to play a critical role in the production of S sleep. This system projects to the RAS, hypothalamus, and limbic forebrain structures. Jouvet hypothesized that the following mechanism controls S sleep. Activation of the raphé center inhibits the arousing action of the RAS which allows the medial thalamus to drive the cerebral cortex in the S sleep patterns. Destruction of the raphé system inhibits the inhibition of the RAS, thereby resulting in an animal which is either waking or in D sleep. If the controlling system for S sleep is the raphé nuclei, then serotonin would be the presumed neuro-transmitter involved in S sleep. Biochemical studies are consonant with this view of the role of the raphé system in sleep and wakefulness.

Jouvet's view of the D-sleep system implicates the *locus caeruleus* (l.c.) and norepinephrine in D sleep. Activation of l.c. neurons via release of norepinephrine results in the phenomena of D sleep. The critical neurons involved in the control of D sleep are in the reticular formation. In waking and S sleep, these neurons are inactive. As the animal moves into D sleep, the activity of these neurons increases significantly and remains strong throughout periods of D sleep. In addition, these neurons show localized bursts of activity immediately preceding rapid eye movements and PGO spikes. With an increase in the activity of reticular neurons, there is a concomitant decrease in the activity of l.c. neurons. This reciprocal relationship between the activity of reticular neurons and l.c. neurons is most easily explained by assuming that the two groups of neurons directly influence each other in a predominantly inhibitory fashion.

11

Learning and memory

11

I sometimes feel, in reviewing the evidence on the localization of the memory trace, that the necessary conclusion is that learning just is not possible.

(Karl S. Lashley, 1950, pages 477–478)

Learning is the most important thing that people do. Language, society, and culture are all learned and depend on the learning of each new individual to exist. The current emphasis on man as a naked ape—an animal with many genetically determined characteristics and behavioral tendencies—tends to ignore this obvious fact. Homo sapiens are qualitatively different from all other primates because of what they can learn. Apes learn much more than rats, who learn a great deal more than the fly. It is largely for this reason that experimental psychology has emphasized the study of learning. The classic question in physiological psychology has become the location and nature of the engrams—the physical memory traces that must develop in the brain whenever learning occurs. Karl Lashley's despairing quotation above reflects the fundamental difficulty of the search for the engram.

Learning is broadly conceived as change in behavior resulting from experience. The processes of learning and memory can only be inferred and measured from changes in the behavior of the organism. Hence, investigations attempting to determine the physiological basis of learning must use a situation in which behavioral changes can be demonstrated, and must look for biological processes which can account for the observed behavior. Learning obviously does not include all changes in behavior; for example, it would be difficult to define death, certainly a profound behavioral change, as an example of learning. Many attempts have been made at a definition of learning (see Kimble, 1961) and most have emphasized that it is a behavioral change occurring as a result of practice. More specific definitions have insisted that learning is the relatively permanent behavioral change resulting from reinforced practice or observation (Kimble, 1961). Definitions of this type exclude short-term changes such as fatigue or adaptation and developmental changes such as imprinting or certain sexual behaviors. Nevertheless, all definitions of learning are somewhat vague.

In an attempt to reduce the confusion over what learning is, many workers are beginning to use the term *behavioral plasticity*, first suggested by William James (1890) to refer to all meaningful changes in behavior. Particular kinds of learned behaviors may then be given more

Written in collaboration with Dr. Michael Patterson, Department of Physiology, Kirksville College of Osteopathic Medicine.

specific definitions. Three broad categories of behavioral plasticity may be defined:

1. *Habituation* is simply a decrease in response to repeated stimulation, and its opposite, *sensitization*, is an increase in response to repeated stimulation.
2. *Classical* or Pavlovian *conditioning* is the category in which a "neutral" stimulus such as a tone is paired with some unconditioned stimulus that elicits a response. Nothing the organism does can change the paired occurrence of the two.
3. *Instrumental learning* describes the situation in which the animal must perform some response to obtain reward or avoid punishment. Instrumental learning can be construed broadly to include all forms of complex learning ranging from pushing a lever for food to language acquisition.

Habituation is a more elementary aspect of behavioral plasticity than classical and instrumental learning. It requires only that a stimulus be repeated; conditioning involves some form of association between stimuli. To simplify, we will treat habituation separately but group together both classical and instrumental conditioning in analyzing the physiological basis of learning.

Learning and memory are intimately related. Since learning can be seen only in terms of behavioral changes which result from some type of stimulation, the effects of the stimuli on the nervous system must be stored for some time before they can result in changed behavior. Hence, any measure of learning must depend upon memory or storage processes to bridge the time between the nervous system change and the output of altered behavior. In the same fashion, any study of the storage mechanisms responsible for memory is dependent upon some change in the nervous system, or learning. Thus, although any study may look primarily at learning processes, the storage mechanism of memory is involved. Any study that attempts to measure memory of necessity depends also upon the learning process which occurred earlier.

Each of us knows much about our own capacities, or lack of them, for learning and remembering. One of the most obvious features of memory is that it can have different durations. Some items are experienced and immediately forgotten, like the details of a complex modern painting that is seen only for a moment; other items are remembered for relatively brief periods of time—the telephone number you look up, dial, and forget; some memories seem to be virtually permanent. Memories can be identified as having at least three different time courses. Considerable modern research on human memory supports this intuitive idea. A model diagram illustrating the three aspects of human memory and how they might interact is shown in Figure 11.1.

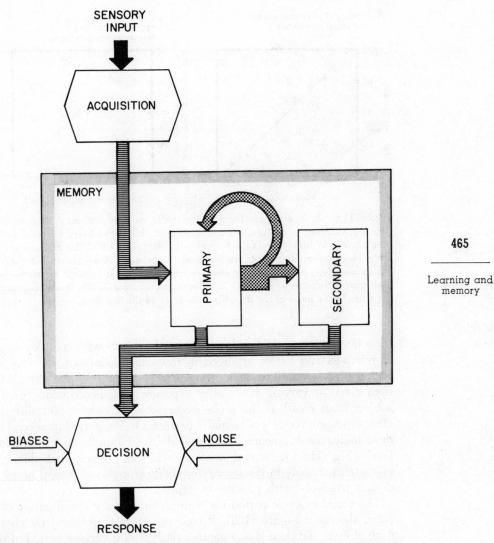

SENSORY INPUT

ACQUISITION

MEMORY

PRIMARY

SECONDARY

BIASES

DECISION

NOISE

RESPONSE

Figure 11.1 Hypothetical scheme of the processes in human memory. Very short-term iconic memory occurs in the sensory acquisition phase. Some portion of that information is placed in primary memory (short-term) and some portion of this goes into secondary or permanent store. (From Norman, D. A. *Memory and Attention; An Introduction to Human Information Processing*. New York: Wiley, 1969.)

George Sperling at Harvard obtained convincing evidence for the existence of very short-term sensory memory, which has come to be called *iconic memory*. The surprising fact about iconic memory is that it is virtually perfect. No matter how bad you think your own memory is, you have perfect iconic memory. Unfortunately, it remains perfect only

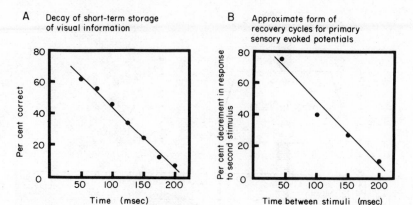

A   Decay of short-term storage
     of visual information

B   Approximate form of
     recovery cycles for primary
     sensory evoked potentials

Figure 11.2 A, Time decay function for iconic memory. (From Averbach, E., and Sperling, G. Short term storage of information in vision. In Cherry, C. (ed.) *Information Theory.* Washington, D.C.: Butterworth, 1961, pp. 196–212.) B, Recovery cycle for evoked potentials to light flash stimuli in primary visual cortex (of cat). Two flashes are given with a varying short interval between and amplitude of the second flash plotted relative to the first. The degree of decrease in amplitude of response to the second is an index of the strength of the trace of the first flash.

for a few milliseconds. Sperling presented subjects with complex displays of numbers and letters arranged in rows and columns for a very brief period of a few milliseconds, using a tachistoscope. Probe stimuli were then given at varying times after exposure to indicate which item the subject must recall. If the probe occurred within about 50 milliseconds after exposure, recall was virtually perfect. Over a period of several hundred milliseconds, accuracy of recall decayed rapidly to a much lower level (Fig. 11.2A). Several lines of evidence suggest that this iconic memory exists only in the sensory modality stimulated (visual here) and decays passively with passage of time.

The recovery cycle period for neurons in primary visual cortex of the cat is shown in Figure 11.2B. A recovery cycle is obtained by giving a flash of light and then giving another flash after a varying period of time. Amplitude or amount of response to the second stimulus is compared with response to the first stimulus. As seen in Figure 11.2B, the response to the second flash decreases as the time between flashes is shortened. Whatever the mechanism of the recovery cycle, it is an index of the degree to which a trace of the first stimulus remains in the primary visual system. The correspondence between Sperling's iconic memory decay and the recovery cycle for evoked response to flash in the visual cortex is quite striking.

William James (1890) defined memories that last for a matter of seconds, the briefly remembered telephone number, as *primary memories.* These are short-term memories of successive events in our environment that seem to result in a continuous flow of experience. Peterson charac-

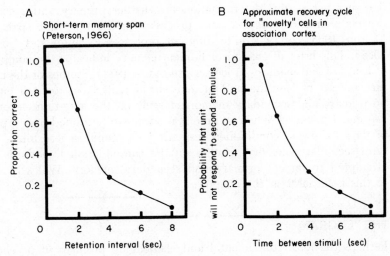

A
Short-term memory span
(Peterson, 1966)

B
Approximate recovery cycle
for "novelty" cells in
association cortex

Figure 11.3 A, The time "decay" function for primary memory. (From Peterson, L. R. Short-term verbal memory and learning. *Psych. Rev.* 73 (3), 1966, pp. 193–207. Copyright 1966 by the American Psychological Association. Reprinted by permission.) B, Recovery cycles for neurons in association cortex (of cat) to two flashes of light compiled as in Fig. 11.2B.

terized primary memory in a series of experiments in which the subject had to recall letters for varying lengths of time while counting backward to prevent rehearsal. The "decay" of this kind of primary memory is shown in Figure 11.3A. Unlike iconic memory, primary memory occurs across sensory modalities—there can be auditory recall of visual stimuli as well as visual recall. Recovery cycles for responses of neurons in association cortex of cat for two successive light flash stimuli are shown in Figure 11.3B. These association area recovery cycles have the same form even if the two stimuli are of different modalities, such as sound and light. Calloway noted that the same form and time course of recovery cycle can be obtained for brain potentials recorded from the scalp overlying association cortex in humans. The correspondence of these association area recovery cycles and the decay of primary memory is intriguing.

Well learned memories persist almost for a lifetime. William James termed these permanent memories *secondary* memory. The diagram of Figure 11.1 indicates some of the possible interrelationships between the three hypothetical forms of memory. In acquisition, sensory input is stored very briefly in the sensory system and encoded into the short-term primary memory store. Some memories are also stored in the permanent secondary memory. In the "decision" process, the output of the memory is combined with the subject's biases, and noise, to determine response.

The diagram of Figure 11.1 is only hypothetical; it serves merely to emphasize the fact that memory has several time constants. The evidence does not yet permit determination of whether primary and secondary aspects of memory are the same process over different time spans (see Melton, 1963), or two quite different processes (Waugh and Norman, 1965). This brief discussion of human memory indicates the complexity of learning and memory processes (see Voss, 1974). Studies of the neural mechanisms of learning and memory in animals have focused entirely on primary and secondary memory, largely on the long-term secondary aspects of memory. When an animal is successfully trained over a period of days to give a conditioned response to a stimulus, it exhibits long-term secondary memory. Studies on the consolidation hypothesis have attempted to dissect primary and secondary memory. We will return to this issue later in the chapter.

THE "ENGRAM"

Perhaps the most fundamental and challenging problem in psychology and the neurosciences is the nature of the *engram*, the set of physical processes and changes in the brain that form the basis of learning. Karl Lashley was the first to conceptualize the issue clearly. As noted above, he ended his brilliant lifelong search for the engram with the somewhat ironic suggestion that learning is impossible.

Experimental analysis of the location and nature of the engram is extraordinarily difficult. Given the limitation of present techniques, a paradox of sorts exists. All forms of learning must involve alterations somewhere between the input and the output of the central nervous system. The known forms of specific interaction between neurons occur at synapses. Consequently, learning may be assumed to involve changes at synapses. In order to analyze the synaptic mechanisms underlying learning, the critical synapses, those where learned changes occur, must be identified. Present techniques permit identification and analysis of synapses only in systems that involve one set of synaptic junctions— monosynaptic pathways. However, monosynaptic pathways do not, by definition, form new associations.

The neurology of learning

The two general research strategies currently employed to study the neurology of learning, whether the manipulations and/or measures involve lesions, anatomy, chemistry, or electrophysiology, are use of "model" biological systems and more-or-less intact behaving animals. The objective is to describe the physical-chemical processes of the nervous system that form the basis of learning. Learning is obviously not a unitary phenomenon. Broadly construed, it is reflected in changes in behavior as a result of experience. As noted above, a simple dichotomy can be made between habituation and sensitization, which imply decreases or increases in already existing responses to particular stimuli, and "associative" learning, which involves development of response to a previously neutral stimulus as a result of temporal association, for example, classical and instrumental conditioning.

The model-systems approach has been particularly successful for study of habituation and sensitization. Similarly, impressive advances have been made in analysis of the neural control of behavioral responses and response sequences in invertebrates (see Kandel, 1975). In most instances, analysis has been possible because the output (and input) neurons controlling the behavior can be identified and are few in number, relative to brain control systems in higher animals. Further, the behavior sequences are often relatively inflexible. To oversimplify greatly, it might be argued that two general strategies have evolved for adaptation of behavior to environment. One is to develop relatively simple "fixed action patterns" elicited by external and internal stimuli and rely on evolution to change these action patterns when the environment changes. This can be done with economy of neurons. Many invertebrates exemplify this strategy. The alternative strategy is to add to simpler fixed actions by developing the capacity for behavioral adaptation within the individual. Higher vertebrates have greatly developed capabilities for learning, which find their ultimate expression in human learning. Perhaps because of this, they have developed brains with a great many more neurons, making analysis more difficult.

NEURAL MECHANISMS OF HABITUATION

If a drop of water falls on the surface of the sea just over the flower-like disc of a sea anemone, the whole animal contracts vigorously. If, then, a second drop falls within a few minutes of the first, there is less contraction, and finally, on the third or fourth drop, the response disappears altogether (Jennings, 1906). Here in this marine polyp with the primitive nerve net is clearly exhibited one of the most pervasive phenomena of the animal kingdom—decrement of response with repeated stimulation. Almost every species studied, from amoeba to man, exhibits some form of response decrement when the stimulus is frequently repeated or constantly applied (Harris, 1943). The ubiquity of the phenomenon plus its obvious survival value suggests that this kind of plasticity must be one of the most fundamental properties of animal behaviour.

(Sharpless and Jasper, 1956, page 655)

With these words Sharpless and Jasper introduced their now classic study of habituation of the EEG arousal response. Their study had a profound impact on physiological psychology and served to kindle the interest of neural scientists in brain mechanisms of habituation. *Habituation* is a decrease in response to repeated stimulation and *sensitization* is an increase in response as a result of stimulation. Virtually all behavioral responses, as well as autonomic and EEG responses and signs of arousal, habituate rapidly and to a profound degree. In contrast, activity in primary sensory systems shows relatively little habituation. The processes responsible for habituation of behavioral responses probably occur largely after the primary sensory pathways of the brain and before the motoneurons that move muscles—somewhere between initial processing of sensory information and the execution of decisions to respond. Sensitization, the increase in response that often occurs when strong stimuli are given, may be similarly localized, although some evidence indicates that sensitization may be prominent even in the higher levels (thalamus and cortex) in primary sensory systems.

Greater progress has been made in analysis of the basic neuronal mechanisms underlying habituation than in more complex forms of behavioral plasticity such as classical and instrumental conditioning. The major reasons for this progress lie in the widespread occurrence of habituation, in its simplicity, and in the reliability with which the behavioral properties of habituation can be specified and determined (Thompson and Spencer, 1966). Habituation occurs both in spinal reflexes of the vertebrate and for responses of simpler animals. Consequently neural mechanisms of habituation can be studied in simplified systems.

Phenomena resembling behavioral habituation and sensitization have been known for many years to occur in reflexes of the transected spinal cord (Sherrington, 1906). As noted earlier, behavioral habituation is simply response decrement as a result of repeated stimulation. For example, if a moderate electric shock is delivered to the foot of a normal but restrained animal for the first time, the animal will show marked struggling and leg flexion movements. However if the stimulus is repeated a few times, the responses decrease considerably and may even disappear. Habituation is commonly differentiated from response decrements due to trauma, growth, aging, etc. In the example above, if the shock to the foot is withheld for a period of time after habituation and then given again, the response will reappear with normal strength. This spontaneous recovery is a common control used to show that habituation is a *reversible* response decrement. Habituation usually is distinguished from receptor adaptation and muscle fatigue.

Response decrements due to altered sensitivity of receptors are often termed *receptor adaptation,* and response decrements due to decremental effects occurring at the neuromuscular junctions of muscles are often termed *muscular fatigue.* Habituation has been characterized as being due to central rather than peripheral processes (Harris, 1943). As we noted, almost all responses of the intact organism initially elicited by a given stimulus, ranging in complexity from leg flexion to exploratory and play behavior (Welker, 1961), show habituation with repeated stimulation.

Response sensitization may be defined simply as an increased response strength to a given stimulus as a result of some other, usually strong, stimulus. The galvanic or electrodermal skin reflex (EDR) is a good case in point. Suppose we were to measure the EDR activity of sweat glands in the palm of the hand in response to a sound of moderate intensity. The response would probably be of relatively low amplitude and somewhat irregular in occurrence. If a strong shock were delivered to the skin, the sound alone now would evoke a much larger EDR response; the response would have been sensitized. The response increase due to sensitization is distinguished from conditioning in that no pairing of shock and sound is necessary to produce the effect. Sensitization itself typically habituates; after a number of shock presentations the response to the sound decreases to the initial weak level. In fact, it seems to decay spontaneously following a sensitizing stimulus.

Spinal reflex habituation

Sherrington (1906) was perhaps the first to study systematically these types of changes in spinal reflexes. He did not term response decrements habituation, but rather referred to them as fatigue. However, he was careful to define fatigue only as a response decrement due to repeated stimulation.

If hind limb reflexes are employed, the spinal cord is usually cut in the mid-thoracic region. Various hind limb muscles and nerves may be dissected out for particular types of stimulation and response measures. The basic procedure involves electrical shock to skin or cutaneous (skin) nerves and measurement of the flexion reflex response strength. If a cutaneous stimulus is given every few seconds, the flexion reflex response typically decreases in strength (habituation). If a strong shock is given to some other portion of the skin or to another afferent nerve, responses to the original test stimulus increase in strength for a period of time (sensitization).

Prosser and Hunter (1936) completed a careful study of flexion reflex habituation in the chronic spinal rat. The animals were suspended in a hammock, skin or nerves of the hind limb were shocked, and the hind limb flexion reflex was recorded. Brief trains of shocks were given every ten seconds or so. If the shock was withheld, the response returned to normal strength in a period of minutes. Prosser and Hunter ruled out the possibility that the response decrement was due to receptor adaptation; the same habituation and recovery occurred when they stimulated afferent nerves rather than skin. Hence the habituation effect must be central to the afferent nerve at the point stimulated, and could not be due to receptor adaptation. Muscle fatigue appeared to be unlikely be-

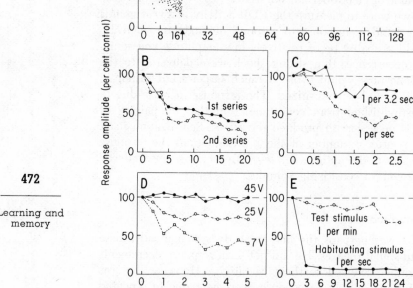

Learning and
memory

Figure 11.4 A, Characteristics of habituation (zero min to arrow) and spontaneous recovery (arrow to 128 min) of the hind limb flexion reflex of the spinal cat in response to repeated skin shocks. Stimuli were brief trains of shocks (5 in 50 msec) delivered every 10 sec during habituation and every 3 min during spontaneous recovery (except for a 12 min period of no stimuli at about 100 min). In this and all subsequent figures the response measured is tension developed by contraction of the tibialis anterior muscle, expressed as per cent mean initial control response amplitude. B, Effect of repeated habituation and spontaneous recovery series on degree of habituation. Response recovered to control level following first habituation series and was then rehabituated (second series). Conditions as in A. Data are averages of 10 trial blocks. C, Effect of stimulus frequency on habituation. Single shocks given 1 per 3.2 sec in one habituation series and 1 per sec in the other to the saphenous nerve. Data are averages over 16-sec periods of time. D, Effect of stimulus intensity on habituation. Brief trains of shocks (as in A) were delivered every 10 sec to the saphenous nerve with spontaneous recovery allowed after each series. Voltages refer to output of stimulator and were attenuated, but in the same ratios, when delivered to the nerve. Data averaged over 3 trial blocks. E, Stimulus generalization of habituation. Single shocks to two separate branches of the saphenous nerve. The habituating stimulus was given to one branch at 1 per sec and the test stimulus was given to the other branch at 1 per min. Data are averages over 3 trial blocks for response to the test stimulus, and averages over the same periods of time for response to the habituating stimulus. (From Thompson, R. F., and Spencer, W. A. Habituation: A model phenomenon for the study of neuronal substrates of behavior. *Psych. Rev.* **73**, 1966, pp. 16–43. Copyright 1966 by the American Psychological Association. Reprinted by permission.)

cause electric shocks to the nerves that innervated the muscles produced a muscle response that did not decrease when the reflex response was habituated.

The extent to which spinal flexion reflex habituation resembles habituation of responses in the intact organism is determined by the extent to which both phenomena follow the same set of laws. Thompson and Spencer (1966) surveyed the behavioral literature on response habituation and identified nine parametric characteristics of response habituation in intact animals. They found that spinal flexion reflex habituation exhibited the same nine parametric features. An example of habituation and spontaneous recovery of the spinal flexion reflex is shown in Figure 11.4A. Brief trains of shocks were given every 10 seconds to skin of the hind leg during habituation training, and once every 3 minutes during recovery. Individual responses are shown to illustrate response variability. Note that the response habituation has an approximately exponential form, and the spontaneous recovery has a long and variable time course.

Examples of four of the parametric features of flexion reflex habituation that parallel response habituation of the intact animal are shown in Figure 11.4. The effects of repeated habituation and spontaneous recovery series on habituation are shown in Figure 11.4B. After the first habituation series, the response was allowed to recover to control level and then rehabituated. In the second habituation series the response exhibits greater habituation. This might be viewed as long-term memory for habituation. The same holds true for most behavioral responses of the intact animal. In Figure 11.4C the effect of stimulus frequencies is shown. Habituation is more rapid when the stimulus is given more frequently. The effect of stimulus strength is illustrated in Figure 11.4D. In general, the weaker the stimulus, the greater the degree of habituation. Finally, Figure 11.4E illustrates stimulus generalization of habituation. An habituating stimulus is given once per second to an afferent nerve and a test stimulus is interposed once per minute to another afferent nerve. As the response to the habituating (1 per second) stimulus develops, a small but significant degree of habituation develops for the response to the 1 per minute test nerve (that is, habituation generalizes to the test channel). These examples illustrate that the parametric features of repeated habituation, stimulus frequency, stimulus strength, and stimulus generalization of the spinal flexion reflex are parallel to comparable habituation effects of the intact animal.

The possible synaptic mechanisms underlying flexion reflex habituation in the acute spinal cat have been studied in a series of experiments (Spencer, Thompson, and Neilson, 1966a, b, c; Thompson and Spencer, 1966).

In initial experiments the flexion reflex of the muscle was habituated to repeated skin shock, as in the studies by Sherrington, Prosser and

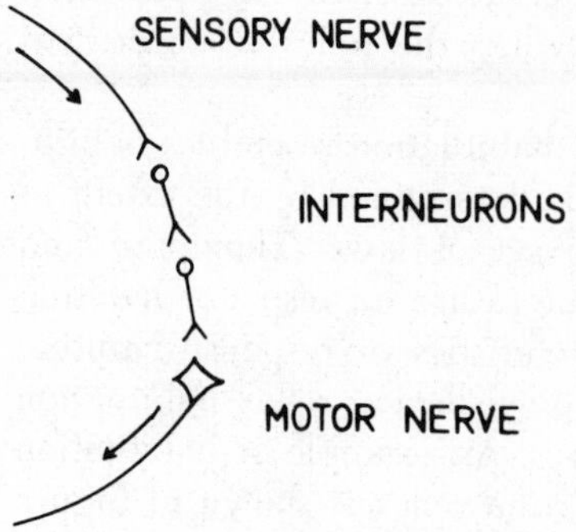

SENSORY NERVE

INTERNEURONS

MOTOR NERVE

Figure 11.5 Simplified diagram of flexion reflex pathway in spinal cord model of habituation. Pathway involves receiving sensory fibers (from skin), at least one group of interneurons, and the motoneurons going out to muscles. Habituation has been shown not to occur in sensory fibers or motoneurons and must therefore involve the interneurons.

Hunter, and others described above. An example of habituation and spontaneous recovery of the flexion reflex was shown in Figure 11.4A. In agreement with previous studies it was found that stimulation of the skin afferent nerve produced the same habituation as did stimulation of the skin itself. Furthermore, measurement of the afferent nerve response demonstrated no decrease in the afferent nerve volley during repeated stimulation, thus showing that the muscle response habituation cannot be due to any decrease in the incoming nerve activity.

The possibility that flexion reflex (muscle response) habituation was due to muscle fatigue or changes at neuromuscular junctions was ruled out by recording efferent nerve responses. The same response habituation occurs when the motor nerve response is measured. These findings indicated that the processes responsible for response decrement occur centrally, in the grey matter.

A greatly simplified drawing of the flexion reflex pathway in the spinal cord is shown in Figure 11.5. The process responsible for habituation could occur at the terminals of the incoming sensory fiber, someplace in the interneurons or at the outgoing motoneuron. In a series of experiments, the details of which are too complex for this discussion, afferent terminals and motoneurons were ruled out as the site of the habituation process (see Spencer, Thompson, and Neilson, 1966c; Groves, Glanzman, Patterson, and Thompson, 1970). Consequently, habituation must occur in the interneurons.

In more recent experiments the author and his associates have studied patterns of response of spinal interneurons during habituation in spinal cat (Groves and Thompson, 1970; 1973). Two separate categories of interneurons exhibited plasticity of response to repeated stimulation and a third category showed no plasticity of response. These are illustrated in relation to sensitization and habituation of the behavioral spinal flexion reflex in Figure 11.6. One type of neuron (type H) shows only habituation and another type shows sensitization (type S). The habituating interneurons lie more dorsally in the spinal grey and have different functional properties than the sensitizing interneurons. Groves and Thompson (1970) developed a general dual-process theory of habituation on the basis of these data. This theory indicates that even at the simple level of the spinal cord two different types of interneurons seem to code the processes of habituation and sensitization; this will be discussed below.

In higher animals habituation occurs at interneurons, both in the spinal cord and in the brain. Unfortunately, the synaptic mechanisms underlying processes of change like habituation are very difficult to analyze in interneurons—it is almost impossible to identify the critical interneurons where the changes first develop. Ideally, a monosynaptic pathway is required; that is, a pathway where the incoming fibers can be identified and cross only one synapse to the output neuron.

Greatest progress in analysis of the basic synaptic processes of habituation has come from two simplified neuronal systems where habituation occurs across a single synapse. One of these is in an invertebrate—the *aplysia* or sea hare. Eric Kandel and associates have analyzed habituation across a single synapse in this simple animal (see Kandel, 1975; Pinsker et al., 1970). Another preparation that shows habituation at a single synapse in the vertebrate central nervous system is the isolated frog spinal cord. The author and his associates (Farel, Glanzman, and Thompson, 1973) have analyzed possible mechanisms of habituation in this simple vertebrate system.

In brief, results agree in both *aplysia* and isolated frog spinal cord. Habituation is due to changes localized to the synapses being activated by the repeated stimulus. No interneurons or synaptic inhibition from other neurons are involved. Figure 11.7 illustrates this point. One theory of the mechanism of habituation (Fig. 11.7A) assumes that the fibers being stimulated activate interneurons that build up activity and induce inhibition on the output neuron. All possibilities like this that involve interneurons acting to cause inhibition were ruled out experimentally in both the *aplysia* and frog cord preparations. Consequently, the only possibility left is that habituation develops at the synapse being stimulated by the habituation stimulus (Fig. 11.7B). This kind of direct decrease in synaptic transmission as a result of repeated activation is termed *synaptic depression*. It is probably due to a decrease in release of the synaptic transmitter substance from the presynaptic terminals, although this is not yet proved.

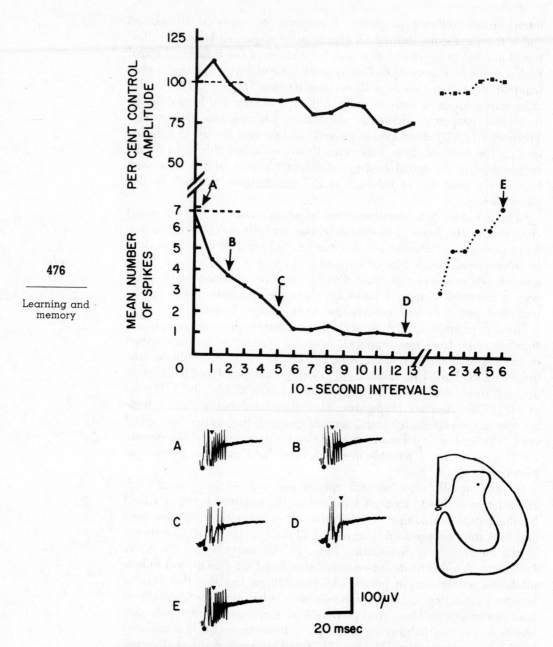

Figure 11.6 Examples of interneurons (in spinal cord) that appear to mediate habituation and sensitization. On the left, the upper graph represents amplitude of reflex response and the lower graph represents discharges of interneuron to a repeated stimulus (2 per sec, rate; recovery plotted 1 per 15 sec). Insets show discharges of the interneuron at various times, and location of interneuron in spinal cord. This type of interneuron (type H) shows only habituation, no matter how strong the stimulus or how much sensitization is shown by the reflex response. (From Groves, P. M., and

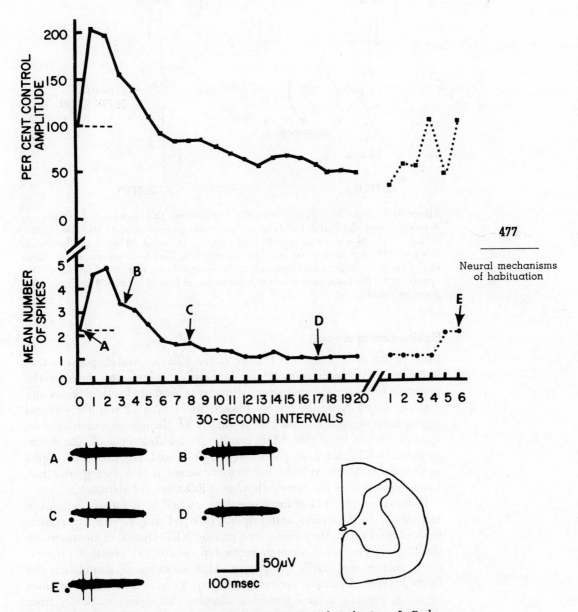

Thompson, R. F. A dual-process theory of habituation: Neural mechanisms. In Peeke, H. V. S., and Herz, M. J. (eds.). *Habituation, Physiological Substrates* II. New York: Academic Press, 1973, pp. 175–205.) On the right, the same kinds of information are represented about a different type of interneuron that exhibits clear sensitization as well as habituation. (From Groves, P. M., DeMarco, R., and Thompson, R. F. Habituation and sensitization of spinal interneuron activity in acute spinal cat. *Brain Res.* 14, 1969, pp. 521–525.)

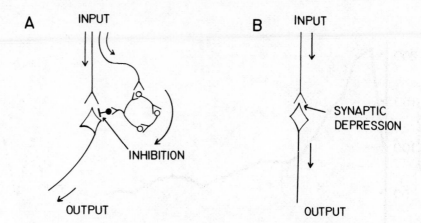

A INPUT

B INPUT

SYNAPTIC
DEPRESSION

INHIBITION

OUTPUT

OUTPUT

Figure 11.7 Two hypothetical synaptic mechanisms that explain habituation. A, A reverberating circuit that builds up activity leading to postsynaptic inhibition on the output neuron as a result of repeated activation of the input. When it can be tested, this possibility has been ruled out experimentally. B, The development of some form of depression or decreased transmission at the synapse being repeatedly activated. This appears to be the basic mechanism of habituation, at least in simplified systems where it can be tested.

Habituation of arousal

Perhaps the most prominent feature of the EEG arousal response is that it habituates in both animals and humans. A common example is the orienting response. When a novel stimulus is presented suddenly, an animal (or man) typically orients toward the source of stimulus—points appropriate receptors toward it. A variety of changes in autonomic responses, such as heart rate, EDR, respiration, and brain waves, also occur, as noted in Chapter 9. In particular, EEG arousal, the shift from alpha or slow waves to low-voltage, fast activity waves, occurs during orienting. Upon repetition of the novel stimulus, EEG arousal habituates.

Habituation of EEG arousal was first studied in detail in the classic experiment by Sharpless and Jasper (1956). Using repeated presentations of brief tones, they found that cortical EEG arousal of the normally sleeping cat (recorded through implanted electrodes) becomes progressively shorter and finally disappears. After cessation of stimulation the arousal response exhibits spontaneous recovery over a period of minutes or hours. Further, a strong sudden stimulus that differs markedly from the habituating stimulus causes dishabituation of the EEG arousal to the original stimulus. One very interesting aspect of Sharpless and Jasper's experiment was the specificity of the EEG arousal habituation in terms of stimulus characteristics. If the EEG arousal response of the sleeping animal was habituated to presentations of a 500-cycle tone to the point at which no arousal occurred, a 1000-cps tone would elicit strong EEG

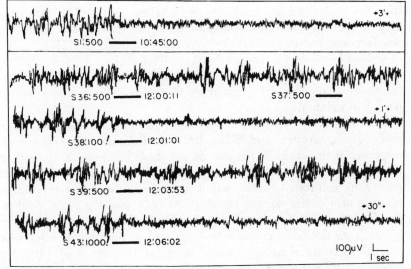

Neural mechanisms
of habituation

Figure 11.8 Cortical electrograms from the suprasylvian gyrus of a normal cat showing typical habituation of the arousal reaction to a 500-cycle tone after about 30 trials. In the first tracing the response to the first presentation of the 500-cycle tone is shown (SI: 500). The solid bar shows the duration of the stimulus followed by the time in hours, minutes, and seconds (10:45:00). In the second tracing are shown the 36th and 37th trials (S36 and S37). Then a novel tone of 100 cycles is presented in the 38th trial (S38:100!) followed by a repetition of the habituated tone (S39:500) and then another novel tone (S43:1000!). The figures at the right above the EEG traces indicate the duration of the activation in each trial. (From Sharpless, H., and Jasper, H. H. Habituation of the arousal reaction. *Brain* **79**, 1956, pp. 655–680.)

arousal (Fig. 11.8). However, if a 600-cps tone was presented after habituation to the 500-cps tone, no EEG arousal occurred. In behavioral terminology this could be described as an auditory frequency generalization gradient for EEG arousal.

The human alpha blocking response, which resembles EEG arousal in the cat, has been shown to habituate to tactile, auditory, and visual stimulation by Sokolov and his associates in the Soviet Union (Sokolov, 1960). Glickman and Feldman (1961) demonstrated that peripheral receptors are probably not involved in habituation of EEG arousal to sensory stimulation. They induced cortical EEG arousal by electrical stimulation through electrodes implanted in the midbrain reticular formation in animals. Under these conditions habituation of EEG arousal occurred just as it did in earlier experiments using tones.

Following Sharpless and Jasper's studies great interest developed in habituation as a fundamental form of behavioral plasticity. As noted above it occurs for virtually all behavioral responses and for many brain responses as well. A number of investigators have reported *evoked response* habituation to various types of stimuli at most levels of the CNS, from first-order sensory nuclei to the cerebral cortex. The first experiment to report evoked response habituation was that of Hernández-Peón, Scherrer, and Jouvet (1956); they recorded responses to click stimulation at several levels of the auditory system. Trains of clicks were delivered once every two seconds for long periods of time and evoked responses of the cochlear nucleus (the first relay of the auditory system) were reported to habituate.

Careful studies by Worden and associates (see Worden and Marsh, 1963; Marsh, Worden, and Hicks, 1962) demonstrated that click evoked responses at the cochlear nucleus do not show habituation. Instead, amplitudes of responses at this first relay nucleus in the auditory system are rigidly controlled by the physical properties of the sound stimulus. Because of acoustic factors, the intensity of a sound is often weaker at the floor of a test cage. If an animal gradually became bored and rested his head on the floor, cochlear nucleus evoked response to click would decrease because of reduced sound intensity. Webster et al. (1965) did report a rapid initial decrease in amplitude of sound evoked responses in cochlear nucleus under carefully controlled acoustic conditions to stimuli given faster than 1 per sec but this probably represents a primary recovery cycle phenomenon more than habituation.

In an extensive and careful study Wickelgren (1968) found that habituation of evoked responses to auditory stimuli was not prominent below the level of the thalamus and cortex in the auditory system. This appears to be a general finding in all sensory systems—the ascending relay nuclei do not exhibit habituation (Thompson and Spencer, 1966). However, recent multiple unit studies indicate that some neurons, even at the level of the cochlear nucleus, may show response decrement to repeated sounds (Buchwald and Humphrey, 1973). It would be most surprising if there were marked habituation in sensory systems. If our sensory systems habituated to sensory stimuli, we would rapidly cease to have sensation—a most unadaptive state of affairs. However, behavioral responses, and phenomena that seem to be related to the probability of behavioral responding, such as EEG arousal and autonomic signs of orienting, show marked habituation. It is very adaptive to cease *responding* to arousing stimuli that have no particular significance.

Theories of habituation

On the basis of the studies on properties of spinal interneurons showing habituation and sensitization of response to repeated stimulation noted above, Groves and Thompson (1970) developed a general dual-process theory of habituation (Figs. 11.9 and 11.10). The central idea is that in the intact animal two independent processes of habituation and sen-

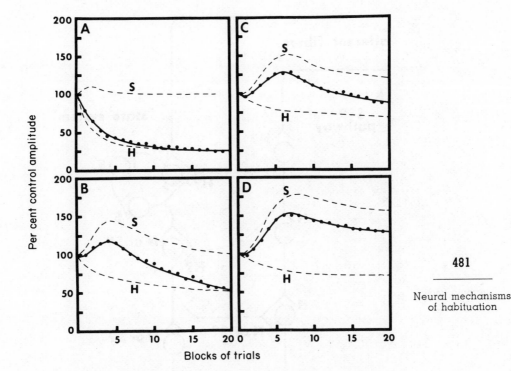

Figure 11.9 Basic idea of dual-process theory of habituation. Processes of sensitization and habituation (broken lines) occur to varying extents as a function of stimulus and training conditions and interact to produce final behavioral outcome (solid lines and dots are actual behavioral results for flexion reflex). (From Groves, P. M., and Thompson, R. F. Habituation: A dual-process theory. *Psych. Rev.* **77**, 1970, pp. 419–450. Copyright 1970 by the American Psychological Association. Reprinted by permission.)

sitization develop to repeated stimulation. Presumably these are mediated by different neural systems and mechanisms. The behavioral response to repeated stimulation is the net result of the interaction of these two processes. With strong stimuli, sensitization will predominate and with weak stimuli habituation will be most prominent; see Figure 11.9 for examples. This dual-process view permits predictions of the form of habituation in a wide range of phenomena, including orienting responses of intact humans.

The dual-process theory of habituation may be contrasted with Sokolov's model-comparator theory. Sokolov's model is indicated in Figure 11.11. He developed the model to account for results of his work on human orienting. In essence, he assumed that the cerebral cortex forms a model of a repeated stimulus. The reticular formation serves as a model-comparator amplifier—if the stimulus changes the reticular formation produces an increase in arousal. Sokolov's model accounts particularly

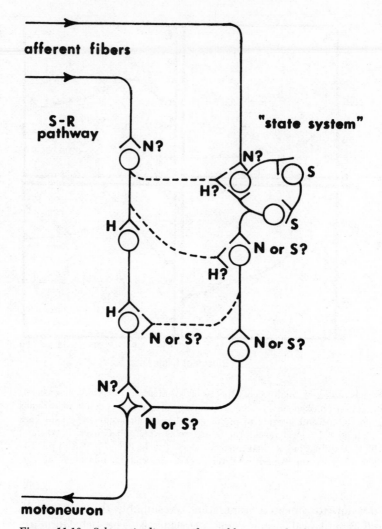

afferent fibers

S-R pathway

"state system"

motoneuron

Figure 11.10 Schematic diagram of possible neuronal substrates of habituation and sensitization. (N indicates nonplastic synapses; H indicates habituation synapses; S indicates sensitizing synapses.) (From Groves, P. M., and Thompson, R. F. Habituation: A dual-process theory. *Psych. Rev.* 77, 1970, pp. 419–450. Copyright 1970 by the American Psychological Association. Reprinted by permission.)

well for the interesting phenomena of sensitization or dishabituation to a stimulus that is reduced in intensity. To a person used to hearing a moderately loud stimulus, a reduction or absence of stimulation is very arousing. City dwellers find the silence of the forest "deafening"! These interesting phenomena can also be explained in the dual-process theory (Thompson et al., 1973). Although the reader can no doubt guess the author's bias, it would be premature to assess the relative success of the

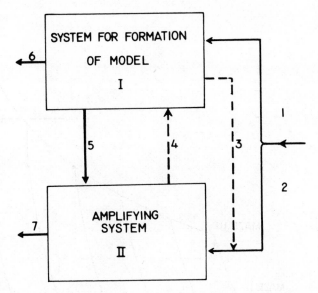

Figure 11.11 Sokolov's model of habituation involving comparator and amplifier components. A model develops against which are compared new stimuli. If they differ from the habituating stimulus an increased response will result. (From Sokolov, E. N. Neuronal models and the orienting reflex. In Brazier, M. A. B. (ed.). *The Central Nervous System and Behavior*. New York: Josiah Macy Jr. Foundation, 1960, pp. 187–276.)

dual-process theory and Sokolov's model-comparator theory at present. The interested reader is urged to consult the recent two-volume work on habituation edited by Peeke and Herz (1973) for extensive discussion of these issues.

LEARNING—THE SEARCH FOR THE ENGRAM

The work of Karl Lashley at Harvard began the search for the engram. Lashley was initially an "S-R" behaviorist. Following Watson's general point of view, Lashley assumed that learning consisted in the establishment of a series of specific new reflex pathways from stimulus to response. These new discrete connections through the brain were termed *engrams*. Lashley further assumed that these connections involved the cerebral cortex—early work in Pavlov's laboratory indicated that conditioned responses could not be learned by dogs after removal of the cerebral cortex.

Lashley's work culminated in his famous 1929 monograph, "Brain mechanisms and intelligence." He trained rats on three mazes varying in difficulty from easy to very difficult and then removed portions of the cerebral cortex. The lesions varied systematically in location and size, ranging from about 10 per cent to more than 50 per cent of the cortex.

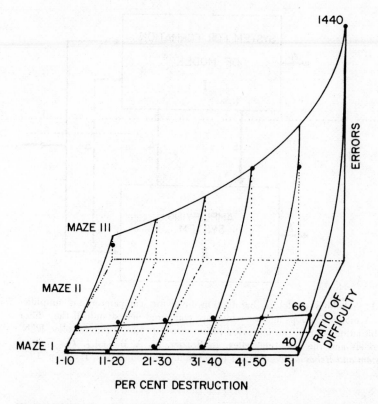

1440

ERRORS

MAZE III

MAZE II

RATIO OF DIFFICULTY

66

MAZE I

40

1-10   11-20   21-30   31-40   41-50   51

PER CENT DESTRUCTION

Figure 11.12 Results of Karl Lashley's search for the engram. Errors by groups of rats on three mazes of increasing difficulty (I, II, III) after various sizes of cortical lesions are plotted. Amount of damage was critical and location in cortex was not, but large effects occurred only with the most difficult maze. (Redrawn from Lashley, K. S. *Brain Mechanisms and Intelligence*. Chicago: Univ. of Chicago Press. Copyright © 1929 by the University of Chicago Press.)

Animals were then retrained on the mazes. The results of the experiment are shown in Figure 11.12. There is a clear effect of size of lesion which varies as a function of maze difficulty. Animals with large lesions could do relatively well on the easiest maze but were virtually unable to learn the most difficult maze. Even more important, the location of the lesion on the cerebral cortex made no difference. These results led Lashley to formulate his *principles of mass action*—the amount of cortex removed is critical—and *equipotentiality*—all areas of the cortex are equally important. These unexpected results, especially the finding that the particular area of cortex destroyed was unimportant, still pose a fundamental problem for analysis of the engram. If the engram for a particular learned behavior were located in a particular place in the brain, the powerful armamentarium of modern electrophysiology and biochemistry

484

Learning and
memory

could be brought to bear on the mechanisms of engram formation. Unfortunately Lashley's demonstration that the engram cannot be localized remains generally true today.

A few more words are in order about the engram. It is a purely hypothetical change in the brain as a result of learning; no one has ever found an engram. On the other hand, the engram must exist. All behavior simply reflects the actions of the nervous system. The nervous system, in turn, is nothing more than a highly complicated physical-chemical system. Consequently, any changes in behavior due to learning must reflect changes in the nervous system, which means physical-chemical alteration. These are the "engrams." Clearly, however, an engram does not develop at one particular locus in the brain. Perhaps the most successful theoretical view of the general nature of the engram is Hebb's theory (1949) of cell assemblies. The basic idea is that the changes that occur during learning develop among interconnections throughout wide areas of the brain. A particular kind of learning involves development of particular circuits, but they are widespread and the individual elements (neurons) may participate in many engrams.

The fact that the engram does not appear to be localized should not be taken to mean that there is no functional localization in the brain. There obviously is. One of the most important qualifications of Lashley's equipotentiality hypothesis was pointed out by Walter Hunter at Brown University. A complex task like maze-learning involves visual, auditory, tactile, and kinesthetic cues for the animal. If he were blinded and deafened, he would not do as well. For purposes of analysis of the engram, tasks that involve only a single sensory modality are simpler.

Actually, all natural learning that occurs in the "real" world would probably involve more than one modality. Humans tend to recode visual information in verbal terms for storage. Even animal learning studies in the laboratory usually use a sense modality for reward or punishment that differs from the training stimulus (CS) modality. Food reward or electric shock punishment are commonly used for visual and auditory discriminations. In some very interesting work John Garcia et al. (1968) has shown that certain types of punishment work much better for certain types of stimulus training cues. A natural example is "bait-shyness"; once poisoned, wild animals avoid such baits in the future. Specifically, Garcia used either the size or the flavor of food pellets as the CS and paired these with shock punishment or sickness due to X-radiation in rats. The measure of conditioning was amount of decrease in food consumption in response to either of the food cues. The results were striking (Fig. 11.13). The shock punishment was very effective in reducing eating when paired with pellet siize but ineffective when paired with flavor. In contrast, X-radiation sickness was effective in reducing eating when paired with flavor but not when paired with size. Garcia argues that the effective pairings of cues and punishments "go together" in terms of cen-

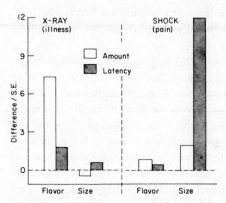

Figure 11.13 Rats were trained with taste (flavor) or size to avoid food pellets. Punishment was X-radiation sickness or electric shock. They learned to avoid X-rays by taste (bait-shyness) and shock by size but could not associate taste and shock or size and sickness. (Redrawn from Garcia, J. et al. Cues: Their relative effectiveness as a function of the reinforcer. *Science* **160**, 1968, pp. 794–795. Copyright 1968 by the American Association for the Advancement of Science.)

tral neural convergence of the afferent inputs. The pathways for taste relate to pathways involved in aftereffects of eating (sickness)—both gustatory and visceral receptors converge in a brain stem nucleus (*N. fasciculus soletarius*). In contrast, the pathways for external sense receptors for vision and hearing relate more closely to external sources of punishment like foot shock and tend to converge in certain regions of the forebrain and cerebral cortex.

There have been a large number of studies in which various portions of the brain have been damaged in an attempt to locate the critical brain structures for particular learned tasks. These studies have provided a great amount of information about the possible functions of the damaged areas but have not provided answers to the fundamental question of the locus of the engram. Only a very brief overview of this huge body of literature is presented here.

Destruction of the lower relay nuclei in the primary sensory systems essentially eliminates learning based on sensory information. This comes as no great surprise—if an animal's eyes are removed he cannot learn responses to visual stimuli. There is a relatively clear effect of removing the visual area of the cerebral cortex in animals from rat to man. As Lashley first demonstrated, pattern vision is lost following complete destruction of visual cortex. Animals can still discriminate brightness but not pattern, for example, vertical stripes vs. horizontal stripes.

There is a fundamental problem of interpretation in all this work insofar as learning is concerned. Does destruction of the visual cortex destroy the learned engrams for visual pattern discrimination or does it merely remove the sensory coding mechanisms that serve to analyze the physical properties of the visual stimulus quite independent of learning. You will remember the work of Hubel and Wiesel showing that neurons in visual cortex code edges, lines and even "angles" and "tongues," and that this coding seems to be present at birth. In the author's view, this latter alternative is more likely. Destruction of visual cortex is analogous to removing the eyes—it eliminates the prewired stimulus coding of patterned visual stimuli necessary for the animal to learn to respond to the correct pattern.

Robert Thompson at Louisiana State University completed a systematic study of effects of brain lesions on visual pattern discrimination in rat (Thompson and Thorne, 1973). His experiment was modeled on Lashley's original approach except that he systematically made lesions throughout the entire brain, rather than just cerebral cortex, and used a very specific visual task. He found, as expected, that destruction of visual cortex prevented learning. More important, there was one other area that seemed to be critical. Damage to a region of the brain at the junction of the midbrain and thalamus in an area sometimes termed the posterior nucleus of the thalamus in rats seemed also to cause marked impairment. This is a most intriguing result. The area is not visual in function but may have some general significance for visual learning. Robert Thompson's unexpected finding is one of the few indications of a localized region in the brain, other than sensory systems, that can produce a clear deficit in learning.

More complex aspects of visual discrimination appear to involve association areas of the cortex, at least in primates and man. They seem to be involved in particular complex aspects of visual function such as very complex pattern discrimination and spatial orientation rather than visual learning per se (see Chapter 12).

Results of damage to the auditory cortex are less clear than those for visual cortex. There is some impairment in sound localization and rather complicated partial deficits in auditory frequency and "pattern" discrimination (see Thompson, 1967 and Neff, 1961, for further discussion). The auditory cortex is clearly involved in more complex aspects of auditory discrimination but auditory learning per se cannot be said to have its home in the auditory cortex or lower auditory relay nuclei.

To summarize, complex sensory learning requires the sensory areas of the cerebral cortex. However, these areas do not appear to be the critical regions for sensory learning. What regions of the brain are essential for learning? Pavlov believed that the cerebral cortex was critical for the formation of conditioned reflexes, at least in higher vertebrates. However, several investigators have succeeded in conditioning decorticate dogs and cats to sounds and lights (Bromily, 1948). Learning requiring utilization of more complex sensory cues is difficult for the decorticate animal because of the absence of the elaborate sensory analyzing mechanisms of the cerebral cortex. It is a mistake to conclude that, because conditioning can occur in decorticate animals, the cerebral cortex is not important for learning. All the learning of any importance done by humans most definitely does require the cerebral cortex. A decorticate human is little more than a reflex machine. Language, comprehension, all aspects of learning that have adaptive value are abolished if the cerebral cortex is destroyed. Nonetheless the point remains that the basic physical-chemical mechanisms of engram formation can occur below the level of the cerebral cortex.

There has been little systematic study of the learning capacities of the decerebrate animal. Lower animals who are normally "decerebrate" can exhibit simple learning—the earthworm can learn a T maze (Yerkes, 1906). Incidental observations by Bard and Macht (1958) on chronic decerebrate cats which had all neural tissue above the level of the midbrain and hypothalamus removed suggest that very simple learning may occur in this preparation.

Recovery of function

An interesting aspect of the effect of brain lesions on learning is that organisms generally show marked long-term recovery from the immediate loss. The studies reviewed above indicating that removal of visual cortex in higher animals led to permanent loss of pattern vision must be qualified in at least two respects. First, if the tissue is removed in infancy many aspects of visual function return as the animal matures (Doty, 1961; Wetzel et al., 1965). Second, if lesions are done in several stages, i.e., first one hemisphere and then the other, recovery of visual function can be markedly improved (D. Meyer, 1958; P. Meyer, 1963).

The recovery from infant lesions is not limited to vision—similar recovery of function following infant brain damage has been found for many types of tasks, even those involving association cortex (see Thompson, 1967; P. Meyer, 1973 for reviews). Perhaps the most striking recovery of all is in human language. Removal of the left "language" hemisphere in children under the age of about 10-12 usually is followed by complete recovery of speech (see Chapter 12 for details).

An important aspect of recovery of function following brain damage is the possibility that we may learn more about the formation of engrams by examining how they reconstitute themselves following damage (see Eidelberg and Stein, 1974). Recent work on this approach has emphasized the anatomical reorganization and regrowth of brain systems following damage. Contrary to the older view, there is considerable regrowth of nerve tissues in the central nervous system following damage. However, for a variety of reasons the original tissue is not regenerated; rather, new fibers grow and new synaptic terminals are formed. The classical demonstration of the occurrence of this *sprouting* of new connections was done in spinal cord (McCouch et al., 1958).

We will describe one recent and intriguing example of sprouting by Lynch, Cotman, and associates in the Department of Psychobiology at the University of California at Irvine to illustrate the phenomenon (see Lynch, 1974; Cotman et al., 1973). They utilized the fact that different pathways to the hippocampus involved different synaptic transmitters. Specifically, a pathway from septum appears to be an acetylcholine (ACh) system—the synaptic transmitter from these fibers to hippocampal neurons is ACh. They go only to certain layers of the hippocampus and their terminations can be identified easily by use of a stain for the enzyme AChE. Another pathway projecting to other layers of the hippocampus and originating in the entorhinal cortex does not involve ACh as a transmitter. Lynch and Cotman destroyed this latter non-ACh path in rats and stained the hippocampus for AChE at varying times after lesion. They found a marked increase in the presence of AChE in the layers of hippocampus normally innervated by the lesioned (non-ACh) path. The effect was apparent at 4 days in adults and by 48 hours in infant rats and developed to a profound degree over the course of a few days.

In brief, what appears to have happened is as follows. The non-ACh terminals from the entorhinal pathway began degenerating immediately after lesion. The ACh pathway from the septum sprouted new ACh fibers and terminals which grew out and came to establish ACh synapses on the layers of the hippocampus that were "freed up" by the degeneration of synaptic terminals from the non-ACh pathway. This striking example of sprouting in the brain illustrates the rapidity with which new and possibly functional synapses can form, even in the adult brain. What role such sprouting may play in behavior, particularly in the formation of engrams, remains to be determined but the possibilities are most intriguing.

Gerald Schneider at MIT has described the possible growth or at least expansion of certain anatomical pathways to account for the marked recovery of function in animals with lesions in infancy. He used hamsters and replicated the earlier work showing that visual discrimination learning was much superior when cortical area 17 was removed from both hemispheres in infancy, compared to adult lesions. These animals with lesions in infancy showed alterations in visual pathways involving a subcortical visual center, the superior colliculus (Schneider, 1973; 1974).

In the case of sprouting in the spinal cord, functional connections are established which lead to aberrant behavior—the exaggerated flexion reflexes characteristic of long-term chronic spinal animals and humans. Whether the sprouting that occurs in various brain systems following damage is actually related either to normal recovery of function or to the process of engram formation remains to be determined.

Spinal conditioning

Spinal conditioning has been a subject of much controversy in psychology. In view of our greatly increased recent understanding of synaptic mechanisms involved in spinal reflexes, we would have a much better chance of analyzing the synaptic basis of learning if conditioning could be demonstrated to occur in the acute neurally isolated spinal cord. An important series of papers by Shurrager, Culler, and colleagues (e.g., Shurrager and Culler, 1940) reported classical conditioning of the hind limb flexion reflex in the acute spinal dog. Subsequent experiments by another group (Kellogg, 1947) reported entirely negative results. The negative findings of Kellogg and colleagues have tended to receive greater weight. This is perhaps unfortunate in view of the extreme importance of spinal conditioning as a model system. Kellogg's experiments did not reproduce the procedures of Shurrager. In fact they seem designed in such a way as to load the dice against the possible development of conditioning.

More recent studies have reported positive results (Buerger and Dawson, 1968; Fitzgerald and Thompson, 1967). An example of a recent study from the author's laboratory is shown in Figure 11.14 (Patterson, Cegavske, and Thompson, 1973). Cats were anesthetized, spinal cord sectioned and hind limb nerves (below the level of section) dissected out for stimulation and recording, and the animal paralyzed and allowed to recover from anesthesia. Paralysis prevents spontaneous movements —the behavioral response is the reflex discharge conducted out the motor nerves to muscles. As seen in Figure 11.14 animals given paired CS and US cutaneous stimuli (a classical conditioning paradigm) show significant conditioning whereas animals given unpaired stimuli or CS alone show no conditioning.

Spinal conditioning, per se, is probably of no importance in the normal behavior of the intact mammal. Its significance lies in the fact that the spinal cord can serve as a simplified model system where some degree of analysis of the basic neural processes underlying learning could be achieved. There is no necessary reason why the spinal cord should not exhibit plasticity. Anatomically it is not a simple neural structure but contains a very complex core of interneurons resembling that of higher brain structures.

Brain stimulation

Electrical stimulation of the brain has been widely used as a tool to search for the engram. The now classical experiments by Loucks (1933) and Brogden and Gantt (1942) were among the first successful attempts to combine electrical stimulation of the brain with behavioral conditioning procedures. Loucks demonstrated that animals could easily be conditioned to respond to an electrical stimulus (conditioned stimulus)

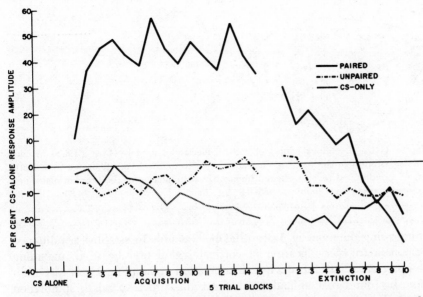

Figure 11.14 Spinal conditioning. The hind limb flexion reflex (actually amplitude of motor nerve volley) was conditioned in acute paralyzed spinal cats. Unpaired (CS and US not paired in time) and CS-only controls did not show learning. (From Patterson, M. M., Cegavske, C. F., and Thompson, R. F. Effects of a classical conditioning paradigm on hind-limb flexor nerve response in immobilized spinal cats. *J. Comp. Physiol. Psychol.* **84**, 1973, pp. 88–97. Copyright 1973 by the American Psychological Association. Reprinted by permission.)

delivered through electrodes implanted in the auditory area of the cortex. Loucks and colleagues were able to demonstrate that if a repeated electrical stimulus was given to the auditory cortex, paired with shock to the foot, the leg flexion response became conditioned to electrical stimulation of the auditory cortex. More recently, Doty and colleagues (e.g., Doty and Rutledge, 1959) and others have confirmed and extended these observations. They found that electrical stimulation of several regions of the cortex, including auditory, visual, somatic-sensory, and suprasylvian areas, could serve as the conditioned stimulus. The animal would learn to flex his leg upon presentation of the cortical stimulus.

In view of Penfield's work, it is not surprising that animals can be conditioned to electrical stimulation of the sensory cortex. Patients report buzzing sounds when the auditory cortex is electrically stimulated, light flashes when the visual cortex is stimulated, and tingling in the appropriate body regions when the somatic-sensory cortex is stimulated (Penfield and Rasmussen, 1950). The brain stimulus apparently can serve as a conditioned stimulus in a somewhat analogous manner to a peripheral stimulus.

It would seem that animals can be trained to respond to electrical stimulation of almost any region of the cerebral cortex. In an extensive

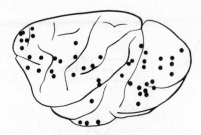

Figure 11.15 Locations (dots) of cortical electrodes used by Doty (1965) as conditioned stimuli in the monkey (macaque). All were effective. (Redrawn from Doty, R. W. Conditioned reflexes elicited by electrical stimulation of the brain in macaques. *J. Neurophysiol.* **28**, 1965b, pp. 623–640.)

study using the monkey, Doty (1965b) was able to establish conditioned responses to every location of cortical stimulation he used, including the prefrontal and infratemporal association areas (Fig. 11.15). In addition, he found that animals could be trained to respond to stimulation of one location but to not respond to stimulation of another point (i.e., discrimination). If both electrodes were in the visual cortex, animals could discriminate between electrodes less than 1 mm apart. This finding is consistent with the fact that animals can discriminate between peripheral visual stimuli that activate different areas of the retina (i.e., pattern discrimination). Much more unexpected is the finding that monkeys can also discriminate between electrodes placed close together in the so-called "silent" prefrontal association area of the cortex.

Results of brain stimulation studies indicate that stimulation almost anywhere in the brain can serve as a conditioned stimulus. These findings are most interesting and may someday have very real practical benefits. Some aspects of vision may someday be restored to the blind by direct stimulation of the visual cortex. However this approach has not taken us much farther in the search for the engram.

Brain activity during learning

With the advent of the techniques and instruments to record the electrical activity of the brain, it was believed that an ideal tool had been found to search for the engram.

EEG-alpha blocking. Investigations of the relations between electrical measures of brain activity and learning represent one of the most vigorous and rapidly growing fields in the study of brain and behavior. Most studies have been concerned with the electrical activity of the cerebral cortex, particularly with EEG arousal and evoked responses. Two quite different approaches to the problem have been used. The more direct but less common method has been simply to record brain activity during the course of a standardized learning experiment, usually either classical or instrumental conditioning. Much more frequently the brain activity itself has been used as the response to be conditioned. Thus if a stimulus elicits some kind of neural activity such as EEG arousal, a neutral stimulus is paired with the first until the neutral stimulus alone elicits EEG arousal. This latter method has been characterized as *sensory-sensory conditioning* or *neural conditioning* because no behavioral responses or measures are used; stimuli are presented and brain activity is recorded. We will use the somewhat neutral term, *EEG conditioning*, here.

EEG conditioning was first reported by Durup and Fessard (1935). They observed that when a camera shutter click had been paired with a light flash, the latter being used to induce EEG-alpha block (EEG arousal), the click alone could serve to block alpha activity. While there is not complete agreement concerning the comparability of EEG spindling in the cat or dog and EEG-alpha in man (see discussion in Chapter 10), it is probably possible to compare "EEG arousal" in the experimental animal with "EEG-alpha blocking" in humans. We will consider both animal studies in which EEG arousal was conditioned and human studies in which EEG-alpha blocking was conditioned.

Durup and Fessard's procedure has served as the prototype for most subsequent experiments on EEG conditioning. A typical human experiment might be carried out as follows (Fig. 11.16). Subjects exhibiting good alpha activity are selected (usually about one-third of normal adults show clear alpha activity). During the experiment the various stimuli are presented only at times when the EEG shows clear alpha activity. The response to be conditioned is blocking of this alpha activity by the stimuli; the blocking appears as a sudden shift from alpha waves to the low-voltage fast activity of EEG arousal. A steady or flickering light is commonly used as the UCS; presentation of the light during a period of EEG alpha activity produces alpha blocking. A tone is commonly used as the CS. One problem in EEG conditioning is that initially almost any type of stimulus causes alpha blocking. Thus the first few presentations of the tone CS alone will cause alpha blocking, the response to be conditioned to the tone! Consequently a series of habituation trials of tone presentaion are always given before the conditioning procedure itself. The tone is repeatedly presented until it no longer causes alpha blocking. Tone is then paired with light for a series of trials, and the tone is then given alone in a series of test trials. Typically, with these procedures, after paired presentations of tone and light, the tone alone will cause alpha blocking in a large proportion of cases.

In evaluation of the current status of EEG conditioning, several problems that are somewhat unique to this field must be considered (see Diamond and Chow, 1962). If the EEG-alpha blocking response to tone

Procedure	Resulting EEG to tone CS ( )

Initial tone presentation

Habituation training to
tone presentations

Pairings of tone CS
and light UCS

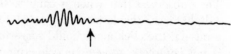

Figure 11.16 Typical conditions used in human EEG conditioning. A series of tones is presented, unpaired with light, until tone alone does not cause alpha blocking. Tone and light are then paired for a few trials until alpha blocking is again elicited by tone. (From Thompson, R. F. *Foundations of Physiological Psychology*. New York: Harper & Row, 1967.)

is habituated, and a series of paired tone-lights presented, the alpha blocking response to tone reappears, albeit somewhat variably. All studies are consistent in reporting this observation. However, if only a series of lights are presented instead of tone-light pairings, the alpha blocking response also reappears. Consequently, it would seem that conditioned alpha blocking resembles sensitization more closely than it resembles conditioning. This is *not* to say that the phenomenon is uninteresting and undeserving of careful and extensive investigation. It is a reversible change in the behavior of an index of neural activity as a result of experience or training. The degree and specificity of the changes that can be induced in alpha blocking, as in a careful and extensive early study by Jasper and Shagass (1941), emphasize this point.

A number of experimenters have analyzed changes in EEG arousal during the course of actual behavioral conditioning. Chow (1961) completed an extensive and careful analysis of EEG arousal changes in the temporal lobe during learning of visual discriminations by monkeys. His findings were somewhat disappointing. Only transient EEG arousal occurred and only during the initial acquisition phase of the experiment. Morrell (1961) concluded on the basis of a survey of the literature that EEG arousal is more widespread on the cortex during initial stages of training and gradually becomes limited to the sensory cortical field of the CS (i.e., auditory cortex for tone CS) and also to the motor cortex if the CS serves to elicit a motor response.

The most general finding of such studies has been that EEG arousal occurs at the beginning of learning, but tends to disappear as learning proceeds. *There is no close correlation between the degree of EEG arousal and the degree of learning.* In this connection we might recall the studies of Bradley (see Chapter 9; and Key and Bradley, 1959) in which animals with permanent EEG synchrony (spindling), induced by prior administration of atropine, exhibited normal learning in several types of learning situations. EEG arousal is not a necessary concomitant of learning, or very closely correlated with degree of learning.

Evoked responses. The general picture of cortical evoked response changes associated with learning resembles the EEG literature in many ways. Results of most studies are consistent in indicating that on the first few paired CS-UCS conditioning trials, cortical evoked responses to the CS increase markedly in amplitude, at least in situations in which the unconditioned stimulus is shock or other aversive stimulation. As in EEG studies there have been two types of conditioning procedures: *sensory-sensory* in which the evoked response amplitude itself serves as the conditioned response, and *conventional conditioning* in which evoked responses are also measured.

An experiment by Galambos, Sheatz, and Vernier (1956) was one of the first to report conditioned changes in evoked responses, and is a prototype of many subsequent experiments. Electrodes were implanted in auditory and visual areas of the cortex and a variety of subcortical regions in cats. The animals were given loud clicks once every three seconds for a period of days until the evoked response was reported to have habituated. A series of about ten strong shocks to the chest were then paired with clicks. Evoked response amplitudes increased markedly. If the shocks were then withheld the response to click diminished to the initial level. Examples of these data are shown in Figure 11.17. Repeated series of conditioning and extinction were obtained. Conditioning was also established in animals paralyzed with Flaxedil and artificially respirated. This control rules out the possibility of muscular response artifacts in the data.

There have been numerous experiments of this type in which the effects on neural evoked responses of pairing a response-evoking stimulus such as a click or a flash with shock or other aversive stimulus have been studied. The general consensus of such experiments is that when the click or other neutral response-evoking stimulus is paired with shocks there tends to be an increase in the amplitude of the evoked response. In general, it is the later components of gross evoked responses, particularly cortical responses, that exhibit the greatest degree of change. It must be emphasized that in most experiments no attempts were made to ascertain whether the evoked response increase reflected a conditioning process or a sensitization process. The reader may consult Morrell (1961)

EXTINGUISHED   CONDITIONED

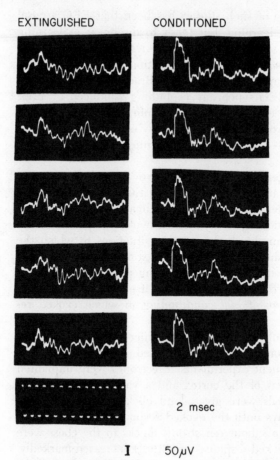

2 msec

I   50μV

Figure 11.17 Cochlear nucleus responses to successive identical click stimuli before ("extinguished") and after ("conditioned") application of three shocks to a cat. The increase in response magnitude after shocks as noted here was observed eight times in this animal. (From Galambos, R., Sheatz, G., and Vernier, V. G. Electrophysiological correlates of a conditioned response in cats. *Science* **123**, 1956, pp. 376–377. Copyright 1956 by the American Association for the Advancement of Science.)

and Thompson, Patterson, and Teyler (1972) for extensive reviews of the literature.

Several experiments have been oriented more toward correlating the changes in neural evoked responses with measures of behavioral conditioning. In an interesting experiment by Buchwald, Halas, and Schramm (1966), the technique of integrating massed unit discharges was employed to measure amount of nerve discharge activity during the course of conditioning. They implanted small (500 μ tip) steel electrodes in several locations in the auditory pathway and cortex (a tone CS was used), in the somatic-sensory pathway and cortex (they used a hind limb shock UCS), and in the reticular formation, and recorded unit hash activity during classical conditioning of the hind limb flexion reflex in normal cats. They reported that activity in response to the tone CS increased in the auditory system and reticular formation when the UCS was first given, and continued to increase during training. In contrast, little or no activity was present in the somatic-sensory system in response to the CS prior to the appearance of overt conditioned responses. No backward conditioning controls were used to investigate possible sensitization effects in this situation.

Studies by Hall and Mark (1967) indicate that emotional factors may play an important role in changes in evoked response amplitude when shock is used for training. They found that evoked responses in higher auditory structure to sound stimuli could be increased following shock, presumably due to fear. Using a conditioned fear technique (see discussion in Chapter 9), they found that wherever circumstances were such that the animals displayed conditioned fear, brain evoked responses to sound were larger. In short, whenever the animals were fearful, whether due to immediate effects of shock or to conditioned fear, evoked potentials increased. This suggests that evoked potential changes in amplitude may reflect emotional state of the animal more than any direct index of the developing memory trace.

Recent work by E. Roy John and associates (1973) indicates that waveforms of evoked responses may be more relevant to learning than amplitude. In an ingenious long-term series of experiments, cats were trained to make one kind of response—lever-press to avoid shock—if, for example, a 2 per sec light flash was given, and another response— jumping over a hurdle—if, for example, a 4 per sec light flash was given. After the animals had been very well trained in both tasks, characteristic late evoked potentials appeared in many brain regions. As shown in Figure 11.18, these potentials had different waveforms. The cats would sometimes behave correctly and sometimes incorrectly. Each time, just before the response was made, the correct waveform appeared that was characteristic of the *behavior* rather than the flash frequency. The details of these experiments are complex and involve computer analysis of individual brain responses. However, the overall result is clear and most interesting (see Fig. 11.18). John interprets the characteristic waveforms as the *memory readout potential*—a potential that reflects what he believes to be the very complex encoding by statistical ensembles of neurons of the learned behaviors. Alternatively they may reflect the initial events of a "motor" nature as the animal prepares to make one response or the other.

Karl Pribram at Stanford University has done most intriguing studies of the kinds of differential brain activity present during learning of difficult discriminations by monkeys for food reward (see Pribram, 1969). An example, shown in Figure 11.19, illustrates the effect of intention to respond. Potentials were recorded from the visual cortex. The monkey was given differing visual stimuli. Response to the correct stimulus

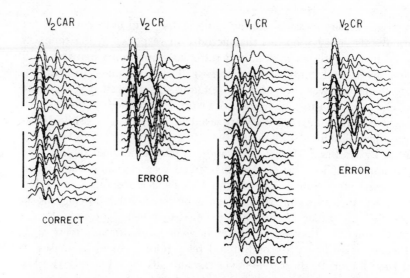

V₂ CAR   V₂ CR   V₁ CR   V₂ CR

CORRECT   ERROR   CORRECT   ERROR

Figure 11.18 Forms of brain evoked potentials to light flashes of two different frequencies (V_1 and V_2) in cats well trained to make two different behavioral responses (CAR = conditioned avoidance response; CR = conditioned lever press) to the two different flash rates. They often made errors in behavior. However, the waveforms of the brain potentials were typically characteristic of the behavior that would occur rather than the frequency of light flash. (From John, E. R. et al., Neural readout from memory. *J. Neurophysiol.* **36**, 1973, pp. 893–924.)

yielded a peanut; wrong responses were not rewarded. There are slight differences in the brain response to the differing stimuli ("stimulus events" column) but marked differences in brain responses in the visual cortex just prior to the animal making a response ("response events" column).

Analysis of single neuron activity in the brain during the course of learning is an enormously difficult but promising approach to the search for the engram. In a pioneering study, Jasper, Ricci, and Doane (1960) completed a very comprehensive analysis of single nerve cell discharges during the course of shock avoidance conditioning in monkeys. A flashing light served as the CS and hand shock as the UCS. The animal could avoid shock by withholding his hand when the light occurred. The monkeys were maintained in "living" chairs arranged in such a way that they could not reach the chronically implanted electrode equipment. Cell discharges from the motor cortex and the parietal cortex were studied during the development of a conditioned response and a differential response (shock avoidance for the 10 per sec light but no shock for a higher frequency light flash). Cells studied in the motor cortex tended to increase their firing rates prior to and during the actual occurrence of a conditioned hand withdrawal. Cell activity did not change in response to the higher differential frequency if no behavioral response occurred. Thus, as might be expected, cell discharges of the motor cortex tended

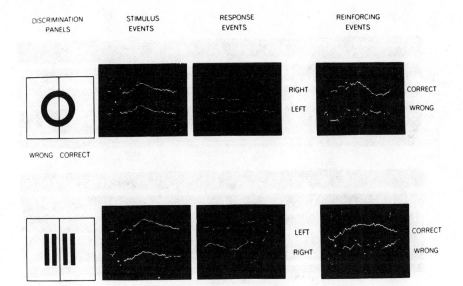

Figure 11.19 Results of visual-discrimination experiment are shown in the waveforms recorded from the striate (visual) cortex of a monkey. The waves are those recorded after he has learned the task described in the text. Under "stimulus events" are waveforms that appear immediately after the monkey has been shown a circle or stripes. The records under "response events" were generated just prior to the moment when the monkey actually responded by pressing either the left-hand or the right-hand half of the panel. The records under "reinforcing events" were produced when the monkey was rewarded with a peanut if he was correct or not rewarded if he was wrong. The correct response was to press the right-hand half of the panel on seeing a circle, the left-hand half on seeing stripes. A slight difference in the "stimulus" waveforms indicates whether the monkey has seen stripes or a circle. After he has learned his task well, sharp differences appear in the response and reinforcing panels. The response waveforms, which are actually "intention" waves, show one pattern (the one with the sharp peak) whenever the monkey is about to press the right-hand half of the panel, regardless of whether he has seen a circle or stripes. If he has actually seen stripes, of course, pressing the right-hand half of the panel is the wrong response. Thus the waveforms reflect his intention to press a particular half of the panel. They could hardly reveal whether his response is going to be right or wrong because at this point he still "thinks" he is about to make the correct response. (From Pribram, K. The neurophysiology of remembering. Copyright © 1969 by Scientific American, Inc. All rights reserved.)

to correlate with the occurrence of an actual behavioral movement. Cells of the parietal cortex, in contrast, tended to increase discharge rates during the CS period of the trial when a CR was given, but not during the actual occurrence of the CR (Fig. 11.20). On the other hand, they tended to be inhibited during presentation of the differential stimulus when no behavioral response was given.

A number of laboratories are now engaged in systematic analysis of changes in neuronal activity that develop during the course of learning

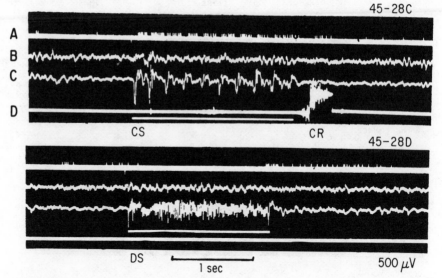

Figure 11.20 Two records of the same single nerve cell in parietal association cortex. The unit firing is increased and driven by the CS (above); unit is inhibited by the differential stimulus (below). A, microelectrode data; B, surface record from parietal cortex; C, surface record from occipital cortex; D, EMG and switch signal (CR). (From Jasper, H. H., Ricci, G. F., and Doane, B. Patterns of cortical neuronal discharge during conditioned responses in monkeys. In Wolstenholme, G. E. W., and O'Connor, C. M. (eds.) *Ciba Foundation Symposium, Neurological Basis of Behaviour.* London: Churchill, 1958, pp. 277–290.)

discrete responses under carefully controlled behavioral conditions—the work of Pribram's group at Stanford (1966), James Olds and associates (Olds et al., 1972) at the California Institute of Technology, E. Roy John's studies (John et al., 1973) in New York, the experiments of Woody and associates (Woody and Engel, 1972) at the University of California at Los Angeles, the studies of Cohen (1969) and associates at Virginia, and the author's laboratory at Harvard University (Thompson, Patterson, and Teyler, 1972; Thompson et al., 1973) provide current examples. The recent literature on this aspect of the search for the engram is large, complex, and difficult to assess. The reader may wish to consult a recent review of the neurophysiology of learning for a current summary (Thompson, Patterson, and Teyler, 1972). We will give just a few examples here.

Olds' ingenious experimental situation is illustrated in Figure 11.21. A rat with several microelectrodes permanently implanted in the brain is given a loud sound followed by delivery of a food pellet. Another wire is used to record head movements. As the procedure is repeated, the animal becomes conditioned to give head movements (e.g., looks toward the food dispenser) when the tone comes. After the food appears, the animal goes to it and eats. The basic training situation is thus classical conditioning of head movement to sound, using a food reward. Animals

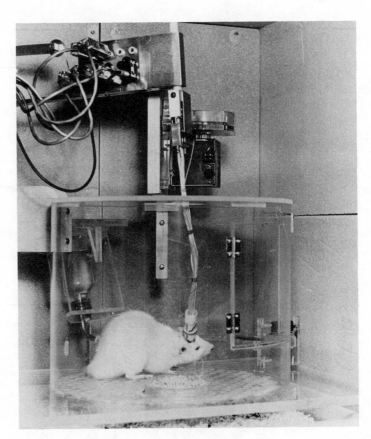

Figure 11.21 A, Cage with counterbalanced arm. B, Cage diagram. (From Olds, J. Multiple unit recordings from behaving rats. In Thompson, R. F., and Patterson, M. M. (eds.) *Bioelectric Recording Techniques, IA.* New York: Academic Press, 1973, pp. 165–198.)

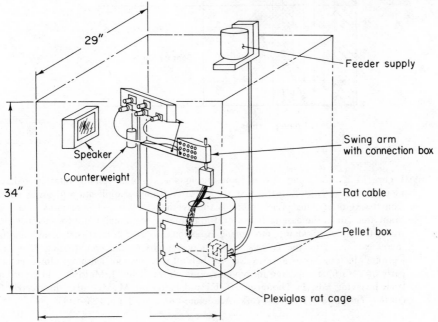

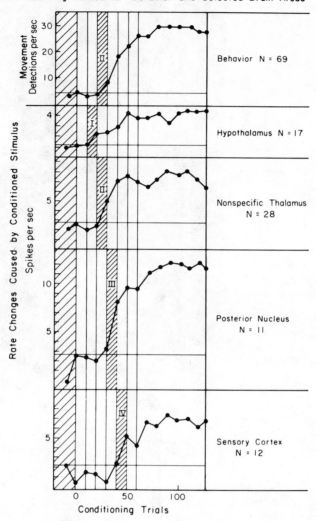

Figure 11.22 Learning curves representing average unit spiking rates or behavior identification rates during the first second after stimulus application given as change from background rates. Each point is the average for a number of units in a given brain area (or in the case of behavior, for a number of animals) and for ten successive trials. During conditioning, movement in response to the CS increased. Unit spike rate increases caused by the CS also rose to new highs during conditioning. The "unit learning" in some cases appeared to lag behind the behavior learning. However, very early unit learning appeared in hypothalamus. (From Olds, J. Multiple unit recordings from behaving rats. In Thompson, R. F., and Patterson, M. M. (eds.) *Bioelectric Recording Techniques, IA*. New York: Academic Press, 1973, pp. 165–198.)

were run for a number of hours until consistent conditioning had occurred; then they were given extinction training with no food reward. Single neuron activity was surveyed throughout the brain. Learned responses of neurons were categorized as those showing very short latency increases in responses.

Examples of single neuron learning curves are given in Figure 11.22. The unit in the posterior nucleus of the thalamus is particularly dramatic —there is an enormous increase in activity after training (which disappears after extinction). In one experiment Olds et al. studied 443 units —31 showed clear learned changes. Most of these were in the posterior nucleus of the thalamus, brain stem reticular formation, and one region of the hippocampus. The greatest number were in the posterior nucleus. This, incidentally, is an interesting correspondence with the lesion studies of Robert Thompson, mentioned above, showing that destruction of this region produces severe impairment in visual discriminations. Olds suggests that the posterior nucleus may be a region of early "nonspecific" learning.

There are a number of requirements for a particular kind of preparation to be maximally useful for analysis of the neurophysiology of learning. Ideally, the learning should occur in a single training session so activity of neurons can be held and tracked through the learning process; the behavior that is conditioned should show no sensitization or other nonassociative processes that can become confounded with the learning process; the characteristics of the learned behavior should be well known and under good control by the experimenter. That is, if learning can reliably be varied by changes in stimulus conditions, the critical brain events can be separated from neural processes that relate more to changes in performance. More detailed discussion of these issues is given in Thompson, Patterson, and Teyler (1972).

The critical requirement is that it must be possible to separate learning and performance. One example, taken from recent studies by Michael Gabriel and associates, illustrates the point well (see Gabriel, Wheeler, and Thompson, 1973a, b). Gabriel used shock avoidance learning of a running response to a tone CS by rabbits and recorded neural activity from "limbic" cortex during single session learning, and in subsequent tests of response to tone frequencies other than the training CS frequency. The results were striking. First, no neural response occurred to the tone CS early in training. However, as learned performance began to occur, learned activity developed in the limbic cortex. Upon tests of behavioral response to the CS and to other tone frequencies, animals tended initially to respond to all frequencies and then stopped responding to frequencies other than the training frequency. However, the brain response was relatively selective to the training frequency throughout. In other words, when the animals were first tested to tones other than the training CS frequency, the brain response predicted the behavioral

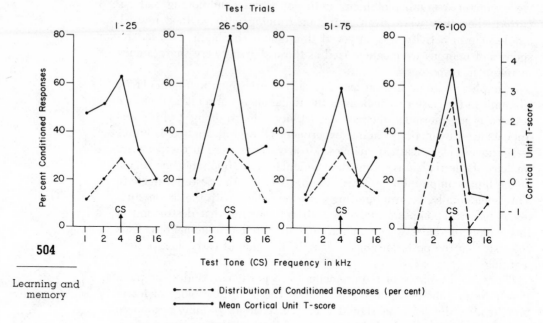

Per cent Conditioned Responses

Cortical Unit T-score

Test Tone (CS) Frequency in kHz

504

Learning and
memory

●- - - - -● Distribution of Conditioned Responses (per cent)
●————● Mean Cortical Unit T-score

Figure 11.23 Examples of neuronal activity (in nonspecific or limbic cortex of rabbit) that show stimulus control and predict the subsequent behavior that develops. Animals are trained (shock avoidance) to 2 k Hz tone and then tested to 0.5, 1, 2, 4, and 8 k Hz tones. Before training there is no brain response (multiple unit activity). During training it develops to the 2 k Hz tone. At the beginning of testing, the brain response shows clear generalization gradients to other tones, even before the animals' behavior does. As testing continues, behavior becomes selective and closely parallels brain activity. (Unpublished data of Gabriel, Wheeler, and Thompson, 1974.)

performance that subsequently developed; see Figure 11.23 for an example. Finally, Gabriel (personal communication) found that when the animals are first *extinguished*—that is, given CS without shock until they stopped responding—the brain response does not extinguish, rather it remains. When the animals are tested the next day, again without shock, the performance shows *spontaneous recovery* to a level predicted from the continued presence of the brain response. In short, the recorded brain events that developed with learning seemed to reflect the underlying associative process in the brain rather than merely correlating with the behavioral performance of the animal.

The distinction between learning and performance is exceedingly critical in studies of brain correlates of learning. The studies by Gabriel illustrate ways that underlying learning and measured performance can be dissected by changes of stimulus conditions (i.e., test tone frequency) or training conditions (extinction tests). In more general terms, the student must remember the importance of the distinction between learning and performance. Learning is assumed or inferred to occur in the brain as a person or animal learns something. However, many other processes may be occurring, such as fear, arousal, habituation, or fatigue, that are different from learning but very strongly affect the performance of the subject at any particular time in the experiment.

In surveying the vast literature on electrophysiological correlates of learning in higher vertebrates, we note that a few general and consistent findings do emerge. During the initial phases of learning, the cortex is widely activated by the training stimuli. Later in training, gross cortical activity seems to subside to the primary sensory cortex associated with the stimuli and the motor cortex associated with the response. Such redistribution of cortical activity usually is preceded by activity increases in various subcortical "nonspecific" systems. Brain activity changes start prior to the appearance of the overt responses, even in the final common path—the motoneurons. During conditioning, marked evoked potential waveform similarities appear in many brain regions. The secondary evoked potential components may reflect learning processes more closely than primary sensory components. However, in aversive situations, much of the change in evoked potential activity may reflect nonspecific fear and other performance variables rather than learning. Slow potential shifts often accompany learning (see Rowland and Dines, 1973) but may reflect motivational state. The nature and locations of changes in the responses of single neurons during learning are at present complex, uncertain, and impossible to summarize. However, there is no question that recording of the activity of single neurons, or small groups of neurons, is the approach of choice in future research.

THE CONSOLIDATION HYPOTHESIS

At the beginning of this chapter we noted that human memory appears to have several different durations or time courses. The animal studies just reviewed have been concerned largely with long-term secondary or permanent memory. At the beginning of the century Müller and Pilzecker (1900) first suggested the consolidation hypothesis—the idea that there is a short-term memory trace which becomes consolidated into permanent memory. The first modern explications of this view were by Hebb and Gerard in 1949. Independently they both suggested that short-term memory is an active, fragile, short-duration process that sets the stage or serves as the initial event in the development of permanent memory. The current evidence for this general hypothesis of two types of interference effects on prior learning in animals as well as humans is overwhelmingly strong. There is no question that very recent learning is extremely susceptible to interference and loss (e.g., by electroconvulsive shock, ECS) but the older well-learned habits are almost impervious to loss. The arguments that rage over the consolidation hypothesis are of two types. First—Are there in fact two processes that are independent, or one continuous process, or two processes which are interdependent, that is, long-term storage requires the short-term consolidation process? Second—Are the interference effects of trauma or ECS on learning and subsequent memory, or on retrieval of memory, or simply on performance?

The classical experiment is that by Duncan (1949). He trained rats to avoid shock to the feet in a shuttle-box situation. A light, presented 10 seconds before shock, served as the CS; the animals received one trial per day for 18 days. A total of nine groups of animals were used in the experiment. Rats in eight of the groups received an electroconvulsive (ECS) shock after each day's trial; the trial-ECS interval ranged from 20 seconds to 14 hours. In the ninth group the clips were placed on the animal's ear for delivery of the ECS, but the ECS was not actually delivered. The results of this experiment are illustrated in Figure 11.24 in which performance is plotted as a function of time between learning trial and ECS each day. As seen, the closer the ECS is to the learning trial the more deleterious effect it has on performance. If the two are separated by more than an hour there appears to be no effect of the ECS on learning. In a variety of subsequent experiments and observations, ECS, epileptic convulsions, hypoxia, depressant drugs, *spreading depression*, and anesthetics have been reported to have similar effects. All these procedures produced marked transient changes in the state of brain activity. It has been hypothesized that relatively short-term electrical activity, perhaps some sort of reverberating circuits in which activity cycles in closed loops around chains of neurons, represents the initial storage of the "memory trace." During the half hour or so of reverberation more permanent memory traces would then be laid down. Procedures that interfere with electrical activity should have a progressively greater effect on learning as they are applied closer in time to the learning trials.

It has been suggested that the supposed interference effects of ECS on recent learning may be nothing other than conditioned fear (Coons and Miller, 1960). Thus the ECS could simply act as a strong negative reinforcer. Actually Duncan ran the necessary control for this possibility in his original experiment: control animals were given the ECS through the feet instead of across the head (when given through the feet it does not produce convulsions or coma). Results tended not to support the conditioned fear hypothesis but were somewhat ambiguous. Other investigators have attempted to separate conditioned fear and memory loss effects (Brady, 1951; Brady and Hunt, 1952; Hudspeth, McGaugh, and Thomson, 1964). To oversimplify an extensive and complex literature: it does appear that ECS effects are not due solely to conditioned fear.

There are still other nonconsolidation interpretations of ECS effects. Lewis and Maher (1965) argued that the seizure activity and performance impairment effects of the ECS become conditioned to the apparatus and

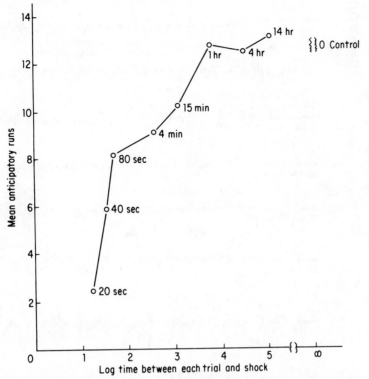

Figure 11.24 Effect of electroconvulsive shock (ECS) on performance in a simple shock avoidance learning task in rats. Anticipatory runs are "correct" (i.e., shock is avoided)! Parameter is time after trial (1 trial per day) that ECS is given. (From Duncan, C. P. The retroactive effect of electroshock on learning. *J. Comp. Physiol. Psychol.* **42**, 1949, pp. 32–44.)

The consolidation
hypothesis

cues associated with the ECS. Indeed, Lewis and his associates have shown that ECS impairment of learning can be strikingly reduced if subsequent tests of learning are made under quite different circumstances than the original ECS conditions. However, this cannot be the entire explanation for ECS effects on memory since a number of well controlled studies have shown marked ECS impairment of consolidation when the convulsive shock is given to anesthetized animals (McGaugh and Alpern, 1966). ECS produces profound effects on memory of recent events in humans when given together with general anesthesia.

Rather inconsistent results have been obtained in studies attempting to determine the exact time course of ECS effects on memory. This seems due largely to the fact that task and ECS variables (particularly intensity, duration, and mode of application of the ECS) all influence the form of retrograde amnesia. An unexpected influence of prior foot shock on ECS effectiveness is suggested in an interesting study by Chorover and

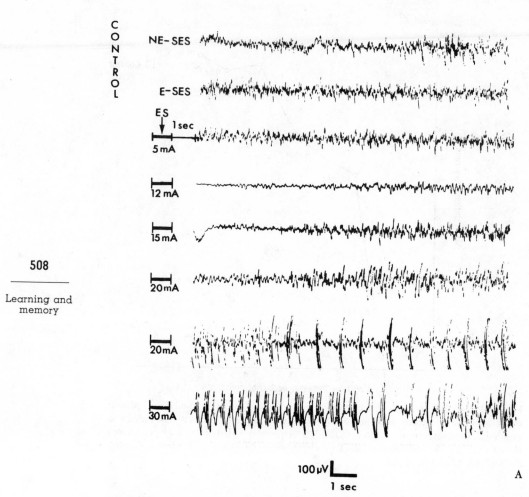

Figure 11.25 A, Mouse ECoG recordings from middorsal cortex, following trans-corneal ES of different intensities. Top two tracings represent control recording taken from a nonetherized sham electroshock (NE-SES) and an etherized sham electroshock (E-SES) animal, respectively. For all animals receiving ES, a 1.0 sec interval, during which there was amplifier blockage, was omitted following the termination of ES. ES intensities are indicated below the ES stimulus marker for each tracing. In the par-

DeLuca (1969). They found that brain ECS threshold was significantly raised by immediately prior foot shock. The peripheral stimulation of shocking the foot seems to protect against the development of brain convulsions. Chorover and DeLuca hypothesize that foot shock increases brain arousal, which serves to protect the subject from the effects of ECS.

More recent ECS studies have been concerned with identification of the variables critical for ECS impairment of short-term memory. It was initially thought that the behavioral seizure was necessary for retrograde

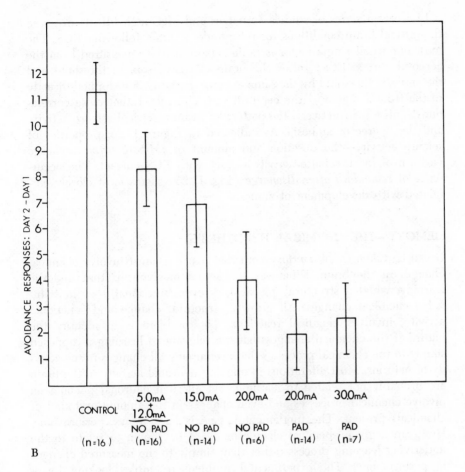

B

ticular examples shown for the 12 and 15 mA intensities, the initial depression of ECoG voltage was due to prolonged amplifier blockage. Note primary afterdischarge spikes (PAD) in 20 and 30 mA data. B, The effects of transcorneal ES current intensities on retrograde amnesia (RA) for an active avoidance response in mice. The magnitude of RA is directly related to current intensity. (From Zornetzer, S. F., and McGaugh, J. L. Retrograde amnesia and brain seizures in mice: A further analysis. *Physiol. and Behav.* **7**, 1971, pp. 841–845.)

amnesia. Following effective ECS, otherwise normal animals show full-blown "grand-mal" type seizures with tonic and clonic contractions of muscles analogous to a human grand-mal epileptic seizure. The behavioral seizure, of course, is produced by seizure or convulsive activity of the brain. However, it appears that the seizure behavior, per se, can be induced by ECS effects on brain stem and spinal cord independent of retrograde amnesia effects on short-term memory (see McGaugh and Herz, 1972).

In a recent series of studies Zornetzer and McGaugh (1970) explored the critical brain conditions for retrograde amnesia following ECS. The most important single factor is brain seizure activity measured from the cerebral cortex. Ether raises the brain electrical seizure threshold and the amnesia threshold by the same amount. If the ECS is applied directly to the frontal region of the cerebral cortex in rats, rather close correlations can be seen between the pattern of brain electrical seizure activity and the degree of amnesia. As indicated in Figure 11.25, properties of seizure activity—the duration and amount of *primary after discharge* (a form of brain seizure activity)—vary with ECS current. The occurrence of *secondary after discharge* (Fig. 11.25) seems most closely correlated with development of amnesia.

MEMORY—THE CHEMICAL HYPOTHESIS

It can be taken as an *a priori* truth that learning must involve chemical changes in the brain. Whatever the actual mechanisms that underlie learning, whether structural, physical, or even functional, they must involve chemical changes. All growth, structural change and functional activity, involves chemical reactions. The problem is to identify the nature of the chemical changes that are relevant to learning as opposed simply to the chemical processes that accompany all changes in the activity of neurons. Most alterations in ongoing neuronal activity in the brain are probably not related to learning. Yet all such neuronal phenomena involve chemical processes and even changes in the amount and kind of chemicals present. The fundamental issue is learning vs. performance. How can a given chemical change or effect be shown to relate to the underlying learning process rather than simply to the measured changes in performance? The experimental problem resembles looking for a needle in a haystack when you are not sure which of an almost infinite number of haystacks has the needle.

It is possible to make many guesses about the nature of the chemical changes that underlie learning. Indeed there have been a great many specific chemical theories of learning. Unfortunately, so little is known about the subject that no very good evidence supports any particular theory. Two general classes of chemical theories that make sense are (1) *transmitter theory* and (2) *protein and RNA theory*. Transmitter theories are based on the fact that synaptic transmission is largely a chemical process in the mammalian brain (see Chapter 5). Since learning must involve changes in the interactions among neurons, and since the important interactions among neurons occur at synapses, then learning involves changes in chemical synaptic transmission. This is a very reasonable approach. Unfortunately, most chemical synaptic transmitter substances in the brain have not been identified yet with certainty. One substance that seems clearly to be a central synaptic transmitter is acetylcholine (ACh); see Chapter 5. We will examine ACh hypotheses of learning below.

Protein theories of learning are also reasonable, at least in general terms. All structural changes, all growth and development, involve proteins. Proteins are the fundamental chemical building blocks of neurons and, in fact, of all tissues. The problem is that almost an infinite number of possible proteins could be involved. How do we decide which brain proteins to study?

Another interesting issue concerns the turnover of proteins in the brain. Proteins are continuously forming and disappearing. The approximate half-life of most proteins in the brain is about two weeks. Any given protein molecule does not exist much more than a month. This means that you grow a completely new brain every month or so, at least insofar as proteins are concerned! If learning involved formation of particular unique protein molecules, memories would only persist for a month. Although some of us may have poor memories, they are not that poor. When proteins form new structures and processes, these do not disappear. It is the individual protein molecules that turn over, not the new structures and processes. However, this general fact of protein turnover argues strongly against the formation of unique protein molecules as the basic process in memory.

RNA theories of learning really represent the protein theory taken one step back. Since RNA forms proteins (Chapter 2), then changes in protein involve changes in the production of protein, hence in the RNA mechanisms of synthesis. Further, there could be permanent changes in RNA that lead to production of new unique proteins, which themselves turn over.

The most reasonable way in which RNA and protein mechanisms of learning could work would be to change the structures and chemical processes that comprise synapses between neurons. This view leads back to the much earlier and more direct theory that learning involves synaptic growth and change; of course it also leads directly to the transmission theories of learning noted above. Unfortunately, these hypothetical changes in synapses during learning have not yet been identified.

The majority of studies of drug actions *on* learning and performance have been done in the context of the consolidation hypothesis. As noted above, it is generally assumed that long-term secondary or permanent memory is coded by some chemical and/or structural change at synapses which probably involves protein synthesis. Consequently, the emphasis in chemical studies of permanent memory storage has been on drugs and other substances that interfere with the synthesis of proteins. Short-term memory, on the other hand, usually is conceived as some type of circulating electrical activity which leads ultimately to consolidation of permanent memory. Chemical studies of short-term memory have emphasized effects of drugs that have more direct actions on neuronal activity.

It can be argued that if some sort of electrical reverberation is involved in short-term memory storage, substances which increase electrical activity ought to improve learning. Early experiments by Hull and Lashley showed that caffeine and strychnine did improve maze learning performance in rats. McGaugh and his colleagues have completed an extensive series of experiments showing comparable effects of strychnine-like substances and of picrotoxin. These drugs lead to increased neural activity by blocking, to some extent, synaptic mechanisms of inhibition. In the initial experiments (McGaugh and Petrinovich, 1959) the drugs were given prior to learning trials. The direct effects of these drugs on performance in maze running may be confounded with possible effects on consolidation. Consequently in subsequent experiments the drugs were given immediately *after* each learning trial. Significant facilitation of learning was still obtained. However, it could be argued that improvement with post-trial injections is due to a rewarding effect of the drugs rather than any direct effect on memory storage.

Westbrook and McGaugh (1963) attempted to circumvent this possibility in an ingenious adaptation of the *latent learning* paradigm. In brief, four groups of rats were trained in a maze learning situation (one trial per day). Two groups were given immediate post-trial injection of a strychnine-like drug and the other two groups were given saline injections. One drug group and one saline group were given no food reward in the alley goal box during the first 5 days (trials). The other groups were rewarded throughout. Scores of the food-rewarded drug group and the food-rewarded saline group improved over the first five days, but the no-food drug group and no-food saline group did not. However, when reward was given to all groups on trials 5 to 10, the drug effect clearly separated the groups; both drug groups did significantly better than the saline groups. The essential point here is that if the drug injections were rewarding, the drug group given no food reward during the first 5 days should have exhibited improved performance (i.e., the drug would reward performance). Because no such result occurred, it would seem that drug effects on maze performance cannot be attributed solely to possible reward value of drug injection.

McGaugh and Krivanek (1970) completed an extensive analysis of convulsant drug facilitation of positive reinforcement learning situations using the post-trial injection technique. Essentially, they trained mice on a black-white visual discrimination task, at 3 trials per day with food reward. Strychnine sulfate injections usually were given after the third trial. Hence, most animals were *never* trained or tested while under the direct influence of the drug. Independent groups of animals were trained using various doses of the drug, with the important control (no drug) group receiving saline injections. Other groups received the drug at various times both before and after training (note that the pre-trial injected groups *were* trained under the drug effect). Figure 11.26 depicts the results of this experiment. Notice that relative to the saline group, animals receiving strychnine or other drugs in various doses did show fewer errors to criterion performance and that the largest effect was at the

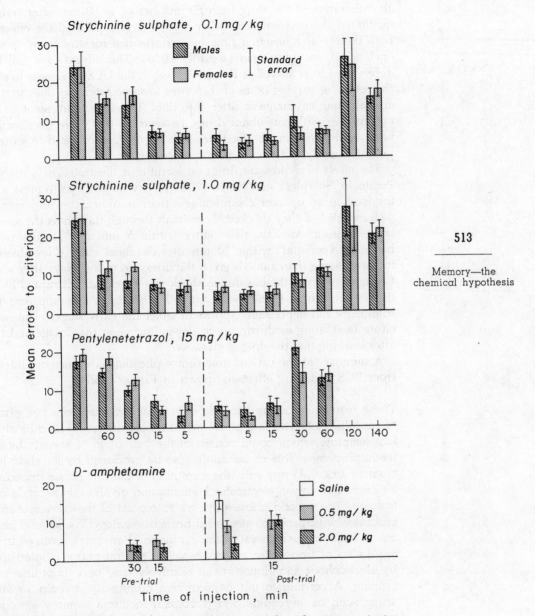

Figure 11.26 Facilitating effects of various drugs on number of errors to criterion of discrimination learning in mice as a function of injection 60, 30, 15, or 5 min before or immediately, 5, 15, 30, 60, 120, or 240 min after each daily training trial. (Data for strychnine sulphate (Krivanek and McGaugh, 1968); data for pentylenetetrazol (Krivanek and McGaugh, 1969); data for D-amphetamine (McGaugh and Krivanek, 1970). Figure from McGaugh, J. L., and Herz, M. J. *Memory Consolidation.* San Francisco: Albion, 1972.)

lower and higher doses. In the time series (Fig. 11.26) notice that the administration of the drug from 60 min before to 60 min after training facilitated the performance. Other studies have replicated the effects of both dosage and injection time on performance for strychnine, pentylenetetrazol, and picrotoxin (see Fig. 11.26). The subject's sex and food deprivation level as well as the shock level of the UCS all appear to affect the results of varying doses of the drugs to some extent, as does strain of animals and environment after injection. The important point of the experiments with convulsant drugs, however, is that there does seem to be at least some genuine facilitation of learning, as opposed to an interpretation solely in terms of performance factors.

The effect of depressant drugs on learning is illustrated in a study by Pearlman, Sharpless, and Jarvik (1961). They trained rats to press a bar for food in an operant conditioning situation. When the response was well established they shocked the animals through the bar as the animals were pressing. Animals given ether within 5 min and sodium pentabarbital (Nembutal) within 10 min after the shock showed less decrease in bar-pressing than animals given the drugs up to four days after shock. Learning to avoid the bar due to shock was apparently disrupted by the depressant drugs. From these and other studies, it is apparent that stimulants and depressants appear to affect the early stages of memory, either facilitating or disrupting it, depending upon the dosage and time after learning that the drug is given.

A summary of the various time-course phenomena of memory inferred from ECS and drug effects is shown in Figure 11.27.

These results, considered together, suggest that there are two phases of consolidation. This first phase might be considered to be a biochemical template which could consist of the activation of specific biosynthetic processes. This phase might also be produced by the short-term memory trace. At any rate, the formation of the first phase appears to be prevented by an electroshock stimulation given eight seconds after training. The second phase appears to consist of the development of processes which are the structural basis of memory. The second phase could, for example, consist of the synthesis of enzymes involved in the regulation of transmitter substances. The second phase is interrupted by electroshock stimulation given relatively long periods of time after training. According to this general and admittedly speculative view, drugs such as strychnine and picrotoxin facilitate memory storage—and prevent retrograde amnesia produced by ECS—by activating or reactivating the memory template formed during the first minute or so after training.

The template or first phase-appears to be temporary. Amnesia cannot be prevented by injecting strychnine after the normal consolidation period has passed.

The period of time over which strychnine can be injected and still

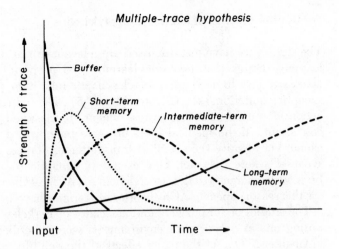

Multiple-trace hypothesis

Strength of trace →

Buffer

Short-term memory

Intermediate-term memory

Long-term memory

Input   Time →

Figure 11.27 Schematic model of a multiple-trace hypothesis of memory storage. (Redrawn from McGaugh, J. L. A multi-trace view of memory storage processes. In Bovet, D., Bovet-Nitti, F., and Oliverio, A. (eds.) *Attuali orientamenti della ricerca sull'apprendimento e la memoria.* Rome: Accademia Nazionale dei Lincei, 1968, pp. 13–24.)

prevent amnesia coincides fairly well with the period of intermediate memory reported by Barondes and Cohen (1966). These investigators, as well as others, including Agranoff (1965) and Flexner et al. (1967), have shown that consolidation is disrupted by the protein synthesis inhibitor puromycin [see below, p. 523]. According to these findings, puromycin does not interfere with acquisitions when it is injected before training. But with pretrial injections the animals forget within a few hours. Since short-term memory is presumed to decay within seconds or minutes after an experience, I interpret this forgetting as due to a decay or decline of intermediate memory. Normally the intermediate memory curve would not be accessible for study because intermediate memory would be replaced by a consolidated memory trace. It is possible that the intermediate memory processes induce memory consolidation. It is also possible that the intermediate memory process merely parallels consolidation and provides for retrieval while consolidation is occurring.

[Figure 11.27] shows another speculative representation of the various memory traces I have discussed. As plotted, they are all initiated by an experience. However, each has a different asymptote and each has a different time course. At different times following training different traces provide a basis for retrieval. It could be that each process is based on a different mechanism and that the kind and number of traces might vary from species to species and from individual to individual . . .

(McGaugh, 1968, pages 22–23)

The studies we have just discussed are relevant to transmitter theories of learning. Drugs that facilitate learning and/or performance generally act at synapses to decrease or block synaptic inhibition, particularly post-synaptic inhibition (see Chapters 4 and 5). The actual mechanisms of action of these facilitating drugs—which are classified as stimulants or convulsants in the medical literature—are unknown, partly because we cannot yet identify the chemical transmitter substances at the inhibitory synapses where they act. One excitatory synaptic transmitter that has been well characterized is acetylcholine (ACh) (Chapter 5). Perhaps for this reason, specific ACh theories of learning have been developed.

The studies of Rosenzweig and associates of Berkeley on the effects of raising rats in rich or poor environments were described in some detail in Chapter 5. One of the major effects of the rich life, as the reader may recall, was an increase in the number of dendritic spine synapses on nerve cells in the cerebral cortex. These studies actually were initiated on the basis of the acetylcholine hypothesis of learning. In earlier experiments, the "maze-bright" rats bred by Tryon to be super maze learners (see Chapter 2) had been found to have more cholinesterase in the cerebral cortex than did the "maze-dull" strain. Subsequently, the same type of effect was found for rich rats relative to poor rats. The studies on the Tryon strains indicated a genetic difference in both maze-learning and cholinesterase control in brain. In the rich-rat/poor-rat studies, the investigators always used littermate pairs for rich and poor groups to control for genetic factors. These experiments seemed to suggest that being raised in the rich environment led to more cholinesterase in brain.

The reason cholinesterase was measured, is, of course, because it is an enzyme that breaks down ACh and related substances. There is a more specific enzyme, acetylcholinesterase (AChE). Actually, in the earlier studies, the investigators meant to measure AChE but the assay method used was not specific for ACh but rather was sensitive to all cholinesterase (ChE). The original rationale was that whenever AChE is present, so is ACh. ChE levels are easier to measure. In more recent studies, refined procedures have been used to measure concentrations of the specific enzyme AChE, with similar results. Rich rats have more AChE, and presumably more ACh, in cortical brain tissue than do poor rats (see Rosenzweig, 1970).

In experiments more specifically aimed at learning, adult rats were housed in cages with an operant Skinner-box arrangement and required to solve visual discrimination problems. Yoked control animals were kept in similar boxes without the lever and given a free pellet whenever the learning rats obtained one. Trained animals had higher ChE and AChE levels in cerebral cortex than the yoked control animals.

These experiments are most suggestive. Rosenzweig argues that the rich environment leads to greater "primary" learning during growth.

There is more to do and more to learn in the rich environment. There is also, of course, more activity, more social interaction, more stimulation, and a list of other differences. Most important, of course, is the fact that the animals and their brains are undergoing growth and development processes. Further, the rich rats may, in fact, be the normal rats and the poor rats may be abnormally deprived of the many kinds of stimulation and interaction with other animals and the environment that normally occurs in the wild state. Their brains may have retarded development.

The learning environment shows the influence of a more specific situation. As Rosenzweig notes (1970) it is still necessary to control for differences in visual stimulation and behavioral responding between the learning animals and the yoked controls. However, the results are certainly suggestive. Assuming that the greater AChE content represents a learning effect, what can we conclude? First, it is likely that increased AChE means increased ACh in cortical neurons. ACh is present both in nerve cells and at synapses, but we can make the further assumption that the increase occurs at synapses where ACh is the transmitter. Two possible explanations are increased numbers of synapses and increased ACh at given synapses. Because of the increase in dendritic spines, at least in rich rats, the answer is likely to be increased numbers of synapses. How does this relate to learning? We cannot even begin to answer this question at present.

J. Anthony Deutsch at the University of California at San Diego has done some rather complicated experiments aimed at testing the notion that learning occurs at ACh synapses in the brain. The basic technique he uses is to inject animals at various times after learning with a substance called DFP that inactivates AChE. Because this substance inactivates AChE, which itself normally breaks down ACh at the postsynaptic site during synaptic transmission (Chapter 5), then ACh would remain at the synapse. If enough remains, a kind of synaptic block occurs—the ACh causes sustained depolarization of the postsynaptic neuron and the neuron stops firing spikes. This is called *depolarization block*. At lower concentrations, DFP only partially inactivates AChE, with the result that more than the normal amount of ACh is present at synapses. Deutsch argues that this should facilitate transmission, and hence retention, of learned habits. This latter point is, of course, an hypothesis, not an established fact. From these possible mechanisms Deutsch argues that small doses of the inactivators should facilitate poor retention and impair good retention.

An example of some of Deutsch's experiments is shown in Figure 11.28 (Deutsch, 1973). In brief, rats are trained to run from a shock grid in a Y maze to the lighted one to avoid shock. They are then injected with small doses of DFP at 14 days after training or 28 days after training and immediately retrained. Control animals are injected with peanut oil (PO), the vehicle—that is, the substance in which the DFP is dissolved when it is injected.

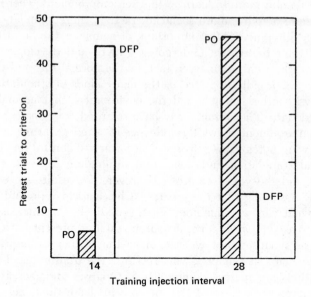

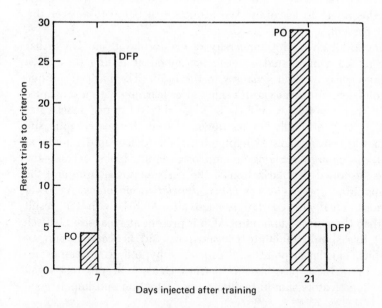

Figure 11.28 The effect of injection of the anticholinesterase DFP (diisopropyl fluorophosphate) and PO (peanut oil), the drug vehicle, on well retained or almost forgotten habits. Trials to criterion are plotted against time between retest and original training. It can be seen that when controls remember well, DFP-injected animals forget. When controls forget, DFP-injected animals remember well. (Data from Deutsch and Leibowitz, 1966; Wiener and Deutsch, 1968. Figure redrawn from Deutsch, J. A. (ed.) *The Physiological Basis of Memory.* New York: Academic Press, 1973, pp. 59–76.)

The reason for the two time intervals is that normal animals remember the task well after 14 days but poorly after 28 days. As can be seen, control animals given peanut oil (PO) at 14 days show good retention but animals given PO at 28 days show very poor retention. In contrast, experimental animals given DFP at 14 days show poor retention but others injected at 28 days show good retention.

Deutsch explains these seemingly paradoxical results in the following way. Where memory is good, after 14 days, the critical synapses are functioning well and DFP causes too great an increase in ACh, which interferes. At 28 days, the hypothetical memory synapses are not doing very well and DFP, by increasing the level of ACh, causes them to do better. In brief, old memories can be facilitated by injecting drugs that interfere with ACh synaptic transmission by partial inactivation of the breakdown enzyme AChE. This kind of inference is, of course, several stages removed from the experimental finding. The major DFP effects are on the behavioral expression of retention, not on original learning, and could involve retrieval processes and performance variables, as well as hypothetical ACh memory synapses.

To summarize, studies of ACh as a possible synaptic transmitter in learning and memory are usually consistent, at least, with the notion that ACh is indeed a synaptic transmitter in the brain and more specifically in the cerebral cortex. However, they have not yet revealed much about the role of ACh synapses in learning. We do not yet know which synapses in the brain use ACh as a transmitter and hence cannot do specific chemical or anatomical studies of changes that might occur with learning.

Protein and RNA approaches to learning

One aspect of protein theories of learning that has captured the popular interest is *memory transfer*—the possibility that memory in the form of protein molecules can be extracted from a donor brain and injected into another to transfer whatever was learned by the donor brain. In a recent television movie, a lady scientist-spy was injected with a brain extract from a murdered colleague and relived his memories to solve the case. The possibility of memory transfer led *Time* to its famous final solution for what to do with old college professors—grind them up and feed them to the students.

Memory transfer was first reported by McConnell and colleagues (1962) at the University of Michigan in studies where they ground up trained planaria (a flatworm) and fed them to naive planaria. The naive planaria were reported to exhibit the trained response. Subsequently, Allen Jacobson and his associates (Babich et al., 1965) reported similar findings in rats. We will take Jacobson's study as a prototype. Rats were trained to approach a food cup upon hearing the click of the food dispenser. They learned to approach the food cup, even in the absence of the click. Brains from the trained rats and naive control rats were ground up, treated with RNA extraction procedures (which extracted RNA and many other substances as well), and injected into naive recipient rats. The recipients of trained brain extract were reported to approach the food cup upon presentation of the click more than recipients of naive brain extract.

Unfortunately, it has not been possible for many other groups to replicate this experiment (see Luttges et al., 1966; Chapouthier, 1973) and even Jacobson cannot now obtain the effect (Jacobson and Schlechter, 1970). The earlier positive reports of memory transfer led to similar experiments in many laboratories. Among the more interesting are those of Ungar and associates (see Chapouthier, 1973; Ungar, 1970). They have reported memory transfer in rats on such tasks as habituation to sound, choice of lighted alley in a maze, and extinction of a conditioned response. Interestingly, Ungar quickly found that it was not necessary to use crude protein or RNA extract from trained brains. In fact, the critical substances from the trained brains were smaller peptide molecules. While proteins are composed of peptides, many other substances are themselves peptides. An example is ACTH, the stress hormone released by the adrenal gland (see Chapter 9). In this context it is interesting to recall that Levine (1971) was able to alter dramatically both habituation and extinction of conditioned responses by increased blood levels of ACTH in rats (see Chapter 9). This of course, raises the question of whether the peptides that Ungar extracts code "learning" or, rather, relate to hormonal substances that are formed due to stress and other factors in the trained rats. This point is a specific illustration again of the general problem of distinguishing between learning and performance. Hormones more likely influence performance variables rather than basic processes of learning.

Another general problem in this intriguing area of memory transfer is the great difficulty in replication of experiments. Typically, a given laboratory can replicate its own results but others cannot. In some instances (e.g., Jacobson) even the same experimenter cannot replicate his own experiments. Jacobson and Schlechter (1970) note one instance in which "two skilled chemists, working side by side, obtained quite different results in identical transfer experiments" (1970, p. 127).

A careful study by Donald Stein and associates at Clark University (Frank, Stein, and Rosen, 1970) illustrates many of the experimental problems in memory transfer. Donor mice were given one trial in a shuttle box by placing them in a white section and allowing them to move to a dark section, whereupon they were shocked.

If the animals were to be put in the test again, they would avoid going to the dark section. Control donors were placed in the maze but not shocked. Stress control animals were rolled back and forth in a small jar and not placed in the maze. Both brain and liver were taken from these three groups of mice, homogenized and injected into naive re-

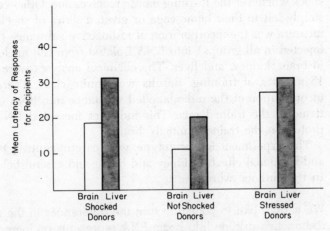

Figure 11.29 Transfer of "memory." Rats were trained (shocked donors), not trained (not shocked donors), or given a nonlearning kind of stress (stressed donors), and their brains and livers ground up and injected into recipient rats, who were then tested in the training situation (step-through latency). The longer the latency, the greater the "memory." Note that recipients of ground-up liver from both trained and untrained-stressed groups showed the best "memory." (Graph constructed from data in Frank, Stein, and Rosen, 1970.)

cipient mice. The injected mice were then placed in the white part of the alley and the time they waited before going to the dark section was measured. The results are shown in Figure 11.29. It is absolutely clear from these results that there was no transfer of any learned behavior. Both brain and liver extracts from both previously trained and previously stressed mice yielded greater latencies in the test. Indeed, the most effective "memory" was from the liver extract of the stressed (but not trained) donors. It is unlikely that if memory molecules exist, they are concentrated in the liver. As the authors note, the only reasonable interpretation is in terms of generalized stress effects producing hormones or related chemicals in the brains and livers of both the trained and stressed donors.

Analysis of possible changes in proteins, RNA, and other chemicals in the nervous system following learning is a less dramatic but more reasonable approach to the chemistry of learning and memory. The fundamental problem faced in such studies is again the learning performance distinction. An example from the careful studies of Glassman and associates at the University of North Carolina (Glassman, 1967) illustrates the point. The training apparatus is a box with a grid floor and a small shelf above. A mouse is placed on the floor and given a series of trials of combined light and buzzer (CS) for 3 seconds, followed by shock. The mouse learns to jump to the platform to escape shock. A yoked control mouse is placed in another box without a shelf and given paired CS—

shock whenever the learning mouse receives one. Other control mice were simply left in their home cage or given a series of shocks. The chemical measure was the incorporation of radioactive substance (which had been injected in all groups) into RNA isolated from cell nuclei and ribosomes in brain, kidney, and liver. The chemical analyses were done after only 15 minutes of training. Results were quite clear. There was increased incorporation of the radio-labelled substance into RNA only in the brain tissue of the trained rats. This indicates increased RNA production of protein in the trained animals' brains.

This experiment is a prototype, with careful controls for general tissue and hormonal effects (kidney and liver) and careful behavioral controls. In the authors' words:

We should like to conclude that the differences in the incorporation of radioactive uridine into brain RNA represents an increase in RNA synthesis that is part of the molecular basis of learning. Good sense, however, compels caution, and alternative hypotheses are considered.

(Zemp et al., 1966, pages 1430–1431)

Two possible problems can be raised. One, of course, is that the trained animals exhibited a different performance—they jumped to a shelf. The increased RNA activity in their brains may reflect this performance, which was not what the mice learned; they already knew how to jump. They learned the association between CS and jumping to avoid shock. The other, more subtle, problem concerns the yoked control animals. They were given a series of classical conditioning trials of CS followed by strong shock. It is certain they learned that CS signaled shock. Measures such as crouching, muscle-tensing, increased heart rate, etc., would reveal the existence of classically conditioned fear. In other words, the yoked control animals also learned something, but it was different from what the training animals learned.

Victor Shashoua at Harvard Medical School has developed an ingenious technique of training goldfish and subsequently analyzing RNA and protein changes in brain (Shashoua, 1970). A small styrofoam float is secured to the ventral surface of the fish. It then floats upside down. After a period of one to three hours and much effort, the fish learns to swim right side up with the float attached. Comparisons of brain RNA and proteins between trained and naive fish reveal changes in RNA and the formation of certain new proteins as a result of the float procedure. The problem, of course, is to provide the proper controls for the greatly increased stress, muscular activity, and other factors that are associated with the task, but not the learning per se. Shashoua is trying such controls as forcing animals to swim against strong currents and using large floats so the animal cannot learn to swim right side up.

Chemical studies designed to interfere with the formation of protein synthesis, and hence memory storage, typically use substances that act on RNA (ribose nucleic acid), the substance necessary for the synthesis of proteins. Dingman and Sporn (1961) injected 8-azaGuanine (an RNA inhibitor) in rats. In one experiment the treated animals had a significantly greater mean number of errors in maze-learning than did control animals. However, in other experiments run by Dingman and Sporn, there were no significant differences between groups. Flexner et al. (1963) injected an antibiotic substance, puromycin, which markedly inhibits protein synthesis in cells. They found that subcutaneous injection of the substance had no effect, but direct injection in the ventricles of the brain, or in the hippocampus, did cause significant impairment of learning. If given during the course of learning a particular task, the treatment abolished learning of that task, but did not impair previous learning or prevent subsequent learning from taking place.

Bernard Agranoff and associates have undertaken an extensive program of studies on effects of puromycin on memory in the goldfish. This animal was selected partly because a very simple and reliable automated learning and memory task had been developed for goldfish by Bitterman and because large numbers of fish can be run easily. The fish is in a two-part tank. When light is turned on in the part of the tank where the fish happens to be, it must swim to the other compartment to avoid shock. Animals were trained, then given brain injections of puromycin at varying times, and tested on how well they retained the learned response. Results are shown in Figure 11.30. Injection within 30 min after initial learning caused marked impairment of retention. Injection just before initial learning did not impair learning but did block retention. Agranoff interprets these results to indicate that short-term learning—the initial acquisition of the response by the fish—is not affected by blocking protein synthesis. However, the conversion of short-term learning to long-term retention is prevented by interference with protein synthesis.

Some caution is necessary in interpreting the effects of puromycin on retention. Macrides and Chorover (1968) found that brain injection of puromycin in the hippocampus induces prolonged seizure activity, lasting several days. Hence interference might be due to this abnormal brain activity rather than to actions of the drug on protein synthesis. Flexner and Flexner (1968) reported a most puzzling reversal of puromycin blocking of memory. You will remember their earlier report that learned behaviors in mice were not retained after puromycin injection. If saline is injected into the same brain area (hippocampus) up to 60 days after puromycin blocking, the supposedly forgotten behavior reappears! It is as though an abnormal brain state were "cured" by the saline.

Barondes and associates have used another type of RNA-protein synthesis inhibitor called *cycloheximide*. This substance exerts more potent inhibition on formation of proteins than puromycin and does not appear to induce seizure activity. In one study (Barondes and Cohen, 1968), mice were injected with cycloheximide and effects on learning and retention of a T maze were studied. Injected animals learned normally and

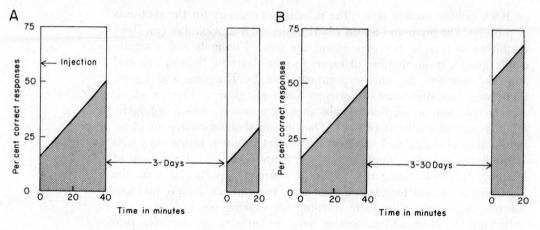

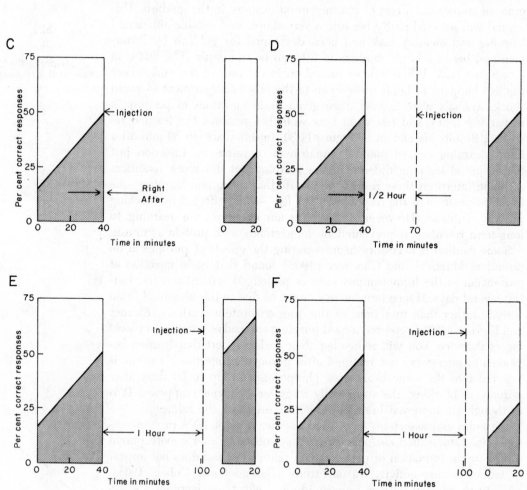

◄ Figure 11.30 A, Injection prior to training did not affect the rate at which goldfish learned to solve the shuttle-box problem. But puromycin given at this point did suppress the formation of long-term memory, as shown by the drop in the scores three days afterward. B, Normal learning rate of goldfish in 30 shuttle-box trials is shown by the black curve. Whether the last 10 trials were given three days after the first 20 (the regular procedure) or as much as a month later, fish demonstrated the same rate of improvement. C, Injection immediately after the first 20 trials erased all memory of training. The fish scored at the untrained level. D, Injection half an hour after the first 20 trials cut the level of correct responses to half the level without such injection. E, Injection with puromycin one hour after completion of 20 learning trials did not disrupt memory. Goldfish given the antibiotic at this point scored as well as those in the control group in the sequence of 10 trials that followed three days afterward. F, Environmental factor in the formation of lasting memory was seen when fish remained in training (instead of "home") tanks during the fixation period. Under these conditions fixation did not occur. Puromycin given at end of period still erased memory.

remembered up to three hours but showed marked deficits in longer term retention.

It is relatively easy to summarize the general results of studies concerned with changes in biochemical substances of the brain resulting from learning. The original experiment on RNA by Hydén and Egyhazi (1962) and most studies since then have reported changes in amount of RNA, types of RNA, amount and kind of proteins, and related chemical alterations in the nervous and brain tissues of animals subjected to learning procedures. However, to date it has not been possible to identify which changes are related to learning and which to performance, stress, and other variables operating in the learning situations. Similarly, drugs that interfere with RNA and protein synthesis do much more than interfere with learning. They can disrupt almost all physiological processes of the organism.

Learning involves altered responses to stimuli. Because the nervous system is composed of elements interconnecting through synapses, it would seem fairly clear that learning results in altered patterns of interaction among the myriad nerve cells from input stimuli to behavioral output. The mechanisms and character of altered synaptic organization must be specified for an understanding of the neural basis of learning. At present RNA and protein hypotheses can offer no help in solving this more general problem. However, it is likely that changes in synaptic efficacy during learning involve increased or decreased activity in excitatory and inhibitory neurons, with associated changes in protein. Because synaptic transmission is chemically mediated, a variety of chemical as well as structural alterations are likely to participate in neural changes during learning. The study of the chemical and structural bases of learning in the nervous system has only begun.

In this chapter we have emphasized the search for the engram. This question has two major experimental aspects. One has to do with finding the engram: What regions and systems of the brain subserve learning

Memory—the
chemical hypothesis

and memory? The other has to do with the actual mechanisms of learning: What are the physical-chemical changes that form the engrams of memory? Studies addressing these issues have used animals as experimental models. Simple models like *aplysia* or spinal cord have been most valuable in analysis of mechanisms underlying simple learning like habituation and sensitization. Learning in higher vertebrates is more appropriate for study of the brain systems involved in learning. Our ultimate interest is to determine how learning occurs in the human brain. The most appropriate experimental subject would be human. There is a large, complex, and often inconclusive clinical literature on effects of brain damage on learning and higher processes in humans. The next best model, and one that can be manipulated experimentally, is the brain of the monkey or ape.

In Chapter 12, we will explore the brain systems that underlie the more complex aspects of learning, and the related processes of language and thought in primates and man.

Summary

Obviously, learning processes and memory processes are related. These processes can be inferred and measured only from changes in an organism's behavior. Any measure of learning is dependent upon storage processes (memory) to bridge the interval between a change in the nervous system and the output of altered behavior. In addition, measures of memory are dependent upon previous learning processes.

The process of memory has been defined in terms of three different time courses. Iconic memory is very short-term sensory memory which has a duration of a few milliseconds. It appears to exist only in the sensory modality stimulated and to decay passively over time. Primary memory lasts for a period of seconds and occurs across sensory modalities. Secondary memory is relatively permanent. At the present time, it is not yet possible to determine whether primary and secondary aspects of memory are two different processes or one process which occurs across different time spans.

Habituation and sensitization are two categories of behavioral plasticity. Nearly all behavioral responses habituate rapidly. It appears that the processes responsible for habituation of behavioral responses occur generally after the primary sensory pathways of the brain and before the motoneurons. Habituation is characterized by a reversible response decrement. In general, habituation is more rapid and pronounced with weaker and more frequent stimulation.

Studies of the synaptic mechanisms underlying flexion reflex habituation in the acute spinal cat have clarified habituation mechanisms. The process responsible for habituation occurs in the interneurons. Two distinct categories of interneurons were found, one which exhibited plasticity of response to repeated stimulation and the other that exhibited an absence of plasticity. In higher animals, habituation occurs at the interneurons in the spinal cord and brain. Studies of *aplysia* and isolated frog spinal cord agree that habituation is the result of changes localized to synapses which are activated by the repeated stimulus itself. This decrease in synaptic transmission resulting from repeated activation is termed *synaptic depression.*

The EEG arousal response habituates in animals and man. The human alpha-blocking response habituates to tactile, auditory, and visual stimulation. Studies of habituation of arousal suggest that evoked response habituation to a variety of stimuli occurs at most levels of the CNS. In general, the ascending relay nuclei do not exhibit habituation in sensory systems.

Two different theories that attempt to account for habituation have been developed, the dual-process theory and the model-comparator theory. According to the dual-process theory, the two independent processes of habituation and sensitization develop to repeated stimulation in the intact animal. These processes are presumed to be mediated by different neural systems and mechanisms. The net result of the interaction of these two processes is the behavioral response to repeated stimulation. This theory predicts that sensitization predominates with strong stimuli, and habituation with weak stimuli. In contrast, the model-comparator theory views the cerebral cortex as forming a model of a repeated stimulus. The reticular formation serves as a model-comparator amplifier. If there is a change in the stimulus, the reticular formation produces an increase in arousal.

Lashley began the search for the engram, that set of physical processes and changes in the brain, which forms the basis of learning. He developed two principles, the *principle of mass action* and the *principle of equipotentiality.* While the engram is a hypothetical change in the brain as a result of learning, the engram must exist. Any changes in behavior due to learning must reflect changes in the nervous system, that is, physical-chemical alterations. These alterations are the "engrams." Hebb's theory of cell assemblies is one view of the nature of the engram. According to this model, changes during learning develop among interconnections throughout wide areas of the brain. A particular kind of learning involves the development of particular circuits, but the neurons in these circuits may participate in numerous engrams.

We have no knowledge of the locus of the engram at the present time. Numerous attempts have been made to locate the critical brain structures for particular learned tasks by damaging various regions of the brain. In humans, all learning of any significance requires the cerebral cortex. However, the basic physical-chemical mechanisms of engram formation can take place below the level of the cerebral cortex.

Brain stimulation has been frequently used as a tool in the search for the engram. It appears that stimulation of any region of the brain can serve as a CS which is somewhat analogous to a peripheral stimulus.

There are two approaches to electrical correlates of learning in the brain: (1) recording of brain activity during a learning experiment, and (2) utilization of brain activity as a response to be conditioned (EEG conditioning). In evoked-response studies, attempts have been made to correlate evoked responses with measures of behavioral conditioning. Emotional factors may be important in the changes which occur in evoked response amplitude when shock is the UCS. The evoked potential changes in amplitude may reflect the animal's emotional state more than being taken as an index of the developing memory trace. More recent evidence indicates that the waveforms of the evoked responses may be more relevant to learning than the amplitude.

In higher vertebrates, there are a few consistent findings on the electrophysiological correlates of learning. While the cortex is widely activated by the training stimuli during the initial phases of learning, later in training gross cortical activity is evidenced only in the primary sensory cortex and motor cortex. This redistribution of cortical activity usually is preceded by increases in activity in various subcortical "nonspecific" systems. In addition, the changes in brain activity are initiated prior to the overt responding. In many brain regions, distinctive evoked potential waveform similarities appear during conditioning. The secondary evoked potential components may reflect learning processes more closely than the primary sensory components. However, in aversive situations, much of the change in evoked potential learning may be the result of nonspecific fear and performance variables, and not of learning.

The consolidation hypothesis argues that there is a short-term memory trace which is consolidated into permanent memory. Presently, the evidence implicates two types of interference effects on prior learning. Very recent learning is highly susceptible to interference and loss; well learned habits are essentially unsusceptible to any loss.

One class of hypotheses about memory argues that learning involves chemical changes in the brain. The major issue is the identification of the nature of the chemical changes pertinent to learning in contrast with the chemical processes that are associated with all changes in neuronal activity. Two general categories of chemical theories are the transmitter theories, and the protein and RNA theories of learning. The transmitter theories are based on the existence of chemical synaptic transmission in the mammalian brain. Since learning must involve changes in neural interactions, and the most significant neuronal interactions occur at the synapse, then learning must involve changes in chemical synaptic transmission. The difficulty is that most chemical synaptic transmitter substances have not been identified with any significant degree of confidence.

Acetylcholine is one excitatory synaptic transmitter substance which has been well characterized. Various studies have suggested that raising animals in a rich environment results in an increase in brain cholinesterase. Other studies have attempted to investigate the hypothesis that learning occurs at ACh synapses in the brain. The studies have consistently indicated that ACh levels in the cerebral cortex can be altered by experience. However, the studies have revealed little about the role of ACh synapses in learning.

While the protein theories of learning appear reasonable on the grounds that proteins are the basic chemical building blocks of neurons, two factors raise problems for such hypotheses. There are a very large number of proteins which could be implicated in learning. In addition, the fact of regular and rapid protein turnover suggests that unique protein molecules could not be the basic process in memory since the turnover implies that memory duration could be no longer than approximately one month. The most reasonable manner in which proteins and RNA could be involved in learning would be as mechanisms by which the structures and chemical processes composing the synapses would be modified.

The fundamental problem in analyzing the protein and RNA approaches to learning is the distinction between learning and performance. In general, studies analyzing changes in biochemical substances in the brain which result from learning find changes in the amount of RNA, types of RNA, amounts and kinds of proteins and related chemical changes in brain tissues. However, the distinction between changes related to learning and those related to performance variables has not yet been made.

12

Complex processes:
thought and language

12 The study of comparative grammar is not the most direct approach to physiology of the cerebral cortex, yet Fournié has written, "Speech is the only window through which the physiologist can view the cerebral life." Certainly, language presents in a most striking form the integrative functions that are characteristic of the cerebral cortex and that reach their highest development in human thought processes.

(Lashley, 1960, page 507)

Inclusion of a chapter on such complex processes as thought and language in a text on physiological psychology is as much a gesture of optimism as a necessary consequence of current knowledge. Relatively little is known about the neural basis of many aspects of these phenomena. Even definitions and distinctions of such processes as thought and language are difficult in humans. People invariably talk to themselves when they think and sometimes think when they talk. We will not attempt to set forth precise definitions at this point, but instead will assume the common-sense meanings of the terms.

Texts on the subject of thinking often overlook the whole range of ordinary ongoing thought processes ranging from idle thought to daydreaming, night dreaming, and fantasy. People engage in daydreaming much of the time they are awake and night dreaming about one-quarter of each night's sleep (Chapter 10). Other types of behavior such as meditation are considered by some to be an aspect of thinking. Research on thinking in humans and other animals has been limited almost entirely to what might be termed directed thinking—information processing, problem-solving, and concept formation.

The diagram of Figure 12.1 from Norman (1969) is a convenient model of human information processing. For purposes of discussion it may be considered a vastly oversimplified flowchart of thinking, particularly if the entire diagram were included in a larger box of the biologically determined structures and functional properties of the individual. Physical stimuli activate sensory systems which analyze and process the input into the languages of the brain. _Iconic_ or very short-term _storage_ occurs here. The processed information is still "raw" information, that is, it has not yet been evaluated. It then enters the storage system(s), presumably first short-term or primary store and later permanent or secondary store (see Chapter 11). About at this point, information is selected. Humans remember and respond only to a small fraction of the potentially effective stimuli they receive. As you read this you have a variety of tactile and pressure sensations from sitting in a chair or lying down. If you attend, you will feel your heart beat and a variety of small sensations from your abdomen, mouth, and other body regions, as well as background sounds, sights, and odors. Most of these ongoing stimulus experiences are not selected or remembered.

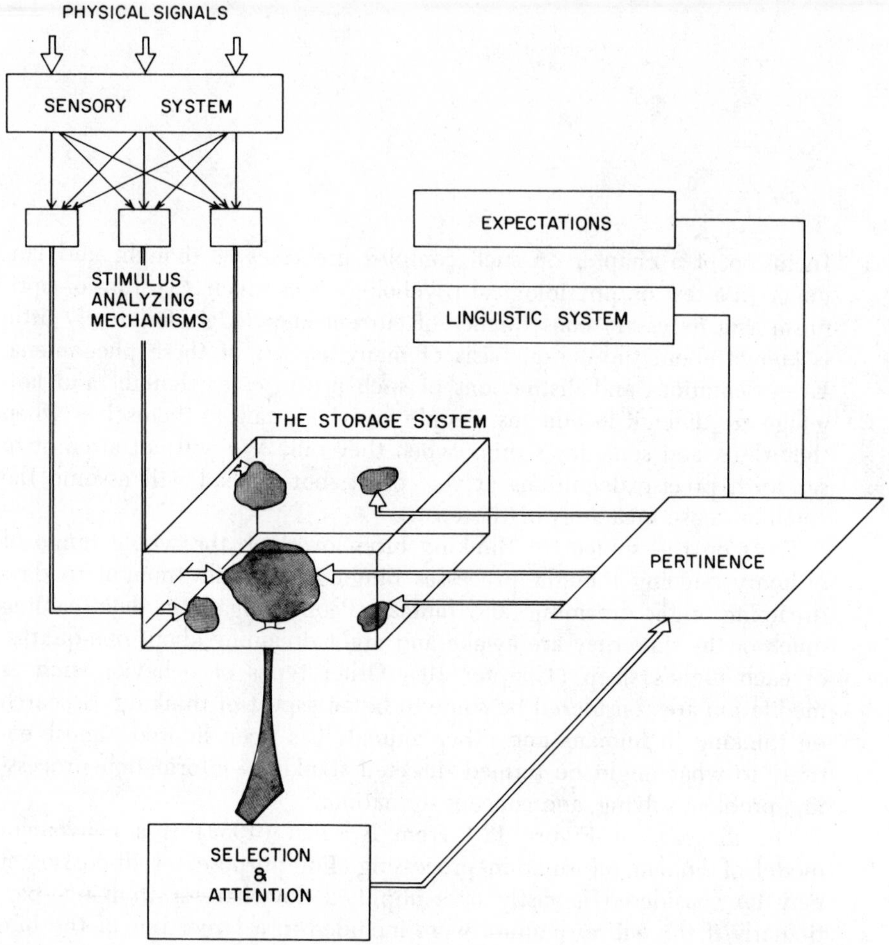

Figure 12.1 Hypothetical schema of human thinking or information processing. This approach to thinking views the memory storage system(s) as central. (Redrawn from Norman, D. A. *Memory and Attention: An Introduction to Human Information Processing.* New York: Wiley, 1969.)

Humans evaluate what is important, or pertinent (see Fig. 12.1), on the basis of the permanent memory store of information they process. This, of course, includes a language system and the expectations or motives humans may have at the time new information is accessed. These various systems and processes interact with new information to determine what is stored in permanent memory. They also determine the overt responses, if any, to new stimuli.

The basic point of Figure 12.1 is, of course, that processes such as learning and memory, attention, language, and thought do not occur in isolation. In fact, distinctions among these processes may be entirely artificial. Attention and learning, for example, may always be a single complex process in the brain. There is no reason to assume that simply because there are different words in the English language for different aspects of complex processes, these words really refer to different things or processes. Words are often merely convenient but fictional abstractions. To be more specific, there is recent evidence in human studies that *attention* does not occur prior to the development of long-term memory storage. If so, it may be impossible to distinguish attention from memory. Although the brain generates words like attention and memory, there is no necessary reason to conclude that these words refer to different brain processes. Keeping this caveat in mind, we will treat human memory, thought, and language separately as a matter of convenience.

Actually, the one category of complex human performance that most closely fits the notion of a separate process or function in the brain is language itself. Comparison of human cognition with that of our closest relative, the chimpanzee, shows the enormous qualitative jump provided by language. It is almost impossible to separate language from any other aspect of complex human abilities. Our chimpanzee cousins are very good at learning complex visual discriminations and solving complex problems. However, there is simply no comparison with humans; humans can code and record problems in verbal terms. In spite of the fact that language pervades all human activities, the brain substrates of language appear to be very recent and very specialized areas of the cerebral cortex. The anatomy, the functional organization, and the behavior of language are all quite new in evolution and quite specialized. Unlike the elusive engram for learning in general, language function appears to be specifically localized in certain regions of the human cerebral cortex.

LEARNING AND MEMORY IN THE HUMAN BRAIN

The amount of information stored in the normal adult human brain is almost without limit. Memory is among the most unique qualities of Homo sapiens. This is partly due to language. However, much more than simply a vocabulary is retained. Some portion of daily experience seems to be remembered almost indefinitely. It is possible that language provides a matrix that facilitates retention of experience. Certainly, we seem to recode visual stimuli into the verbal mode when we make an effort to store information. Memory of general experience, independent of language, seems to be stored by higher animals, at least from the level of carnivore to man. Higher mammals depend largely upon experience to survive.

We noted in Chapter 11 that human memory can be characterized in terms of several time course events. Iconic memory is very short-term memory lasting less than a second (see Fig. 11.2A). The parallel form and duration of the recovery cycle for evoked potentials recorded from the primary visual cortex in cat was also noted (Fig. 11.2B). The recovery cycle, the amplitude of response to the second of two identical stimuli relative to the amplitude of response to the first stimulus, is a simple measure of the persistence of effects of the first stimulus on a particular brain system, in this case, the primary visual system. Iconic memory is sense-modality specific. We might speculate (and it is only a guess) that iconic memory is localized to the primary sensory regions of the cerebral cortex.

The next longer duration of memory is primary or short-term memory, lasting a few seconds, the briefly remembered telephone number. We noted that this process in humans and the recovery cycle for evoked potentials recorded from association areas in cat and man have the same form and duration. It has been suggested by Sperling, who discovered iconic memory, that iconic memory is likely a separate process, independent of primary memory and not necessarily for it. By the same token, recovery cycles of association cortex evoked responses are unchanged after removal of visual cortex. We might guess that primary memory involves certain association regions of the cerebral cortex.

As noted in Chapter 11, it is not entirely clear whether primary and long-term or secondary permanent memory are two processes or one, or whether primary memory is necessary for permanent memory. The reader is urged to consult Norman (1969) and Voss (1974) for clear and readable discussions of these and other issues in human learning and memory. Wickelgren (1973) recently reviewed the evidence regarding the issue of the possible distinction between short-term and long-term memory, or as he puts it, "the long and the short of memory." He notes three types of evidence that favor the existence of two distinct processes. First, and most obvious, the form of the retention (remembering) curve is quite different for the two. Second, close degrees of similarity between things learned interfere with long-term storage but not short-term storage. Third, certain types of human brain damage, particularly to temporal regions of the brain, are extremely selective in severely impairing long-term storage without impairing short-term storage. (We will review this latter data below.) Consequently, current evidence does favor the view of two separate processes of short-term and long-term memory storage.

The little information we have about the brain mechanisms of learning and memory in humans has been obtained from unfortunate experiments of nature where persons have suffered brain damage, either from injury and disease, or as a result of necessary brain surgery.

ICONIC

536

Complex processes:
thought and
language

short
term
memory

Wernicke-Korsakoff disease

Wernicke-Korsakoff disease produces a very clear and pronounced defect in memory. Adams and associates (Adams, 1969) completed an extensive study on 219 patients with the disease and did extensive neuroanatomical studies on 53 terminal cases. The disease is characteristic of severe alcoholism and appears to be due almost entirely to extreme thiamine deficiency—it is not due to the ingestion of alcohol but rather to the lack of ingestion of food, particularly that containing B vitamins. If the disease is diagnosed early enough, the symptoms can be reversed with massive doses of B vitamins. The symptoms of Wernicke-Korsakoff disease are quite striking. Adams summarizes the positive diagnostic (i.e., the characteristics that define the disease) features as follows:

1. An inability to form new memories, that is, anterograde amnesia (prolonged practice does not help).
2. A loss of past memories, which had been formed before the beginning of the illness, that is, retrograde amnesia.
3. Confabulation, that is, fabrications about past events in response to questions or in spontaneous conversation.
4. Paucity of information and meagerness of content in conversation.
5. Loss in insight, that is, lack of or incomplete awareness of the memory defect.
6. Apathy, indifference, and incapacity to adopt a set or to persevere in complex activities.

The negative [diagnostic] features of the syndrome were identified as follows:

1. Preservation of normal capacity to think, solve problems, etc.; in the end stages of the disease intelligence test scores are probably little if at all reduced from premorbid level despite gross memory defects.
2. Preservation of an alert, attentive, wide-awake state of mind.
3. Ability to perceive, imagine, speak, and calculate with customary speed and efficiency.
4. Adequate cooperation and motivation in test procedures.
5. Correct deportment.
6. Lack of other neurological signs of cerebral deficit (EEG and CSF normal).

(Adams, 1969, pages 98–99)

In sum, patients have normal or near normal intelligence, motivation, perception, numerical, and verbal abilities, but severely impaired permanent memory for events both before and after onset of the disease. Interference with long-term memories formed after disease or damage is common in temporal lobe damage, as we will see below. However, loss of well learned memories prior to disease is unusual and may be characteristic of diseases that cause widespread damage to the brain, particularly the cerebral cortex.

The findings of Adams and associates on the brain damage that develops in such patients illustrates the difficulties in assigning functions to particular parts of the human brain on the basis of clinical data. It is stated widely in neurology and pathology tests that the common feature of brain damage in Wernicke-Korsakoff disease is severe damage to the mammillary bodies. Many neurologists have consequently localized long-term memory to the mammillary bodies. This is a region of the hypothalamus that receives the major projection from the hippocampus via the fornix (see Chapter 9). This observation does not really fit well with the animal data, except insofar as some animal studies report certain types of impairment in learning with hippocampal damage.

Adams and associates were able to rule out the involvement of the mammillary bodies in memory impairment in Wernicke-Korsakoff disease. While it was true that every patient with the disease had damage to the mammillary bodies, several such patients had *no memory impairment whatsoever*. Structures most likely to be damaged in the disease are those surrounding the third ventricle. The closer a structure is to the ventricle, the more likely it is to be damaged. Why this should be so for damage due to vitamin deficiency is unclear, but it is so. In the study by Adams, the medial dorsal nucleus of the thalamus was the one critical structure—degree of memory loss correlated closely with degree of damage to this nucleus. The medial dorsal nucleus is a major relay in the limbic system (Chapter 9) and also has extensive projection to frontal cortex in primates and man. Whether other structures are also involved in the disease, as seems likely, and whether subtle chemical changes occurred in tissues that appeared normal under the microscope, cannot be determined from Adams' work. Many more careful anatomical chemical studies of this type are needed on complex human brain disease syndromes involving memory.

The temporal lobes

A classical and dramatic example of seemingly permanent memory impairment following bilateral removal of portions of the temporal lobe has been studied by Brenda Milner in Montreal (1966):

This young man (H.M.) . . . had had no obvious memory disturbance before his operation, having, for example, passed his high school examinations without difficulty. . . . [He sustained] a minor head injury . . . at the age of seven. Minor [seizures] began one year later, and then, at the age of 16, he began to have generalized seizures which, despite heavy medication, increased in frequency and severity until, by the age of 27, he was no longer able to work . . . his prospects were by then so desperate that . . . the radical bilateral medial temporal lobe [surgery] . . . was performed. The patient was drowsy for the first few postoperative days but then, as he became more alert, a severe memory impairment was apparent. He could no longer recognize the hospital staff, apart from [the surgeon], whom he had known for many years; he did not remember and could not relearn the way to the bathroom, and he seemed to retain nothing of the day-to-day happenings in the hospital. . . . His early memories were seemingly vivid and intact, his speech was normal, and his social behaviour and emotional responses were entirely appropriate.

There has been little change in this clinical picture during the years which have elapsed since the operation . . . there [is no] evidence of general intellectual loss; in fact, his intelligence as measured by standard tests is actually a little higher now than before the operation. . . . Yet the remarkable memory defect persists, and it is clear that H.M. can remember little of the experience of the past . . . years. . . .

Ten months after the operation the family moved to a new house which was situated only a few blocks away from their old one, on the same street. When examined . . . nearly a year later, H.M. had not yet learned the new address, nor could he be trusted to find his way home alone, because he would go to the old house. Six years ago the family moved again, and H.M. is still unsure of his present address, although he does seem to know that he has moved. [The patient] . . . will do the same jigsaw puzzles day after day without showing any practice effect, and read the same magazines over and over again without finding their contents familiar. . . .

Even such profound amnesias as this are, however, compatible with a normal attention span . . . On one occasion, he was asked to remember the number "584" and was then allowed to sit quietly with no interruption for 15 minutes, at which point he was able to recall the number correctly without hesitation. When asked how he had been able to do this, he replied,

"It's easy. You just remember 8. You see, 5, 8, and 4 add to 17. You remember 8; substract it from 17 and it leaves 9. Divide 9 in half and you get 5 and 4, and there you are: 584. Easy."

In spite of H.M.'s elaborate mnemonic scheme, he was unable, a minute or so later, to remember either the number "584" or any of the associated complex train of thought; in fact, he did not know that he had been given a number to remember . . .

One gets some idea of what such an amnesic state must be like from H.M.'s own comments . . . Between tests, he would suddenly look up and say, rather anxiously,

"Right now, I'm wondering. Have I done or said anything amiss? You see, at this moment everything looks clear to me, but what happened

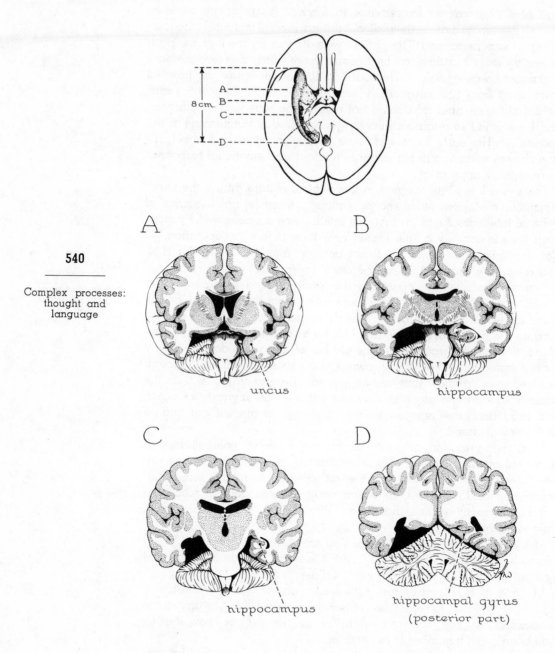

Figure 12.2 Diagrammatic cross sections of the human brain, showing the estimated extent of removal in Dr. Scoville's medial temporal lobe ablation. All operations were bilateral, single-stage procedures but here, for illustrative purposes, one side has been left intact. (From Milner, B. The memory defect in bilateral hippocampal lesions, *Psychiat. Res. Rep.* **11**, 1959, pp. 43–52.)

just before? That's what worries me. It's like waking from a dream; I just don't remember."

(Milner, 1966, pages 112–115)

The primary loss shown by this patient was in the formation of new permanent memory. His iconic memory and short-term or primary memory were intact and seemingly normal, or nearly so. Furthermore, his permanent memory for well learned events prior to surgery was intact. He could no longer convert immediate memory into long-term storage. However, the speech areas were not damaged.

Brenda Milner's studies of H.M. have become a classic illustration both of selective loss of long-term memory and how to do clinical research properly. The approximate regions of the brain removed in H.M. are shown in Figure 12.2. Both temporal lobes were removed, including the cerebral cortex and portions of the hippocampus and amygdala. The syndrome exhibited by H.M. is of great interest both in terms of the abilities he lost and the abilities he retained. Jerzy Konorski, a renowned Polish neuropsychologist, developed a method of testing memory for

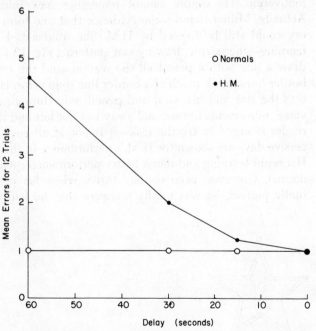

Figure 12.3 Effect of bilateral medial temporal lobe resection on the ability to compare stimuli that are separated by a short time interval. The graph shows the mean error scores of patient H. M. for five tasks, as a function of the intratrial interval. Six errors would be chance performance. (Prisko, 1963; figure modified from Milner, B. Memory and the medial temporal regions of the brain. In Pribram, K. H., and Broadbent, D. E. (eds.) *Biology and Memory*. New York: Academic Press, 1970, pp. 29–50.)

single events, termed *delayed paired comparisons,* which Milner used on H.M. Successive stimuli are presented one at a time with variable time (usually 0 to 60 seconds) between presentations and the subject is asked each time whether the last two are the same or different. Stimuli can be tones, color shades, nonsense forms, words, etc. Normal subjects average about one error for every 12 trials even when time intervals between stimuli were as long as 60 seconds. The performance of H.M. is shown in Figure 12.3. His error score increased dramatically as time interval was increased and at 60 seconds he was performing not much better than chance (6 errors for 12 trials is chance). Thus, H.M. can register new perceptual information quite normally in short-term store. However, the information ceases to be available to him in about 30 seconds—the approximate maximum time limit for short-term store duration.

It is important to emphasize that H.M. had no loss of knowledge or skills acquired prior to surgery, no reduction in intelligence measured by IQ tests, no perceptual difficulty, no impairment of short-term primary memory, no impairment of verbal ability, and no deficit in attention or motivation. He simply cannot remember new information very long. Actually, Milner found some evidence that one form of long-term memory could still be formed by H.M. She used a task that tapped motor learning—the mirror drawing star pattern (Fig. 12.4). The subject must draw a line with a pencil all the way around the star between the two border lines. Each touch of a border line is an error. However, the subject sees the star and his hand and pencil only through a mirror, which reverses movements toward and away but not left and right. The interested reader is urged to try the task—it is not at all easy at first! Three successive days are shown for H.M.'s performance of the task in Figure 12.5. His rapid learning and much better performance each day are essentially normal. However, even on day three, when his performance was virtually perfect, he was totally unaware that he had ever done the task

Figure 12.4 A mirror-reversed drawing star task. The subject views the star through a mirror such that movements toward and away are reversed but left and right are not. Subject must draw a pencil line between two star borders without touching a border. Each border touch is an error. (Redrawn from Milner, B. Les troubles de la mémoire accompagnant des lésions hippocampiques bilatérales. In *Physiologie de l'hippocampe.* Paris: Centre National de la Recherche Scientifique, 1962, pp. 257–272.)

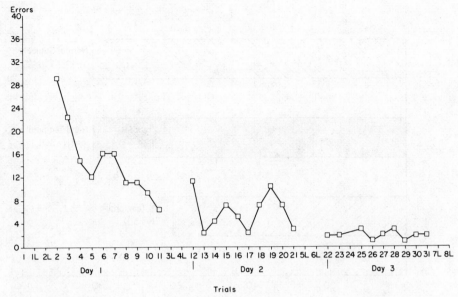

Figure 12.5 Mirror-drawing performance of H. M. showing normal learning over the three-day period. (Modified from Milner, B. Les troubles de la mémoire accompagnant des lésions hippocampiques bilatérales. In *Physiologie de l'hippocampe*. Paris: Centre National de la Recherche Scientifique, 1962, pp. 257–272.)

before and it had to be explained to him again. A normal subject, of course, remembers the task in terms of his verbal report as well as of his motor performance.

In essence, H.M. has normal abilities to develop long-term storage of learned motor skills. There appears to be a complete dissociation between his *perceptual-verbal-awareness* memory and his *perceptual-motor* memory. This is a most important finding and deserves great emphasis. It would seem to argue that the brain substrates for motor-skill learning and memory are entirely different than those for verbal awareness. Does H.M. remember the mirror task or not?—By one measure, his own verbal report, not at all; by another measure, his own motor performance, perfectly.

H.M.'s brain damage was bilateral; both temporal lobes were removed. Milner and her associates have evaluated the effects of damage to left versus right temporal lobe in a series of patients. The reader may recall from our discussion of the Sperry and Gazzaniga studies on split-brained humans in Chapter 3 that verbal abilities are localized in the left hemisphere and spatial abilities in the right hemisphere, with particular focus in the so-called speech areas. Milner has focused on memory rather than speech per se, and her series of patients had damage to temporal lobes but not to the speech areas. The tasks Milner and her colleagues used are of great importance. One was a modification of the Peterson short-term

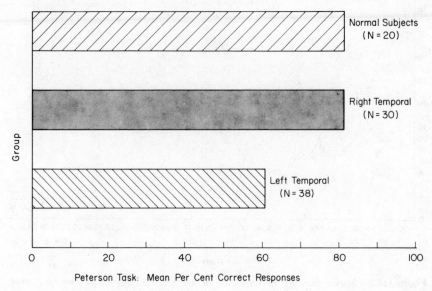

Figure 12.6 Verbal memory defect after left temporal lobectomy. Corsi's (1969) results for Peterson and Peterson task requiring recall of three consonants after a short distracting activity. (From Milner, B. Disorders of learning and memory after temporal lobe lesions in man. *Clinical Neurosurg.* **19**, 1972, pp. 421–446.)

memory paradigm using verbal material—the subject has to recall a group of three consonants (e.g., X, B, J) after an interval of 3 to 18 seconds while counting backward from a given number (e.g., 357). This is a test of short-term memory for verbal material. Performances of normal subjects, patients with right temporal lobe damage, and left temporal lobe damage are shown in Figure 12.6. The normals and right temporals performed the same and the left temporals showed a marked deficit.

A further analysis of the left temporal patient group permitted some evaluation of the importance of the hippocampus in the short-term memory task. It was possible to match patients on amount of temporal lobe cerebral cortex removed with varying degrees of removal of the hippocampus (Fig. 12.7). The results of this analysis on the Peterson task are shown in Figure 12.8. The more hippocampus removed, the greater the deficit.

Patients with right temporal lobes removed performed normally on short-term memory for verbal material. Could they be shown to have a deficit in short-term spatial memory? Milner and associates utilized an ingenious test developed by Michael Posner at the University of Oregon (see Fig. 12.9). The subject is shown a drawing of a line with a circle part way along the line. The drawing then is covered, and after a rest

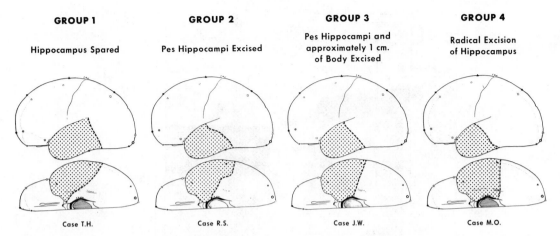

Hippocampus Spared

GROUP 2

Pes Hippocampi Excised

GROUP 3

Pes Hippocampi and approximately 1 cm. of Body Excised

GROUP 4

Radical Excision of Hippocampus

Case T.H.

Case R.S.

Case J.W.

Case M.O.

Figure 12.7 Brain maps based on the surgeon's drawings at the time of operation, showing representative left temporal lobectomies in four groups of patients classed according to the extent of hippocampal destruction. Lateral surface *above,* medial surface *below; stippled area* indicates extent of cortical excision. (From Milner, B. Memory and the medial temporal regions of the brain. In Pribram, K. H., and Broadbent, D. E. (eds.) *Biology and Memory.* New York: Academic Press, 1970, pp. 29–50.)

Learning and memory in the human brain

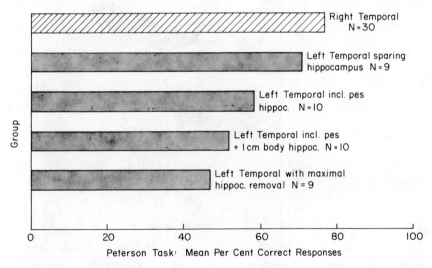

Figure 12.8 Verbal memory defect after left temporal lobectomy as related to medial extent of temporal lobe resection. These data for the Peterson task show the progressive reduction in the mean number of consonant trigrams correctly recalled with increasing destruction of the left hippocampus. No impairment is seen after right temporal lobectomy, regardless of whether or not the hippocampus was excised. (From Milner, B. Memory and the medial temporal regions of the brain. In Pribram, K. H., and Broadbent, D. E. (eds.) *Biology and Memory.* New York: Academic Press, 1970, pp. 29–50.)

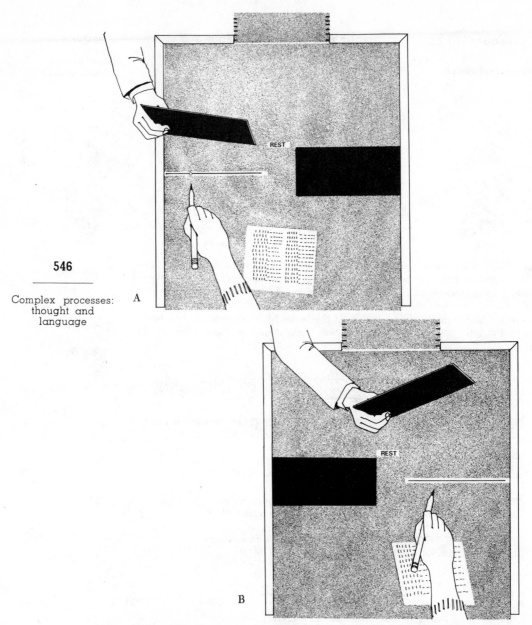

A

B

Figure 12.9 Drawings illustrating the procedure adapted by Corsi from Posner (1966) to test memory for the exact position of a small circle situated at various distances along an 8-inch line. A, The patient marks the circle indicated on the exposed line. B, After a short intratrial delay, he attempts to reproduce this position, from memory as accurately as possible, on a similar 8-inch line. The sign "REST" means that the patient did nothing during the interval, in contrast to "WORK" trials in which a distracting activity was interpolated. (From Milner, B. Hemispheric specialization: Scope and limits. In Schmitt, F. O., and Worden, F. G. (eds.). *The Neurosciences: Third Study Program.* Copyright © 1974, and reprinted by permission of The M.I.T. Press, Cambridge, Massachusetts.)

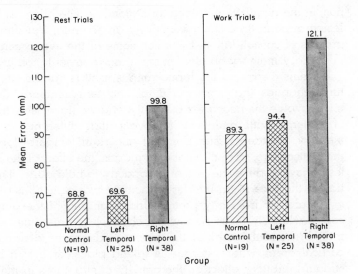

Figure 12.10 Results of the Posner task, showing impaired memory for position after right temporal lobectomy but not after left. The score is the total error (in millimeters) for four trials, without regard to sign, averaged across three retention intervals. (From Milner, B. Disorders of learning and memory after temporal lobe lesions in man. *Clinical Neurosurg.* **19**, 1972, pp. 421–446.)

period, the subject must indicate the location of the circle on a test line. The performance of normals, the left temporals (now the control lesion group), and the right temporals are shown in Figure 12.10. As predicted, the left temporals and normals are the same but the right temporals make many more errors. Interestingly, analysis in terms of amount of hippocampus damaged revealed no effect, in contrast to the verbal short-term memory task for the left temporal lobe removal group. The critical factor for right temporal lobe removal effect on the spatial short-term memory task was amount of temporal cerebral cortex removed.

It is not easy to form unambiguous conclusions from these studies. It was clear that H.M., with bilateral removal of both temporal lobes, was unable to form new permanent memories, except for motor skills. This does not mean that his long-term memory "center" had been removed—after all, he retained everything he had learned prior to surgery. More likely, some part of the brain systems critically involved in translating short-term store into long-term store was destroyed. In contrast, the patients with lesions limited to one side or the other appeared to show more deficit of modality-specific (e.g., verbal versus spatial) short-term memory. However, in the normal person, both processes occur and the Peterson task may depend in part on both.

Milner draws the following conclusions:

The data reviewed in this chapter have focused attention on the role of the medial temporal lobe structures, and particularly the hippocampus, in the acquisition of long term memory. The bilateral hippocampal lesion appears to disturb selectively an essential transition process, or process of consolidation, by which some of the evanescent information in primary memory obtains an enduring representation in the brain.

It seems clear that the hippocampus itself is not the site of the structural changes that correspond to long term memory. Such learning must involve the neocortex primarily, and we have seen, from the study of patients with unilateral removals, that different material-specific memory disorders result from left and right temporal lobe lesions. In these disorders, as in the global amnesias, the effect of the hippocampal lesion is to reduce the patient's capacity to hold quite simple information in the face of an interfering activity that claims his attention.

We are far from any precise understanding of the underlying processes whereby these behavioral changes are mediated. It is possible that, in normal learning, the hippocampus acts to prime activity in cortical areas where storage is taking place, or that it has a downstream inhibitory effect on the activity of structures in the lower brain stem . . . thereby reducing the interfering effect of new sensory input . . . Nor do we know whether the deficit after bilateral lesions should be regarded as a failure of storage (as I have always supposed), or as a failure to inhibit inappropriate responses at the time of retrieval, as Warrington and Weiskrantz . . . maintain. Only future research can decide among these hypotheses.

(Milner, 1972, page 443)

Studies of effects of frontal lobe damage in monkeys and apes have stressed a particular kind of memory impairment termed *delayed response*. This literature will be examined in more detail below in the context of functions of the association areas of the cerebral cortex. One of the problems in comparing human and infrahuman primate lesion studies has been to show a loss in man in tasks comparable to *delayed response*. In brief, a monkey is shown two or more food wells, one is baited, they are all covered, a period of time elapses, and the monkey must remember which well was baited. Monkeys with frontal lobe damage show severe deficits in this simple temporal memory task. However, the task is too easy for brain-damaged humans. Brenda Milner (personal communication, 1973) recently developed some ingenious tests for temporal memory function in human patients with damage to either the left or right frontal lobe. Arguing by analogy from the general separation of functions in the human brain (left–verbal, right–spatial), Milner developed two temporal memory tasks. For verbal, she showed the patient a series of cards, one at a time, with time intervals between. Each card had an "interesting" word on it (motivation is a problem with frontal brain-damaged humans). At a certain point in the series of cards, a card having two of the previously shown words on it would be exhibited and the patient was required to say which of the two words had been shown more recently. Results were striking. Left frontal damage patients had great difficulty with the task but right frontal patients did as well as normals.

To tap spatial-temporal memory, Milner used the same type of test except each card had a modern abstract painting on it. The paintings could not easily be recoded verbally. The test card had two of the previously shown paintings and the patient was to identify which painting he had seen more recently. In this task, the right frontal lobe damaged patients showed a deficit and the left frontal patients did as well as normal subjects.

In short, memory for the temporal ordering of past experience seems to depend more on the frontal lobes. Temporal lobe patients had no great difficulties with these tasks. Further, the general segregation of the human brain into verbal–left hemisphere and spatial–right hemisphere occurs even in the frontal lobes.

Brain substrates of short-term and long-term memory

In terms of differential effects of brain damage on short-term and long-term memory, Milner's studies of H.M. are perhaps the clearest dichotomy in the literature. H.M. had normal short-term memory but virtually no long-term memory (except for motor skills).

There have been a few reports of the opposite kind of syndrome—impairment of short-term memory but not long-term memory (see Warrington and Weiskrantz, 1973). The case of K.F. was studied in detail by Warrington and Shallice (1972). K.F. was profoundly deficient in the ability to repeat brief strings of letters or numbers presented to him verbally. He could recall only one item correctly. However, his performance was nearly normal when the same items were presented visually. Examples of this very specific defect of short-term memory are shown in Figure 12.11. Even at very short delays, K.F. was severely impaired. Control tests indicated no impairment of auditory perception or motor speech. Luria and his associates (Luria et al., 1967) in the Soviet Union have similarly reported on patients showing specific defects in short-term memory for auditorily presented verbal items, without impairment of short-term memory for the same materials presented visually. Such patients have difficulty with spoken language but not in reading.

In contrast, some patients have also been described who have defects in short-term visual memory for digits, letters, and nonsymbolic line stimuli, but not with auditory memory of verbally presented sounds or words. These patients typically have severe reading impairment but no difficulty with spoken language (see Warrington and Weiskrantz, 1973).

These impairments all appear to be due to damage to the left hemisphere. The approximate locations on the left hemisphere of lesions pro-

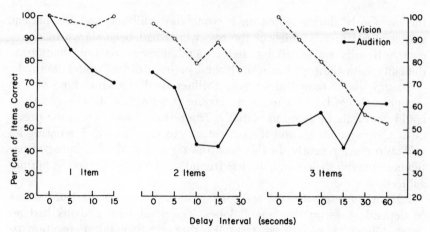

Figure 12.11 Post-operative recall after varying delay intervals of single, two, or three letters presented visually or auditorily. Broken line indicates visual and solid line indicates auditory recall. (Redrawn from Warrington, E. K., and Shallice, T. Neuropsychological evidence of visual storage in short-term memory tasks. *Quart. J. Exp. Psychol.* **24,** 1972, pp. 30–40.)

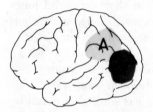

Figure 12.12 Provisional anatomical foci for auditory (A) and visual (V) short-term memory deficits. (Redrawn from Warrington, E. K., and Weiskrantz, L. An analysis of short-term and long-term memory defects in man. In Deutsch, J. A. (ed.) *The Physiological Basis of Memory.* New York: Academic Press, 1973, pp. 365–395.)

ducing these modality-specific impairments in short-term memory are shown in Figure 12.12. It is of great importance to note that these short-term memory defects appear independent of long-term memory, at least in the case of K.F. He was given a series of verbal learning tasks, presented in the auditory mode and exhibited normal long-term memory in the face of markedly impaired short-term memory! We may provisionally assume that the regions of posterior association cortex shown in Figure 12.12 are critically involved in short-term memory for auditory and visually presented materials. Putting this together with Milner's studies of H.M., where long-term memory requires the temporal lobes, we may begin to see some degree of pattern or localization of memory function in humans. However, a more comprehensive analysis must include speech and language functions. Indeed, the modality-specific short-term memory defects described above could be redescribed as language impairments—defects in comprehension of spoken or written language—as well as defects in short-term memory. We will return to the issue of the brain substrate of language and speech after a brief review of the association cortex in higher animals and man.

ASSOCIATION AREAS OF THE CEREBRAL CORTEX AND THOUGHT

The association areas of the cerebral cortex are the regions that seem most specialized for mediation of complex processes like thought and language. These regions of cortex have expanded enormously in phylogenetic development of mammals. There is little association cortex in the rat, but in man the bulk of the cortex is association rather than sensory or motor. In the late 19th and early 20th centuries a kind of "switchboard" theory of cortical function was popular. Sensory information was believed to project to sensory fields of the cortex, relayed directly to association areas where it was "associated, integrated, and evaluated" and then relayed to motor cortex to control movements. It was assumed that subcortical systems, other than those concerned with autonomic activity, served primarily to get information to the cortex and movements from it. Many years ago Lashley (1950) disposed of any rigid interpretation of this type by showing that severing the motor cortex from sensory areas by deep vertical cuts appeared to have little effect on a monkey's behavior. However, as we will see later in our discussion of brain correlates of human language, such *cortical-cortical* connections appear to be of crucial importance in the human brain.

Most information concerning the possible functions of association cortex has come from studies of the behavioral effects of removing it. Association cortex has been the favored target of assaults by physiological psychologists in recent years. The primate, particularly the rhesus monkey, has been the subject of choice in most lesion-behavior studies. The rhesus has a large amount of association cortex, and is readily adaptable to behavioral training and testing procedures and has an all-too-human disposition, particularly when displeased. It might be well to describe the most common technique used for behavioral testing of primates, namely the Wisconsin General Test Apparatus (see Fig. 12.13) developed and standardized by Harlow. The monkey remains in a cage facing the investigator. A stimulus tray in front of the animal can be pushed forward so that he can reach objects on it through the bars of his cage. The objects are placed over the food wells, one of which is baited with a raisin, peanut, or other reward. The experimenter can slide the tray back and interpose an opaque screen while baiting the wells. To take a simple example of discrimination learning, suppose the monkey is required to discriminate between a cube and a pyramid. The experimenter always baits the food well underneath the cube, but varies the relative positions of the two objects in a random fashion. The monkey soon learns to push the cube away to obtain the reward.

551

Association areas of
the cerebral cortex
and thought

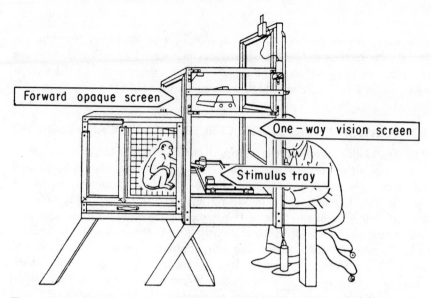

Figure 12.13 The Wisconsin General Testing Apparatus (WGTA) used to test monkeys in a variety of discrimination and learning problems. (From Harlow, H. F. Behavioral contributions to interdisciplinary research. In Harlow, H. F., and Woolsey, C. N. (eds.) *Biological and Biochemical Bases of Behavior.* Madison: Univ. of Wisconsin Press, 1958, pp. 3–23.)

Behavioral tests that have been used extensively in evaluating effects of cortical damage include *discrimination learning,* particularly visual discriminations, *learning sets, delayed response,* and *delayed alternation.* We have just described the basic procedures for visual discrimination. The animal is required to respond to one object but not another. *Learning set* is an interesting "higher order" type of discrimination learning task (see Harlow, 1949). The monkey is given a long series of six-trial tests on simple visual discriminations. Each test employs a different pair of dissimilar objects. Thus on the first test the animal is given six trials of training on two dissimilar objects, one of which is always correct. If his first trial response is to the wrong object, he has to wait until the next trial. After six trials on this pair of objects, he is given six trials on a different pair of objects, and so on. A normal adult human usually will solve the problem on the second trial of each test; no information is available telling which object is correct on trial one. If the correct object is first chosen, it will always be correct in the next five trials. If the incorrect object is chosen on the first trial the other object will always be correct on subsequent trials. Thus performance over a long series of such six-trial tests will always be about 50 per cent correct on trial one and 100 per cent on trials two to six. Rhesus monkeys (and small children) typically improve gradually on their performance of trials two to six over a long period of time with a great many different test objects. This gradual improvement on trials two to six is what has been called by Harlow *learning set.*

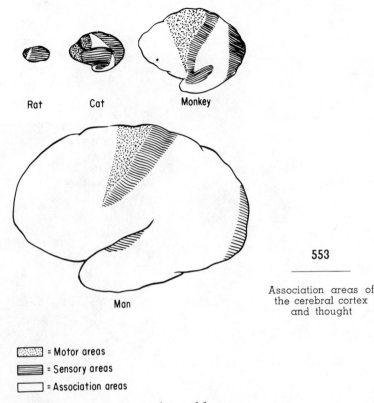

Rat   Cat   Monkey

Man

▨ = Motor areas

▤ = Sensory areas

▢ = Association areas

553

Association areas of
the cerebral cortex
and thought

Figure 12.14 Approximate scale drawings of the cerebral hemispheres of four mammals. Note both the increase in size and relative increase in amount of "association" cortex. (From Thompson, R. F. *Foundations of Physiological Psychology.* New York: Harper & Row, 1967.)

The *delayed response* test was first developed by Hunter (1913). The method in common use today for primates is to bait one of two food wells while the monkey watches and then place two identical objects over the food wells and require the monkey to wait for varying periods of time, usually from 0 to 30 sec, before pushing the tray within reach. An opaque screen is often placed in front of the monkey during the period of delay. In colloquial terms, the monkey has to "remember" which object the food is under. Delayed alternation is an elaboration of the delayed response test. On the first trial, two identical objects are usually baited. After the monkey makes the first choice an opaque screen is interposed and only the object opposite the one chosen on the first trial is baited. If the monkey gets this correct, the opposite object is next baited, and so on. If the monkey chooses the incorrect object, he is required to repeat the trial until he eventually chooses that object. Varying periods of delay are used between successive choices in the delayed alternation test. Again, in colloquial terms, all the monkey has to do is

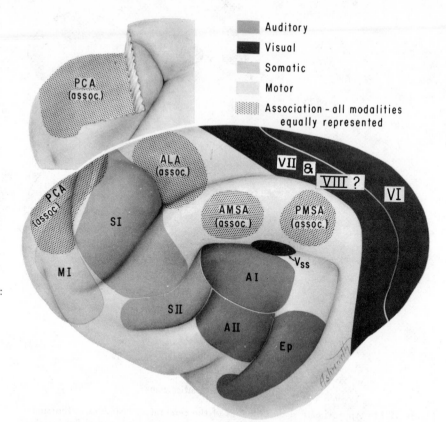

Auditory
Visual
Somatic
Motor
Association - all modalities equally represented

Figure 12.15 Primary and association evoked response regions of the cerebral cortex of the cat. Primary areas are modality specific, but association responses are evoked by all types of stimuli. VI, VII, VIII, Vss, visual areas; AI, AII, Ep, auditory areas; SI, SII, MI, sensory-motor areas; PCA, ALA, AMSA, PMSA, association response areas. (From Thompson, R. F., Johnson, R. H., and Hoopes, J. J. Organization of auditory, somatic sensory, and visual projection to association fields of cerebral cortex in the cat. *J. Neurophysiol.* **26,** 1963, pp. 343–364.)

"remember" which object the bait was under on the last trial and choose the opposite object on the next trial.

The extent of association cortex visible on the lateral surface of the brain in rat, cat, monkey, and man are shown in Figure 12.14. Much of the association cortex, particularly in monkey and man, tends to be electrically "silent," in the sense that peripheral stimuli like sounds and lights do not evoke neural activity. Certain regions of association cortex can be activated by all varieties of stimuli—they are *polysensory*. Much of the association cortex of cat and dog is of this type (see Fig. 12.15). The primate association cortex also has posterior and anterior polysensory areas but they are less extensive *relative* to silent association cortex. The extent of polysensory association cortex in man is not known. These poly-

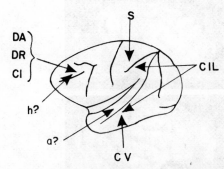

Figure 12.16 "Localization of function" in association areas of the primate cortex in terms of the results of lesion experiments. Abbreviations are: a, complex auditory; CI, conditioned inhibition, CV, complex visual discriminations; CIL, complex intersensory learning; DA, delayed alternation; DR, delayed response; h, hyperactivity; S, somesthetic discriminations. (Modified from Chow, K. L., and Hutt, P. J. The "association cortex" of *Macaca mulatta:* A review of recent contributions to its anatomy and functions. *Brain* **76**, 1953, pp. 625–677.)

555

Association areas of
the cerebral cortex
and thought

sensory areas seem to play a special role in coding the significance of stimuli to the organism.

Certain regions of silent association cortex in primates can be categorized as having complex functions that are modality specific. The extensive lesion-behavior studies of Pribram and his associates at Stanford have demonstrated functional specialization of posterior association cortex for somesthesis, vision and hearing; see Figure 12.16.

The frontal lobes

One most impressive aspect of the human brain is the relatively great size of the frontal lobes, particularly the cortex anterior to the motor area. Almost all conceivable functions have been attributed at one time or another to the frontal lobes; such functions range from sensory-motor integration to higher thought processes, the will, emotions, and intelligence. A tremendous amount of research has been done on the possible behavioral functions of the frontal lobes; see the symposium on the *Frontal Granular Cortex and Behavior*, edited by Warren and Akert (1964).

The locations of the frontal granular cortex (Brodmann's areas 7–12) are indicated in Figure 12.17 for cat, dog, squirrel monkey, and rhesus monkey. The relative amount of this frontal granular cortex increases from cat to rhesus, and is considerably greater still in man. A large portion—but not all—of the frontal granular cortex receives direct projections from the dorsomedial nucleus of the thalamus (Akert, 1964).

The most consistent and clear-cut behavioral deficit exhibited by monkeys after frontal lesions is severe and long-lasting impairment in delayed response performance. This was first demonstrated in the clas-

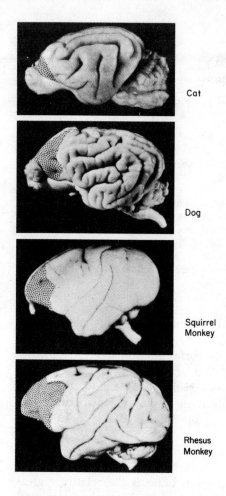

Cat

Dog

Squirrel
Monkey

Rhesus
Monkey

Figure 12.17 Relative locations of the frontal granular cortex in four mammals (brains not to scale). (From Warren, J. M., and Akert, K. (eds.). *The Frontal Granular Cortex and Behavior*. New York: McGraw-Hill, 1964.)

sic study by Jacobsen (1935) and has been confirmed in dozens of subsequent studies. A carefully designed experiment by French and Harlow (1962) is typical. Monkeys were trained pre-operatively in a simple delayed response task. At the start of a given trial an opaque screen was present in front of the animal. After raising the opaque screen, the experimenter placed a reward in one of two food wells and placed identical wooden blocks over the two food wells when the monkey had given some sign of attending to the reinforcement. Both food wells were immediately covered and five seconds allowed to pass. The object tray was then advanced and the monkey allowed to displace one block only and obtain (or fail to obtain) the reward. Pre-operative performance of a group of

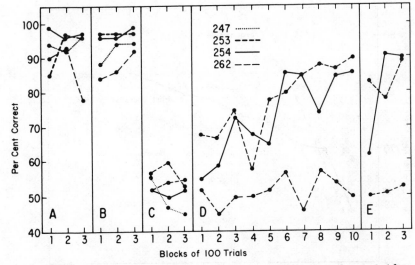

Figure 12.18 Performance of monkeys with lesions removing frontal area 9 (done between B and C) on delayed reaction. A, Last 300 trials of initial training. B, Pre-operative retests. C, Early post-operative retests. D, Interim post-operative retests. E, Late post-operative retests. (From French, G. M., and Harlow, H. F. Variability of delayed-reaction performance in normal and brain damaged rhesus monkeys. *J. Neurophysiol.* **25**, 1962, pp. 585–599.)

Association areas of
the cerebral cortex
and thought

four monkeys trained to criterion on this task is shown in Figure 12.18. Data are plotted in blocks of 100 trials; the performance shown is for the last 300 trials of training. Part D of Figure 12.18 illustrates retesting of these same animals after a period of six months had elapsed in which they were given no training. This control demonstrates that the monkeys did not forget the performance during the six-month period. Between portions B and C of the figure, animals all received bilateral ablations of area 9 of the prefrontal granular cortex. Their initial performance, shown in portion C of the figure, is at a chance level for the first 300 trials. In portion D they are shown on intermediate post-operative test performance in over 1000 trials of training. As can be seen, there is significant improvement in the performance. Figure 12.18E illustrates the last of a very long series of post-operative training trials. Note that two animals perform moderately well and one animal still responds at chance level. This partial recovery of delayed response performance is obtained only after very extensive post-operative training; few studies have reported even this much recovery of function. Although the delayed response deficit is most characteristic of frontal damage, lesions to certain regions of limbic forebrain structures can also impair delayed response.

Another task that shows marked impairment after frontal lesion is delayed alternation. An example from an experiment by Stamm (1964) is shown in Figure 12.19. Four animals were trained pre-operatively in the delayed alternation task. In this experiment, the animals faced a

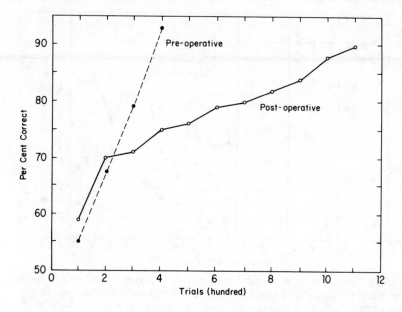

Figure 12.19 Per cent correct performance by a group of monkeys on a delayed alternation task before and after frontal lesions. (From Stamm, J. S. Retardation and facilitation in learning by stimulation of frontal cortex in monkeys. In Warren, J. M., and Akert, K. (eds.) *The Frontal Granular Cortex and Behavior*. New York: McGraw-Hill, 1964.)

testing tray consisting of two rectangular boxes, each covered with an aluminum slide. By pushing the slide forward the monkey could find a peanut in the box. A sliding opaque panel was interposed between the monkey and testing tray between subsequent trials, and the intertrial interval was approximately 7 seconds. Both boxes were initially baited and, after the subject had retrieved a peanut from one box, the reward was placed in the opposite box. During subsequent trials, the box opposite to that just previously rewarded was baited. When an error was made, the peanut remained in the same box for succeeding trials until it was found by the monkey. A correct response was scored when the animal shifted to the opposite box after it had obtained a reward, whereas repetitive responses to one side were scored as a single error.

Per cent of correct responses in pre-operative training and in post-operative relearning of the task is shown in Figure 12.19. Note that by 400 pre-operative trials the animals had attained virtually perfect performance. They were then subjected to bilateral ablation of dorso-lateral frontal cortex. Following operation, their performance was down to nearly a chance level and improved only very slowly, appearing to stabilize after a thousand trials at a slightly lower level than pre-operative performance. Thus there is an initial loss of the delayed alternation performance following frontal lesion, but after extensive retraining there is considerable recovery. Delayed alternation deficits also seem unique to the frontal lobes, other neocortical regions not being essential to the task. However, lesions in rhinencephalic regions and the caudate nucleus can also cause marked impairment in this task (Rosvold, Mishkin, and Szwarcbart, 1958).

There has been a good bit of comparative work analyzing the effect of prefrontal ablations in dog and cat on a variety of tasks, particularly by Konorski and his many associates in Poland, and by Warren and associates at Pennsylvania State University. Lawicka and Konorski (1959) were able to demonstrate severe and permanent deficits in delayed response performance by dogs following ablation of frontal cortex. This clear-cut deficit in performance was also demonstrated with cats, and has been extensively analyzed in subsequent work of Konorski and his colleagues. They have also demonstrated a variety of deficits in conditioned response performance following prefrontal lesions in dogs. Particular kinds of deficits that are most pronounced are those involving conditioned inhibition, that is, situations in which the animal has been conditioned to respond to one stimulus but not to another. Following lesion, animals typically seem to respond to both positive and negative stimuli. Brutkowski (1964) completed a very extensive analysis of the effects of prefrontal lesions on conditioning and has suggested that the kind of response inhibition that is most impaired by frontal lesion might be termed *inhibition of affective behavior,* or *drive inhibition.*

Warren and associates have completed a very extensive series of experiments testing effects of prefrontal lesions in cats on most of the types of learning situations that have been used in primate investigations. He has found that prefrontal lesions impair retention but do not prevent post-operative solution of the double-alternation problem by cats (see Warren, 1964). Cats are impaired on delayed response following lesions but rather less so than are dogs or primates. In addition, a variety of discrimination learning deficits appeared in cats following frontal lesions. However, these deficits all disappear after extensive post-operative training. Warren also finds that frontal cats are seriously and permanently impaired in discrimination reversal learning (in which objects that have been rewarded are subsequently not rewarded).

Perhaps the most difficult aspect of an understanding of frontal lobe function has to do with the inferred meanings of the various operative deficits. It is almost unanimously the opinion that ablation of prefrontal cortex in the primate and carnivore leads to severe and long-lasting deficits in delayed response performance. However, there is little to no agreement in the interpretation of this deficit. The initial conclusion that immediate or short-term memory resides in the frontal lobes has been questioned in a variety of ways. Delay does seem to play a rather general role in the frontal lobe syndrome. Mishkin and Weiskrantz (1958) showed that deficits were still present if, instead of making a delay between

Association areas of the cerebral cortex and thought

baiting the food well and the animal's response, the delay was introduced between the animal's response and delivery of the reward.

Pribram and associates have developed a comprehensive and ingenious series of experiments which seem to support the general notion that in frontal monkeys a given set of responses that had proved useful in the past tend to persevere when reinforcement cue changes are introduced *between* problems, but that there is an increased tendency to shift to other types of responses when such changes occur *within* problems (see Pribram et al., 1964).

The student encounters another difficulty in understanding frontal lobe function comparative data on the effects of lesions in animals and man. For many years it appeared that no symptoms of human frontal damage paralleled the classical deficits seen in monkeys. However, studies by Milner (1972) and Teuber (1964) have obtained deficits in frontal humans in tasks resembling some of those that show deficits in frontal animals. We described Milner's demonstration of impaired temporal memory with frontal humans above. You will recall that verbal temporal memory required the left frontal lobe and spatial temporal memory depended on the right temporal lobe.

Teuber presents considerable data indicating that many complex aspects of sensory-motor function are impaired in frontal man. Thus the ability to maintain correctly perceived upright position during changes in posture is severely depressed in frontal patients. Visual searching tasks, in which the subject has to engage in order to find an object embedded in a group of dissimilar objects, exhibit marked impairment. Teuber summarizes his conclusions as follows:

We have only to look at the forced movements of the hyperkinetic bifrontal monkey or the curious forced grasping and groping of human frontal lobe disease to be impressed at the need for an analysis of frontal symptoms which stresses the motor element. But it is a particular aspect of motor control that needs to be stressed; it is that aspect which may permit us to give a physiologic meaning to the forbidden concept of "voluntary" movement, in contrast to forced, or reflex movement.

(Teuber, 1964, page 439)

Some understanding of frontal lobe function is suggested by the original observations by Jacobsen on chimpanzees which led to the use of the procedure in man. When normal well trained chimps make a mistake on a task such as delayed response, they give every sign of being angry. Chimps with frontal lobotomy exhibit no such emotional reaction when they miss. Authorities on the organization and function of the frontal cortex (see, for example, Pribram, 1971) emphasize that it can legitimately be considered the highest level of the limbic forebrain system. We noted this in our earlier discussion of emotion and the limbic system (Chapter

9). The frontal lobe is the one major region of the cerebral cortex where information from the internal environment of the body and the external environment of the major senses converge, even though remotely. Pribram emphasizes that the tasks showing clearest deficits with frontal damage are those involving conflict in response tendencies or sets. He summarizes the frontal syndrome in the following terms:

Taken together, these analyses of the delayed alternation and reaction tasks suggest that frontal lobe damage impairs those brain processes in which coding of perturbations of states is an essential element. These processes occur in the operations of short-term memory that involve context-sensitive decisions, rather than in well established context-free operations, and are reflected in both problem solving and in emotional behavior. Viewed prospectively, the defect shows in problem solving: the organism is not able to regulate his behavior on the basis of the perturbing events that signal changes in context. Viewed restrospectively, the defect shows in emotional expression: the organism has failed to monitor, register, and evaluate perturbations that continuously complicate context and so add to the troubling present. In the temporal domain this loss of context-sensitive operations is reflected in the fact that the stream of happenings is not segmented and so runs together in a present which is forever, without past or future. The organism becomes completely a monitor at the mercy of his momentary states, instead of an actor on them.

(Pribram, 1971, pages 347–348)

561

Association areas of
the cerebral cortex
and thought

Interestingly, the so-called "typical" signs of frontal damage in man, such changes in mood and attitude as euphoria, superficiality, facetiousness, and so on, seem to be relatively rare in cases in which the brain damage is limited to the frontal lobes (Teuber, 1964). However, one rather dramatic aspect of the "typical" frontal syndrome in man seems to be widely substantiated. This is the lack of responsiveness to chronic pain (see discussion by Barber, 1959). Indeed about the only current justification for performing lobotomy in man would appear to be relief of chronic incurable pain, such as that resulting from terminal cancer. When questioned, such patients usually report the presence of pain, but otherwise act as though it does not bother them, in spite of the fact that their pain thresholds are normal.

The posterior association cortex

Most studies on the behavioral functions of posterior regions of the infrahuman association cortex have emphasized the temporal lobe. This is due, in large part, to the very dramatic findings of Klüver and Bucy (1937) indicating that total destruction of the temporal lobes in the rhesus monkey produces a variety of symptoms including some deficits they characterized as "psychic blindness." Their animals, you may remember, did not distinguish between edible and inedible objects (putting both in the mouth), were no longer afraid of stimuli such as rubber snakes that invariably produce intense fear reactions in normal monkeys, were abnormal in sexual behavior, and showed marked deficits in many types of visual discriminations. We discussed these changes in emotional behavior in Chapter 9. Here we emphasize the learning and performance deficits. Klüver and Bucy actually resected the temporal lobe, removed it entirely. This procedure includes a great deal more than just the temporal neocortex: rhinencephalic cortex, the amygdala, and portions of the hippocampus are removed as well. However, more recent experiments with lesions limited to cortical tissue have reproduced many aspects of the syndrome, including visual deficits and changes in response to fear-producing stimuli (Blum, Chow, and Pribram, 1950; Riopelle et al., 1958; Meyer, 1958). The visual deficit is particularly severe in pattern and color discrimination, but surprisingly enough may be minimal or nonexistent in object recognition and visual acuity tasks (Chow, 1952a, b). The results are in marked contrast to the effects of large lesions of the lateral surface of the occipital cortex, which can produce marked visual field deficits and some decrease in acuity without significantly impairing pattern discrimination (Harlow, 1959b). On the other hand, impairment in delayed response performance, the *sine qua non* of the frontal animal, does not occur in the animal with temporal lesions.

Learning set performance seems to be rather severely impaired following temporal neocortical lesions. Riopelle et al. (1953) found that if temporal animals were trained on *learning set* problems, their initial performance was comparable to that of normal animals, but with practice the normal animals improved considerably more than did the temporals. Chow (1954) found that if the lesion was made after training it caused severe impairment in retention of learning set performance. Meyer (1958) completed an extensive analysis of this effect. Animals were well trained prior to lesion. He found that initial impairment in learning set performance following lesion was marked, but that there was some degree of recovery, and indeed one animal eventually reached preoperative performance levels. These results, together with the previous findings, would seem to suggest that temporal lesions produced their greatest effects in complex visual tasks.

As noted above, Pribram (1954) emphasized the fact that complex discriminations based on various types of sensory information are selectively impaired by lesions of differing location within the posterior association cortex of the primate, the effective locus depending upon the sensory modality (Fig. 12.16). Pribram (see Pribram, 1971; Spinelli and Pribram, 1966) has suggested that these regionally distinct and modality-specific effects might result from the association areas exerting their influences downstream via corticofugal afferent pathways which could

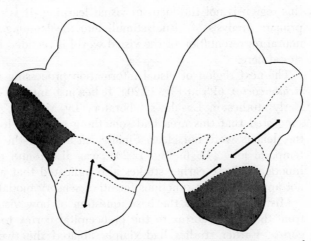

Figure 12.20 Hypothetical pathways before and after a crossed striate-inferotemporal lesion. See text for full explanation. (From Mishkin, M. Visual mechanisms beyond the striate cortex. In Russell, R. W. (ed.) *Frontiers in Physiological Psychology*. New York: Academic Press, 1966, pp. 93–119.)

563

Association areas of
the cerebral cortex
and thought

alter the functional activity of the primary sensory systems. Results of an interesting study by Spinelli and Pribram (1966) concerning the effects of long-term electrical stimulation of posterior association cortex seem consistent with this view. A small, transistorized stimulator was implanted in a dental cement plug attached to the skull in monkeys. Stimulating electrodes were placed on the inferior temporal cortex, or the parietal center, or the precentral gyrus, in different groups of animals, and continuous low level electrical stimulation was given for periods of weeks. The group receiving inferotemporal stimulation learned visual discriminations significantly faster than did the other groups. This finding is consistent with the fact that lesions of the inferotemporal area, but not the other areas, impair visual discrimination learning.

Mortimer Mishkin, at the National Institute of Mental Health in Washington, D.C., has completed a very careful lesion-anatomical-behavioral analysis of the pathways from primary visual cortex to association areas in the monkey. The critical brain areas are shown in Figure 12.20. The striate cortex (S in Fig. 12.20) is the primary visual cortex—the region receiving direct projections from the eyes via the thalamus. As noted in Chapter 6, the primary visual cortex has a detailed retinal projection from the eyes— destruction of a particular region of this cortex is like having the corresponding region of the retina in the eye destroyed. That particular region of the animal's visual field is essentially blind. Actually, the animal behaves as though he can see nothing in that part of his visual world (except for large differences in brightness). If the entire occipital pole, region S, is destroyed in both hemispheres, the animal is completely without pattern vision; that is, he is functionally blind. As noted in Chapter 11, this region is not the locus of visual learning. It is rather a stage in the primary analysis of visual stimuli into the languages of the brain. The neural representation of the visual world is recoded but not permanently stored here.

The next region of visual information processing is the so-called *prestriate cortex* (PS in Fig. 12.20). It lies just anterior to the striate cortex. Early studies in Lashley's laboratory by Mishkin, Pribram and Chow suggested that this area had something to do with visual function but the deficits were not clear. Finally, an area on the inferior part of the temporal lobe (IT in Fig. 12.20), was also found to have some visual functions. These earlier studies also indicated that areas PS and IT did not appear to have functions for other sensory modalities.

Mishkin addressed the basic question of how visual information gets from the striate cortex to the preoccipital cortex to the inferotemporal cortex. Earlier studies had simply ablated the two preoccipital areas or the two inferotemporal areas. The problem with this direct approach is that it is very difficult on any given animal's cortex to determine the exact boundaries of cortex to remove. The exact histological borders must be established by microscopic study of dead cortex cut in slices—they vary considerably from animal to animal. Mishkin hypothesized that the pathways projected from each striate cortex to its adjacent prestriate region (Fig. 12.20). The two prestriate regions then project to each other via the corpus callosum and each in turn projects to the inferotemporal cortex on its own side (see Fig. 12.20).

To test this hypothesis Mishkin performed a series of cortical lesions on a group of monkeys trained on visual pattern discriminations in the Wisconsin General Test Apparatus. Animals were retrained after each lesion. In the first stage (Fig. 12.21A) half the animals had their left frontal cortex removed (a control) and the other half their left inferotemporal area removed. They relearned the visual pattern discriminations relatively easily (Fig. 12.21). Half of each of these groups then had their left striate cortex removed and the remainder their right striate cortex removed. There are now four different groups of animals (Fig. 12.21B). The hypothetical remaining connectors are shown. The controls

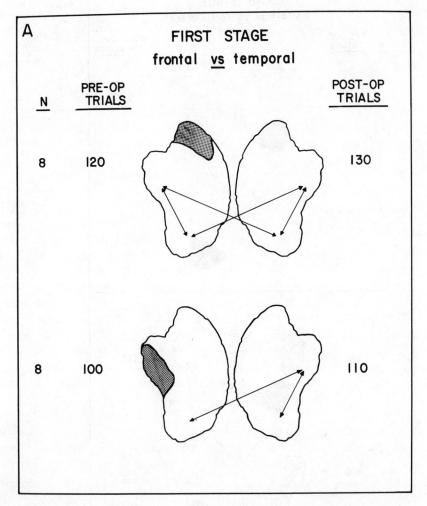

A

FIRST STAGE
frontal vs temporal

N

PRE-OP
TRIALS

POST-OP
TRIALS

8   120   130

8   100   110

565

Association areas of
the cerebral cortex
and thought

Figure 12.21   A, Discrimination retention before and after the first-stage lesion. B, Discrimination retention before and after the second-stage lesion. C, Discrimination retention before and after the third-stage lesion. In these figures, N equals number of animals; arrows denote hypothetical connections left intact by the lesions; scores are group medians and include the 100-trial criterion run; an underlined score denotes impairment; and F indicates failure to relearn within the limits of training. (From Mishkin, M. Visual mechanisms beyond the striate cortex. In Russell, R. W. (ed.) *Frontiers in Physiological Psychology.* New York: Academic Press, 1966, pp. 93–119.)

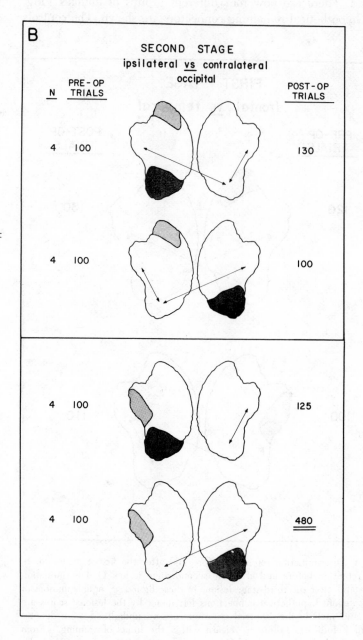

Figure 12.21   (*continued*)

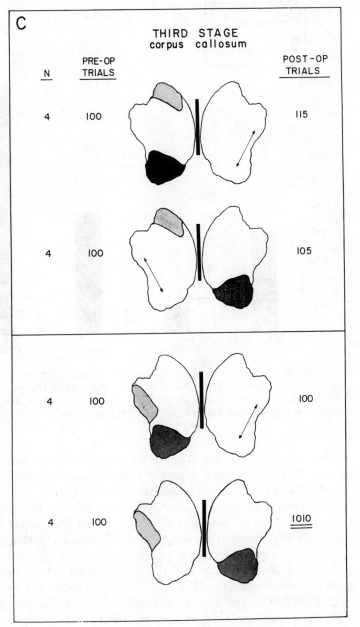

567
―――――

Association areas of
the cerebral cortex
and thought

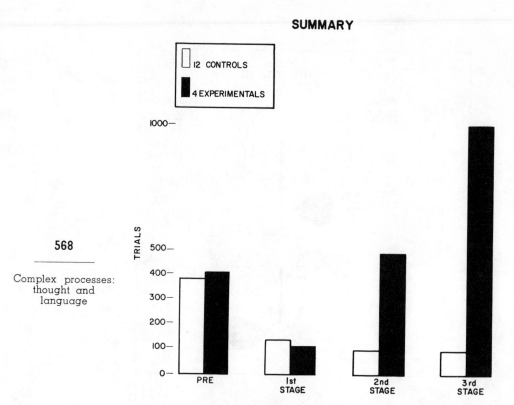

Figure 12.22 Recapitulation of results, comparing the experimental animals with all others on initial learning (PRE) and on retention after each of the three lesions. (From Mishkin, M. Visual mechanisms beyond the striate cortex. In Russell, R. W. (ed.) *Frontiers in Physiological Psychology.* New York: Academic Press, 1966, pp. 93–119.)

in this and the remaining stage of the experiment had one intact hemisphere. After the second stage the two experimental groups were able to relearn the visual task. The animals with one inferotemporal lesion and a striate lesion on the other side had some difficulty but did relearn.

The last stage in the experiment was to cut the corpus callosum. If Mishkin's hypothesis is correct, the one remaining pathway from preoccipital to opposite temporal cortex should be destroyed in the appropriate experimental group and the animals should have great difficulty with the visual task (Fig. 12.21C). This is precisely what happened (see Fig. 12.22). The result is particularly satisfying because the animals with the severe visual deficit had one intact striate and prestriate cortex and one intact inferotemporal cortex. However, they were in opposite hemispheres and the interconnections between them via the corpus callosum were severed.

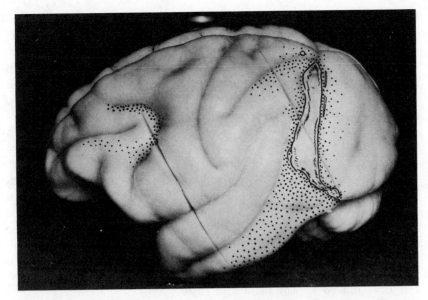

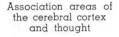

569

Association areas of
the cerebral cortex
and thought

Figure 12.23 Photograph of the brain of an operated monkey, showing the unilateral prestriate lesion (outlined) and the cortical distribution of degenerating fibers (stippled). In addition to heavy degeneration in the inferotemporal cortex, this preoccipital lesion led to degeneration in (a) the prefrontal area, particularly the prefrontal "eyelids," (b) intact portions of the prestriate region, including the area around the intraparietal sulcus, and possibly (c) the striate area, though only few scattered fibers were noted here. (From Mishkin, M. Visual mechanisms beyond the striate cortex. In Russell, R. W. (ed.) *Frontiers in Physiological Psychology.* New York: Academic Press, 1966, pp. 93–119.)

Finally, careful anatomical studies of the location of degenerating nerve terminals following ablation of the prestriate cortex verified the hypothetical pathways. Figure 12.23 shows an ablation of one prestriate area and the dots indicate degenerating fibers. There is massive fiber projection to the inferotemporal cortex, some to cortex just in front and above the prestriate area, and distinct projections to the frontal cortex to a region believed to be involved in motor control of the eyes. There is also projection from one prestriate area via the corpus callosum to the corresponding prestriate area in the other hemisphere.

These studies have chased the engram for visual pattern-learning several steps farther into the association cortex but they have not yet nailed it down. Actually, it is more likely that the inferotemporal cortex is a further stage in processing or recording of visual stimuli rather than the locus of permanent visual pattern-learning storage. It may be the analog of the visual short-term memory area in the human cortex. Compare Figures 12.20 and 12.12. However, it does not seem to be the critical locus of permanent visual memory storage. Judged from the fragmentary human brain damage data reviewed above, interconnections between temporal cortex and limbic structures like the amygdala and hippocampus may be essential links in permanent memory. There are connections from the tip and base of the temporal lobe to the amygdala and hippocampus in monkey. It is probably via pathways such as these that Pribram and his associates can influence visual discriminations by electrical stimulation of the inferotemporal cortex (see above).

These studies by Mishkin are among the first clear-cut demonstrations of the critical importance of cortical-cortical connections mediating complex functions in infrahuman animals. We might expect that such pathways interconnecting various cortical areas within the hemisphere and between the hemispheres will be of even greater importance in man than in monkey. Humans have a much larger and more elaborated association cortex that subserves far more complex functions. The trend of primate brain evolution might well be toward even greater specificity and importance of cortical-cortical interconnections. As will be seen in the section on the cortical substrates of speech and language below, this does indeed appear to be the case.

Findings on humans in whom the temporal lobes have been removed (see above) or electrically stimulated are rather consistent with the other primate literature. Of greatest importance, damage or electrical inactivation of the left temporal lobe produces severe loss of speech. We will defer discussion of speech functions to the later section on language. We have already described Milner's studies of temporal lobe functions in memory. She also studied a series of patients with *right* temporal lobe damage in the general area corresponding to the speech area of the left hemisphere (Milner, 1954). She found striking and consistent impairment of complex visual discrimination tasks, particularly those in which attention has to be given to many aspects of a complex picture. Perhaps the best-known experiments on the human temporal lobe are those of Penfield and Rasmussen (1950). Electrical stimulation of the exposed temporal lobes in epileptic patients may produce complex auditory and visual hallucinations, and even "reactive" memories:

Dream produced by stimulation. The thyraton stimulation intensity was now increased from 16 to 10 and a monopolar electrode substituted for the usual bipolar. The frontal, parietal, and temporal lobes were explored with negative result, omitting the sensorimotor and the responding portion of the temporal lobe. After 10 such negative stimulations, the electrode was applied to the first temporal convolution near **MG3.** This produced the usual fading away of sounds. Point **MG4** was then stimulated. The patient made a little inarticulate sound. After stimulation was over she said, "I had a dream. I wasn't here." She explained that it was not like the dreams she had had before.

Without warning, the same point was restimulated. The patient said, "Dream," and after stimulation was over, she seemed to find it difficult to explain for a time. Finally she said it was gone, that she seemed to be here but things sounded different and that she heard a lot of funny sounds.

Music produced by stimulation. After talking with her a little while point **MG4** was stimulated again with no warning. "I hear people coming in," she said, "I hear music now, a funny little piece." Stimulation was continued. She became more talkative than usual, explaining that the music was something she had heard on the radio, that it was the theme song of a children's program. Afterward she complained of feeling nauseated. After an interval, the same point was restimulated again with no warning. She said, "Another dream. People were coming in and out and I heard boom, boom, boom. I don't remember the rest." And a little later, following a short stimulation, "It's a dream. There are a lot of people. I don't seem to see them, I hear them. I don't hear them talking. I just hear their feet." Stimulation just below **MG2** caused fading of sounds. Patient was then given usual warning of stimulation, but no stimulus was applied. She reported, "Nothing."

(Penfield and Jasper, **Epilepsy and the Functional Anatomy of the Brain,** pages 460–461. © 1954 by Little, Brown and Company.)

A word of caution. Such experiences and "memories" evoked by electrical stimulation have been obtained only from epileptic patients, who, of course, have abnormal brains. Further, the "memories" so obtained have not been checked for accuracy or reality. Nonetheless, the fact that complex subjective experiences can be evoked by electrical stimulation only of the temporal lobe is of great interest.

Thus there is a general correspondence between the effects of damage to posterior association cortex in monkey and man. As we noted, complex sensory discriminations and learning set are impaired in the monkey. In man damage to comparable regions in the nondominant right hemisphere produces loss of awareness of visual-sensory orientation; such persons are often unable to orient themselves in space. Penfield provides a clear example:

In one patient the [speech equivalent] area on the nondominant side was removed completely. . . In the years that followed the operation, the patient's epileptic attacks stopped. He was able to earn his living, but he had a penalty to pay. With his eyes closed, he had no conception of his position in space. On leaving his house in the village where he lived, he seemed to be well oriented until he turned a street corner. After that he was lost. To get back home, it was necessary for him to ask the direction from a passerby.

(Penfield, 1969, page 151)

In his brilliant book *The Organization of Behavior,* which we mentioned earlier in our discussion of learning, Hebb (1949) proposed a theory of how the brain might develop neural coding of perception and concepts. In essence he suggested that during development after birth the organism learns to perceive visual objects as a result of numerous experiences with simple forms. Lines and other simple stimuli are coded by complex interconnecting groups of neurons, which he termed *cell assemblies,* and these in turn interconnect with one another in still more complex ways to form *phase sequences,* which code squares, triangles, and other more complex forms. As learning continues these processes are elaborated into very complex coding of concepts in association cortex. A somewhat different view has been developed by Konorski (1967), Thompson et al. (1970), and others. Konorski suggested that even very complex concepts could be represented by single neurons in the cerebral cortex which he termed *gnostic* cells (from the Greek *gnosis,* knowledge). Actually these two ideas are not contradictory. Gnostic cells could very well develop through learning by means of the complex assemblages of neurons that Hebb envisaged.

The work of Hubel and Wiesel (1959) seems to support the idea that single neurons code concepts, at least in visual perception. As we saw in Chapter 6, single neurons in the visual cortex code angles and forms, and this coding is apparently present at birth. In a very real sense these visual form-coding cells are *concept,* or *gnostic,* cells; they respond to a category of stimuli in the same sense that human subjects learn to respond to a category such as triangle in simple concept-learning experiments. Even more complex types of concept-coding cells have been reported in recent times. For example, Gross et al. (1969) described a neuron in the inferotemporal association cortex of the monkey that responded only to a form resembling a monkey's hand; the more the stimulus silhouette resembled a hand, the more the cell fired. This might be termed a "hand-concept" gnostic cell. This observation fits nicely with Mishkin's studies described above.

Thompson et al. (1970) have observed cells in the association cortex of the cat that could serve to "code" the concept of number. As an example, a series of stimuli were presented, one after the other, and the cell fired mostly on the sixth presentation. This was independent of the nature of the stimulus (sound or light), the intensity of the stimulus, and the time between successive stimuli. The response was in terms of only the number of stimuli. Color, shape, and number seem to form an increasingly difficult series of concepts. Color is coded at the level of the eye, form is coded at the level of the visual cortex, and number may be coded in the association cortex. It is important to keep in mind that the evidence regarding such concept-coding or gnostic neurons is still preliminary and tentative. There are single neurons in the cerebral cortex that *could* serve to code angle, hand, and number, but it remains to be determined whether or not such neurons are, in fact, performing these functions.

Furthermore, there must be many thousands of neurons activated by each successively more abstract aspect of stimuli. The brain is an enormously complex set of overlapping sets of neural networks, each involving thousands or millions of neurons. The notion that any one unique neuron exists to code the highest abstractions—that a "Papal neuron" exists someplace in the brain—is simply not feasible.

LANGUAGE

Language is the unique property of the species Homo sapiens. Although many animals communicate in ways ranging from chemicals in fish and insects to elaborate behavior patterns like the nectar dance of the bee, it would be a great mistake to draw close analogies with human speech. Language is a system of communication that has a *syntax*—a set of formal rules and structure for the sequencing of sounds or symbols. As Hockett demonstrated in a systematic analysis of animal communication (1960), none of these even begins to qualify as language.

The modern field of psycholinguistics has done much to clarify the essential properties of language. Noam Chomsky at Massachusetts Institute of Technology has been particularly influential in developing the field. Chomsky hypothesized that languages have two kinds of *structure*, surface structures that relate to the particular forms and sequences of words in a given language and "deep structure," a more fundamental kind of organization or syntax that may be common to all languages.

To oversimplify greatly, all but the last of the following sentences have differing surface structures but the same deep structure; the last sentence has a different deep structure:

Virginia eats the cookie.
The cookie was eaten by Virginia.
Virginia ate the cookie.
The cookie ate Virginia.

It is important to emphasize that this kind of linguistic analysis is formal rather than empirical. It is based on the formal grammatical or syntactical structures of languages rather than upon empirical evidence. Psycholinguists (see, for example, Deese, 1970) have attempted to develop support for this view by comparing language development of children in unrelated language cultures like English and Japanese.

Roger Brown, at Harvard University, undertook an extensive analysis of the acquisition of language by three children (*A First Language*, 1973). In his view there is a common semantic and grammatical order of progression across children learning any language in what he terms

Stage I, natural language acquisition. However, his finding and the results of other recent studies do not in general support the linguistic theory of Chomsky. In essence, Chomsky's view asserts that the more linguistically complex a sentence is, the more psychologically complex it is. As Brown summarizes it,

> The positive experimental results accumulated over some years can no longer be taken as a proper test of the original hypothesis for the reason that the sentences studied do not differ exclusively, or necessarily at all, in the number of optional transformations entering into their respective derivations. The small number of negative results, reported by Fodor and Garrett (1966) and involving besides the separable verb case the movement of sentence adverbials and the optional deletion of redundant predicate elements, are the only proper tests of the hypothesis. And so the general hypothesis has come tumbling down, though, of course, the experimental results themselves have other interesting aspects.

(Brown, 1973, pages 405–406)

Chomsky's theory has a considerable appeal to those of us interested in the brain mechanisms of language. Actually, the notion of some universal aspects to language is not negated by the failure of Chomsky's more specific hypothesis relating grammatical and psychological complexity. Eric Lenneberg has written a most interesting book, *Biological Foundations of Language.* He notes some of the implications and corollaries of Chomsky's view of the universality of "deep grammar." Thus, although particular sounds differ in different languages, each language has about 40 sounds. Apparently, the deep structure of all languages is similar. All children are said to develop a similar, initial, universal "deep grammar." Perhaps most surprising is the fact that languages show little sign of evolution or development. All languages, from English to obscure dialects of isolated aborigines, have the same degree of complexity and similar general properties. It is as though man came into the world equipped with a well elaborated, complex and biologically determined language system. In short, man appears to have predetermined speech centers in the brain. This last conclusion is true, as we will see below.

Language and the ape

Can apes learn language? For many years attempts to teach chimpanzees spoken language failed completely. Chimpanzees are simply not predisposed to talk. However, more recently, two attempts to teach language to chimps have met with some degree of success. The Gardners, in Nevada, have trained a chimp named Washoe in the American Sign Language (Gardner and Gardner, 1971). They approached her training just as one would teach spoken language to a child. They lived with her, constantly talked (in finger signs) to her and rewarded her for appropriate signs. Washoe learned over 100 signs and has strung them together in phrases as long as five signs. Examples are given in the following passage from the Gardners:

A listing of Washoe's phrases, together with the contexts in which they occurred, is striking because the phrases seem so apt. For play with her companions, she would sign, "Roger you tickle, you Greg peekaboo," or simply "catch me" or "tickle me." She indicated destinations with phrases such as "go in," "go out," or "in down bed." Other phrases produced descriptions: "drink red" for her red cup, "my baby" for her dolls, "listen food" or "listen drink" for the supper bell, and "dirty good" for the toilet chair. Asking for access to the many objects that were kept out of sight and out of reach by the various locked doors in her quarters, Washoe signed, "key open food" at the refrigerator, "open key clean" at the soap cupboard, and "key open please blanket" at the bedding cupboard. Combinations with "sorry" were frequent, and these were appropriate for apology and irresistible as appeasements: "please sorry, sorry dirty, sorry hurt, please sorry good," and "come bug-love sorry sorry."

These examples of apt phrases are by no means exceptional; there were hundreds of other such phrases, and particular phrases were observed repeatedly, as their appropriate situation recurred.

Any participant in this project saw and responded to "go out" and "tickle me" far more often than he would care to remember.

Washoe also produced variants that left the key phrase unchanged while emphasizing her request. For example,

soda pop, which Washoe referred to as "sweet drink," was requested by all of the following: "please sweet drink, more sweet drink, gimme sweet drink, hurry sweet drink, please hurry sweet drink, please gimme sweet drink," and by variations in the order of these signs. . . .

About half of the longer combinations were formed by adding appeal-signs to shorter combinations as in "please tickle more, come Roger tickle," and "out open please hurry." In the remaining cases, the additional signs introduced new information and new relations among signs. Most of the signs added were proper names or pronouns. Sometimes the effect was to specify more than one actor as in "you me in, you me out, you me Greg go," and "Roger Washoe out." . . . "You me drink go" and "you me out look" are examples of combinations which specify agent, action, and a destination or object. There were also apologies, such as "bug-love me good," which specified an action, an agent, and an attribute. Finally, a number of Washoe's combinations specified both the subject and the object of an action, as in "Roger Washoe tickle," "you tickle me Washoe," and "you peekaboo me."

(Gardner and Gardner, 1971, pages 166–167, 176)

David Premack (1970) has used quite a different approach with his star pupil, Sarah. He uses a variation of the Wisconsin General Test Apparatus with plastic cutout forms to represent words. A little blue triangle, for example, represents "apple." Sarah has learned over 120 words including nouns, verbs, adjectives, and adverbs, and uses them "correctly." One interesting difference between Washoe and Sarah is that Washoe "talks" spontaneously but Sarah does not.

Do these highly trained apes possess language? They certainly utilize what they have learned very well indeed to communicate needs and desires to the experimenter. However, as any dog owner will testify, dogs also communicate a great deal about their needs by using behaviors available to them—pointing with nose at the food dish, scratching at the door, many variations of canine vocalizations, etc. Returning to Hockett's criteria noted above, the answer is not clear. Roger Brown comes to the qualified conclusion that Washoe exhibits Stage I language resembling that of the children he studied in some ways but also differing in some ways. Word order or syntax is much less important to Washoe than to human children. However, Washoe constantly uses sign language to initiate interactions to get what she wants and to comment on events. Sarah never does. However, Sarah has reached the stage of solving very complex linguistic problems. Her behavior resembles a problem-solver more than a speaking individual. Perhaps the simplest conclusion is that they have indeed learned language, but not as people do.

The importance of these chimpanzee studies for us relates to the question of the brain substrates of speech and language. There is a major difference. Normal humans learn speech by hearing it spoken. This is not necessary—deaf children can also learn language. However, if Homo sapiens were a deaf species, there would probably be no language. We seem to have very specialized regions of the brain that subserve the auditory learning of speech and language. Judged by the chimpanzee studies to date, chimps have rather well developed capacities for abstract and symbolic thought—their association cortex is large. However, they obviously have not evolved the specialized speech areas of man.

Human brain mechanisms of language

Essentially all information about the brain mechanisms of language has come from studies on unfortunate patients who have suffered damage to

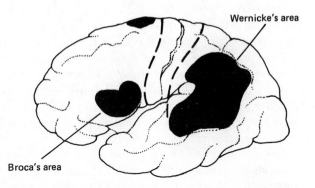

Wernicke's area

Broca's area

Figure 12.24 Approximate locations of "speech" areas in human brain. Broken line outlines primary somatic-motor and somatic-sensory areas. (Redrawn from Fig. X-4 from Penfield, Wilder, and Roberts, Lamar. *Speech and Brain-Mechanisms*. Copyright © 1959 by Princeton University Press, p. 201. Reprinted by permission of Princeton University Press.)

the speech areas (*aphasia*). Approximate locations of the major regions of the cerebral cortex involved in language are shown in Figure 12.24. In the normal adult, language is localized entirely to one hemisphere of the brain—the left for 97 per cent of all people (all right-handed and most left-handed individuals). Penfield orders the severity of general damage to the various areas as follows. Damage to the superior area (in the general region of the supplementary motor cortex) causes speech difficulties or aphasia for only a few weeks. Damage to *Broca's area* causes much more prolonged aphasia but recovery usually occurs. Many authorities believe that a major aspect of damage to Broca's area has to do more with motor control of words and word sequences than with the conceptual aspects of language. The most devastating and permanent aphasias result from damage in a rather large region of the left posterior association cortex termed *Wernicke's area*. An adult with severe injury of this entire region is likely to remain permanently aphasic.

In young children the effect of brain damage on language is dramatically different. If the entire dominant (left) hemisphere is destroyed, the child is completely aphasic, but usually recovers over a period of months and ultimately develops perfectly normal language.

Penfield and Jasper (1954) have observed the effects of electrical stimulation of the cerebral cortex on language function in epileptic patients when recording for abnormal brain foci. You may remember that stimulation of certain regions of human cortex evokes sensation or even detailed experiences or "memories." In the case of the language areas the electrical stimulus acts to block normal language function. Their stimulation maps of the speech areas agree well with the clinical brain damage literature. In the case of individuals with early brain damage to language regions of the dominant hemisphere, language function develops in the corresponding regions of the other hemisphere of the brain.

The clinical literature on aphasia is enormously complex and difficult to interpret in terms of localization of function or relation to known brain systems (see Schuell, Jenkins and Jiménez-Pabón, 1964 and Lenneberg, 1967 for extensive reviews). Norman Geschwind, a neurologist at Harvard Medical School, has recently summarized the aphasia literature in very clear reviews (1966, 1972).

The characteristic result of damage to Broca's area is very slow poorly articulated speech. Such patients typically produce little speech. It is apparently not only a difficulty with motor control of the tongue, since small grammatical words and endings are omitted. In contrast, the patient with damage to Wernicke's area can produce rapid, well articulated sound and even proper phrases and sequences of words easily, but not language. The "speech" of such a patient has the correct rhythm and general sound of normal speech but in fact conveys no information. These patients show an essentially total failure to understand both spoken and written language, although basic hearing and vision are normal.

Geschwind has elaborated Carl Wernicke's earlier view of brain function in language in terms of the interconnections among the various sensory receptive and association areas and the speech areas. Indeed, he has renamed the aphasias the *disconnection syndromes* to emphasize the importance of the connecting pathways. In brief, Geschwind's view is as follows. Wernicke's area (see Fig. 12.25) is the critical region for the conceptual formation and production of language. If a phrase is to be spoken, it originates in Wernicke's area, is transmitted by a fiber bundle called the arcuate fasciculus to Broca's area where the correct sequence of articulations is aroused and transmitted to the motor cortex for speech. If a word spoken by someone else is to be understood, it projects from the primary auditory cortex (called *Heschl's gyrus* in man) to Wernicke's area. If a written word is seen, and understood (Fig. 12.25), it projects to the primary visual cortex (the striate cortex), then to a visual association area, then to a region called the angular gyrus that is said to integrate visual and auditory information, and then to Wernicke's area. If a spoken word is to be spelled, it projects from the auditory area to Wernicke's area to the angular gyrus. If a written word is to be spoken it passes from striate cortex to visual association cortex to the angular gyrus to Wernicke's area to Broca's area and to the motor cortex. To further complicate this picture, auditory and visual information projects from one hemisphere to the other via the corpus callosum.

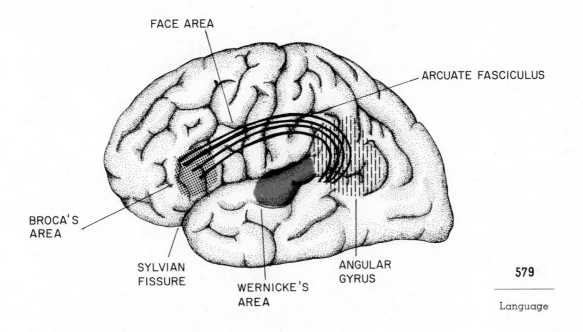

FACE AREA

ARCUATE FASCICULUS

BROCA'S
AREA

SYLVIAN
FISSURE

WERNICKE'S
AREA

ANGULAR
GYRUS

Figure 12.25 Primary language areas of the human brain are thought to be located in the left hemisphere, because only rarely does damage to the right hemisphere cause language disorders. Broca's area, which is adjacent to the region of the motor cortex that controls the movement of the muscles of the lips, the jaw, the tongue, the soft palate, and the vocal cords, apparently incorporates programs for the coordination of these muscles in speech. Damage to Broca's area results in slow and labored speech, but comprehension of language remains intact. Wernicke's area lies between Heschl's gyrus, which is the primary receiver of auditory stimuli, and the angular gyrus, which acts as a way-station between the auditory and the visual regions. When Wernicke's area is damaged, speech is fluent but has little content, and comprehension is usually lost. Wernicke's and Broca's areas are joined by a nerve bundle called the arcuate fasciculus. When it is damaged, speech is fluent but abnormal, and patient can comprehend words but cannot repeat them.

This rather complicated hypothesis about the brain substrates of speech was developed on the basis of a few patients showing very specific and selective disorders of speech and language function. We will give a few examples to illustrate. First, a lesion limited to the arcuate fasciculus interconnecting Wernicke's area and Broca's area (Fig. 12.25) produces what is called *conduction aphasia*. The patient has perfect comprehension of spoken and written language, but speech is severely abnormal and resembles that of patients with damage to Wernicke's area—fluent words but no sense. Repetition of spoken language is grossly impaired.

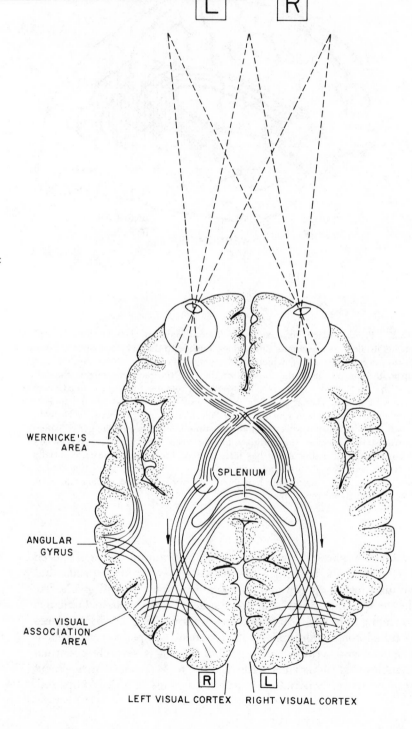

L R

Complex processes:
thought and
language

WERNICKE'S
AREA

SPLENIUM

ANGULAR
GYRUS

VISUAL
ASSOCIATION
AREA

R L

LEFT VISUAL CORTEX RIGHT VISUAL CORTEX

◀ **Figure 12.26** Classic case, of a man who lost the ability to read even though he had normal visual acuity and could copy written words, was described in 1892 by Joseph Jules Dejerine. Post-mortem analysis of the man's brain showed that the left visual cortex and the splenium were destroyed as a result of an occlusion of the left posterior cerebral artery. The splenium is the section of the corpus callosum that transfers visual information between the two hemispheres. The man's left visual cortex was inoperative making him blind in his right visual field. Words in his left visual field were properly received by the right visual cortex, but could not cross over to the language areas in the left hemisphere because of the damaged splenium. Thus words seen by the man remained as meaningless patterns. (From Geschwind, N. Language and the brain. Copyright © 1972 by Scientific American, Inc. All rights reserved.)

Both Broca's and Wernicke's areas are normal but Wernicke's no longer controls Broca's.

A patient, described many years ago by the French neurologist Dejerine, had lost the ability to read and write but could understand spoken language and could speak. This disorder is called *alexia* (inability to read) with *agraphia* (inability to write). Autopsy revealed a lesion in the left angular gyrus, the auditory-visual association area. Words and letters were seen correctly but were meaningless visual patterns since the visual pattern must first be connected to the auditory form before the word can be understood. The auditory pattern of hearing a word must be transformed into the visual pattern before it can be spelled and rewritten. However, heard words could be processed through the auditory cortex and Wernicke's area for understanding, and thence to Broca's area for speech.

Another of Dejerine's patients awakened one morning to discover he could not read. He was found to be blind in the right half of his visual field, due to occlusion (blocking) of a cerebral artery (e.g., a "stroke"). The visual cortex of the left hemisphere was completely destroyed. This explains the half-blindness but not the inability to read. The patient could speak and comprehend spoken language. Vision in the right side of his visual field was normal. The patient could also write. Post-mortem examination revealed that in addition to destruction of the left visual cortex, the posterior region of the corpus callosum, that carries visual information between the hemispheres, was also destroyed. Consequently, although visual information got to the right visual cortex and association area, it could not cross to the left angular gyrus, the critical region for integration of visual and auditory function, or to the left Wernicke's area (Fig. 12.26).

A striking case studied by Geschwind and his colleagues involved a woman who suffered from accidental poisoning from carbon monoxide.

She had extensive brain damage and was totally helpless for the period of nine years she was studied. She never spoke a word spontaneously and showed no evidence of understanding words. In Geschwind's words,

She could, however, repeat perfectly sentences that had just been said to her. In addition she would complete certain phrases. For example, if she heard "Roses are red," she would say "Roses are red, violets are blue, sugar is sweet and so are you." Even more surprising was her ability to learn songs. A song that had been written after her illness would be played to her and after a few repetitions she would begin to sing along with it. Eventually she would begin to sing as soon as the song started. If the song was stopped after a few bars, she would continue singing the song through to the end, making no errors in either words or melody.

On the basis of Wernicke's model we predicted that the lesions caused by the carbon monoxide poisoning lay outside the speech and auditory regions, and that both Broca's area and Wernicke's area were intact. Postmortem examination revealed a remarkable lesion that isolated the speech area from the rest of the cortex. The lesion fitted the prediction. Broca's area, Wernicke's-area and the connection between them were intact. Also intact were the auditory pathways and the motor pathways to the speech organs. Around the speech area, however, either the cortex or the underlying white matter was destroyed. The woman could not comprehend speech because the words did not arouse associations in other portions of the cortex. She could repeat speech correctly because the internal connections of the speech region were intact. Presumably well-learned word sequences stored in Broca's area could be triggered by the beginning phrases. This syndrome is called isolation of the speech area.

(From Language and the brain, N. Geschwind, pages 80–81. Copyright © 1972 by Scientific American, Inc. All rights reserved.)

Geschwind also completed anatomical studies of 100 normal human brains, comparing a portion of Wernicke's area for the two hemispheres. On the average, the left region was one-third larger than the right. Juhn Wada, of the University of British Columbia, published similar findings and also found that the left Wernicke's area was larger in human infants (that had died soon after birth). It would appear that a larger left Wernicke's area is genetically determined.

It is not yet possible to fit the various reports on humans with critical brain damage into a consistent pattern, let alone put it together with the experimental monkey data. A few observations do seem to fit. The location of the presumed region for short-term visual memory in the human brain (Fig. 12.12) corresponds roughly with the location of the angular gyrus, believed by Geschwind to form the visual-auditory association area.

The studies of Mishkin on the projections to the inferotemporal cortex of the monkey have certain formal similarities to Geschwind's disconnection syndromes. Visual information must first be relayed from striate (primary visual) cortex to prestriate visual association cortex. It can then relay to the inferotemporal region on the same side, or cross the corpus callosum to the other prestriate cortex and then to the inferotemporal cortex. We might speculate that the monkey inferotemporal area is homologous to the human Wernicke's area, but this is a completely untestable hypothesis.

Perhaps the most significant result from the studies on aphasia is the critical importance of the cortical-cortical connections in the human brain. It seems quite possible that many complex human attributes and abilities, in addition to language, may depend upon particular pathways interconnecting specific regions of the cortex and subcortical structures. The studies of primate visual function and human speech both began with a Lashlian mass action view—the more cortex removed the greater the deficit—and have now come back to much more connectionistic ideas of critical areas and pathways interconnecting them. Given the existence of several critical areas and pathways, it is easy to misinterpret imprecise lesion data in terms of global effects like mass action.

Several recent studies have explored possible scalp-recorded evoked potential correlates of language function in man. For the most part they have been concerned with asymmetries of response between left and right hemispheres. Buchsbaum and Fedio (1970) compared responses of left and right occipital regions to visually presented verbal and nonsense stimuli. When stimuli were presented to the direct dominant pathway—left hemiretina to left cortex—differences were greater than when stimuli were presented via the direct route to the right hemisphere. Asymmetric evoked responses to word stimuli have been reported by Morrell and Salamy (1971). Responses are longer to the same word over the left temperoparietal region (Wernicke's area?) than over the right. McAdam and Whitaker (1972) report that slow negative potentials over Broca's area are larger in the left hemisphere than the right when a subject spontaneously pronounced polysyllabic words. Matsumiya et al. (1972) showed that responses to verbal sounds were not only larger over Wernicke's area on the left side but that the difference between responses on the two sides was greater with meaningful than with nonmeaningful verbal stimuli.

In a recent study done by Timothy Teyler in the author's laboratory at Harvard, scalp-evoked potentials recorded from the approximate regions overlying Wernicke's areas of the two hemispheres were compared for different meanings of the same stimulus words. More specifically, the subjects were given (on a preprogrammed tape) the phrase "to rock" (a verb) or "a rock" (a noun) and then a click stimulus to evoke the brain potential.

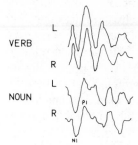

VERB L

VERB R

NOUN L

NOUN R

Figure 12.27 Average scalp-recorded evoked response to an ambiguous word (*rock*). Right (R) and left (L) hemisphere responses to the verb and noun meanings of the word. Note the similarity between hemispheres and the differences between meanings. Calibration: 200 msec, 5 V. (Redrawn from Teyler, T. J., et al. Human scalp-recorded evoked-potential correlates of linguistic stimuli. *Bull. Psychon. Soc.* 1, 1973, pp. 333–334.)

As seen in Figure 12.27, the waveforms can be quite different for the two meanings of the same stimulus word. In another phase of the experiment, the subjects were simply given the word "rock" and asked to think of one or the other meaning and indicate later which. Results appeared to be consistent with those obtained when the subject was instructed in the meaning.

These studies can be said to constitute a new and potentially very exciting field of research in the area of "neurolinguistics." Stimuli can be selectively presented to the two hemispheres using visual tachistoscopic devices and dichotic listening tasks, and scalp brain potentials can be recorded and computer analyzed from the various brain regions believed to be involved in the processing and production of speech. To date, most of our information on the neural basis of language has come from clinical studies of human patients suffering brain damage. It may be that with the newer approaches we can learn much about the neurology of speech and language from normal subjects.

Summary

Relatively little is known about the neural basis of many aspects of the complex processes of thought, language, and attention. Psychologists have developed various models of human information-processing which are basically flowcharts of thinking. According to these models, iconic storage takes place when physical stimuli activate the sensory systems which analyze and process the input. At this time, information is selected and evaluated on the basis of the intersection of the short-term and permanent memory stores. Processes such as learning and memory, attention, language, and thought do not occur in isolation; consequently, the distinctions usually made among these processes may be artificial.

Current evidence on the neural aspects of learning and memory favors the view that short-term and long-term memory storage are two separate processes. Most of the evidence on brain-damaged individuals, such as those with Wernicke-Korsakoff disease, is consistent with such a view. This disease produces a clear and pronounced memory defect characterized by anterograde and retrograde amnesia. The brain structures surrounding the third ventricle appear to be closely involved in this disorder.

Temporal lobe damage also results in memory disorders although they are of a different nature than those associated with Wernicke-Korsakoff disease. When the temporal lobes are removed bilaterally, the patient's iconic and short-term memory remain intact, but he is unable to convert immediate memory into long-term storage. The patient can, however, develop long-term storage of learned motor skills. This suggests that the brain substrates for motor skill learning and memory are different from those for verbal awareness. Unilateral temporal damage results in deficits of modality-specific short-term memory. Patients with left temporal damage show a pronounced deficit on verbal short-term memory tasks, while those with right temporal damage show a deficit on spatial short-term memory tasks. For the left temporal patients, the deficit was more pronounced the greater the amount of hippocampus removed. The critical factor in the spatial short-term memory deficits is the amount of right temporal cerebral cortex removed.

Frontal lobe damage in monkeys and apes produces a delayed response memory impairment. In humans with unilateral frontal lobe damage, those with left frontal damage show deficits on verbal memory tasks while right frontals show deficits on spatial-temporal memory tasks. The general distinction of the brain by hemispheres (verbal–left, and spatial–right) holds even in the frontal lobes.

From the studies of brain-damaged individuals it appears that short-term memory defects are independent of long-term memory. Regions of the posterior association cortex appear to be critically involved in short-term memory for auditorily and visually presented stimuli.

The association areas of the cerebral cortex seem to be the regions most specialized for the mediation of complex processes such as language and thought. Four behavioral tasks have been used to evaluate the complex effects of cortical damage in animals: discrimination learning, learning sets, delayed response, and delayed alternation. There is a tendency, especially in man and monkey, for much of association cortex to be electrically "silent." While much of association cortex in dog and cat is polysensory, primate association cortex has far less extensive polysensory areas in comparison with the "silent" association cortex. These polysensory areas appear to play a role in the coding of the significance of stimuli to an organism.

The amount of frontal granular cortex increases significantly from cat to man. A large portion of frontal granular cortex receives direct projections from the dorso-medial nucleus of the thalamus. Frontal lesions in monkeys produce marked behavioral deficits in delayed response and delayed alternation test performance. While the impairment in delayed response performance is severe and long-lasting, the deficit in delayed alternation performance is initially severe but recoverable with retraining. There is also a severe deficit in delayed response performance by dogs and cats following frontal cortex ablation, although cats are impaired to a lesser extent than dogs or primates. In dogs there are also deficits in conditioned response performance following prefrontal lesions. The major difficulty with the results obtained from various species following frontal lesions is the problem of interpretation and comparative data from humans. Several investigators have obtained deficits in frontal humans relating to complex aspects of sensory-motor functioning. The frontal lobe is one major region of the cerebral cortex where information from the internal and external environments converges.

Studies of the posterior association cortex have emphasized the temporal lobes. Total destruction of the temporal lobes in rhesus monkeys results in a variety of symptoms including "psychic blindness." Learning set performance is severely impaired following temporal neocortical lesions. The greatest effects of temporal lesions appear to be on complex visual tasks such as pattern discrimination and color problems.

Mishkin's studies were the first clear demonstrations of the crucial importance of the cortical-cortical connections in mediating complex functions in species other than man. Although it is impossible to investigate experimentally, it would be expected that the pathways interconnecting various cortical areas within the hemisphere and between the hemispheres would be of even greater importance in man than in monkey. There is a general correspondence between the effects of damage to posterior association cortex in monkey and man.

Language is a system of communication with syntax. Chomsky's form of linguistic analysis is based upon the formal grammatical structures of language and not upon empirical evidence. His model of language structure, as a theory of language processing difficulty, has not been experimentally substantiated. However, the notion of particular universal aspects to language appears to have more credence than Chomsky's views of grammatical and psychological complexity. Man does seem to possess predetermined speech centers in the brain.

Several chimps have been taught language, one in the form of American Sign Language (ASL), the other in terms of plastic forms representing words. Interestingly, Washoe, the chimp learning ASL, talks spontaneously, while Sarah, who is learning language via plastic forms, behaves more like a problem-solver and does not talk spontaneously. Chimps have not evolved the specialized brain regions subserving the learning of speech and language.

Almost all our knowledge concerning putative brain mechanisms of language has come from studies of aphasic individuals. In the normal adult, language is localized entirely in one hemisphere, usually the left one. There is a stark contrast between aphasia in adults and in children. In adults, the most permanent and profound aphasias result from damage to Wernicke's area. Damage to Broca's area, while affecting the motor control of words and word sequences, seems to be less prolonged with recovery generally possible. If the left hemisphere is completely destroyed during childhood, the child becomes completely aphasic for a time, but usually recovers normal language functioning over a period of months as the other intact hemisphere takes over the language functions.

There are distinct differences in the characteristics of damage to Broca's and Wernicke's areas. Little speech is produced after damage to Broca's area, with the speech produced being slow and poorly articulated. In contrast, aphasics with damage to Wernicke's area produce rapid, well articulated sounds and word sequences, but their speech is not language and conveys no information. These individuals are unable to understand written or spoken language.

Geschwind has called the aphasias the *disconnection syndromes* because of the significance he believes the connecting pathways have in normal language functioning. He views Wernicke's area as crucial for the conceptual formation and production of language. Lesions of the arcuate fasciculus which connects Wernicke's area with Broca's area produce conduction aphasia since Wernicke's area no longer controls Broca's area. Lesion of the left angular gyrus, which Geschwind views as an integrating mechanism for visual and auditory information, results in *alexia* with *agraphia*. Perhaps one of the most significant results of the aphasic studies is the importance they give to the cortical-cortical connections in the human brain.

A recent attempt to investigate language functioning in man has been to record scalp-evoked potentials in relation to linguistic stimuli. In general, these studies have found asymmetries in the resulting waveforms between the left and right hemispheres. It appears that there may be not only a left-right asymmetry but also differences between responses on the two sides to meaningful as opposed to nonmeaningful, or nonsense, verbal stimuli. The waveforms may also be different for varying meanings of the same stimulus word.

Glossary

Absorption spectra Relative absorption of light energy as a function of wavelength. Refers here to photochemical substances in the eye.

Acetylcholine (ACh) A chemical substance known to be a synaptic transmitter at the neuromuscular junction and believed to be a transmitter at many places in the brain.

Acetylcholinesterase (AChE) Enzyme that breaks down acetylcholine (ACh) into acetyl and choline.

Action potential The all-or-none spike discharge that travels down the axon of a nerve cell.

Adaptive radiation Evolution of particular forms of creatures to fill available ecological niches.

Addiction (drug) Behaviorally—habitual use of drug. Subjectively—extreme need for drugs. Pharmacologically—occurrence of withdrawal symptoms upon cessation of use.

Adenohypophysis Anterior pituitary gland.

Adipsia Absence of drinking, usually as a result of hypothalamic damage.

Adrenal cortex Outer region or cortex of the adrenal gland. Releases adrenocorticosteroids.

Adrenal medulla Inner region of adrenal gland. Releases norepinephrine.

Adrenocortical steroids Hormones released from adrenal cortex, particularly in response to stress.

Agonistic behavior Fighting; can refer to flight, defense, or attack behavior.

Agraphia Inability to write language, usually as a result of a cerebral lesion.

Alexia Inability to read, usually a result of cerebral damage.

Allele One of a pair of corresponding genes.

Alpha blocking Sudden shift of the cortical EEG alpha rhythm to a low-voltage, high-frequency, flat-appearing arousal response. Usually the result of presenting a sudden peripheral stimulus, particularly a light.

Amacrine neuron Association type neuron having no long axon. The term is general, but in this text is used specifically for association type neurons in the retina of the eye.

Amphetamine A stimulant drug—dexedrine. It is addicting and in large doses can mimic symptoms of paranoia.

Angiotensin II Thirst substance produced by kidney.

Aphagia Absence of eating, usually as a result of hypothalamic damage.

Aphasia Inability to speak language, usually as a result of cerebral damage.

Apical dendrite Dendritic process from neuron that rises above soma; characteristic of pyramidal type neurons in cortex.

Archicortex Old cortex, as in more primitive vertebrates like reptiles.

Arousal response A change in the EEG waves of the cerebral cortex to a pattern of low-voltage, fast, irregular activity.

Athetoid movements Slow, repeated involuntary movements of the limb, usually due to damage to portions of the basal ganglia in humans. *See also* choreiform movements.

Autonomic nerve fibers Peripheral nerve fibers of the autonomic nervous system that innervate glands and smooth muscle, contrasted with somatic nerve fibers to striated muscles or from skin, muscle, and joint receptors.

Averaged evoked potential An average or mean potential computed from a series of individual brain potentials (electrical changes) evoked by a stimulus.

Axon The process of a neuron that conducts the action potential to other neurons (or muscles or glands).

Axon hillock The initial part or initial segment of the axon, where the spike or action potential is first initiated.

Axoplasmic transport The movement of substances down (or up) the axon of a nerve cell in the interior axoplasm. Both active transport and passive (i.e., diffusion) occur.

Barbiturates A class of depressant narcotic-hypnotic drugs derived from barbituric acid. Nembutal and pentothal are examples. Their effects range from mild sedation to deep coma, and they are addicting.

Behavior genetics Field of study concerned with the genetic determinants of behavior.

Betz cell Large pyramidal type cells in the motor area of the cerebral cortex in higher mammals. Axons from Betz cells descend toward the spinal cord in the pyramidal tract. This tract, however, includes many axons from other cortical neurons as well; Betz cell axons make up only one to two per cent of pyramidal tract fibers.

Binocular vision Overlap of the visual fields of the two eyes. Frogs have none, all mammals have some, and man has virtually total.

Biofeedback   A general term referring to information about brain or body that is fed back to the brain. The entire central nervous system, and the peripheral nervous system as well, can be viewed as a series of biofeedback systems. Also refers to a set of techniques for providing an animal or person with additional information about his ongoing body and brain events, for example, visual or auditory signalling of the state of the brain EEG, as in "alpha" training.

Blood-brain barrier   A barrier which prevents many chemical substances from passing from blood to brain. Not present in other tissues (e.g., liver). Location of barrier not known for certain, but probably at small blood vessels in central nervous system. A critical problem when studying effects of injected drugs and chemicals on the brain. Many do not cross the barrier. A way to by-pass it is to inject substances directly into the brain ventricles (i.e., into the cerebrospinal fluid).

Bouton   The end terminal from an axon fiber that forms a synapse on another cell. Also called *presynaptic terminal* or *ending*.

Broca's area   The so-called motor speech area lies just anterior to the motor face area of the human cerebral cortex, usually only on the left hemisphere. Damage causes severe impairment of speech production but not ideation. Recovery from damage limited to Broca's area is usually good.

Cerebrospinal fluid   The fluid within the brain and spinal cord that is in direct contact with the nerve (and glial) cells. It is "inside" the blood-brain barrier. It serves a variety of functions, many not clearly understood, but including a protective hydraulic system cushioning brain inside skull, for exchange of ions and nutrients with neurons, etc.

Cerveau isolé   An animal (or human) who has sustained a complete transection of the brain stem, generally in the region of the midbrain. Refers to the part of the brain above the transection.

Choreiform movements   Jerky irregular movements of the limbs, usually due to damage to basal ganglia. *See also* athetoid movements.

Circadian rhythms   From the Latin *circa,* about, and *dies,* a day. A 24-hour cycle or rhythm such as the normal sleep-waking cycle of adult humans. There are many biological rhythms ranging in time periods from seconds to months.

Circuit of Papez   An anatomical circuit in the brain interconnecting a number of limbic structures. In brief, it is as follows: hippocampus projects via fornix to mammillary bodies of hypothalamus, which project to anterior nucleus of thalamus, which connects to cingulate gyrus of cerebral cortex, which projects back to hippocampus.

Classical conditioning   The conditioning procedure first developed by Pavlov. A supposedly neutral stimulus (the *Conditioned Stimulus* or *CS*), usually a sound or light, is paired with a stimulus that evokes a response

(*Unconditioned Stimulus* or *US*), for example, food for salivation, air puff to eye for eyeblink, etc. Pairing CS and US usually leads to the CS coming to evoke the response initially evoked only by the US. CS onset must precede US onset for conditioning to develop. Control procedures are necessary to be sure the response that comes to be elicited by the CS is not due to sensitization—an increased general responsiveness due to repeated presentations of the US and CS, independent of pairing.

Cochlear microphonic   Electrical activity of the cochlea that follows closely the frequency of auditory stimuli applied to the ear. Believed to be generated by bending of the hair cells.

Columnar organization   In cerebral cortex, the functional vertical columns of cells that appear to exist in visual and somatic-sensory areas. A given column represents a particular aspect of a stimulus, for example, touch, joint angle, visual orientation.

Conditioned emotional response (CER)   An emotional response conditioned to a neutral stimulus as a result of pairing with an aversive stimulus, for example, fear of tone due to pairing with shock.

Conduction aphasia   A form of speech defect believed to be due to damage to the arcuate fasciculus, a pathway that interconnects Wernicke's and Broca's areas. Characterized by inability to speak intelligently, but with no defect in ability to read.

Cone   Color receptor in the retina of the eye.

Consolidation hypothesis   Notion that learning occurs in two (or more) phases. The initial short-term memory phase is easily disrupted by electroconvulsive shock or other brain trauma. However, if not disrupted, it is consolidated into longer term memory that is relatively impervious to disruption.

Contact comfort   Concept developed by Harlow to explain observation that infant monkeys respond more to the contact feel of a surrogate (artificial) mother than to other aspects such as food dispensing.

Corpus callosum   Large band of nerve fibers interconnecting two hemispheres of cerebrum.

Corticotropin releasing factor (CRF)   Endocrine hormone released by hypothalamic neurons to act on adenohypophysis (pituitary gland) that in turn releases ACTH that acts on the cortex of the adrenal gland to in turn release its hormones, the corticosteroids.

Cranial nerves   Sensory and motor nerves interconnecting brain and receptors, the muscles and glands of head.

Cross-tolerance   For some drugs, tolerance (fact that repeated doses must be progressively increased to yield some effect) developed to one drug is found to exist for some others. Mescaline and LSD exhibit cross-tolerance.

Crossing over In chromosomes, pieces of two will link and cross over, so each new chromosome consists of parts of two old chromosomes.

Cytoarchitectonics Characterization of areas of cerebral cortex in terms of their appearance in cross section, that is, in terms of visual characteristics of the layers.

Dark adaptation If eyes are in dark after being in light, receptors become progressively more sensitive to faint light.

Delayed alternation Technique for measuring ability to perform patterns of successive responses, for example, go left, wait, go right, wait, go left, etc.

Delayed response test Test of short-term memory. One of several objects is labeled, for example, by hiding reward under it, and subject must remember for varying lengths of time which object is correct (i.e., has the reward).

Dendrite Receptive processes of the neuron. Extensions of the cell body that receive synaptic inputs from other neurons.

Dendritic spines Small spines on dendrites of nerve cells that are believed to be sites of synapses receiving inputs from other nerve cells.

Deoxyribonucleic acid (DNA) Nucleic acid that forms the genetic material, the genes, that make up the chromosomes in the nucleus of each cell.

Depolarization Change in the potential level (voltage) of a nerve cell membrane that moves from the resting level (about -70 mV) toward zero. During depolarization the inside of the membrane becomes more positive than at rest. Sufficient depolarization usually leads to the development of the all-or-none spike action potential.

Determination In embryology, once cells have been induced to develop in certain ways, for example, induction of nervous tissue by notochord, determination is said to have occurred.

Discrimination learning Refers to technique or process of learning to discriminate between different stimuli.

Dopamine One of the biogenic amines, a substance found in nerve cells and believed to be a synaptic transmitter in the basal ganglia. Dopamine is formed from the naturally occurring amino acid tyrosine, and in turn is also converted to norepinephrine.

Down's syndrome Technical term for the disorder commonly called mongolism, characterized by moderate to severe mental retardation and a variety of other physical defects. Believed due to chromosome abnormality that can occur in mother at time that chromosomes of ovum (egg) are formed by reduction division.

Ectoderm One of the three germinal layers of cells of the embryo—cells from ectoderm come to form skin and nervous system.

Electrodermal response (EDR) Modern term for activity of sweat glands in skin, usually of palms. Older terms were GSR, galvanic skin response, or PGR, psychogalvanic response. Activity of sweat glands is accompanied by changes in voltage and resistance of skin. It occurs to both physical and "psychological" stimuli and is often used as an index of arousal or emotion, as in a lie detector.

Electromyography Study of the electrical activity of muscles, usually by inserting insulated recording needle electrodes into muscles.

Electron microscopy (EM) Use of focused electron beam to yield extremely high magnification of objects. Many structural details of neurons can be seen only with use of EM.

Encéphale isolé Animal preparation where brain is severed from spinal cord. Refers to fact that brain is "isolated" from spinal cord.

Endocrine glands Glands, such as pituitary, adrenal, ovary, and testes, that release hormones directly into the blood stream.

Endoderm One of three germinal layers of cells of the embryo—cells from endoderm come to form internal organs.

Epicritic Term suggested by Head to refer to discrete qualities of somatic-sensory stimulation, for example, light or localized touch, light pressure, sharp pain. *See also* lemniscal system.

Equipotentiality, Principle of Developed by Lashley to explain the fact that the impairment in complex learning tasks (e.g., maze learning) following damage to the cerebral cortex seems to be independent of the location of the lesion. Instead it is dependent only on the amount of tissue removed (principle of mass action).

Eugenics Application of selective breeding techniques to humans.

Excitatory postsynaptic potential (EPSP) A brief depolarizing potential evoked in a neuron (usually in the cell body and/or dendrites) by the action of excitatory synapses from other neurons. If the EPSP is sufficiently large the cell will generate a spike action potential.

Exocrine glands Duct glands like sweat or tear glands that release secretions into ducts or channels separate from blood—contrasted to endocrine glands that secrete into the blood stream.

Extensor muscle Muscle that causes extension or straightening of limbs when they contract—opposite of flexor muscle.

Extrafusal fibers The contractile fibers of striated or skeletal muscles that exert tension as they contract.

Extrapyramidal motor system All descending "motor" systems of brain and spinal cord except the pyramidal system.

Extrapyramidal tract fibers Fibers of all motor systems except pyramidal tract. They are grouped into discrete regions of the fiber systems (white matter) of the spinal cord.

Fixed action pattern Stereotyped response patterns, particularly in lower animals, that are released by particular stimuli or combinations of external and internal conditions—for example, attack response of stickleback fish against appropriately sized red objects.

Flexor muscle Muscle that causes a limb to bend or flex when it contracts; opposite of an extensor muscle.

Fornix Discrete fiber pathway of limbic forebrain system that projects primarily from hippocampus to mammillary bodies of hypothalamus.

Fovea Region on retina onto which projects the center of gaze or visual stimulus fixation point. It has the greatest concentration of receptors, maximal visual acuity, and the greatest density of innervation of retinal neurons. It occupies about 2° of visual angle in the retina but projects to roughly half the visual cortex.

Frequency A fundamental physical measurement of the rate at which change occurs in time, for example, for acoustic stimuli the frequency of tone is measured in Hz (Hertz, or the number of cycles per second).

Gamma motoneurons Motoneurons that send their axons to the intrafusal muscle fiber-stretch receptor system in muscles. They activate the gamma afferent fibers, which in turn activate alpha motoneurons.

Gamma system Collectively, the stretch receptor-intrafusal fiber system of muscles, together with the gamma motoneurons and the gamma afferent fibers projecting into the spinal cord (and brain for cranial nerves) to activate alpha motoneurons. The gamma motoneurons activate the intrafusal fiber-stretch receptor system and are in turn activated by many descending and reflex motor paths.

Ganglia Generally refers to collections of nerve cells that lie outside the central nervous system (e.g., autonomic ganglia). However, there are exceptions; for example, basal ganglia are collections of nerve cell bodies in the cerebrum.

Genotype The underlying genetic constitution of an organism. Contrasted with the phenotype—the outward expression of the genotype. A person with one "sickle-cell" gene and one normal gene appears almost normal (phenotype) but carries one sickle-cell gene (genotype).

Glial cell Nonneural cell of nervous system. The mammalian brain contains perhaps ten times as many glial cells as neurons. They are believed to serve various structural and biochemical functions, many of which are as yet unclear.

Golgi bodies Small organelles found only in nerve cells and secretory cells. Believed to play some role in formation-secretion of substances from cells.

Golgi tendon organs Receptors in tendons of muscles that are activated by any increase in muscle tension—either due to stretch or to contraction.

(Note: no relation to Golgi bodies; both were named after the illustrious neuroanatomist.)

Grey matter   Regions of central nervous system containing nerve cell bodies (e.g., cerebral cortex) that look grey. Areas composed of nerve fibers appear whiter.

Habituation   Decrease in response to repeated stimulation, excluding receptor adaptation and muscle fatigue, at stimulus frequencies, for example, 2 per second or slower, well below those that might produce neuronal refractoriness. Behavioral response habituation exhibits a number of properties or parameters relating to stimulus and training variables that serve to define habituation more precisely.

Heritability   Percentage of variance in a trait that is due to genotype differences. To oversimplify, a trait that has high heritability is under strong genetic control.

Heschl's gyrus   A region of cerebral cortex in the human brain, lying in the depth of the sylvian fissure, that serves as the primary auditory receptive area of the cortex.

Histology   Refers generally to microscopic study of tissue.

Homeostasis   Tendency of a system to remain constant. Temperature regulation in warm-blooded animals is a classical example.

Huntington's chorea   A degenerative brain disease of genetic origin.

Hybrid   Offspring of a cross between two breeds—for example, hybrid corn.

Hybrid vigor   Fact that, at least in plants, hybrid offspring are more vigorous than either parent strain.

Hyperphagia   Increase in eating above normal levels. Damage to the ventromedial nucleus of the hypothalamus leads to increased eating and obesity.

Hyperpolarization   An increased negativity of the nerve membrane potential, for example, a shift to greater negativity from the resting level of −70 mV. In a nerve cell body hyperpolarization is usually associated with postsynaptic inhibition.

Iconic memory   Very short-term memory, usually considered to last less than a second. Iconic memory is surprisingly accurate and complete but decays rapidly.

Imipramine   A drug used to treat severe depression. Seems to act to prevent chemical breakdown of norepinephrine in brain.

Imprinting   Refers to observation that newly hatched precocial birds tend to fixate behaviorally on the first stimulus objects they see.

Induction   In embryology, the process whereby one tissue causes or induces another to develop in a particular way, for example, notochord induces neural tissue from ectoderm.

Infantile amauratic idiocy An hereditary metabolic disease resulting in mental deficiency in infants. Also termed Tay-Sachs disease.

Inhibitory postsynaptic potential (IPSP) Hyperpolarization (usually) in a neuron cell body and/or dendrites due to the action of an inhibitory synapse from another neuron. Occurrence of the IPSP prevents or inhibits the cell from being excited by excitatory synaptic influences.

Instrumental learning General category of learning where the response of the organism plays some role in determining the occurrence or nature of subsequent reinforcement—for example, pigeon pecking at a key to receive food or dog flexing leg to avoid shock.

Intrafusal fibers Muscle fibers in striated or skeletal muscles that contain stretch receptors. They do not contribute directly to tension exerted by muscle, but rather lead to increased (or decreased) activity of gamma afferent fibers, which activate alpha motoneurons to cause contraction of extrafusal muscle fibers. *See* gamma system.

Intravenous anesthetics Anesthetics administered in solution directly into blood stream (e.g., into veins).

Iodopsin Refers to group of photosensitive chemical substances in color receptors (cones) in retina of eye.

Isometric For muscles, refers to a contraction in which the muscle remains at constant length, for example, isometric exercises when muscles are "tensed" but limbs not moved.

Juvenile amauratic idiocy An hereditary metabolic disease resulting in mental deficiency that develops between the ages of 2 and 10.

Klinefelter's syndrome Condition where person has *XXY* sex chromosomes. They are usually categorized as females with many male characteristics.

Learning set Term introduced by Harlow to refer to the fact that animals get progressively better at learning general types of problems even though particular stimuli are changed. Learning to learn.

Lemniscal system A component of the ascending somatosensory system in the brain that projects via the medial lemniscus, a pathway in the lower brain. This system subserves the more discrete or epicritic aspects of somatic-sensory stimulation.

Locus caeruleus A region of the brain stem believed to include norepinephrine-containing neurons and believed by some to play an important role in the regulation of sleep.

MAO inhibitors Substances that inhibit the action of monoamine oxidase, an enzyme critical in the breakdown of biogenic amines (e.g., norepinephrine) in the nervous system. They are used clinically to treat severe depression.

Mass action, Principle of   Developed by Lashley to refer to the fact that the amount of cortex removed is more important than location, in terms of effects on complex learning tasks. *See* equipotentiality, principle of.

Median eminence   A region of the hypothalamus that releases hormones into the local blood supply to the anterior pituitary or adenohypophysis. These hypothalamic hormones, in turn, cause the adenohypophysis to release its hormones into the general circulation.

Mesoderm   One of three germinal layers of cells of the embryo—cells from mesoderm come to form skeletal muscles.

Messenger RNA   A form of ribonucleic acid involved in transferring the genetic code from the genes to the ribosomes, where proteins are made.

Mutation   A change at the level of the gene or chromosome that usually leads to a change in phenotype. Mutations can be "spontaneous" or induced (e.g., by x-rays) and are ultimately the only mechanism that can yield completely new characteristics in organisms. Most mutations, but obviously not all, are harmful.

Myelin sheath   The fatty insulating sheath that surrounds most larger nerve fibers in vertebrates.

Neocortex   Literally, "new cortex"—refers generally to the cerebral cortex in higher animals, excluding certain regions of old (paleo- or archi-) cortex.

Nerve   Generally refers to collections of nerve fibers outside central nervous system.

Neural tube   The initial nervous system in the embryo formed by folding of the neural plate.

Neurohypophysis   One of the two portions of the pituitary gland, also termed the *posterior pituitary*. The neurohypophysis does not, in fact, manufacture its own hormones but serves as a store and releasing region for hormones manufactured in the hypothalamus.

Neuron   A nerve cell, including the soma (cell body) and all its processes, for example, axon and dendrites.

Nictitating membrane   The "third eyelid" present in many animals.

Nissl bodies   Small organelles in the nerve cell body composed of ribosomes (the RNA present in the cell outside the nucleus).

Nissl method   Staining technique that stains Nissl bodies in the cell bodies of neurons; that is, it is a stain selective for nerve cell bodies.

Node of Ranvier   Periodic constrictions of the myelin sheath covering a nerve fiber. Conduction in myelinated fibers "jumps" from node to node, thus increasing conduction velocity relative to fibers without myelin.

Norepinephrine   A substance present in many nerve cells. It is a synaptic transmitter at autonomic ganglia, is released by the adrenal gland (it is also called *Noradrenaline*), and may be a transmitter in brain as well.

Notochord A rod-like cord of mesoderm that develops in the early embryo and induces overlying ectoderm to differentiate into nervous tissue.

Nucleus In neuroanatomy, nucleus refers to collections of nerve cell bodies inside central nervous system, for example, caudate nucleus. In cellular biology it, of course, refers to the central dense region of a cell.

Opsin A complex protein that complexes with retinene to form rhodopsin (photochemical in rods in eye for black-white vision). Other forms of opsin are present in the color receptor photochemicals of the cones.

Optic chiasm Point at which the optic nerves from the two eyes join and resort into the optic tracts. In humans, half of each optic nerve comprises each optic tract, such that information from the left half of each retina projects to the left side of the brain and vice versa.

Pacinian corpuscle Large specialized pressure receptors distributed throughout the body.

Parasympathetic Portion of the autonomic nervous system. Generally characterized as serving maintenance functions as opposed to the "emergency reactions" of the sympathetic portion of the autonomic nervous system.

PGO spikes Large brain wave "spikes" that can be recorded from the Pons, lateral Geniculate body and Occipital cortex regions of brain during D (deep or paradoxical) sleep. They occur in conjunction with rapid eye movements.

Phenothiazine derivatives Anti-psychotic drugs used to treat mental illness, particularly schizophrenia. A common example is chlorpromazine.

Phenotype The outward expression of gene actions as a result of growth, development, and interactions with the environment. Contrasted with the underlying genotype.

Phenylketonuria (PKU) An hereditary disease involving an abnormality in metabolism of an amino acid, phenylalanine, normally present in food. It results in severe mental deficiency but can be prevented if the infant is maintained on a special diet.

Pitch The perceived or judged tone of a sound. It is, of course, related to acoustic frequency but not linearly. The relation between pitch and frequency can be described as a semi-log or power function. Pitch compresses frequency—for example, a tone twice as high as another in frequency sounds less than twice as high.

Polygenetic system A system, trait, or characteristic determined by more than one pair of genes; for example, some authorities suggest that intelligence may involve as many as 70 different gene loci.

Postsynaptic inhibition Synaptic process whereby the postsynaptic cell is inhibited by being (usually) hyperpolarized. Major synaptic inhibitory process in the central nervous system. Believed due to the presynaptic terminals releasing inhibitory synaptic transmitter substances to act on the postsynaptic cell receptor regions.

Postsynaptic receptor region Region of cell body or dendrites receptive to transmitter released by a given presynaptic terminal.

Power law Law developed by S. S. Stevens to describe relation between stimulus intensity and subjective judgment of intensity. It has the form $\psi = K\phi^n$, where ψ is judged experience, ϕ is physical intensity, and K and n are constants.

Precocial Refers to birds like chickens that are able to fend for themselves at hatching.

Prestriate cortex The visual association cortex. A strip of cortex lying just beyond the primary visual (striate) cortex (area 17). It has Brodmann's numbers 18 and 19 and is believed to relay more complex aspects of visual experience.

Presynaptic excitation Process whereby one pathway is believed to act on the axon terminals of another pathway prior to the synaptic terminals to *increase* the excitatory action of the second pathway. Hypothetical mechanism of action is to induce hyperpolarization in second pathway fibers.

Presynaptic inhibition Process whereby one pathway is believed to act on the axon terminals of another pathway prior to the synaptic terminals to *decrease* the excitatory action of the second pathway. Hypothetical mechanism of action is to induce partial depolarization in second pathway fibers.

Primary after discharge In brain EEG, a pattern of electrical activity immediately following an electrical brain seizure, for example, following electroconvulsive shock.

Propagated action potential The moving spike discharge or action potential that travels rapidly along an axon to its synapses on other nerve cells or on target muscle or gland cells.

Protein Class of biochemical substances composed of large molecules made up of chains of amino acids. They form the building blocks of all tissue.

Protopathic Subdivision of somatic-sensory system, named by Head, which conveys diffuse touch, pain, and temperature sensations to higher brain regions. Equivalent to the spino-thalamic system.

Psychosurgery Human brain surgery done primarily to treat psychological or behavioral problems rather than brain pathology.

Pyramidal cell Nerve cells having cell bodies with the shape of a pyramid. The largest cells in the cerebral cortex and in hippocampus are pyramidal cells. They characteristically send their axons out to other regions of the brain.

Pyramidal tract Technically a bundle of fibers named for its pyramidal shape in the brain stem. Cell bodies lie in the cerebral cortex and fibers project down to lower brain regions and to spinal cord. It is a major motor system.

Pyramidal tract fibers Nerve fibers coursing through the pyramidal tract. *See* pyramidal tract.

Random assortment In genetics, the fact that during reduction division to form the ovum or sperm, the two members of each pair of chromosomes have an equal chance of assorting into a given cell.

Raphé nuclei Group of nuclei in brain stem believed to contain serotonin and to play an important role in sleep.

Raphé system The raphé nuclei and their widespread fiber projections to more anterior regions of the brain.

Rauwolfia alkaloids A group of naturally occurring (and now synthesized) plant biochemicals particularly effective in tranquilizing. Reserpine is the most important active substance in Rauwolfia.

Receptor cells The sensory cells that receive and transform physical stimuli into biological signals.

Receptor potential The electrical potential associated with the activity of a receptor cell, for example, when it responds to a physical stimulus.

Recruiting waves EEG waves recorded (usually) from the cerebral cortex in response to repeated electrical stimulation of the medial thalamus. They typically grow in amplitude, or "recruit," during the first few waves.

Renin Substance produced by kidney and involved in regulation of water content of body.

Reserpine A tranquilizer substance—the active ingredient of Rauwolfia. Believed to act on brain serotonin.

Resting membrane potential The resting voltage level across a nerve cell membrane when it is not actively responding, for example, to input from other neurons. The value is typically about −70 mV (approximately 7/100 of a volt).

Reticular activating system (RAS) An ascending system believed to originate in the brain stem reticular formation that activates or "arouses" electrical activity in cerebral cortex. The RAS is a functional concept rather than an exactly specified anatomical system. It is believed to play a crucial role in regulation of sleep and waking and in behavioral arousal.

Reticular formation A mixture of nerve cells and fibers in the lower or ventral portion of the brain stem, the tegmentum, extending from spinal cord to thalamus and giving rise to important ascending and descending systems. *See* reticular activating system.

Retina The layers of cells of the back of the eye that contain the photoreceptor cells and nerve cells of the eye.

Retinene A portion of the photochemical substance rhodopsin in the rods of the retina at the back of the eye. Rhodopsin is composed of retinene, which is closely related to Vitamin A, and a protein called opsin.

Retinotopic projection The fact that the retina of the eye projects anatomically and functionally in a topographically organized fashion to the visual areas of the cerebral cortex.

Retrograde degeneration analysis An anatomical method of tracing neural pathways by destroying the axon terminals and then locating the cell bodies of origin showing degenerative changes.

Rhodopsin The photochemical substance of the rods in the retina of the eye responsive to gradations of light intensity; composed of retinene and opsin.

Ribonucleic acid (RNA) A type of nucleic acid involved in the synthesis of proteins in cells.

Ribosomes Specialized organelles in cell bodies that serve as the site of protein synthesis in the cell. They are composed of RNA.

Rod Receptor cell in retina sensitive to light. Rods detect low levels of illumination (scotopic vision) and, in primates, code black-white vision. Color (photopic vision) is subserved by cones.

Sacral nerves The autonomic nerves at the lower end of the spinal cord that form the sacral portion of the parasympathetic system.

Scotopic vision Vision sensitive to dim levels of illumination and coding black-white (e.g., shades of grey). Subserved by rods.

Sensitization In learning, sensitization is an increase in response as a result of presenting stimuli, not dependent upon pairing; that is, it is a simple form of behavioral plasticity not involving associative learning.

Sensory-motor integration The author's euphemism for the term *perception.*

Septal area A region of the limbic forebrain system. Has been implicated in rewarding electrical self-stimulation of the brain. It is closely connected to the hippocampus.

Serotonin A biogenic amine, also termed 5HT (5-hydroxytryptamine). It is formed from the naturally occurring amino acid tryptophan, is present in brain, particularly in the raphé system, and has been implicated as a synaptic transmitter and as playing a role in psychosis. Brain levels of serotonin are dramatically altered by tranquilizers like reserpine.

Sham rage A term used to describe rage behavior that does not include directed attack. A cat with all brain tissue above hypothalamus destroyed will show autonomic and behavioral signs of rage but is incapable of an integrated and directed attack. It has also been described to occur as a result of hypothalamic stimulation in intact cats.

Sign stimulus   In ethology, a stimulus that serves as a trigger or releasing stimulus to elicit a fixed action pattern.

Soma   The cell body of a nerve cell.

Somatic nerves   The nerves going to and from brain and spinal cord that control striated muscles and receive sensory information from body and specialized receptors. Contrasted with visceral nerves that relate to the autonomic portion of the nervous system.

Spectral sensitivities   Sensitivity of visual receptors to different wavelengths (spectra) of light energy. The human eye is much more sensitive to green than to red or blue.

Spike discharge   The all-or-none spike discharge of a nerve cell that usually starts at the axon hillock and travels out the axon at a constant velocity (a few meters per second). *See* action potential.

Spike discharge threshold   The membrane voltage level at which a neuron will develop an all-or-none spike discharge. Typically a few millivolts more positive than the resting level. The cell must be depolarized from resting level (of about -70 mV) to the spike discharge level (about -60 mV), usually by synaptic actions from other neurons.

Spindle organs   The stretch receptors in intrafusal fibers of muscle. Contain the gamma afferent fibers and the terminations of gamma motoneuron fibers. The spindle organs code degree of stretch (but not necessarily tension) on the muscle.

Spinothalamic system   That portion of the somatic-sensory system conveying diffuse touch, pain, and temperature to the brain. Also termed the *protopathic system.*

Spontaneous recovery   In learning, after a conditioned response is extinguished it generally recovers to some degree in the absence of further training.

Spreading depression   In cerebral cortex, physical or chemical trauma induces a depression of activity to the point where it becomes nonfunctional for a period of minutes. The depression often spreads quite widely from the region of trauma. In smooth-brained animals like rat, an entire cortical hemisphere may become depressed.

Stellate cell   Neurons, for example, in cerebral cortex, with short branching axons and dendrites. Also called Golgi Type II or association neurons.

Striate cortex   The primary visual receiving area of the cerebral cortex. Called striate because of a pronounced stripe (the stripe of Gennari) running horizontally in the cortex.

Sympathetic division   One of the two major divisions of the autonomic portion of the nervous system. It has been characterized as serving emergency functions, for example, mobilizing bodily reactions to deal with sudden stress.

Synapse The point of interaction between nerve cells. The synapse has a number of characteristic features easily identified in electron microscopy, for example, a presynaptic terminal containing vesicles, a synaptic space, and a specialized postsynaptic membrane. At least in supposedly chemical synapses, there is always a small space between the presynaptic and postsynaptic sides of the synapse.

Synaptic depression A decrease in the efficacy of transmission at a synapse, usually as a result of prior activation. A decrease in synaptic efficacy not due to presynaptic or postsynaptic inhibition.

Synaptic potential The electrical potential recorded (usually) from the postsynaptic neuron that is generated by the activity of synapses acting on the neuron.

Tay-Sachs disease An hereditary metabolic disease that results in severe mental retardation in infants. *See also* infantile amauratic idiocy.

Thyroxin The hormone secreted by the thyroid gland. It regulates growth and metabolic rate.

Tolerance In relation to drugs, fact that progressively larger doses of the drug must be given to yield the same effect. Drugs that show large tolerance effects are usually, but not always, addicting.

Transduction In sensory reception, refers to the process whereby a physical stimulus is transformed into a biological signal at sensory receptors.

Transfer RNA A form of RNA outside the nucleus of a cell that is most directly involved with the synthesis of proteins.

Transmitter breakdown enzyme A chemical that breaks down or inactivates a synaptic transmitter substance, for example, acetylcholinesterase breaks acetylcholine down into acetyl and choline, thus rendering it inactive.

Turner's syndrome An individual with XO sex chromosomes—that is, only the one female X and no second X (normal female) or Y (normal male). Such individuals are phenotypic females of short stature with diminished sexual characteristics.

Ventrobasal complex That portion of the thalamus (a large nuclear region of the cerebrum) concerned with relaying somatic-sensory information to the somatic-sensory areas of the cerebral cortex.

Volatile anesthetics Any anesthetic that can act in gaseous form.

Wernicke-Korsakoff disease A severe degenerative brain disease usually resulting from chronic alcoholism.

Wernicke's area The region of cerebral cortex in the left temporal area that is critical for speech in the human brain.

White matter Nervous tissue composed of fibers covered with myelin. It has a white appearance in contrast to the greyish look of regions containing cell bodies.

Bibliography

Adametz, J. H. Rate of recovery of functioning in cats with rostral reticular lesions. *J. Neurosurg.*, 1959, **16**, 85–98.

Adams, M. S., and Neel, J. V. Children of incest. *Pediatrics*, 1967, **40**, 55–62.

Adams, R. D. The anatomy of memory mechanisms in the human brain. Pp. 91–106 in Talland, G. A., and Waugh, N. C. (eds.), op. cit., 1969.

Adolph, E. F., Barker, J. P., and Hoy, P. A. Multiple factors in thirst. *Am. J. Physiol.*, 1954, **178**, 538–562.

Agranoff, B. W. Molecules and memories. Pp. 13–22 in *Perspectives in biology and medicine*, **2**, 1965.

————. Memory and protein synthesis. *Sci. Am.*, 1967, **216**, 115–122.

Ahlskog, J. E., and Hoebel, B. G. Overeating and obesity from damage to a noradrenergic system in the brain. *Science*, 1973, **182**, 166–169.

Akert, K. Comparative anatomy of frontal cortex and thalamofrontal connections. Pp. 372–396 in Warren, J. M., and Akert, K. (eds.), op. cit., 1964.

Akert, K., and Andersson, B. Experimenteller beitrag zur physiologie des nucleus caudatus. *Acta Physiol. Scand.*, 1951, **22**, 281–298.

Allen, W. F. Formatis reticularis and reticulo spinal tracts, their visceral functions and possible relationships to tonicity and clonic contractions. *J. Wash. Acad. Sci.*, 1932, **22**, 490–495.

Alpern, M., Laurence, M., and Wolsk, D. *Sensory processes.* Belmont, Cal.: Wadsworth, 1967.

Anand, B. K., and Brobeck, J. R. Hypothalamic control of food intake in rats and cats. *Yale J. Biol. Med.*, 1951, **24**, 123–140.

Andersson, B. The effect of injections of hypertonic NaCl solutions into different parts of the hypothalamus of goats. *Acta Physiol. Scand.*, 1953, **28**, 188–201.

Andersson, B., and Wyrwicka, W. The elicitation of a drinking motor conditioned reaction by electrical stimulation of the "drinking area" in the goat. *Acta Physiol. Scand.*, 1957, **41**, 194–198.

Aserinsky, E., and Kleitman, N. Regularly occurring periods of eye motility and concomitant phenomena during sleep. *Science*, 1953, **118**, 273–274.

Averbach, E., and Sperling, G. Short term storage of information in vision. Pp. 196–212 in Cherry, C. (ed.), *Information theory.* London: Butterworth, 1961.

Babich, F. R., Jacobson, A. L., Bubash, S., and Jacobson, A. Transfer of response to naive rats by injections of ribonucleic acid extract from trained rats. *Science*, 1965, **149**, 656–657.

Bandler, R. J., Chi, C. C., and Flynn, J. P. Biting attack elicited by stimulation of the ventral midbrain tegmentation of cats. *Science*, 1972, **177**, 364–366.

Barber, T. X. Toward a theory of pain: Relief of chronic pain by prefrontal leucotomy, opiates, placebos, and hypnosis. *Psychol. Bull.*, 1959, **56**, 430–460.

Bard, P. A diencephalic mechanism for the expression of rage with special reference to the sympathetic nervous system. *Am. J. Physiol.*, 1928, **84**, 490–515.

Bard, P., and Macht, M. B. The behavior of chronically decerebrate cats. Pp. 55–71 in Wolstenholme, G. E. W., and O'Connor, C. M. (eds.), *Ciba Foundation Symposium, Neurological basis of behavior*. London: Churchill, 1958.

Bard, P., and Mountcastle, V. B. Some forebrain mechanisms involved in expression of angry behavior. *Assn. Res. Nerv. Dis. Proc.*, 1947, **27**, 362–404.

Barondes, S. H., and Cohen, H. D. Puromycin effect on successive phases of memory storage. *Science*, 1966, **151**, 594–595.

———. Memory impairment after subcutaneous injection of acetoxycycloheximide. *Science*, 1968, **160**, 556–557.

Basmajian, J. V. *Muscles alive: their functions revealed by electromyography*. Baltimore: Williams and Wilkins, 1967.

———. Electromyography: Single motor unit training. In Thompson, R. F., and Patterson, M. M. (eds.), op. cit., **IC**, 1974.

Basmajian, J. V., Baeza, M., and Fabrigar, C. Conscious control and training of individual spinal motor neurons in normal human subjects. *J. new drugs*, 1965, **5**, 78–85.

Békésy, von, G. The variation of phase along the basilar membrane with sinusoidal vibrations. *J. acoust. Soc. Am.*, 1947, **19**, 452–460.

Békésy, von, G., and Rosenblith, W. A. The mechanical properties of the ear. Pp. 1075–1115 in Stevens, S. S. (ed.), *Handbook of experimental psychology*. New York: Wiley, 1951.

Bennett, E. L., Diamond, M. C., Krech, D., and Rosenzweig, M. R. Chemical and anatomical plasticity of brain. *Science*, 1964, **146**, 610–619.

Berger, H. Über das elektrenkephalogramm des menschen. *Arch. Psychiat. Nervenkr.*, 1929, **87**, 527–570.

Berlyne, D. E. The influence of the albedo and complexity of stimuli on visual fixation in the human infant. *Brit. J. Psychol.*, 1958, **49**, 315–318.

———. Conflict and arousal. *Sci. Am.*, 1966, **215**, 82–87.

Bickford, R. G., Galbraith, R. F., and Jacobson, J. L. The nature of averaged evoked potentials recorded from the human scalp. *Electroencephalog. clin. Neurophysiol.*, 1963, **15**, 720.

Blakemore, C., and Cooper, J. F. Development of the brain depends on the visual environment. *Nature* (London), 1970, **228**, 477–478.

Blass, E. M., and Kraly, F. S. Medial forebrain bundle lesions: specific loss of feeding to decreased glucose utilization in rats. *J. comp. physiol. Psychol.*, 1974, **86**, 679–692.

Blum, J. S., Chow, K. L., and Pribram, K. H. A behavioral analysis of organization of parieto-temporo-preoccipital cortex. *J. comp. Neurol.*, 1950, **93**, 53–100.

Bogen, J. E. The other side of the brain: an appositional mind. *Bull. Los Angeles Neurological Socs.*, 1969, **34**, 135–162.

Bogen, J. E., and Gazzaniga, M. S. Cerebral commissurotomy in man: Minor hemisphere dominance for certain visuospatial functions. *J. Neurosurg.*, 1965, **23**, 394–399.

Bolles, R. C. *Theory of motivation*. New York: Harper and Row, 1967.

Bonvallet, M., Dell, P., and Heibel, G. Tonus sympathique et activité électrique corticale. *Electroencephalog. clin. Neurophysiol.*, 1954, **6**, 119–144.

Bradley, P. B. The central action of certain drugs in relation to the reticular formation of the brain. Pp. 123–149 in Jasper, H. H. (ed.), *Reticular formation of the brain*. Boston: Little, Brown, 1958.

————. Intermediation between administered drugs and behavioral effects: The electro-physiological approach. Pp. 338–344 in de Reuck, A. V. S., and Knight, J. (eds.), *Ciba Foundation Symposium, Animal behavior and drug action*. Boston: Little, Brown, 1964.

Brady, J. V. The effect of electro-convulsive shock on a conditioned emotional response: the permanence of the effect. *J. comp. physiol. Psychol.*, 1951, **44**, 507–511.

————. Ulcers in "executive" monkeys. *Sci. Am.*, 1958, **199**, 95–100.

————. Motivational-emotional self-stimulation. Pp. 413–430 in Sheer, D. E. (ed.), *Electrical stimulation of the brain*. Austin, Texas: Univ. of Texas Press, 1961.

Brady, J. V., and Hunt, H. F. The effect of electro-convulsive shock on a conditioned emotional response: a control for impaired hearing. *J. comp. physiol. Psychol.*, 1952, **45**, 180–182.

Brazier, M. A. B. *The electrical activity of the nervous system*. New York: Macmillan, 1960.

————. The analysis of brain waves. *Sci. Am.*, 1962, **206**, 142–153.

Bremer, F. *Cerveau isolé* et physiologie du sommeil. *Comp. Rend. Soc. biol.*, 1935, **118**, 1235–1241.

————. *Bull. l'Acad. roy. med. Belgique*, 1937, **2**, 6ᵉ Série, 68–86.

Brodal, A. *Neurological anatomy*. 2d ed. New York: Oxford Univ. Press, 1969.

Brogden, W. J., and Gantt, W. H. Intraneural conditioning: cerebellar conditioned reflexes. *Arch. neurol. Psychiat.*, 1942, **48**, 437–455.

Bromily, R. B. Conditioned responses in a dog after removal of neocortex. *J. comp. physiol. Psychol.*, 1948, **41**, 102–110.

Brooks, V. B., and Stoney, S. D., Jr. Motor mechanisms: The role of the pyramidal system in motor control. *Ann. Rev. Physiol.*, 1971, **33**, 337–392.

Brown, J. J., Curtis, J. R., Lever, A. F., Robertson, J. I. S., deWardener, H. E., and Wing, A. J. Plasma renin concentration and the control of blood pressure in patients on maintenance haemodialysis. *Nephron*, 1969, **6**, 329–349.

Brown, J. S. *The motivation of behavior.* New York: McGraw-Hill, 1961.

Brown, R. *A first language: The early stages.* Cambridge, Mass.: Harvard Univ. Press, 1973.

Bruner, J. S. *Processes of cognitive growth: Infancy,* **III**, 1968, Heinz Werner Lecture Series. Worcester, Mass.: Clark Univ. Press—Barre Pub., 1968.

Brush, F. R. (ed.). *Aversive conditioning and learning.* New York: Academic Press, 1971.

Brutkowski, S. Prefrontal cortex and drive inhibition. Pp. 242–270 in Warren, J. M., and Akert, K. (eds.), op. cit., 1964.

Buchanan, A. R. *Functional neuro-anatomy.* 4th ed. Philadelphia: Lea and Febiger, 1957.

Buchsbaum, M., and Fedio, P. Hemispheric differences in evoked potentials to verbal and nonverbal stimuli in the left and right visual fields. *Physiol. Behav.*, 1970, **5**, 207–210.

Buchwald, J. S., Halas, E. S., and Schramm, S. Changes in cortical and subcortical unit activity during behavioral conditioning. *Physiol. Behav.*, 1966, **1**, 11–22.

Buchwald, J. S., and Humphrey, G. L. An analysis of habituation in the specific sensory systems. Pp. 1–75 in Stellar, E., and Sprague, J. M. (eds.), *Progress in physiological psychology,* **5**. New York: Academic Press, 1973.

Buchwald, N. A., and Hull, C. D. Some problems associated with interpretation of physiological and behavioral responses to stimulation of caudate and thalamic nuclei. *Brain Res.*, 1967, **6**, 1–11.

Buerger, A. A., and Dawson, A. M. Spinal kittens: Long-term increases in electromyograms due to a conditioning routine. *Physiol. Behav.*, 1968, **3**, 99–103.

Burt, C. The genetic determination of differences in intelligence: A study of monozygotic twins reared together and apart. *Brit. J. Psychol.*, 1966, **57**, 137–153.

Campbell, B. A., Ballantine, P., II, and Lynch, G. Hippocampal control of behavioral arousal: Duration of lesion effects and possible interactions with recovery after frontal cortical damage. *Exp. Neurol.*, 1971, **33**, 159–170.

Campbell, B. A., and Lynch, G. S. Cortical modulation of spontaneous activity during hunger and thirst. *J. comp. physiol. Psychol.*, 1969, **67**, 15–22.

Chang, H. T., Ruch, T. C., and Ward, A. A., Jr. Topographical representation of muscles in motor cortex of monkeys. *J. Neurophysiol.*, 1947, **10**, 39–56.

Chapman, R. M. Kappa waves and intellectual abilities. *Electroencephalog. clin. Neurophysiol.*, 1972, **33**, 254.

Chapouthier, G. Behavioral studies of the molecular basis of memory. In Deutsch, J. A. (ed.), op. cit., 1973.

Cherry, E. C. Some experiments on the recognition of speech, with one and with two ears. *J. acoust. Soc. Am.*, 1953, **25**, 975–979.

Chi, C. C., and Flynn, J. P. Neural pathways associated with hypothalamically elicited attack behavior in cats. *Science*, 1971, **171**, 703–705.

Chorover, S. L., and DeLuca, A. M. Transient change in electrocorticographic reaction to ECS in the rat following footshock. *J. comp. physiol. Psychol.*, 1969, **69**, 141–149.

Chow, K. L. Conditions influencing the recovery of visual discriminative habits in monkeys following temporal neocortical ablations. *J. comp. physiol. Psychol.*, 1952a, **45**, 430–437.

————. Further studies on selective ablation of associative cortex in relation to visually mediated behavior. *J. comp. physiol. Psychol.*, 1952b, **45**, 109–118.

————. Effects of temporal neocortical ablation on visual discrimination learning sets in monkeys. *J. comp. physiol. Psychol.*, 1954, **47**, 194–198.

————. Anatomical and electrographical analysis of temporal neocortex in relation to visual discrimination learning in monkey. Pp. 507–525 in Delafresnaye, J. F. (ed.), *Brain mechanisms and learning*. Oxford: Blackwell, 1961.

Chow, K. L., and Hutt, P. J. The "association cortex" of *macaca mulatta*: A review of recent contributions to its anatomy and functions. *Brain*, 1953, **76**, 625–677.

Clark, W. E. L. *The hypothalamus*. London: Oliver and Boyd, 1938.

Clegg, P. C., and Clegg, A. G. *Hormones, cells and organisms*. Stanford: Stanford Univ. Press, 1969.

Clemente, C. D. Forebrain mechanisms related to internal inhibition and sleep. *Cond. Refl.*, 1968, **3**, 145–174.

Cohen, D. H. Development of a vertebrate experimental model for cellular neurophysiologic studies of learning. *Cond. Refl.*, 1969, **4**, 61–80.

Cohen, S. *The beyond within. The LSD story.* New York: Atheneum, 1970.

Coombs, J. S., Eccles, J. C., and Fatt, P. Excitatory synaptic action in motoneurones. *J. Physiol.*, 1955, **130**, 374–395.

Coons, E. E., and Miller, N. E. Conflict *vs.* consolidation of memory traces to explain "retrograde amnesia" produced by ECS. *J. comp. physiol. Psychol.*, 1960, **53**, 524–531.

Cooper, J. R., Bloom, F. E., and Roth, R. H. *The biochemical basis of neuropharmacology.* 2d ed. New York: Oxford Univ. Press, 1974.

Corsi, P. M. Verbal memory impairment after unilateral hippocampal excisions. Paper presented at the 40th annual meeting of the Eastern Psychological Assoc., Philadelphia, April 1969.

Cotman, C. W., Matthews, D. A., Taylor, D., and Lynch, G. Synaptic rearrangement in the dentate gyrus: Histochemical evidence of adjustments after lesions in immature and adult rats. *Proc. Nat. Acad. Sci.*, 1973, **70**, 3473–3477.

Davidson, J. Activation of the male rat's sexual behavior by intracerebral implantation of androgen. *Endocrinology*, 1966, **79**, 783.

Davis, H. Excitation of auditory receptors. Pp. 565–585 in Field, J., Magoun, H. W., and Hall, B. E. (eds.), *Handbook of physiology, Neurophysiology*, I. Washington, D.C.: Am. Physiol. Soc., 1959.

———. Some principles of sensory receptor action. *Physiol. Rev.*, 1961, **41**, 391–416.

———. A model for transducer action in the cochlea. *Cold Spring Harbor Symp. on Quant. Biol.*, 1965, **30**, 181–190.

Davis, H., Benson, R. W., Covell, W. P., Fernández, C., Goldstein, R., Katsuki, Y., Legouix, J. P., McAuliffe, D. R., and Tasaki, I. Acoustic trauma in the guinea pig. *J. acoust. Soc. Am.*, 1953, **25**, 1180–1189.

Decke, E. Effects of taste on the eating behavior of obese and normal persons. Cited in S. Schachter, *Emotion, obesity and crime.* New York: Academic Press, 1971.

Deese, J. *Psycholinguistics.* Boston: Allyn and Bacon, 1970.

Delay, J., and Deniker, P. Trente-huit cas de psychoses traitées par la cure prolongée et continue de 4560 RP. Le Congrès des Al. et Neurol. de Langue Fr. In *Compte rendu du Congrès.* Paris: Masson et Cie, 1952.

Dethier, V. G., and Bodenstein, D. Hunger in the blowfly. *Zeits. f. Tierpsychol.*, 1958, **15**, 129–140.

Deutsch, J. A. *The structural basis of behavior.* Chicago: Univ. of Chicago Press, 1960.

———. Appetitive motivation. Chapter 4 in McGaugh, J. L. (ed.). *Psychobiology. Behavior from a biological perspective.* New York: Academic Press, 1971.

———. (ed.). *The physiological basis of memory.* New York: Academic Press, 1973.

———. The cholinergic synapse and the site of memory. Pp. 59–76 in Deutsch, J. A. (ed.), op. cit., 1973.

Deutsch, J. A., and Leibowitz, S. F. Amnesia or reversal of forgetting by anticholinesterase, depending simply on time of injection. *Science*, 1966, **153**, 1017.

DeValois, R. L. Analysis and coding of color vision in the primate visual system. Pp. 567–580 in *Sensory receptors.* Cold Spring Harbor, N.Y.: Cold Spring Harbor Lab. of Quant. Biol., 1965.

DeValois, R. L., and Jacobs, G. H. Primate color vision. *Science,* 1968, **162,** 533–540.

DeWeid, D. Effects of peptide hormones on behavior. In Ganong, W. F., and Martini, J. L. (eds.), *Frontiers in Neuroendocrinology.* New York: Oxford Univ. Press, 1969.

Diamond, I. T., and Chow, K. L. Biological psychology. Pp. 158–241 in Koch, S. (ed.), *Psychology: A study of a science,* **4.** New York: McGraw-Hill, 1962.

Dilger, W. Nest material carrying behavior of F_1 hybrids between *Agapornis fischeri* and *A. roseicollis. Anat. Rec.,* 1959, **134,** 554.

Dingman, W., and Sporn, M. B. The incorporation of 8-azaguanine into rat brain RNA and its effect on maze learning by the rat: An inquiry into the biochemical basis. *J. psychiat. Res.,* 1961, **1,** 1–11.

Dobzhansky, T. *Mankind evolving: The evolution of the human species.* New Haven: Yale Univ. Press, 1962. (Pb, Bantam Books, 1970).

———. *Heredity and the nature of man.* New York: Harcourt, Brace and World, 1964.

Doty, R. W. Functional significance of the topographical aspects of retinocortical projection. Pp. 228–247 in Jung, J., and Kornhuber, H. (eds.), *The visual system: Neurophysiology and psychophysics.* Berlin: Springer-Verlag, 1961.

———. Ability of *macaques* to discriminate locus of electrical stimuli applied to neocortex. *XXIII Int. Cong. physiol. Sci.,* abstract, 1965a.

———. Conditioned reflexes elicited by electrical stimulation of the brain in macaques. *J. Neurophysiol.,* 1965b, **28,** 623–640.

Doty, R. W., and Rutledge, L. T. Generalization between cortically and peripherally applied stimuli eliciting conditioned reflexes. *J. Neurophysiol.,* 1959, **22,** 428–435.

Downer, J. L. Interhemispheric integration in the visual system. Pp. 83–100 in Mountcastle, V. B. (ed.), *Conference on Interhemispheric Relations and Cerebral Dominance.* Baltimore: Johns Hopkins Press, 1962.

Drachman, D. A., and Arbit, J. Memory and the hippocampal complex. II. Is memory a multiple process? *Arch. Neurol.* (Chicago), 1966, **15,** 52–61.

Duffy, E. *Activation and behavior.* New York: Wiley, 1962.

Duncan, C. P. The retroactive effect of electroshock on learning. *J. comp. physiol. Psychol.,* 1949, **42,** 34–44.

Durup, G., and Fessard, A. L'électroencéphalogramme de l'homme. *Année psychol.,* 1935, **36,** 1–32.

Eason, R. G., Harter, M. R., and White, C. T. Effects of attention and arousal on visually evoked cortical potentials and reaction time in man. *Physiol. Behav.,* 1969, **4,** 283–289.

Eccles, J. C. *The physiology of nerve cells.* Baltimore: Johns Hopkins Press, 1957.

————. The behavior of nerve cells. Pp. 28–47 in Wolstenholme, G. E. W., and O'Connor, C. M. (eds.), *Ciba Foundation Symposium, Neurological basis of behavior.* London: Churchill, 1958.

————. *Facing reality: philosophical adventures by a brain scientist.* New York: Springer, 1970.

————. *The understanding of the brain.* New York: McGraw-Hill, 1973.

Eccles, J. C., Eccles, R. M., and Lundberg, A. Synaptic actions on motoneurones in relation to the two components of the group I muscle afferent volley. *J. Physiol.,* 1957, **136,** 527–546.

Eccles, J. C., Ito, M., and Szentágothai, J. *The cerebellum as a neuronal machine.* New York: Springer, 1967.

Eibl-Eibesfeldt, I. *Ethology: The biology of behavior.* Trans. by Erich Klinghammer. New York: Holt, Rinehart, and Winston, 1970.

Eidelberg, E., and Stein, D. G. (eds.). Functional recovery after lesions of the nervous system. *Neurosciences Research Program Bltn.,* 1974, **12** (2).

Emmers, R. Interaction of neural systems which control body water. *Brain Res.,* 1973, **49,** 323–347.

Epstein, A. N. The lateral hypothalamic syndrome: Its implications for the physiological psychology of hunger and thirst. Pp. 263–317 in Stellar, E., and Sprague, J. M. (eds.), op. cit., 1971.

Epstein, A. N., and Teitelbaum, P. Regulation of food intake in the absence of taste, smell, and other oropharyngeal sensations. *J. comp. physiol. Psychol.,* 1962, **55,** 753–759.

Evarts, E. V. Pyramidal tract activity associated with a conditioned hand movement in the monkey. *J. Neurophysiol.,* 1966, **29,** 1011–1027.

————. Relation of pyramidal tract activity to force exerted during voluntary movement. *J. Neurophysiol.,* 1968, **31,** 14–27.

Fantz, R. L. Form preferences in newly hatched chicks. *J. comp. physiol. Psychol.,* 1957, **50,** 422–430.

————. The origin of form perception. *Sci. Am.,* 1961, **204,** 66–72.

Farel, P. B., Glanzman, D. L., and Thompson, R. F. Habituation of a monosynaptic response in the vertebrate central nervous system: lateral column-motoneuron pathway in isolated frog spinal cord. *J. Neurophysiol.,* 1973, **26,** 1117–1130.

Farrell, B. Scientists, theologians, mystics swept up in a psychic revolution. *Life,* 1966, March 25. Life Educational Reprint 22.

Fechner, G. *Elements of psychophysics,* 1860. Trans. by H. E. Adler. New York: Holt, Rinehart and Winston, 1966.

Fehmi, L. G., Adkins, J. W., and Lindsley, D. B. Electrophysiological correlates of visual perceptual masking in monkeys. *Exp. Brain Res.,* 1969, **7,** 299–316.

Feldberg, W., and Myers, R. D. A new concept of temperature regulation by amines in the hypothalamus. *Nature*, 1963, **200**, 1325.

Feldman, S. M., and Waller, H. J. Dissociation of electrocortical activation and behavioral arousal. *Nature*, 1962, **196**, 1320–1322.

Ferrier, D. *Functions of the brain.* 2d ed. London: Smith and Elder, 1886.

Fisher, A. E., and Coury, J. N. Cholinergic tracing of a central neural circuit underlying the thirst drive. *Science*, 1962, **138**, 691–693.

Fitzgerald, L. A., and Thompson, R. F. Classical conditioning of the hind-limb flexion reflex in the acute spinal cat. *Psychon. Sci.*, 1967, **8**, 213–214.

Fitzsimons, J. T. The physiology of thirst: A review of the extraneural aspects of the mechanisms of drinking. Pp. 119–201 in Stellar, E., and Sprague, J. M. (eds.), op. cit., 1971.

———. The renin-angiotensin system in the control of drinking. Pp. 195–212 in Martini, L., Motta, M., and Fraschini, F. (eds.), *The hypothalamus.* New York: Academic Press, 1970.

Flexner, J. B., Flexner, L. B., and Stellar, E. Memory in mice as affected by intracerebral puromycin. *Science*, 1963, **141**, 57–59.

Flexner, L. B., and Flexner, J. B. Studies in memory: the long term survival of peptidylpuromycin in mouse brain. *Proc. Nat. Acad. Sci.* 1968, **60**, 923–927.

Flexner, L. B., Flexner, J. B., and Roberts, R. B. Memory as analyzed with antibiotics. *Science*, 1967, **155**, 1377–1383.

Flynn, J. P. The neural basis of aggression in cats. Pp. 40–60 in Glass, D. C. (ed.), op. cit., 1967.

Flynn, J. P., Vanegas, H., Foote, W., and Edwards, S. Neural mechanisms involved in a cat's attack on a rat. Pp. 135–173 in Whalen, R. E., Thompson, R. F., Verzeano, M., and Weinberger, N. M. (eds.), *The neural control of behavior.* New York: Academic Press, 1970.

Fodor, J., and Garrett, M. Some reflections on competence and performance. Pp. 135–162 in Lyons, J., and Wales, R. J. (eds.), *Psycholinguistics papers.* Edinburgh: Univ. of Edinburgh Press, 1966.

Fonberg, E. The role of the hypothalamus and amygdala in food intake, alimentary motivation and emotional reactions. *Acta Biologiae Experimentalis* (Warsaw), 1969, **29**, 335–358.

Fox, S. S., and O'Brien, J. H. Duplication of evoked potential waveform by curve of probability of firing of a single cell. *Science*, 1965, **147**, 888–890.

Frank, B., Stein, D. G., and Rosen, J. Interanimal "memory" transfer: Results from brain and liver homogenates. *Science*, 1970, **169**, 399–402.

French, G. M. Locomotor effects of regional ablation of frontal cortex in rhesus monkeys. *J. comp. physiol. Psychol.*, 1959, **52**, 18–24.

French, G. M., and Harlow, H. F. Variability of delayed-reaction performance in normal and brain-damaged rhesus monkeys. *J. Neurophysiol.*, 1962, **25**, 585–599.

French, J. D. The reticular formation. *Sci. Am.*, 1957, **196**, 54–60.

French, J. D., Van Amerongen, F. K., and Magoun, H. W. An activating system in the brain stem of the monkey. *Arch. neurol. Psychiat.*, 1952, **68**, 577–590.

French, J. D., Verzeano, J., and Magoun, H. W. An extralemniscal sensory system in the brain. *Arch. neurol. Psychiat.*, 1953, **69**, 505–518.

Fritsch, G., and Hitzig, E. Ueber die elektrische Erregbarkeit des Grosshirns. *Arch. anat. Physiol. wiss. Med.*, 1870, **37**, 300–332.

Fuster, J. M. Effects of stimulation of brain stem on tachistoscopic perception. *Science*, 1958, **127**, 150.

Gabriel, M., Wheeler, W., and Thompson, R. F. Multiple-unit activity of the rabbit cerebral cortex in single-session avoidance conditioning. *Physiol. Psychol.*, 1973a, **1**, 45–55.

———. Multiple unit activity of the rabbit cerebral cortex during stimulus generalization of avoidance behavior. *Physiol. Psychol.*, 1973b, **1**, 313–320.

Galambos, R., Sheatz, G., and Vernier, V. G. Electrophysiological correlates of a conditioned response in cats. *Science*, 1956, **123**, 376–377.

Ganz, L., Fitch, M., and Satterburg, J. A. The selective effect of visual deprivation on receptive field shape determined neurophysiologically. *Exp. Neurol.*, 1968, **22**, 614–637.

Garcia, J., McGowan, B. K., Ervin, F. R., and Koelling, R. A. Cues: Their relative effectiveness as a function of the reinforcer. *Science*, 1968, **160**, 794–795.

Gardner, B. T., and Gardner, R. A. Two-way communication with an infant chimpanzee. Pp. 117–184 in Schrier, A., and Stollnitz, F. (eds.), *Behavior of nonhuman primates*. New York: Academic Press, 1971.

Gardner, E. *Fundamentals of neurology*. 5th ed. Philadelphia: W. B. Saunders, 1968.

Gazzaniga, M. S. The split brain in man. *Sci. Am.*, 1967, **217**, 24–29.

———. *The bisected brain*. New York: Appleton-Century-Crofts, 1970.

Geldard, F. A. *The human senses*. 2d ed. New York: Wiley, 1972.

Gerard, R. W. Physiology and psychiatry. *Am. J. Psychiat.*, 1949, **106**, 161–173.

Geschwind, N. Disconnexion syndromes in animals and man. *Brain*, 1966, **88**, 237–294.

———. Language and the brain. *Sci. Am.*, 1972, **226**, 76–83.

Gibson, J. J. *The senses considered as perceptual systems*. Boston: Houghton-Mifflin, 1966.

Gibson, W. E., Reid, L. D., Sakai, M., and Porter, P. B. Intracranial reinforcement compared with sugar-water reinforcement. *Science*, 1965, **148**, 1357–1359.

Glass, D. C. (ed.). *Neurophysiology and emotion*. New York: Rockefeller Univ. Press, 1967.

Glassman, E. (ed.). *Molecular approaches to psychobiology.* Belmont, Cal.: Dickenson Pub. Co., 1967.

Glickman, S. E., and Feldman, S. M. Habituation of the arousal response to direct stimulation of the brain stem. *Electroencephalog. clin. Neurophysiol.*, 1961, **13**, 703–709.

Globus, A., Rosenzweig, M. R., Bennett, E. L., and Diamond, M. C. Effects of differential experience on dendritic spine counts in rat cerebral cortex. *J. comp. physiol. Psychol.*, 1973, **82**, 175–181.

Globus, A., and Sheibel, A. B. The effect of visual deprivation on cortical neurons—a golgi study. *Exp. Neurol.*, 1967, **19**, 331–345.

Gold, R. M. Hypothalamic obesity: The myth of the ventromedial nucleus. *Science*, 1973, **182**, 488–490.

Goodman, L. S., and Gilman, A. (ed.). *The pharmacological basis of therapeutics.* 2d ed. New York: Macmillan, 1956.

Grady, K. L., Phoenix, C. H., and Young, W. C. Role of the developing rat testes in differentiation of the neural tissue mediating mating behavior, *J. comp. physiol. Psychol.*, 1965, **59**, 176–182.

Graff, H., and Stellar, E. Hyperphagia, obesity and finickiness. *J. comp. physiol. Psychol.*, 1962, **55**, 418–424.

Granit, R. *Sensory mechanisms of the retina.* London: Oxford Univ. Press, 1947.

———. *Receptors and sensory perception.* New Haven, Conn.: Yale Univ. Press, 1955.

Granit, R., and Kaada, B. R. Influence of stimulation of central nervous structures on muscle spindles in cat. *Acta physiol. Scand.*, 1952, **27**, 130–160.

Grastyan, E., and Karmos, G. The influence of hippocampal lesions on simple and delayed instrumental conditioned reflexes. Pp. 225–234 in *Physiologie de l'hippocampe.* Paris: Centre National de la Recherche Scientifique, 1962.

Gray, G. W. The great ravelled knot. *Sci. Am.*, 1948, **179**, 26–39.

Green, D. M., and Swets, J. A. *Signal detection theory and psychophysics.* New York: Wiley, 1966.

Grings, W. W. Recording of electrodermal phenomena. In Thompson, R. F., and Patterson, M. M. (eds.), **IC**, op. cit., 1974.

Gross, C. G. Locomotor activity under various stimulus conditions following partial lateral frontal cortical lesions in monkeys. *J. comp. physiol. Psychol.*, 1963, **56**, 232–236.

Gross, C. G., Bender, D. B., and Rocha-Miranda, C. E. Visual receptive fields of neurons in inferotemporal cortex of the monkey. *Science*, 1969, **166**, 1303–1305.

Gross, C. G., and Zeigler, H. P. (eds.). *Readings in physiological psychology: Learning and memory.* New York: Harper and Row, 1969a.

———. *Readings in physiological psychology: Motivation.* New York: Harper and Row, 1969b.

619

Bibliography

————. *Readings in physiological psychology: Neurophysiology/Sensory processes.* New York: Harper and Row, 1969c.

Grossman, S. P. Eating or drinking elicited by direct adrenergic or cholinergic stimulation of hypothalamus. *Science*, 1960, **132**, 301–302.

————. *A textbook of physiological psychology.* New York: Wiley, 1967.

Groves, P. M., DeMarco, R., and Thompson, R. F. Habituation and sensitization of spinal interneuron activity in acute spinal cat. *Brain Res.*, 1969, **14**, 521–525.

Groves, P. M., Glanzman, D. L., Patterson, M. M., and Thompson, R. F. Excitability of cutaneous afferent terminals during habituation and sensitization in acute spinal cat. *Brain Res.*, 1970, **18**, 388–392.

Groves, P. M., and Thompson, R. F. Habituation: A dual-process theory. *Psychol. Rev.*, 1970, **77**, 419–450.

————. A dual-process theory of habituation: Neural mechanisms. Pp. 175–205 in Peeke, H. V. S., and Herz, M. J. (eds.), op. cit., 1973.

Guedel, A. E. *Inhalation anesthesia.* 2nd ed. New York: Macmillan, 1951.

Haider, M., Spong, P., and Lindsley, D. B. Attention, vigilance, and cortical evoked potentials in humans. *Science*, 1964, **145**, 180–182.

Hailman, J. P. How an instinct is learned. *Sci. Am.*, 1969, **221**, 98–106.

Hall, C. S. What people dream about. *Sci. Am.*, 1951, **184**, 60–63.

Hall, R. D., and Mark, R. G. Fear and modification of acoustically evoked potentials during conditioning. *J. Neurophysiol.*, 1967, **30**, 893–910.

Hammel, H. T. Regulation of internal body temperature. *Ann. Rev. Physiol.*, 1968, **30**, 641–710.

Hardy, J. D. (ed.). *Temperature: Its measurement and control in science and industry*, 3, Part 3. New York: Reinhold, 1963.

Harlow, H. F. The formation of learning sets. *Psychol. Rev.*, 1949, **56**, 51–65.

————. Behavioral contributions to interdisciplinary research. Pp. 3–23 in Harlow, H. F., and Woolsey, C. N. (eds.), *Biological and biochemical bases of behavior.* Madison, Wis.: Univ. of Wisconsin Press, 1958.

————. Love in infant monkeys. *Sci. Am.*, 1959a, **200**, 68–74.

————. The development of learning in the rhesus monkey. *Am. Scientist*, 1959b, **47**, 459–479.

————. Heterosexual affectional system in monkeys. *Am. Psychol.*, 1962, **17**, 1–9.

————. *Learning to love.* New York: Ballantine, 1973.

Harlow, H. F., McGaugh, J. L., and Thompson, R. F. *Psychology.* San Francisco: Albion, 1971.

Harris, G. W., and Michael, R. P. The activation of sexual behaviour by hypothalamic implants of oestrogen. *J. Physiol.*, 1964, **171**, 275–301.

Harris, J. D. Habituatory response decrement in the intact organism. *Psychol. Bull.*, 1943, **40**, 385–422.

Hartmann, E. *The biology of dreaming.* Springfield, Ill.: Charles C. Thomas, 1967.

620

Bibliography

Hawkes, J., and Woolley, L. *History of mankind.* **I:** *Prehistory and the beginnings of civilization.* New York: Harper and Row, 1963.

Hebb, D. O. On the nature of fear. *Psychol. Rev.,* 1946, **53,** 259–276.

———. *The organization of behavior.* New York: Wiley, 1949.

———. *A textbook of psychology.* Philadelphia: W. B. Saunders, 1966.

Hécaen, H., Ajuriaguerra, J. de, and Angelerues, R. Apraxia and its various aspects. In Halpern, L. (ed.), *Problems of dynamic neurology.* Jerusalem: Hebrew Univ. Hadassah Med. School, 1963.

Held, R. Plasticity in sensory-motor systems. *Sci. Am.,* 1965, **213,** 84–94.

Held, R., and Hein, A. Movement-produced stimulation in the development of visually guided behavior. *J. comp. physiol. Psychol.,* 1963, **56,** 872–876.

Held, R., and Richards, W. (eds.). *Perception: Mechanisms and models. Readings from Scientific American.* San Francisco: W. H. Freeman, 1972.

Hernández-Peón, R., Jouvet, M., and Scherrer, H. Auditory potentials at cochlear nucleus during acoustic habituation. *Acta neurol. Lat.-Am.,* 1957, 3, 144–156.

Hernández-Peón, R., Scherrer, H., and Jouvet, M. Modification of electrical activity in cochlear nucleus during "attention" in unanesthetized cats. *Science,* 1956, **123,** 331–332.

Heron, W. The pathology of boredom. *Sci. Am.,* 1957, **196,** 52–56.

Hess, E. H. Space perception in the chick. *Sci. Am.,* 1956, **195,** 71–80.

Hess, E. H., and Polt, J. M. Pupil size as related to interest value of visual stimuli. *Science,* 1960, **132,** 349–350.

Hess, W. R., and Akert, K. Experimental data on role of hypothalamus in mechanism of emotional behavior. *Arch. neurol. Psychiat.,* 1955, **73,** 127–129.

Heston, L. L. Psychiatric disorders in foster home children of schizophrenic mothers. *Brit. J. Psychiat.,* 1966, **112,** 819–825.

Hetherington, A. N., and Ranson, S. W. The spontaneous activity and food intake of rats with hypothalamic lesions. *Am. J. Physiol.,* 1942, **136,** 609–617.

Higgins, J. V., Reed, E. W., and Reed, S. C. Intelligence and family size: A paradox resolved. *Eugen. Qu.,* 1962, **9,** 84–90.

Hind, J. E., Rose, J. E., Davies, P. W., Woolsey, C. N., Benjamin, R. M., Welker, W. S., and Thompson, R. F. Unit activity in the auditory cortex. Pp. 201–210 in Rasmussen, G. L., and Windle, W. F. (eds.), *Neural mechanisms of the auditory and vestibular systems.* Springfield, Ill.: Charles C. Thomas, 1961.

Hinde, R. A. *Animal behaviour, a synthesis of ethology and comparative psychology.* 2nd ed. New York: McGraw-Hill, 1970.

Hirsch, H. V. B., and Spinelli, D. N. Visual experience modifies distribution of horizontally and vertically oriented receptive fields in cats. *Science,* 1970, **168,** 869–871.

———. Modification of the distribution of receptive field orientation in cats by selective visual exposure during development. *Exp. Brain Res.*, 1971, **13**, 509–527.

Hirsch, J. (ed.). *Behavior-genetic analysis.* New York: McGraw-Hill, 1967.

Hirsch, J., and Boudreau, J. C. Studies in experimental behavior genetics: I. The heritability of phototaxis in a population of *Drosophila melanogaster. J. comp. physiol. Psychol.*, 1958, **51**, 647–651.

Hobson, J. A., McCarley, R. W., Pivik, R. T., and Freedman, R. Selective firing by cat pontine brain stem neurons in desynchronized sleep. *J. Neurophysiol.*, 1974, **37**, 497–511.

Hochberg, J. *Perception.* New York: Prentice-Hall, 1964.

Hockett, C. D. The origin of speech. *Sci. Am.*, 1960, **203**, 88–111.

Hodgkin, A. L. Ionic movements and electrical activity in giant nerve fibres. *Proc. roy. Soc. Series B*, 1958, **148**, 1–37.

———. *The conduction of the nervous impulse.* Liverpool: Liverpool University Press, 1964.

Hodgkin, A. L., and Huxley, A. F. A quantitative description of membrane current and its application to conduction and excitation in nerve. *J. Physiol.*, 1952, **117**, 500–544.

Hoebel, B., and Teitelbaum, P. Hypothalamic control of feeding and self-stimulation. *Science*, 1962, **135**, 375–376.

Hofmann, A. Psychotomimetic drugs: Chemical and pharmacological aspects. *Acta physiol. pharmac. néer.*, 1959, **8**, 240–258.

Horn, G. Electrical activity of the cerebral cortex of the unanesthetized cat during attentive behavior. *Brain*, 1960, **83**, 57–76.

Hubbard, R., and Wald, G. Cis-trans isomers of vitamin A and retinene in the rhodopsin system. *J. gen. Physiol.*, 1952–53, **36**, 269–315.

Hubel, D. H., and Wiesel, T. N. Receptive fields of single neurones in the cat's striate cortex. *J. Physiol.*, 1959, **148**, 574–591.

———. Receptive fields, binocular interaction and functional architecture in the cat's visual cortex. *J. Physiol.*, 1962, **160**, 106–154.

———. Receptive fields and functional architecture in two nonstriate visual areas (18 and 19) of the cat. *J. Neurophysiol.*, 1965, **28**, 229–289.

Hudspeth, W. J., McGaugh, J. L., and Thomson, C. W. Aversive and amnesic effects of electro-convulsive shock. *J. comp. physiol. Psychol.*, 1964, **57**, 61–64.

Humphrey, M. E., and Zangwill, O. L. Cessation of dreaming after brain injury. *J. neurol. neurosurg. Psychiat.*, 1951, **14**, 322–325.

Hunter, W. S. The delayed reaction in animals and children. *Behav. Monogr.*, 1913, **2**, 1—86.

Hurvich, L. M., and Jameson, D. An opponent-process theory of color vision. *Psychol. Rev.*, 1957, **64**, 384–404.

Hydén, H., and Egyhazi, E. Nuclear RNA changes in nerve cells during a learning experiment in rats. *Proc. Nat. Acad. Sci.*, 1962, **48**, 1366–1372.

Isaac, W., and DeVito, J. L. Effect of sensory stimulation on the activity of normal and prefrontal lobectomized monkeys. *J. comp. physiol. Psychol.*, 1958, **51**, 172–174.

Isaacson, R. L. (ed.). *The neuropsychology of development.* New York: Wiley, 1968.

Jacobs, H. L., and Sharma, K. N. Taste versus calories: Sensory and metabolic signals in the control of food intake. *Ann. N.Y. Acad. Sci.*, 1969, **157**, Art. 2, 1084–1125.

Jacobsen, C. F. Functions of the frontal association area in primates. *Arch. neurol. Psychiat.*, 1935, **33**, 558–569.

Jacobson, A. L., and Schlechter, J. M. Chemical transfer of training: Three years later. In Pribram, K. H., and Broadbent, D. E. (eds.), op. cit., 1970.

Jaffe, J. H. Drug addiction and drug abuse. Pp. 276–313 in Goodman, L. S., and Gilman, A. (eds.), *The pharmacological basis of therapeutics.* 4th ed. New York: Macmillan, 1970.

James, W. *The principles of psychology.* New York: Henry Holt, 1890.

Jarvik, L. F., Klodin, V., and Matsuyama, S. S. Human aggression and the extra Y chromosome: Fact or fantasy? *Am. Psychol.*, 1973, **28**, 674–682.

Jarvik, M. E. Drugs used in the treatment of psychiatric disorders. Pp. 151–203 in Goodman, L. S., and Gilman, A. (eds.), *The pharmacological basis of therapeutics.* 4th ed. New York: Macmillan, 1970.

———. The psychopharmacological revolution. *Psychology Today*, 1967, **1**, 51–59.

Jasper, H. H., Ricci, G., and Doane, B. Patterns of cortical neuronal discharge during conditioned responses in monkeys. Pp. 277–290 in Wolstenholme, G. E. W., and O'Connor, C. M. (eds.), *Ciba Foundation Symposium, Neurological basis of behavior.* London: Churchill, 1958.

———. Microelectrode analysis of cortical cell discharge during avoidance conditioning in the monkey. Pp. 137–155 in Jasper, H. H., and Smirnov, G. D. (eds.), *The Moscow colloquium on electroencephalography of higher nervous activity. Electroencephalog. clin. Neurophysiol.*, 1960, Suppl. 13.

Jasper, H. H., and Shagass, C. Conditioning the occipital alpha rhythm in man. *J. exp. Psychol.*, 1941, **28**, 373–388.

Jennings, H. S. *Behavior of the lower organisms.* New York, 1906.

Jerison, H. J. *Evolution of the brain and intelligence.* New York: Academic Press, 1973.

John, E. R. *Mechanisms of memory.* New York: Academic Press, 1967.

John, E. R., Bartlett, F., Shimokochi, M., and Kleinman, D. Neural read-out from memory. *J. Neurophysiol.*, 1973, **36**, 893–924.

John, E. R., Herrington, R. N., and Sutton, S. Effects of visual form on the evoked response. *Science*, 1967, **155**, 1439–1442.

Jouvet, M. The states of sleep. *Sci. Am.*, 1967, **216**, 62–72.

Jouvet, M., and Michel, F. Recherches sur l'activité électrique cérébrale au cours du sommeil. *Comptes Rendus Société Biologie*, 1958, **152**, 1167–1170.

Julien, R. *A primer of drug actions*. San Francisco: W. H. Freeman, 1975.

Kaada, B. R., Anderson, P., and Jansen, J. Stimulation of amygdaloid nuclear complex in unanesthetized cats. *Neurol.*, 1954, **4**, 48–64.

Kandel, E. R. *The cellular basis of behavior: An introduction to behavioral neurobiology*. San Francisco: W. H. Freeman, 1975.

Katz, B. *Nerve, muscle and synapse*. New York: McGraw-Hill, 1966.

Keesey, R. E., and Powley, T. L. Self-stimulation and body weight in rats with lateral hypothalamic lesions. *Am. J. Physiol.*, 1973, **224**, 970–978.

Kellogg, W. N. Is "spinal conditioning" conditioning? A reply to "a comment." *J. exp. Psychol.*, 1947, **37**, 263–265.

Kennedy, G. C. The role of depot fat in the hypothalamic control of food intake in the rat. *Proc. roy. Soc. Series B*, 1953, **140**, 578–592.

Kennedy, J. L., Gottsdanker, R. M., Armington, J. C., and Gray, F. E. A new electroencephalogram associated with thinking. *Science*, 1948, **108**, 527–529.

Key, B. J., and Bradley, P. B. The effect of drugs on conditioned arousal responses. *Electroencephalog. clin. Neurophysiol.*, 1959, **11**, 841.

Khavari, K. A., and Russell, R. W. Acquisition, retention, and extinction under conditions of water deprivation and of central cholinergic stimulation. *J. comp. physiol. Psychol.*, 1966, **61**, 339–345.

Kim, C., Choi, H., Kim, J. K., Kim, M. S., Huh, M. K., and Moon, Y. B. Sleep pattern of hippocampectomized cat. *Brain Res.*, 1971, **29**, 223–236.

Kimble, D. P. Hippocampus and internal inhibition. *Psychol. Bull.*, 1968, **70**, 285–295.

―――. Possible inhibitory functions of the hippocampus. *Neuropsychologia*, 1969, **7**, 235–244.

Kimble, G. A. *Hilgard and Marquis' conditioning and learning*. New York: Appleton-Century-Crofts, 1961.

King, F. A., and Myers, P. M. Effects of amygdaloid lesions upon septal hyperemotionality in the rat. *Science*, 1958, **128**, 655–656.

Kinsbourne, M. Cognitive deficit: Experimental analysis. Chapter 7 in McGaugh, J. L. (ed.), *Psychobiology: Behavior from a biological perspective*. New York: Academic Press, 1971.

Klüver, H., and Bucy, P. C. "Psychic blindness" and other symptoms following bilateral temporal lobectomy in rhesus monkeys. *Am. J. Physiol.*, 1937, **119**, 352–353.

Konorski, J. *Integrative activity of the brain: An interdisciplinary approach*. Chicago: Univ. of Chicago Press, 1967.

Krivanek, J., and McGaugh, J. L. Effects of pentylenetetrazol on memory storage in mice. *Psychopharmacologia* (Berlin), 1968, **12**, 303–321.

—————. Facilitating effects of pre- and posttrial amphetamine administration on discrimination learning in mice. *Agents and Actions*, 1969, **1**, 36–42

Kuffler, S. W. Discharge patterns and functional organization of mammalian retina. *J. Neurophysiol.*, 1953, **16**, 37–68.

Kupfermann, I., Castellucci, V., Pinsker, H., and Kandel, E. R. Neuronal correlates of habituation and dishabituation of the gill-withdrawal reflex in *Aplysia. Science*, 1970, **167**, 1743–1745.

Lacey, J. I., Kagan, J., Lacey, B. C., and Moss, H. A. The visceral level: Situation determinants and behavioral correlates of autonomic response patterns. Pp. 161–196 in Knapp, P. H. (ed.), *Expression of the emotions in man*. New York: Int. Univ. Press, 1963.

Lacey, J. I., and Lacey, B. C. The law of initial value in the longitudinal study of autonomic constitution: Reproductibility of autonomic responses and response patterns over a four-year interval. *Ann. N.Y. Acad. Sci.*, 1962, **98**, 1257–1290.

Lack, D. *Darwin's finches*. Cambridge: Cambridge Univ. Press, 1947.

Lashley, K. S. Studies of cerebral function in learning. V. The retention of motor habits after destruction of the so-called motor areas in primates. *Arch. neurol. Psychiat.*, 1924, **12**, 249–276.

—————. *Brain mechanisms and intelligence*. Chicago: Univ. of Chicago Press, 1929.

—————. In search of the engram. Pp. 454–482 in *Symp. Soc. exp. Biol.*, No. 4. New York: Cambridge Univ. Press, 1950.

—————. The problem of serial order in behavior. Pp. 506–528 in Beach, F. A., Hebb, D. O., Morgan, C. T., and Nissen, H. W. (eds.), *The neuropsychology of Lashley: Selected papers of K. S. Lashley*. New York: McGraw-Hill, 1960.

Laursen, A. M. Corpus striatum. *Acta physiol. Scand.*, 1963, Suppl. 211, **59**, 1–106.

Lawicka, W., and Konorski, J. The physiological mechanism of delayed reactions. III. The effects of prefrontal ablations on delayed reaction in dogs. *Acta biol. Exp.*, 1959, **19**, 221–231.

Lehrman, D. S. The physiological basis of parental feeding behavior in the ring dove (*Streptopelia risoria*). *Behaviour*, 1955, **7**, 241–286.

—————. Behavioral science, engineering, and poetry. Pp. 459–472 in Tobach, E., Aronson, L. R., and Shaw, E. (eds.), op. cit., 1971.

Lele, P. P., and Weddell, G. The relationship between neurohistology and corneal sensibility. *Brain*, 1956, **79**, 119–154.

LeMagnen, J. Peripheral and systemic actions of food in the caloric regulation of intake. *Ann. N.Y. Acad. Sci.*, 1969, **157**, 1126–1157.

Lenneberg, E. H. *Biological foundations of language*. New York: Wiley, 1967.

Lerner, I. M. *Heredity, evolution, and society*. San Francisco: W. H. Freeman, 1968.

Lettvin, J. Y., Maturana, H. R., McCulloch, W. S., and Pitts, W. H. What the frog's eye tells the frog's brain. *Proc. inst. Radio Engr.*, 1959, **47**, 1940–1951.

Levine, S. Stimulation in infancy. *Sci. Am.*, 1960, **202**, 80–86.

———. Stress and behavior. *Sci. Am.*, 1971, **224**, 26–31.

Levine, S., and Brush, F. R. Adrenocortical activity and avoidance learning as a function of time after avoidance training. *Physiol. Behav.*, 1967, **2**, 385–388.

Levy-Agresti, J., and Sperry, R. W. Differential perceptual capacities in major and minor hemispheres. *Proc. Nat. Acad. Sci. U.S.*, 1968, **61**, 1151.

Lewis, D. J., and Maher, B. A. Neural consolidation and electroconvulsive shock. *Psychol. Rev.*, 1965, **72**, 225–239.

Licklider, J. C. R. Basic correlates of the auditory stimulus. Pp. 985–1039 in Stevens, S. S. (ed.), *Handbook of experimental psychology*. New York: Wiley, 1951.

Lindsley, D. B. Psychological phenomena and the electroencephalogram. *Electroencephalog. clin. Neurophysiol.*, 1952, **4**, 443–456.

———. The reticular system and perceptual discrimination. Pp. 513–534 in Jasper, H. H. (ed.), *Reticular formation of the brain*. Boston: Little, Brown, 1958.

———. Attention, consciousness, sleep and wakefulness. Pp. 1553–1593 in Field, J. (ed.), *Handbook of physiology, Neurophysiology*, III. Washington, D. C.: Am. Physiol. Soc., 1960.

Lindsley, D. B., Bowden, J., and Magoun, H. W. Effect upon EEG of acute injury to the brain stem activating system. *Electroencephalog. clin. Neurophysiol.*, 1949, **1**, 475–486.

Lindsley, D. B., and Cutts, K. K. Electroencephalograms of "constitutionally inferior" and behavior problem children: Comparison with those of normal children and adults. *Arch. neurol. Psychiat.*, 1940, **44**, 1199–1212.

Lindsley, D. B., and Henry, C. E. The effects of drugs on behavior and the electroencephalograms of children with behavior disorders. *Psychosom. Med.*, 1942, **4**, 140–149.

Lindsley, D. B., Schreiner, L. H., Knowles, W. B., and Magoun, H. W. Behavioral and EEG changes following chronic brain stem lesions in the cat. *Electroencephalog. clin. Neurophysiol.*, 1950, **2**, 483–498.

Lindsley, D. B., Schreiner, L. H., and Magoun, H. W. An electromyographic study of plasticity. *J. Neurophysiol.*, 1949, **12**, 197–216.

Lindsley, D. B., and Wicke, J. D. The electroencephalogram: autonomous electrical activity in man and animals. Pp. 3–83 in Thompson, R. F., and Patterson, M. M. (eds.), **IB**, op. cit., 1974.

Lindzey, G. Some remarks concerning incest, the incest taboo, and psychoanalytic theory. *Am. Psychol.*, 1967, **22**, 1051–1059.

Lindzey, G., Lykken, D. T., and Winston, H. D. Infantile trauma, genetic

factors, and adult temperament. *J. abnorm. soc. Psychol.*, 1960, **61,**
7–14.

Livingston, R. B. Some brain stem mechanisms relating to psychosomatic
functions. *Psychosom. Med.*, 1955, **17,** 347–351.

Longo, V. G. *Neuropharmacology and behavior.* San Francisco: W. H.
Freeman, 1972.

Lorente de Nó, R. Cerebral cortex: cytoarchitecture. Pp. 274–301 in Fulton, J. F. (ed.), *Physiology of the nervous system.* New York: Oxford
Univ. Press, 1938.

Lorenz, K. *King Solomon's ring.* London: Methuen, 1952.

————. *On aggression.* New York: Harcourt Brace and World, 1966.

Loucks, R. B. Preliminary report of a technique for stimulation or destruction of tissues beneath the integument and the establishing of a
conditioning reaction with faradization of the cerebral cortex. *J. comp.
Psychol.*, 1933, **16,** 439–444.

Luce, G. G., and Segal, J. *Sleep.* New York: Coward-McCann, 1966.

Luria, A. R., Sokolov, E. N., and Klimkowski, N. Towards a neurody-
namic analysis of memory disturbances with lesions of the left temporal lobe. *Neuropsychologia*, 1967, **5,** 1–10.

Luttges, M., Johnson, T., Buch, C., Holland, J., and McGaugh, J. L.
An examination of "transfer of learning" by nucleic acid. *Science*, 1966,
151, 834–837.

Lynch, G. The formation of new synaptic connections after brain damage
and their possible role in recovery of function. Pp. 228–233 in Eidelberg, E., and Stein, D. G. (eds.), op. cit., 1974.

Lynn, R. *Attention, arousal, and the orientation reaction.* New York:
Pergamon Press, 1966.

MacLean, P. D., and Ploog, D. W. Cerebral representation of penile erection. *J. Neurophysiol.*, 1962, **25,** 29–55.

Macrides, F., and Chorover, S. L. Neuroelectrical disturbances produced
by intracerebral injection of puromycin dihydrochloride in rats. Paper
presented at the Eastern Psychological Assoc. meeting, 1968.

Magoun, H. W. Central neural inhibition. Pp. 161–193 in Jones, M. R.
(ed.), *Nebraska symposium on motivation.* Lincoln, Neb.: Univ. of
Nebraska Press, 1963a.

————. *The waking brain.* Springfield, Ill.: Charles C. Thomas, 1963b.

Magoun, H. W., and Rhines, R. An inhibitory mechanism in the bulbar
reticular formation. *J. Neurophysiol.*, 1946, **9,** 165–171.

Malmo, R. B. Activation: A neuropsychological dimension. *Psychol. Rev.*
1959, **66,** 367–386.

Mandell, A. J., and Mandell, M. P. (eds.). *Psychochemical research in
man.* New York: Academic Press, 1969.

Mandler, G. Emotion. In *New directions in psychology.* New York: Holt,
Rinehart and Winston, 1962.

Manosevitz, M., Lindzey, G., and Thiessen, D. D. (eds.). *Behavior genetics. Method and research.* New York: Appleton-Century-Crofts, 1969.

Margules, D. L., and Olds, J. Identical "feeding" and "rewarding" systems in the lateral hypothalamus of rats. *Science,* 1962, **135,** 374–375.

Mark, V. H., and Ervin, F. R. *Violence and the brain.* New York: Harper and Row, 1970.

Marsh, J. T., Worden, F. G., and Hicks, L. Some effects of room acoustics on evoked auditory potentials. *Science,* 1962, **137,** 281–282.

Marshall, J. F., Turner, B. H., and Teitelbaum, P. Sensory neglect produced by lateral hypothalamic damage. *Science,* 1971, **174,** 523–525.

Mason, J. W., Brady, J. V., and Sidman, M. Plasma 17-hydroxycorticosteroid levels and conditioned behavior in the rhesus monkey. *Endocrinology,* 1957, **60,** 741–752.

Matsumiya, Y., Tagliasco, V., Lomboroso, C. T., and Goodglass, H. Auditory evoked response: Meaningfulness of stimuli and interhemispheric asymmetry. *Science,* 1972, **175,** 790–792.

Maturana, H. R., Lettvin, J. Y., McCulloch, W. S., and Pitts, W. H. Anatomy and physiology of vision in the frog (Rana pipiens). *J. gen. Physiol.,* 1960, **43,** 129–175.

Mayer, J. Genetic, traumatic and environment factors in the etiology of obesity. *Physiol. Rev.,* 1953, **33,** 472–508.

McAdam, D. W., and Whitaker, H. A. Language production: Electroencephalographic localization in the normal human brain. *Science,* 1971, **172,** 499–502.

McClearn, G. E. Behavioral genetics. *Ann. Rev. Genetics,* 1970, **4,** 437–468.

McClearn, G. E., and DeFries, J. C. *Introduction to behavioral genetics.* San Francisco: W. H. Freeman, 1973.

McCleary, R. A. (ed.). *Genetic and experiential factors in perception, research and commentary.* Glenview, Ill.: Scott, Foresman and Co., 1970.

————. Where we stand today. Pp. 138–141 in McCleary, R. A. (ed.), op. cit., 1970.

McCleary, R. A., and Moore, R. Y. *Subcortical mechanisms of behavior.* New York: Basic Books, 1965.

McConnell, J. V. Memory transfer through cannibalism in planarium. *J. Neuropsychiat.,* 1962, **3,** Suppl. 1, 542–548.

McCouch, G. P., Austin, G. M., Liu, C. N., and Liu, C. Y. Sprouting as a cause of spasticity. *J. Neurophysiol.,* 1958, **21,** 205–223.

McFie, J., and Piercy, M. F. Intellectual impairment with localized cerebral lesions. *Brain,* 1952, **75,** 292–311.

McGaugh, J. L. A multi-trace view of memory storage processes. Pp. 13–24 in Bovet, D., Bovet-Nitti, F., and Oliverio, A. (eds.), *Attuali orientamenti della ricerca sull'apprendimento e la memoria.* Roma: Accademia Nazionale dei Lincei, 1968.

McGaugh, J. L., and Alpern, H. P. Effects of electroshock on memory: Amnesia without convulsions. *Science,* 1966, **152,** 665–666.

McGaugh, J. L., and Herz, M. J. *Memory consolidation.* San Francisco: Albion, 1972.

McGaugh, J. L., and Krivanek, J. Strychnine effects on discrimination learning in mice: Effects of dose and time of administration. *Physiol. Behav.,* 1970, **5,** 1437–1442.

McGaugh, J. L., and Petrinovich, L. The effect of strychnine sulfate on maze learning. *Am. J. Psychol.,* 1959, **72,** 99–102.

McGinty, D. J., and Sterman, M. B. Sleep suppression after basal forebrain lesions in the cat. *Science,* 1968, **160,** 1253–1255.

McLennan, H. *Synaptic transmission.* Philadelphia: W. B. Saunders, 1963.

Melton, A. W. Implications of short-term memory for a general theory of memory. *J. verb. learn. verb. behav.,* 1963, **2,** 1–21.

Mettler, F. A. (ed.). *Psychosurgical problems.* New York: The Blakiston Co., 1952.

———. Cortical subcortical relations in abnormal motor functions. Pp. 445–497 in Yahr, M. D., and Purpura, D. P. (eds.), *Neurophysiological basis of normal and abnormal motor activities.* New York: Raven Press, 1967.

Mettler, F. A., Ades, H. W., Lipman, E., and Culler, E. A. The extrapyramidal system. *Arch. neurol. Psychiat.,* 1939, **41,** 984–995.

Meyer, D. R. Some psychological determinants of sparing and loss following damage to the brain. Pp. 173–192 in Harlow, H. F., and Woolsey, C. N. (eds.), *Biological and biochemical bases of behavior.* Madison, Wis.: Univ. of Wisconsin Press, 1958.

Meyer, P. M. Analysis of visual behavior in cats with extensive neocortical ablations. *J. comp. physiol. Psychol.,* 1963, **56,** 397–401.

———. Recovery from neocortical damage. Pp. 115–129 in French, G. M. (ed.), *Cortical functioning in behavior, research and commentary.* Glenview, Ill.: Scott, Foresman and Co., 1973.

Miller, G. A., and Taylor, W. G. The perception of repeated bursts of noise. *J. acoust. Soc. Am.,* 1948, **20,** 171–182.

Miller, N. E. Studies of fear as an acquirable drive. I. Fear as motivation and fear-reduction as reinforcement in the learning of new responses. *J. exp. Psychol.,* 1948, 38, 89–101.

———. Learning of visceral and glandular responses. *Science,* 1969, **163,** 434–445.

Milner, B. Intellectual function of the temporal lobes. *Psychol. Bull.,* 1954, **51,** 42–62.

———. Psychological defects produced by temporal lobe excision. *Res. Pub. Assn. nerv. ment. Dis.,* 1958, **36,** 244–257.

———. The memory defect in bilateral hippocampal lesions. *Psychiat. Res. Rep. Am. Psychiat. Ass.,* 1959, **11,** 43–52.

———. Les troubles de la mémoire accompagnant des lésions hippocampiques bilatérales. Pp. 257–272 in *Physiologie de l'hippocampe*. Paris: Centre Nationale de la Recherche Scientifique, 1962.

—————. Amnesia following operation on the temporal lobes. Pp. 112–115 in Whitty, C. W. M., and Zangwill, O. L. (eds.), *Amnesia*. London: Butterworths, 1966.

—————. Memory and the medial temporal regions of the brain. Pp. 29–50 in Pribram, K. H., and Broadbent, D. E. (eds.), op. cit., 1970.

—————. Disorders of learning and memory after temporal lobe lesions in man. *Clinical Neurosurgery*, 1972, **19**, 421–446.

—————. Hemispheric specialization: Scope and limits. Pp. 75–89 in Schmitt, F. O., and Worden, F. G. (eds.), *The neurosciences, third study program*. Cambridge: MIT Press, 1974.

Milner, P. M. *Physiological psychology*. New York: Holt, Rinehart and Winston, 1970.

Mishkin, M. Visual mechanisms beyond the striate cortex. Pp. 93–119 in Russell, R. W. (ed.), *Frontiers in physiological psychology*. New York: Academic Press, 1966.

Mishkin, M., and Weiskrantz, L. Effects of delaying reward on visual-discrimination performance in monkeys with frontal lesions. *J. comp. physiol. Psychol.*, 1958, **51**, 276–281.

Money, J. (ed.). *Sex research, new developments*. New York: Holt, Rinehart and Winston, 1965.

Money, J. Psychosexual differentiation. Pp. 3–23 in Money, J. (ed.), op. cit., 1965.

Money, J., and Erhardt, A. A. *Man and woman, boy and girl: Differentiation and dimorphism of gender identity*. Baltimore: Johns Hopkins Press, 1972.

Morgane, P. J. Maturation of neurobiochemical systems related to the ontogeny of sleep behavior. Pp. 141–162 in Clemente, C. D., Purpura, D. P., and Mayer, F. E. (eds.), *Sleep and the maturing nervous system*. New York: Academic Press, 1972.

Morison, R. S., and Dempsey, E. W. A study of thalamocortical relations. *Am. J. Physiol.*, 1942, **135**, 280–292.

Morrell, F. Electrophysiological contributions to the neural basis of learning. *Physiol. Rev.*, 1961, **41**, 443–494.

Morrell, L. K., and Salamy, J. G. Hemispheric asymmetry of electro-cortical responses to speech stimuli. *Science*, 1971, **174**, 164–166.

Moruzzi, G. Summary statement. Pp. 241–243 in Akert, K., Bally, C., and Schadé, J. P. (eds.), *Progress in brain research*, **13**, *Sleep mechanisms*. Amsterdam: Elsevier, 1965.

Moruzzi, G., and Magoun, H. W. Brain stem reticular formation and activation of the EEG. *Electroencephalog. clin. Neurophysiol.*, 1949, **1**, 455–473.

Mountcastle, V. B. Modality and topographic properties of single neurons of cat's somatic sensory cortex. *J. Neurophysiol.*, 1957, **20**, 508–534.

Mountcastle, V. B., Poggio, G. F., and Werner, G. The relation of tha-

lamic cell response to peripheral stimuli varied over an intensive continuum. *J. Neurophysiol.*, 1963, **26**, 807–834.

Müller, G. E., and Pilzecker, A. *Experimentelle Beiträge zur Lehre vom Gedächtniss.* Leipzig, 1900.

Munn, N. L. *The evolution of the human mind.* Boston: Houghton-Mifflin, 1971.

Murray, E. J. *Sleep, dreams, and arousal.* New York: Appleton-Century-Crofts, 1965.

Myers, R. D. Temperature regulation: Neurochemical systems in the hypothalamus. Pp. 506–523 in Haymaker, W., Anderson, E., and Nauta, W. J. H. (eds.), *The hypothalamus.* Springfield, Ill.: Charles C. Thomas, 1969.

————. Hypothalamic mechanisms of pyrogen action in the cat and monkey. Pp. 131–153 in Wolstenholme, G. E. W., and Birch, J. (eds.), *Ciba Foundation symposium on pyrogens and fever.* London: Churchill, 1971a.

————. Primates. Pp. 283–326 in Whittow, G. C. (ed.), *Comparative physiology of thermoregulation,* **2.** New York: Academic Press, 1971b.

Nauta, W. J. H. Hypothalamic regulation of sleep in rats: An experimental study. *J. Neurophysiol.*, 1946, **9**, 285–316.

Nauta, W. J. H., and Karten, H. J. A general profile of the vertebrate brain with sidelights on the ancestry of the cerebral cortex. In Schmitt, F. O. (ed.), *The neurosciences, second study program.* New York: Rockefeller Univ. Press, 1970.

Neff, W. D. Neural mechanisms of auditory discrimination. Pp. 259–278 in Rosenblith, W. A. (ed.), *Sensory communication.* New York: Wiley, 1961.

Nirenberg, M. W. The genetic code: II. *Sci. Am.*, 1963, **208**, 80–94.

Noback, C. R. *The human nervous system.* New York: McGraw-Hill, 1967.

Norgren, R., and Leonard, C. Ascending central gustatory pathways. *J. comp. Neurol.*, 1973, **150**, 217–238.

Norman, D. *Memory and attention; an introduction to human information processing.* New York: Wiley, 1969.

Olds, J. Pleasure centers in the brain. *Sci. Am.*, 1956, **195**, 105–116.

————. Self-stimulation of the brain. *Science*, 1958, **127**, 315–323.

————. Hypothalamic substrates of reward. *Physiol. Rev.*, 1962, **42**, 554–604.

————. Multiple unit recordings from behaving rats. Pp. 165–198 in Thompson, R. F., and Patterson, M. M. (eds.), **IA**, op. cit., 1973.

Olds, J., Allan, W. S., and Briese, E. Differentiation of hypothalamic drive and reward centers. *Am. J. Physiol.*, 1971, **221**, 368–375.

Olds, J., Disterhoft, J. F., Segal, M., Kornblith, C. L., and Hirsh, R. Learning centers of rat brain mapped by measuring latencies of conditioned unit responses. *J. Neurophysiol.*, 1972, **35**, 202–219.

Olds, J., and Milner, P. Positive reinforcement produced by electrical stimulation of septal area and other regions of rat brain. *J. comp. physiol. Psychol.*, 1954, **47**, 419–427.

Ornstein, R. E. *The psychology of consciousness.* San Francisco: W. H. Freeman, 1972.

————. (ed.). *The nature of human consciousness. A book of readings.* San Francisco: W. H. Freeman, 1973.

Papez, J. W. A proposed mechanism of emotion. *Arch. neurol. Psychiat.*, 1937, **38**, 725–743.

Patten, B. M. *Human embryology.* 2d ed. New York: McGraw-Hill, 1953.

Patterson, M. M., Cegavske, C. F., and Thompson, R. F. Effects of a classical conditioning paradigm on hind-limb flexor nerve response in immobilized spinal cats. *J. comp. physiol. Psychol.*, 1973, **84**, 88–97.

Patton, H. D. Reflex regulation of posture and movement. Pp. 167–198 in Ruch, T. C., and Fulton, J. F. (eds.), *Medical physiology and biophysics.* Philadelphia: W. B. Saunders, 1960.

Pavlov, I. *Conditioned reflexes.* New York: Oxford Univ. Press, 1927.

Pearlman, C. A., Sharpless, S. K., and Jarvik, M. E. Retrograde amnesia produced by anesthetic and convulsant agents. *J. comp. physiol. Psychol.*, 1961, **54**, 109–112.

Peeke, H. V. S., and Herz, M. J. (eds.). *Habituation, II, Physiological substrates.* New York: Academic Press, 1973.

Penfield, W. Consciousness, memory, and man's conditioned reflexes. In Pribram, K. H. (ed.), *On the biology of learning.* New York: Harcourt, Brace and World, 1969.

Penfield, W., and Jasper, H. *Epilepsy and the functional anatomy of the human brain.* Boston: Little, Brown, 1954.

Penfield, W., and Rasmussen, T. *The cerebral cortex of man.* New York: Macmillan, 1950.

Penfield, W., and Roberts, L. *Speech and brain mechanisms.* Princeton: Princeton Univ. Press, 1959.

Peterson, L. R. Short-term verbal memory and learning. *Psychol. Rev.*, 1966, **73**, 193–207.

Pfaff, D. W., Diakow, C., Zigmond, R. E., and Kow, L.-M. Neural and hormonal determinants of female mating behavior in rats. Pp. 621–646 in Schmitt, F. O., and Worden, F. G. (eds.), *The neurosciences, third study program.* Cambridge: MIT Press, 1974.

Phillips, C. G., and Porter, R. The pyramidal projection to motoneurones of some muscle groups of the baboon's forelimb. Pp. 222–245 in Eccles, J. C., and Schadé, J. P. (eds.), *Progress in brain research, 12, Physiology of spinal neurons.* Amsterdam: Elsevier, 1964.

Phillips, D. S., Denney, D. D., Robertson, R. T., Hicks, L. H., and Thompson, R. F. Cortical projections of ascending nonspecific systems. *Physiol. Behav.*, 1972, **8**, 269–277.

Pinsker, H., Kupfermann, I., Castellucci, V., and Kandel, E. R. Habituation and dishabituation of the gill-withdrawal reflex in *Aplysia. Science,* 1970, **167,** 1740–1742.

Poggio, G. F., and Mountcastle, V. B. A study of the functional contributions of the lemniscal and spinothalamic systems to somatic sensibility. Central nervous mechanisms in pain. *Bull. Johns Hopkins Hosp.,* 1960, **106,** 266–316.

———. The functional properties of ventrobasal thalamic neurons studied in unanesthetized monkeys. *J. Neurophysiol.,* 1963, **26,** 775–806.

Polyak, S. *The retina.* Chicago: Univ. of Chicago Press, 1941.

Posner, M. I. Components of skilled performance. *Science,* 1966, **152,** 1712–1718.

Powley, T. L., and Keesey, R. E. Relationship of body weight to the lateral hypothalamic feeding syndrome. *J. comp. physiol. Psychol.,* 1970, **70,** 25–36.

Premack, D. The education of Sarah. *Psychol. Today,* 1970, **4,** 54–58.

Pribram, K. H. Toward a science of neuropsychology (method and data). In Patton, R. A. (ed.), *Current trends in psychology and the behavioral sciences.* Pittsburgh: Univ. of Pittsburgh Press, 1954.

———. Interrelations of psychology and the neurological disciplines. Pp. 119–157 in Koch, S. (ed.), *Psychology: A study of a science,* **4.** New York: McGraw-Hill, 1962.

———. Some dimensions of remembering: Steps toward a neuropsychological model of memory. In Gaito, J. (ed.), *Macromolecules and behavior.* New York: Appleton-Century-Crofts, 1966.

———. The neurophysiology of remembering. *Sci. Am.,* 1969, **220,** 73–86.

———. *Languages of the brain: Experimental paradoxes and principles in neuropsychology.* Englewood Cliffs, N. J.: Prentice-Hall, 1971.

Pribram, K. H., Ahumada, A., Hartog, J., and Roos, L. A progress report on the neurological processes disturbed by frontal lesions in primates. Pp. 28–55 in Warren, J. M., and Akert, K. (eds.), op. cit., 1964.

Pribram, K. H., and Broadbent, D. E. (eds.). *Biology of memory.* New York: Academic Press, 1970.

Prisko, L. Short-term memory in focal cerebral damage. Unpublished doctoral dissertation, McGill Univ., 1963.

Prosser, C. L., and Hunter, W. S. The extinction of startle responses and spinal reflexes in the white rat. *Am. J. Physiol.,* 1936, **117,** 609–618.

Ranson, S. W. Somnolence caused by hypothalamic lesions in monkeys. *Arch. neurol. Psychiat.,* 1939, **41,** 1–23.

Ranson, S. W., and Clark, S. L. *The anatomy of the nervous system.* 10th ed. Philadelphia: W. B. Saunders, 1959.

Reichlin, S. Neuroendocrinology. *N.E. J. Med.,* 1963, **329,** 1182–1191.

Resnick, O. The role of biogenic amines in sleep. Pp. 109–116 in Clemente, C. D., Purpura, D. P., and Mayer, F. E. (eds.), *Sleep and the maturing nervous system.* New York: Academic Press, 1972.

Riesen, A. H. Arrested vision, in which chimpanzees raised in the dark shed light on the relationship between visual experience and visual development. *Sci. Am.*, 1950, **183** 16–19.

Riggs, L. A., Ratliff, F., Cornsweet, J. C., and Cornsweet, T. N. The disappearance of steadily fixated visual test objects. *J. Opt. Soc. Am.*, 1953, **43**, 495–501.

Riopelle, A. J., Alper, R. G., Strong, P. N., and Ades, H. W. Multiple discrimination and patterned string performance of normal and temporal-lobectomized monkeys. *J. comp. physiol. Psychol.*, 1953, **46**, 145–149.

Riopelle, A. J., and Churukian, G. A. The effect of varying the intertrial interval in discrimination learning by normal and brain-operated monkeys. *J. comp. physiol. Psychol.*, 1958, **51**, 119–125.

Robertson, R. T., and Lynch, G. S. Orbitofrontal modulation of EEG spindles. *Brain Res.*, 1971, **28**, 562–566.

Rodin, J. Effects of distraction on performance of obese and normal subjects. Unpublished doctoral dissertation, Columbia Univ., 1970.

Roe, A., and Simpson, G. G. (eds.). *Behavior and evolution.* New Haven: Yale Univ. Press, 1958.

Romer, A. S. Phylogeny and behavior with special reference to vertebrate evolution. Pp. 48–75 in Roe, A., and Simpson, G. G. (eds.), op. cit., 1958.

Rose, J. E., and Woolsey, C. N. Cortical connections and functional organization of the thalamic auditory system of the cat. Pp. 127–150 in Harlow, H. F., and Woolsey, C. N. (eds.), *Biological and biochemical bases of behavior.* Madison, Wis.: Univ. of Wisconsin Press, 1958.

Rosenzweig, M. R. Evidence for anatomical and chemical changes in the brain during primary learning. In Pribram, K. H. and Broadbent, D. E. (eds.), op. cit., 1970.

Ross, L. D. Cue- and cognition-controlled eating among obese and normal subjects. Unpublished doctoral dissertation, Columbia Univ., 1969.

Rosvold, H. E., Mirsky, A. F., and Pribram, K. H. Influence of amygdalectomy on social behavior in monkeys. *J. comp. physiol. Psychol.*, 1954, **47**, 173–178.

Rosvold, H. E., Mishkin, M., and Szwarcbart, M. K. Effects of subcortical lesions in monkeys on visual-discrimination and single-alternation performance. *J. comp. physiol. Psychol.*, 1958, **51**, 437–444.

Routtenberg, A., and Lindy, J. Effects of the availability of rewarding septal and hypothalamic stimulation on bar pressing for food under conditions of deprivation. *J. comp. physiol. Psychol.*, 1965, **60**, 158–161.

Rowland, V., and Dines, G. Cortical steady potential shift in relation to the rhythmic electrocorticogram and multiple unit activity. In Thompson, R. F., and Patterson, M. M., **IA,** op. cit., 1973.

Ruch, T. C. The cerebral cortex: Its structure and motor functions. Pp. 249–276 in Ruch, T. C., and Fulton, J. F. (eds.), *Medical physiology and biophysics.* Philadelphia: W. B. Saunders, 1960.

Rushton, W. A. H. The cone pigments of the human fovea in colour blind and normal. *Visual problems of color* (Symposium), **1**. New York: Chemical Pub. Co., 1961, 77–109.

Russell, R. W. Biochemical substrates of behavior. Pp. 185–246 in Russell, R. W. (ed.), *Frontiers in physiological psychology*. New York: Academic Press, 1966.

Sartre, J. P. *Nausea*. Trans. by Lloyd Alexander. New York: New Directions Publ. Corp., 1964.

Schachter, S. Cognitive effects on bodily functioning: Studies of obesity and eating. Pp. 117–144 in Glass, D. C. (ed.), op. cit., 1967.

——. Some extraordinary facts about obese humans and rats. *Am. Psychol.*, 1971, **26**, 129–144.

Schachter, S., and Singer, J. E. Cognitive, social, and physiological determinants of emotional state. *Psychol. Rev.*, 1962, **69**, 379–399.

Scheibel, M. E., and Scheibel, A. B. Structural substrates for integrative patterns in the brain stem reticular core. Pp. 31–55 in Jasper, H. H. (ed.), *Reticular formation of the brain*. Boston: Little, Brown, 1958.

——. Some structurofunctional correlates of development in young cats. *Electroencephalog. clin. Neurophysiol.* Suppl., 1963, **24**, 235–246.

——. Structural organization of non-specific thalamic nuclei and their projection towards cortex. *Brain Res.*, 1967, **6**, 60–95.

Schildkraut, J. J., and Kety, S. S. Biogenic amines and emotion. *Science*, 1967, **156**, 21–30.

Schlosberg, H. Three dimensions of emotion. *Psychol. Rev.*, 1954, **61**, 81–88.

Schneider, G. E. Early lesions of superior colliculus: Factors affecting the formation of abnormal retinal projections. *Brain Behav. Evol.*, 1973, **8**, 73–109.

——. Anomalous axonal connections implicated in sparing and alteration of function after early lesions. Pp. 222–227 in Eidelberg, E., and Stein, D. G. (eds.), op. cit., 1974.

Schneider, G. E., and Nauta, W. J. H. Formation of anomalous retinal projections after removal of the optic tectum in the neonate hamster. *Anat. Rec.*, 1969, **163**, 258. (Abstr.)

Schreiner, L. H., Lindsley, D. B., and Magoun, H. W. Role of brain stem facilitory systems in maintenance of spasticity. *J. Neurophysiol.*, 1949, **12**, 207–216.

Schuell, H., Jenkins, J. J., and Jiménez-Pabón, E. *Aphasia in adults: Diagnosis, prognosis, and treatment*. New York: Hoeber, 1964.

Schull, W. J., and Neel, J. V. *The effects of inbreeding on Japanese children*. New York: Harper and Row, 1965.

Scott, J. P. Genetics and the development of social behavior in dogs. *Am. Zoologist*, 1964, **4**, 161–168.

——. *Early experience and the organization of behavior*. Belmont, Cal.: Wadsworth, 1968.

Selye, H. *The physiology and pathology of exposure to stress.* Montreal: Acta, Inc., 1950.

------. *The stress of life.* New York: McGraw-Hill, 1956.

------. *Stress without distress.* New York: Lippincott, 1974.

Semmes, J., Weinstein, S., Ghent, L., and Teuber, H. L. *Somatosensory changes after penetrating brain wounds in man.* Cambridge, Mass.: Harvard Univ. Press, 1960.

Sharpless, S., and Jasper, H. H. Habituation of the arousal reaction. *Brain,* 1956, **79,** 655–680.

Shashoua, V. E. RNA metabolism in goldfish brain during acquisition of new behavioral patterns. *Proc. Nat. Acad. Sci.,* 1970, **65,** 160–167.

Sherrington, C. S. *The integrative action of the nervous system.* New York: Charles Scribner's Sons, 1906.

------. The physical basis of mind. Pp. 1–4 in Laslett, P. (ed.), *The physical basis of mind.* New York: Macmillan, 1950.

Sholl, D. A. *The organization of the cerebral cortex.* London: Methuen, 1956.

Shurrager, P. S., and Culler, E. Conditioning in the spinal dog. *J. exp. Psychol.,* 1940, **26,** 133–159.

Sidman, R. L., and Sidman, M. *Neuroanatomy, a programmed text.* Boston: Little, Brown, 1965.

Siegel, J., and Gordon, T. P. Paradoxical sleep: Deprivation in the cat. *Science,* 1965, **148,** 978–980.

Simpson, G. G. *The major features of evolution.* New York: Columbia Univ. Press, 1953.

------. The study of evolution: Methods and present status of theory. Pp. 7–26 in Roe, A., and Simpson, G. G. (eds.), op. cit., 1958.

Siqueland, E. R. Conditioned sucking and visual reinforcers with human infants. Paper presented Eastern Regional meeting, Society for Research in Child Development, Worcester, Mass., April 1968.

Skinner, J. E., and Lindsley, D. B. Electrophysiological and behavioral effects of blockage of the non-specific thalamo-cortical system. *Brain Res.,* 1967, **6,** 95–118.

Smith, B. M. The polygraph. *Sci. Am.,* 1967, **216,** 3–9.

Smith, J. M. *The theory of evolution.* Baltimore: Penguin, 1958.

Smith, R. L. The ascending fiber projections from the principal sensory trigeminal nucleus in the rat. *J. comp. Neurol.,* 1973, **148,** 423–446.

Smith, S. M., Brown, H. O., Toman, J. E. P., and Goodman, L. S. The lack of cerebral effects of d-tubocurarine. *Anesthesiology,* 1947, **8,** 1–14.

Snowden, C. T. Motivation, regulation and control of meal parameters with oral and intragastric feeding. *J. comp. physiol. Psychol.,* 1969, **69,** 91–100.

Sokolov, E. N. Neuronal models of the orienting reflex. Pp. 187–276 in Brazier, M. A. B. (ed.), *The central nervous system and behavior.* Trans. 3rd Conf. Josiah Macy, Jr. Found. New York, 1960.

————. Higher nervous functions: The orienting reflex. *Ann. Rev. Physiol.*, 1963a, **25**, 545–580.

————. *Perception and the conditioned reflex.* Oxford: Pergamon Press, 1963b.

Spencer, W. A., Thompson, R. F., and Neilson, D. R., Jr. Response decrement of flexion reflex in acute spinal cat and transient restoration by strong stimuli. *J. Neurophysiol.*, 1966a, **29**, 221–239.

————. Alterations in responsiveness of ascending and reflex pathways activated by iterated cutaneous afferent volleys. *J. Neurophysiol.*, 1966b, **29**, 240–252.

————. Decrement of ventral root electrotonus and intracellularly recorded post-synaptic potentials produced by iterated cutaneous afferent volleys. *J. Neurophysiol.*, 1966c, **29**, 253–274.

Sperling, G. The information available in brief visual presentations. *Psychol. Monogr.*, 1960, **74**, Whole No. 498.

Sperry, R. W. The eye and the brain. *Sci. Am.*, 1956, **194**, 48–52.

Spinelli, D. N. Receptive field organization of ganglion cells in the cat's retina. *Exp. Neurol.*, 1967, **19**, 291–315.

Spinelli, D. N., Hirsch, H. V. B., Phelps, R. W., and Metzler, J. Visual experience as a determinant of the response characteristics of cortical receptive fields in cats. *Exp. Brain Res.*, 1972, **15**, 289–304.

Spinelli, D. N., and Pribram, K. H. Changes in visual recovery function produced by temporal lobe stimulation in monkeys. *Electroencephalog. clin. Neurophysiol.*, 1966, **20**, 44–49.

Spong, P., Haider, M., and Lindsley, D. B. Selective attentiveness and cortical evoked responses to visual and auditory stimuli. *Science*, 1965, **148**, 395–397.

Sprague, J. M., and Chambers, W. W. Control of posture by reticular formation and cerebellum in intact anesthetized and unanesthetized, and in decerebrate cat. *Am. J. Physiol.*, 1954, **176**, 52–64.

Sprague, J. M., Chambers, W. W., and Stellar, E. Attentive, affective and adaptive behavior in the cat. *Science*, 1961, **133**, 165–173.

Stamm, J. S. Retardation and facilitation in learning by stimulation of frontal cortex in monkeys. Pp. 102–125 in Warren, J. M., and Akert, K. (eds.), op. cit., 1964.

Starzl, T. E., Taylor, C. W., and Magoun, H. W. Ascending conduction in reticular activating system, with special reference to the diencephalon. *J. Neurophysiol.*, 1951, **14**, 461–497.

Stellar, E., and Sprague, J. M. (eds.). *Progress in physiological psychology*, 4. New York, Academic Press, 1971.

Stent, G. S. *Molecular biology of bacterial viruses.* San Francisco: W. H. Freeman, 1963.

Sterman, M. B., McGinty, D. J., and Adinolfi, A. M. (eds.). *Brain development and behavior.* New York: Academic Press, 1971.

Stern, C. *Principles of human genetics.* 3d ed. San Francisco: W. H. Freeman, 1973.

Stevens, S. S. On the psychophysical law. *Psychol. Rev.*, 1957, **64**, 153–181.

Stevens, S. S., and Davis, H. *Hearing*. New York: Wiley, 1938.

Stevens, S. S., and Volkmann, J. The relation of pitch to frequency: A revised scale. *Am. J. Psychol.*, 1940, **53**, 329–353.

Stiles, W. S. The average colour-matching functions for a large matching field. *Visual problems of color* (Symposium), 1. New York: Chemical Pub. Co., 1961, 213–249.

Stoll, W. A., LSD-25, a hallucinatory agent of the ergot group. *Swiss Arch. Neurol.*, 1947, **60**, 279.

Stunkard, A. J., Van Itallie, T. B., and Reis, B. B. The mechanism of satiety: Effect of glucagon on gastric hunger contractions in man. *Proc. Soc. Exp. Biol. Med. N.Y.*, 1955, **89**, 258–261.

Talland, G. A., and Waugh, N. C. (eds.). *The pathology of memory.* New York: Academic Press, 1969.

Tasaki, I. *Nervous transmission.* Springfield, Ill.: Charles C. Thomas, 1953.

Taub, E., Bacon, R. C., and Berman, A. J. Acquisition of a trace-conditioned avoidance response after deafferentation of the responding limb. *J. comp. physiol. Psychol.*, 1965, **59**, 275–279.

Teitelbaum, P. Sensory control of hypothalamic hyperphagia. *J. comp. physiol. Psychol.*, 1955, **48**, 156–163.

———. Random and food-directed activity in hyperphagic and normal rats. *J. comp. physiol. Psychol.*, 1957, **50**, 486–490.

———. Disturbances of feeding and drinking behavior after hypothalamic lesions. Pp. 39–65 in Jones, M. R. (ed.), *Nebraska symposium on motivation.* Lincoln, Neb.: Univ. of Nebraska Press, 1961.

———. The encephalization of hunger. Pp. 319–350 in Stellar, E., and Sprague, J. M. (eds.), op. cit., 1971.

Teitelbaum, P., and Epstein, A. N. The lateral hypothalamic syndrome. *Psychol. Rev.*, 1962, **69**, 74–90.

Teitelbaum, P., and Stellar, E. Recovery from the failure to eat produced by hypothalamic lesions. *Science*, 1954, **120**, 894–895.

Teuber, H. L. The riddle of frontal function in man. Pp. 410–444 in Warren, J. M., and Akert, K. (eds.), op. cit., 1964.

Teyler, T. J., Roemer, R. A., Harrison, T. F., and Thompson, R. F. Human scalp-recorded evoked-potential correlates of linguistic stimuli. *Bull. Psychon. Soc.*, 1973, **1**, 333–334.

Teyler, T. J., Roemer, R. A., and Thompson, R. F. Habituation of the pyramidal response in unanesthetized cat. *Physiol. Behav.*, 1972, **8**, 201–205.

Teyler, T. J., Roemer, R. A., Thompson, J. K., Thompson, R. F., and Voss, J. F. The role of sensory biofeedback in EMG response learning in an interactive man-machine system. In Mostofsky, D. I. (ed.), *Behavioral control and modification of physiological activity.* New York: Appleton-Century-Crofts, 1974.

638

Bibliography

Thiessen, D. D. *Gene organization and behavior.* New York: Random House, 1972.

Thompson, R. F. *Foundations of physiological psychology.* New York: Harper and Row, 1967.

―――. (ed.). *Physiological psychology: Readings from Scientific American.* San Francisco: W. H. Freeman, 1971.

Thompson, R. F., Groves, P. M., Teyler, T. J., and Roemer, R. A. A dual-process theory of habituation: Theory and behavior. Pp. 239–271 in Peeke, H. V. S., and Herz, M. J. (eds.), *Habituation, I, Behavioral studies.* New York: Academic Press, 1973.

Thompson, R. F., Johnson, R. H., and Hoopes, J. J. Organization of auditory, somatic sensory, and visual projection to association fields of cerebral cortex in the cat. *J. Neurophysiol.,* 1963, **26,** 343–364.

Thompson, R. F., Mayers, K. S., Robertson, R. T., and Patterson, C. J. Number coding in association cortex of cat. *Science,* 1970, **168,** 271–273.

Thompson, R. F., and Patterson, M. M. (eds.). *Bioelectric recording techniques.* Volumes **IA, IB,** and **IC.** New York: Academic Press, 1973–1974.

Thompson, R. F., Patterson, M. M., and Teyler, T. J. Neurophysiology of learning. *Ann. Rev. Psychol.,* 1972, **23,** 73–104.

Thompson, R. F., and Shaw, J. A. Behavioral correlates of evoked activity recorded from association areas of the cerebral cortex. *J. comp. physiol. Psychol.,* 1965, **60,** 329–339.

Thompson, R. F., and Spencer, W. A. Habituation: A model phenomenon for the study of neuronal substrates of behavior. *Psychol. Rev.,* 1966, **173,** 16–43.

Thompson, R., and Thorne, B. M. Brainstem reticular lesions: Amnestic effects on learned habits in the rat. *Physiol. Psychol.,* 1973, **1,** 61–70.

Tobach, E., Aronson, L. R., and Shaw, E. (eds.). *The biopsychology of development.* New York: Academic Press, 1971.

Tower, S. S. Pyramidal lesion in the monkey. *Brain,* 1940, **63,** 36–90.

Treisman, A. M. Selective attention in man. *Brit. Med. Bull.,* 1964, **20,** 12–16.

Truex, R. C., and Carpenter, M. B. *Strong and Elwyn's human neuroanatomy.* 5th ed. Baltimore: Williams and Wilkins, 1964.

Tryon, R. C. Individual differences. Pp. 330–365 in Moss, F. A. (ed.), *Comparative psychology.* Revised ed. New York: Prentice-Hall, 1942.

Tunturi, A. R. A difference in the representation of auditory signals for the left and right ears in the iso-frequency contours of the right middle ectosylvian cortex of the dog. *Am. J. Physiol.,* 1952, **168,** 712–727.

Ungar, G. Role of proteins and peptides in learning and memory. In Ungar, G. (ed.), *Molecular mechanisms in memory and learning.* New York: Plenum Press, 1970.

Ursin, H. The effect of amygdaloid lesions on flight and defense behavior in cats. *Exp. Neurol.*, 1965, **11**, 61–79.

Uttal, W. R. *The psychobiology of sensory coding.* New York: Harper and Row, 1973.

Valenstein, E. *Brain control. A critical examination of brain stimulation and psychosurgery.* New York: Wiley, 1973.

Valenstein, E. S., Cox, V. C., and Kakolewski, J. W. Re-examination of the role of the hypothalamus in motivation. *Psychol. Rev.*, 1970, **77**, 16–31.

Valenstein, E. S., and Meyers, W. J. Rate-independent test of reinforcing consequences of brain stimulation. *J. comp. physiol. Psychol.*, 1964, **57**, 52–60.

Vandenberg, S. G. Hereditary factors in normal personality traits (as measured by inventories). Pp. 65–104 in Wortis, J. (ed.), *Recent advances in biological psychiatry*, 9. New York: Plenum Press, 1967.

———. Primary mental abilities or general intelligence? Evidence from twin studies. Pp. 146–160 in Thoday, J. M., and Parkes, A. S. (eds.), *Genetic and environmental influences on behavior.* New York: Plenum Press, 1968.

Vander, A. J., Sherman, J. H., and Luciano, D. S. *Human physiology: The mechanisms of body function.* New York: McGraw-Hill, 1970.

van Lawick-Goodall, J. *In the shadow of man.* Boston: Houghton-Mifflin, 1971.

Vaughan, E., and Fisher, A. E. Male sexual behavior induced by intracranial electrical stimulation. *Science,* 1962, **137**, 758–760.

Verzeano, M. Evoked responses and network dynamics. Pp. 27–54 in Whalen, R. E., Thompson, R. F., Verzeano, M., and Weinberger, N. M. (eds.), *The neural control of behavior.* New York: Academic Press, 1970.

Vittorino, M. A., and Trabucchi, C. Graphic modifications using LSD_{25} in a schizophrenic group. Pp. 275–284 in Volmat, R., and Wiart, C. (eds.), *Art and psychopathology.* Amsterdam: Excerpta Medica Foundation, 1969.

Von Bonin, G., and Bailey, P. *The neocortex of macaca mulatta.* Urbana, Ill.: Univ. of Illinois Press, 1947.

Von Holst, E., and Von Saint Paul, V. Electrically controlled behavior. *Sci. Am.,* 1962, **206**, 50–59.

Voss, J. F. *Psychology as a behavioral science.* Pacific Palisades, Cal.: Goodyear, 1974.

Wald, G. Retinal chemistry and the physiology of vision. *Visual Problems of Color* (Symposium), 1. New York: Chemical Pub. Co., 1961, 15–67.

Wald, G., Brown, P. K., and Smith, P. H. Iodopsin. *J. gen. Physiol.*, 1955, **38**, 623–681.

Walshe, F. M. R. On the mode of representation of movements in motor cortex, with special reference to "convulsions beginning unilaterally." (Jackson). *Brain*, 1943, **66**, 104–139.

Warren, J. M. The behavior of carnivores and primates with lesions in the prefrontal cortex. Pp. 168–191 in Warren, J. M., and Akert, K. (eds.), op. cit., 1964.

Warren, J. M., and Akert, K. (eds.). *The frontal granular cortex and behavior.* New York: McGraw-Hill, 1964.

Warrington, E. K., and Shallice, T. Neuropsychological evidence of visual storage in short-term memory tasks. *Qu. J. Exp. Psychol.*, 1972, **24**, 30–40.

Warrington, E. K., and Weiskrantz, L. Amnesic syndrome: Consolidation or retrieval? *Nature* (London), 1970, **228**, 628–630.

———. An analysis of short-term and long-term memory defects in man. In Deutsch, J. A. (ed.), op. cit., 1973.

Washburn, S. L., and Shirek, J. Human evolution. Pp. 10–21 in Hirsch, J., (ed.), op. cit., 1967.

Watson, J. B., and Rayner, R. Conditioned emotional reactions. *J. exp. Psychol.*, 1920, **3**, 1–14.

Waugh, N. C., and Norman, D. A. Primary memory. *Psychol. Rev.*, 1965, **72**, 89–104.

Wayner, M. J., and Carey, R. J. Basic drives. *Ann. Rev. Psychol.*, 1973, **24**, 53–80.

Webster, W. R., Dunlop, C. W., Simons, L. A., and Aitken, L. M. Auditory habituation: A test of a centrifugal and a peripheral theory. *Science*, 1965, **148**, 654–656.

Weinberger, N. M. Attentive processes. Pp. 129–198 in McGaugh, J. L. (ed.), *Psychobiology. Behavior from a biological perspective.* New York: Academic Press, 1971.

Weisenburg, T., and McBride, K. E. *Aphasia: A clinical and psychological study.* New York: Commonwealth Fund, 1935.

Welker, W. I. An analysis of exploratory and play behavior in animals. Pp. 175–226 in Fiske, D. F., and Maddi, S. R. (eds.), *Functions of varied experience.* Homewood, Ill.: Dorsey Press, 1961.

———. Principles of organization of the ventrobasal complex in mammals. *Brain, Behav. Evol.*, 1973, **7**, 253–336.

Weller, G. M., and Bell, R. Q. Basal skin conductance and neonatal state. *Child Dev.*, 1965, **36**, 647–657.

Westbrook, W. H., and McGaugh, J. L. Drug facilitation of latent learning. *Psychopharmacologia*, 1963, **5**, 440–446.

Wetzel, A. B., Thompson, V. E., Horel, J. A., and Meyer, P. M. Some consequences of perinatal lesions of the visual cortex in the cat. *Psychon. Sci.*, 1965, **3**, 381–382.

Wever, E. G., and Bray, C. W. The nature of acoustic response; the relation between sound frequency of impulses in the auditory nerve. *J. exp. Psychol.*, 1930, **13**, 373–387.

Whalen, R. E. (ed.). *Hormones and behavior*. Princeton, N. J.: D. Van Nostrand, 1967.

Whalen, R. E. Hormones and behavior. Pp. 3–20 in Whalen, R. E. (ed.), op. cit., 1967.

Whitfield, I. C., and Evans, E. F. Responses of auditory cortical neurons to stimuli of changing frequency. *J. Neurophysiol.*, 1965, **28**, 655–672.

Wickelgren, W. A. The long and the short of memory. *Psychol. Bull.*, 1973, **80**, 425–438.

Wickelgren, W. O. Effect of acoustic habituation on click-evoked responses in cats. *J. Neurophysiol.*, 1968, **31**, 777–785.

Wiener, N. I., and Deutsch, J. A. Temporal aspects of anticholinergic- and anticholinesterase-induced amnesia for an appetitive habit. *J. comp. physiol. Psychol.*, 1968, **66**, 613–617.

Wiesel, T. N., and Hubel, D. H. Comparison of the effects of unilateral and bilateral eye closure on cortical unit responses in kittens. *J. Neurophysiol.*, 1965, **28**, 1029–1040.

Wolf, G., and DiCara, L. V. Impairments in sodium appetite after lesions of gustatory thalamus: Replication and extension. *Behav. Biol.*, 1974, **10**, 105–112.

Wolstenholme, G. E. W., and O'Connor, M. (eds.). *Growth of the nervous system*. Boston: Little, Brown, 1968.

Woody, C. D., and Engel, J., Jr. Changes in unit activity and thresholds to electrical microstimulation of central-pericruciate cortex of cat with classical conditioning of different facial movements. *J. Neurophysiol.*, 1972, **35**, 230–241.

Woolsey, C. N. Organization of somatic sensory and motor areas of the cerebral cortex. Pp. 63–81 in Harlow, H. F., and Woolsey, C. N. (eds.), *Biological and biochemical bases of behavior*. Madison, Wis.: Univ. of Wisconsin Press, 1958.

———. Organization of cortical auditory system. Pp. 235–258 in Rosenblith, W. A. (ed.), *Sensory communication*. New York: Wiley, 1961.

———. Cortical localization as defined by evoked potential and electrical stimulation methods. Pp. 17–27 in Schaltenbrand, G., and Woolsey, C. N. (eds.), *Cerebral localization and organization*. Madison, Wis.: Univ. of Wisconsin Press, 1964.

Worden, F. G., and Marsh, J. T. Amplitude changes of auditory potentials evoked at cochlear nucleus during acoustic habituation. *Electroencephalog. clin. Neurophysiol.*, 1963, **15**, 866–881.

Yerkes, R. M. Modifiability of Hydroides dianthus V. *J. comp. Neurol.*, 1906, **16**, 441–450.

Young, W. C., Goy, R. W., and Phoenix, C. H. Hormones and sexual behavior. *Science*, 1964, **143**, 212–218.

Zangwill, O. L. Asymmetry of cerebral hemisphere function. Pp. 51–62 in Garland, H. (ed.), *Scientific aspects of neurology*. London: E. and S. Livingstone, 1961.

Zeigler, H. P. Trigeminal deafferentation and feeding behavior in the pigeon: Sensorimotor and motivational effects. *Science,* 1973, **182,** 1155–1158.

————. Feeding behavior in the pigeon: A neurobehavioral analysis. In Goodman, I., and Schein, M. (eds.), *Birds: Brain and behavior.* New York: Academic Press, 1974.

Zeigler, H. P., and Karten, H. J. Brain mechanisms and feeding behavior in the pigeon (Columbia livia): I. Quinto-frontal structures. *J. comp. Neurol.,* 1973, **152,** 59–82.

Zeigler, H. P., and Karten, H. J. Central trigeminal structures and the lateral hypothalamic syndrome in the rat. *Science,* 1974, **186,** 636–637.

Zemp, J. W., Wilson, J. E., Schlesinger, K., Boggan, W. O., and Glassman, E. Brain function and macromolecules, I. Incorporation of Uridine into RNA of mouse brain during short-term training experience. *Proc. Nat. Acad. Sci.,* 1966, **55,** 1423–1431.

Zornetzer, S. F., and McGaugh, J. L. Effects of frontal brain electroshock stimulation on EEG activity and memory in rats: Relationship to ECS-produced retrograde amnesia. *J. Neurobiol.,* 1970, **1,** 379–394.

————. Retrograde amnesia and brain seizures in mice: A further analysis. *Physiol. Behav.,* 1971, **7,** 841–845.

Zuckerman, Sir S. Hormones. *Sci. Am.,* 1957, **196,** 76–87.

Suggested readings

Chapter 1

Dobzhansky, T. *Mankind Evolving*. New York: Bantam Books, 1970.

Hawkes, J. and Woolley, Sir L. *History of Mankind, Vol. I, Prehistory and the Beginnings of Civilization*. New York: Harper and Row, 1963.

Jerison, H. J. *Evolution of the Brain and Intelligence*. New York: Academic Press, 1973.

Munn, N. L. *The Evolution of the Human Mind*. Boston: Houghton-Mifflin, 1971.

Roe, A. and Simpson, G. G. (eds.). *Behavior and Evolution*. New Haven: Yale University Press, 1958.

Thompson, R. F. (ed.). *Physiological Psychology: Readings from Scientific American*. San Francisco: Freeman, 1971. Sections I and II, pp. 1–84.

Chapter 2

Hirsch, J. (ed.). *Behavior-Genetic Analysis*. New York: McGraw-Hill, 1967.

Isaacson, R. L. (ed.). *The Neuropsychology of Development*. New York: Wiley, 1968.

Manosevitz, M., Lindzey, G., and Thiessen, D. D. (eds.). *Behavior Genetics. Method and Research*. New York: Appleton-Century-Crofts, 1969.

McClearn, G. E. and DeFries, J. C. *Introduction to Behavioral Genetics*. San Francisco: Freeman, 1973.

Sterman, M. B., McGinty, D. J., and Adinolfi, A. M. (eds.). *Brain Development and Behavior*. New York: Academic Press, 1971.

Thiessen, D. D. *Gene Organization and Behavior*. New York: Random House, 1972.

Thompson, R. F. (ed.). *Physiological Psychology: Readings from Scientific American*. San Francisco: Freeman, 1971. Sections I and II, pp. 1–84.

Tobach, E., Aronson, L. R., and Shaw, E. (eds.). *The Biopsychology of Development*. New York: Academic Press, 1971.

Wolstenholme, G. E. W. and O'Connor, M. (eds.). *Growth of the Nervous System*. Boston: Little, Brown, 1968.

Chapter 3

Brodal, A. *Neurological Anatomy.* 2d Ed. New York: Oxford University Press, 1969.

Gazzaniga, M. S. *The Bisected Brain.* New York: Appleton-Century-Crofts, 1970.

Noback, C. R. *The Human Nervous System.* New York: McGraw-Hill, 1967.

Ornstein, R. E. (ed.). *The Nature of Human Consciousness. A Book of Readings.* San Francisco: Freeman, 1973.

Ornstein, R. E. *The Psychology of Consciousness.* San Francisco: Freeman, 1972.

Sidman, R. L. and Sidman, M. *Neuroanatomy, A Programmed Text.* Boston: Little, Brown, 1965.

Thompson, R. F. (ed.). *Physiological Psychology: Readings from Scientific American.* San Francisco: Freeman, 1971. Section III, pp. 87–124.

Chapter 4

Eccles, John C. *The Understanding of the Brain.* New York: McGraw-Hill, 1973.

Hodgkin, A. L. *The Conduction of the Nervous Impulse.* Liverpool: Liverpool University Press, 1964.

Katz, B. *Nerve, Muscle and Synapse.* New York: McGraw-Hill, 1966.

Thompson, R. F. (ed.). *Physiological Psychology: Readings from Scientific American.* San Francisco: Freeman, 1971. Sections III and IV, pp. 87–170.

Thompson, R. F. *Foundations of Physiological Psychology.* New York: Harper and Row, 1967. Chapters 6–9.

Thompson, R. F. and Patterson, M. M. (eds.). *Bioelectric Recording Techniques.* Volumes IA, IB, and IC. New York: Academic Press, 1973–1974.

Chapter 5

Cohen, S. *The Beyond Within. The LSD Story.* New York: Atheneum, 1970.

Cooper, J. R., Bloom, F. E. and Roth, R. H. *The Biochemical Basis of Neuropharmacology.* 2d Ed. New York: Oxford University Press, 1974.

Julien, R. *A Primer of Drug Actions.* San Francisco: Freeman, 1975.

Longo, V. G. *Neuropharmacology and Behavior.* San Francisco: Freeman, 1972.

Mandell, A. J. and Mandell, M. P. (eds.). *Psychochemical Research in Man.* New York: Academic Press, 1969.

McLennan, H. *Synaptic Transmission.* Philadelphia: Saunders, 1963.

Thompson, R. F. (ed.). *Physiological Psychology: Readings from Scientific American.* San Francisco: Freeman, 1971. Section V, pp. 172–218.

Chapter 6

Alpern, M., Laurence, M., and Wolsk, D. *Sensory Processes*. Belmont, CA: Wadsworth, 1967.

Geldard, F. A. *The Human Senses*. 2d Ed. New York:Wiley, 1972.

Gross, C. G. and Zeigler, H. P. (eds.). *Readings in Physiological Psychology. Neurophysiology/Sensory Processes*. New York: Harper and Row, 1969.

Thompson, R. F. (ed.). *Physiological Psychology: Readings from Scientific American*. San Francisco: Freeman, 1971. Section VI, pp. 220–280.

Uttal, W. R. *The Psychobiology of Sensory Coding*. New York: Harper and Row, 1973.

Chapter 7

Basmajian, J. V. *Muscles Alive*. 2d Ed. Baltimore: Williams and Wilkins, 1967.

Gibson, J. J. *The Senses Considered as Perceptual Systems*. Boston: Houghton-Mifflin, 1966.

Granit, R. *Receptors and Sensory Perception*. New Haven: Yale University Press, 1955.

Held, R. and Richards, W. (eds.). *Perception: Mechanisms and Models. Readings from Scientific American*. San Francisco: Freeman, 1972.

McCleary, R. A. (ed.). *Genetic and Experiential Factors in Perception*. Glenview, IL: Scott Foresman, 1970.

Thompson, R. F. (ed.). *Physiological Psychology: Readings from Scientific American*. San Francisco: Freeman, 1971. Section VI, pp. 220–280.

Thompson, R. F. *Foundations of Physiological Psychology*. New York: Harper and Row, 1967. Chapters 11–13.

Chapter 8

Brown, J. S. *The Motivation of Behavior*. New York: McGraw-Hill, 1961.

Deutsch, J. A. "Appetative Motivation." Chapter 4 in McGaugh, J. L. (ed.). *Psychobiology. Behavior from a Biological Perspective*. New York: Academic Press, 1971.

Gross, C. G. and Zeigler, H. P. (eds.). *Readings in Physiological Psychology. Motivation*. New York: Harper and Row, 1969b.

Hinde, R. A. *Animal Behavior; a Synthesis of Ethology and Comparative Psychology*. 2d Ed. New York: McGraw-Hill, 1970.

McCleary, R. A. and Moore, R. Y. *Subcortical Mechanisms of Behavior*. New York: Basic Books, 1965.

Stellar, E. and Sprague, J. M. *Progress in Physiological Psychology*. Volume 4. New York: Academic Press, 1971.

Thompson, R. F. (ed.). *Physiological Psychology: Readings from Scientific American.* San Francisco: Freeman, 1971. Section VII, pp. 282–324.

Chapter 9

Brush, F. R. (ed.). *Aversive Conditioning and Learning.* New York: Academic Press, 1971.

Glass, D. C. (ed.). *Neurophysiology and Emotion.* New York: Rockefeller University Press, 1967.

Mark, V. H. and Ervin, F. R. *Violence and the Brain.* New York: Harper and Row, 1970.

Money, J. (ed.). *Sex Research, New Developments.* New York: Holt, Rinehart and Winston, 1965.

Selye, H. *Stress without Distress.* New York: Lippincott, 1974.

Thompson, R. F. *Physiological Psychology: Readings from Scientific American.* San Francisco: Freeman, 1971. Section VII, pp. 282–324.

Valenstein, E. *Brain Control. A Critical Examination of Brain Stimulation and Psychosurgery.* New York: Wiley, 1973.

Whalen, R. E. (ed.). *Hormones and Behavior.* Princeton, NJ: D. Van Nostrand, 1967.

Chapter 10

Hartmann, E. *The Biology of Dreaming.* Springfield, IL: Charles C Thomas, 1967.

Luce, G. G. and Segal, J. *Sleep.* New York: Coward-McCann, 1966.

Lynn, R. *Attention, Arousal, and the Orientation Reaction.* New York: Pergamon, 1966.

Sokolov, E. *Perception and the Conditioned Reflex.* New York: Pergamon, 1963.

Thompson, R. F. (ed.). *Physiological Psychology: Readings from Scientific American.* San Francisco: Freeman, 1971. Section VIII, pp. 326–358.

Thompson, R. F. *Foundations of Physiological Psychology.* New York: Harper and Row, 1967. Chapter 14.

Weinberger, N. M. "Attentive processes." Chapter 5 *in* McGaugh, J. L. (ed.). *Psychobiology. Behavior from a Biological Perspective.* New York: Academic Press, 1971.

Chapter 11

Deutsch, J. A. (ed.). *The Physiological Basis of Memory.* New York: Academic Press, 1973.

Gross, C. G. and Zeigler, H. P. (eds.). *Readings in Physiological Psychology. Learning and Memory.* New York: Harper and Row, 1969a.

John, E. R. *Mechanisms of Memory.* New York: Academic Press, 1967.

Kandel, E. R. *The Cellular Basis of Behavior: An Introduction to Behavioral Neurobiology.* San Francisco: Freeman, 1975.

McGaugh, J. L. and Herz, M. J. *Memory Consolidation.* San Francisco: Albion, 1972.

Pribram, K. H. and Broadbent, D. E. (eds.). *Biology of Memory.* New York: Academic Press, 1970.

Thompson, R. F. (ed.). *Physiological Psychology: Readings from Scientific American.* San Francisco: Freeman, 1971. Section IX, pp. 360–398.

Thompson, R. F. *Foundations of Physiological Psychology.* New York: Harper and Row, 1967. Chapters 15 and 17.

Chapter 12

Brown, R. *A First Language.* Cambridge, MA: Harvard University Press, 1973.

Geschwind, N. "Language and the Brain." *Scientific American,* **226.** 1972. Pp. 76–83.

Kinsbourne, M. "Cognitive Deficit: Experimental Analysis." Chapter 7 in McGaugh, J. L. (ed.). *Psychobiology: Behavior from a Biological Perspective.* New York: Academic Press, 1971.

Lenneberg, E. H. *Biological Foundations of Language.* New York: Wiley, 1967.

Pribram, K. H. *Languages of the Brain.* Englewood Cliffs, NJ: Prentice-Hall, 1971.

Thompson, R. F. (ed.). *Physiological Psychology: Readings from Scientific American.* San Francisco: Freeman, 1971. Section X, pp. 400–429.

Author Index

Subject Index

Slow-wave sleep, 114, 122
Soma, neuron, 93
Somatic nerves, 95–96
Somatic-sensory-motor cortex, 227
Somatic-sensory system, 223ff
Spectral sensitivity, 201
Spike discharge, 129–131
Spinal conditioning, 490, 491
Spinal cord, 87, 99–100
Spinal motoneuron, 93, 94
Spinal reflexes, 99
    habituation, 471–477
Spindle organ, 258
Spinothalamic tract, 225
Split-brain studies, 69–76
Sprouting, 489
Stimulants, 170, 178–179
Stimulus coding, 193ff
Stimulus intensity, 195ff
Stimulus quality, 195ff
Stimulus transduction, 196
Stress, 381ff
Striate cortex, 204, 564
Substantia nigra, 102, 168
Supraspinal activity, 99
Surgical anesthesia, 173
Sympathetic division, autonomic nervous system, 97–98, 375
Synapse, 94–95, 155, 160–162
    chemical, 155–165
    general features, 136–137
Synaptic activity, 129
Synaptic depression, 475, 478
Synaptic potential, 138–139
Synaptic transmission, 136–144
Synaptic transmitters, 165–168
    See also ACh and Biogenic amines
Synergists, 254

T

Tabula rasa, 61, 64
Tay-Sachs disease, 46, 47
Tectum, 102
Tegmentum, 102
Telencephalon, 91
Temperature control, 303ff
Temporal lobes, 538–548
    effects of removal, 570

effects of stimulation, 570
    in infrahumans, 561
Thalamus, 88, 91, 100, 103–104
Theta waves, 118, 119
Thin rat syndrome, 321
Thirst, 307ff
Thymus gland, 353
Thyroid gland, 353
Tight junctions, 143
Tolerance, 185
Transmitter breakdown enzyme, 164
Transmitter substance, 162–163
Transmitter theories of learning, 510, 516–519
Trigeminal system, role in eating, 326
Turner's syndrome, 48

V

Ventrobasal complex, 225
Ventromedial hypothalamus feeding center, 319
Vertebrate brain, divisions of, 88–91
Vesicles, 160–161, 162
Violence, brain mechanisms in humans, 399ff
Visual cortex, 204
Visual discrimination, lesion effects on, 487
Visual pathways, 71–72
Visual receptive fields, simple, complex, and hypercomplex, 207ff
Visual stimulus coding, 205ff
Vitamin A in vision, 200
Volatile anesthetics, 169

W

Waking EEG patterns, 414, 415
Wernicke-Korsakoff disease, 537–538
Wernicke's area, damage, 577, 578–582
White matter, definition, 87, 95
Wisconsin General Test Apparatus (WGTA), 551–552, 564

X

XXY syndrome, 33
XYY syndrome, 32–33, 49, 63

Speech - can't talk of a human distinction based on language.

Broca's.

motor ← [diagram] → Wernicke's area.

homeostatis - faces organisms
hypothalamus works as a hub around which the nervous system revolves.

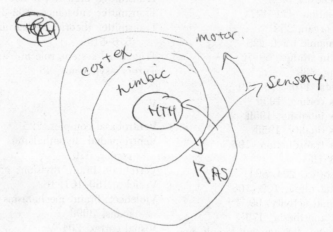

cortex
limbic
HTH
motor
sensory
RAS

sensory — Reward
+ medial forebrain bundle
— dorsal longitutindal fascud.

Detection ⇄ Orientation
satiety ← motor

when stimuli is too high becomes negatively reinforced.

76 77 5 4 3